THE HANDBOOK OF CHILD LIFE

THE HANDBOOK
OF
CHILD LIFE

A Guide for Pediatric Psychosocial Care

Edited by

RICHARD H. THOMPSON, Ph.D.

Dean of the School of Arts & Sciences
The College of New Rochelle
New Rochelle, New York

CHARLES C THOMAS • PUBLISHER, LTD.
Springfield • Illinois • U.S.A.

Published and Distributed Throughout the World by

CHARLES C THOMAS • PUBLISHER, LTD.
2600 South First Street
Springfield, Illinois 62704

©2009 by CHARLES C THOMAS • PUBLISHER, LTD.

ISBN 978-0-398-07831-7 (hard)
ISBN 978-0-398-07832-4 (paper)

Library of Congress Catalog Card Number: 2008026862

Printed in the United States of America
CR-R-3

Library of Congress Cataloging-in-Publication Data

The handbook of child life : a guide for pediatric psychosocial care /
edited by Richard H. Thompson
   p. ; cm.
Includes bibliographical references and index.
ISBN 978-0-398-07831-7 (hard) -- ISBN 978-0-398-07832-4 (pbk.)
   1. Clinical child psychology--Handbooks, manuals, etc. 2. Child devel-
opment--Handbooks, manuals, etc. 3. Child health services--Handbooks,
manuals, etc. I. Thompson, Richard H.
   [DNLM: 1. Child Psychology--methods. 2. Child Development. 3.
Child Health Services--organization & administration. 4. Child Welfare--
psychology. 5. Child, Hospitalized--psychology. WS 105 H23536 2009
RJ503.3.H358 2009
   618.92'89--dc22
                                      2008026862

CONTRIBUTING AUTHORS

Kimberly Eury Allen, MS, CCLS, is the Child Life Manager and Hematology/Oncology Child Life Specialist of the Medical College of Georgia's Children's Medical Center.

Jacqueline Bell, B.S. CCLS, is the Child Life Manager for the Baystate Children's Hospital in Springfield, Massachusetts. She has also been the Child Life Director for the University of Nebraska Medical Center and the University of Massachusetts Children's Medical Center in Worcester, Massachusetts.

Christina D. Brown, MS, CCLS, is Director of Child Life and Family Centered Care at Dell Children's Medical Center in Austin Texas. She has over twenty-five years of experience as a child life specialist/administrator and bereavement coordinator and is a Past President of both the Child Life Council and the Association for the Care of Children's Health.

Janet Cross, M.Ed., CCLS, is the director of Child Life Services and Family Resource Center at Monroe Carell Jr. Children's Hospital at Vanderbilt in Nashville, Tennessee. Janet worked as a child life specialist at Vanderbilt for ten years before assuming the leadership of the department in 1992 and is a past Senior Chairperson for the Child Life Certifying Committee.

Kathryn "Kat" Davitt, MOT, CCLS, OTR, is the Community Program Manager at Cook Children's Medical Center. Previously she was a clinical child life specialist with greater than 10 years experience in rehabilitation settings and is the current Secretary on the Child Life Council Executive Board.

Priti P. Desai, Ph.D., MPH, CCLS, is Assistant Professor in the Child Development and Family Relations Department at East Caro- lina University. She formerly worked at Children's HealthCare of Atlanta, Kennedy Krieger Institute and the Johns Hopkins Children's Center as a child life specialist and is a past executive board member of the Child Life Council.

LeeAnn Derbyshire Fenn, M.Sc., CCLS, is an Associate Clinical Professor, Department of Pediatrics, McMaster University, Hamilton Ontario, Canada. She is a former Director in the Child Life Studies Diploma Programme in the Faculty of Health Sciences at McMaster University.

Laura L. Gaynard, Ph.D., CCLS, is Adjunct Associate Professor, Department of Family and Consumer Studies, University of Utah. She was formerly the director of child life departments in several major teaching hospitals and served on the Child Life Council Board in a variety of roles.

Joy Goldberger, MS, CCLS, is education coordinator at the Johns Hopkins Children's Center in Baltimore, MD. Her career has included a variety of clinical and leadership roles, most significantly initial work with infants and toddlers, collaboration in a range of contexts with colleagues within the Child Life Council and the former ACCH, and as coordinator of the internship and other training programs at Hopkins.

Melissa Hicks, MS, CCLS, LPC, RPT, is the Program Director for Support and Educational Programs at the Camp Sunshine House in Atlanta, GA. She co-founded Wonders & Worries, formerly worked at the Johns Hopkins Children's Center, and Children's Healthcare of Atlanta and has served as President and Certification Chairperson of the Child Life Council.

Maggie Hoffman is the Director of Project DOCC - Delivery of Chronic Care. Project DOCC's mission is to use the experience of family caregivers to enhance health care practice and inform more responsive policies so that individuals with chronic illness/disability and their families have the services needed to live successfully in the community.

Ellen C. Hollon, MS, CCLS, was former director of the Child Life/Child Development Department at Children's Medical Center Dallas, TX, where she had been since 1994. She previously directed child life departments at Rainbow Babies & Children's Hospital in Cleveland, OH, and Rush-Presbyterian St. Luke's Medical Center in Chicago, IL and is a past President of the Child Life Council.

Peggy O. Jessee, Ph.D., CCLS, is Professor Emeritus at The University of Alabama. She was a faculty member in Child Life at The University of Alabama for 25 years, editor of the *CLC Bulletin*, and a board member of the Association for the Care of Children's Health and the Child Life Council.

Beverley H. Johnson is the President and Chief Executive Officer of the Institute for Family-Centered Care in Bethesda, Maryland.

Dene G. Klinzing, Ph.D., CCLS, is Professor of Individual and Family Studies and former Dean of the College of Human Resources at the University of Delaware. She served as Co-editor of *Children's Health Care* with Dennis R. Klinzing and was a board member of ACCH.

Dennis R. Klinzing, Ph.D., is Professor and Chair of the Department of Communication Studies at West Chester University. He served as Co-editor of *Children's Health Care* with Dene G. Klinzing and was a former board member of ACCH.

Kathleen McCue, MA, LSW, CCLS, is the Children's Program Director at The Gathering Place, a community-based support center for individuals and families touched by cancer. She is adjunct faculty in Child Life at the University of Akron, a former director of child life in two major children's hospitals, and a Past President and Past Secretary of the Child Life Council.

Sharon M. McLeod, MS, CCLS, CTRS, is Senior Clinical Director for the Division of Child Life at Cincinnati Children's Hospital Medical Center. She is a Past President of the Child Life Council.

Anne Luebering Mohl, Ph.D., CCLS, is a Child Life Specialist at The Johns Hopkins Children's Center, Baltimore, Maryland.

Melodee Moltman, MS Ed., CCLS, is Associate Professor and the current Director of Psychology-Child Life at Utica College in Utica, New York where she has taught for 27 years. She has presented papers on international issues in child life and has served as a consultant to child life programs in Kuwait.

Lois Pearson, M.Ed., CCLS, is a Child Life Specialist in the Intensive Care Unit of Children's Hospital of Wisconsin in Milwaukee. She has been a child life specialist for more than 25 years and is a lecturer in child life at Edgewood College in Madison, Wisconsin.

Cynthia Rosen is the Education Coordinator in the Child Life and Education Services Program at Schneider Children's Hospital at North Shore and a consultant to the Long Term Follow-up program at the Cancer Center for Kids at Winthrop University Hospital. She has worked on Long Island for 15 years as educational advocate for children with special needs and their families.

Linda Skinner, B.Ed., CCLS, is the Professional Practice Chief of Child Life and School Services at the IWK Health Centre in Halifax, Nova Scotia,

Canada. She has served as the President of the Canadian Association of Child Life Leaders and Board Member of Child Life Council.

Charles W. Snow, Ph.D., is Professor Emeritus, Department of Child Development and Family Relations, East Carolina University, Greenville, NC. He is formerly Coordinator of the Child Life Program at East Carolina University.

Vickie L. Squires, M.M.Ed., CCLS, LPC, has been the Manager of Child Life and Child Development Services at CHRISTUS Santa Rosa Children's Hospital in San Antonio, Texas for over 20 years. She has served as the Secretary on the Child Life Council Executive Board and is the Child Life Studies faculty member for Texas State University in San Marcos, Texas.

Richard H. Thompson, Ph.D., CCLS, is Dean of the School of Arts & Sciences at The College of New Rochelle. He was formerly a faculty member in Child Life at Wheelock College in Boston and is a Past President of the Child Life Council.

Joan C. Turner, Ph.D., CCLS, is an Assistant Professor in the Department of Child and Youth Study at Mount Saint Vincent University in Halifax, Nova Scotia. She was formerly a Child Life Specialist at Winnipeg's Health Sciences Centre and is currently the Associate Editor of the *Child Life Bulletin/FOCUS.*

Patricia Weiner, MS, is on the adjunct faculty of Bank Street College of Education, New York, NY and is the Educational Consultant to the Making Headway Foundation. After 25 years of child life, special education and administrative work at the North Shore- Long Island Jewish Health System on Long Island, NY, she became the first Director of the Child Life Program at Bank Street College of Education.

Claire M. White, MS, CCLS, is an Assistant Professor of Child Life at Wheelock College, Boston, Massachusetts.

Jerriann Myers Wilson, M.Ed., CCLS, retired after 43 years of child life work with 34 years as Child Life Director at The Johns Hopkins Hospital. She is Associate Professor Emeritus, Pediatrics, at the Johns Hopkins University School of Medicine and was the first President of the Child Life Council.

Susan Wojtasik, MA, CCLS, is the former Director of the Child Life

Departments at Bellevue and Schneider Children's Hospitals in New York, and is a former faculty member in the Child Life graduate programs at Bank Street College of Education in New York City.

TO MY FAMILY

LYNN, BRENNA, AND HALEY

INTRODUCTION

It has been said that the moral test of a society is how it treats its most vulnerable citizens. Those who enter the field of child life daily encounter those in our society who are among the most vulnerable . . . vulnerable because of their age and their ways of interpreting the world, vulnerable because of their physical circumstances, vulnerable because of the unfamiliar they encounter, vulnerable at times because of additional barriers such as language, poverty or prejudice. Yet, the child life specialist understands that each individual, despite the vulnerabilities he or she may bring to an encounter, also brings strength and resiliency. The task of the child life specialist is to build upon those strengths to minimize individual vulnerability and maximize the growth of the individual. The goal of this text is to assist in this process, drawing upon the expertise of leading figures in the field to help provide child life specialists, and other allied health professionals, with the knowledge and skills they will need to accomplish this important task.

This text was conceived several years ago through a conversation with Doctor Peggy Powers, my faculty colleague at the time at Wheelock College. We began with an outline of topics we felt would address the most important aspects of the practice of child life, a list that was modified more than once in the subsequent years. We then set about contacting our respected friends and colleagues in the field of child life, asking them to contribute a chapter and, in most cases, pairing them with one or more additional authors with whom they may or may not have already had a working relationship. Having assigned the topic for each, we gave them the further guidelines that the book be geared toward an audience beyond the introductory level, that it include information on the state of the art in the given area, and that, wherever possible, it demonstrated application of the content in practice through case studies.

We are grateful to each of the authors for the collaborative spirit with which they approached this project, for care with which they prepared their chapters, and for their patience with the editing process. On behalf of the authors, I would also to acknowledge the many, many individuals who have contributed to the preparation of this book through their reading and review of the text, through their support of the process and in many other ways too numerous to list. I am certain the list is incomplete, but it includes Patricia Azarnoff, Peg Belson, Pat Collins, Donna Doerr, Della Ferguson, Laurie Fraga, Evelyn Hausslein, Muriel Hirt, Mary Ann Janda, Stephanie Kirylych, Jill Koss, Erin Munn, Michele O'Neill, Sheila Palm, Stefi Rubin, Renee Ruggiero, Rebecca Smith, Bev Stone, Gina Tampio (nee Fortunato), and Richard Wayne.

CONTENTS

Page

Contributing Authors v
Introduction xiii

Chapter

1. THE STORY OF CHILD LIFE 3
   Susan Pond Wojtasik and Claire White

2. THEORETICAL FOUNDATIONS OF CHILD LIFE
   PRACTICE 23
   Joan C. Turner

3. RESEARCH IN CHILD LIFE 36
   Richard H. Thompson and Charles W. Snow

4. THERAPEUTIC RELATIONSHIPS IN CHILD LIFE 57
   Kathleen McCue

5. COMMUNICATION AND CHILD LIFE 78
   Dene G. Klinzing and Dennis R. Klinzing

6. FAMILY-CENTERED CARE AND THE IMPLICATIONS FOR
   CHILD LIFE PRACTICE 95
   *Jacqueline L. Bell, Beverley H. Johnson, Priti P. Desai, and
   Sharon M. McLeod*

7. ASSESSMENT AND DOCUMENTATION IN CHILD LIFE . . 116
   Ellen Hollon and Linda Skinner

8. PARADIGMS OF PLAY 136
    Peggy O. Jessee and Laura Gaynard

9. PSYCHOLOGICAL PREPARATION AND COPING 160
    Joy Goldberger, Anne Luebering Mohl, and Richard H. Thompson

10. PROGRAM ADMINISTRATION AND SUPERVISION 199
    Jerriann Myers Wilson and Janet Cross

11. CHILD LIFE INTERVENTIONS IN CRITICAL CARE AND
    AT THE END OF LIFE 220
    Lois J. Pearson

12. WORKING WITH GRIEVING CHILDREN AND
    FAMILIES 238
    Chris Brown

13. CHRONIC ILLNESS AND REHABILITATION 257
    Melissa Hicks and Kathryn Davitt

14. THE EMERGENCY DEPARTMENT AND AMBULATORY
    CARE 287
    Vickie L. Squires and Kim Eury Allen

15. CHILD LIFE AND EDUCATION ISSUES: THE CHILD
    WITH A CHRONIC ILLNESS OR SPECIAL HEALTHCARE
    NEEDS 310
    Patricia L. Weiner, Maggie Hoffman and Cynthia Rosen

16. CHILD LIFE: A GLOBAL PERSPECTIVE 327
    Melodee Moltman, Priti P. Desai and LeeAnn Derbyshire Fenn

Index 353

THE HANDBOOK OF CHILD LIFE

Chapter 1

THE STORY OF CHILD LIFE

Susan Pond Wojtasik and Claire White

INTRODUCTION

Discovering the story of childhood and the social and environmental conditions contributing to the health and illness of children is a challenging enterprise. Children are given scant space in the historical record. The modern reader is understandably puzzled and distressed by the indifference, indeed the harshness, with which children have been treated in earlier times. Today, knowledge of children's needs, and efforts to meet those needs, are taken quite seriously. Child life has played, and is continuing to play, a significant role in this new benevolence toward children, especially children in hospitals and other healthcare settings.

The history of how we became a people knowledgeable about and sympathetic to the complexity of childhood, in particular with respect to issues of health and disease, covers a very brief time span. Although theories of the contribution of microbes to the spread of disease and studies leading to improved infant nutrition occurred in the eighteenth century, a specific focus on children's health in the United States did not take hold until the mid-nineteenth century when the first children's hospital began caring for patients

in Philadelphia (Brodie, 1986). Some years later scientific interest in the causes and cure of diseases in children, as well as interest in their general welfare, led to the academic institution of pediatric medicine. Nursing schools and social welfare agencies also have their roots in the middle to late nineteenth century and were agents of change in promoting the well-being of children (Dancis, 1972; Brodie, 1986; Colón, 1999).

The Industrial Revolution, which caused the migration of thousands of families from rural areas in this country and thousands more from abroad, caused a crisis in the cities. Men, women and children were paid small wages for long hours of work. Families lived in hovels without access to clean food or water and without even a semblance of sanitation. Disease epidemics were common, and large numbers of babies succumbed to the lethal "summer diarrhea" every year (Colón, 1999).

In the midst of this misery, philanthropists and professionals responded with investigations and programs to help children live and grow. As a deeper understanding of the nature of childhood was probed by professionals interested in the development of intelligence, emotional response, and social relationships, the care of children came to

3

include these elements as well. These aspects of child development have engaged the energies of child life specialists since the early decades of the twentieth century.

"THEY PLAY WITH YOU HERE"

The story of child life begins in the early twentieth century when large numbers of children began to be hospitalized. Children were understandably terrified at being in an unfamiliar place where many children cried and where everyone was a stranger. The children were there, of course, for their own good, for the treatment of illness or accident that would restore them to health.

There was, however, no way for the children to comprehend this. They often faced empty days in which there was nothing to do but wait for the next dreaded examination or treatment. The children were so obviously miserable that in some instances recommendations were made to institute a program of activities to engage the children's interest when they were admitted and while they waited in their cribs for what would happen next.

Some critics of non-medical activities for children argued that a child sick enough to be in the hospital was too sick to play. Surely the hospital, the place where grave illnesses and impending death were the very reasons for being there, was no place for frivolity, for games, for laughter. But children need play like they need air to breathe, no matter what their circumstances.

Play is fundamental to the very structure and meaning of childhood. This is true even in the most onerous of circumstances, perhaps especially in times of great distress. Frank McCourt (1996), in his memoir *Angela's Ashes*, describes his childhood as miserable, immersed in poverty, neglect, the

death of siblings, drunkenness, living conditions of almost unimaginable squalor. He was furious at it. Yet when he and his brothers played at romps and adventures he could say with unbridled enthusiasm, "We had a grand time!"

The preponderance of opinion was ultimately on the side of the child, and programs of play and education were introduced into pediatric hospital care as early as the 1920's (Rutkowski, 1986). Play leaders taught volunteers and nursing students how to communicate with children primarily through play, helped children understand the strange ways of the hospital and the people who work there, and prepared children for what was going to happen to them in their own hospital stay. These play leaders, with their volunteers and students, helped normalize the hospital experience.

There was a sense of urgency in this work based on an understanding that childhood is a time of such rapid development that not a day should go by without attention to the basic imperative to grow. As was noted in an article appearing in 1937:

> Children come to us at a formative period. They are developing rapidly, each day brings vast changes in them. We can do dreadful things to a child during even a twenty-four-hour stay, and we can change his entire outlook on life for better or worse during an eight-months' stay in a hospital. Any program of patient's care naturally begins with excellent medical and nursing care. In addition to that we must safeguard him in every way, physically and mentally. His day should approach the day of a normal child as nearly as is possible under the circumstances. (Smith, 1937, p.1)

By 1950 ten hospitals in the United States and Canada had implemented play programs on their children's wards (Rutkowski, 1986). The stage was set to address systematically the multiple emotional insults experienced by children when they are hospitalized. New scientific discoveries and methods of treatment continually change the face of pediatric medicine, and child life practice has developed to meet the changing needs of sick children. Preparation for medical encounters, supporting family centered care, pain management, coping with grief and loss are as fundamental to child life practice today as is play. Nevertheless, play continues as a central experience in the hospital lives of children. It is a mode of healing.

Play liberates laughter. It blows up and deflates, builds up and knocks down. It takes bits of this and that and makes a new thing. It imitates life and elaborates on it. It can be quite earnest and intense when a child is laboring to come to grips with something important, or it can be as flippant and irreverent as a thumb of the nose.

We value play in the hospital not only for the sheer fun of it, but also for the opportunities it affords for "playing out" emotionally laden hospital experiences in order to come to terms with them. This playing out is analogous to the work we adults do when we think through a problem, play with an idea, imagine a series of scenarios before taking action. It is with this kind of play that we create who we are and who we will become.

THE GROUND WE STAND ON

Humanizing healthcare for children was passionately embraced by its practitioners, but the success of such a revolutionary undertaking depended on validation of its presuppositions by others. Without the scientific enquiries and the advocacy for children's health and well-being by the relatively new division of medicine called "pediatrics," a stable context for child life programs could not exist. The development of

interest in the behavioral aspects of pediatrics opened the way for making hospitalization a more child-friendly experience (Bakwin, 1941; Spitz, 1945). The insights of early to mid-twentieth century developmentalists and child psychologists provided a firm theoretical rationale for child life practice (Erikson, 1963; Winnecott, 1964; Piaget & Inhelder, 1969; Bowlby, 1982), and the structure of the multidisciplinary organization that came to be known as the Association for the Care of Children's Health added the impact of many voices from nursing, social work, pediatric medicine and psychiatry to help sustain and focus the ongoing work of child life specialists (Brooks, 1975).

Pediatrics: Developmental Medicine

In the late nineteenth century a sufficient body of knowledge existed about the health maintenance and the diseases of children for a new division of medical practice devoted exclusively to the care of infants and children to be established. Pediatrics in the United States has a very short history indeed, beginning, officially, when Abraham Jacobi, M.D., became the first Professor of Pediatrics in 1870 at Columbia University in New York City. Although Jacobi remained a general practitioner all his life, he had an unusual interest in and knowledge of the diseases of children and was a great advocate in the field of children's health. His interests were not limited to the diagnosis and treatment of disease but were wide-ranging, taking on issues of proper nutrition, preventive care, and the social aspects of illness. He began a tradition of concern for children's health that has had a profound and enduring effect on the well-being of children (Abt, 1965; Dancis, 1972; Colón, 1999).

In the first half of the twentieth century, city hospitals were filled with children sick from the poverty and filth that corrupted their food and drink just as certainly as they were sick from rheumatic fever, tuberculosis, diphtheria, polio, meningitis and other diseases (Dancis, 1972; Colón, 1999). The advent of pediatrics brought scientific methods to the study of childhood illnesses, but there was still little in the formulary to overcome them. The germ theory was embraced enthusiastically leading to improved standards of cleanliness and the institution of infection control methods (Brenneman, 1931; Bakwin, 1941; Dancis, 1972). However, immunizations were not readily available to children until the outbreak of World War II, and antibiotics were not used in civilian populations in the United States until after that war.

When children became sick from infectious processes, the medical response was an intensification of infection control measures: strict isolation or quarantine, and, in the case of babies, infrequent handling and meticulously aseptic surroundings (Brenneman, 1931). Medical approaches had, however, been dramatically unsuccessful in the care of infants in hospitals and foundling homes. These babies frequently failed to gain weight or to reach normal developmental milestones. They were unusually susceptible to infections. Death rates were high. In a report given before the American Pediatric Society in 1915, H. D. Chapin, a prominent pediatrician and social activist, presented his findings that infant mortality rates in ten urban institutions ranged from thirty-one to seventy-five percent (Spitz, 1945).

"Hospitalism"

René Spitz popularized the term "hospitalism," as a description of this condition of severe physical and developmental decline (1945). Something in the environment was lethal, to be sure, but he didn't think it was primarily pathogens. His solution was the antithesis of the accepted hospital practice of scrupulous asepsis, and this interface of medical and psychological approaches to health and illness fostered the opening of pediatrics to the idea that social and environmental factors, as well as medical management, influence a child's response to treatment.

Spitz made careful observational studies of infants in a foundling home in order to test his hypothesis that it was precisely the absence of mothering and environmental stimulation that led to this alarming susceptibility to disease, physical wasting, and emotional withdrawal. Spitz's studies of the developmental decline in infants raised in even the most well meaning and hygienic foundling home, as compared with those raised in families or in an institution where their prisoner mothers could be with them every day, have been meticulously recorded on film (Spitz, 1947). Pictures of infants in the foundling home must surely be some of the most haunting film footage in the entire library of child studies. The babies raised in the foundling hospital were emaciated, listless, unsmiling, scarcely able to move. Pictures like these are seen these days only where there is social devastation.

Spitz's studies were carried out on babies institutionalized for conditions "other than sickness" (Spitz, 1945). Harry Bakwin, a pediatrician in hospital practice working with sick children, shared Spitz's bias toward humanizing care and was to initiate unlimited parental visits to infants. He also encouraged house staff to develop friendly relationships with the children they treated. The term "T.L.C." (tender loving care) was coined to characterize this relationship (Dancis, 1972).

According to Bakwin (1941), hospitalism "is looked on as a result of repeated infections" (p. 30). Strict infection control policies were instituted which isolated infants from human contact and sensory stimulation.

To lessen the danger of cross infections, the large open ward of the past has been replaced by small, cubicled rooms in which masked, hooded and scrubbed nurses and physicians move about cautiously so as not to stir up bacteria. Visiting parents are strictly excluded, and the infants receive a minimum of handling by the staff. Within recent years attempts at isolation have been intensified, and a short time ago there was devised a box equipped with inlet and outlet valves and sleeve arrangements for the attendants. The infant is placed in this box and can be taken care of almost untouched by human hands. (p. 31)

Bakwin questioned whether these precautions might not be harmful to the child.

Infants confined in hospitals present a fairly well defined clinical picture. A striking feature is their failure to gain properly, despite the ingestion of diets which in the home are entirely adequate for growth. Infants in hospitals sleep less than infants who are at home, and they rarely smile or babble spontaneously. They are listless, apathetic and look unhappy. The appetite is indifferent, and food is accepted without enthusiasm. . . . Infections of the respiratory tract which last only a day or two in a home often persist for months in a hospital. Return home results in defervescence within a few days and a prompt and striking gain in weight. (p. 31)

A satisfactory medical solution never was found for the foundling hospitals. Most were ultimately shut down, and homeless infants were raised in the community by foster families, a solution initially suggested by Chapin (Dancis, 1972). During the struggle to resolve the issues of infant deaths in institutions, however, a great deal was discovered about the needs of infants and, by inference, of all children, for special attention to environmental factors both personal and spatial, in their psychosocial development.

With the exception of infant wards like Bakwin's at Bellevue, which permitted mothers to tend to their children, early twentieth century hospitals were more receptive to the inclusion of volunteers and "play ladies" who could function as "substitute mommies and daddies" than they were to the inclusion of real parents. There were, of course, reasons other than hospital rules that precluded or limited parental visiting, but by many accounts hospitals found parents a nuisance: disruptive of routines and upsetting to children, as well as sources of disease. Even D. W. Winnicott (1964), the champion of mothering on every other count, drew the line at the hospital door. He saw visits as compromising medical care by the practice of parents giving children foods "completely upsetting the investigation on which future treatment is to be based" (p. 222). He was concerned that visiting would undermine the selfless giving of the nurse (sister) who gives all her care and attention to the child only to be usurped by the parent during visiting hour. And there is always a lot of crying when parents come and sad leave-taking when they go.

It would not be so bad if the mothers were contented to go in and see their children for a few minutes and then go out again; but mothers do not feel like this, naturally. As will be expected, they go into the ward and use the whole time that is allowed. Some seem to be almost 'making love' to their child; they bring presents of all kinds, and especially food, and they demand affectionate response; and then they take quite a long time going, standing waving at the door till the child is absolutely exhausted by the effort of saying good-bye. And the mothers are quite liable to go to the Sister on the way out and say something about the child's not being warmly enough clad or not having enough to eat for dinner or something like that. (Winnicott, 1964, p. 223)

Hospitals would look elsewhere, to something less threatening to the hospital system than parents, for help in easing the distress of children.

An Early Play Program

Like a stranger in a foreign land who suddenly hears his own language, the child reaches out to play as an assurance of friendliness in a bewildering situation. (Smith, 1937)

At about the same time that Spitz was carrying out his studies and Bakwin was describing the psychosocial shortcomings of pediatric wards, the first hospital play programs were inaugurated. Although archival material on the origins and early history of child life programs has only recently been accumulated and is still being collected, we have a report on the first years, 1932-1937, of the development of a play program at Children's Memorial Hospital in Chicago written by Anne Smith. Smith does not identify her relationship to the program she describes, but her knowledge of the details of its origins, organization, development and scope might fairly lead one to believe her to be its creator. This was a remarkably vigorous program in which play leaders were asked to respond to the distress of children admitted in large groups for tonsillectomies and to individual children undergoing major surgeries; to provide daily activities for children on the wards, many of them long term patients; to help with parent visiting by setting up toy displays to educate parents on what is suitable to bring to their children; and to set up a program for outpatients receiving bronchoscopies (Smith, 1937).

In addition to their work with patients and parents the director and play leaders taught play techniques to student nurses and nurses on the Children's Memorial staff.

University students and volunteers often joined these classes about play in the hospital and benefited from the clinical supervision of their work with children. To further the normalization of the hospital environment, the play director facilitated the development of a school program for kindergarten and early elementary grades; built and staffed a library; and invited special volunteers to visit with nature projects, handicraft projects and entertainments.

The program was put together by the play director on the basis of clearly identified needs, starting with the most obvious: pandemonium on the days when groups of about fifteen children ages two to twelve were admitted for tonsillectomies. Smith described this scene, noting that "Often their crying and screaming could be heard all down the halls. In their terror, some bit and kicked" (p. 3). The play director engaged these children in simple games, stories and songs immediately after they were admitted and again the next day as they waited to be taken to the operating room, one by one. Because children were said to go easily under anesthesia and to wake up smoothly, the play program was considered a success. As part of their training in play, nurses ran these groups once their efficacy was established.

Group play was highly valued by the play leaders. They saw that children were reassured by the company of each other. Play without equipment was also highly valued, possibly because toys were hard to come by and, in certain of these situations, encumbering. Play was not dependent on toys. Nurses were taught to use play while doing their usual routines and treatments with children. Again, simple finger games, songs, guessing games and stories were planned to engage the child all day long.

Much emphasis was placed on the program's teaching efforts. The entire nursing staff, students and volunteers were all made comfortable with using play as a primary means of communicating good will. The importance of play in the child's daily life was strongly endorsed by Smith, who wrote, "Like a stranger in a foreign land who suddenly hears his own language, the child reaches out to play as an assurance of friendliness in a bewildering situation" (p. 2).

There were no set protocols for this work. Group play was the choice for children newly admitted for surgery and during the waiting time before surgery. Individual projects worked well for some long-term patients. From an eclectic repertoire of activities play leaders could experiment until they found the ones best suited to the task at hand. According to Smith, children were offered opportunities to play in order to prevent their being returned home "marked and scarred psychologically, retarded mentally, or rendered social misfits because of the neglect of stimulating interests and happy co-operation with other children" (p. 9). This sentiment echoes that of the psychoanalytically oriented pediatricians describing the fate of infants who survived long periods of institutional care. As Spitz (1945) states in the opening comments of his article on hospitalism, ". . . physicians and administrators . . . discovered that institutionalized children practically without exception developed subsequent psychiatric disturbances and became asocial, delinquent, feeble-minded, psychotic, or problem children" (p. 54).

Developmental Psychology

Mid-twentieth century concern for the psychological responses of children exposed to war, separation from parents, bodily illness, and confinement in hospital, led to investigations and theoretical constructs about the emotional life of children (Bowlby, 1952; Freud, A., 1952; Prugh, Staub, Kirschbaum, & Lenihan, 1953). These theories of relationships, perceptions of reality, behaviors, and feelings and how these change over a child's lifetime are of fundamental interest to child life studies.

Observations of his own children's infant activities led to Jean Piaget's elegant theory of the development of intelligence (Piaget & Inhelder, 1969). Piaget's work, together with Erikson's interpretations of psychosocial development, has given us a picture of what and how infants, children and adolescents think and feel. The role of the senses in first learning, the limits of cognition at various ages, the importance of play as an interpretive and problem solving activity have illuminated and made accessible to students of development the physical, mental and emotional lives of children that could only be guessed at in earlier times.

The major themes have been laid down for us by Erikson and Piaget. Erikson (1963) took the ancient "ages of man" model to construct an epigenetic theory of psychosocial development from birth to death. Far from the disinterest of the ancients in the first seven years of life, this period was the most interesting to those clinicians and scholars who were drawn to psychoanalytic interpretations of childhood. Infants and toddlers were especially interesting.

The root meaning of the word *infant* is voiceless, speechless. For much of western history the child was considered virtually speechless until the age of seven. The following is from a medieval manuscript describing the ages of man.

> The first age is childhood when the teeth are planted, and this age begins when the child is born and lasts until seven, and in this age that which is born is called an infant, which is as good as saying not talking, because in this age it cannot talk well or form its words perfectly, for its teeth are not yet well arranged or firmly implanted.

. . . After infancy comes the second age . . . and this age lasts until fourteen. (Aries, 1965, p. 21)

We might say that the imperfect speech described here is a metaphor for the persistence of imaginative thought in the speech of young children which to this day confounds adults whose mode of thinking is fully rational. It is at points of dissonance like this that child life becomes the interpreter of the medical system to the child and of the child to his medical caregivers.

Piaget has taught us to listen to children in a new way, to observe their language in play and to tease out the internal logic of their imaginative constructs. We can then see with utmost seriousness and sympathy how children gradually develop the capacity to separate fantasy from reality, to see something from the point of view of another, to manipulate symbols instead of real objects, to distinguish between proximity and causality, to learn that something hidden may not be gone forever.

John Bowlby, James and Joan Robertson

John Bowlby began his work on attachment and separation issues in the early 1950s. Bowlby was interested in the theoretical aspects of the observed reactions of young children to brief separations from their mothers or mother surrogates. These observations provided some of the first clinical evidence for the considerable emotional complexity of infants and toddlers. His work, drawing upon ethological studies as well as clinical research in human bonds, led to his conclusion that human attachment, most commonly seen in mother-infant bonds, but also prevalent throughout the life span, constituted a primary and singular component of human life independent of

other needs or gratifications. This is a fundamental part of the human condition and, as we have seen in the foundling hospital stories, is necessary for life. This innate need for social intimacy has been extraordinarily important to the understanding of human nature. Interruptions in love relationships, particularly the early ones, pose significant challenges to healthy psychological development (Bowlby, 1982).

A close associate of Bowlby's in his early years of research was James Robertson. Robertson and his wife, Joan, filmed children's responses to brief separations from parents under a variety of circumstances. Of special interest to child life studies is the film, *A Two-Year-Old Goes to the Hospital* (1953). A child is hospitalized for several days for a hernia operation. Her parents can make only a few visits, and she expresses the full range of feelings and behaviors associated with separation and the fear of abandonment: protest, despair, detachment. We do not see in this child the marasmic faces of the foundlings, but traces of their distress flicker across the face of this otherwise vivacious toddler. To add the stresses of separation to the stresses inherent in hospitalization is to place a great emotional burden on a very small child. These studies led to the suggestion that elective hospitalizations be postponed until after the age of three years.

THE CHILD LIFE MOVEMENT

Emma Plank: Child Life Speaks Out

In 1962, Emma Plank's publication, *Working with Children in Hospitals*, described the work of the Child Life and Education Department at Cleveland Metropolitan Hospital. She called her staff "child-care workers" and vividly describes the substance of their clinical tasks in the hospital. There is a resistance to generalization in this text. Plank depends on the anecdote to show what the child-care worker can do. One child with no family ties needs an especially close and trusting relationship; a gang of small boys, far from needing the permissive atmosphere usually desired on the ward, are gotten firmly in hand; a child's misunderstanding is untangled; a four-year-old is prepared for amputation of her leg.

She is careful to note the individual differences of children's responses to illness and hospitalization and to stress initial and ongoing assessments of these responses. It is through knowing the child and developing a carefully thought out and continually reviewed plan of care that child-care work will succeed.

There are some general principles here that need to be applied in an individual manner. For very young children, the fear of abandonment is more alarming than the illness itself or its treatment. Plank applauds hospitals which provide rooming in for mothers with very small children. She also applauds the advance of more liberal visiting hours and notes the comforting attention staff members give to children who cry when the time is up. The maintenance of trust in relationships is reinforced by truth-telling, no matter how difficult that may be. Parents are not to sneak away; children are not to be deceived about the possibility of pain or even loss.

The child's day should be as normal as possible with opportunities for play and schooling away from medical interventions. The child's day has a structure and plan, which is basic to his sense of being in a reasonable world even when the day's plan includes going to x-ray or surgery. To illustrate the importance of these arrangements to a child's well-being, Plank (1962) says the following:

It is nice to have entertainments during holidays or at regular intervals, such as a week-

ly movie or puppet plays, given by a volunteer service. But a healthy child's day is not built around entertainment, and a sick child's should be even less. Children do not need diversion to get well, but rather opportunities to participate with all available emotional and intellectual energy in daily living. (p. 73)

Plank continues by stating the goals of a child life and education program:

1. To provide a setting for children of all ages where they can find play and activities that interest and absorb them, counteract their loneliness and anxiety, and help to turn the passivity of the patient into the activity of the growing child.
2. To give children a chance to interact with others away from their cubicle, to form relationships to adults as well as to other children, to help them work through the basic fears inherent in illness and hospitalization, to reassure them about or prepare them for procedures and surgery.
3. To help school-age children to continue with some of their schoolwork while hospitalized.
4. To arrange specific opportunities for play under direction of a skilled worker where fantasies or traumatic experience in relation to hospitalization can be played out and worked through.
5. To provide an area where parents can visit and play with their child as part of an ongoing program. At the time when parents have to leave, the child finds himself with others and can be more easily reassured.
6. To help children at mealtimes to accept hospital food or limiting diets, by providing food groupings at mealtimes with a chance for conversation and informality. (p. 73)

Plank speaks of the common experiences and special problems that need to be assessed and planned for in each hospital admission by the "staff." She does not mean by this the child life and education staff alone but the whole of pediatrics. She is convinced that the child's needs will be served only when there is a coordinated effort and ease of communication among all professionals working with children. The work of the person on the child-care side of the interface between normalization and medical treatment must be included in the total care of the child.

What's in a Name?

We will speak throughout this document of "child life" as the designated name of the professional service and its practitioners whose goals have been to help children engage and subdue fears, misconceptions, anger and profound sadness that hospital experiences provoke, to protect and enhance their developmental integrity, and, whenever possible, use the experiences of illness and hospitalization to build strengths rather than compromise them. But as Rubin (1992) pointed out, the eclectic nature of the staff and programs, made it hard to find a name inclusive enough to take into account all that child life does. Recreation therapy was too narrow and misleading, so was teacher, so was play lady, although that's what the children often called us.

What the programs and the people who staffed them were called both reflected and determined what people thought of them. For the child the program and its people would always be play providers, sources of pleasure and safety. This is no mean thing. D.W. Winnicott (1964), pediatrician and child analyst, was to go so far as to say, "Play is the continuous evidence of creativity, which means aliveness" (p.144). The child

analysts and psychologists understood play to be both the child's language and means of learning about and interpreting the world. Cut off from play, the young child is lost in an unintelligible environment. But the word "play" is a two-edged sword, appealing to children and people knowledgeable about the intellectual and psychological development of children, but easily denigrated by administrators on tight budgets and medical staff on tight schedules.

Environments

When Doctor F. C. Robbins hired Emma Plank to organize the Child Life and Education Department at Cleveland Metropolitan Hospital, one of his goals was to change the drab, stark spaces in which the children stayed. The huge wards with only utilitarian furnishings provided an efficient environment, but hardly an appealing one. Entrusted with improving the hospital environment for children, Plank carved playrooms out of the available space where children could engage in meaningful activities away from medical care. Here the task of living was fully engaged.

In its 1960 report and recommendations for the care of hospitalized children, the American Academy of Pediatrics stated that all pediatric units should have a playroom stocked with appropriate supplies of toys, games, books. The playroom should be placed near the nurses' station for ease of supervision or, if that wasn't feasible, there should be an effort made to recruit volunteers to supervise the playroom.

We have seen that in the early play program at Children's Memorial Hospital, 1932-1937, play without equipment and play in any setting where the children could be gathered seemed to be the norm. There is no mention of a special room for play. This recommendation for space and supplies indicates an acknowledgement by the Academy of the importance of play in the daily lives of children in the hospital.

It takes, however, both space and equipment and a staff whose full attention can be invested in using the playroom to help children cope effectively with the hospital experience. The state of playrooms that have not been managed by child life has often been a sorry story. Volunteers could seldom take on the full-time responsibility of supervising a playroom. Without supervision, toys were broken or lost. Children felt neither safe nor fulfilled in what could often be a state of chaos, without boundaries or rules. Unsupervised playrooms, some with a dirty doll or two for decoration, stopped being used altogether by children and parents and were sometimes taken over by staff as a place to have lunch or take a break.

As child life matured it assumed responsibility for playrooms and equipment, and in 1985, the Academy, in its chapter on child life, acknowledged playroom management as one of the tasks of child life. A well-stocked and well-managed playroom is far more than a place to play. It offers sanctuary, a safe place away from hospital routines and treatments. It's a safe place to just hang out and fool around or talk it over or play it out.

In the 1980s great emphasis was placed on making the entire pediatric unit feel like a safe and friendly place. Walls were brightened, pictures were hung, the stark, white uniform was no longer required of nurses, treatment rooms were hung with mobiles and instruments were made less conspicuous.

In some institutions quite elaborate efforts were made to bring the huge scale of the hospital down to human size, to child size. Many of these environments were well designed to make children feel both comfortable and pleasurably stimulated. But adults often mistakenly assume that they know what children like and will, for instance, apply liberal doses of cartoon characters to corridor walls and the windows of nurses' stations. Olds (1986), designer of children's hospital environments, warns that primary colors can become strident if overused in the assumption that "that's what children like."

Child Life and the Founding of ACCH

Child life was formative in the creation of the multidisciplinary organization ultimately known as the Association for the Care of Children's Health (ACCH) whose members where dedicated to promoting and providing developmentally based psychosocial care to sick children. ACCH throughout its history has fostered a veritable explosion of services for children and families in healthcare settings. Principle among these are support for child life programs and the development of family centered care programs.

In 1965 a group of forty professionals working in play and education programs in twenty-three hospitals scattered throughout the United States and Canada gathered in Boston to discuss "Patient Recreation in Pediatric Settings" (Brooks,1975). Although this title would suggest a modest agenda, these participants were in fact inaugurating a revolution in pediatric healthcare. Emma Plank (1962), speaking of her own program at Cleveland Metropolitan General hospital stated, "We asked ourselves how we can best serve the child who is about to enter the hospital; what we can do for him when he is there; and how to help him to return to normal living" (p. 2). This would serve well as the definition of the work we still strive to do.

By the end of this first conference there was a consensus concerning the need to create an organization that would provide a forum for the discussion of experiences and problems in their own program areas and that would promote appropriate attention to the growth and developmental needs of hospitalized children. Representatives from six participating hospitals were chosen as founders, and an interim committee was chosen to study the establishment of a permanent organization and to plan a conference for the following year (Brooks, 1975).

Because their numbers were small and because, although essential to the well-being of children, their work was not central to the mission of medical care, the founders were persuaded that their hope of achieving their goals could best be served by inviting the participation of other pediatric professionals.

At the second conference in 1966 representatives from pediatrics, surgery, nursing and social work joined in the discussions of psychosocial issues and formed, with the original group of recreation, play and education specialists, an association briefly named The Association for the Well-Being of Hospitalized Children and Their Families. Although this first name has the virtue of being an almost perfect description of the organization's purpose, it was a mouthful. After two other failed attempts at naming, the organization became the Association for the Care of Children in Hospitals (ACCH)-- until its mission expanded and it became the Association for the Care of Children's Health (also ACCH).

By the time of the third conference, in Philadelphia, more potential participants applied than could be accommodated. The hard work of the founders and their multidisciplinary colleagues had provided the groundwork for a functional organization, and 1967 saw officers and a board of directors elected, by-laws accepted, and standing committees formed. ACCH membership increased dramatically, and conference sites moved across the continent from their east coast origins to the Midwest and on to record-breaking attendance in San Francisco

in 1970. In 1972, the meetings were held in Canada for the first bilingual conference (Brooks, 1975).

In 1975 ACCH drew members from forty-five states and the District of Columbia, all ten Canadian provinces, and several foreign countries. Membership had grown from 40 in 1965 to 1,200 in 1975. The number of child life programs also increased dramatically during this ten year period from 10 in 1950 to 170 in 1975 (ACCH, 1984).

ACCH as Identity and Context for Child Life

The richly multidisciplinary environment of ACCH, which included nurses, psychologists, social workers, physicians, and, in 1978, parents, was an excellent medium for the work of self-definition for child life. Child life specialists always formed a large percentage of the ACCH membership and consistently held leadership positions in the organization until it ceased operations in 1999.

The rapid growth of ACCH in the sixties and seventies reflected a corresponding growth in child life programs. Because child life practice was the clearest embodiment of the goals of ACCH at this time, its quarterly journal Children's Health Care, annual conference presentations, and local membership chapters were filled with contributions from the ranks of child life professionals. ACCH provided a forum and a publishing house for child life initiatives, and child life benefited from the organization's linkages to the Society of Pediatric Psychology, the Academy of Child Psychiatry (now the American Academy of Child and Adolescent Psychiatry, AACAP), and the American Academy of Pediatrics (AAP). Child life leaders represented ACCH on the Academy of Pediatrics' Hospital Care Committee.

The Child Life Position Statement, 1979

During the 1970s child life began in earnest to develop the philosophical, theoretical and ethical ground of its work, to define the necessary skills and knowledge of its practitioners and to determine educational requirements for practice. In 1979, *The Child Life Position Statement* was drafted and ratified by ACCH. This had been preceded by more than a decade of discussion and debate resulting in the consolidation of the many aspects of child life work into a single statement and the many tasks of child life workers into a many-faceted but single job description.

This position statement was a hard won consensus that rested securely on child life's past and became the cornerstone of all future conceptual developments. It contained a rationale for child life programs based on the observed emotional damage to children caused by stress factors, interruptions of development, regression and the loss of self-esteem. Essential components of child life programs were listed as abundant play opportunities for self-expression, mastery and understanding of medical experiences; familiarization with the hospital milieu; maintaining family relationships and providing empathic support to parents; the provision of essential life experiences; and providing opportunities to retain self-esteem and appropriate independence. It was believed that, with appropriate support, a child's hospital experience might even be a positive one, providing an opportunity for enhanced development.

The *Position Statement* also included staffing standards and job descriptions for child life personnel. To be a child life specialist required a bachelor's degree, supervised experience in a healthcare setting and competencies in growth and development, family dynamics, play and activities, interpersonal communication, developmental observation and assessment, the learning process, group process, behavior management, the reactions of children to hospitalization, to illnesses and to medical terminology, supervisory skills (ACCH, 1979).

The child life program should be autonomous, have a budget for staff and supplies, be given adequate space for activities and storage, and assume responsibility for training and supervising volunteers in its service. Child life staff should be on an equal footing with other clinical team members.

Child Life Speaks for Itself: The Child Life Council

During the sixties and seventies the child life membership met as a study section at ACCH annual meetings to talk among themselves about their mission, identity, policies, and practices. Times allotted for these discussions were short and sometimes in conflict with other study sections that members were interested in attending. Frustration ran high. There was just too much to do at the one time in the year when everyone could get together.

As in the first years of ACCH, child life brought together an interdisciplinary task force to consider the feasibility of establishing a Child Life Council under the auspices of ACCH. Child life felt the need to return to one of its original goals in calling its first meeting in 1965: to provide a forum for the discussion of experiences and problems in their own program areas.

In 1980, Gene Stanford, a leader in the field of child life, challenged the fledgling organization to enter adulthood by achieving three things: a clearly defined role, clearly defined qualifications, and control of who can enter the profession. The Child Life Council was established in 1982 to take on these and other professional issues. At its first meeting the Council elected officers, approved by-laws and held two days of meetings prior to the ACCH annual conference. In order to be eligible for Council membership, child life professionals were required to maintain their membership in ACCH. As an early and highly symbolic act of independence, the Child Life Council revised and reissued the *Child Life Position Statement* under its own imprimatur in 1983.

Child life continued to benefit from the rich mix of disciplines and parents that comprised ACCH, and it was ACCH that secured and administered the grant that made child life's major research project possible. Over time, however, as Council membership increased and the demands of professionalization intensified, the focus on child life issues began to overshadow interest in interdisciplinary issues. In 1992 the Child Life Council (CLC) became incorporated as a free-standing organization. Membership in ACCH was now an option rather than a requirement for Council members.

Academic Programs

As the profession emerged, leaders in the field called for educational programs designed specifically to train child life practitioners. Course offerings related to working with hospitalized children are found in the Wheelock College Catalog in the 1960s. Specific programs of study (or majors) in child life are documented as being formally established in the 1970s. Among the first colleges and universities to offer child life programs were: Wheelock College, Boston, MA, established 1972; Mills College, Oakland, CA, established 1977; and Utica College of Syracuse University, NY, established 1978. Several other academic settings offering formalized training programs were established throughout the 1970s and 1980s.

By the late 1980s the profession still lacked a unified standard of preparation for entrance into the field.

In order to achieve high quality and maximum effectiveness in the profession, standards for the profession were developed over a period of time from 1987 to 1992. *The Standards for Academic and Clinical Preparation Programs in Child Life* was written and approved by the Child Life Council in 1992. The standards were revised in 2001 in order to reflect the growth of the profession and its practitioners. The standards serve as a guide for anyone wishing to pursue academic or clinical training in child life.

It is not the intent for the standards to establish a rigid formula. The standards include curriculum recommendations for academic programs. The child life profession continues to draw practitioners from a variety of educational backgrounds. The Child Life Council currently lists 32 academic programs that offer coursework in child life (S. Clay-Robison, personal communication, August 13, 2003). Some of these programs offer comprehensive child life majors (coursework and integrated internships) and some offer a course on the hospitalized child within another major (e.g., child development, child & family studies, or child psychology).

CHILD LIFE COMES OF AGE

Defining the Tasks

CLC continued work begun in the seventies on creating a core curriculum for academic programs, formulating a theoretical and philosophic base, articulating a code of ethics, defining professional competence, describing a method of program evaluation, and dealing with issues of membership, by-laws, and meeting the standards of regulatory bodies. Much of the material in the *Official Documents of the Child Life Council* published in 1994 was developed in the eighties. These documents *(Standards for Academic and Clinical Preparation Programs in Child Life, Standards for Clinical Practice, Child Life Competencies, Code of Ethical Responsibilities, and Child Life Philosophic Base)* stand as the self-proclaimed authority for holding child life accountable for its actions.

The annual conference agenda expanded to make room for presentations on program development, clinical practice and administrative issues such as documentation in the medical record and data collection. Even as it secured its sense of self, the profession was changing. The conference business meetings were wonderfully exciting. The membership engaged in outspoken and energized discussions of such things as staff/patient ratios, how to conduct program reviews, whether and how to pursue certification, how to continue to welcome people from diverse academic and professional backgrounds into the ranks of child life practitioners.

A collection of articles entitled, *Child Life: An Overview*, published by ACCH in 1986 was both a recapitulation of accomplishments in the second decade of child life's existence and a spur to consolidate and move on. Thompson and Stanford's *Child Life in Hospitals* (1981), which put flesh on the bones of the *Position Statement*, and the first edition of *Guidelines for the Development of Child Life Programs* (1984), which articulated the fundamentals of establishing programs were benchmarks in standardizing practice in a rapidly expanding profession. Although these texts were descriptive rather than prescriptive they provided vivid pictures of best practice in the living, breathing corridors of real hospitals. They would prove invaluable guides to establishing standards.

Descriptive literature was voluminous in this period and included books on such topics as emotional care, parenting in the hospi-tal, techniques in medical preparation, hospital play, and chronicity. Hospital-based child life programs produced monographs on programming for each developmental stage, on family issues, on outpatient, intensive care, and isolation areas. And as it had from its inception the ACCH journal, *Children's Health Care*, provided a lively forum of ideas.

Credibility

Program Review Guidelines: Self-study and Peer Review

The CLC piloted a set of questions in outline form called the *Program Review Guidelines* in the U.S and Canada in 1985 and published the document in 1987. The process of self-study and peer review which it inaugurated was an important stepping stone toward reaching program standardization. The *Guidelines* were inclusive of a broad spectrum of program elements and helped participants in the self-study determine which of these possible elements were included in their programs and which they would hope to include as their programs developed.

In addition to this self-study, CLC offered hospitals the opportunity to have their child life programs reviewed by experienced child life professionals who could give an outside opinion on strengths and opportunities for growth. This review provided an opportunity for child life to show the hospital leadership what they were doing and what could still be done for children and families.

Credentialing

Certification of child life specialists was highly desired by the Child Life Council membership. The lack of appropriate education and experience could compromise the work of even the most well-meaning practitioner. The establishment of competencies, requirements for completion of a basic curriculum in child studies, and development of properly supervised internships were all geared to assuring that children and families would be well served by the profession.

In 1986 a credentialing tool was approved, and the Child Life Certifying Commission was established to examine the credentials of aspirants to the profession. This was inevitably a cumbersome, time-consuming and somewhat subjective process. In 1998, the credentialing process changed to certification by examination. Successful candidates certified by either method may use the initials, CCLS, (certified child life specialist) in addition to their academic degree as part of their professional designation. However, by 2004 everyone was required to be certified by examination.

Research: The Phoenix Project

The credibility of any practice depends on its demonstrated efficacy. Although there have been innumerable accolades of the good child life does for children and families, to survive in the scientific marketplace of ideas requires more than anecdotal acclaim. Richard Thompson's twenty-year review of the research literature on hospitalized children has both bolstered the idea that psychosocial services were necessary to children in hospitals and shown up the paucity of well-designed studies in this area (Thompson, 1985).

A research project under the auspices of ACCH with John Wolfer, a psychologist, as Principal Investigator was initiated in 1983 to examine the efficacy of child life interventions in reducing stress and accelerating healing. This project was carried out at the newly opened Phoenix Children's Hospital. Control data were collected from children

and families before the child life team began its work. Subsequently, children were provided with a range of child life services, and their responses were compared with those of children hospitalized during the control period. The research focused on "helping children understand and master potentially upsetting health care experiences" (Wolfer, Gaynard, Goldberger, Laidley, & Thompson, 1988). On most measures the children receiving child life interventions responded more favorably than did children who did not have access to child life.

The project also produced a teaching tool for child life staff and students and all audiences interested in children's healthcare. *Psychosocial Care of Children in Hospitals: A Clinical Practice Manual* (Gaynard, Wolfer, Goldberger, Thompson, Redburn, & Laidley, 1990) describes the practices and teaching tools used with children by the researchers.

A Place at the Table

Child life was also making contributions to and getting affirmation from outside organizations. The Joint Commission on the Accreditation of Healthcare Organizations invited the Council to contribute to its developing standards for the psychosocial care of pediatric patients. Members of the Child Life Council were appointed to attend Joint Commission meetings and to represent ACCH as a liaison member of the American Academy of Pediatrics Committee on Hospital Care. This Committee's 1985 recommendations include an entire chapter on child life and describe it as an essential component in the comprehensive care of sick children in pediatric units. The Canadian Pediatrics Society passed a resolution in 1978 recommending that "all hospitals that have pediatric units have organized facilities for play available under the direction of a child life worker for both inpatient and outpatient facilities." And in 1985 the American Academy of Pediatrics commented in its journal, *Pediatrics*, that child life is "one of the most progressive, useful and humane programs to be initiated in recent years" (p. 467).

CHILD LIFE IN THE LONG RUN

The Changing Nature of Children's Healthcare

The AAP Committee on Hospital Care in its 1994 report noted dramatic shifts in the nature of children's healthcare and in healthcare financing over the previous twenty years. Fundamental changes in hospital reimbursement practices by both federal agencies and private insurers brought about significant decreases in hospital funding. At the same time hospital costs were rising, paying for medical and surgical advances that greatly reduce morbidity and mortality. Advances in radiology, nuclear medicine, chemotherapy, dialysis, surgery and many other technologies and pharmaceuticals have produced long remissions and cures for diseases and defects once considered hopeless. These advances are as profound as were the immunizations and antibiotics of a previous generation.

In hospital practice the length of a patient's stay has been shortened, inpatient admissions present more complex and severe medical problems, more beds are filled by chronically ill children hospitalized for episodic treatments, and more surgeries and procedures involving increasingly advanced technologies are done in special outpatient areas.

The kinds of health issues confronting pediatrics today–chronic diseases, congenital and neonatal anomalies, multiple trauma, mental and developmental problems–comprise what is called the *new morbidity*. Success in treating many of the children suffering from these morbidities depends on complex technology and frequent medical interventions. Family life becomes medicalized. The lives of children whose afflictions are not amenable to cure need support and palliation to sustain them through their every day lives. The challenges to families living with the new morbidly are challenges to child life professionals as well.

Parents and Families

The inclusion of parents in the hospital care of their children has been incremental and hard won, with pockets of resistance all along the way. Even when parents were allowed to visit on a fairly open basis, they often felt as dislocated as their children, not knowing what was permitted and what was not. But gradually parents began to take ownership of their rights to be with their children and to be the primary decision makers in their children's care. Indeed the term "visitor" has become virtually obsolete when discussing the presence of parents in the hospital.

In 1978 ACCH opened its membership to parents of sick children. By the 1990s parents were beginning to assume leadership roles in ACCH and were joining as full partners in efforts to change healthcare policies and practices to include consideration of how life is really lived by families with a child with multiple healthcare requirements.

Child life has always made common cause with parents, advocating for extended visiting and overnight sleeping accommodations in the early days, and working with parents and siblings who are living with the new morbidity, whose daughter or brother will live their lives in the context of healthcare. Parents as members of advisory boards and as teachers of medical personnel have raised the consciousness of the medical community to the complex dimensions of raising a chronically ill child at home and at school, as well as in the hospital.

In 1992 ACCH published a set of comprehensive guidelines for the hospital care of children and their families (Johnson, Jeppson, & Redburn, 1992). It undertook to articulate the hospitals' responsibilities in providing psychosocial care for both children and families and is a landmark in the development of family centered care. Initiatives in family centered care continue unabated to enable families to be full participants in their sick child's care and to enable the healthcare system to understand and respond to needs for change in the delivery of that care.

The Changing Role of Child Life in Healthcare

Child life specialists increasingly staff outpatient areas, emergency rooms, and day surgery programs. In large institutions where there are neonatal and pediatric intensive care units, transplant units and special treatment units such as dialysis and burn centers, child life is present. Outreach efforts are addressed to children on home care protocols, in hospice programs, in community-based healthcare centers, in programs addressing school re-entry, and in private practice. Wherever child life is practiced, however, its essential core of service remains the same. As the American Academy of Pediatrics states in its report and recommendations from the Hospital Care Committee (2000), there are three essential responsibilities that child life specialists must undertake:

(1) providing play experiences; (2) presenting developmentally appropriate information about events and procedures; and (3) establishing therapeutic relationships with children and parents to support family

involvement in each child's care. . . . Child Life Programs have become a standard in large pediatric settings and should not be withheld regardless of reimbursement. (p. 1156)

The tasks of meeting the non-medical needs of sick children and their families in the context of the new morbidity may seem overwhelming to the child life specialist whether working in the hospital or the community. It may be helpful to keep firmly in mind the three child life responsibilities stated above. These are our priorities.

Vision to Action

In 1996 a group of child life administrators, clinicians and educators elected from the CLC membership met to grapple with issues of what the future might hold for child life specialists. This process was called *Vision to Action* and the proceedings were shared with the general membership at the Child Life Conference when it was next convened. Conference members were invited to continue the discussion at this meeting. Given the continuing crisis in healthcare costs and the shortened length of in-hospital stays, what was the conventionally trained child life specialist to do?

Child life specialists have adapted in-hospital practice to a broad range of patients and settings (e.g., chronically ill children in multiple settings; children treated at home and at school; children in hospital and community clinics; in special camps, in hospice and in private practice settings). Because of child life's demonstrated adaptability within healthcare, it seemed reasonable that the education, experience and training of child life specialists enabled them to mitigate the distress of children in a number of situations beyond healthcare. What about shelters for homeless families? What about family court?

What about children traumatized by terrorist activity or its threat?

In the spring of 1997, Mission, Vision and Values statements were published in the Child Life Council newsletter (Fenn, 1997). The *Values Statement* basically reaffirms the values child life has endorsed from its inception: an understanding of and respect for infants, children, youth and families, their individuality and complexity, their diversity and community; an understanding of the need for play as an essential part of childhood, as a healing modality in itself and as a method of child life practice; an understanding of the importance of therapeutic relationships; an understanding of communication as a task of interpretation of the child and family to the hospital and the hospital to the child and family; an appreciation of the theoretical foundations of practice, of professional collaboration, of professional standards of practice, of research.

The *Mission Statement* affirms the profession's intent to provide meaningful interventions in traumatic situations involving children and their families which will mitigate the impact of the trauma and preserve basic developmental pathways and family support systems. The Vision Statement reinforces and expands the Mission Statement. "The philosophy and practice of child life will be applicable to any healthcare setting and transferable to other environments or situations in which the potential for infants, children and youth to cope, learn and master is placed at risk" (p. 1).

At its annual conference in the late spring of 2002, the Child Life Council celebrated its twentieth anniversary. Of its 2,400 members, 720 attended the conference to exchange information, to teach and to learn, to sustain and support each other in the professional life we have chosen. Instead of facing diminished opportunities to give service as the number of inpatient pediatric beds declines, the child life profession has undertaken the challenge to serve the growing number of children and families in other settings who need support and empowerment. In our demonstrated capacity to maintain traditional programs and establish new ones, in our resilience and creativity in overcoming obstacles, in our ability to establish and meet goals, it is clear that child life has evolved into a mature and fruitful profession over its nearly forty-year history.

REFERENCES

Abt, I. (1965). *History of pediatrics.* Philadelphia: W. B. Saunders.

American Academy of Pediatrics. (1960). *Committee on hospital care: Care of children in hospitals.* Evanston: Author.

American Academy of Pediatrics. (1985). Committee on hospital care: Child life programs for hospitalized children. *Pediatrics, 76,* 467-470.

American Academy of Pediatrics. (1993). Committee on hospital care: Child life programs. *Pediatrics, 91,* 671-673.

American Academy of Pediatrics. (2000). Committee on hospital care: Child life services. *Pediatrics, 106,* 1156-1159.

Aries, P. (1965). *Centuries of childhood.* New York: Vintage Books.

Association for the Care of Children's Health. (1984). *Guidelines for the development of child life programs.* Washington, DC: Author.

Association for the Care of Children's Health. (1986). *Child life: An overview.* Washington, DC: Author.

Association for the Care of Children's Health. (1979). *Child life position paper.* Washington, DC: Author.

Bakwin, H. (1941). Loneliness in infants. *American Journal of the Diseases of Children, 63,* 30-40.

Bowlby, J. (1982). Attachment and loss: Retrospect and prospect. *American Journal of Orthopsychiatry, 52,* 664-678.

Bowlby, J. (1952). *Maternal care and mental health.* Geneva: World Health Organization.

Brennemann, J. (1931). The infant ward. *American Journal of the Diseases of Children, 43*, 577-584.

Brodie, B. (1986). Yesterday, today and tomorrow's pediatric world. *Children's Health Care, 14*, 168-173.

Brooks, M. (1975). The growth and development of ACCH. *Journal of the Association for the Care of Children in Hospitals, 4*, 1-7.

Canadian Pediatric Society. (1978). *Resolution passed on the child in hospital.* Ottawa, Ontario: Author.

Child Life Council. (1983). *Child life position paper.* Rockville, MD: Author.

Child Life Council. (2001). *Child life position paper.* Rockville, MD: Author.

Child Life Council. (2001). *Directory of child life programs.* Rockville, MD: Author.

Child Life Council. (1994). *Official documents of the child life council.* Rockville, MD: Author.

Child Life Council. (1997). *Operating principles: Mission, vision and values.* Rockville, MD: Author.

Child Life Council. (1987). *Program review guidelines.* Rockville, MD: Author.

Child Life Council. (2001). *Standards for the academic and clinical practice programs in child life.* Rockville, MD: Author.

Colon, A. R. (1999). *Nurturing children.* Westport, CT: Greenwood Press.

Dancis, J. (1972). *History of a pediatrics department.* New York: New York University School of Medicine, Department of Pediatrics, Bellevue Medical Center.

Erikson, E. (1963). *Childhood and society.* New York: Norton Press.

Fenn, L. (1997). Mission, vision and values statements for the child life profession. *Child Life Council: Bulletin, 14*, 1-2.

Freud, A. (1952). The role of bodily illness in the mental life of children. In *The psychoanalytic study of the child.* New York: International Universities Press.

Gaynard, L., Wolfer, J., Goldberger, J., Thompson, R. H., Redburn, L., & Laidley, L. (1990). *Psychosocial care of children in hospitals: A clinical practice manual.* Bethesda, MD: ACCH.

Johnson, B., Jeppson, E., & Redburn, L. (1992). *Caring for children and families: Guidelines for hospitals.* Bethesda, MD: ACCH.

McCourt, F. (1996). *Angela's ashes.* New York: Simon and Schuster.

Olds, A. (1986). Psychological considerations in humanizing the physical environment of pediatric outpatient and hospital settings. In *Child life: An overview.* Washington, DC: ACCH.

Piaget, J., & Inhelder, B. (1969). *The psychology of the child.* New York: Basic Books.

Plank, E. (1962). *Working with children in hospitals.* Cleveland: Western Reserve Press.

Prugh, D., Staub, E., Sands, H., Kirschbaum, R., & Lenihan, E. (1953). A study of the emotional reactions of children and families to hospitalization and illness. *American Journal of Orthopsychiatry, 23*, 70-106.

Robertson, J. (1958). *A two-year-old goes to the hospital: A scientific film record.* (film). Nacton, UK: Concord Film Council.

Robertson, J. (1958). *Young children in hospitals.* New York: Basic Books.

Rubin, S. (1992). What's in a name? Child life and the play lady legacy. *Children's Health Care, 21*, 4-13.

Rutkowski, J. (1986). A survey of child life programs. In *Child life: An overview.* Washington, DC: ACCH.

Smith, A. (1937). *They play with you here, The Modern Hospital, Report on the development of play at the Children's Memorial Hospital, Chicago, IL.* Unpublished paper.

Stanford, G. (1980). Now is the time: The professionalization of child life workers. *Children's Health Care, 8*, 55-59.

Spitz, R. (1945). Hospitalism: An inquiry into the genesis of psychiatric conditions in early childhood. *Psychoanalytic Study of the Child, 1*, 53-74.

Spitz, R. (1947). *Grief: A peril in infancy.* (film). New York: New York University Film Library.

Thompson, R. (1985). *Psychosocial research on pediatric hospitalization and health care.* Springfield, IL: Charles C Thomas.

Thompson, R. H. & Stanford, G. (1981). *Child life in hospitals: Theory and practice.* Springfield, IL: Charles C Thomas.

Winnecott, D. W. (1964). *The child, the family and the outside world.* London: Penguin Books.

Wolfer, J., Gaynard, L., Goldberger, J., Laidley, L., & Thompson, R. (1988). An experimental evaluation of a model child life program. *Children's Health Care, 16*, 244-254.

Chapter 2

THEORETICAL FOUNDATIONS OF CHILD LIFE PRACTICE

JOAN C. TURNER

INTRODUCTION

As human beings, we each have our own informal theories of human nature, development and helping. These theories are typically derived from a combination of our life and educational experiences. Whereas informal theories are important in our daily lives, as child life practitioners we draw from a collective source of formal theories to shape and drive our contemporary practice. Theories are our way of making sense of the world around us; theories guide us in our interactions with others, help us to analyze our observations and experiences and offer us solutions to many of the choices that we face caring for children and families. Theories are important to the work that we do–without theory it would be difficult to determine and articulate why and how things happen the way they do.

The following chapter presents an overview of the traditional theoretical bases that have been used to build exemplary child life practice. Starting with play, this chapter will progress through cognitive theories, social learning, attachment, temperament, stress and coping, psychosocial development and systems theories. A general overview of each

theory, combined with examples of application from the current literature, will be presented.

Play as Healing Modality

Although not a formal theory, the perspective of play as a conceptual framework for assessment, planning, intervention, relationship-building, and advocacy is a foundation of child life practice. Play is described as a healing modality through which child life practitioners promote growth and development of infants, children and youth (Child Life Council, 2002). Therapeutic properties of play, such as creative thinking, catharsis, fantasy and mastery, are utilized by child life specialists as a means to allow children to become active participants in the environment, express thoughts and feelings and practice emotional control over difficult issues. As a review of therapeutic play and related theory is offered in a Chapter 8, the focus here is limited to a general overview of the application of play as a mode to promote normal growth and development in child life practice.

There are many possible definitions of play. Common characteristics of play include the notion of play as a pleasurable activity, as child directed rather than goal oriented, requiring active engagement and promoting physical, social and cognitive development as the child explores and experiences his or her world. Cognitive theorists Piaget (1962) and Vygotsky (1976) both view play as the child's method for learning about the world, promoting development through experience and interaction. Similarly, psychodynamic theorists, such as Erikson (1963) view play as an important part of personality development through mastery of issues or social conflicts that arise as children develop.

Child life practice requires a broad view of all types of play. Two widely accepted ways of looking at play during childhood include the categories of Parten (1932, as cited in Mulligan, 1996) and the stages of Piaget (1962). Parten provides an observation guide to describe play in terms of the level of social interaction involved. Solitary, onlooker, parallel, associative and cooperative play are categories describing the levels of social interaction observed in children's play. As a stage theorist, Piaget described changes in play parallel to changes in cognitive development. Sensorimotor, symbolic or representational play and games with rules are categories of play observed during the early stages of childhood. Table 1 illustrates examples of developmentally appropriate child life practice using the Piagetian perspective to develop opportunities for individual and group programs.

In child life practice, the combination of play-based observations and interventions is fundamental. Observations of children during play provide insight into social patterns of interaction that are informative relative to prior experiences with play, social skill development, peer relationships, cognitive and physical strengths and limitations, as well as competence with social or healthcare-related situations. Based on their observations, child life specialists can develop individualized and group-based activities and programs. Often child life resources provide for the advantage of structuring the environment to offer a variety of opportunities for both individual play and peer or group play. For example, child life specialists act in an important advocacy role to support both indoor and outdoor playgrounds, play decks and play gardens, as well as access to gymnasiums and sports fields to support the physical aspects of growth and development.

A number of articles describing the promotion of play as a method of practice are available (Haiat, Bar-Mor & Shochat, 2003; Jessee, Wilson & Morgan, 2000). Others illustrate the value of related program components such as camps (Thomas & Gaslin, 2001; Cox, 2004), music therapy (Kennelly & Brien-Elliott, 2001), humor (Dowling, 2002), children's literature (Manworren & Woodring, 1998), gardens (Jackson, 2004), pet therapy (Kaminski, Pellino & Wish, 2002) and companion animals (Heimlich, 2001). Typically, these papers are developed within a framework promoting the role of play to support continued growth and development.

Cognitive Theories

Three cognitive theories that contribute to our understanding of children's thinking are Piagetian, Information Processing and Vygotskian. Piagetian theory tends to be a highly visible influence in academic and professional publications in pediatric practice in general. A model of information processing, in combination with developmental and stress-coping theories, was developed and applied by Gaynard, Wolfer, Goldberger, Thompson, Redburn and Laidley (1990) for their experimental child life program. Vygotsky is included here in response to the striking absence of reference to his work in the child life literature and due to the relevance of this sociocultural perspective to cur-

Table 1
DEVELOPMENTALLY APPROPRIATE PLAY OPPORTUNITIES

Age	Piaget: stages of play	Developmentally Appropriate opportunities Facilitated by Child Life Staff
Birth - 1 year	Sensorimotor	Tactile, visual, auditory, and kinetic stimulation such as positive touch, face-to-face contact, singing and talking, and rocking or swinging; walks in a stroller, tummy time and positioning for exploratory play through grasping, reaching, sitting, crawling, standing and walking; opportunities to experience cause-effect relationships; introduce colorful toys, books and changes in the environment: light, sound, textures
1- 3 years	Symbolic representational	Imitation facilitated through opportunities for parallel play, use of props for symbolic play and exploration of sensory materials such as paint, play dough, sand, water, big blocks; increased exposure to language through talking, books, music, pictures and peer play
4 - 5 years	Preoperational	Increased opportunities for both independent activities and associative play in groups. For example, playrooms set up to allow for choice of activity, tone of activity (passive–quiet, active–physical) and individual or group play
6 - 12 years	Games with rules	Exposure to familiar, novel and 'safe' activities, ideas and friends can be facilitated through structured opportunities for appropriate interactions with materials and peers, e.g. bingo, tic tac toe, board and card games; emerging development of language and understanding of new concepts is encouraged through the introduction of stimulating interactive programs such as health related games or experiments and music or magic tricks

rent child life practice. These three theories advance our knowledge base through perspectives on how changes in thinking occur. This review of cognitive theory allows for speculation on the role of the child life specialist as an agent of change relative to the continued growth and development of children.

Piagetian Theory

Piaget's characterization of the ways children think reflects a maturational process of development (Ginsburg & Opper, 1979). Over a predictable sequence of stages, from the sensorimotor period of birth to about two years through the formal operational stage initiated in early adolescence, Piaget depicts the development of cognitive skills in relation to the interaction of maturational processes and experience.

With a focus on the individual child as an active agent experiencing the world, Piaget described learning as taking place as children encounter new experiences, for example, during play. *Assimilation* is described as the process whereby children exposed to new information transform it to fit into their existing way of thinking. When a context of disequilibria between a child's current thinking and the new information occurs, *accommodation* is said to take place whereby the information is adapted or organized in a new way. The resulting state of *equilibrium* is described as resulting from the challenge to a child's existing understanding and allows for the potential of growth or learning to take place.

Typically, the stages of Piaget's theory of cognitive development are applied as a framework from which educators plan age-appropriate activities and instruction. Careful consideration for the relationship between the developmental cognitive characteristics and the process of learning may produce effective programs designed to meet individual, rather than generic, requirements of children. For example, Jessee, Wilson and Morgan (2000) offer a comprehensive review of cognitive development in their discussion of medical play in the early childhood classroom; Vessey, Braithwaite and Wiedmann (1990) provide guidelines for the development of effective activities designed to enhance school-aged children's knowledge of their internal bodies.

Information Processing Theory

Information processing theory suggests a number of mechanisms involved in the way a child thinks. Rather than a stage theory, information processing theory is developed within the analogy of a computer system, with concepts such as encoding, generalization, automatization and strategy construction key to the process of learning for children and adults (Seigler, 1998). Information processing theorists assert that children's thinking is greater than we generally assume relative to adult thinking. The processes are the same as abilities develop with maturation

and experience, with variation reflecting differences in degree rather than kind. For example, as thinking develops children are able to integrate and sort greater amounts of information with greater speed and memory.

The influence of the social world on children's thinking coincides with increasing knowledge and the development of functional structures (e.g., brain development). Like Piaget, information processing theory considers children to be active agents, striving to develop strategies for problem solving by processing information and learning ways to reach goals based on successful strategies. In contrast to Piaget, information processing focuses on the small, precise steps involved in problem solving. For example, relative to the sorting of relevant and irrelevant information, knowledge is encoded and organized for future use. As new strategies for problem solving become more familiar they may take on an automatic style. That is, the child does not have to stop and think about something because it becomes a part of their processing. However, social influences can introduce stress or emotional responses that may interfere with the ability of the individual to apply previously successful skills or strategies to novel situations.

Accordingly, Gaynard et al. (1990) developed an integrative model of information processing under stress whereby child life specialists are depicted as actively promoting the processing of information rather than merely serving as transmitters of information. For example, the authors illustrate the importance of facilitating effective processing of cognitive and sensory information under potentially stressful conditions (e.g., hospitalization, illness). Transactions consisting of complete and accurate information presented in a developmentally appropriate manner with special consideration for the influence of the child's emotional response on the processing of information are techniques illustrated by the authors.

Vygotskian Theory

Vygotsky was a Russian contemporary of young Piaget whose work did not emerge as an influence on contemporary developmental theory until the past 25 years. This theory, embedded in the social-cultural context, acknowledges the influence of context on children's developing knowledge of the world. Children's thinking is said to reflect a combination of maturation and learning from the social and cultural context (Vygotsky, 1976). For example, cultural and educational systems have the shared goal of assisting children in the acquisition of skills and knowledge necessary for the development of competence within a particular culture, with guidance and assistance provided by skilled members of the culture (e.g., caregivers and teachers). In particular, the cultural context is considered to influence *what* children learn and *how* they learn it.

Within the context of learning, children's thinking is described as reflecting the integration of where they are cognitively with the demands of the given context (immediate or cultural). A number of terms are associated with this perspective. The "zone of proximal development" (ZPD) describes the difference between a child's actual developmental level when acting independently and the potential level a child may reach under effective guidance. "Scaffolding" refers to the use of appropriate guidance techniques that allow for the presentation of enough challenge to advance the child to the next level, as well as recognize and adapt characteristics of the environment to promote learning or information processing.

A skilled scaffolder, such as a child life specialist, is able to assess the child's ZPD, consider the context of healthcare settings and related demands placed on children and present interventions that assist children in their ability to learn and cope. For example,

a child life specialist may observe a child personalize a medical doll prior to admission for day surgery. The child life specialist may engage the child in the activity to gain rapport and ask for the child's ideas related to the reason for the admission. The inclusion of carefully presented information, open-ended questions, and the introduction of healthcare materials (from wristband and hospital pajamas to stethoscope and anesthetic mask) can promote an extension of the child's ideas through manipulation of the ideas leading to the construction of new knowledge. Further, simple adjustments to the immediate contextual demands, observed by the child life specialist to interfere with the child's ability to cope, could be suggested and implemented. For example, some boys are distressed when asked to wear a hospital *gown* prior to surgery. The simple adjustment of removing the stressor by allowing the child to wear pajama bottoms under the gown may better allow that child to learn during the events that occur prior to entering the operating room.

Social Learning Theory

Social learning theory describes the child as an active participant in learning within the environment and larger systems. One central concept of the theory, observational learning, explains the transmission of information resulting in a change in behavior as a consequence of experience or *modeling* (Bandura, 1977). Four main processes of learning: attention, retention, imitation and reinforcement involve the interaction of behavioral and cognitive components. From the perspective of a child life specialist, attention to these processes is key to the manner in which environments and interventions are planned to provide opportunities for children and families to observe competent models.

Modeling interventions are typically developed using delivery modes that capture the attention of the target audience. Picture books (Manworren & Woodring, 1998) and puppets (Zimmer, 1990) are frequently used with younger children; videotapes and peer support groups are used with school-age children and youth. The presentation of information is designed to facilitate the retention of information through entertainment, repetition and opportunities for imitation. Positive reinforcement may take the form of observing successful outcomes, making new friends, gaining new information and coping strategies, or expressing feelings under comfortable and safe conditions. Feelings of increased self-esteem and mastery are often the stated goals of related interventions (Hart, Mather, Slack & Powell, 1992).

Attachment Theory

Attachment theory provides a perspective to child life specialists from which to clarify the central role of the parent-child relationship to the well being of the developing child. Due to the physical, cognitive and social limitations of infancy, the adult influences the organization of the attachment relationship as it develops over time and across situations (Bowlby, 1973). The notion of attachment reflects the relationship between the quality of care provided by a caregiver (parent or surrogate) as it affects the child's confidence in the availability of the caregiver (Ainsworth, Blehar, Waters & Wall, 1978). The development of a secure relationship promotes exploration of the social and physical environment as the child experiences the caregiver's ability to be sensitive to and respond to his/her needs in a contingent manner. *Insecure* attachment relationships reflect the child's experience of a pattern of inconsistent or dismissive responses to his/her bouts for attention during times

of discomfort, distress or pain. As the child develops, shifts in the relationships are apparent. Eventually, the child emerges as a partner in the ongoing relationship and is more able to anticipate or forecast not only the care provided by the parent, but also potentially threatening events that may occur.

For young infants, early threats to a sense of security are loss of support, loud noises, and sudden movement. Restricted in both discriminating perception and physical movement, the response of young infants is limited to crying, muscle tension, and diffuse movements. These attachment behaviors or "signals" elicit a protective response in the caregiver whose role is to identify and respond to the threat and return the infant to a state of comfort. As children grow and develop, they become able to influence the organization of the relationship. The expanded repertoire now includes active contact behaviors (e.g., clinging, following) and the ability to communicate through language. By the time children are three or four years of age, they are able to use this cognitive capacity to predict, plan, influence, communicate, and negotiate with the caregiver. With these changes, children are able to perceive a need for proximity maintenance (protection) and respond through eliciting attachment behaviors. The organization of expectancies and patterns, referred to as "working models," is facilitated through cognitive advances. That is, the dyadic relationship itself becomes represented internally through the child's capacity to believe in the existence of the caregiver without the physical presence of that caregiver (Bowlby, 1969/1982).

Conditions of consistency, comfort and predictability are provided in pediatric healthcare settings in part through promotion of child life services designed to sustain relationships between the parent and child.

For example, basic child life interventions include the use of a symbolic object (e.g., a toy, keys, a photograph, blanket) to provide the sense of security otherwise provided by the physical presence of the caregiver. Likewise, the maintenance of a child-family connection during absences is supported through the use of photographs, videotapes, audiotapes and e-mail, as well as separation play activities using stories, dramatic and symbolic play (Gaynard et al., 1990).

Additional literature is available suggesting ways in which security can be promoted during healthcare experiences. Stephens, Barkey and Hall (1999) present a model of working with children and parents, referred to as positioning for comfort, consistent with the notions of protection, security and proximity maintenance as explained in attachment theory. Early research by Bush, Melamed, Sheras and Greenbaum (1986) suggested attachment theory as a framework to investigate the influence of parent-child interactions on children's adaptive and attachment behaviors. Patterns of parental behavior seen to be helpful to children's coping were the use of distraction, information provision and low rates of ignoring. In contrast, maternal agitation and emotion-based reassurance were found to result in maladaptive behaviors in the child as defined by the authors (e.g., crying, diffuse, motor, movement, anger, withdrawal).

Psychosocial Development

Erik Erikson considered the social and cultural environment of the developing individual as the influential factor in the development of personality across the lifespan (Erikson, 1963). Erikson viewed development as a dynamic and continuous process whereby the individual strives to adjust to issues that arise at key interaction points. Typically, the social conflicts identified with-

in the stages of Erikson's theory of psychosocial development are applied as a framework from which caregivers approach age appropriate activities and instruction across the lifespan. Table 2 provides a summary of the psychosocial stages, issues and suggested areas for interventions by child life specialists.

Reference to the application of Erikson's stages can be found in a number of resources available to child life specialists. For example, Carpenter (1998) outlines a framework of a pediatric preparation program using the stages of Erikson's theory to delineate the needs of specific developmental stages. Additionally, Hart, Mather, Slack and Powell (1992) suggest interventions developed to assist with negotiation of Erickson's developmental crisis.

Temperament Theory

Child life professionals can apply temperament theory as an organizing framework to describe individual characteristics of the child observed in relation to specific characteristics of the environment (McLeod & McClowery, 1990). Considered to be genetic in origin, temperament qualities such as adaptability, irritability, activity level, emotionality and fearfulness may account for some individual differences in behavior. Environmental factors, however, are considered to influence the expression of these traits (Chess & Thomas, 1986). Referred to as *goodness of fit*, the challenge for child life professionals involves providing a supportive environment that *matches* the needs of the child with the demands of the healthcare setting, Thus, maladaptive behaviors observed in the child are believed to result from a lack of sensitivity to the child and an increase in stress.

McLeod and McClowery (1990) present an effective demonstration of the application

Table 2
APPLICATION OF ERIKSON'S PSYCHOSOCIAL THEORY TO CHILD LIFE PRACTICE

Age	Psychosocial stage	Issues	Child Life Interventions
Birth - 1 year	Trust vs. mistrust	Separation from caregivers Unfamiliar environment, routines, and people	Prompt consistent care; encourage parent involvement to meet both physical and emotional needs
1 - 3 years	Autonomy vs. Doubt	Reduced autonomy Lack of opportunities for self-control Separation anxiety	Encourage normalization through play and exploration of environment and materials
4 - 5 years	Initiative vs. Guilt	Limitations on sense of control and independence Magical thinking and egocentric thought resulting in misunderstanding, fear	Increase opportunities for control; maintain routines; assess understanding and provide age-appropriate explanations
6 - 12 years	Industry vs. Inferiority	Separation from normal activities associated with home, school and peers Concrete literal thought resulting in misunderstanding, reduced self-esteem	Promote opportunities for peer interaction, parental support; Structure and provide activities that allow for success; support connections to home and school
13 - 17 years	Identity vs. Role confusion	Limitations related to privacy, peer relationships, independent activity and decision making Concern with perspective of others, body image	Provide opportunities for choice, control, self-expression and relationship building. Allow for privacy but also promote peer interactions

of temperament theory and research in an explanatory model supporting child life practice. Three commonly referred to temperament types, "easy," "difficult," and "slow-to-warm-up," are illustrated in case scenarios with a caution against the oversimplification of generalities when working with individuals. An "easy" child, characterized by adaptability and positive mood, may show anxious behavior at times that can be addressed by interventions such as planning, preparation and expressive activities. The comfort level of a "difficult" child, perhaps described as manipulative, demanding, highly active and/or loud, can be facilitated through interventions related to increased choices and control, positive feedback and activities designed to increase the child's self esteem. The "slow-to-warm" child may need extra time and attention in order to adjust to new situations. Activities developed to increase familiarity and provide encouragement for individual children should be considered characteristic of exemplary child life programs.

Stress and Coping Theories

The theory of Lazarus and Folkman (1984) is frequently described in child life and related literature as a framework for explaining children's coping. Coping is defined as "constantly changing cognitive and behavioral efforts to manage specific external and or internal demands that are appraised as taxing or exceeding the resources of the person" (Lazarus & Folkman, 1984, p. 141). The role of the child life specialist is to determine what type of information and coping strategies are most effective in decreasing a child's experience of stress.

This theory focuses on the individual viewpoint or appraisal of a stressful situation recognizing that individuals use different coping responses in different situations. Approaches to assessing coping strategies require an understanding of two types of strategies: emotion-based and problem-based. Emotion-based strategies are characterized by behavior aimed to regulate the emotion responses to a problem such as reappraisal of the situation and tension release; problem-based strategies are characterized by efforts to change the situation or solve the problem, for example information seeking. The child's thought processes and level of understanding influence the evaluation of the meaning of a given situation and in turn influence the child's behavior. The responsibility of a child life practitioner includes providing the child with information on what to expect, how to cope and ways to participate or assert some control in the situation (Gaynard et al., 1990). Hart et al. (1992) discuss the application of a range of play-based activities designed to address specific needs of children related to, for example, self expression, tension-release and pain management activities. Additionally, Blaine (1999) suggests practical distraction materials and techniques to facilitate coping during stressful procedures.

Systems Theories

An understanding of the interaction among the child, the family, and the environment is central to the work of child life specialists. Two theories have emerged as frameworks to support the attention of the child life practitioner to extend beyond the child in isolation and focus on the child in the context of family relations and the social environment. First, family systems theory informs child life practice by providing a perspective on the socialization of the child and drawing attention to many aspects of the context of family as a socializing agent. Additionally, the ecological theory of Bronfenbrenner (1979) contributes to the study of families through the examination of development in the context of both immediate and distal systems. While both theories acknowledge the influence of the wider social systems, ecological theory explains the interdependence of the systems.

To be consistent with both theories, child life specialists must be particularly attune to the nature of the hospital or healthcare system as a social institution that serves as an *immediate* context influencing the hospitalized child and his or her family. To run efficiently, the healthcare system is formally organized by rules, schedules, codes of practice, regulations and social norms. As a result, families are placed in a unique culture or psychological environment as they interact with the social organization, patterns of relationships and style of management particular to each healthcare setting. Similar to the notion of goodness of fit described in temperament theory, systems theories offer opportunities for further examination of the family's response, adjustment and adaptation to change within the family and/or the wider social system within which it is embedded. The role of the child life specialist reflects a need to both assess family responses and support families in the process of navigating the system in order to meet the needs of the child.

Family Systems Theory

Family systems theory promotes the examination of the family as a whole in terms of individual family members, their relations within the family, and the relations among members as the family strives to maintain balance in the face of development and change (Friedman, 1998). Each family is considered to represent more than a simple tabulation of family members. Each member is viewed from the perspective of complex relations with other family members in terms of dyads, triads and so on, with each of these relations among family members viewed as an integral subsystem. The notion of complexity arises from the interdependency of subsystems and the circularity of influence that each subsystem has on other subsystems, as well as on the system as a whole. That is, when change occurs the whole system is affected and reacts in a manner that serves to sustain balance.

As families are imbedded in wider social systems, each is influenced by outside events to varying degrees. Additionally, families are faced with change that occurs naturally as a consequence of typical growth and development. Regardless of the source, the consequence is that the challenge of coping with change is ongoing in the course of family life. Family systems theory demonstrates how characteristics of families, such as openness, permeability, and flexibility, vary in degree and influence the family's capacity to adjust to change.

Therefore, child life specialists are educated to recognize and understand that events, such as the diagnosis of illness or the traumatic injury of a child, impact the whole family. To this end, assessment and interventions are carried out with consideration of the impact on all family members, as well as related systems. Family systems theory provides a framework for child life professionals to observe the transactional nature of family responses to situational events and plan interventions to meet the unique needs of individual families. As such, child life specialists strive to develop relationships, not only with the child, but parents, siblings and other primary figures in the life of the child. Many of these interventions focus not only on supporting the family's ability to cope within the healthcare system, but to also transition smoothly back into life outside the protective walls of the healthcare environment.

Ecological Theory

In 1979, Bronfenbrenner offered a new theoretical perspective emphasizing the interdependence of persons and the environment. Bronfenbrenner (1979) illustrated the process of human development using an analogy of Russian nesting dolls, with the individual contained within his/her immediate setting, surrounded by interconnected levels representing the relations between settings, events occurring in external settings, and the different subcultures or cultures of the greater environment. Currently, an illustration using a series of overlapping circles is more commonly portrayed to represent relations and transitions among the microsystem, mesosystem, exosystem and macrosystem. Emphasis upon extending attention beyond the immediate context of the developing child by observing within the context of society draws attention to environmental interconnections and their impact on growth and development.

According to ecological theory, it is the perceptions of, and transactions with, the environment that influence development. Microsystems refer to the immediate settings within which the child develops. The home is typically the first setting that comes to mind. Additionally, child care and schools, or for chronically ill children the hospital or rehabilitation setting, are microsystems where children spend a good deal of time as they develop and begin to experience relations away from home. Within each setting, the child experiences many relationships with others, from primary care givers to incidental persons in the environment. As well, experiences extend to the mesosystem. The mesosystem represents the links between two or more microsystems and the relations between or among these settings, for example, the interactions between school and home, hospital and home, or among all three.

Bronfenbrenner further extends the notion of the ecology of human development to illustrate the exosystem and macrosystem. The exosystem represents those systems separate from the individual but which have an effect on the microsystems containing the developing child, for example, the parent's workplace, financial institution, or local pharmacy. The macrosystem refers to the greater social system of culture and subcultures and the reality of consistencies or inconsistencies in belief systems or ideologies between cultures. The healthcare system consists of a body of beliefs and practices that may or may not be supportive of, or consistent with, the beliefs or needs of a family with an ill or injured child.

From the child life literature, Gaynard et al. (1990) apply a systems framework for the assessment of the child's vulnerability to stress relative to the context of the healthcare system, called *the stress potential assessment process.* An illustration of the relationship between systems includes a series of overlapping circles, each representing a system of potential influences on the child's ability to

adjust and adapt to change, be it physical, psychological or environmental change. This model draws the attention of the child life practitioner towards the interaction of child variables, family variables and healthcare variables during the dynamic and ongoing process of assessment. The skill of the child life specialist in building relationships and observing the systems that influence the child affects the type and level of interventions designed to promote positive development and coping of the child and family.

According to Bronfenbrenner (1979), a balance between the individual and systems in the environment serves to support positive developmental outcomes. As Bronfenbrenner's theory encourages us to view the individual within a set of interacting ecosystems, so too should child life practice include attention to these systems that ultimately influence the growth and development of the child. Current child life practice supports the participation of practitioners in the policy and procedures activities of the larger healthcare system as advocates for the unique needs of children and families, for example through development of family friendly policy and procedures. Current trends also demonstrate the role of the child life specialist liaising with systems beyond the walls of the hospital by providing and coordinating services in subsystems such as homes, schools and the greater community.

SUMMARY

The ability of child life professionals to articulate and justify to others the meaning and underlying functions of clinical interventions and programs supports the ongoing development of the profession. A recent hospital-based study by Cole, Diener, Wright and Gaynard (2001) revealed that some healthcare professionals perceived of child life specialists as providers of *entertainment and activity*. As the role of child professionals goes much beyond this simple view, the finding underscores the need for educational strategies to encourage better understanding of the function and goals of specific child life activities. Theories are a helpful tool in the explanation of *why* we support and promote specific interventions and policies. To this end, one can imagine theories as representing a common language between professions.

As child life specialists strive to maintain their professional status and recognition, attention must be paid to practice standards firmly supported by current theory and research. The synthesis of theory and practice is a skill that is initiated within the curriculum of our educational foundations and put into practice as we move through practicum, internship and professional experiences. Child Life Council curriculum recommendations include theoretical foundations in, for example, human development, play, attachment, stress and coping, social learning and family systems (CLC, 2002). In practice, the responsibility of child life supervisors should include an emphasis on core clinical skills through ongoing clarification of connections between theory and practice. Child life competencies grounded in theoretical perspectives can equip practitioners with explanatory frameworks that allow for connections between theory and practice to be advanced—or in times of economic struggles, for the status quo to be maintained.

To revisit theory allows for a level of detachment from our personal response and current practice milieu to ground us in the conceptual framework of our profession. This review of the theoretical foundations of child life practice serves as a reflection process where we can step back and evaluate (or reevaluate) our own reactions, rationales and practice through a different lens.

REFERENCES

Ainsworth, M., Blehar, M., Waters, E., & Wall, S. (1978). *Patterns of attachment: A psychological study of the strange situation.* Hillsdale, NJ: Erlbaum.

Blaine, S. (1999). Coping kits and distraction techniques. *Child Life Focus, 1.*

Bowlby, J. (1973). *Attachment and loss volume 2: Separation, anxiety and anger.* Penguin Books: England.

Bandura, A. (1977). *Social learning theory.* Englewood Cliffs, NJ: Prentice-Hall.

Bowlby, J. (1969/1982). *Attachment and loss volume I: Attachment.* The Hogarth Press: London.

Bronfenbrenner, U. (1979). *The ecology of human development.* Cambridge, MA: Harvard University Press.

Bush, J. P., Melamed, B. G., Sheras, P. L., & Greenbaum, P. (1986). Mother-child patterns of coping with anticipatory medical stress. *Health Psychology, 5,* 137-157.

Carpenter, K. (1998). Developing a pediatric patient/parent hospital preparation program. *AORN Journal, 67,* 1042-1046.

Chess, S., & Thomas, A. (1984). Origins and evolution of behavior disorders. New York: The Guilford Press.

Child Life Council (2002). *Official documents of the child life council.* Rockville, MD: Child Life Council, Inc.

Cox, E. R. (2001). Shedding the layers: Exploring the impact of the burn camp experience on adolescent campers' body image. *Journal of Burn Care and Rehabilitation, 25,* 141-147.

Dowling, J. S. (2002). Humor: A coping strategy for pediatric patients. *Pediatric Nursing, 28,* 123-131.

Erikson, E. (1963). *Children and society.* New York: Norton.

Friedman, M. M. (1998). *Family nursing: Research, theory, and practice (4th ed.).* Appleton & Lange: Connecticut.

Gaynard, L., Wolfer, J., Goldberger, J., Thompson, R., Redburn, L. & Laidley, L. (1990). *Psychosocial care of children in hospitals: A clinical practice manual for the ACCH child life research project.* Bethesda, MD: Association for the Care of Children's Health.

Ginsburg, H., & Opper, S. (1979). *Piaget's theory of intellectual development.* New Jersey: Prentice-Hall, Inc.

Haiat, H., Bar-More, G., & Shochat, M. (2003). The world of the child: A world of play even in the hospital. *Journal of Pediatric Nursing, 18,* 209-214.

Hart, R., Mather, P., Slack, J., & Powell, M. (1992). *Therapeutic play activities for hospitalized children.* St. Louis, MO: Mosby Year Book.

Heimlich, K. (2001). Animal assisted therapy and the severely disabled child: A quantitative study. *Journal of Rehabilitation, 67,* 48-54.

Jackson, A. (2004). Increasing interaction with nature: An option to consider for sick and chronically ill children. *Child Life Bulletin, 22,* 11-14.

Jessee, P. O., Wilson, H. & Morgan, D. (2000). Medical play for young children. *Childhood Education Summer,* 215-218.

Kaminski, M., Pellino, T., & Wish, J. (2002). Play and pets: the physical and emotional impact of child life and pet therapy for hospitalized children. *Children's Health Care, 31,* 321-335.

Kennelly, J., & Brien-Elliott, K. (2001). The role of music therapy in pediatric rehabilitation. *Pediatric Rehabilitation, 4,* 137-143.

Lazarus, R. S., & Folkman, S. (1984). *Stress, appraisal and coping.* New York: Springer.

Manworren, R., & Woodring, B. (1998). Evaluating children's literature as a source for patient education. *Pediatric Nursing, 24,* 548-553.

McLeod, S. M., & McClowry, S. G. (1990). Using temperament theory to individualize the psychosocial care of hospitalized children. *Children's Health Care, 19,* 79-85.

Mulligan, V. (1996). *Children's play.* Don Mills, ON: Addison-Wesley Publishers Limited.

Piaget, J. (1962). *Play, dreams and imitation in childhood.* New York: W.W. Norton & Co.

Siegler, R. S. (1998). *Children's thinking.* Englewood Cliffs, New Jersey: Prentice-Hall.

Stephens, B. K., Barkey, M. E., & Hall, H. R. (1999). Techniques to comfort children during stressful procedures. *Advances in Mind-Body Medicine, 15,* 49-60.

Thomas, D., & Gaslin, T. C. (2001). "Camping it up" self esteem in children with hemophilia. *Issues in Comprehensive Pediatric Nursing, 24,* 253-263.

Vessey, J. A., Braithwaite, K. B., & Wiedmann, M. (1990). Teaching children about their internal bodies. *Pediatric Nursing, 16,* 29-33.

Vygotsky, L. (1976). *Mind in society.* Cambridge, MA: Harvard University Press.

Zimmer, L. (1999). Partnering with puppets: A therapeutic tool. *Child Life Focus, 1.*

Chapter 3

RESEARCH IN CHILD LIFE

RICHARD H. THOMPSON AND CHARLES W. SNOW

INTRODUCTION

The profession of child life exists within medical environments, where decisions about clinical practices are based largely upon supportive research findings. However, the relationship between the practice of child life and research findings is not always direct or clear. The extent to which child life specialists are aware of, or apply the findings of research is uncertain. O'Byrne, Peterson, and Saldana (1997) report, for example, that child life specialists are second only to nursing, among members of the medical team, in terms of responsibility for the preparation of children for medical events. However, the results of their survey of pediatric hospitals in the United States also indicate that, regardless of who is responsible for preparation, the programs implemented are not always based upon the lessons that can be derived from the research literature.

To date, only a relatively small amount of research directly related to the profession and practice of child life has been generated, although far more research of relevance to the field has been conducted by members of other professions, including pediatric psychology and nursing. The relative lack of child life research is not surprising, given the more recent introduction of child life to the healthcare team, the small numbers of child life specialists in comparison to other professions, and the absence of academic supports, such as doctoral programs in child life that would formally encourage research. These factors, coupled with the inherent difficulties of conducting research within the medical environment, complicate the production of additional work.

Nevertheless, despite these barriers, an encouraging number of studies have appeared in recent years that have examined the growth of the child life profession (Snow & Triebenbacher, 1996), perceptions of child life specialists (Cole, Diener, Wright, & Gaynard, 2001), factors associated with job satisfaction (Holloway & Wallinga, 1990; Munn, Barber, & Fritz, 1996), and the practice of child life in hospitals (Pass & Bolig, 1993; Krebel, Clayton, & Brown, 1996) and in community-based programs (Chernoff, Ireys, DeVet, & Kim, 2002). The presence of this work is commendable and should be fostered because research such as this has the capacity to evaluate and inform practice, as well as to test existing forms of practice that may have been taken for granted.

The purpose of this chapter is to provide a concise overview of research in areas most relevant to the practice and profession of child life, whether generated by child life specialists or others on the healthcare team. This review will necessarily be limited in its scope. The primary focus will be on work appearing since the mid-1980s. For reviews of research prior to this time, see Thompson (1985) and Vernon, Foley, Sipowitz, and Schulman (1965). In addition, the work reviewed in this chapter will be limited to empirically-based studies, primarily quantitative in nature. The topics addressed have been selected as those areas where a "critical mass" of studies appears, where the topics have direct relevance to the practice of child life, and where the focus is on evaluating efficacy of approaches and guiding practice. Some of the research findings reviewed in other chapters will not be duplicated here.

RESEARCH SPECIFIC TO CHILD LIFE

As noted, the volume of research literature specifically related to the profession of Child Life is quite limited. It encompasses four principal areas: (1) the growth and development of the profession, including the expansion of Child Life over time; (2) professional issues, including the activities engaged in by child life specialists, perceptions of their work, and factors associated with job satisfaction; (3) research describing and documenting the work done by child life specialists in specific settings, such as outpatient clinics and emergency departments; and (4) research addressing the efficacy of child life work.

The Development of the Profession

As the profession of child life developed over the second half of the twentieth centu-

ry, a number of surveys were conducted investigating the prevalence and functioning of programs in the United States and Canada (Dombro, 1967a, 1967b; McCue, Wagner, Hansen, & Rigler, 1978; Rutkowski, 1978; Mather & Glasrud, 1981; Ricks & Faubert, 1981). Questions addressed by these studies include characteristics of the programs, staffing patterns, areas of the hospital served, and the educational preparation of the people in the field. The earliest of these studies were summarized by Larsen (1980).

More recently, Snow and Triebenbacher (1996) conducted a survey of employment trends and practices in child life – a study that also included analysis of data published in the 1990 and 1994 directories of child life programs (Association for the Care of Children's Health, 1990; Child Life Council, 1994). The directory analysis indicated growth in the profession over this four-year period. When program additions and deletions were accounted for (74 programs were added to the 1994 directory, but another 56 were deleted), there was a net gain of 18 child life programs and of 164.9 full-time equivalent positions.

The data gathered from the 205 programs responding to the survey also reflected growth in the field, partially offset by losses. In the year prior to the survey (1995), 27 percent of the programs reported adding at least one new position, for a total of 83 positions. However, an additional 16 percent of the institutions reported losing one or more positions, totaling 24 positions in all.

Additional information on the characteristics of child life specialists was gathered. One-third of the respondents had academic training in child life, with others (in order of frequency) trained in child development, education, and therapeutic recreation. A substantial number (43%) held master's degrees, and nearly 80 percent held either professional or provisional certification in child life. Staff turnover was an issue for some, but not all programs. Although the majority of programs (59%) reported no turnover, rates of change in others were high, yielding an overall annual turnover rate of 42 percent. Most common reasons for job change were pursuit of a new career, family-related issues, acceptance of another child life position, or return to school. Job dissatisfaction or "burnout" accounted for only 8.5 percent of the turnover.

Professional Issues

A second group of studies examines the nature of the work engaged in by child life specialists, perceptions of the nature and importance of this work, and factors associated with job satisfaction and possible burnout. Two observational studies investigated the nature of child life work and interactions with children, their families, and staff members (Gaynard, Hausslein, & DeMarsh, 1989; Giles, Bradbard, & Endsley, 1987). Not surprisingly, each found the nature of the work to involve substantial, direct social interaction with children.

Gaynard et al. (1989) observed five child life specialists in four separate hospital settings for a total of approximately 100 hours. Nearly half of the total observed time (46%) was spent in direct service with children and families. Of this direct service time, half was devoted to patient support (defined as developing relationships that facilitate emotional expression and holding therapeutic conversations), with an additional 23 percent of the time spent in therapeutic play. Preparation and other activities each occupied less than 10 percent of the child life specialists' direct service time. Of the time not devoted to direct service, most was spent on administrative duties or in meetings. Time spent in contact with other members of the healthcare team represented less than 10 percent of the child life specialists' time, with interactions with nurses, students, and volunteers most frequent, and contact with physicians and social workers limited.

Giles et al. (1987) observed the interactions of child life interns (rather than professionals) with hospitalized children ranging in age from 1 to 15 years. The observed work of the interns was characterized as facilitating and modeling interaction with children. Less effort was devoted to involvement of parents in their children's play.

As these studies indicate, child life specialists are highly visible on inpatient units, with their interaction focused on children and, to a lesser extent, their families. Despite this visibility, perceptions or understanding of the nature and importance of their work, as well as the degree of power they hold, differ among various members of the healthcare team. Cole et al. (2001) examined these differences in a study that was a partial replication of Gaynard's (1985) investigation. Gaynard's earlier research, which surveyed the perceptions of healthcare professionals in hospitals throughout the northeastern United States, found that child life specialists' views of their own work differed from that of their colleagues. For example, child life specialists frequently noted their role as a member of the healthcare team – a role infrequently cited by others. Conversely, other professionals frequently mentioned the role of child life in "amusing and entertaining" patients, while child life specialists did not perceive themselves in this role. Overall, Gaynard (1985) found child life specialists to be ranked highly in terms of their "importance" to the physical and psychosocial well-being of the patient (exceeded only by physicians and nurses), but low in power.

Cole et al. (2001) focused on a single hospital, similarly surveying perceptions of role, importance, and power as perceived by child life specialists and others. Discrepancies in views of child life specialists' roles persisted, with child life specialists noting their role in preparation, patient and family support, and advocacy more frequently than other professionals, while mentioning entertainment of patients less often than others. As in the earlier study (Gaynard, 1985), the importance of the child life specialist was rated highly, though ratings differed by position. Child life specialists and hospital administrators rated the importance of child life more highly than did physicians and nurses. However, the frequency of contact that a respondent had with child life specialists was associated with a tendency to increase ratings of the importance of child life. Regardless of the relatively high rating of child life importance, child life specialists were viewed as having little power.

Ambiguity of roles fulfilled by child life, the discrepancies in perceptions about their work and its importance, and the limited power associated with the position are conditions that might result in higher levels of job dissatisfaction and burnout. Several studies have investigated the degree to which child life professionals experience dissatisfaction, as well as factors that might mitigate their negative effects (Holloway & Wallinga, 1990; Munn, Barber, & Fritz, 1996; Snow & Triebenbacher, 1996). Despite the emotional nature of the work of child life specialists, it appears that members of the profession are less susceptible than others to burnout characterized by emotional exhaustion, depersonalization, and lower sense of personal accomplishment (Maslach & Jackson, 1981). For example, Snow and Triebenbacher (1996) found burnout to be infrequently cited as a reason for job turnover. Holloway and Wallinga (1990) found that child life specialists were comparable to other human service professionals in terms of emotional exhaustion, but were substantially lower in ratings of "depersonalization," and were

higher than others in "personal accomplishment" – resulting in lower overall burnout.

Nevertheless, several factors are associated with increased levels of burnout or job dissatisfaction, among these being "role ambiguity," or a lack of clarity about the duties and responsibilities of a position. Holloway and Wallinga (1990) found role ambiguity to be associated with levels of burnout among child life specialists, with high levels of ambiguity associated with greater exhaustion and depersonalization and lesser feelings of personal accomplishment. In addition, burnout was associated with perceived adequacy of salary, perceived ability to fulfill the demands of the job, and number of years in the current position.

In a survey of child life specialists from the United States and Canada, Munn et al. (1996) found levels of role ambiguity to be a good predictor of emotional exhaustion and job satisfaction. In addition, they found that the lack of supervisory support was a good predictor of job dissatisfaction and intentions to leave a child life position.

Practice in Specific Clinical Settings: Nature and Impact of Work

During the beginnings of the profession, child life specialists worked within inpatient pediatric units of hospitals. Through the years child life services have been expanded to include a variety of inpatient as well as outpatient and community-based locations. In the late 1970s, researchers began to examine the practice and effects of child life in specific areas of the hospital, including intensive care units (Cataldo, Bessman, Parker, Pearson, & Rogers, 1979; Pearson, Cataldo, Tureman, Bessman, & Rogers, 1980) and outpatient clinics (Williams & Powell, 1980).

Within a few years, the studies encompassed emergency departments (Alcock, Berthiaume, & Clarke, 1984; Alcock, Feldman, Goodman, McGrath, & Park, 1985; Alcock, Goodman, Feldman, McGrath, Park, & Cappelli, 1985; Krebel, Clayton, & Graham, 1996) and, most recently, have expanded to community-based support programs (Chernoff et al., 2002). The findings of these studies provide evidence that the presence of child life professionals enhances the play behavior of children, increases parent-child interaction, reduces the level of negative behaviors exhibited by children, and may facilitate the adjustment of children and their families to a variety of medical settings and conditions.

Intensive Care Unit

A pair of related studies (Cataldo et al., 1979; Pearson et al., 1980) examined the effects of providing supervision and play materials to children in the intensive care unit. In each case, the behavior of children who were awake and alert in the ICU were observed in three successive periods – prior to a period of interaction with a child life specialist, during the period of interaction itself, and after the interaction was concluded. In each study, the presence of the child life specialist greatly increased children's positive affect and interaction with materials, while decreasing negative behaviors. Cataldo et al. (1979) found that immediately following the conclusion of the session and the withdrawal of the child life specialist, children displayed a moderately high level of interactions with toys, when given the opportunity. In contrast, however, Pearson et al. (1980) found the level of interaction with toys to decrease in the longer term following an interaction with a child life specialist. Thirty to forty-five minutes after the conclusion of the child life session, the children's level of activity was lower than in the pre-intervention period.

Ambulatory Clinic

Williams and Powell (1980) compared the behavior of children in an outpatient setting when supervision was either present or absent. Increases in positive behavior, and a corresponding decrease in negative behavior of children, were noted when the area was supervised. Withdrawal of the supervision was found to result in a return to increased negative behavior, even when play materials remained.

Emergency Department

The involvement and impact of child life services in the emergency department has been the subject of several research projects. Krebel, Clayton, and Graham (1996) surveyed hospitals regarding the availability of child life services to children and families in the emergency department, finding that only 14 percent had a full-time child life specialist devoted to this area, with an additional 14 percent providing child life services to the area through consults. Alcock and colleagues conducted a series of studies on the effects of child life presence on the responses of children and their families in the emergency department (Alcock, Berthaiume, & Clarke, 1984; Alcock, Goodman et al., 1985; Alcock, Feldman, et al., 1985). One of the studies (Alcock, Goodman et al., 1985) considered the impact of child life presence on the environment and waiting behaviors of children and families in the emergency department. When a child life specialist was not available, children were observed more frequently in passive behavior (defined as, "not interacting with the environment and not playing, painting, or reading" p. 176) than when a child life specialist was present. In addition, parents were observed playing with their children more when a child life specialist was present.

A more targeted emergency department intervention was examined by Alcock, Feldman et al. (1985). In this study, children entering the emergency department for sutures were observed either with or without the benefit of a child life intervention. Children and families in the intervention condition were approached by the child life specialist who provided basic information including anticipated waiting time, who would be performing the procedure, and the location of services the family might need while in the emergency department, such as bathrooms and telephones. Information about the procedure was provided verbally and through a play demonstration. The child life specialist supported parent involvement during the procedure, with most parents choosing to remain with their child while it was performed, and provided instruction in coping techniques to both parent and child. Although few significant group differences were found in this study, those that emerged suggested benefits of the child life intervention. The presence of child life was found to be most effective for patients 11 to 14 years of age who required six or more sutures. Those in this category who had contact with the child life specialist reported significantly lower levels of anxiety than among those who had not. In addition, parent satisfaction was significantly higher among those who received the child life intervention.

Community-Based Programming

In recent years, the work of child life specialists has reached beyond the walls of the hospital. Chernoff et al. (2002) evaluated the effectiveness of one such program – a community-based support program for children with one of four chronic illnesses (diabetes, sickle cell anemia, cystic fibrosis, or asthma) and for their mothers. This program, intended to reduce emotional problems potentially associated with these conditions, was provided by child life specialists and by mothers who had experience with such medical conditions. The program consisted of regular contact, in person and via telephone, as well as special family events. Measures of adjustment increased for participants in the program over the period of intervention, while they declined for a control group during the same period. The effects of the program were most evident among children who initially had lower levels of physical self-esteem.

Research on Efficacy of Child Life Programs and their Components

Most of the empirical research guiding the practice of child life specialists is focused on specific forms of intervention, such as preparation for medical events, instruction in coping skills, or the use of play-based activities. The majority of this research, which is reviewed in a later section of this chapter, is conducted and implemented by other disciplines including nursing and pediatric psychology. Child life draws from the work of each of these disciplines, combining these elements in the services it delivers. Although research examining the effectiveness of individual elements of child life programming is quite common, studies directly addressing the efficacy of the constellation of services that constitute child life programming are rare, with only two such studies identified (Carson, Jenkins, & Stout, 1985; Wolfer, Gaynard, Goldberger, Laidley, & Thompson, 1988).

Carson et al. (1985) conducted a small-scale experimental study of child life programming, implemented by students, for a group of children from 4 to 15 years of age hospitalized for accidents that necessitated the use of traction. The play-based programming model was designed to promote cognitive, social, and emotional stimulation, as well as interactions with family members and other patients. In addition, the students communicated with children and their families about the patient's progress and development. The results indicated that patients involved in the child life programming experienced a substantial reduction in state anxiety from the beginning to end of their hospital stay, while subjects in the control group displayed increased levels of anxiety. The difference in state anxiety scores of the control and experimental groups at discharge were characterized by the researchers as "moderately significant" ($p<.20$, $N=10$). Self-esteem scores did not differ between groups.

The most comprehensive assessment of the efficacy of child life programming conducted to date is found in Wolfer et al. (1988). In this quasi-experimental study, implemented under the sponsorship of the Association for the Care of Children's Health (ACCH), a model child life program was developed and implemented by experienced child life specialists at Phoenix Children's Hospital in Phoenix, Arizona. The child life program consisted of a comprehensive set of interventions, including group and individualized play experiences, stress-point preparation for impending events, and parent involvement in the care of their children. Although the program that was developed served the full pediatric population from infants through adolescents, a subset of children ages 3 to 13 were selected for inclusion in the study.

Children who participated in this program ($N=68$) were evaluated on a wide range of stress, coping, adjustment, and surgical recovery measures. Their scores were contrasted with those of a control group of children ($N=160$) who had been hospitalized prior to the implementation of the child life program when child life services were minimal. The researchers found that children who had participated in the child life program faired significantly better than control group children on 18 of the 21 outcome variables assessed.

A related group of studies has examined the effects of varying or contrasting approaches to the delivery of child life services on targeted outcomes (e.g., amount of play or verbalizations, or anxiety levels). Pass and Bolig (1993) compared the play behavior of children participating in a child life program that was either playroom, group play-focused or individual, non-playroom focused. The observed play behavior of children in hospital playrooms apparently did not differ as a result of program focus. Jessee, Strickland, Leeper, and Hudson (1987) examined the potential impact on anxiety reduction of incorporating nature-based experiences into child life activities, but found no significant differences in the anxiety levels between groups. Finally, Froehlich (1984) compared two approaches to eliciting verbalizations from children regarding their hospital experiences – music therapy sessions or participation in medical play. Children who had participated in the music therapy sessions were found to provide more involved responses to questions posed about hospitalization than did children who participated in medical play.

CHILDREN'S REPSONSES TO HOSPITALIZATION AND HEALTHCARE ENCOUNTERS

Effects of Hospitalization on Children's Behavior

Early research on the psychosocial aspects of pediatric healthcare addressed the issue of whether hospitalization (especially hospitalization for surgery) was associated with negative behavioral change in children. In their 1965 review of the literature,

Vernon, Foley, Sipowitz, and Schulman (1965) noted a bias in this research, observing that it considered only the possibility of the experience resulting in either no behavioral change or change in a negative direction, rather than allowing for the possibility of positive change or growth. In their continued research on the topic, Vernon, Schulman, and Foley (1966) partially remedied this omission through development of the Post-Hospital Behavior Questionnaire. In completing this measure, the parent indicates whether a number of specified behaviors that potentially indicate emotional distress occur more or less frequently than they did prior to hospitalization.

Vernon and colleagues (1965) reviewed other studies indicating that children, especially older infants through preschoolers, experience a degree of emotional distress in response to hospitalization. Thompson (1985) also found evidence in the research literature that hospitalization results in behavioral change or in other potential indicators of emotional distress during the period of treatment and following discharge. Anxiety was the most commonly reported emotional response of children to hospitalization in studies reviewed by Thompson (1994). Other responses that were reported include aggression, attitudinal and affective changes, and disturbances in sleep or eating.

Obviously, not all children are affected by hospitalization and medical treatment in the same way. There are numerous factors that potentially affect the emotional responses of children to healthcare encounters. The age of the patient appears to be one of the critical variables (Kain, Mayes, O'Connor, & Cicchetti, 1996). Accumulating evidence indicates that the period of time between 6 months and 4 years is the age when children are most vulnerable to hospitalization and medical encounters (King & Ziegler, 1981; Mabe, Trieber, & Riley, 1991; McClowry, 1988; Thompson, 1985).

Gender is another factor that has been considered as potentially affecting children's responses to healthcare encounters. Although gender differences have been reported within individual studies, the results have not consistently related gender to variations in children's responses to hospitalization (Thompson, 1985; Eiser & Eiser, 1990). Other factors that apparently affect the amount of stress children experience in medical encounters include parental anxiety, temperament of the child (Kain et al, 1996), and previous medical experiences (Dahlquist, Gil, Armstrong, DeLawyer, Greene, & Wuori, 1986; Kain et al., 1996).

The severity of a child's condition, or the intrusiveness of the treatment received, may also affect the child's response. Saylor, Pallmeyer, Finch, Eason, Trieber, and Folger (1987) found that the number of physical stressors a child experiences (e.g., pain, vomiting, sleep disturbance) was the most consistently significant predictor of psychological distress during hospitalization. Rennick, Johnston, Dougherty, Platt, and Ritchie (2002) reported that children who were more severely ill, and those who had more invasive procedures during hospitalization, had more medical fears, a lower sense of control over their health, and responses that lasted for a longer period of time.

Zurlinden (1985) classified factors associated with children's adjustment to hospitalization, using a three-dimensional hospital crisis model consisting of (1) age of the patient, (2) balancing factors (e.g., perceptions of events, social supports, coping skills), and (3) hazards of hospitalization (loss of control, uncertain limits, separation, the unknown, harm or injury). Although additional information is needed, the research studies reviewed above tend to support Zurlinden's model. However, researchers have not explored the ways in which the various factors interact to influence children's responses to hospital experiences.

The research literature indicates that behavioral change is not an uncommon result of hospitalization or medical care, yet in most instances the change is of relatively brief duration. Thompson and Vernon (1993) conducted a meta-analysis of 26 studies that had used the Vernon Posthospital Behavior Questionnaire. They concluded that, in the absence of interventions designed to reduce psychological upset, negative behavioral change tended to increase significantly following hospitalization. However, this effect had largely disappeared within two weeks. Nevertheless, studies have consistently identified a small percentage of children for whom disturbances persist beyond a period of six months (Thompson, 1985; Rennick et al., 2002). For such children, the stressors of hospitalization, illness, and the accompanying, invasive treatment may have resulted in symptoms of post-traumatic stress disorder.

Stress-Coping Responses

Other researchers have examined the behavior of children during hospitalization and medical care, viewing the behavior exhibited as evidence of children's attempts to cope with stressful circumstances, rather than as a positive or negative response. This line of research is based upon the work of Lazarus and colleagues regarding stress and coping (Lazarus & Folkman, 1984). According to the Lazarus model, stress is viewed as "a relationship between the person and environment that is appraised by the person as taxing or exceeding his or her resources" (p. 21). Under such circumstances, the individual uses coping strategies or behaviors to manage the relationship between the person and the environment. Coping efforts, according to Lazarus and Folkman, may be either emotion-focused (i.e., directed toward regulation of one's emotional responses to a

potentially stressful circumstance) or problem-focused (with efforts directed toward managing or changing the situation). Researchers such as LaMontagne (1985, 1987, 2000) suggest that by recognizing that children's coping is a dynamic process, and by understanding and appreciating the appraisals children make of their circumstances, healthcare professionals are in a better position to support children's coping efforts and reduce their levels of stress.

Varying forms of coping behavior have been identified among children, with the most basic distinction being made between strategies that are *active* (i.e., vigilantly seeking information, support) or *avoidant* (e.g., restricting their access to information about the event, avoiding discussion of the events). Strategies or approaches selected may vary within the individual, with differing circumstances, and over time. LaMontagne (1985), for example, found some children to be "combination copers," who had acquired much information about the nature of an impending surgery, but denied any knowledge of post-operative complications or potential negative effects of surgery.

Ritchie and colleagues (Ritchie, Caty, & Ellerton, 1984) developed an observational instrument for identifying and documenting coping behaviors, which consists of forty items distributed among six subscales: seeking information, direct action, inhibition of action, seeking or accepting help or comfort from others, movement toward independence or growth, and intrapsychic efforts. An observation of hospitalized preschool children using this instrument (Ritchie et al., 1988) indicated that information seeking and direct action behaviors were most common and that more coping behaviors were observed in situations categorized as "low stress" rather than "high stress." The latter finding may, in part, have been due to greater constraints placed on children by healthcare professionals during high stress events. In a separate study, Ellerton, Ritchie, and Caty (1994) found that children's self-reported pain during the "high stress" event of a venipuncture was correlated with the number of coping behaviors they used, with attempts to protect themselves, and with the occurrence of helpful interventions by nurses during the event.

Studies have also examined the relationship between children's observed coping behaviors and other factors, including locus of control, age, type of illness, and the amount of information children acquired related to a procedure or event. For example, studies by LaMontagne (1984, 1985, 1987) revealed that children who were classified as "active copers" had greater internal locus of control than did children identified as either "avoidant" or as using a combination of active and avoidant approaches to coping. Moreover, LaMontagne found some evidence that preferred coping approaches may vary with age. In this research, older children were more likely to use active coping modes, while children categorized as "avoidant" tended to be younger. Spirito, Stark, and Tyc (1994) concluded that acutely ill children (ages 7 to 17) were more likely than their chronically ill peers to use avoidant coping strategies. Peterson and Toler (1986) discovered that children who used the active coping strategy of "information seeking" were likely to have acquired more information prior to hospitalization than other children. Information-seeking behavior was also found to be predictive of more adaptive behavior during blood tests.

EFFECTIVENESS OF INTERVENTIONS USED BY CHILD LIFE

Play

Play is, perhaps, the most ubiquitous tool used by child life specialists. It is used to pro-mote continuing development among patients, to normalize medical environments, to facilitate emotional expression, and to enhance children's understanding of medical events. Although play typically occupies most of a child's waking hours, studies indicate that hospitalization tends to, at least temporarily, disrupt play activity. Among the earliest studies to note this effect was that of Tisza, Horwitz, and Angoff (1970) who observed the nature of young children's free play in a hospital playroom. They found an initial lack of play among the observed children in the absence of a parent or parent substitute, such as a playroom supervisor. However, the level of children's play was found to increase over successive days of hospitalization.

Evidence of a suppression of play during hospitalization is also found in the work of Burstein and Meichenbaum (1979). They observed the play of children with a variety of toys (classified as either medical or non-medical) before, during and after hospitalization. A significantly greater amount of play disruption was observed during hospitalization than either before or after. Keilhofner, Barris, Bauer, Shoestock, and Walker (1983) contrasted the playfulness of hospitalized and non-hospitalized preschool children in familiar and unfamiliar setting. In each case the scores of hospitalized children were lower.

The causes of the disruption are not always suggested, but may include anxiety, unfamiliarity of the surroundings, and the absence of adult guidance, as well as physical constraints or the child's medical condition. Whatever the causes may be, research indicates that the presence and involvement of adults is capable of increasing the level or amount of children's play. For example, Tisza et al. (1970) found that the presence of adult supervision in the playroom helped children become more secure, resulting in a corresponding increase in play behavior.

Keilhofner et al. (1983) found that the developmental age for both hospitalized and non-hospitalized children increased when a caregiver was present and involved. Moreover, in studies described above, the presence of child life specialists has been found to increase levels of children's play in settings including the intensive care unit (Cataldo, Bessman, Parker, Pearson, & Rogers, 1979), the emergency department (Alcock, Goodman, Feldman, McGrath, Park, & Cappelli, 1985), and outpatient clinics (Williams & Powell, 1980).

The question remains whether play engaged in spontaneously or facilitated by an adult is used by children to address their fears or concerns and whether that form of play is effective in reducing levels of distress. Evidence from correlational studies suggests that the relationships between children's emotional states, their selection of play materials, and the potential benefits of this activity are complex. For example, studies have found that higher levels of play with medical toys prior to hospitalization are associated with lower distress following discharge (Burstein & Meichenbaum, 1979; Tarnow & Gutstein, 1983). However, as these studies are correlational in design they cannot be viewed as conclusive evidence that medical play causes a reduction in anxiety. It is equally probable that children's selection of medical toys is an indicator of their relative comfort in approaching the impending medical events. Support for this interpretation comes from studies conducted in pediatric dental care settings. Researchers found that greater use of toy dental equipment was associated with less anxious behavior in *prior* dental visits (McTigue & Pinkham, 1978; Pinkham & Kerber, 1979).

Use of experimental research techniques might provide more conclusive evidence regarding the value of play in the reduction of children's distress associated with hospitalization and medical events. However, studies using the experimental paradigm are few in number, and their results are mixed. Fosson, Martin, and Haley (1990) considered five- to ten-year-old children who were hospitalized for a minimum of ten days. Children included in the study were provided with a single 30-minute session of either medical play or an attention control condition of viewing television with an investigator. Anxiety scores of both groups of children declined from admission to discharge, with a greater reduction noted among children in the medical play condition. However, the difference in anxiety scores between the medical play and control conditions was not significant.

Rae, Worchel, Upchurch, Sanner, and Daniel (1989) compared the effects of medical play with several other experimental conditions. Subjects in this study (who were five to ten years of age experiencing a brief hospitalization) were assigned to one of four groups – therapeutic play (with medical equipment, reflection, and interpretation), diversionary play (e.g., games and puzzles), verbal support, or a condition of no contact. Children in the first three conditions participated in two 30-minute sessions. A significant reduction was noted in self-reported fears of children in the therapeutic play group. However, no significant differences were found among the experimental groups on five other dependent variables.

Clatworthy (1981) provided hospitalized children with daily 30-minute play sessions involving both medical and non-medical play equipment. The levels of anxiety of children involved in the play sessions remained stable over the course of hospitalization, while those of children not involved in the play actually increased. The difference, however, failed to achieve a conventional level of significance.

Each of these studies provides limited evidence of the potential benefits of play for children in healthcare settings. That the results are not greater may be due to several factors, including the limited nature of the intervention provided (ranging from a single 30-minute session to 30 minutes daily), the difficulty of studying the phenomenon of play in healthcare settings, and the fact that play is provided in many forms in medical settings apart from the research protocol. Nevertheless, additional research should be pursued to better understand the potential effects of this most common child life approach.

In summary, the few studies that have directly addressed the value of play in medical settings suggest that:

- Hospitalization and its attendant stressors may suppress or disrupt children's play, at least temporarily
- The presence and involvement of adults can increase the level or amount of children's play
- Unless children are excessively anxious, they may engage in play related to their condition
- Spontaneous selection of play relevant to ones condition may be associated with reductions in distress, and
- Systematically providing children with opportunities for therapeutic play may provide benefits, although the results may be limited.

Preparation

Of the primary psychosocial interventions used by child life specialists, none has received as much research attention as has the preparation of children and their families for healthcare encounters, with the earliest of this research dating back to the 1950s. This body of research has examined varying forms and components of the preparation process, including the presentation of information, both procedural and sensory, the providing of emotional support, use of modeling techniques, instruction in coping skills, and the application of combinations of these approaches. The effectiveness of these preparation approaches in reducing stress among children experiencing medical procedures will be briefly reviewed and summarized here. A more complete review of the research in this area is provided in Chapter 8.

Overall, the preponderance of the evidence from the scores of studies conducted on preparation of children for healthcare experiences over the past fifty years supports the effectiveness of interventions, although this research is not without its methodological limitations (Vernon et al., 1965; Thompson, 1985; Whelan & Kirkby, 1998; O'Connor-Von, 2000; Rape & Bush, 1994; Yap, 1988). Further evidence of the efficacy of preparation efforts comes from a small series of meta-analyses, or studies designed to reveal trends that may be found in groups of related research reports. For example, Saile, Burgmeier, and Schmidt (1988) conducted an analysis of 75 studies on preparation. They concluded that preparation had a small, but significant effect in reducing children's distress. They also noted that the benefits of preparation appeared to be greater among children facing major operations or a series of treatments (as opposed to minor procedures or single events). Vernon and Thompson (1993) considered 22 studies investigating interventions designed to reduce the post-hospital distress of hospitalized children. Sixteen of these studies involved preparation, with the remaining six assessing parent presence during procedures. Significant positive effects were found for the interventions. A few researchers have concluded that, in general, psychological preparation compares favorably with pharmacological treatment of stress among pediatric patients (Jay, Elliott, Katz, & Siegel, 1987; Mansson, Fredrikson, & Rosberg, 1992; Rape & Bush, 1994).

Early preparation studies indicated the effectiveness of specific interventions, including the combination of approaches referred to as "stress-point preparation" (Wolfer & Visintainer, 1975, 1979; Visintainer & Wolfer, 1975; Wolfer et al., 1988). This intensive approach identifies periods of particular difficulty during hospitalization and prepares the child and family for each by providing information, opportunities for rehearsal, and emotional support. However, only a few studies have directly compared the relative effectiveness of various individual approaches to preparation. In studies where direct comparisons have been made, basic verbal information has been found to be less effective in comparison to sensory information (Johnson, Kirchhoff, & Endress, 1975), to more specific information (Edwinson, Arnbjornsson, & Ekman, 1988), or to information provided in combination with instruction in coping skills (Campbell, Kirkpatrick, Berry, & Lamberti, 1995). Zastowny, Kirschenbaum, and Meng (1986) compared the effectiveness of providing children and their parents with information, anxiety reduction techniques (e.g., relaxation), or instruction in the use of coping skills (with parents given information on their role as "coping coaches" for their children) on their distress responses before, during, and after surgery. Coping skills training was the method that best helped children adapt to their hospitalization. These results are consistent with the perceptions of a panel of "experts" who rated preparation in coping skills, overall, as the most effective approach (O'Byrne et al., 1997). Other comparisons, however, have reported no significant difference between approaches of providing sensory information and coping instruction

(Dahlquist et al., 1986; Siegal & Peterson, 1980, 1981).

PARENT PRESENCE AND PARTICIPATION IN THE CARE OF THEIR CHILDREN

Research conducted prior to 1985 on parental roles and involvement during the hospitalization of a child primarily addressed topics such as the effects of parents "rooming in" during a hospital stay, parents' desires to participate during their child's hospitalization, and factors that are related to that participation (Thompson, 1985). Much of this research was conducted with families whose child faced acute hospitalization for relatively brief periods. Since the 1980s, there have been major shifts in conditions for which children are hospitalized and in the rights and services accorded to parents in the hospital. Over the past decades an increasing proportion of the pediatric hospital population has consisted of children with complicated, chronic conditions or those hospitalized with severe, acute conditions. Recent research suggests that families in these categories may benefit from targeted, supportive interventions, whether their children are hospitalized repeatedly for chronic conditions (Burke, Kauffmann, Wong, & Harrison, 2001) or for sudden, unplanned admissions (Melnyk & Feinstein, 2001).

Parents of children with chronic conditions develop impressive expertise in their child's medical status and care, which may or may not be recognized and utilized during periods of an inpatient stay. Research by Balling and McCubbin (2001) indicates that parents of chronically ill children want to participate actively in the care of their children when hospitalized. Moreover, they expressed concern that a lower quality of care is given to their children in the hospital than at home due to the understaffing and overwork of nurses.

Since the right of parents to remain with a child during hospitalization has become an accepted practice (Roberts, Maieron, & Collier, 1988), research activity has shifted away from the global effects of rooming-in to an examination of parent presence and participation during specific events. The largest body of research in recent years on parent participation in medical events has examined the practice of allowing parents to be present during the induction of anesthesia in their children. A portion of this research addresses the level of acceptance of this practice by parents and professional staff. Blesch and Fisher (1996) found the practice to be accepted by parents, physicians, and nursing staff. However, researchers have found that attitudes toward parental presence differ between professionals in the United States and the United Kingdom, with greater use and acceptance of parent participation found among surgeons (Kain, Fernandes, & Touloukian, 1996) and anesthesiologists (Kain, Ferris, Mayes, & Rimar, 1997) in the United Kingdom.

Researchers have also studied the effects of parent presence during anesthesia induction. Kain, Mayes, Caramico, Silver, Spieker, Nygren, Anderson, and Rimar (1996) compared the responses of children whose parents were either present or absent during anesthesia induction. Overall, there were no significant differences in the behavioral or physiological responses of the children in the two groups. Additional analyses indicated that parent presence had a positive effect on one of the physiological measures (children's serum cortisol levels) for three subgroups of children: children older than age four, children whose parents had low trait anxiety levels, and children whose temperament assessment indicated low baseline levels of activity. Although this research does not consistently demonstrate that parental presence contributes to the reduced anxiety of children, there are positive effects upon children in some cases, as well as reduced anxiety and increased satisfaction among parents who have participated.

The effects of parent presence during anesthesia were contrasted with use of a preoperative sedative by Kain, Mayes, Wang, Caramico, and Hofstadter (1998). Children given the sedative were rated as less anxious in response to the procedure than either children whose parents were present or a control group of children who were given neither intervention. However, the percentage of children whose compliance during inductions was rated as "poor" was larger among the control group than either the sedative or parent-present group. As an extension of this study, Kain, Mayes, Wang, Caramico, Krivutza, and Hofstadter (2000) examined whether a combined approach of sedation and having parent presence is more effective than the use of sedatives alone. The combined approach was found to be no more effective at reducing children's anxiety than sedation alone. Parents who had been present for their child's induction, however, had lower levels of anxiety following separation from their child and higher levels of satisfaction with the overall care of their child and with the separation process than did parents who had not been present. Cameron, Bond, and Pointer (1996) also reported a reduction in anxiety among parents who were present during anesthesia induction. Kain (2000) notes the potential importance of such findings for the efforts of healthcare providers to improve patient and parent satisfaction.

Additional research has considered the potential effects of the presence of family members during critical, intrusive medical procedures, particularly those occurring in the pediatric intensive care unit (PICU) or the emergency department. Sacchetti, Lichenstein, Carraccio, and Harris (1996) surveyed parents and emergency department staff regarding their attitudes toward parent presence during a range of procedures including lumbar puncture, nasogastric tube placement, intubation, and removal of an object from the child's eye. More than 90 percent of the parents and staff surveyed favored allowing parents to be present. Powers and Rubenstein (1999) report similar results. The level of support among staff members for parental presence may vary with their personal experience with the practice (Sacchetti, Carraccio, Leva, Harris, and Lichenstein, 2000) and with the degree of intrusiveness of the procedure. Beckman, Sloan, Moore, Cordell, Brizendine, Knoop, Goldman, & Geninatti (2002) found the majority of emergency department physicians and nurses they surveyed to be supportive of parent presence, regardless of the procedure. However, the proportion expressing support for the practice declined as the intrusiveness of the procedure increased.

A survey of parents conducted by Boie, Moore, Brummett, and Nelson (1999) reflected a similar pattern of acceptance, with the majority stating a preference to be present during each of a variety of emergency department procedures. However, a decline was noted in the desire to be present as intrusiveness increased. Also, in regard to resuscitation of the child, most parents (83.4%) said they would want to be present if their child were likely to die. Given the degree of support for the practice by parents and staff, and the relative absence of evidence that the presence of family members negatively affects the care of the child, rigid continuance of exclusionary policies is unwarranted.

CONCLUSIONS AND RECOMMENDATIONS

Generalizations based on the current review of research related to child life theory and practice are made with some degree of caution due to limitations in both quantity and quality of existing studies. We will identify some of the gaps in the literature in connection with our summary of the findings of our review. The methodological problems in child life research along with recommendations for future research will be considered in separate sections below.

Summary and Conclusions

Although studies on new topics (e.g., parent presence and participation in medical procedures) continue to emerge, the findings of research we reviewed do not diverge markedly from the studies on the same issues covered in earlier reviews. Recent studies on the development of the field of child life practice reveal some of the growing pains associated with the growth of a relatively new profession. Problem areas identified by child specialists include role ambiguity and limited power in comparisons to other healthcare providers. Yet child life professionals, as a group, do not appear to be especially demoralized in the face of such obstacles.

The cumulative evidence generally supports the efficacy of child life practice. Child life specialists clearly provide important services that have a positive impact on children and their families who undergo hospitalization and painful medical procedures. However, additional studies are needed to identify and define the components of "best" child life practices. Also, as child life services continue to expand into non-traditional settings such as dental offices, emergency departments, and centers for sexually abused children there is an increasing need for summative and formative program evaluation studies in those areas.

Studies included in our review also tend to confirm reports published in previous reviews that hospitalization is typically stressful to children. The amount of stress appears to be mediated by various factors including age, parental anxiety, personality factors, medical history, and degree of physical stressors encountered. The most obvious symptoms of psychosocial stress of appear to be short-lived. However, additional studies are needed to assess both short-term and long-term residual psychosocial effects of hospitalization as well as how various factors interact to affect the level of stress.

Through the years researchers have identified some of the strategies hospitalized children and adolescents use to cope with the stress of hospitalization and painful medical procedures. Individual differences in coping behaviors have been attributed to a variety of factors including age, personality, and previous medical encounters. Additional studies are needed to identify other factors associated with variations in coping style and how child life professionals can best identify and facilitate children's stress reduction responses.

Research studies consistently show that hospitalization tends to suppress or disrupt children's natural tendency to play. The findings also indicate that presence and involvement of adults can increase the level or amount of children's play. Overall, research findings tend to support basic child life philosophy and practices that promote play as a critical component of children's healthcare. Further studies are needed to identify the conditions that influence play as well as the context and types of play (e.g. structured or unstructured) that are most beneficial to pediatric patients of various ages.

Child life specialists use a variety of procedures in preparing children to cope with painful medical procedures. Studies consistently indicate that, in general, preparation has a significant effect in reducing the stress associated with healthcare experiences. However, some procedures appear to be more effective (e.g., stress point preparation and instruction in coping skills) than others. Additional studies are needed to determine which preparation procedures works best for whom under what circumstances.

In a relatively new line of research, investigators are studying the effects of parental presence on pediatric patients during medical procedures as well as parent participation in preparation of the child for the event. On the basis of the limited studies available, it appears that parental presence has positive effects on the patient and contributes to parent satisfaction. Investigators should continue to explore ways in which parents can best assist in the psychosocial caring for their children as well as well as benefit from the process.

Methodological Problems

In general, the quality of research in the field of child life does not differ markedly from investigations in other areas related to the psychosocial care of children's health (e.g., see La Greca & Varni, 1993; Gottleib, 1990). The problems include but are not limited to small sample size, lack of comparable control groups, failure to randomize, use of broad categorical groupings of subjects (age and medical conditions), inadequate information about reliability and validity of assessment instruments and procedures, failure to control possible mediating variables, and heavy reliance on patient and parent reports. Many studies are one-dimensional and do not consider possible influence of multiple variables. Long-term follow-up studies are rare. In spite of these problems that may limit generalizations of findings, fatal methodological flaws that totally nullify the results of a published report are rare.

Recommendations

How can we encourage more and better research that addresses the deficiencies identified above as well as new lines of inquiry? Clearly, the difficulties associated involved in controlling multiple variables, conforming to ethical guidelines, limited subject availability (especially for control/comparisons groups), problems in finding suitable measuring instruments, along with time constraints and limited resources are deterrents to the proliferation of child life research. This means that all professionals in the field need to be more resourceful in identifying resources and forming alliances to provide a support system for research endeavors.

Even though their numbers may be limited, child life academicians typically have more institutional incentives than clinicians to conduct research. These professionals need to become more involved in networking with child life clinicians, as well as nurses and other healthcare professionals when appropriate. As the field of child life expands, there will be a need for doctoral programs in child life to provide educational and research underpinnings of the profession.

A recommendation made by La Greca and Varni (1993) offers a strategy for improving the quality and quantity of child life research. They suggest solving some of the problems associated with sample size and matching subjects by conducting multisite studies involving several investigators. This approach is not intended to discourage or discount individual or single site investigations. However, through a combination of resources and efforts, cooperating investigators with varying degrees of clinical and research expertise could participate in research endeavors that might otherwise not be possible.

REFERENCES

Alcock, D., Berthaiume, S., & Clarke, A. (1984). Child life intervention in the emergency department. *Children's Health Care, 12,* 130-136.

Alcock, D., Feldman, W., Goodman, J. T., McGrath, P. J., & Park, J. M. (1985). Evaluation of child life intervention in emergency department suturing. *Pediatric Emergency Care, 1,* 111-115.

Alcock, D., Goodman, J., Feldman, W., McGrath, P. J., Park, M., & Cappelli, M. (1985). Emergency and waiting behaviors in emergency waiting areas. *Children's Health Care, 13,* 174-180.

Association for the Care of Children's Health. (1990). *Directory of child life programs in North America* (8th ed.). Bethesda, MD: Author.

Balling, K., & McCubbin, M. (2001). Hospitalized children with chronic illness: Parental caregiving needs and valuing expertise. *Journal of Pediatric Nursing, 16,* 110-119.

Beckman, A. W., Sloan, B. K., Moore, G. P., Cordell, W. H., Brizendine, E. J., Knoop, K. J., Goldman, M. J., & Geninatti, M. R. (2002). Should parents be present during emergency department procedures on children, and who should make the decision? A survey of emergency physician and nurse attitudes. *Academic Emergency Medicine, 9,* 154-158.

Blesch, P., & Fisher, M. L. (1996). The impact of parental presence on parental anxiety and satisfaction. *AORN Journal, 63,* 761-768.

Boie, E. T., Moore, G. P., Brummett, C., & Nelson, D.R. (1999). Do parents want to be present during invasive procedures performed on their children in the emergency department? A survey of 400 parents. *Annals of Emergency Medicine, 34,* 70-74.

Burke, S. O., Kauffmann, E., Wong, C., & Harrison, M. B. (2001). Effects of stress-point intervention with families of repeatedly hospitalized children. *Journal of Family Nursing, 7*, 128-158.

Burstein. S., & Meichenbaum, D. (1979). The work of worrying in children undergoing surgery. *Journal of Maternal Child Psychology, 7*, 121-132.

Cameron, J. A., Bond, M. J., & Pointer, S. C. (1996). Reducing the anxiety of children undergoing surgery: Parental presence during anesthetic induction. *Journal of Pediatrics and Child Health, 32*, 51-56.

Campbell, L. A., Kirkpatrick, S. E., Berry, C. C., & Lamberti, J. J. (1995). Preparing children with congenital heart disease for cardiac surgery. *Journal of Pediatric Psychology, 20*, 318-328.

Carson, D. K., Jenkins, J., & Stout, C. B. (1985). Assessing child life programs: Study model with a small number of subjects. *Children's Health Care, 14*, 123-125.

Cataldo, M. F., Bessman, C. A., Parker, L. H., Pearson, J. E. R., & Rogers, M. D. (1979). Behavioral assessment for pediatric intensive care units. *Journal of Applied Behavioral Analysis, 12*, 83-97.

Chernoff, R. G., Ireys, H. T., DeVet, K. A., & Kim, Y. J. (2002). A randomized, controlled trial of a community-based support program for children with chronic illness: Pediatric outcomes. *Archives of Pediatrics and Adolescent Medicine, 156*, 533-539.

Child Life Council, Inc. (1994). *Directory of child life programs* (9th ed.). Bethesda, MD: Author.

Clatworthy, S. (1981). Therapeutic play: Effects on hospitalized children. *Children's Health Care, 9*, 108-113.

Cole, W., Diener, M., Wright, C., Gaynard, L. (2001). Health care professionals' perceptions of child life specialists. *Children's Health Care, 30*, 1-15.

Dahlquist, L. M, Gil, K. M., Armstrong, D., Delawyer, D., Greene, P., & Wuori, D. (1986). Preparing children for medical examinations: The importance of previous medical experience. *Health Psychology, 5*, 249-259.

Dombro, R. H. (1967a). Child life programs in ninety-two pediatric departments of general hospitals in the United States and Canada. In J. A. Haller, J. L. Talbert, & R. H. Dombro

(Eds.), *The hospitalized child and his family*. Baltimore, MD: Johns Hopkins Press.

Dombro, R. H. (1967b). Child life programs in ninety-one children's hospitals in the United States and Canada. In J. A. Haller, J. L. Talbert, & R. H. Dombro (Eds.), *The hospitalized child and his family*. Baltimore, MD: Johns Hopkins Press.

Edwinson, M., Arnbjornsson, E., & Ekman, R. (1988). Psychologic preparation program for children undergoing acute appendectomy. *Pediatrics, 82*, 30-36.

Eiser, C., & Eiser, J. R. (1990). The effects of personal and family hospital experience on children's heath beliefs, concerns, and behavior. *Social Behavior, 5*, 307-314.

Ellerton, M. L., Ritchie, J. A., & Caty, S. (1994). Factors influencing young children's coping behaviors during stressful encounters. *Maternal-Child Nursing Journal, 22*, 74-82.

Fosson, A., Martin, J., & Haley, J. (1990). Anxiety among hospitalized latency-age children. *Journal of Developmental and Behavioral Pediatrics, 11*, 324-327.

Froehlich, M. A. (1984). A comparison of the effect of music therapy and medical play therapy on the verbalization behavior of pediatric patients. *Journal of Music Therapy, 21*, 2-15.

Gaynard, L. L. (1985). Child life specialists as perceived by health care specialists. *University Microfilms, International, 46*, (O8B), 2611B. (International Microfilm No. DES85-23416)

Gaynard, L., Hausslein, E., & DeMarsh, J. P. (1989). Child life specialists: Report of an observational study. *Children's Health Care, 18*, 75-81.

Giles, H. W., Bradbard, M. R., & Endsley, R. (1987). Child life interns' contributions to pediatric care in a community hospital. *Journal of Research in Childhood Education, 2*, 80-88.

Gottleib, S. (1990). Documenting the efficacy of psychosocial care in the hospital setting. *Developmental and Behavioral Pediatrics, 11*, 328-329.

Holloway, D., & Wallinga, C. R. (1990). Burnout in child life specialists: The relation of role stress. *Children's Health Care, 19*, 10-18.

Jay, S., Elliott, C. H., Katz, E., & Siegel, S. E. (1987). Cognitive-behavioral and pharmacologic interventions for children's' distress during painful medical procedures. *Journal of Consulting and Clinical Psychology, 55*, 860-865.

Jessee, P., Strickland, M. P., Leeper, J. D., & Hudson, C. J. (1987). The effect of nature-based experiences on children's adjustment to the hospital: A comparative study. *Journal of Environmental Education, 19*, 10-15.

Johnson, J. E., Kirchhoff, K. T., & Endress, M. P. (1975). Altering children's distress behavior during orthopedic cast removal. *Nursing Research, 24*, 404-410.

Kain, Z. N. (2000). Perioperative psychological issues in children. *American Society of Anesthesiologists Newsletter, 64*.

Kain, Z. N., Fernandes, L. A., & Touloukian, R. J. (1996). Parental presence during induction of anesthesia: The surgeon's perspective. *European Journal of Pediatric Surgery, 6*, 323-327.

Kain, Z. N., Ferris, C. A., Mayes, L. C., & Rimar, S. (1997). Parental presence during induction of anesthesia: Practice differences between the United States and Great Britain. *Paediatric Anaesthology, 6*, 187-193.

Kain, Z. N., Mayes, L. C., Caramico, L. A., Silver, D., Spieker, M., Nygren, M. M., Anderson, G., & Rimar, S. (1996). Parental presence during induction of anesthesia: A randomized controlled trial. *Anesthesiology, 84*, 1060-1067.

Kain, Z. N., Mayes, L. C., O'Connor, T. Z., & Cicchetti, D.V. (1996). Preoperative anxiety in children: Predictors and outcomes. *Archives of Pediatric and Adolescent Medicine, 150*, 1238-1245.

Kain, Z. N., Mayes, L. C., Wang, S. M., Caramico, L. A., & Hofstadter, M. B. (1998). Parental presence during induction of anesthesia versus sedative premedication: Which intervention is more effective? *Anesthesiology, 89*, 1147-1156.

Kain, Z. N., Mayes, L. C., Wang, S. M., Caramico, L. A., Krizutza, D. M., & Hofstadter, M. B. (2000). Parental presence and a sedative premedicant for children undergoing surgery: A hierarchical study. *Anesthesiology, 92*, 939-946.

Keilhofner, G., Barris, R., Bauer, D., Shoestock, B., & Walker, L. (1983). A comparison of play behavior in hospitalized and nonhospitalized children. *The American Journal of Occupational Therapy, 37*, 305-312.

King, J., & Ziegler, S. (1981). The effects of hospitalization on children's behavior: A review of the literature. *Children's Health Care, 10*, 20-28.

Krebel, M. S., Clayton, C., Graham, C. (1996). Child life programs in the pediatric emergency department. *Pediatric Emergency Care, 12*, 13-15.

La Greca, A. M., & Varni, J. W. (1993). Editorial: Interventions in pediatric psychology: A look toward the future. *Journal of Pediatric Psychology, 18*, 667-679.

LaMontagne, L. L. (1984). Children's locus of control beliefs as a predictor of preoperative coping behavior. *Nursing Research, 33*, 76-85.

LaMontagne, L. L. (1985). Facilitating children's coping. *AORN Journal, 42*, 718-723.

LaMontagne, L. L. (1987). Children's preoperative coping: Replication and extension. *Nursing Research, 36*, 163-167.

LaMontagne, L. L. (2000). Children's coping with surgery: A process-oriented perspective. *Journal of Pediatric Nursing, 15*, 307-312.

Lazarus, R., & Folkman, S. (1984). Stress, appraisal, and coping. New York: Springer.

Mabe, P. A., Treiber, F. A., & Riley, W. T. (1991). Examining emotional distress during pediatric hospitalization for school-aged children. *Children's Health Care, 20*, 162-169.

Mansson, M. E., Fredrikson, B., & Rosberg, B. (1992). Comparison of preparation and narcotic-sedative premedication in children undergoing surgery. *Pediatric Nursing, 18*, 337-342.

Maslach, C., & Jackson, S. E. (1981). The measurement of experienced burnout. *Journal of Occupational Behavior, 2*, 99-113.

Mather, P. L., Glasrud, P. H. (1981). Child life workers: Who are they and what are they doing? *Children's Health Care, 10*, 11-15.

McClowry, S. G. (1988). A review of the literature pertaining to the psychosocial responses of school-aged children to hospitalization. *Journal of Pediatric Nursing, 3*, 296-311.

McCue, K., Wagner, M., Hansen, H., & Rigler, D. (1978). A survey of a developing health care profession: Hospital "play" programs. *Journal of the Association for the Care of Children in Hospitals, 7*, 15-22.

McTigue, D. J., & Pinkham, J. (1978). Association between children's dental behavior and play behavior. *Journal of Dentistry for Children, 45,* 218-222.

Melnyk, B. M., & Feinstein, N. F. (2001). Mediating functions of maternal anxiety and participation in care on young children's posthospital adjustment. *Research in Nursing and Health, 24,* 18-26.

Munn, E. K., Barber, C. E., & Fritz, J. (1996). Factors affecting the professional well-being of child life specialists. *Children's Health Care, 25,* 71-91.

O'Bryne, K. K., Peterson, L., & Saldana, L. (1997). Survey of pediatric hospitals' preparation programs: Evidence of the impact of health psychology research. *Health Psychology, 16,* 147-154.

O'Connor-Von, S. (2000). Preparing children for surgery: An integrative research review. *AORN Journal, 71,* 334-343.

Pass, M. D., & Bolig, R. (1993). A comparison of play behaviors in two child life program variations. *Children's Health Care, 22,* 5-17.

Pearson, J. E. R., Cataldo, M., Tureman, A., Bessman, C., & Rogers, M. C. (1980). Pediatric intensive care unit patients: Effect of play intervention on behavior. *Critical Care Medicine, 8,* 64-67.

Peterson, L., & Toler, S. M. (1986). An information seeking disposition in child surgery patients. *Health Psychology, 5,* 343-358.

Pinkham, J. R., & Kerber, P. E. (1979). Association between school-age children's dental behavior and play behavior. *Pediatric Dentistry, 1,* 221-224.

Powers, K. S., & Rubenstein, J. S. (1999). Family presence during invasive procedures in the pediatric intensive care unit: A prospective study. *Archives of Pediatrics and Adolescent Medicine, 153,* 955-958.

Rae, W. A., Worchel, F. F., Upchurch, J., Sanner, J. H., & Daniel, D. A. (1989). The psychological impact of play on hospitalized children. *Pediatric Nursing, 14,* 617-627.

Rape, R. N. & Bush, J. P. (1994). Psychological reparation for pediatric oncology patients undergoing painful procedures: A methodological critique of the research. *Children's Health Care, 23,* 51-67.

Rennick, J. E., Johnston, C., Dougherty, G., Platt, R., & Ritchie, J. (2002). Children's psychological responses after critical illness and exposure to invasive technology. *Journal of Developmental and Behavioral Pediatrics, 23,* 133-144.

Ricks, F., & Faubert, T. (1981). Canadian child life/non-medical programs in hospitals. *Children's Health Care, 10,* 16-19.

Ritchie, J. A., Caty, S., & Ellerton, M. L. (1984). Coping in preschool hospitalized children: Toward the development of an observation instrument. *Nursing Papers* (Special Supplement), 38-48.

Ritchie, J., Caty, S., & Ellerton, M. L. (1988). Cooing behaviors of hospitalized preschool children. *Maternal-Child Nursing Journal, 17,* 153-171.

Roberts, M. C., Maieron, M. J., & Collier, J. (1988). *Directory of hospital psychosocial policies and programs.* Washington, DC: Association for the Care of Children's Health.

Rutkowski, J. (1978). A survey of child life programs. *Journal of the Association for the Care of Children in Hospitals, 6,* 11-16.

Saile, H., Burgmeier, R., & Schmidt, L. R. (1988). A meta-analysis of studies on psychological preparation of children facing medical procedures. *Psychology and Health, 2,* 107-132.

Sacchetti, A., Carraccio, C., Leva, E., Harris, R. H., Lichenstein, R. (2000). Acceptance of family member presence during pediatric resuscitations in the emergency department: Effects of personal experience. *Pediatric Emergency Care, 16,* 85-87.

Sacchetti, A., Lichenstein, R., Carraccio, C., & Harris, R. H. (1996). Family member presence during pediatric emergency department procedures. *Pediatric Emergency Care, 12,* 268-271.

Saylor, C., Pallmeyer, T., Finch, A., Eason, L., Trieber, F., & Folger, C. (1987). Predictors of psychological distress in hospitalized pediatric patients. *Journal of the American Academy of Child and Adolescent Psychiatry, 26,* 232-236.

Siegal, L. J., & Peterson, L. (1980). Stress reduction in young dental patients through coping skills and sensory information. *Journal of Consulting and Clinical Psychology, 48,* 785-787.

Siegal, L. J., & Peterson, L. (1981). Maintenance effects of coping skills and sensory information on young children's responses to repeated dental procedures. *Behavior Therapy, 12,* 530-535.

Snow, C. W., & Triebenbacher, S. L. (1996). Child life program employment trends and practices. *Children's Health Care, 25,* 211-220.

Spirito, A., Stark, L. J., & Tyc, V. L. (1994). Stressors and coping strategies described during hospitalization by chronically ill children. *Journal of Clinical Child Psychology, 23,* 314-322.

Tarnow, J. D., & Gutstein, S. E. (1983). Children's preparatory behavior for elective surgery. *Journal of the American Academy of Child Psychiatry, 22,* 365-369.

Thompson, M. L. (1994). Information-seeking coping and anxiety in school-age children anticipating surgery. *Children's Health Care, 23,* 87-97.

Thompson, R. H. (1985). *Psychosocial research on pediatric hospitalization and health care: A review of the literature.* Springfield, IL: Charles C Thomas.

Thompson, R. H., & Vernon, D. T. A. (1993). Research on children's behavior after hospitalization: A review and synthesis. *Developmental and Behavioral Pediatrics, 14,* 28-35.

Tisza, V. B., Hurwitz, I., & Angoff, K. (1970). The use of a play program by hospitalized children. *Journal of the American Academy of Child Psychiatry, 9,* 515-531.

Vernon, D. T. A., Foley, J.M., Sipowitz, R.R., & Schulman, J. L. (1965). *The psychological responses of children to hospitalization and illness.* Springfield, IL: Charles C Thomas.

Vernon, D. T. A., Schulman, J. L., & Foley, J. M. (1966). Changes in children's behavior after hospitalization. *American Journal of the Diseases of Children, 111,* 581-593.

Vernon, D. T. A., & Thompson, R. H. (1993). Research on the effect of experimental interventions on children's behavior after hospital-ization: A review and synthesis. *Journal of Developmental and Behavioral Pediatrics, 14,* 36-44.

Visintainer, M. A., & Wolfer, J. A. (1975). A psychological preparation for surgical pediatric patients: The effect on children's and parents' stress responses and adjustment. *Pediatrics, 56,* 187-202.

Whelan, T. A., & Kirkby, R. J. (1998). Advantages for children and their families of psychological preparation for hospitalization and surgery. *Journal of Family Studies, 4,* 35-51.

Williams, Y. B, & Powell, M. (1980). Documenting the value of supervised play in a pediatric ambulatory clinic. *Journal of the Association for the Care of Children's Health, 9,* 15-20.

Wolfer, J., Gaynard, L., Goldberger, J., Laidley, L. N., & Thompson, R. (1988). An experimental evaluation of a model child life program. *Children's Health Care, 16,* 244-254.

Wolfer, J. A., & Visintainer, M. A. (1975). Pediatric surgical patients' and parents' stress responses and adjustment. *Nursing Research, 24,* 244-255.

Wolfer, J. A., & Visintainer, M. A. (1979). Prehospital psychological preparation for tonsillectomy patients: Effects on children's and parents' adjustment. *Pediatrics, 64,* 646-655.

Yap, J.N. (1988). A critical review of pediatric preoperative preparation procedures: Processes, outcomes, and future directions. *Journal of Applied Developmental Psychology, 9,* 359-389.

Zastowny, T. R., Kirschenbaum, D. S., & Meng, A. L. (1986). Coping skills training for children: Effects on distress before, during, and after hospitalization for surgery. *Health Psychology, 5,* 531-547.

Zurlinden, J. (1985). Minimizing the impact of hospitalization for children and their families. *Maternal Child Nursing, 10,* 178-182.

Chapter 4

THERAPEUTIC RELATIONSHIPS IN CHILD LIFE

KATHLEEN McCUE

Child life has borrowed many concepts from a wide variety of fields and professions, and incorporated them into the overall language and practice of what we currently define as child life. However, there is probably no component of child life that is as vague and generalized as the concept of "therapeutic relationships." In the statement of Mission, Vision and Values of Child Life, one of the values of the profession of child life is titled "Therapeutic Relationships." In the official documents of the Child Life Council (1990), the value is stated as follows: "We are committed to relationships built on trust, respect and professional competence which contribute to the development of confidence, resilience, and problem-solving skills that enable individuals and families to deal effectively with challenges to development, health and well-being." This statement seems to capture a very important essence of the profession, and most individuals in child life would agree with it. However, the concept itself is difficult to operationalize and measure, and certainly difficult to teach to new professionals in the field. The actual definition, scope, and applicability of the concept of therapeutic relationships are subject to many interpretations and representations. In this chapter, we will examine the history and usage of this concept in the professions that provide direct human services, and will attempt to synthesize the ways in which it applies to child life.

On the most primary level, it would seem logical to start with definitions of each of the terms used in the phrase, "therapeutic relationship." According to Webster (2001), "therapeutic" means "relating to or dealing with healing, especially with remedies for disease." It also means "providing or assisting in a cure." It comes from the word "therapy" meaning "remedial treatment of bodily, mental or social disorders or maladjustments." The word "relationship" is "the state of being related" while "relation" is "the state of being mutually interested or involved." Thus, a therapeutic relationship would seem to be a state of mutual interest or involvement that has to do with healing or curing. This healing may be purely physical, such as in healing a fracture or a disease, or it may be psychological or developmental healing. The healing referred to in the child life values speaks to developmental or psychosocial issues such as confidence, resilience and the management of challenges and might be more appropriately referred to as a "psychotherapeutic relationship" to exclude one that simply heals the body. However, for efficiency we will continue to use the phrase that is the title of this chapter, "therapeutic relationships." The concept of a healing involvement will be addressed throughout this chapter as we attempt to clarify the meaning of therapeutic relationships in child life. Also throughout this chapter, for ease of language, children and adults who receive child life services will be referred to as patients or clients, and the word children will refer to infants, children and adolescents.

One significant factor in using the classic definitions of "therapy" and/or "therapeutic" is that they are based on a reactive response to a problem. There must be a problem, something that needs fixing, in order to heal something. Although child life can certainly function reactively, a large portion of the work done in child life is proactive and preventive. In the early history of child life, as the profession was developing, the vast majority of interventions, those based on play, normalization of the environment, and enhancement of general coping, were directed at preventing certain negative developmental and psychosocial consequences. In one of the earliest studies of the child life profession, Wolfer, Gaynard, Goldberger, Laidley and Thompson (1988) defined child life relationships with children and families as "supportive" rather than "therapeutic." These relationships involved expressions of positive affect, affirmation and the provision of aid or assistance. Over time, as the visibility and reliability of child life increased, child life specialists were called in more and more often to provide services to a child or family member who was demonstrating existing problematic responses. So an additional issue to be addressed is whether it is meaningful to refer to a therapeutic relationship in a preventive or development-enhancing situation.

Look at some examples of these two types of interventions. General preparation for a procedure, in its broadest scope, is a proactive or preventive intervention. Working with a child who is referred or identified because of non-compliance or high anxiety is reactive. General play in a playroom or at bedside to maintain normal development is proactive. Play sessions specifically designed to help a child who has regressed language or motor skills is reactive. Are there, then, two different types of relationships the child life professional may have with a child depending on the situational goal or intention of the professional? Are all preventive/proactive interventions really supportive in nature and all intentional, reactive, problem-based interventions therapeutic? And should we, as a profession, place more emphasis on one type of relationship over the other? As we look at different types of child life programming, these questions will be addressed.

It would probably be helpful to limit the scope of this discussion by acknowledging that there are many possible parameters of "therapeutic." There are therapeutic environments, therapeutic contacts, therapeutic intentions, therapeutic locations, therapeutic activities and therapeutic personalities. Many of these categories may well apply to child life, but are beyond the scope of this chapter. Here we will be speaking only of the interactive relationship between the child life specialist and one or more other people; that is, when the child life specialist is in a state of mutual involvement with a child, parent/family member or other professional.

We have already begun to contrast "therapeutic relationships" with "supportive relationships." It is also important to acknowledge the terms "professional relationships," and "clinical relationships" and examine the interrelationships and differences between all these labels. These terms are sometimes used interchangeably, but actually probably represent overlapping but separate concepts. Many professions have examined at some length the scope and responsibilities that are encompassed by the total range of their professional services. These have been described in articles, codes of ethics, professional textbooks and well as the lay literature. All professions that involve service to the others have developed standards for how both clients and coworkers should be treated. Education, law, the business community as well as health and mental health have these standards. Even some vocational groups, for example, plumbers and salespeople, have made statements about their ethical responsibilities to their clients. However, in the non-professional categories, these standards are usually not nationalized, are dependent on support from individual employers, and reflect more personal ethical values than industry norms. For the purposes of this chapter, child life will be considered a profession, and will be examined in the context of similar or related professions. Therefore, the relationship a child life specialist has with a child or adult is a professional relationship, regardless of other relationship possibilities.

Discussions of professional relationships tend to focus on those activities by the professional that are expected behavior, and those that may be dangerous or harmful to the client. Most professions have established a list of behaviors, activities and roles that pose a danger to the accomplishment of the goals of the service. This list provides the parameters of the professional relationship, and individuals in the profession make a commitment to abide by the rules of the profession. Violations of the standards on the list may be illegal, may be against licensure rules and/or may put the client or the therapeutic relationship into jeopardy. Categories such as confidentiality, sexual relations, respect and dignity, competence per standards and law, and representation of the profession to the public are often included in the discussion of professional relationships for the helping professions. Boundary violations

are specific violations of the standards of a professional relationship, and will be discussed in detail later in this chapter.

Clinical relationships, on the other hand, reflect the simple fact that a professional and a client are in a relationship in which some sort of clinical service is provided by the professional to the client. There is no implication of interpersonal trust, integrity, or empowerment in the reality of a clinical relationship. A clinical relationship is hierarchical and assumes some knowledge or ability of the clinician is being transferred to the client or patient. The factors of trust, warmth, interpersonal positive regard and focus on empowerment of the client or patient are all more definitional of a supportive relationship. Many professionals include factors that are part of a supportive relationship in their definition of a therapeutic relationship. As the reader progresses through this chapter, it will become clear that when the term "therapeutic relationship" is used, a positive, trusting interpersonal connection is implied. However, it is not mandated simply by the phrase. Often, in reading professional literature, authors use terms such as clinical relationship or therapeutic relationship when they are really referencing the integrity and trust of a supportive relationship. All these types of relationships have potential to be part of the repertoire of child life professionals.

From the discussion above, we can probably define each of the possible relationships in a way that would be generally agreeable to most service-based or health care professionals. Below are these definitions. Remember, these are generic definitions, and not meant to specifically define these terms as they are utilized in child life.

PROFESSIONAL RELATIONSHIPS: All relationships that are established in connection with the specific profession engaged in by any individual. This includes relationships with clients or patients, their families and friends, other professionals, other coworkers, administrators, buyers, vendors, volunteers and students, and any other persons which a professional would encounter in his or her day-to-day work. All professional relationships may be categorized as either clinical or non-clinical:

- *Clinical Relationships:* Those relationships existing within the scope of a health or service profession, which are based on the accepted practice of that profession and are developed specifically with the assigned patients or clients, as well as with their families and friends.
- *Non-clinical Relationships:* Those relationships existing within the scope of the profession which are established with coworkers, colleagues, vendors, volunteers, entertainers and any other individuals that are involved, directly or indirectly, with those served by a clinical relationship. When a relationship with one of these individuals expands to include the provision of some direct clinical service, such as consultation, supervision or referral, the relationship, for that period of time, shifts from non-clinical to clinical.

SUPPORTIVE RELATIONSHIPS: Those relationships, both clinical and non-clinical, which advocate for psychosocial coping and adjustment. The word support comes from the Latin verb "to carry." These relationships usually include expressions of positive affect, affirmation and the provision of aid or assistance. Supportive relationships promote the interest of or the cause of the individual/family served. In the health fields and especially the mental health fields, factors such as trust, respect, advocacy, and interpersonal warmth are often included in the definition of supportive relationships. By general definition,

there is no specific requirement that a supportive relationship be therapeutic.

THERAPEUTIC RELATIONSHIPS: Those relationships, both clinical and non-clinical, in which a goal for providing some sort of healing is established. The word "therapeutic" comes from the Greek word "therapeutikos," meaning, (1) relating to the treatment of disease or disorder and (2) providing or assisting in a cure. This healing is usually developed in response to an identified problem or risk. Healing can also refer to making whole or restoring to health. In health care, the problem or risk is usually clearly identified, measurable and related to a disease. In mental health, prevention or empowerment may be aspects of the healing goal. A common component in most definitions of therapeutic relationships is a clear intention by the professional to have some specified impact on the client or patient. Intrapsychic processes may occur as part of any relationship, but an expected component of a therapeutic relationship is the recognition of and attention to these internal processes. By general definition, there is no specific requirement that a therapeutic relationship be supportive.

Let's use a dentist to illustrate the interactions between these types of relationships. We are, as patients, in a professional relationship with our dentist. The success of this professional relationship depends on how well the dentist abides by the standards and ethics of dentistry. We are also all in a clinical relationship with our dentist, but not necessarily a therapeutic one. Our dentist may not be healing anything, but may simply be providing an assessment, and perhaps even preventive services. If our dentist is very unlikable and abrupt, but does provide a healing service, then it is probably a therapeutic relationship, albeit not necessarily a supportive one. If our dentist is warm, trusting, helps us to handle our fears, does good dental work that results in healing, and follows all the standards, ethics and requirements of his profession, we are in a professional relationship, a clinical relationship, a therapeutic relationship, and a supportive relationship. By this description, it is possible to maintain a professional relationship and a clinical relationship without the therapeutic component. It is also possible for a dentist to omit the supportive relationship and still maintain professional responsibilities. However, a disruption of the professional relationship will endanger the clinical and therapeutic relationships. It is also possible, from this perspective, to have a supportive relationship without a professional one. This dentist might be an individual we respect and use to talk about personal problems, even though we do not use him in the capacity of a dentist.

The next challenge, and things become even more complex here, is to determine what the interface is between therapeutic relationships and therapy. Does a therapeutic relationship, by definition, only exist as a component of therapy? In other words, can you have a therapeutic relationship outside of the realm of therapy? The corollary question, "Is child life a therapy?" will be addressed, but unfortunately not totally answered, later in this chapter. And even more confusing, can you have successful therapy without the existence of a therapeutic relationship? It is these complexities with which we struggle as we attempt to understand therapeutic relationships in the context of child life.

HISTORY OF THERAPEUTIC RELATIONSHIPS

Although many professions provide services, interact with children and families, and find it important to define relationships with their clients, not all of these professions utilize the term or concept of therapeutic relationships. In the realm of health care and mental health, the concept is used frequently. It is especially common to find a reference to therapeutic relationships in any service or profession that, by definition, provides therapy. Most professions that engage in therapy, no matter what the type, would agree that a therapeutic relationship either always is or can be part of the therapy process.

Think about the different types of therapists with which you are familiar; there are physical therapists, speech therapists, psychotherapists, massage therapists, respiratory therapists, just to name a few. Do they all depend on therapeutic relationships to engage in competent practice? Certainly most of them work toward healing in some sort of problem-based and reactive manner. But this does not imply that a supportive relationship is also necessary. It would seem that the more technical and concrete the activities of the therapist, the less need there is for, or the less use there is of, supportive relationships. Let's start with the respiratory therapist. What type of relationship is important while providing an inhalation treatment for asthma? By definition, if the therapist is assisting in opening an airway, then a healing is taking place and a therapeutic relationship exists. The treatment will be just as effective regardless of the warmth and kindness of the therapist toward the patient. But what if the therapist has the opportunity to address issues of non-compliance, or fear of death, or generalized depression due to disease? Perhaps healing is needed in one of these areas also. In these cases, either a supportive relationship is needed, or there needs to be a component of support and trust in the therapeutic relationship to provide opportunities for healing to occur in relation to the psychosocial topics.

Any time the interaction between therapist and client goes beyond technical, mechanical, rehearsed tasks, there is potential to make use of a supportive component in the relationship. In the standards of practice for physical therapy (2001), there is not a single mention of "therapeutic relationships" in the patient management, practice patterns, professional conduct, or code of ethics sections. The only references to relationships between therapist and client indicate that "therapists shall act in a trustworthy manner toward patients" and "therapists shall not engage in sexual relationships with any patient" which are more descriptions of a professional relationship than a therapeutic one. Interestingly, in speaking to a highly competent and experienced physical therapist prior to reading these standards, she was convinced that therapeutic relationships were a core concept in her profession and would be clearly defined in the standards.

At the other end of the spectrum of therapies, the psychotherapist probably utilizes both therapeutic relationships and supportive relationships most of the time in clinical practice, but there may be types of psychotherapy, such as therapy for personal growth and self-awareness that are not really working on solving a problem. And there may be types of therapy, such as behavioral or cognitive therapies, that do not depend on any supportive elements. From this discussion it would seem that there is a continuum of different therapies, some that use therapeutic relationships extensively and some that use them at a lesser level, and that also within each therapy specialty there is also a continuum of situations in which a therapeutic relationship would or would not enhance healing. It also becomes clear that it is very difficult, perhaps even impossible, to separate out the supportive, trust-based aspects of relationship from those that are considered therapeutic. Although child life is occasionally called a therapy, the roots of child life lay more in the fields of education and child development. It seems evident that there is

much about child life that goes beyond what might be expected in the typical therapeutic relationship.

Because child life is, at least in part, a psychosocial profession, and more closely aligned to the mental health fields than to the physical health professions, it makes the most sense to look at ways in which psychiatry, psychology, counseling and social work handle the concept of therapeutic relationships. Ultimately, child life will probably take its direction from these fields in continuing to define its therapeutic relationships. Even within these closely related professions, there is a range of expectations regarding therapeutic relationships. For example, look at the historical information available on psychotherapy. Michael Kahn (1991) gives a clear and concise summary of the history of therapeutic relationships in his book, *Between Therapist and Client: The New Relationship.* He describes Freud's early dismissal of the relationship, referred to as "bedside manner," stating that it was irrelevant in the therapeutic process. Psychoanalytic theory justified a practice that was supposedly devoid of relationship. However, Kahn points out that Freud himself did not practice a non-responsive therapy, but was actually quite active with his patients. It was the followers of Freud who tried to implement his theories and stay completely invisible, physically and personally, to their patients.

Then, in the 1940s, an entirely different approach to clinical relationships emerged, fueled by the humanist movement and an American psychologist named Carl Rogers. The theories behind the work of Rogers led to a therapy that required warmth, genuineness, and positive regard from the therapist toward the patient. Over time, in an effort to equalize the power in the client-therapist relationship, therapists moved to an even more open relationship with patients, offering loving support, the sharing of feelings, and sometimes confrontation. This range of approaches still exists today in the many professions that practice psychotherapy. There are therapists who will tell you that the relationship is irrelevant in the therapy process, and that a competent therapist can practice her or his profession quite well without ever developing what we think of as a "supportive relationship" with the client or patient. And at the other end of the spectrum, there are therapists, in all the therapeutic professions, who will state unequivocally that the one most significant element of change and healing is, simply, the therapeutic relationship. Regardless of the place one falls along this theoretical continuum, Kahn states that there are two reasons to make a careful study of the clinical relationship. First, it is risky not to. There are many potential damages that can be done to the client/family when the ground rules of the clinical situation are not known and respected. And second, the clinical relationship is a potentially powerful tool to use in the work we all do with clients.

So, what is the connection between the profession of child life and the concept of therapeutic relationships? Comparing and contrasting various aspects of child life with psychotherapeutic processes and professions will best shed light on this question. The following areas will be covered:

1. Review of various concepts related to therapeutic relationships that have been identified from several professions and psychosocial theories, with emphasis on their application to child life.
2. Identification of a typology of child life programming
3. Examination of the ways in which relationship may interface with each of the types of child life.

Finally, at the end of this chapter, a review of ways in which child life specialists develop their multiple relationship skills will be offered. Thus we will not only move toward an understanding of what these myriad relationships are, but also how they are acquired.

CONCEPTS IN THERAPEUTIC RELATIONSHIPS

Types of Relationships

One way to examine therapeutic relationships is to look at the different types of relationships that might exist between individuals. In a fairly simple paradigm, Varcarolis (1994) delineates three types of relationships: friendship (social), intimate, and therapeutic (professional). It might be useful to add casual and business (professional) to this list, although they are less likely to interface with child life. Varcarolis defines friendship as when "Mutual needs are met during social interaction." Roles shift during friendships, and may include advice giving and meeting dependency needs, such as loaning money and helping with jobs. Intimate relationships involve a partnership with an emotional commitment to one another. Interaction between these individuals is personal and intimate, on social, emotional and/or physical levels. Varcarolis, who is writing from a nursing perspective, identifies that neither of these relationships is appropriate for the professional and/or therapeutic relationship. The therapeutic relationship moves through several stages, but its goal is to prepare the client and/or family for the time when they no longer need the professional. The previous two relationships embrace the possibility or even the probability that they will exist for an extremely extended period of time, as long as is mutually agreeable. Taking responsibility for ending the relationship is one of the expectations for a professional relationship within nursing, and thus impacts the establishment and course of the therapeutic relationship. Gary Schoener (1998), a psychologist, describes the relationship between therapist and client as a fiduciary contract – that is, an agreement between unequals in which one person has more power and more responsibility.

Determining the type of relationship child life has with those it serves has always been a difficult task. Although the profession is now over forty years old, it is still developing its identity. Due to the small size of the profession, and the lack any national licensure that would legally mandate standards, each employer is still free to internally establish its own description of the child life role. There are those who still see child life as a friend to children and a nice perk, but far from a profession. There are those who see child life as only an educator, and would not see the purpose in establishing a therapeutic relationship. More and more, however, employers are using the same standards that the profession has set for itself through the Child Life Council. These standards clearly include the development of a therapeutic relationship as a key value. And when this is the case, that is, a professional and therapeutic relationship exists, then it becomes a boundary violation to establish a second (or dual) relationship such as friend, business partner, or family member. The reality that a therapeutic relationship does not allow for any secondary relationship to be safely pursued with the client is a major challenge to the establishing identity of child life.

Phases of Therapeutic Relationships

Within the specific realm of the therapeutic relationship, there are often thought to be stages or phases that help to define appropriate goals and maintain the dynamic of the relationship. Although each profession might describe the process in a somewhat different manner, Stuart and Sundeen (1995) identify three most commonly conceived phases in a therapeutic relationship. The first phase is the initiation or orientation phase. The most important goal for this phase is that trust is established. This phase usually includes some sort of introduction, the establishment of the purpose of the interaction, and a mutual decision about the plans and logistics for continued interaction. Some theorists divide this first phase into two subsections, an introduction section and a beginning or contractual section. The next phase is the working phase. At this point the professional works toward achievement of goals as established in the initiation phase. The final phase is the termination phase. During this phase, the focus is on ending the relationship, not on establishing new material. Closure for both the client and the professional is important here and is usually achieved by summarizing the previous interactions and accomplishments.

Phases in the progress of relationships between parents of children with chronic illness and health care providers were also identified by Thorne and Robinson (1989). They recognized three phases, with the development of a guarded alliance between family members and professionals being the final step in an ongoing relationship. Following up on this work, Knafl, Breitmayer, Gallo and Zoeller (1992) also documented this development of an alliance and described it as a blend of technical and interactional competencies. The study emphasized that although parents valued and needed provider's expertise, it was the compassion and respect that were consistent components when describing outstanding health care encounters. In other words, the therapeutic or healing component of the encounter was highly significant but it was the supportive component that made it outstanding. The alliance phase as defined by these two studies could not be achieved without a therapeutic relationship that meets identified healing needs along with a strong supportive connection.

The child life specialist has traditionally not needed to establish such clarity in the phases of a relationship she or he develops with a child or adult. Historically, the child life specialist worked with hospital inpatients. The relationship was developed as close to the time of admission as could be established by the specialist, remained a working relationship all during the hospital stay, and terminated at discharge. As health care has changed, and as the role of the child life specialist has expanded, these external limitations are less relevant. In the inpatient setting, the specialist may have had a fixed number of beds for which to be responsible. The case load, by definition, never exceeded that number of children. Now, child life specialists work in outpatient areas in which children may return again and again for years. Even in the inpatient settings, as relationships develop with children who are managing chronic illnesses, there is the potential to see children over and over again during repeated admissions. Specialists also work in less traditional settings outside the hospital, in a manner that more resembles the social worker or psychotherapist.

In all these situations, it becomes the responsibility of the professional to take charge of both beginning and terminating relationships. If the child life specialist does not purposefully take charge of the phase of relationship, the "open" cases will soon become much more numerous than can be successfully managed, and a lesser quality of service will be the outcome. If the specialist struggles to appropriately terminate relationships, boundary violations, as will be discussed in an upcoming section, are a clear

risk. Child life has also learned that therapeutic relationships can be established in a fairly short period of time. Look at child life services in the emergency department. In the space of a few hours, a specialist must complete an introduction including the establishment of trust, must work through the professionally appropriate tasks to assist each individual patient and family group with their specific challenges, and must terminate with closure that empowers both the child and the supporting family to deal with additional problems without the support of the specialist.

Theoretical Foundations

In the earlier history section of this chapter, groundwork was presented on the development of the concept of the therapeutic relationship in mental health. It is probably not particularly useful to divide psychotherapeutic theory by individual professions. In reality, all the mental health professions, including psychiatry, psychology, social work, counseling, play therapy, art therapy, and others, have emerged from the same theoretical roots. Whether child life is partially or fundamentally a mental health profession will be discussed in the next section. To whatever extent child life embraces the tenants of one or more of the various mental health professions, then the same theories that influenced the development of these fields have equivalent importance to child life.

There are three primary theoretical bases for most of the clinical mental health work done today. Two have already been discussed; they include psychoanalytic theory, initiated by Sigmund Freud and expanded by many others, and the humanist movement as represented by Carl Rogers. A third major theoretical category is that of learning theory, and entire therapeutic approaches have developed based on these constructs.

There are other important therapeutic traditions, including existential psychology, Gestalt therapy, cognitive therapy, and even advice-giving counseling. All of these approaches to therapeutic intervention have both theoretical and application components, and all require significant study and clinical training in order to be able to be implemented to their fullest potential. Those individuals who pursue careers in any of the mental health professions have had comprehensive education in one or more of the areas above. It is theory that, in a very major way, guides the clinician to the appropriate level and type of therapeutic relationship.

Although individuals who practice child life have sometimes had training in one or more of the theories and philosophies above, they rarely fully embrace one particular theoretical approach to their work. More often child life specialists are eclectic, knowing a little about several approaches to clinical work. They may be behaviorists when they set up a reinforcement schedule for a child, humanists when they give a child with interrupted self-image unconditional positive regard, and psychoanalytic when they interpret the meaning of a child's symbolic painting. The fact that many theories are embraced partially, but none fully, is one of the factors that makes the definition of therapeutic relationships so difficult in child life. Earlier in this chapter caution was expressed about considering child life a therapy in and of itself. This eclectic nature of child life does not allow for the tight, theoretical parameters that are a condition of almost all therapies. Establishing such specific parameters would be restrictive, and child life should carefully consider the advantages and limitations before moving further in that direction.

Trust

In the section describing the phases of a therapeutic relationship, it was stated that the most important goal in the first phase is the establishment of trust. The concept of trust should be very familiar to every child life specialist. All educational curriculums for child life teach Erik Erikson's (1963) eight stages of psychosocial development and every child life professional knows that Erikson defines the very first stage as the stage of "Trust versus Mistrust." Erikson believed that this stage was the most crucial in a human being's development, as it allowed the child to establish a sense of hope and the expectation that the world is a good place. It was acknowledged by Erikson that experiences in both trust and mistrust could and should occur during that first year, but that a baby should emerge from this stage with a favorable balance of trust over mistrust. More recent theorists go a step further by suggesting that experiences in mistrust are more useful after the first twelve months. Arnold Gesell (1952) theorized that positive, trusting relationships would develop best when the parent consistently followed the cues of the baby. Theorists agree that if trust is not established in the first year of life, it will be very difficult to establish later, and will always be more fragile than it might have been if integrated in the child's first few months.

So, if trust is so pivotal in the development of a human, what is the role of trust in the work of the child life specialist and what is the connection between trust and relationship? Although it is possible to trust an object ("I trust this medicine to cure me," "I trust this rope to not break"), the trust we are concerned with involves person-to-person interrelationships. When one loses trust in an object (the medicine doesn't work after all, the rope breaks), one simply avoids that object in the future. When one loses trust in another person, not only is the relationship in jeopardy, but also anything that person is connected to or representative of will be impacted by the loss of trust. Trust is defined as having confidence in another person, or accepting another person as being true and reliable without being able to or seeing the need to verify it. Trust in a professional, which, as we have established, includes child life, means that one should be able to expect certain knowledge and certain professional behavior. Trust is the very core of positive human interactions, and is an absolutely necessary component of a supportive relationship. It becomes a component of a therapeutic relationship in that, if trust is lacking, the client may well terminate the relationship and select an individual with equivalent abilities who does provide the trust factor. How long would you remain with that dentist we discussed earlier, no matter how good he is, if you did not trust him?

Long ago, as a new child life specialist, I found myself working with a two-year-old child I'll refer to as Ronnie, hospitalized for an acute medical condition. This little boy had experienced significant negative events over his first 24 hours in the hospital, but was now with me in the playroom, and was beginning to relax and develop a trusting relationship that I hoped would allow me to support him successfully throughout the rest of his stay. His mother had mentioned to me that she would need to leave to pick up a sibling from school, and I had worked with her on appropriate methods of saying "goodbye." As I was sitting on the floor with Ronnie, his mother stood up behind him, and before I could stop her, put her finger to her lips in a silent "shusssh," and backed out the door. For a brief moment, I thought everything would be all right, and that the relationship I had begun would survive this challenge. However, after a moment, Ronnie glanced over his shoulder and froze. He did not see his mother. He looked at me again, then back to the empty space behind him, and then began crying with a despair that was heartbreaking. This child, who had been playing so trustingly with me, now could not

be comforted by me or anyone else. He continued to express his distress until the mother returned a couple of hours later. Most importantly, for the rest of his hospitalization, he would have nothing to do with me. I had lost his trust, and it was complete and final. All opportunities to help him accept medical personnel, to support him through procedures, to enhance his development, were as lost as the trust. Thus I learned not only the necessity of trust in a relationship, but also the power of mistrust to undermine the best of intentions. Trust carries with it responsibility, and the potential to do significant harm.

Communication Skills

The foundation of any therapeutic relationship is dependent on the communication skills of the therapist. This is such an important concept for child life that an entire chapter in this book has been devoted to the topic. The authors have stated unequivocally that "It is through the effective use of communication that child life specialists facilitate interpersonal relationships with children, staff and family members. . . ." The current chapter will hopefully provide some clarity as to what a therapeutic relationship is, but the chapter on communications will help the reader gain insight as to how to establish one.

Boundaries

A concept in all professional relationships, which also certainly impacts therapeutic relationships, is that of boundaries. Boundaries are those limitations or barriers that keep some things in and keep other things out. Peterson and Solomon (1998) point out that those interpersonal boundaries operate on a continuum. When they are too tight, individuals are prevented from engaging in open and giving relationships. When they are too loose, an individual is robbed of the sense of being a unique person whose needs and wants are separate from others.

Peterson and Solomon describe three ways in which boundaries are established for professionals. First, there is licensure or certification. When given official sanction by society or by a governing body, the professional receives society's permission to engage in activities that might not usually be allowed but are for the good of the client. For example, it is not considered appropriate for a typical citizen to observe the genitals of someone else's child. In fact, it is called child pornography. However, it is acceptable for a child life specialist, by way of his or her credential, and with the goal of providing some positive, helpful intervention, to observe and even interact with a child who is not clothed.

The next boundary method is the development of ethical standards for each profession. Child life, through the Child Life Council, has established a code of ethical responsibility for its members that clearly states expected behaviors for members of the profession, or at least those professionals who are members of the profession's only organization. Principle 10 of that code states that the child life specialist shall assess and amend any personal relationships or situations that may interfere with professional effectiveness, objectivity or otherwise negatively impact children and families. The principle goes on to state that a minimum of two years following the conclusion of a professional role shall lapse before any personal relationship is permitted to develop with children or family members. Thus a very clear boundary between personal relationships and professional ones has been drawn for child life specialists.

Finally, boundaries are developed by the implied definitional assumption that profes-sional relationships are to be kept professional, not personal. As long as there is clarity about what type of relationship one has with one's client, boundaries can be maintained.

In 1996, in response to concerns about boundary violations in nurses, the National Council of State Boards of Nursing developed a conceptual framework of professional boundaries. In this document is a continuum of connectedness that helps us all to understand the interaction between professional boundaries and therapeutic relationships. It is called "The Zone of Helpfulness." An adjusted version of the nursing concept, with examples more appropriate to child life, may be seen in Figure 1.

In the center of this zone is the area of most potential for a therapeutic relationship. If one moves too far to the left, there is potential for under-involvement and the neglect of professional responsibilities. Too far to the right, and the relationship becomes over-involved, with the need to maintain the relationship taking priority over the needs of the client. This template does not require that the professional embrace a particular style or even theory, but rather be aware of one's place on a relationship continuum. The most important point in any discussion of boundaries in child life is that when professional boundaries are violated, therapeutic relationships and all other relationships are permanently impacted.

Transference and Countertransference

The concept of transference is one of the most important contributions Sigmund Freud made to the understanding of human behavior. In its most basic conceptualization, Freud theorized that when people enter therapy, the way that they see and respond to their therapist will be influenced by two factors; they will see the relationship in light of

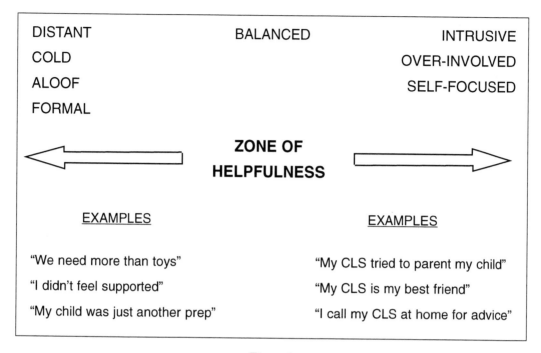

DISTANT	BALANCED	INTRUSIVE
COLD		OVER-INVOLVED
ALOOF		SELF-FOCUSED
FORMAL		

ZONE OF HELPFULNESS

EXAMPLES

"We need more than toys"

"I didn't feel supported"

"My child was just another prep"

EXAMPLES

"My CLS tried to parent my child"

"My CLS is my best friend"

"I call my CLS at home for advice"

Figure 1
Zone of Helpfulness for Professionals

their earlier ones, especially very early childhood relationships, and they will have a tendency to replay those earlier situations. In other words, clients will transfer onto their therapist their previous patterns of behavior and response. It has become clear over the years since this theory was developed that it applies not only to clients of psychotherapists but to all of us in many of our relationships. So it is not surprising that child life specialists would be the recipients of transference responses from adults with whom they work, and also with children. Several years later, Freud saw similar responses in the therapists toward their clients, and titled this countertransference. This concept has produced much controversy among therapists, but the most common use of the term now refers to all the feelings and attitudes about the client that occur in the professional. Although Freud saw transference as the

vehicle by which the work of therapy was done, he had little good to say about countertransference. However, when understood and used as a tool, both transference and countertransference can be useful to the child life specialist.

It does not take long for a child to begin acting toward a child life specialist the same way he or she acts toward a parent. This is transference in its most simple manifestation. Children easily transfer their reaction patterns to a variety of adults in their lives. These patterns provide wonderful clues as to how a child learns, responses to challenges, and copes with stress. By paying close attention to transference reactions, the child life specialist can map out a plan for intervention that fits the style of that individual child, and has the potential to be effective both in the institution and at home. The stronger the relationship between the child life specialist and the child, the more the transference reaction is likely to occur. Transference can also occur between a parent and a child life specialist. Parents may react toward the professional the same way they have reacted toward other authority figures in their lives. If the child life specialist is much younger than the parent, the parent may transfer reactions they have to a younger sibling or even to an adolescent child onto the specialist. As long as these reactions are understood in the light of normal transference, they become working tools for the specialist.

Countertransference is more challenging for the child life specialist. There will always be children who "push your buttons," whose behavior or attitude or demeanor produce emotional responses in you that are less than professional. Perhaps you have a hard time with the child who bullies others, or with the child who whines and complains a lot. Any pattern of responses on the part of the specialist is an opportunity for personal growth and discovery. The first step in dealing with countertransference is to recognize that a pattern is occurring or that you are having a strong reaction to a particular characteristic of a child. Then, the specialist must find a way to accept that this reaction may be coming as much from the professional's own values, judgments and personal experiences as from the child. The next step is to find an outlet to openly discuss your reaction with a supervisor or peers in an environment that feels safe and free of judgment. At the very least, the mature child life specialist will want to be able to recognize and control countertransference reactions so that they do not interfere with therapeutic work. At best, specialists may utilize this countertransference in their work with children and may address and even resolve some powerful experiences from their own early lives.

TYPOLOGY OF CHILD LIFE

With so many different types of relationships, and so many different standards, the reader may be quite confused at this point about what really constitutes a therapeutic relationship. A great deal of this confusion comes from the fact that, as mentioned earlier, child life still embraces many different types of programming, coming from many different professional and theoretical backgrounds. The first person to attempt to describe these differences was Rosemary Bolig (1983). She listed five basic approaches to child life programming, including (a) diversion, (b) activity/recreation, (c) child development, (d) therapeutic, and (e) comprehensive. She stated that the child life program elements and strategies offered are typically related to the educational background of program staff and administrators. In the twenty-five years since the publication of this typology, many of Bolig's observations continue to be valid. However, a few adjustments to her typology theory may be useful to describe the current profession of child life.

The Child Life Council and the certification process have educated the health care community to the potential benefits of child life. National standards are available to hospital administrators, and JCAHO now places expectations on health care facilities that mesh well with the goals and objectives of the more comprehensive child life programs. However, without national licensure, and with only minimal outcome-based research, it is still up to each hospital administration to determine what typology of child life programming will be supported. Bolig felt that program typology was determined mostly by educational background of child life professionals. This educational background is a major factor, but certainly not the only one. Hospital administrators and medical/psychosocial personnel, community expectations, and budget all influence the type of program a hospital may have. The most sophisticated and comprehensive child life director may not be able to implement the type of program he/she desires due to limitations involving the factors above.

There are a few other considerations to be added to the five program types described by Bolig. It is not clear if the typology "educational" is included in any of the initial five. Some child life programs focus primarily on providing both academic and health-related education to patients. Child life specialists in such programs must usually be certified teachers, and may receive additional educational certifications such as diabetes instructor. Although no child life program is completely educational in nature, if that is the primary function of the staff, then it should probably be its own typology category. Second, there are still programs in which the child life specialist is primarily a nice and friendly person who solves problems, acts as patient advocate and promotes the institution. These programs are typically one-person programs, and often are administratively managed by the volunteer department, public relations, or some similar administrative area. Again, the specialist may have some opportunity to play with or prepare children, and may attempt to incorporate more comprehensive child life skills into day-to-day work, but these are not the person's primary functions. Next, it would be useful to add the word "entertainment" to the category called "diversion." This category applies to the child life program whose primary function is to take children's minds off the hospital experience by developing the most interesting and pleasurable events possible, filling as much time as possible in a child's day. Finally, since we have seen that the term "therapeutic" can apply to almost any professional orientation, and since Bolig

was referring to psychoanalytic and humanistic theory in her use of the word "therapeutic," change the category "therapeutic" to "psychotherapeutic" to better indicate a mental health focus. An amended typology, without judgment as to value or usefulness, might be listed as follows: (a) friend/advocate, (b) diversion/entertainment, (c) activity/recreation, (d) education, (e) child development, (f) psychotherapeutic, and (g) comprehensive. It must be clearly understood that these categories are not mutually exclusive, and one can find some components of all categories in most child life programs.

Problem-solving activities and preventive activities can be part of every category. It also should be understood that to be a truly comprehensive program, all of the components must be interwoven in a seamless matrix that is constantly adjusted to meet the needs of each individual patient.

THE INTERFACE BETWEEN TYPOLOGY AND RELATIONSHIP

Now that we have a model for child life typology, it becomes a bit easier to examine how therapeutic relationships might be part of the profession. Consider the four earlier-described relationship types. If you will recall, these are professional relationships, supportive relationships, clinical relationships and therapeutic relationships. We will examine these relationship types from the perspective of the seven categories above.

One category is easy to summarize, and that is the category of professional relationships. If an individual is doing work as a child life professional, calling herself or himself a child life specialist, representing the field of child life, then it becomes incumbent upon that person to maintain existing standards of a professional relationship. No matter what type of program is offered, a professional is responsible for maintaining standards. For child life, those standards are implied by the standards set by other similar professions, and stated by the Child Life Council. They are not nationally mandated by licensure or by law, as they are in other, more established professions. These standards include ethics, boundaries, and the responsibility for a certain level of professional practice. Even if the child life specialist is only paid to walk around with coffee for parents and toys for children, the same standards apply. No matter what the typology of a program, it is still not professional to take a teenage patient to his driving test, go to the movies with the family of a patient, talk to a child or parent about one's own personal problem, or date the parent of a child you are seeing. The only way a child life specialist could be exempt from these standards is to acknowledge that he or she is not a professional.

Although it is a bit more difficult to determine clinical relationships, it can be simply stated that a clinical relationship exists in any type of child life program in which clinical services are provided. There are probably differences of opinion as to what constitutes clinical service, but most would agree that general advocacy, entertainment and probably education are not clinical services, and so do not involve a clinical relationship. The typology of activities/recreation in and of itself is not clinical, but recreation therapy, as a healing modality, certainly is clinical. The use of this relationship category is only significant in that it helps to define one possible label for the type of service provided. Since it does not imply any standards or make any statements about child life as a profession, this relationship category is only marginally useful in child life. It becomes important only if the child life professional misuses the term clinical to have a broader definition than described here.

The concept of supportive relationships is an interesting one, as it has meaning to the general population from common usage. Friends, family members, even casual acquaintances may find themselves in supportive relationships. The ability to establish supportive relationships is probably one of those subtle "X-factor" skills that many individuals in child life have when they enter the profession. It is a skill that is very hard to teach, although it can be refined by personal awareness and both personal and professional maturity. Certainly, the entire spectrum of child life types can be enhanced by the establishment of supportive relationships. In our dentist analogy earlier, it was clear that although a dentist could do his work without a supportive relationship, such a relationship would add a positive dimension to the interaction between professional and client. It was also pointed out that without a supportive relationship, a client is more likely to avoid or even terminate the contact with a professional. Some types of child life programming, however, are more dependent on supportive relationships than others. Diversion, activities, education and arguably child development may well be able to be provided without consistent establishment of supportive relationships. As long as the relationship is not punitive or intimidating, a neutral relationship will not prohibit these types of child life. However, in those typologies that are more clinical in nature, supportive relationships are an integral part of the work, and become inseparable from therapeutic relationships.

And so finally, we return to look at therapeutic relationships as they apply to different types of child life. As we have stated earlier, all the types of child life programming have the potential to be therapeutic, that is, to provide some healing or problem solving. So, any of the typology categories may well include therapeutic relationships. Whether the problem is developmental, psychosocial, functional or logistic, the relationship that allows the child life specialist to assist the patient or a family member in solving that problem is a therapeutic one. For those types of child life programs, such as diversion/ entertainment, activity/recreation or child developmental that focus more on prevention and maintenance of wellness, the use of a therapeutic relationship is, by definition, less significant. This does not mean the relationships established are less supportive or less humanistic and it certainly does not mean that the relationships are less important.

It also seems clear that it is more effective to be therapeutic if there is also a supportive relationship in place. Let's use an unlikely example. The child life program fits into the first typology, that of simply being nice and helpful. One child life specialist is assigned to get coffee and water for families in the surgery waiting area, and provide toys for waiting siblings. No specific preparation, therapeutic play or other more clinical duties are assigned. However, a parent seems upset because she must find the billing office but is worried about leaving the waiting area. The supportive child life specialist will sit down with that parent, plan some sort of coverage in case the child's parent is needed in the waiting room, provide clear directions to the billing office, and perhaps even provide a beeper number in case the parent becomes delayed. A therapeutic relationship has developed, a problem has been identified and solved, and there also seems to be a supportive relationship established built on trust and caring. But what if the child life specialist is a nasty, frustrated person? The specialist still could give the directions and explain what would happen if the parent were called. But what if the specialist tells the parent to stop worrying and do what she needs to do, minimizes her possible role with her post-surgical child, states that "anyone can find their way around this hospital?" Would the

problem still be solved? If so, the relationship is a therapeutic one. Is a supportive relationship established? Clearly not. The risk here is that even though there is potential for a therapeutic relationship, the problem may not be solved, the healing may not occur, because the supportive relationship hasn't occurred. The parent may dislike the specialist so much that she doesn't trust her directions or her assessment of the situation, and so doesn't leave to take care of the billing problem.

Even though we have established definitional differences between therapeutic and supportive relationships, in practice the two may be so interwoven as to be inseparable. In fact, there probably is almost always considerable overlap between supportive and therapeutic relationships in child life. At the 2005 Child Life Council Conference on Professional Issues, a graphic model of the interactions between types of relationships was presented. This model is mobile, and can be adjusted to the realities of any child life program, and actually to any health care or mental health profession. Figure 2 represents what might be a standard depiction of professional relationships in health care in general and a depiction of professional relationships in child life. Notice that there is some mixture of supportive and therapeutic components in the general health care model, but the therapeutic component is the larger. Also notice that there are only minimal non-clinical relationships in the general model. Child life, on the other hand, has a much larger percentage of supportive relationships and almost all therapeutic relationships overlap with the supportive ones. Child life also has a higher percentage of non-clinical relationships than most other health care personnel.

As we bring this discussion of the interaction between relationship types to a close, it must be acknowledged that no one set of definitions, no one graphic model, will be ac-

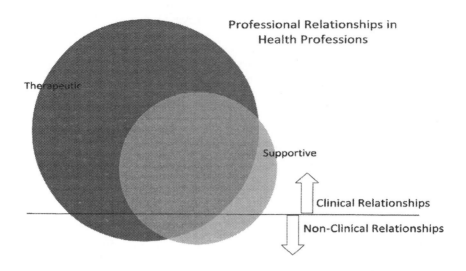

Professional Relationships in
Health Professions

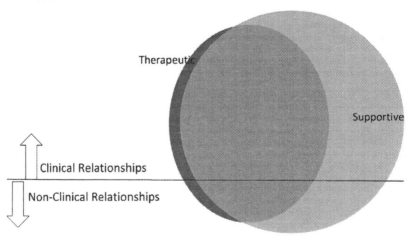

Professional Relationships in
The Child Life Profession

Figure 2

ceptable to all those in child life. Some professionals believe that since the roots of child life came from play and child development, the professional focus should be on developing supportive relationships. Some professionals, especially those that came out of one of the more traditional therapies, like social work, psychology or art therapy, are more inclined to see all of the work of a child life specialist as therapeutic in nature. Whatever approach any individual, or program, or institution may take, it is still important for us to acknowledge both our roots and our current function. Child life should not have to apologize for the importance of the supportive nature of its work, nor should it have to hide or avoid the therapeutic components of the profession.

DEVELOPING RELATIONSHIP SKILLS

Even though we have talked at length about what these child life relationships are, we haven't addressed how they are acquired and how they can impact the professional, especially over time. Therapeutic relationships are not a static entity; they change and are challenged over the career of the child life specialist. Usually the change is in the direction of positive development, as the specialist becomes more seasoned in her work and more able to personally reflect on the purpose and function of child life. However, a change in supervisory administration, a catastrophic experience in either one's personal or work life, or even a work overload can have a negative impact on the professional's ability or willingness to develop therapeutic relationships. One could devote another entire chapter to the growth and development of a child life specialist, but for the sake of brevity, we will examine three areas that contribute to the ability of the specialist to develop both therapeutic and supportive relationships. These areas are (1) pre-professional training, (2) on-the-job training, and (3) personal growth.

The first steps in learning to establish and differentiate professional relationships, both therapeutic and supportive, occur in an individual's personal life prior to formal education. Then, college education, specific career education, and clinical training through practicum and internship experiences all add to the emerging sense of what a therapeutic relationship might entail. The pre-professional now knows the theory behind the development of therapeutic relationships, but has had only minimal opportunity to examine such relationships. Even clinical training, as important as that is, is a protected experience that rarely mimics the true demands on a professional.

The actual job world is the second area in which the professional can learn about relationships. It is finally the place where the new child life specialist can gain real competence in the art of developing, maintaining and utilizing the variety of relationships that are part of the field of child life. Through modeling, child life specialists can watch other more experienced professionals, both in child life and in related professions, do the work they do so well with children and families. Newcomers to child life should take every opportunity possible to watch nurses, psychotherapists, educators and others build relationships that allow them to do healing work with children and adults. Slow down and try to see the nuances, and observe from a place of openness and non-judgment. Hopefully, at the same time that there are opportunities to model the behavior of others, there is also someone in the new specialist's life who can act as a mentor. Mentors are most effective when they are outside the supervisory role, and can, through discussion and demonstration, help the new professional critically examine the scope of therapeutic relationships that are being developed, keeping in mind professional limitations, supportive roles and clinical responsibilities. Mentors may be within or outside the profession of child life, and can occur all during the career of a child life specialist. Finally, during a person's work life, there are always official supervisors who have specific responsibility for helping the new child life specialist learn to establish the best possible relationships, and the continuing child life specialist deepen her or his knowledge of this important component of child life. Even if the supervisor is outside the profession, there is often the possibility of peer supervision to explore these issues.

One would think that the above opportunities to develop insight into therapeutic relationships would be enough. Well, they are not! It would be remiss to leave the topic of professional development with referring to the personal growth that is an integral part of the most successful child life specialists. In order to really understand and utilize therapeutic relationships, one must not only develop a significant level of personal maturity but also a willingness to be purposeful, intentional and undefended in one's work. Some individuals develop these abilities naturally, some work on them in structured personal development activities such as journaling or retreat work, and some seek group or individual counseling to achieve such growth. If we in child life truly believe that creative and expressive activities help a person to cope more successfully, handle stress and develop the most positive interpersonal relationships possible, we should be open to exploring as many of these modalities as possible in our own lives.

SUMMARY

We have now examined therapeutic relationships in child life from numerous perspectives. A therapeutic relationship has been defined as being involved with another person in a way that provides healing. Therapeutic relationships, then, apply primarily to situations in which there is a problem or deficit to be addressed or repaired. It seems clear that such a definition, although linguistically simple, is inadequate to cover the range of relationships that exist between child life professionals and those they serve. This type of relationship does not, by definition, include the supportive, humanistic component that is so important in many types of child life programming. It also omits reference to the significant child life work that has to do with preventive or proactive interventions. All the previous information on relationships would lead one to the conclusion that an ideal and truly comprehensive child life relationship includes all the components of a supportive relationship, all the components of a therapeutic relationship, and specific reference to maintaining normalcy and preventing development of negative psychosocial sequellae. And all this should be done in situations that involve both clinical and non-clinical relationships. It is this combination of relationships that sets child life apart from other professions, including both the traditional therapist as well as the friendly support person. The child life specialist who omits the purposeful, goal-directed, intentional nature of the therapeutic relationship will lose as many opportunities as the one who omits the trusting, client-centered genuineness of the supportive relationship. However, the all-encompassing nature of the described comprehensive child life relationship must include the following caveat. Complex relationships such as this offer the professional much flexibility to determine which relationship is useful at which time, and to transition back and forth between modalities. Therefore, the components of a professional relationship, including standards, conduct, boundaries and expectations must be maintained at the highest level of consciousness at all times. All these terms play an important role in defining the ways that individuals in child life interact with others, and each should be used appropriately in any discussion of the profession.

A review of seven different, overlapping types of child life programs has been provided, with attention to the place of therapeutic relationships in each of the program types. Therapeutic relationships are useful in some of the categories, and absolutely mandated in others. However, there is no clinical work of child life that is likely to have maximum success without the warmth, trust and positive regard that is included in the supportive part of the relationship.

The final section of this chapter is perhaps the most important, as it discusses the ways in which child life specialists can develop and maintain the important relationships described in the earlier parts of the chapter. Obviously, all of the education available pre- and post-graduation is important, especially the development of appropriate communication skills. But personal growth, self-awareness, willingness to let down defenses and be vulnerable, and a strong desire for honest feedback will lead the specialist to the most powerful, most professional, most useful relationships possible with the children and adults who are the recipients of child life services.

REFERENCES

American Physical Therapy Association. (2001). *Physical therapy: Guide to physical therapist practice.* Alexandria, Virginia.

Bolig, R. (1983). Play in hospital settings. In T., Yawkey & T., Pellegrini (Eds.), *Child's play: Developmental and applied.* Hillsdale, NJ: Erlbaum.

Child Life Council. (1990). *Official documents of the Child Life Council.* Bethesda, Maryland.

Erikson, E. H. (1963). *Childhood and society.* New York: Norton.

Gesell, A. (1952). *Infant development: The embryology of human behavior.* New York: Harper.

Kagel, J. D. & Giebelhausen, P. N. (1994). Dual relationships and professional boundaries. *Social Work, 39,* 3-9.

Kahn, M. (1991). *Between therapist and client: The new relationship.* New York: Freeman.

Knafl, K., Breitmayer, B., Gallo, A., & Zoeller, L. (1992). Parent's views of health care providers: An exploration of the components of a positive working relationship. *Children's Health Care, 21,* 90-95.

Mensh, I. (1966). *Clinical psychology.* New York: Macmillan.

Peterson, E., & Solomon, D. (1998). Maintaining healthy boundaries in professional relationships: A balancing act. *Home Care Provider, 3,* 314-8.

Schoener, G. R. (1998). *Boundaries in professional relationships.* Minneapolis: Walk-In Counseling Center.

Stuart, G. W. & Sundeen, S. J. (1995). *Principles and practices of psychiatric nursing* (5th Ed.). New York: Mosby.

Thorne, S., & Robinson, C. (1989). Guarded alliance: Health care relationships in chronic illness. *Image, 21,* 153-157.

Varcarolis, E. M. (1994). *Foundations of psychiatric and mental health nursing* (2nd Ed.). Philadelphia: Saunders.

Wolfer, J., Gaynard, L., Goldberger, J., Laidley, L., & Thompson, R. (1988). An experimental evaluation of a model child life program. *Children's Health Care, 16,* 244-254.

Chapter 5

COMMUNICATION AND CHILD LIFE

Dene G. Klinzing and Dennis R. Klinzing

INTRODUCTION

Communication is a fundamental component of child life practice. It is through the effective use of communication that child life specialists facilitate interpersonal relationships with children, staff, and family members and help to create and maintain family-centered care (Klinzing & Klinzing, 1977). Further, McConnell (2000) argues that effective communication helps to improve healthcare outcomes, task coordination, worker satisfaction, and that it saves time and energy, and increases patient comfort.

During our many years of experience in the field of health communication we have observed that those who choose child life as a profession tend to have personalities, attitudes, and values that equip them well to be good communicators. However, sometimes missing from the communication repertoire of child life specialists is a thorough understanding of the complexity of human communication and knowledge of communication concepts and research findings that can serve to inform and improve communication. In this chapter we will examine these elements. More specifically, we will study

the process, transactional, and symbolic nature of communication; we will consider several important features of verbal communication including abstraction, labeling, fact inference confusion, and jargon; we will discuss the sources of nonverbal messages and we will review misconceptions about listening and consider how correcting them can improve listening. Each of these topics will be grounded by applications to child life and examples of exemplary practice. First, some comments about the literature that pertains to communication in child life.

LITERATURE:
HEALTH COMMUNICATION
AND CHILD LIFE

The field of health communication is broad, expansive, and interdisciplinary. It includes the study of interaction that occurs with patients and health professionals in all healthcare settings as well as media influences in healthcare and public health campaigns. Because of this broad focus, research findings and writings that bear on health communication can be found in a wide array of journals (see Table 1). While none of the

Table 5-1
JOURNALS WITH COMMUNICATION CONTENT

- *American Journal of Emergency Medicine.* (1983-). Philadelphia, PA: Centrum Philadelphia.
- *AORN. Association of Operating Room Nurses.* Denver, CO: Association of Operating Room Nurses.
- *Children's Health Care.* (1973-). Mahwah, NJ: Lawrence Erlbaum.
- *Communication Quarterly.* (1953-). West Haven, CT: Eastern Communication Association.
- *Communication Reports.* (1988-). Pullman, WA: Western Communication Association.
- *Communication Research.* (1995-). Thousand Oaks, CA: Sage.
- *Critical Care Nursing Quarterly.* (1987-). Frederick, MD: Aspen.
- *Family Practice News.* (1971-). Short Hills, NJ: International Medical News Group.
- *Health Communication.* (1989). Mahwah, NJ: Lawrence Erlbaum.
- *JAMA. The Journal of the American Medical Association.* (1848-). Chicago, IL: American Medical Association.
- *Journal of Advanced Nursing.* (1976-). Oxford, England: Blackwell Scientific.
- *Journal of Applied Communication Research.* (1973 -). Annandale, VA: National Communication Association.
- *Journal of Communication.* (1951-). Oxford, England: International Communication Association.
- *Journal of Family Practice.* (1974-). New York, NY: Appleton and Lange.
- *Journal of Health and Social Behavior.* (1989-). New York: American Sociological Association.
- *Nurse Practitioner.* (1975-). Springhouse, PA: Springhouse.
- *Nursing Economics.* (1983-). Pitman, NJ: Jannetti.
- *Nursing Management.* (1990-). Harrow, Middlesex, England: Viking House.
- *Nursing Research.* (1952-). Philadelphia, PA: Lippincott, Williams and Wilkins.
- *Pediatric Nursing.* (1900-) Pitman, NJ: Jannetti.
- *Pediatrics.* (1948-). Evanston, IL: American Academy of Pediatrics.
- *Qualitative Health Research.* (1991-). Newbury Park, CA: Sage.

journals listed in the table focus specifically on communication in child life, they often contain information that can be generalized, adapted, and applied to the communication encounters faced by child life specialists. Indeed, our strategy in writing this chapter has been to search various journals as well as books for such information. Our literature search was not confined to recent publications because many important findings have been published in previous years. We have integrated the results of our literature review throughout the chapter.

THE COMPLEXITY OF HUMAN COMMUNICATION

Human communication is often seen as a simple, uncomplicated event. Someone speaks and a message is sent. Another listens and a message is received. What could be simpler? Well, as is the case with many things that seem uncomplicated at first glance, there is more, much more to the story.

Process

Human communication is not a linear, static event as is indicated in the view of a speaker sending a message and a listener receiving the message. Rather, human communication is a process that involves dynamic, ongoing, and constantly changing interaction. Burgoon and Ruffner (1978) have provided a health related comparison that illustrates how communication is a process. They have related the process of communication to the process of digestion and have observed that:

. . . to explain digestion, we could list the elements of the digestive process just as the organs involved: the mouth, stomach, small and large intestines, pancreas, and liver. But these elements of the digestive process must work together, interacting and changing to meet different needs. Like digestion, the process of communication also involves change, interaction, adaptation and on going function. (p. 8.)

Extending this illustration we can observe that the elements of communication include speaker, listener, message, channel, feedback and context and each of these elements change, interact, and adapt in ongoing functions. Further, just as a problem with one of the elements of the digestive process can cause the digestive system to become upset, a problem with one of the elements of the communication process can cause a communication breakdown. Thus, the process nature of communication not only contributes to its complexity, but also it contributes to its vulnerability.

Recognizing that communication is a complex process that is vulnerable to breakdowns has an important implication for child life specialists. It reveals the presence of "Murphy's Law" (if something can go wrong it will) in all communication. This is not to say that successful communication is impossible. Rather, it alerts us to the potential for communication failures to occur and the need to take measures to prevent or reduce the failures. The measures to be taken include recognizing when an element of communication may cause a problem and then acting to prevent or correct the problem. We can see these measures in action when a child life specialist recognizes that the message about a medical treatment may frighten or confuse a child and then modifies her preparation explanation to suit the age, ability, and sensitivity of the child. Similarly, we have seen a child life specialist recognize

that the hallway context of a conversation was reducing her ability to communicate with a parent and then move the discussion to a private office. Awareness of communication elements, interactions, problems and subsequent actions taken to address the problems does not guarantee communication success but it can reduce the likelihood of communication failure.

Transaction

Human communication is a transactional activity, one in which participants reciprocally influence each other. The most obvious form of this reciprocal influence is verbal behavior, what people say to one another. For example, during staff meetings we can hear participants influence one another through verbal behavior when they exchange information and ideas, when they argue and disagree, and when they reach agreement on a course of action. However, participants in communication also influence one another by means less obvious than verbal behavior. They do so through nonverbal behaviors such as facial expressions, posture, gesture, movement, and vocal variations. Have you ever modified a statement in mid-sentence or simply stopped talking when you saw a colleague grimace or drop his or her jaw as you were making a remark during a staff meeting? If so, you were influenced by nonverbal behavior. The influence of nonverbal behavior may be even subtler. Slight head nods, forward leans, and barely audible "uh hums" can cause us to continue talking while their opposites can cause us to stop. Although the influence of nonverbal behavior can be considerable, even when it is subtle, there are situations in which nonverbal behavior may have little or no effect. This lack of effect occurs when someone ignores or is not sensitive to nonverbal signals. For example, we have probably all encountered individuals who did not respond to our attempts to signal our need to end a conversation by repeatedly glancing at our watch or walking backward and away from them.

Recognizing that communication is a transaction in which what others and we do as well as what others and we *say* can exert influence. This is especially important in child life because the emotionally charged climate in healthcare settings increases the impact of the messages that are exchanged. A word, a facial expression, or a gesture can have critical effects in conversations with children who are ill, their parents, or other members of the healthcare team. By recognizing the transactional nature and dimensions of such conversations, child life professionals are enabled to identify and attend to aspects of communication that may go unnoticed and unattended by others. In other words, knowledge of communication as transaction can enable child life professionals to observe glances and nods and to notice sighs and hesitations of speech that may be missed by others and to make appropriate adjustments when this happens. For example, the information gathered from "informed observation" can be used to adjust words and actions to the fit the situation, to avoid medical acronyms when speaking with children and parents, to repeat messages when explanations are greeted by puzzled looks, and to maintain distance during a conversation when the other takes steps away. While attention to the transactional nature of communication may not eliminate misunderstandings, it can help child life specialists to contribute to communication success by recognizing, and accommodating to the multiple messages that are exchanged during conversations.

Context

The place where a communication occurs can have an unexpectedly powerful effect on outcome of communication. Evidence of this assertion can be found in the communication failures that litter the landscape as a result of meetings that have been held in hot, poorly ventilated rooms; conversations that have occurred in noisy hallways, and interviews that have been held in offices with ringing phones. Our previous discussions of process and transaction in communication highlight the complexity and fragility of communication and strongly urge that measures be taken to see that context does not interfere with effectiveness in communication. How can child life professionals do this? The distractions that are so frequently a part of context need to be recognized and whenever possible steps need to be taken to eliminate them. For example, in each of the preceding communication failures a room change could have eliminated the distractions of context. Of course, sometimes such changes are not possible. When this occurs, the context problem should be acknowledged rather than ignored and the other elements of communication that can be changed should be changed. Meetings in hot rooms may be shortened, conversations in noisy hallways may require loud talk or close quarters, and ringing phones can be redirected until interviews are completed. In other words, the key to having context work for rather than against communication success is the ability to recognize and adapt to its very considerable influence.

Symbolic

Humans have the unique ability to engage in symbolic activity; to use symbols (words) to stand for objects, actions, concepts and feelings. This seemingly simple activity has enormous consequences. It enables adults to have abstract thought and thereby accounts for the ability of humans to consider the past and plan for the future.

Without it, our existence would be confined to the present, and our communication would be limited to the signals displayed by other species such as the raised tail danger signal of the white tail deer.

The symbolic activity involved in human communication contributes significantly to its complexity. This is because the meaning of the symbols we use as we communicate does not reside in the symbols themselves but in the people who use them. As a result, even common symbols can have varied meanings. For example, the word "hospital" can frighten a child for whom it means a place filled with frightening instruments and needles while to a child life specialist the word simply means a workplace. Even though standardized usage and dictionary definitions of symbols exist, varied meanings abound in human communication. Thus, the possibility always exists that the words we use will not mean the same thing to another person that they mean to us.

Child life specialists can profit from knowledge of the symbolic nature of human communication by recognizing the potential to misunderstand or be misunderstood, especially when talking with children, and then taking measures to reduce misunderstandings. These measures may range from choosing and using words that do not frighten or confuse children to planning preparation explanations that recognize and accommodate the potential for misunderstanding of such explanations.

VERBAL COMMUNICATION IN CHILD LIFE: PROBLEMS AND SOLUTIONS

Although verbal communication has considerable power, it does not always function as a positive force in human interaction.

Some of the features of verbal communication that can lead to problems include: fact/inference confusion, allness statements, word/thing confusion and jargon. Fortunately there are remedies for these problems that may be especially helpful in child life.

Fact Inference Confusion

There are two basic types of statements that we use as we communicate with one another, statements of fact and statements of inference. DeVito (1978) has offered the following distinctions between the two:

1. Statements of fact may be made only after observation while statements of inference may be made at any time.
2. Statements of fact are limited to what is observed while statements of inference go beyond what has been observed.
3. Only the observer may make statements of fact while statements of inference may be made by anyone.
4. Statements of fact may only be made about the past or the present while statements of inference may be made about anytime- past, present or future.
5. Statements of fact approach certainty while statements of inference involve varying degrees of probability.
6. Statements of fact are subject to standards of verifiability while statements of inference are not subject to such standards.

This listing reveals that there are distinct differences between statements of fact and statements of inference. However, during conversations, statements of inference are often mistaken for statements of fact. This occurs because there are no grammatical, syntactical, or other verbal distinctions between the two types of statements. Further, tone of voice and inflection can make an inference sound like a fact. As a result, inferential statements can assume the weight of fact, even though no evidence is offered to support them. When this occurs, further discussion may reveal support for fact sounding inferential statements and conversations can proceed and be productive. However, when further discussion does not reveal support for "fact sounding" inferential statements, the result can be unreasoned discussions, illogical conclusions, disagreements, arguments, and conflicts. Further, during the "heat" of a deteriorating conversation it can be difficult to determine that a problematic inferential statement is the source of the deterioration.

In order to combat the problems that can be created by fact inference confusion three suggestions are offered. First, we must be alert and able to detect when others and we are inferring. Second, we must try to determine the degree of probability that inferences are correct. Third, we need to offer or request evidence to support inferences that are made.

These suggestions can be especially useful during the stressful situations that child life specialists face with worried parents. For example, parents of sick children often share their fears about their child's condition during conversations. Careful listening during these conversations can make it possible to detect when parent's fears are based on unsupported inferences that need to be addressed by a physician who can provide facts about the child's illness. Detecting and addressing unsupported inferences can also prove useful in staff and team meetings because it can help reveal the need for facts and evidence as issues are addressed. Of course, tact must be exercised when support for inferences is requested or the request may be seen as a challenge rather than an appeal.

Allness Errors

In the early 1930s a scientist named Alfred Korzybski observed that while we can never know *all* about something, the structure of our language tends to lead us to think that we can. It does this by inviting us to use absolutes rather than relative terms as we describe and discuss our observations and experiences. Because absolutes require fewer words and less discrimination, they are simply easier to use than relative terms. Korzybski (1933) labeled the tendency to use absolutes the "allness error." Allness errors are a problem in communication because they obscure and devalue differences and promote a dogmatic, judgmental attitude. Examples of allness errors are easy to find because they occur each time we use the words all, every, none, and never. While these words may be found in many types of conversations, they are often found in abundance when frustration and hostility dominate an interaction and they take the form of statements like: "You always . . .", "You never . . . ," "All physicians, nurses, aids, etc. are . . . ," and "Every one of you is . . . ," or, "None of you. . . ." Most of us have probably used one or more of the above phrases at one time or another and it is very likely that we have heard others do so as well.

Because even an occasional "allness error" can create problems, we need to try to remove them from our communication repertoire. The elimination of allness errors may be initiated by a two-step procedure. The first step requires a determined, persistent effort to recognize when others and we make allness errors. This may be accomplished by carefully listening for allness errors as we talk with children, family members, and other staff and team members throughout the course of a workday. When allness errors are detected, step two comes into play. It requires the insertion of linguistic qualifiers such as: some, many, few, most, usually sometimes, or often, to replace allness statements. For example, a child life specialist appropriately uses linguistic qualifiers when saying to a child who is about to have a finger stick, "some children find it helpful to blow the hurt away when they are having a finger stick." While it may be tempting to insert linguistic qualifiers for others when they make allness errors, such behavior will likely be seen as presumptive or worse and it is therefore not recommended. Modeling the insertion of qualifiers when we personally make an allness error is the recommended course of action. The aim of this practice is not just to eliminate allness words, but also to promote the adoption of an attitude that acknowledges the need to qualify statements at an appropriate level of generalization. Thereby, our conversations may depict a more accurate picture of reality and conflicts may be avoided or effectively addressed. Of course, elimination of allness errors is not a "cure all." But, we have found it to be a very useful device in our efforts to improve personal as well as professional communications.

Word-Thing Confusion

"The word is not the thing" is a mantra-like phrase uttered repeatedly by those linguists who believe that word-thing confusion can be quite troublesome in communication (Brown & Van Riper, 1966). They observe that words can stimulate images and feelings that are so intense that they can replace reality. For example, the word surgery can so frighten children and parents with images of pain and suffering that it obscures the reality of pain management, recovery, and the reason for surgery. In situations of such word-thing confusion there is a need to test the words that are stimulating fears against real-

ity (Klinzing & Klinzing, 1985). Children and parents who are terrified by the word "surgery" are ill prepared to make such reality tests on their own. Preparation procedures provide child life specialists with excellent opportunities to identify when children and parents are experiencing word-thing confusion and to help correct the confusion through reality checks. While such checks may not eliminate all fears, they can reduce irrational fears by connecting them to reality. A further value of information about word-thing confusion lies in its potential to sensitize other health professionals to the mental torment that medical terms can cause children and their families and the need to address this problem.

Jargon

Merriam-Webster's Dictionary (2001) offers three different definitions of jargon:

1. Confused unintelligible language.
2. The technical terminology or characteristic idiom of a special activity or group.
3. Obscure and often pretentious language marked by circumlocutions and long words.

The healthcare professions abound with jargon and each of the above definitions can be seen at work in healthcare settings. The first definition applies to the jargon used in healthcare because to most laypersons the language used by health professionals seems confused and unintelligible. Further, medical jargon can frighten, irritate, intimidate, and confuse children and their families and thereby create communication failures (Flynn & Ricca, 2000). Consider the plight of the parents when the pediatric resident tried to explain to them what had been done to alleviate the fever and seizure in their young child. The pediatric resident reported "that the LP was clear gram stain, protein and glucose OK, CBS showed elevated WBC with a shift, calcium and BMP OK, cultures were sent, the CT and MRI were ordered. Neuro was called and an EEG might be done. Sepsis was considered so amp and cefotaxime were started. We considered HSV, and CMV but they were less likely. Do you have any questions?"

The second definition applies to the jargon used in healthcare because when it is used among health professionals it can promote clarity and precision of meaning while providing an economy of language that can save time when time is of the essence. Health professionals have an obvious obligation to be familiar with the specialized terminology of their professions. Less obvious but still important is an obligation to recognize that patients and their families may be confused by medical jargon and that translation may be needed for understanding to occur. Sometimes child life professionals may need to assist in the translation process but care must be exercised so that professional boundaries are not violated.

The third definition of jargon, the use of obscure and pretentious language, has no place in family centered healthcare. Successful communication in healthcare is too important to be compromised by the need to impress.

NONVERBAL COMMUNICATION: CONSIDERATIONS FOR CHILD LIFE SPECIALISTS

Nonverbal communication is the communication that occurs as a result of "all those messages that people exchange beyond words themselves" (Burgoon, Buller, & Woodall, 1996, p. 1). Some of the sources of nonverbal messages include: physical appearance, clothing, facial expression, gaze, gesture, touch, voice, and space. The sheer volume of these elements makes them a very powerful force that can overwhelm the words we exchange. For example, when someone who is six feet, six inches tall, has as scowl on his face, his hands on his hips, and is shouting at you and grabbing your arm, you may not be able to attend to what he is saying but you certainly will know that he is angry. Even subtle nonverbal behaviors can overpower spoken words. When a child utters a softly spoken, hesitant and halting, "I'm OK," to a question about how she feels, should her verbal or the nonverbal response be believed? In order to provide insight about the impact of nonverbal communication in child life, we will consider each of the above listed elements and we will identify implications and applications.

Physical Appearance

The way we look sends messages to others about who we are and these messages have immediate and often enduring effect. While the importance of inner beauty cannot be denied, outer beauty plays a vital role in communication because people tend to respond more favorably to those who are perceived as physically attractive as opposed to those who are seen as physically unattractive. Research shows that physically attractive persons not only score higher than unattractive persons on a wide range of socially desirable evaluations, but also that being physically attractive seems to be an advantage in school, in dating and marriage, on the job, when persuading others, in building self-esteem, when charged with a crime, and during hospitalization (Knapp & Hall, 2002). So, what are the implications of this information for child life professionals? If you are judged as physically attractive you may well enjoy many, readily available opportunities for personal and professional success. But, what if you are judged as physically unattractive? The most frequent answer to this question is that options exist for changing appearance through hairstyle, makeup, clothing, and adornment; thereby improving the nonverbal messages sent by physical appearance. Also, many individuals who have been judged as physically unattractive have risen above the negative image communicated by their physical appearance and forged a life of achievement and satisfaction by displaying competence, skill, and sociability.

It is, of course, especially important for child life specialists to be able to look beyond physical attractiveness because of the likelihood of having to work with children who, for various health related reasons, may not be physically attractive. Also, looking beyond physical attractiveness is inherently a "best practice" because judging others on the basis of beauty is shallow and confining and looking beyond physical beauty provides breadth and depth to our relationships with others.

Clothing

Clothing communicates. It does so because others use what we wear to make judgments about us. Hall and Knapp (2002) have noted that judgments about age, sex, and socioeconomic status using clothing are more accurate than judgments about another's attitudes and beliefs. They also point out that what we wear can affect how we feel about ourselves and that feeling can affect how we communicate. Since clothing has strong communication potential, the choices we make about how we dress can be quite important. We may, of course, choose to ignore the communication potential of what we wear but we do so at some risk. This risk can be particularly troublesome in healthcare settings where professional attire, uni-

forms, and written and unwritten dress codes prevail in spite of the move to casual clothing in many parts of the corporate world. Child life specialists find themselves in a particularly difficult situation with regard to dress. This is because the nature of the work of child life specialists requires casual dress (it would be quite difficult to sit on the floor with a child with while wearing a dress or a suit) while the demands for status require more professional attire. Management of the professional/casual attire dilemma is not an easy task. Some child life programs are choosing to have their staff in scrub clothes. While this protects from messiness, it can increase the risk of role confusion with children and parents. Time spent finding clothing that is both professional and functional is valuable because such dress has the potential to enhance the image and status not only of individual child life specialists, but also the profession of child life as well.

Facial Expression

Hall and Knapp (2002) have observed that the face is a multi-message system. This system can communicate basic emotions and it can help us to manage our interactions with others (Knapp & Hall, 2002). There are six basic emotions that have been shown to appear on the face: surprise, fear, disgust, anger, happiness, and sadness (Ekman & Friesen, 1975). The expression of these emotions can be seen on the faces of children, family members, and coworkers as we talk with them and the facial displays can help to guide the course of conversations. For example, when the expression of sadness covers a child's face we are alerted to the need to consol and comfort the child. However, expressions of emotion can also be masked; as when we "put on a happy face" when we are sad or when hide our anger when we are livid. Therefore, caution must be exercised as facial expressions are interpreted. The task of interpreting facial displays is further complicated by the fact that facial expressions may exhibit more than one emotion; an occurrence referred to by Ekman and Friesen (1975) as facial blends. For example, unexpected receipt of a gift may trigger a simultaneous display of surprise and happiness. Despite the problems of masking and blends, communication of emotion is still the primary function of facial display and as Remland (2000) has noted, "Perhaps no other channel of nonverbal communication is more significant than is the face" (p. 175).

Two additional observations about facial displays may prove useful. The first concerns what is known as the facial feedback hypothesis. This hypothesis was first proposed by Charles Darwin (1872) and contends that that facial expression of an emotion can directly and immediately influence a person's experience of that emotion. Recent research studies lend support to the hypothesis (McHugo & Smith, 1996; McIntosh, 1996) and by extension they may be seen to suggest that helping sick or injured children to smile or laugh may, in fact, help them to feel better. The second observation concerns facial mimicry, the mirroring of facial expressions of another person. A review of research on mimicry shows that mimicry occurs quickly and effortlessly (Dimberg & Ohman, 1996). Even infants have been found to mimic facial expressions they see (Field, Woodson, Greenberg, & Cohen, 1982). The implication of this observation for child life professionals is obvious. Smile. It's contagious and combined with the observation about facial feedback, helpful.

Gaze

Gaze is the term used by communication specialists to describe the way we use our eyes to communicate. It includes: nonrecip-rocal gaze (gaze that is not returned), mutual gaze (when two people look at each other), gaze aversion (when one person looks away from another), and staring (extended, unwelcome looking at another person).

Kendon (1967) and others have identified five functions of gazing behaviors: regulatory, monitoring, cognitive, expressive and relational. The *regulatory* function of gaze can be seen when we extend a glance to another beyond a brief look of recognition, and thereby signal a desire to initiate a conversation and when we avert our gaze we show that communication is not desired. Gaze also plays a role in regulating communication by providing turn taking cues during conversations, as when we look at someone at the end of an utterance to signal that it is their turn to speak. The *monitoring* function of gaze occurs as we try to assess the reactions of others when we speak with them. If the other person is looking at us, we generally assume that he or she is listening to us. And, if the other person averts his or her gaze, we assume that he or she is no longer listening. However, the *cognitive* function of gaze reveals that gaze aversion can be caused by the processing of ideas, not just disinterest (Day, 1964). Thus, we should not automatically assume that someone is not listening to us if they look away as we are speaking to them. They may be engaging in cognitive functioning and trying to process what we have just said. For example, when children avert their gaze during medical preparation sessions, their gaze aversion *may* indicate that they are processing the ideas that are being presented to them. The *expressive* function of gaze occurs as we react to the visual cues provided by the eyes and the brow area of the face. Expression of the emotions of fear and surprise appear to be concentrated in the eye area. As a result, the eyes can provide important clues as to when a child or parent may need emotional support. Gaze also appears to be related to the *relationship* between interactants and their mutual perceptions of dominance, status, power, control, and affection. Summarizing the various findings related to gaze and relationships Knapp and Hall (2002) have said that the unifying thread in these studies is that, "*People tend to look at those with whom they are interpersonally involved. Gazing motivated by hostility or affection both suggest an interest and involvement in the interpersonal relationship*" (p. 360). Because the relational aspect of gaze provides information for assessing and establishing relationships, it is especially important to child life specialists whose responsibilities require the establishment of positive relationships with children, parents and other professionals.

This information about gaze may prove useful in child life because it can help to direct attention to the gaze behavior exhibited by children, parents, and others and because it can provide a stimulus and a direction for an assessment of one's own use of gaze behavior.

Gesture

We are capable of making a vast number of movements with our bodies and each movement has the potential to be a nonverbal cue that communicates something to others. It has been estimated that the number of movements that we are able to make range as high as 700,000 (Birdwhistell, 1970). In order to study this great number of movement cues, researchers have devised various systems to classify them. The most widely used system is one developed by Ekman and Frieson (1969). It categorizes behaviors by function. The categories include the following: emblems, illustrators, adaptors, affect displays and regulators.

An emblem is a nonverbal behavior that can be translated into a verbal message. For example, a headshake back and forth indicates disagreement; an index finger pressed to the lips is a request for quiet, and a thumb up indicates approval. Most North Americans generally understand these and many other emblems. However, the meaning of specific emblems may vary from one culture (e.g., Chinese, Arab, French) or subculture to another (e.g., African-American, Italian-American, Irish-American). Therefore, child life specialists need to be careful when using emblems lest they communicate an unintended or insulting message to someone from another culture.

Illustrators are facial displays, gestures, and movements that accompany our speech. Frowns and pointing are examples of illustrators. Illustrators may help to clarify what is being said or if they become excessive they may become distracting. Knapp (1980) has observed that more illustrators occur when speakers are excited than when they are not and that difficult communication situations tend to stimulate an increased use of illustrators. Thus, when difficult situations occur in child life it is likely that children, parents and family members will use a large number of illustrators as they vent their frustration and anger. Nonjudgmental listening is probably the best response to such behaviors.

Affect displays are facial expressions and body positions that are a result of emotional states. They may accompany or be separate from verbal communication; they may be fleeting or extended behaviors. Further, those who display affect may not be aware of their displays. Affect displays occur continually during communication and they provide information about the feelings and attitudes that communicators have toward the topics being discussed and toward each other. Interpretation of affect displays is difficult because they can be genuine or contrived. Child life specialists need to be sensitive to their own display of affect and be cautious when interpreting the affect displays of others.

Adaptors are behaviors that occur during the course of conversations but are more a means of satisfying physical or emotional needs than behaviors used to accomplish a communication objective. Examples of adaptors include scratching, picking, and rubbing, grooming, and tugging or squeezing oneself. Adaptors seem to be responses to tension and they have been found to vary with level of tension and anxiety (Ekman & Friesen, 1972). Adaptors may provide child life specialists with information about the tension level of children and others with whom they work. However, it is important to recognize that an adaptor such as scratching may be the result of a simple itch.

Touch

Ashley Montagu, a noted anthropologist, argued that touch is necessary for human existence and he reported on numerous studies to support the contention that touch during infancy and childhood is required for subsequent physical and psychological health (Montagu, 1971). A continuing and growing body of scientific research is providing further support for the importance of touch. The Touch Research Institute at the University of Miami School of Medicine has compiled examples of this research.

Touch is not only essential to healthy development but also it is an important aspect of nonverbal communication. Research by Jones and Yarbrough (1985) has revealed that there is a wide range of meaning associated with touch including: positive, negative, playful, controlling, ritualistic, task oriented, and accidental. In addition, there are implicit as well as explicit, culture specific rules or norms which dictate who may touch whom, where, how much, and for how long. Violation of these rules and norms can result in penalties ranging from embarrassment to arrest.

What are the implications for child life specialists of the complexity and risk involved with touch? Two primary implications are apparent. First, because children and their families may attribute various meanings to the use of touch, it may be useful to accompany a touch with an explanation about why that particular touch is necessary. For example, it may be helpful to tell a child why you are holding his arm firmly as it is being sutured, even though the child's loud cries make it difficult for him to hear. Second, because problems can occur when culture specific rules about touch are violated, it is essential to learn the rules about touch that apply in the cultures of the families served by your healthcare facility. This knowledge can be obtained from colleagues, by observing families' use of touch as they interact in a playroom or reception area, or by reading about the culture(s). Jones (1994) admonishes that care should be taken to see that our use of touch does not startle, frighten, offend, or interrupt and that a sincere apology should be offered if it does so. This seems like especially good advice for the practice of touch in child life because the stress that children and families experience in healthcare environs may cause them to react poorly to a touch as innocuous an unexpected tap on the shoulder. This is not to say that the use of touch in child life must be eliminated. In fact, the use of appropriate "positions of comfort" or a gentle touch during a child's procedure can demonstrate how comforting touch can be. Touch can do much to reduce stress, promote calm, and provide comfort. But, it has to be used with knowledge and care.

Voice

"It's not what you said, but how you said it that upsets me." If you have heard or used this statement or similar statements you have experienced the impact that voice can have on communication. A simple change of vocal emphasis can have a dramatic effect on the meaning of what we say. For example, try saying "I really care for you" and emphasize a different word each time you say it. The impact should be obvious. In addition to emphasis, the characteristics of the voice that can influence meaning include rate, tone, pitch, volume, and rhythm. Any variation in these features can communicate. While these variations can be used to confirm or reinforce the meaning of the words we use, they may also serve to contradict or change the meaning of what we say, as indicated in the example above. Furthermore, when vocal behavior contradicts the words that are used, listeners judge the speaker's intention from the voice, not the words (Mehrabian & Weiner, 1967). However, it is important to recognize that the ability to detect and use vocal features to change meaning is a skill that seems to have a developmental component that does not appear until adolescence. If a speaker's words contradict her vocal expression, a young child, unlike most adults, will believe the words (Burgoon, Buller & Woodall, 1996). Thus, a child will not "get it" if the voice is used for sarcasm, irony and contradiction.

Vocal behaviors are also used to regulate the flow of conversations. Knapp (1980) has indicated that this occurs in four ways. First, if we drop our pitch it signals a wish to "yield the floor." Second, vocal cues such as "ah, ah, ah," are a signal that we wish to speak. Third, increasing volume and rate indicates a desire to "maintain one's turn." Fourth "uh-huhs" and "mm-hmms" by a listener tell the speaker to keep talking.

The implications of this information for child life specialists and others who work with children and families are threefold. First, careful attention should be paid to "how something is said" because it can change the meaning for adults and confuse

children. Second, appropriate use should be made of the vocal cues that can be employed to manage the flow of conversation. These cues can be especially valuable in managing conversations with family members who need to be encouraged to talk or who need to listen. Third, research by Buller and Aune (1992) and Remland and Jones (1994) has shown that it can be helpful to match the rate of speech of the other person in a conversation. Besides having more positive attitudes towards same-rate speakers, listeners also are more likely to comply with their requests.

There are, of course, cultural differences in regard to vocal behavior. For example, some cultures (Arab, Israeli, and German) encourage the use high volume when speaking to show strength and authority while other cultures (Thai, Japanese, and Philippine) encourage soft speech to show good manners and education (Ruch, 1989). Knowing that the children and families with whom you work are from a culture that uses voice in a manner different from your own may help to prevent the attribution of negative characteristics to them when they speak with a voice that seems to be too fast or too slow, too loud or too soft, or too high or too low.

Space

The way we use space and distance as we interact has the potential to communicate nonverbal messages. In a now classic work, Edward T. Hall (1966) identified four distances that can communicate messages. These distances are: intimate distance, personal distance, social distance, and public distance. *Intimate distance* ranges from touch to about 18 inches and is reserved for interaction with people with whom we have a positive emotional relationship. If non-intimates invade this space they are met with withdrawal, rebuke, or worse because it is usually perceived as an aggressive act. However, under certain circumstances, such as a medical examination or a visit to the dentist, a non-intimate may be permitted to move into the intimate distance. On the other hand, if an intimate partner avoids the intimate zone, counselors suggest that this may signal a distancing in the relationship (Rothwell, 2000). *Personal distance* ranges from 18 inches to four feet. This is the distance that is normally used for casual conversation. The type of communication that goes on in this range is less personal than that which occurs with intimate distance. Most North Americans feel comfortable carrying on conversations at this distance. If someone tries to close this distance, we back up. If we become backed into a corner while trying to maintain personal distance, we will tense up and look for a way out of the conversation as well as the corner. We may even arrange furniture in our offices and homes to protect our personal distance. *Social distance* ranges from four to about 12 feet. Its closer phase, 4 to 7 feet, is the distance used for professional and business conversations. The far range of social distance, 7 to 12 feet, is used for formal and impersonal encounters such as court hearings. The need to discuss confidential matters may occasionally require that this distance be closed as when a judge asks lawyers to "approach the bench." *Public distance* ranges from 12 feet outward. At this distance it is difficult to carry on a dialog. Thus, public distance is best suited for lectures and public speeches. Although at this distance there is a loss of detail in the face and eyes of listeners, a speaker can still judge listener response from other cues such as silence, laughter, and, of course, applause. In order to make effective use in child life of information drawn from Hall's four distance categories, it must first be recognized that Hall drew these categories from observations of middle-class North Americans and that he cautions against generalizing to other cultures or subcultures. However, Hall (1959, 1996) did observe that some cultures use less personal space than others, and therein resides one explanation of why cross-cultural communication can be problematic. For example, people from Southern European and Middle Eastern cultures tend to stand very close together as they talk. North Americans, as we have seen, need a minimum of 18 inches to three feet for casual conversations. Thus, it can be expected that someone from Southern Europe or the Middle East will try to close distance when speaking to a North American and that the North American will try to maintain distance. Not surprisingly, reports of the results of such conversations indicate that the Southern Europeans and Middle Easterners find the North Americans to be distant and aloof while North Americans find the Southern Europeans and Middle Easterners to be pushy and inappropriately intimate (Hall, 1959). The primary value of Hall's observations is to sensitize us to cultural differences in the use of space and distance. This sensitivity can be quite useful when communicating with children and families from various cultural and ethnic backgrounds because it can help prevent the occurrence of situations like the one just described.

LISTENING

Effective listening is one of the most important and least appreciated elements of human communication. Listening effectively makes it possible for us to understand and be understood. It completes the communication process. Without effective listening communication becomes a soliloquy rather than a dialog. However, in spite of its importance, effective listening is virtually ignored in our educational system and it is taken for granted in workplaces and during social encounters. As a result, many communications fail due to poor listening behavior. We cannot provide a comprehensive analysis of listening in this chapter. However, we can begin to address the problem of poor listening and to promote effective listening in child life by examining some misconceptions about listening and by considering how correcting the misconceptions can improve listening.

Listening Misconceptions

There are four misconceptions about effective listening that we believe deserve attention. First is the mistaken impression that effective listening is a behavior that develops naturally as part of the maturation process rather than a skill that must be learned (Nichols & Stevens, 1957). This mistaken impression helps to account for the lack of attention paid to listening in schools and elsewhere, and it helps to perpetuate the myth that effective listening is synonymous with hearing. In reality, listening is more than just hearing. Larry Barker (1981), a widely recognized authority on listening, argues that the listening process includes four stages: hearing, attention, understanding and remembering. Hearing, the first stage, is the physiological process required for the following stages to occur. Attention, the second stage, directs hearing to particular sounds and blocks out other sounds. For example, as we hear someone speak in an auditorium, we may block out the sound of others who may cough or carry on private conversations. Understanding, the third stage, involves attaching meaning to the sounds to which our attention is directed. The attachment of meaning to sounds is not an easy task. It is the result of experience, association, and context and thus the "word-sounds" we use to communicate can have

various meanings. For instance, think of the meaning that the word "surgery" or "anesthesia" has for a parent of a child who is scheduled for open-heart surgery as compared with the meaning of the words for a vascular surgeon. We also use listening as we hear and observe a pediatric patient engaged in medical play to ascertain a child's understanding of medical experiences. Barker includes a fourth stage in his listening process, remembering. He notes that a listener not only receives and interprets a message but also adds it to memory. However, what is remembered may be different from what was heard. Evidence of the problems associated with the memory phase of listening can be found in virtually every situation that requires patients or parents to recall information that is presented to them and in circumstances involving trauma and stress.

A second misconception about effective listening is that speakers control communication more than listeners. Many people seem to believe that speaking is synonymous with control in communication and that listening is simply a passive response to what is said. In reality, listeners can exert as much, if not more, control over communication than speakers. They do so by choosing whether or not to listen, and if they listen, by choosing how to respond to what a speaker says. Have you ever daydreamed during a meeting? Was the speaker in control? Have you ever heard a shy child expand upon an answer as you nodded and smiled while listening? If so, you have experienced the power that listening can exert on communication. The opportunities to use the power of listening to improve communication in child life abound and awareness of this power is the first step toward its effective use.

A third misconception about listening is that we usually remember most of what we hear. As a matter of fact, research on retention has showed that immediate recall after listening to a ten-minute talk was less than 50 percent and that after twenty-four hours it was less than 10 percent. This report strongly suggests that we do not remember most of what we hear. Further, Barker and Watson (2000) argue that even when we try to listen harder, we do not necessarily listen better. Child life specialists, as well as other health professionals, need to be especially attuned to the limitations of listener retention because of the critical nature of much of the communication that occurs in healthcare. More specifically, not only is it important to recognize one's own retention limitations, but also, there may be times when it is appropriate to help others to recognize the limits of their retention ability. For example, overstressed parents may be helped considerably by the suggestion to write down information provided by a physician rather than relying on their ability to listen and remember what the physician says. The use of objects such as dolls, medical equipment, photographs, or diagrams can help children to listen to what is said during preparation.

A fourth misconception about listening is that noise is a relatively minor problem in listening that is easily managed. This misconception arises from a failure to recognize that noise can be psychological as well physical and that psychological noise can be more difficult to manage than physical noise. The type of noise that we usually think of when we here the word noise is physical noise. It is distracting sounds like hospital paging, rattling food carts, loud talking visitors, and annoying or frightening sounds from medical devices. Physical noise can often be reduced or eliminated by closing doors or moving closer to a patient or family member to carry on a conversation. However, psychological noise is not so easily managed. This is because psychological noise, daydreaming and inattention are difficult to detect. Just because someone looks as though she is listening does not mean that

she is doing so; her mind may be "a thousand miles away." For example, a stressed mother of an ill child may not hear a word that is said, even though she looks attentive. Further, research has indicated that the nonverbal feedback displayed by young children does not always provide an accurate indication of their listening comprehension (Klinzing, 1972). Therefore, instead of trying to detect when someone is distracted by psychological noise it is probably better to assume that distraction is ever-present and to try to compensate for its impact. Such compensations may involve: repeating important messages and supplementing them with written documentation; using examples, and illustrations that are drawn from listeners' experiences and frames of reference during conversations; keeping oral explanations and instructions as uncomplicated as possible; and by modeling good listening behavior.

CONCLUSION

In this chapter we have provided information about the complexity of human communication, we have discussed communication concepts and research findings, and we have offered suggestions about applications of this information in child life. Our aim has been to add to the communication repertoire of child life specialists and thereby further the development of a primary means of meeting the psychosocial needs of pediatric patients and their families. We trust that our explanations will be understood and that our suggestions prove useful.

REFERENCES

Barker, L. L. (1981). *Communication.* Englewood Cliffs, NJ: Prentice-Hall.
Barker, L. L., & Watson, K. (2000). *Listen up.* New York: St. Martin's Press.

Birdwhistell, R. L. (1970). *Kinesics and content.* Philadelphia: University of Pennsylvania Press.

Brown, C. T., & Van Riper, C. (1966). *Speech and man.* Englewood Cliffs, NJ: Prentice-Hall.

Buller, D. B., & Aune, R. K. (1992). The effects of speech rate similarity on compliance: Application of communication accommodation theory. *Eastern Journal of Communication, 56,* 37-53.

Burgoon, J. K., Buller, D. B., & Woodall, W. G. (1996). *Nonverbal communication: The unspoken dialogue* (2nd Ed.). New York: McGraw-Hill.

Burgoon, M., & Ruffner, M. (1978). *Human communication.* New York: Holt, Rinehart and Winston.

Darwin, C. (1872). *The expression of the emotions in man and animals.* University of Chicago Press. London: John Murray.

Day, M. E. (1994). Eye movement phenomenon relating to attention, thought, and anxiety. *Perceptual and Motor Skills, 19,* 443-6.

Dimberg, U., & Ohlman, A. (1996). Behold the wrath: Psychophysiological responses in facial stimuli. *Motivation and Emotion, 20,* 149-182.

DeVito, J. A. (1978). *Communicology: An introduction to the study of communication.* New York: Harper and Row.

Ekman, P., & Friesen, W. V. (1969). Repertoire of nonverbal behavior: Categories, origins, usage, and coding. *Semiotica, 1,* 49-98.

Ekman, P., & Friesen, W. V. (1972). Hand movements. *Journal of Communication, 22,* 353-74.

Ekman, P., & Friesen, W. V. (1975). *Unmasking the face: A guide to recognizing emotions from facial cues.* Englewood Cliffs, NJ: Prentice-Hall.

Field, T., Woodson, R., Greenberg, R., & Cohen, D. (1982). Discrimination and imitation of facial expressions by neonates. *Science, 218,* 179-181.

Flynn, L., & Ricca, J. (2000). For the patient's sake, communicate! *Nursing Management, 31,* 49.

Hall, E. T. (1959). *The silent language.* Garden City, NY: Doubleday.

Hall, E. T. (1966). *The hidden dimension.* Garden City, NY: Doubleday.

Hess, E. (1975). *The tell-tale eye.* New York: Van Nostrand Reinhold.

Jones, S. E. (1994). *The right touch: Understanding and using the language of physical contact.* Cresskill, NJ: Hampton Press.

Jones, S. E., & Yarbrough, A. E. (1985). A naturalistic study of the meanings of touch. *Communication Monographs, 52,* 19-56.

Kendon, A. (1967). Some functions of gaze-direction in social interaction. *Acta Psychologica, 26,* 22-63.

Klinzing, D. G. (1972). Listening comprehension of preschool aged children. *The Speech Teacher, 21,* 86-92.

Klinzing, D. R., & Klinzing, D. G. (1977). *The hospitalized child.* Englewood Cliffs, NJ: Prentice-Hall.

Klinzing, D. R., & Klinzing, D. G. (1985). *Communication for allied health professionals.* Dubuque, IA: William C. Brown.

Korzybski, A. (1933). *Science and sanity: An introduction to non-aristotelian systems and general semantics.* Lancaster, PA: Science Press.

Knapp, M. (1980). *Essentials of nonverbal communication.* New York: Holt, Reinhart and Winston.

Knapp, M., & Hall, J. (2002). *Nonverbal communication in human interaction* (5th ed.). Fort Worth, TX: Harcourt Brace.

McConnell, E. (2000). Communication systems making a caring connection. *Nursing Management, 31,* 49-52.

McIntosh, D. N. (1996). Facial feedback hypotheses: Evidence, implications, and directions. *Motivation and Emotion, 20,* 121-147.

Mehrabian, A., & Weiner, M. (1967). Decoding of inconsistent communications. *Journal of Personality and Social Psychology, 6,* 108-11.

Merriam-Webster's collegiate dictionary (10th ed.). (2001). Springfield, MA: Merriam Webster.

Montagu, A. (1971). *Touching: The human significance of the skin.* New York: Columbia University Press.

Nichols, R. G., & Stevens, L. A. (1957). *Are your listening?* New York: McGraw Hill.

Remland, M. S. (2000). *Nonverbal communication in everyday life.* Boston: Houghton Mifflin.

Remland, M. S., & Jones, (1994). The influence of vocal intensity and touch on compliance gaining. *The Journal of Social Psychology, 134,* 89-97.

Rothwell, J. D. (2000). *In the company of others: An introduction to communication.* Mountain View, CA: Mayfield Publishing.

Chapter 6

FAMILY-CENTERED CARE AND THE IMPLICATIONS FOR CHILD LIFE PRACTICE

Jacqueline L. Bell, Beverley H. Johnson, Priti P. Desai, and Sharon M. McLeod

OVERVIEW

Coping with the stresses of a child's diagnosis and treatment is one of the most daunting challenges a parent faces. When that coping is facilitated through family-centered care practices, the outcome is a collaborative relationship between the family and the healthcare providers. Fostered by mutual respect and founded on family strengths and priorities, this strong partnership enables every member of the healthcare team, with the family "in the driver's seat," to create and implement a comprehensive and dynamic plan of care.

In this chapter we present an overview of family-centered care, outlining its definition and history, its benefits, and its practical applications to child life practice. The heart of the chapter includes "how to" suggestions in support of the nine elements of family-centered care through descriptive scenarios, performance standards of care, and critical feedback regarding the child life specialist's collaboration with families. The next section offers tools that child life specialists may use to evaluate their own programs and individual efforts. We then explore an essential aspect of family-centered care, ensuring cul-

tural competence. The chapter concludes with a vision for the enhancement of family-centered child life practice in the future.

DEFINITION OF FAMILY-CENTERED CARE

Family-centered care is an approach to healthcare that is based on mutually beneficial partnerships between patients, families, and healthcare professionals. These partnerships are integral to the care and support of individual children and their families. They extend beyond the caregiving process. Hospitals and agencies that have made a genuine commitment to family-centered care welcome family participation in program planning and evaluation, as well as in facility design. Families serve not only on parent advisory committees but also are represented, along with clinical and administrative staff, on key hospital or institutional committees.

Seeking to articulate concepts such as these, the Institute for Family-Centered Care brought together families, clinicians, educators, researchers, funders, and other health-

care leaders in 1996 to define the core principles of family-centered care:

1. People are treated with dignity and
   respect.
2. Healthcare providers communicate
   and share complete and unbiased
   information with patients and families
   in ways that are affirming and useful.
3. Individuals and families build on their
   strengths by participating in experiences that enhance control and independence.
4. Collaboration among patients, families,
   and providers occurs in policy and
   program development and professional education, as well as in the delivery
   of care (Institute for Family-Centered
   Care, 1998).

These principles were first published in an
issue of *Advances in Family-Centered Care* and
later formed the basis for the *Patient- and
Family-Centered Care Toolkit* published by the
American Hospital Association and distributed to the chief executive officer of every
hospital in the United States (American Hospital Association, 2004).

Family-centered care is based on the
recognition that the family is the constant in
an individual's life, and that it has significant
influence over an individual's health and
well being. Because of that influence, all families must be supported and encouraged in
their caregiving and decision-making during
hospitalization and other healthcare experiences.

Families play essential roles in healthcare
– whether the patient is a child, an adolescent, or an adult. The word "family" has no
standard definition. A family "can be as temporary as a few weeks, or as permanent as
forever. We become part of a family by birth,
adoption, marriage, or from a desire for
mutual support" (Arango, 1990). Thus, while
family members very often include parents,

grandparents, siblings, and other blood relatives, they may also include friends, significant others, or anyone who is willing to
assume responsibility and reap the rewards
that this role entails.

Each family is unique; each is a culture
unto itself. Healthcare professionals who
practice family-centered care tailor their
approach to each patient and family. They
respect differences, build on and seek to support each family's strengths, and help families secure the resources they need to complement these strengths. The nine elements
and representative scenarios, presented later
in the chapter, will provide helpful insight
into this individualized approach.

HISTORY OF
FAMILY-CENTERED CARE

The evolution of family-centered care and
the development of the child life profession
have many common roots. Both have been
strengthened by the recognition of the
importance of meeting the developmental
and psychosocial needs of children. Both
have been influenced by the roles families
play in promoting the health and well being
of their children. During the last half of the
twentieth century, this new awareness had a
major role in changing the way healthcare is
provided to children and families. Child life
professionals were often in the forefront of
these changes (see Chapter 1).

The foundation for this new family-centered care approach to the delivery of
healthcare for children and families may also
be traced to breakthroughs in medicine and
medical technology. Between 1940 and the
early 1960s, new medical modalities (e.g.,
antibiotics, chemotherapy, pediatric surgery)
became available for children and adolescents. These new treatments were effective.
However, healthcare experiences, particu-

larly hospitalization, were often traumatic for children. Hospitals at that time considered parents and other family members as visitors, and many visitation restrictions were imposed. There were few supportive play programs in hospitals, and little attention was paid to preparing children for procedures. Parents were not encouraged to participate in their child's care.

In the 1950s and early 1960s, research began to emerge about the effects of separating hospitalized children from their families and of depriving them of typical childhood activities. Enlightened healthcare professionals began to realize that play, preparation, and 24-hour visitation for parents would improve clinical and developmental outcomes. In 1965, some of these professionals founded an organization that ultimately came to be known as the Association for the Care of Children's Health (ACCH). ACCH's mission was to provide leadership for "humanizing healthcare for children." While the organization was interdisciplinary from the beginning, it was not until 1978 that parents were invited to join as members. ACCH was the first organization to advocate for the professionalism of child life. In 1987, ACCH articulated eight key elements of family-centered care in a publication entitled *Family-Centered Care for Children with Special Healthcare Needs* (Shelton, Jeppson, and Johnson, 1987). These elements, now revised and expanded, are the basis for the "Best Service/Best Practice" standards discussed later in this chapter (Baystate Children's Medical Center, 1997).

Key legislation in the United States in the fields of education, family support, and healthcare over the last 25 to 30 years has also had an impact on the evolution of family-centered care.

- In 1976, Congress passed The Education for All Handicapped Children Act (P.L. 94-142), mandating publicly supported education for these children in the least restrictive environment. It stipulated that these children have an individualized educational plan developed by a team that includes the child's parents.
- Early in the 1980s, Congress created the Child and Adolescent Service System Program to improve services for children with serious emotional, behavioral, or mental disorders. Family-centered care is an essential aspect of this program.
- To improve systems of care for young children, Congress passed P.L. 99-457, Education of the Handicapped Act Amendments of 1986. Part H – Early Intervention Programs for Handicapped Infants and Toddlers. This legislation recognized the importance of collaborating with families in maximizing the health and development of these children and coordinating services across agencies.
- Congress passed the Individuals with Disabilities Education Act of 1990 (P.L. 101-476); the Developmental Disabilities Assistance; and Bill of Rights Act Amendments of 1990 (P.L. 101-496). With passage of the Mental Health Amendments of 1990 (P.L. 101-63), the Federation for Children's Mental Health was established as a consumer-led organization to assist in building family-centered systems of care.
- Congress passed The Family Preservation and Family Support Act of 1993 (P.L. 103-66) and the Families of Children with Disabilities Act of 1994 (P.L. 103-82). These laws authorized a range of family support services, many of which are offered in the home, that build on family strengths and are planned in collaboration with families.

Contiguous with these new developments in child life, family-centered care, education, and family support, was continued progress in medical care. For example, new technologies made it possible to save the lives of premature or low-birth weight infants. Many of these infants, however, were faced with long-term or repeated hospital stays. Seeking a more active role in their child's care, parents initiated advocacy efforts. They asked for partnerships with healthcare professionals and for support to bring their children home. The resultant parent/professional partnerships were supported by a growing body of research evidence that documented the negative effects of depriving parents of their normal roles during a child's illness. Furthermore, although many of these efforts were initially focused on children with special health needs, they soon spread to include all children and families.

As the family-centered movement grew, some of its leaders came to believe that the conceptual framework could be simplified and made more accessible to those unfamiliar with the field. Thus, in 1996, a group of healthcare professionals, researchers, and families brought together by The Nathan Cummings Foundation outlined four principles (presented earlier in this chapter) that subsequently became central to the Institute for Family-Centered Care's philosophy and approach to changing practice in hospitals, other healthcare settings, and professional education.

In recent years a growing number of professional organizations and agencies have articulated a commitment to family-centered practice. The American Nurses Association and the Society of Pediatric Nurses issued a policy statement that established family-centered care as the standard for nursing practice of children in 1996 and later published a review of the literature that provided the evidence-base for the principles of practice (1996 and Lewandowski & Tesler, 2003). The American Academy of Pediatrics inte-

grated family-centered principles in its national initiatives promoting a medical home for children with special needs and published guidelines on family-centered pediatric home care (Sia, Antonelli, Gupta, Buchanan, Hirsch, Nackashi, et al., 2002; McConnell & Imaizumi, 2001). In 2000, the National Association of Emergency Medical Technicians and the Health Resources and Services Administration of the U.S. Department of Health and Human Services issued a policy statement, "Family-Centered Prehospital Care: Partnering with Families to Improve Care" (National Association of Emergency Medical Technicians, 2000). And finally, shaping the direction for the first decade of the twenty-first century, was *Healthy People 2000* and *Healthy People 2010*, published by the U.S. Department of Health and Human Services, making family-centered care the standard for the care of children with special healthcare needs (U.S. Department of Health and Human Services Maternal and Child Health Bureau). As this history reveals, progress has resulted from a unique synergy between families, healthcare professionals, researchers and policy makers.

BENEFITS OF FAMILY-CENTERED CARE

The benefits of family-centered care may be analyzed from various perspectives – that of patients, their families, healthcare professionals, the institutions of which they are a part, and the healthcare system as a whole (see Table 1). In some cases, the benefits are expressed informally – in the responses of patients, families, healthcare providers and administrators who have seen family-centered care in action and are convinced of its merits. In an increasing number of instances,

Table 1
BENEFITS OF FAMILY-CENTERED CARE

- Improvement in medical and developmental outcomes;
- Greater responsiveness to patient- and family-identified needs and priorities;
- Enhanced patient and family satisfaction and staff and faculty satisfaction as well;
- Creation of a more supportive workplace environment;
- Creation of more effective learning environments for professionals-in-training;
- Wiser use of scarce resources, with a reduction in healthcare costs;
- A cadre of families able to advocate for quality in healthcare and the resources to support quality care; and
- Enhanced competitiveness for the hospital in the marketplace.

Source: From Johnson, B. H., Resource manual for the hospitals moving forward with family-centered care: An intensive training seminar, 2001.

however, the benefits of family-centered care are research-based and have been documented in the literature. This section summarizes some of the key research documenting the impact of family-centered care. It also includes supporting quotes from patients, family members, healthcare professionals and administrators.

From the Patients' and Families' Perspectives

"They really listened to me, even though I'm only twelve. I told them that, 'that medicine always gives me hives,' and they listened."

"I asked them to please wait to ask me the questions when my parents returned. I was nervous and embarrassed. Even at 17, being in the hospital is still scary."

"It assures me I'm included – a part of the process for helping my child get through this experience."

"My opinion, my assessments are as valued as the more educated doctor. I know my child best. My input helps everyone treat my child most appropriately."

For many family-centered practitioners, input such as this – from patients and families alike – attests to the importance of family-centered care. Patients' and families'

responses are now being complemented and validated by research studies that confirm that relationship-based care improves patient outcomes and patient satisfaction (Johnson, 2000). For example, when parents and children are prepared for surgery together, with the parent encouraged to be present for the induction of anesthesia, the parent reports less anxiety and assess the overall experience much more satisfactorily. This research demonstrates that family presence is beneficial to the child and to the parents (LaRosa Nasa & Murphy, 1997; Blesch & Fisher, 1996; Wolfram & Turner, 1996; Powers & Rubenstein, 1999).

Family-centered care recognizes the family as the constant in a child's life and seeks to empower family members at every opportunity. It fosters collaboration with families in the care of individual children and in planning and program development for hospitals and other healthcare settings. At its best, this collaboration is evident in mutually respectful parent/professional partnerships.

Parent participation in care can improve healthcare outcomes. Dunst and colleagues have examined healthcare professionals' help-giving practices and related them to outcomes such as family empowerment, quality of life, and growth in self-confidence and control (Dunst & Trivette, 1996; Trivette,

Dunst, Boyd & Hamby, 1995; Trivette, Dunst & Hamby, 1996). This research demonstrates that the active involvement of people in help-giving/help-receiving relationships is an important factor contributing to positive outcomes. Family-centered practices, such as the sharing of information, facilitation of family/professional collaboration, encouragement of family decision making, and building on family competence and confidence, bring added value to good clinical practice. Participatory involvement in the healthcare experience has been shown to have a powerful effect on empowerment outcomes. These outcomes include belief in one's self and one's ability to have control over important life events and situations.

Parent/professional partnerships can have an impact in all healthcare encounters, including those that are particularly traumatic – for example, an emergency room visit or resuscitation. Too often in hospitals, families are separated from their children during stressful events. For many parents, the loss of their parenting role is more traumatic than their child's illness (Miles & Carter, 1982). When parents are invited to stay with their children, the outcomes can be much more positive. In the videotape, *The Birth of Jacob . . . Celebrating the Life of Jacob*, a mother states that that the respect and support for her and her husband's decision to remain with their son during an unsuccessful resuscitation attempt "has very much helped the grief process" (Institute for Family-Centered Care, 1997).

The benefits of family involvement, in other words, can accrue even when a child's medical outcome is not optimal. For example, Votta, Franche, Sim, Mitchell, Frewen, and Maan (2001) found that parents involved in the decision-making process of removing their child from life-support reported "less dissatisfaction with time spent with their child, fewer negative changes in family functioning, and more positive changes in feelings toward staff" at six to twelve months after the child's death than parents who had not participated in a decision to withdraw life support from their child (p. 17).

Another important element of family-centered care is enhancing family support, particularly the access to peer support and parent-to-parent support. Several recent studies confirm that peer support helps families cope more effectively in caring for children with special needs (Singer, Marquis, Powers, Blanchard, DiVenere, Santelli, Ainbinder, & Sharp, 1999; Ainbinder, Blanchard, Singer, Sullivan, Powers, & Marquis, 1998). This research matched experienced parents with parents of children with newly diagnosed disabilities and found that parent-to-parent support increased parents' confidence and problem-solving capacity. Over 80 percent of the parents interviewed found this program helpful. Interviews with participants also suggested that the kind of support offered through the parent-to-parent program was unique and probably could not come from any other source.

From Healthcare Providers' Perspective

I work collaboratively with families not only because it's the right way to do things, but because it's the most enjoyable, energizing, and satisfying way to provide services.

Ann Wallace, social worker
(Bishop, Woll, & Arango, 1993)

A family-centered approach has a positive impact on providers as well as patients and family members. For example, after reexamining and changing a policy that had not allowed parents to be with their children during anesthesia induction, the Children's Hospital in Boston decided to encourage parent presence during this time. An evaluation of the new program demonstrated that parental participation in post-anesthesia care is not only beneficial to patients and families, but also is rewarding to nurses (Fina, Lopas, Stagnone, & Santucci, 1997).

Another study showed that when emotional support and family-centered care are cornerstones of the culture of a pediatric emergency room, the staff "have more positive attitudes about the impact of ER work than that reported by personnel working in ER cultures that do not emphasize emotional support" (Hemmelgarn, Glisson, & Dukes, 2001, p. 104). This positive attitude may be attributed to the assumption that when staff members provide emotional support to families, they also extend it to each other. Moreover, the intrinsic reward received through positive feedback from families, co-workers, and supervisors may also lead to more positive attitudes. This emotional support may, in turn, lead to improved job performance, less staff turnover due to greater job satisfaction, and the reduction in cost of care. For healthcare providers and families, collaboration equals a "win-win" proposition.

From the Institution's Perspective

Patients and families are making us smarter. There are no surprises on satisfaction surveys when you have consumers involved in meaningful advisory roles.

Jim Conway, Chief Operating Officer, Dana-Farber Cancer Institute, Boston, Massachusetts (Personal Communication, 2001).

Executives of healthcare institutions and third-party payers are continually looking for best practices that provide the highest-quality outcomes at the lowest cost. Fewer visits to clinics, fewer calls to practitioners, fewer visits to the emergency department,

shorter hospital stays, and less frequent re-admissions mean more positive healthcare experiences for children and families. It also equates to fewer dollars and resources spent by the institutions that serve those families. The evidence is mounting that family-centered approaches to care can help reduce costs. For example, the Newborn Individualized Developmental Care and Assessment Program (NIDCAP) uses an approach that combines developmental and family-centered care. Not only did this program save between $90,000 and $129,000 per infant served, it also decreased the number of days the baby received ventilator support and oxygen and promoted more rapid weight gain. In addition, babies nipple fed more quickly, and were discharged home at an earlier date (Als, Lawhon, Duffy, McAnulty, Gibes-Grossman, & Blickman, 1994).

The Transitional Care Center at Rainbow Babies' and Children's Hospital, Cleveland, Ohio, implemented a family-centered approach to care several years ago. Key features of the program included welcoming families 24 hours a day and a commitment to open exchange of information between staff and families. The unit was redesigned in a way that was emotionally and physically supportive of families and their participation in the care and nurturing of their infants. After these changes were made, a 30 to 50 percent decrease in the babies' length of hospital stay was reported. Other effects included fewer re-hospitalizations, reduced use of the emergency department, greater parent satisfaction, and a decrease in maternal anxiety (Forsythe, 1995; Talbert-May, 1995).

In an increasingly competitive healthcare marketplace, institutions also are aware of the importance of patient satisfaction. Here, too, family-centered care can be a real advantage. For example, Pat Sodomka, Chief Operating Officer of the Medical College of Georgia's (MCG) Hospitals and Clinics in Augusta, described the benefits that the hospital has seen as a result of a long-term commitment to family-centered care (Sodomka, 2001) were involved in the development of the vision and values that would guide the planning for MCG's new Children's Medical Center. Subsequently, both a family advisory council and a children's advisory council were created for pediatrics, families were appointed to committees, and a staff position was created for a parent to further family-centered practice throughout the medical center. Family-centered care was included as a specific goal in the hospital's strategic plan. Sodomka believes that family-centered care and the collaboration with families is what enabled the hospital to have the highest family satisfaction scores for 1999 and 2000 among 37 other children's hospitals.

From the Healthcare Systems' Perspective

Family-centered care requires a systemic approach – both at the level of the individual institution and at the level of the nation's overall health infrastructure. This need is being increasingly recognized in reports issued by private and government organizations.

In spring 2001, the Institute of Medicine released a landmark publication, *Crossing the Quality Chasm: A Heath Care System for the 21st Century*, which outlines basic "rules" for healthcare that are consistent with family-centered care and calls for healthcare consumers to participate in the redesign of healthcare. To encourage the implementation of these recommendations, the federal Agency for Healthcare Research and Quality instituted a multimillion dollar funding initiative to place more emphasis on the patient's experience of care and on effective partnerships among clinicians, patients, and families. These initiatives recognize that hav-

ing patients and families informed and actively engaged in healthcare; having care processes tailored to families' priorities, preferences, and values; and having patient needs anticipated and addressed lead to better health outcomes, ensure quality, and promote safety.

THE ROLE OF THE CHILD LIFE SPECIALIST

Child life professionals are ideally positioned to support families in their caregiving roles and to build on parent knowledge and skills about child development. They can prepare families and support their presence in critical care, anesthesia induction, and painful procedures. In addition, many child life professionals have opportunities to foster independence and supportive relationships among children and adolescents and their families. They can assist them in coping with hospitalization, chronic illness or disability. While they support the normal developmental tasks of independence, continuation in schooling, and the development of individuality, they can also support families and their relationship with their children.

Fostering collaborative dialogue with families, promoting communication throughout the experience, and continuously acknowledging the family as an integral part of the healthcare team are strong foundations in quality child life programs. Child life provides a number of interventions that are fundamental to the well being of children and their families, including the following:

• Developmental assessments and play opportunities;
• Preparation and accompaniment for procedures, tests, or surgery;
• Sibling support and education; and
• Parent respite and support groups.

When providing any of these services, it is essential that child life specialists communicate with and collaborate with the child and family in order to create a care plan that best meets the child and family's identified needs and priorities.

As an impetus for change and improvement in the healthcare setting, the child life specialist is often the healthcare provider advocating for and facilitating the development of advisory councils and support groups for patients, parents, and siblings. The role of the child life specialist may also involve encouraging colleagues to revise their beliefs about patient and family empowerment, to progress toward a mentality of "encouraging" rather than "allowing" parents, and to trust that the family is a valuable informational resource in the development of effective, responsive care plans.

BEST SERVICE/BEST PRACTICE: THE NINE ELEMENTS OF FAMILY-CENTERED CARE IN ACTION

Each day brings opportunities for the child life specialist to have a positive impact on children's healthcare outcomes. The nine elements of family-centered care, linked to performance standards for child life specialists, offer an avenue for moving from theory to collaboration, from philosophy to intervention – a genuine effort to develop indicators of exemplary practice. Some of the best service/best practice examples are more fully illustrated through descriptive scenarios that provide important cues to building positive partnerships with children and families.

Element 1. Recognize that the Family is the Constant in the Child's Life, While Healthcare Professionals and Services Systems Often Change.

Performance Standards

- Ask the parents/children daily to identify their priorities for child life/other support, and their assessment of their plan of care and need for support, as these priorities may change over the course of the healthcare experience.
- Inquire daily how they want to be involved in their child's care – preparation, accompaniment for procedures, play outlets, and how you may facilitate each.
- Encourage parent/child to relay information/concerns/assessments.

Descriptive Scenario:

"Good morning, Mr. Finn. How was your night with Sammy?" child life specialist, Mary greets eight-year-old Sammy's father as he is folding up his bedside sleep chair. Still sleeping sounding, Sammy is well known on this unit, as his diagnosis of cystic fibrosis has required numerous admissions. "Tell me what's in store for you and your family today?" Mary whispers.

Although Mary had received morning report from Sammy's primary nurse, inquiring what Mr. Finn's perception of the day's events provides Mary a more comprehensive picture.

"Sam slept on and off. He really needs to sleep a little longer this morning or he will be a bear the rest of the day. Sarah, (mom) will be here soon with Emily and

Dan (siblings). Today we are switching off so I will have Em and Dan. Sarah will go with Sam for his pulmonary function test."

"How can I be of help this morning? Do you need to get off the unit for breakfast or did you receive a parent tray?"

"Well, actually, I did eat, but wanted to check out the parent resource library. Can you peek in on Sam and come get me if he wakes up?"

"Sure. Just before you go, if I remember correctly, Sam's PFT's went pretty well last admission, right? Are you expecting the same this time?"

"I think he will be alright. Sarah and I reviewed everything with him again last night. It's only been 6 months since the last ones, and he remembered 'Silly Sue' right away. She's the respiratory therapist who makes the PFT's almost fun for him."

"Well, it sounds like he's ready for the test. Is there anything else you think I might be able to assist with? We could try the medical play again? And it's cooking day in the playroom. He usually likes getting in on the fun. Can Emily and Dan participate?"

"Thanks for the invite, but I need to run them to some appointments today. They will be back this evening and can play with Sam then. I'll remind Sarah that it's cooking day so she can bring Sam down before his PFT's. He does love the medical play with you. The kit you sent home turned our living room into Finn's hospital."

"Okay, it's a plan. I'll check in on Sam a little later." Both exit the room, closing the door quietly so as not to waken Sam.

Feedback

Mary solicited Mr. Finn's assessment of "how it was going," focused on the family's agenda for the day and their priorities for support, made no assumption that past experience would insure present coping with Sam's test, and provided a variety of child life service choices.

Element 2. Facilitate Parent and Professional Collaboration at all Levels of Healthcare

Performance Standards

- Nurture mutual respect for skills, knowledge, and care.
- Partner daily in the delivery of service – jointly creating the plan of care and evaluating intervention outcomes.
- Proactively seek opportunities to engage parents/youth in planning and evaluating programs, services, and the environment to best meet their needs.

Element 3. Honor the Racial, Ethnic, Cultural, and Socioeconomic Diversity of Families

Performance Standards

- Be aware of personal values, beliefs, and biases when interacting with families.
- Acknowledge and honor diverse family values, customs, and experiences.
- Identify the family's preferred support systems and spiritual resources, and engage appropriate interpreters, cultural consultants, and community support whenever possible.
- Model, teach, and reinforce culturally competent care.

Descriptive Scenario

Fatimah Al-Humeid is a five-month-old female infant admitted to the hospital with seizure disorder and Down Syndrome. Her parents are from Kuwait. Mr. Al-Humeid speaks some English, while his wife speaks only Arabic. Fatimah's twelve-year-old brother, Ahmed, is bilingual in Arabic and English.

Shaneka, a child life specialist, enters Fatimah's room and says," Salaam." They are surprised, smile and return her greeting. Shaneka greets the family verbally, respectful not to extend a handshake. She engages both parents visually, then addresses Mr. Al-Humeid with a brief introduction about her role as a child life specialist and requests that he convey the information to his wife. As Shaneka inquires about Fatimah's developmental milestones, Mr. Al-Humeid appears confused and requests that Ahmed interpret for him. Shaneka politely interjects that she will return with an Arabic interpreter.

With the assistance of the interpreter, Shaneka further reviews her role and discusses a variety of issues with the family. She receives permission to educate Ahmed about his sister's Down Syndrome, diagnosis and treatment, and engages the parents in opportunities to be a part of that education. Mrs. Al-Humeid, now more verbal, expresses her concern that Fatimah is not responding to sounds in her environment or playing as her brother did at the same age. Mr. Al-Humeid expresses surprise, stating he was not aware of this concern. He also confided that "the doctors tell me she has this Down Syndrome, but I do not believe it. My God will heal my daughter." The parents then shared the educational materials they had received about Down Syndrome, with text in both Arabic and English. They agreed to read the information and incorporate the recommendations into their care of Fatimah. Shaneka also reviewed some of the benefits of early intervention with the parents.

As the parents spoke with Shaneka and the interpreter, Fatimah's neurologist, Doctor Parks, entered the room. He engaged Ahmed in a conversation, describing a diagnostic test he had ordered for Fatimah. When Doctor Parks requested that Ahmed interpret this information for his parents, Shaneka caught Ahmed's puzzled expression. She stepped to Doctor Parks' side to let him know that the Arabic

interpreter was available to translate pertinent information and solicit questions. Respecting that a more appropriate option was available to educate the family and obtain the parental consent, Doctor Parks took this opportunity to inquire about other needs or information the family might have. With their medical questions answered, Doctor Parks left. Shaneka inquired about cultural or religious practices specific to their family and opportunities to support them during their stay. Mr. Al-Humeid requested a contact in his religious community, a priest or a mosque in the vicinity. Shaneka agreed to follow-up with chaplaincy services to provide a contact for the family.

Later that afternoon, Shaneka charted her assessment and plan, outlining pertinent family perceptions, concerns, and requests for information and support. Those same points were reiterated at interdisciplinary rounds the next morning, with appropriate referrals made for hearing and speech evaluations.

Feedback

Shaneka was respectful of the family's dynamics, gender and nonverbal spatial boundaries. She learned an Arabic greeting, thus conveying her care and interest in learning about other cultures. She inquired about the parents' perceptions and concerns about their daughter's developmental and health issues. Her awareness of gender roles in parenting helped her appreciate Mr. Al-Humeid's knowledge base in regard to Fatimah's development. Making no gender assumptions however, she guided her questions and discussion to be inclusive of both parents, though her initial comments were directed to Mr. Al-Humeid. She appropriately engaged the Arabic interpreter to assist with her discussion and advocated that her colleague, Dr. Parks, also use this resource rather than the sibling. In so doing, she ensured that parents received accurate information, prevented potential psychosocial harm to Ahmed, and possible risk and liability issues for the hospital. She incorporated sibling education and support into the plan of care. Spiritual and religious expression were fostered and respected. Facilitation of ongoing support was provided through a connection to community resources. Communication of key issues and follow-up needs were documented in the patient record and shared with interdisciplinary team members in a timely manner to assist each in creating a culturally sensitive plan of care.

Element 4. Share Complete and Unbiased Information with Parents on a Continuing Basis and in a Supportive Manner

Performance Standards

- Periodically ask what the patient and family's understanding is of the child's current condition and treatment plan. Determine how they wish to receive information (i.e. verbally, with complementary readings/diagrams, in one-on-one session, in a private space away from other patients and families).
- Reinforce family inquisitiveness regarding diagnosis and treatment through reference to in-house, local, regional and on-line resources, therefore empowering them through education and support.
- Provide information using language that conveys "compassion and respect, which fosters the parent's confidence and care giving abilities." (Knafl, Breitmayer, Gallo, & Zoeller, 1992, p. 94).

Element 5. Implement Comprehensive Policies and Programs that Provide Emotional and Financial Support to Meet Family Needs

Performance Standards

- Collaborate continuously to help the child and family express emotional, educational, spiritual, and financial needs.
- Solicit family recommendations for improvements through verbal exchanges, chart entries, suggestion boxes, issue forums, advisory councils, and discharge surveys.
- Be knowledgeable about unit or clinic resources, both human and written. Orient and encourage family exploration and use of resources.
- Value, respect and facilitate private time for families.
- Respect professional boundaries.
- Bring child/family requests "full circle" – finding answers or acknowledging that the issue is still being addressed.

Element 6. Recognize Individual Family Strengths and Respect Various Methods of Coping

Performance Standards

- Avoid Assumptions.
- Respect the family's coping strategy (unless illegal or physically harmful).
- Facilitate usual forms of coping and offer new strategies.
- Practice "strengths" rather than "deficits" assessments.

Element 7. Understand and Incorporate the Developmental Needs of Infants, Children, and Adolescents and Their Families into Healthcare Systems

Performance Standards

• Know and foster the developmental stages of infants, children, adolescents, and adults.
• Collaborate with the parent and child to identify developmental strengths and needs, their priorities and goals.
• Incorporate the parents' recommendations for fostering their child's developmental growth and emotional well being in the plan of care.
• Proactively address sibling issues with parents to review reactions to the healthcare experience and collaborate in creating supportive interventions.
• Assist families in anticipating new educational opportunities and supportive interventions when the child's previous mental or developmental status has been altered.

Descriptive Scenario

During morning report, nurse Glenna reports to child life specialist, Zoë, "Tom was readmitted last night for the first time in a year. Remember his last visit – days and days in the PICU in status epilepticus? When he came out here to the unit, they had another three weeks before discharge. It was a tough time for them. His parents have sought alternative approaches in the interim, including therapeutic touch, herbal remedies, and aquatic therapy. Tom's mother, Tammy, was anxious last night when they arrived. She was concerned we might find her requests unmanageable. This admission is for dehydration following

a bout with the flu. The whole family had it so mom is really fatigued."

Zoë offers, "How can I help? Child life teamed well with the family during the last admission. His sister, Lauren, came often for play sessions. Tom's primary nurse and I did a school re-entry program with the family after Tom's discharge."

Nurse Glenna continues, "Mrs. Stauffer's primary wish is that Tom lose no ground developmentally while here. They have constructed a supportive schedule for him at home, which should be adaptable here, and she has some great recommendations for 'creating a home-away-from-home' also. A change of routine and environment has her concerned. Let's see how we can help this transition be as seamless as possible. There are no tests scheduled until this afternoon. He is getting I.V. meds. Mr. Stauffer, Sid, is away on business for a week. Lauren is with her grandmother at home, also a little under the weather."

"Thanks for the report. I'll see them now," states Zoë as she leaves the nurses' station.

As Zoë knocks on the Stauffers' door, she hears soothing music. Welcomed in, Zoë scans the room quickly. What is this room? She had played with a child here just yesterday and now it is totally transformed! The lights are dimmed, CD's are lined up next to a boom box, family pictures are taped to the bed rails, and Tom is positioned comfortably with colorful, soft pillows. Zoë can also see that he is resting on flannel sheets, which have a fresh, spring-like smell. Tom has grown since she last saw him, somewhat more alert, still nonverbal, and displays his characteristic arm and hand gestures.

After an exchange of greetings, Zoë inquires how child life can help with the family's transition back into the hospital. Tammy is eager to review Tom's daily schedule, specific cues, and soothing techniques. She requests that these ideas be posted for caregivers at the bedside and incorporated into the cardex and plan of care. Although she has brought several of Tom's favorite toys and CD's, she wonders if Zoë might bring some texture squares and switch toys.

Tammy also shares what she knows about the day's schedule. "Tom will be having therapeutic touch at 11:00. His resident is coming back to observe since he has not seen it done before. Tom's test is this afternoon at 3:00. Could we talk about how we might make that go smoothly also?"

Mrs. Stauffer and Zoë spend another fifteen minutes reviewing preferences and other opportunities for support during this hospital stay. Zoë concludes by saying she will relay this information to the rest of the healthcare team and follow-up later with Mrs. Stauffer when she brings the texture and touch toys back.

Feedback

An initial, thorough review of needs and preferences works to ensure the development of a collaborative plan, which builds on the family's expertise and priorities for support. This proactive engagement honors the core principles of family-centered care of dignity and respect, respectful two-way communication, building on the family's strengths, thus enhancing their control and independence.

Element 8. Encourage and Facilitate Family-to-Family Support and Networking

Performance Standards

- Proactively and regularly solicit information about the family and the child's interest in support and the opportunity to meet with peers.
- Whenever possible, facilitate families meeting other families.

- Encourage exploration and use of institutional, community, national, and Internet resources, groups, and organizations. Provide information about "favorites" identified by other patients and families.
- Recognize that family needs for information and support and interest in connecting with peers change over time.

Element 9. Design Accessible Healthcare Delivery Systems that are Flexible, Culturally Competent, and Responsive to the Needs that Families Identify

Performance Standards

- Value the child, adolescent, and family's input in improving programs and facilities.
- With each family interaction, seek opportunities to be responsive to the family's cues and priorities and their requests for information and support.
- Create a variety of ways for children, youth, and families from diverse backgrounds and with diverse healthcare experiences to participate in planning, implementing, and evaluation systems of care.
- Strive to create collaborative relationships with all patients and families, being flexible and tailoring practices to each individual patient and family's values, beliefs, priorities, and preferences.
- Build on the "Golden Rule" of treating others as you and your family would like to be treated, and on the "Platinum Rule" of treating others as they would like to be treated.

ASSESSING CHILD LIFE PROGRAMS FOR CONSISTENCY WITH FAMILY-CENTERED PRINCIPLES

Each healthcare institution following the standards recommended by the Joint Commission on the Accreditation of Healthcare Organizations (JCAHO) is responsible for ensuring that its policies, practice standards, job descriptions and performance appraisals include family-centered language (JCAHO, 2002). In addition to these important standards, key hospital leaders, in collaboration with advisory councils, may make use of self-assessment tools to evaluate their efforts to achieve family-centered programming. These instruments focus attention on areas such as: the philosophy of care, information and decision-making practices, charting and documentation, and environment and design. Often an eye-opening exercise, completion of the inventory is only the first step. Building a plan of action to support areas where improvement is needed is a rewarding and gratifying experience for the "agents of change." A comprehensive tool developed by the Institute of Family-Centered Care, "Family-Centered Child Life Programs: Key Questions to Ask," can be a useful component of a thorough program assessment. Self-assessment inventories that address broader aspects of pediatric programs are also available from the Institute for Family-Centered Care.

In addition to participating in program assessments, each child life professional should assess his or her own personal interactions with patients and families on a daily basis to ensure that they are consistent with the principles of family-centered care. This review may be done in a variety of ways. The child and family may provide an assessment of their experience, either directly to the specialist or indirectly through a nurse,

physician, guest relations representative or parent advocate. The family may respond to unit-based or institutional phone or written surveys, which include questions evaluating child life service. Additionally, advisory councils' assessments may identify key opportunities for improving child life programming.

CHILD LIFE PROGRAMMING: PROVIDING CULTURALLY COMPETENT CARE

The chapter has provided a comprehensive overview of the practice of family-centered care, but a review of how diversity and spirituality impact our collaboration with families requires a closer look.

The North American society is undergoing dramatic demographic changes. It is expected that racial and ethnic minorities will become the numerical majority in the United States by 2010, with White American families constituting 48 percent of the population (Sue, 1991). This population trend is the result of two notable developments: (1) current immigration patterns and (2) differential birth rates between white, racial and ethnic minority populations. Immigrant populations are those defined as documented and undocumented immigrants and refugees. European immigrants arriving early in the twentieth century were oriented to assimilate into the American culture. More recent immigrants are primarily from Asian, Latino, and other ethnic groups that are more visibly different from White Americans. They may not readily assimilate with the majority culture and are likely to have a greater tendency to hold on to customs and practices of their countries of origin. In the 1990 census data, linguistically isolated households were identified for the first time. In these homes, where no one over 14 years of age speaks English, 30 percent were Asian households and 23 percent were Hispanic households. Additionally, 28 percent of all immigrant households with school-aged children were identified as linguistically isolated (The Center for the Study of Social Policy, the Population Reference Bureau, 1992). These statistics hold significant implications for all professionals who provide care to children both inside and outside healthcare systems. Language and cultural barriers bring profound challenges in providing culturally competent care.

Culturally competent care is sensitive to individual family values and avoids stereotypical models of communication or the assumption that one's own background is the "norm" and the patient and family's background is diverse. Lynch and Hanson (1998) outline important variables that need careful consideration when working with families of any culture.

- Family structure – patriarchal or gender differences in care giving roles; involvement of extended family members.
- Family dynamics – male head of household; importance of elders in decision making.
- Family beliefs – regarding the cause of the illness such as physical imbalance, yin/yang, supernatural forces, or evil spirits.
- Communication styles – verbal/nonverbal, language fluency – spoken and written, use of touch, spatial norms, eye contact/aversion.
- Time orientation – to present rather than future, to being habitually late or fanatically on time.

Incorporating Cultural Competence in Child Life Practice

Using culturally appropriate greetings in the family's chosen language is one sugges-tion. Another is to avoid assumptions through the incorporation of simple statements such as, "I know a little about your cultural background, but I do not know about your individual family and what practices and rituals are important for you. Please tell me how I can respect those and best help meet your needs at this time." Advocating for the unique needs that may be identified with interdisciplinary team members is an essential child life role. The conscientious, consistent use of appropriate interpreters, rather than younger English-speaking family members, will also support a culturally competent practice. Learning and incorporating diverse songs, games, and cultural celebrations into child life programming and environment are also welcoming practices for supporting families from culturally diverse backgrounds.

Culturally competent care also encompasses respect for the family's spiritual and religious foundation. It requires that the child life specialist and each healthcare professional be cognizant of the family's faith traditions and have a firm grasp on his or her own personal beliefs. These shared or divergent beliefs not only impact the family and staff members' perceptions and care of the illness or disability, but also direct the family's daily living habits, interactions, and decision-making about child-rearing, utilization of healthcare, and treatment options.

Spirituality of Parents and Family Members

Parents' child-rearing practices are filtered through their cultural, spiritual and religious lens. This lens is the prism through which they assess and find meaning in their child's illness or injury, treatment plan and day-to-day care.

Families may advocate for specific spiritual and religious therapies as complementary, supplemental or alternative to the medical treatment of their child. Their pursuit of such supportive care may reflect their belief that biomedical interventions address only limited aspects of the person – the body, rather than the soul, mind, and spirit (Barnes, Plotnikoff, Fox, & Pendleton, 2000). Families may turn to their spiritual community to provide a variety of healing therapies. Spiritual traditions may include prayer, pilgrimage, vows to saints or God, anointing, or the use of amulets, icons and other religious objects. Families may seek faith healers for solace and support. Some faith traditions mistrust or even fear physicians. Others believe in a passive resignation to a divine authority. In some instances, the medical community has responded to families' religious beliefs, intervening when a particular belief posed a medical threat to the child. In a culturally-sensitive environment, religious and spiritual beliefs are routinely incorporated into a coordinated plan of care with the family.

Implications for Clinical Practice

Guidelines provided by Barnes, Plotnikoff, Fox, and Pendleton (2000) will assist the child life specialist in integrating spiritual and religious resources into everyday practice.

- Anticipate the presence of religious and spiritual concerns in pediatric care.
- Develop awareness of your own spiritual history and perspectives.
- Become broadly familiar with the religious worldviews of the cultural groups in your patient population.
- Encourage children and families to be your teachers about the specifics.
- Build strategic interviewing skills and ask questions over time.
- Develop a relationship with available chaplain services.
- Build a network of local consultants.

- Refer to family-preferred spiritual care providers.
- Listen for understanding rather than for agreement or disagreement.
(Barnes et al., 2000, p. 903.)

The child life specialist who respects and practices these guidelines, and advocates for their acknowledgment and implementation by other healthcare professionals, is building the foundation for continued dedication to culturally competent and spiritually supportive care.

FUTURE VISIONS

The practice of family-centered care has become the rudder for exceptional child life programs in many healthcare centers, nationally and internationally. Yet the voyage has just begun. As programs seek opportunities to improve care through extending this philosophy to colleagues via education and mentoring, more outcome studies to identify benefits to patient, family, staff and institutions will be crucial. Anecdotal reflections provide profound insight into day-to-day practices, but research will "prove" those perceptions and shoulder far more credibility in academic and medical circles.

A vision for the future of the child life profession that furthers family-centered, culturally competent care would embrace these enhancements.

- Students from diverse backgrounds will be actively recruited to pursue careers in child life.
- Courses supporting cultural competence and spirituality will be incorporated into academic curricula, internships, and continuing education for child life specialists.
- Child life staff, students, and volunteers will be encouraged to become multilingual.

• The practice of family-centered care will be embraced in the multitude of alternative settings where child life specialists practice.

SUMMARY

Child life practice that is responsive to family-identified needs and builds a collaborative plan of care for play, support, and education is synonymous with a sound family-centered approach. In this chapter, we challenge the child life professional to critically review individual, program and institutional practices and policies with patients and families and partner *with* them to create, improve and enhance the healthcare experience for all.

REFERENCES

Adnopoz, J., & Nagler, S. (1993). Supporting HIV infected children in their own families through family-centered practice. In E. S. Morton, & R. K. Grigsby (Eds.), *Advancing family preservation practice.* Newbury Park, CA: Sage.

Ainbinder, J., Blanchard, L., Singer, G. H. S., Sullivan, M., Powers, L., & Marquis, J. (1998). A qualitative study of parent to parent support for parents of children with special needs. *Journal of Pediatric Psychology, 23,* 99-109.

Als, H., Lawhon, G., Duffy, F. H., McAnulty, G. B., Gibes-Grossman, R., & Blickman, J. G. (1994). Individualized developmental care for the very low-weight preterm infant: Medical and neurofunctional effects. *Journal of the American Medical Association, 272,* 853-858.

American Academy of Pediatrics. (2004). Policy statement: Medical home initiatives for children with special needs project advisory committee. *Pediatrics, 113,* 5, 1545-1547.

American Hospital Association and the Institute for Family-Centered Care. (2004). *Patient- and family-centered care toolkit – Strategies for leadership.* Washington, DC: Author. Retrieved April 14, 2007, from http://www.aha.org/aha/issues/Communicating-With-Patients/pt-family-centered-care.html.

American Nurses Association and Society of Pediatric Nurses. (1996). *Statement on the scope and standards of pediatric clinical nursing practice.* Washington D.C.: American Nurses Association.

Arango, P. (1990, November 6). House Memorial 5 Task Force on Young Children and Families. *First steps to a community based coordinated continuum of care for New Mexico children and families.* (Available from Polly Arango, PO Box 338, Algodones, New Mexico, 87001).

Barnard, D., Dayringer, R., & Cassel, C. K. (1995). Toward a person centered medicine: Religious studies in the medical curriculum. *Academic Medicine, 70,* 806-813.

Barnes, L. L., Plotnikoff, G. A., Fox, K. & Pendleton, S. (2000). Spirituality, religion and pediatrics: Intersecting worlds of healing. *Pediatrics, 106,* 899-908.

Baystate Medical Center Children's Hospital. (1997). Best service/best practice – performance standards for the practice of family-centered care.

Beckman, H. B., Markakis, K. M., Suchman, A. L., & Frankel, R. M. (1994). The doctor-patient relationship and malpractice. *Archives of Internal Medicine, 154,* 1365-1370.

Bishop, K., Woll, J., & Arango, P. (1993). *Family/professional collaboration for children with special health needs and their families.* Burlington, VT: Family/Professional Collaboration Project.

Blaylock, B. L. (Summer 2000). Patients and families as teachers: Inspiring an empathic connection. *Families, Systems, and Health, 18,* 161-175.

Blesch, P., & Fisher, M. L. (1996). The impact of parental presence on parental anxiety and satisfaction. *AORN Journal, 63,* 761-768.

The Center for the Study of Social Policy, the Population Reference Bureau. (1992) *The challenge of change. What the 1990 Census tells us about children.* Washington, DC: The Center for the Study of Social Policy.

Dunst, C. J., & Trivette, C. M. (1996). Empowerment, effective helpgiving practices, and family-centered care. *Pediatric Nursing, 22,* 334-337.

Fina, D., Lopas, L. J., Stagnone, A. H., & Santucci, P. R. (1997). Parent participation in the postanesthesia care unit: Fourteen years of progress at one hospital. *Journal of Peri-Anesthesia Nursing, 12,* 152-162.

Forsythe, P. (1995). Changing the ecology of the NICU. *Designing for Child Health, 3,* 11-14.

Forsythe, P. (1998). New practices in the transitional care center improve outcomes for babies and their families. *Journal of Perinatology, 18,* 13-17.

Fulton, R. B., & Moore, C. M. (1995). Spiritual care of the school-age child with a chronic condition. *Journal of Pediatric Nursing, 10,* 224-231.

Hemmelgarn, A. L, Glisson, C., Dukes, D. (2001). Emergency room culture and the emotional support component of family-centered care. *Children's Heath Care, 30,* 93-110.

Hobbs, S. F., & Sodomka, P. F. (2000). Developing partnerships among patients, families, and staff at the Medical College of Georgia Hospital and Clinics. *Journal of Quality Improvement, 26,* 268-276.

Hostler, S. L. (1999). Pediatric family-centered rehabilitation. *Journal of Traumatic Head Injury, 14,* 384-393.

Institute for Family-Centered Care. (1998). Core principles of family-centered health care. *Advances in Family-Centered Care, 4,* 1, 2-4.

Institute of Medicine. (2001). *Crossing the quality chasm: A new heath care system for the 21st century.* Washington, DC: Author.

Ireys, H., Chernoff, R., DeVet, K. D., & Kim, K. (2001). Maternal outcomes of a randomized controlled trial of a community-based support program for families of children with chronic illnesses. *Archives of Pediatric and Adolescent Medicine, 155,* 772-222.

Joint Commission on Accreditation of Healthcare Organizations. (2002). *Accreditation Manual for Hospitals: The Official Handbook.* Oakbrook Terrace, IL: Joint Commission of Healthcare Organizations.

Johnson, B. H. (2001). *Resource manual for the hospitals moving forward with family-centered care: An intensive training seminar.* Bethesda, MD: Institute for Family-Centered Care.

Johnson, B. H. (1999). Family-centered care: Creating partnerships in health. *Group Practice Journal, 48,* 18-21.

Johnson, B. H. (2000). Family-centered care: Four decades of progress. *Families, Systems, and Health, 18,* 133-156.

Johnson, B. H. (Executive Producer). (1997). *The birth of Jacob . . . celebrating the life of Jacob.* [Videotape]. Bethesda, MD: Institute for Family-Centered Care.

Johnson, B. H., Jeppson, E. S., & Redburn, L. (1992). *Caring for children and families: Guidelines for hospitals.* Bethesda, MD: Institute for Family-Centered Care.

Knafl, K., Breitmayer, B., Gallo, A., & Zoeller, L., (1992), Parents' views of healthcare providers: An exploration of the components of a positive working relationship, *Children's Heath Care, 21,* 90-95.

LaRosa Nasa, P. A., & Murphy, J. M. (1997). An approach to pediatric perioperative care: Parent-present induction. *Nursing Clinics of North America, 32,* 183-199.

Levinson, W. (1997). Doctor-patient communication and medical malpractice: Implications for pediatricians. *Pediatric Annals, 26,* 186-193.

Lewandowski, L. A., & Tesler, M. D. (Eds.). (2003). *Family-centered care: Putting it into action, SPN/ANA guide to family-centered care.* Washington, DC: Society of Pediatric Nurses/American Nurses Association.

Lynch, E. W., & Hanson, M. J. (1998). *Developing cross-cultural competence.* Baltimore: Paul H. Brookes.

McConnell, M., & Imaizumi, S. O. (Eds.). (2001). *Guidelines for pediatric home health care.* Evanston, IL: American Academy of Pediatrics.

Miles, M. S., & Carter, M. C. (1982). Sources of parental stress in pediatric intensive care units. *Children's Heath Care, 11,* 65-69.

National Association of Emergency Medical Technicians. (2000). *Family-centered pre-hospital care: Partnering with families to improve care.* Clinton, MS: Author. Retrieved April 14, 2007 from http://www.naemt.org/divisionsAnd Committees/pediatricCommittee/emsc.htm.

Powers, K. S., & Rubenstein, J. S. (1999). Family presence during invasive procedures in the pediatric intensive care unit. *Archives of Pediatrics and Adolescent Medicine, 153,* 955-958.

Resnick, M. D., Bearman, P. S., & Blum, R. W. (1997). Protecting adolescents from harm: Findings from the national longitudinal study on adolescent health. *Journal of the American Medical Association, 278,* 823-832.

Robinson, J. S., Schwartz, M. M., Magwene, K. S., et al. (1989). The impact of fever health education on clinic utilization. *American Journal of Diseases of Childhood, 143,* 698-704.

Schneider, D. (1997). Spiritual care for children with cancer. *Seminars in Oncology Nursing, 13,* 263-270.

Shelton, T. L., Jeppson, E. S., & Johnson, B. H. (1987). *Family-centered care for children with special healthcare needs.* Bethesda, MD: Association for the Care of Children's Health.

Shelton, T. L., & Stepanek, J. S. (1994). *Family-centered care for children needing specialized health and developmental services.* Bethesda, MD: Association for the Care of Children's Health.

Sia, C., Antonelli, R., Gupta, V. B., Buchanan, G., Hirsch, D., Nackashi, J., et al. (2002). American Academy of Pediatrics. Medical Home Initiatives for Children with Special Needs Project Advisory Committee. The medical home. *Pediatrics, 110,* 1, 184-186.

Singer, G. H. S., Marquis, J., Powers, L. K., Blanchard, L., DiVenere, N., Santelli, B., Ainbinder, J. G., & Sharp, M. (1999). A multisite evaluation of parent to parent programs for parents of children with disabilities. *Journal of Early Intervention, 22,* 217-229.

Skipper, J. K., Leonard, R. C., & Rhymes, J. (1968). Child hospitalization and social interaction: An experimental study of mother's feelings of stress, adaptation, and satisfaction. *Medical Care, 6,* 6, 496-506.

Smith, T., & Conant Rees, H. L. (2000). Making family-centered care a reality. *Seminars for Nurse Managers, 8,* 136-142.

Sodomka, P. Keynote Address. Presented at the Patient- and Family Centered Care: Good Values, Good Business Conference; American College of Healthcare Executives Conference; May 17, 2001; Virginia Beach, VA.

Solberg, B. (1996). Wisconsin prenatal care coordination proves its worth: Case management becomes Medicaid benefit. *Inside Preventive Care, 2,* 1,5-6.

Still, J. V. (1984). How to assess the spiritual needs of children and their families. *Journal of Christian Nursing, 1,* 4-6.

Sue, D. W. (1991). A conceptual model for cultural diversity training. *Journal of Counseling and Development, 70,* 99-105.

Talbert-May, A. (1995). *The effects of a non-traditional hospital environment for premature infant care on maternal state anxiety.* Unpublished master's thesis. Case Western Reserve, Cleveland, OH.

Trivette, C. M., Dunst, C. J., Boyd, K., & Hamby, D. W. (1995). Family-oriented program models, helpgiving practices, and parental control appraisals. *Exceptional Children, 62,* 237-248.

Trivette, C. M., Dunst, C. J., & Hamby, D. W. (1996). Characteristics and consequences of helpgiving practices in contrasting human services programs. *American Journal of Community Psychology, 24,* 273-293.

Vander Stoep, A., Williams, M., Jones, R., Green, L., & Trupin, E. (1999). Families as full research partners: What's in it for us? *The Journal of Behavioral Health Services and Research, 26,* 329-344.

Weissbourd, B. (1994). The evolution of the family resource movement. In S. Kagan & B. Weissbourd (Eds.), *Putting families first: American's family support movement and the challenge of change.* San Francisco: Jossey-Bass.

U.S. Department of Health and Human Services Maternal and Child Health Bureau. *Achieving and measuring success: A national agenda for children with special health care needs.* Retrieved April 14, 2007, from http://mchb.hrsa.gov/programs/specialneeds/measuresuccess.htm

U.S. Department of Health and Human Services. *Healthy people 2010. Volume II: Objectives for improving health.* (2nd ed.). Available at: http://www.health.gov/healthypeople/Publication. Accessed January 1, 2003.

Votta, E., Franche, R.-L., Sim, D., Mitchell, B., Frewen, T., Maan, C. (2001). Impact of parental involvement in life-support decisions; a qualitative analysis of parents' adjustment following their child's death. *Children's Heath Care, 30*, 17-25.

Widrick, G., Whaley, C., DiVenere, N., Vecchione, E., Swartz, D., & Stiffler, D. (1991). The medical education project: An example of collaboration between parents and professionals. *Children's Heath Care, 20*, 93-100.

Wolfman, W., & Turner, E. (1997). Effects of parental presence during young children's venipuncture. *Pediatric Emergency Care, 13*, 325-58.

Chapter 7

ASSESSMENT AND DOCUMENTATION IN CHILD LIFE

Ellen Hollon and Linda Skinner

OVERVIEW

The success of child life work is dependent on accurate and ongoing assessment of a child and his or her family as they experience and respond to healthcare encounters and on the accurate recording or documentation of that work. This chapter provides an introduction to the child life assessment and documentation process that is essential in order to communicate with others and maintain a permanent legal record of child life interventions.

Establishing a trusting relationship with the patient, the foundation of child life work, begins with initial information gathering and assessment. In order to make an accurate and valuable assessment, the child life specialist must have extensive knowledge of:

- child growth and development
- the potential impact of stress and hospitalization
- family systems theory and family dynamics
- therapeutic and other forms of play

In addition, the child life specialist must be skilled in:

- establishing supportive relationships
- communicating with children, families and team members
- guiding children in therapeutic play techniques
- gathering information from a variety of sources

The child life assessment process requires information from three sources: the healthcare team, the family and the child.

Each of these sources provides information that is unique and rich. Taken together, a child life specialist is able to build a comprehensive assessment of the needs of the child and family.

Information from the Healthcare Team

The patient record will provide a portion of the information needed for accurate assessment. The admission or history section of the patient's medical record, consult reports, progress notes and letters from referring agencies will all give clues, not only about the medical issues, but also psychosocial information that is vital to the child life specialist. The patient record is not the only source of information, however. The admitting nurse or physician will have information that may not be recorded. This might include information about questions the family asked, whether they appeared apprehensive, how they supported their child, and so on. Though not recorded in the patient's medical record, this information can be invaluable for the child life specialist. It may provide insights about the immediate needs of the family related to their response to the admission, or other events they have encountered. In addition, the child's nurse will have information about upcoming medical procedures related to diagnosis and treatment. Nurses who worked the night shift, for example, may have information about restless nights, nightmares, and parental rooming-in decisions. A positive professional working relationship with members of the healthcare team who fully understand the role of the child life specialist will ensure necessary information is exchanged fully and in a timely manner.

Information from the Family

Establishing a supportive relationship with the family is important for the child life specialist because the members of the family "know their child best." A strong supportive relationship provides a foundation for the family to share pertinent information about the child and the family. Such relationships begin with the child life specialist providing his or her name along with an explanation of the role of child life in the child's healthcare experience.

The next step in building the relationship may involve providing information that helps the family to understand the hospital environment. For example, explanations may be given regarding the roles of interns, residents, medical students and other team members in caring for their child. This information should also include a "menu" of strategies the family can use to have an active role in supporting the child in hospital. Items on the "menu" might include information on:

- methods of providing play opportunities for the child, with a discussion of why play is important in coping with hospital experiences
- roles that family members can play during procedures
- learning supportive distraction techniques, if the family chooses that role
- how to take care of oneself while "living" in a hospital.

Once this initial relationship is developed, the family will be a critical source of information and often the only source of information about:

- recent stresses for the child and family, such as deaths of relatives or pets
- the child's usual responses to stress
- typical coping strategies used by the child

Information from the Child

The child is, of course, the most accurate source for much of the information that the child life specialist requires. Regardless of the child's age, temperament, and other individual attributes, play is the best assessment tool for the child life specialist to communicate with the child (Gaynard, Wolfer, Goldberger, Thompson, Redburn, & Laidley, 1998). Play is a natural activity for children and will help to establish a supportive relationship and facilitate the assessment process. The child life specialist will be able to determine the child's developmental level, emotional state, understanding of his or her healthcare experience, misconceptions the child may have, and other critical information such as questions the child may find difficult to ask.

Sometimes, developing supportive relationships with children in the hospital can be a challenge (Gaynard et al., 1998). Children who are shy, angry, and fearful or who are in significant pain can be difficult to engage. In these circumstances, the child life specialist may begin the relationship by participating in a favorite activity, game or craft. Activities such as these can be the bridge to connect with children and help them to be comfortable in expressing their thoughts and feelings about the hospital experiences. Through play, children can relax and are more likely to ask questions, express concerns, and reveal misconceptions about what is happening.

MODELS FOR ASSESSMENT

A number of models for assessing the child and family may be used. Three such approaches are considered here. Francis (1990) formulates a model of assessment based on both general and specific information about children and their families. Relevant information includes the child's medical condition and developmental level, as well as other issues expected to affect coping for an individual child. Specific environmental factors such as family stressors, culture, and the child's temperament are also taken into account. Medical information considered includes the child's diagnosis and the procedures he or she is expected to experience, along with assessment of the child and family's understanding of this information. The child's previous experiences, both positive and negative, with healthcare, and

his or her coping with those, are to be noted as well. Developmental considerations should include the child's physical, psychosocial and cognitive development.

Similar to the approach outlined by Francis is the Stress Potential Assessment Process developed by Gaynard et al. (1998). This model encourages the child life specialist to formulate a care plan based on consideration of three categories of information: health care, family, and child variables (see Figure 1). By combining an evaluation these variables, the child life specialist assigns a "stress potential" rating to the patient using a scale of 1 to 5, with 1 being low stress potential and 5 indicating the "highest potential for experiencing stress and coping difficulties" (p. 41). The child life specialist draws upon knowledge of child development and family systems functioning with healthcare stressors to assign each child a rating. Child life specialists would likely spend the greatest amount of time with children rated 3 or higher. The child's stress potential is continuously reassessed and may be modified as changes occur in an individual's healthcare encounter, and his or her response to it, or as additional information about the child and family is gleaned. In addition to providing a way of assessing and prioritizing patients, the method may also assist in distribution of child life staff resources.

Yet another model of assessment developed at the IWK Health Centre in Halifax, Nova Scotia, looks at the following critical psychosocial variables to predict possible psychological upset in children experiencing healthcare:

1. Response to health care variables
2. Developmental vulnerability
3. Age
4. Mobility
5. Culture and language
6. Social and family status
7. Family support
   (Skinner & LeBlanc, 2002)

Figure 1
Stress Potential Assessment Process

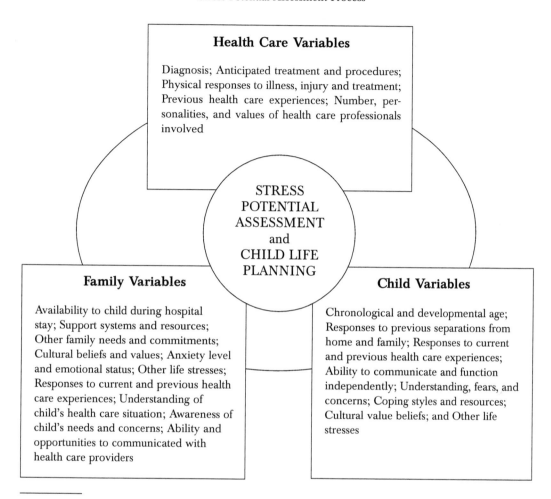

Health Care Variables

Diagnosis; Anticipated treatment and procedures; Physical responses to illness, injury and treatment; Previous health care experiences; Number, personalities, and values of health care professionals involved

STRESS
POTENTIAL
ASSESSMENT
and
CHILD LIFE
PLANNING

Family Variables

Availability to child during hospital stay; Support systems and resources; Other family needs and commitments; Cultural beliefs and values; Anxiety level and emotional status; Other life stresses; Responses to current and previous health care experiences; Understanding of child's health care situation; Awareness of child's needs and concerns; Ability and opportunities to communicated with health care providers

Child Variables

Chronological and developmental age; Responses to previous separations from home and family; Responses to current and previous health care experiences; Ability to communicate and function independently; Understanding, fears, and concerns; Coping styles and resources; Cultural value beliefs; and Other life stresses

From: Gaynard, L., Wolfer, J., Goldberger, J., Thompson, R., Redburn, L., & Laidley, L. (1990) *Psychosocial care of children in Hospitals.* Child Life Council: Bethesda, MD. Reprinted with permission of the Child Life Council.

In the IWK system, two of these variables are considered to be the most critical in the prioritization of child life care provided to patients – Response to Health Care and Developmental Vulnerability. The presence of either of these variables is an indication that the child life specialist must develop an individual plan to help the child cope. Each of the variables used in this system will be considered in turn.

Response to Healthcare Variables

This variable pertains to the child who is having a poor response to healthcare experiences, displaying some form of emotional distress such as fear, anxiety, apprehension, tension, uncertainty or confusion. The child demonstrates this emotional distress through specific thoughts, feelings, behaviors and/or physiological processes (IWK Health Centre Child Life Department, 2005). Children's responses to healthcare are described by Thompson and Stanford (1981) as falling into three categories:

- Active – obvious behaviors like hitting, destroying property or fighting
- Passive – less obvious behaviors like becoming withdrawn, loss of appetite, increased sleeping
- Regressive – developing some new behavior that is not consistent with positive development such as changes in sleep patterns, loss of toileting skills, being restless or anxious

Child life specialists must also examine the range of healthcare variables with which the family may be coping. Gaynard et al. (1998) describe five such variables:

1. Child's diagnosis – whether the illness is acute, chronic, disfiguring, life threatening or terminal, and the degree of uncertainty regarding prognosis
2. Nature of current and anticipated symptoms – duration, degree of life disruption, effect on appearance, degree of discomfort
3. Anticipated treatment and procedures – type, degree of invasiveness and discomfort, frequency, duration, potential side effects
4. Course of child's recovery or deterioration – slow, rapid, variable, or unpredictable
5. Number and type of healthcare professionals involved in the child's care

A child may or may not be able to express feelings verbally, so the child life specialist must design activities to determine the child's reactions and feelings, allowing the child self-expression under circumstances that promote comfort and a sense of emotional safety. *Healthcare play* is a symbolic activity including play with medical equipment that elicits concerns, clarifies misconceptions and discerns coping strategies. A child life specialist may use dolls and real or play medical equipment to facilitate the child "playing out" his or her feelings.

Developmental Vulnerability

Children may be more vulnerable in their responses to a healthcare experience due to an existing developmental delay or as a result of a healthcare experience or treatment that temporarily restricts or impairs the child's ability to interact with his or her environment. For instance, a fractured leg may require traction, which restricts movement and the ability of a child to experience the environment fully.

Several of the vulnerability factors identified by Gaynard et al. (1998), such as the child's ability to communicate fears related to healthcare, can help us to understand why children who are challenged in one or more developmental domain may have a more difficult time coping with healthcare experiences. In comparison to typically developing children, those with developmental delays may not have the same range of skills to help them cope effectively or the language or cognitive ability to understand explanations of upcoming events or procedures. Some children may have verbal abilities, but not the corresponding age-related cognitive capacities. With such children, staff members may assume they understand explanations when, in fact, they do not.

The developmental impact of hospitalization will also be of concern for children who are physically restricted to their rooms, are in traction, or are influenced by other factors that compromise optimal development.

Extra effort will be required by the child life specialist to facilitate coping and continued development.

Age

Very young children are particularly vulnerable to the impact of hospitalization, and attention to their needs should be given priority by the child life specialist, especially if the child's parent is unable to be present during the hospital stay. Separation anxiety is the primary source of stress for children ages six months to three years, and its impact should be considered as the child life specialist begins to plan care for children in this age group. The child life specialist's developmental knowledge can be instrumental in influencing care provided for children in this age group. Minimizing the number of assigned caregivers, for example, offers increased security to an infant or toddler whose trust has been disrupted. Encouraging parents to participate in the non-invasive parts of care, and to provide comfort during the invasive ones, will also help the infant or toddler to feel more secure.

Mobility

Limitations in the child's mobility may negatively impact his or her ability to engage in play and other experiences while hospitalized. Added priority should be given to children who are in isolation or restricted to bed, as accommodations to their environment must be made to insure their positive coping.

Culture and Language

The child and family's cultural background and language may also have an influence on their healthcare experience and should be considered by the child life specialist when planning care. The racial and ethnic group with which the family primarily identifies shapes its behaviors and rituals (Rollins, Bolig, & Mahan, 2005). The healthcare beliefs of that group also have an impact on the family's adaptation to, and coping with, the hospital experience. Additionally, delivery of healthcare information in the family's preferred language is essential to their understanding, but may be impeded unless qualified interpreters are readily available to translate the material.

Social and Family Status

A child in the hospital is a member of family system, however it may be uniquely defined. That system brings to the hospital its own set of influences. When planning child life care, the specialist should seek to understand current stressors influencing the family such as changes in family structure, employment issues faced by the parent, or financial strain.

Family Support

A child's ability to cope successfully with hospitalization is largely influenced by the presence of a supportive parent. Varying circumstances may, in some cases, limit the parent's ability to be present; in these situations, the child life specialist should give priority to supporting the needs of the child whose parent is absent.

In planning and prioritizing their daily work, child life specialists may consider the combination of the factors described above to guide them in deciding which children require their attention, and to what degree. Thorough and ongoing assessment and reassessment are essential to the success of child life work.

Formal Developmental Assessment Tools

Child life specialists are, on occasion, asked by others in the healthcare setting to conduct a more formal developmental assessment on a particular child. The results may assist in confirming a diagnosis, demonstrating a need for referral to an early intervention program for a young child whose development is lagging, or providing a baseline assessment prior to the initiation of a particular treatment, intervention, or surgery. Such assessments should be administered only if the specialist has received appropriate training regarding the administration of such tools. Examples of formal assessments that might be used by child life specialists include the Denver Developmental Screening Test – Second Edition (Denver II), the Hawaii Early Learning Profile (HELP), and the Bayley Scales of Infant and Toddler Development – Third Edition (Bayley-III).

The Denver II is used to screen children ages birth to six in four domains: personal-social, fine motor-adaptive, language and gross motor. It is available in both English and Spanish, and has been validated in both languages. The HELP has been validated in infant, toddler and preschool versions, and includes assessment of multiple domains (cognition, language, gross motor, fine motor, social-emotional, self-help, regulatory and sensory). The Bayley-III assesses children in five major developmental domains: cognitive, language, motor, adaptive behavior, and social-emotional. Each of these assessments relies heavily on parent report and assumes parent presence at the time of test administration – a condition sometimes difficult to obtain in the hospital or other healthcare setting. Most of these tools, however, do not accommodate for a child with disabilities, do not consider cultural influences on the ways that children develop, and are certainly not ideally administered under the circumstance of hospitalization or a stress-producing healthcare experience. Moreover, most of the tools are not standardized in the diverse languages and cultures represented in many healthcare settings.

Benefits of Child Life Assessment for Other Disciplines

In most settings where child life specialists work, they do so in collaboration with a team of other professionals. Each team member brings a unique approach to the child and family's care, and the most successful synthesis of information gathered through this collaboration results in care that is well-planned, thorough and expeditious. Child life specialists often work closely with a social worker and, perhaps, a chaplain, as part of a "family services" team. The shared assessments of each discipline prove to be valuable as they work to coordinate the best possible developmentally-appropriate and family-centered care for children and their families.

Child life specialists participating in formal rounds or a case conference, for example, may be asked to comment on the normative developmental milestones expected from a particular patient and how the experience of healthcare may cause interruptions to that development. Child life specialists may also provide information relative to children's responses and reactions to healthcare based on their developmental level. Additionally, the child life specialist can provide valuable information to other members of the team through documentation of an identified coping plan. Through sharing of the assessment and corresponding care plan for the specific child, the child life specialist can suggest methods and approaches that others can use with the child, facilitating the performance of procedures and examinations.

DOCUMENTATION

Just as the assessment process lays the foundation for child life work, documentation of the clinical care provided allows child life professionals to leave "footprints" of their work. Documentation is one of the most challenging, yet potentially rewarding elements of child life practice. Documentation of the service by a child life group or team demonstrates the quality of service provided to the children, families and the organization. Role ambiguity, overwhelming workload and lack of confidence may be some of the factors that contribute to difficulties that documentation can present for child life specialists. It is ironic that effective documentation can have a positive effect on each of these challenges.

Role Ambiguity

Many child life specialists, especially those new to the field, may not fully appreciate the impact of the work they do on the patient, family and other health professionals. It may also be hard to describe specific interventions and the outcomes of those interventions. For instance, time spent providing emotional support for a child may be difficult to articulate in the patient's medical record. However, a child life specialist may be more comfortable talking about that service as a therapeutic dialogue. The child life specialist may then be more comfortable describing the intervention and the outcomes of the work. Sharing information with others helps clarify the role of the child life specialist and demonstrates pride in the contribution that child life specialists make to the care of children and families.

Workload

Child life specialists often have large case loads. It is not unusual, therefore, for child life specialists to be faced with the choice of either documenting the care they have given or providing additional direct patient care. Child life specialists may see the task of documentation as separate from care - an additional demand on their time that deprives other children of their service. As with other health professionals, the child life specialist must believe that documentation is an integral component of child life care. An intervention is not regarded as complete until it is shared with other team members through the patient record.

Confidence

Effective and efficient documentation is a skill. As with the development of any skill, practice leads to mastery of that skill. Clear guidelines for charting and a vision of what should be shared in the chart will give the child life specialist the confidence to document in an efficient and effective way. The information in the following sections will provide the foundation for quality documentation. The medical record or patient chart is the most commonly used form of documentation. The chart is the legal record that contains history and assessment information, the results of tests and procedures, and a clear record of the patient's plan of care. The chart also serves as a method of communication with all healthcare professionals in order to provide the most comprehensive and appropriate treatment possible. Most child life specialists would agree that recording information, observations and service in the patient record is an opportunity to influence patient care. However, child life specialists may not be aware of additional outcomes of appropriate chart notes.

Benefits of Charting from the Perspective of the Child and Family

Child life specialists contribute a unique perspective and expertise to the care of children and families. The quality of care improves if all caregivers share an understanding of how the child is coping, the child life goals for the child, the nature of interventions planned for the child, and the outcomes of his or her care. The child life specialist acts as an advocate for the child and family by ensuring that team members have information that will make care more effective. For example, some children and families, for whom English is not identified as their primary language, may appear to understand more than they actually do. The child life specialist may be aware of this fact, but failure to share this information with others may result in poor communication between child and family and the members of their healthcare team, resulting in decreased understanding and satisfaction.

Benefits of Charting from the Perspective of the Healthcare Team

Using the example above, charting information on the child and family's understanding is supportive of the team and demonstrates the value of the child life specialist as a supportive member of that team. This valuable piece of information helps team members to determine an appropriate approach that may result in more positive relationship between child and family and the health professional.

Benefits of Charting from the Perspective of the Child Life Specialist

The chart note can be seen an advertisement for the work of the child life specialist. The note indicates that the child life specialist is involved with the child, has assessed valuable information, has a plan to intervene, and is making a significant contribution to the care of this child and family. Charting may not seem as important to the child life specialist as providing direct care for the child and family. However, child life specialists are accountable not only for their immediate actions, but also for the thoughtful planning and reporting of care provided. An audit of the chart should demonstrate that the child life specialist is providing quality child life care for this family and is also a skilled team member. The child life manager can use the chart note as one indicator of the ability of the child life specialist to assess, intervene and evaluate patient care. Absence of a chart note may indicate that the child life specialist did not provide care for the patient, especially if the chart is reviewed retrospectively.

Benefits of Charting from the Perspective of the Child Life Profession

Many pediatric hospitals also serve as academic medical centers, providing practical experience for a number of health disciplines. Chart notes can provide a valuable tool to introduce the child life profession, and educate others about how the child life specialist contributes to care of the patient and family. This increased understanding of child life will be carried by the student to new placements and employment, benefiting child life staff in those subsequent settings, as well as the profession as a whole, as they become advocates for child life service.

Hospital Documentation Standards

Individual hospitals have established basic standards and policies for charting that may include: where the child life specialist should chart, how the healthcare professional is identified and, often, the format to be used for recording information. Common formats used for charting include the SOAP (Subjective, Objective, Assessment, Plan) and APIE (Assessment, Plan, Intervention, Evaluation) methods. No matter which format is used, each comprehensive note must include assessment information, a plan for care and outcomes of that care.

Electronic Charting

Many hospitals are implementing an electronic form of charting where professionals' notes are entered into the record using a computer. There are several products that hospitals may use to manage the patient record electronically, and all of these systems require standard definitions of professional work. The key for the child life team is to ensure that child life specialists are involved in developing the definitions for the care that they provide patients. For instance, each profession will have a menu of outcomes for their care. It is critical for child life specialists to develop standard definitions for each outcome that is listed in the child life outcome menu in order to ensure consistency and clarity.

National Standards

The Joint Commission for Accreditation of Health Organizations in the United States and the Canadian Council on Health Service Accreditation in Canada also set standards for documentation. These standards change periodically, but hospital officials can provide information on current standards.

Child Life Department Standards

The key for successful documentation is the development of a charting policy for the staff in the child life service, even if it is a single child life specialist who provides the service (see Appendix A). The policy should incorporate the institution's standards and set clear expectations for content. It should also provide clear standards for recording the outcomes of child life work. Each form of documentation, including chart notes, service plans, and discharge reports, should include clear statements of outcome. The statement of outcome can be derived from the goals established for the intervention. For example, a goal established may be that "healthcare play is provided in order to increase coping." Therefore, the child life specialist should identify the behaviors that indicate that the child is able to cope better as a result of the play sessions. In this example, the child might be less fearful of equipment and better able to accurately explain what will happen during a procedure or to demonstrate the procedure on a doll. Other child life outcomes could include ongoing development, decreased emotional stress, increased understanding of hospitalization or a specific procedure, or increased adjustment to the hospital setting.

The Child Life Consult

Child life specialists receive consults, or requests for their involvement, verbally and in more formal formats. Some may receive consults on a general hospital consult form. In hospitals where the role of child life is clear and well understood, a general consult may be an adequate means to communicate between professionals and record information for the permanent record. However, if the child life service is new to the hospital, the consult may be of little use because the reason for consultation may not be well understood or articulated by other health professionals. For example, a generic consult form may not give a reason for referral, the service requested or other useful information.

A profession-specific consult form, such as that seen in Appendix B, is a valuable tool to help the child life specialist record service, but the consult form has many other benefits. The clear description of child life interventions teaches all team members about the role of child life and allows other professionals to easily identify a reason for referral. The consult provides an efficient tool to facilitate child life's charting the plan of care and lays the foundation for future notes on the outcomes of care. The most important aspect to consider in using a child life consult form is that it must be developed by child life professionals and approved by the hospital as part of the permanent record. In an electronic health record, a consult for child life services may be generated from a "drop down menu" listing screening criteria for which child life is often consulted. The list in Appendix C is that currently used at Children's Medical Center Dallas.

The use of consults can also help to identify child life work that is not done. For example, in some child life programs the standard is that all children have access to a group play/activity program and those who demonstrate difficulty coping may receive additional individual service. The consult may be used to record those children who are not coping, yet do not receive individual service due to lack of resources. Comparing the number of consults that are filled with the number that are not can be used to demonstrate the need for additional child life resources.

Workload Measurement

Workload measurement (WLM) is a method of measuring the volume of professional activity (Walsh, 2003; Watts, 1986). Many hospitals use this approach in order to measure staff productivity and compare productivity with workers at other hospitals. WLM records the service provided by the child life specialist in direct patient care, indirect patient care and indirect service as well. The time spent in each category is recorded either in real time, average time or weighted units. The input of the child life specialist in the development of the WLM tool is the most important factor to ensure that the system will accurately reflect the work of the profession in that setting. For example, all workload measurement systems for professionals will include a category called assessment. The assessment work is very different in each profession, so the staff members in each define assessment for that profession - when a child life specialist records 30 minutes in the assessment category, everyone is aware of the work that is involved.

The WLM provides a standard method of recording workload that yields uniform data for reporting and for permitting peer group comparisons within facilities, regions, or provinces/states. WLM allows the hospital to identify patient-specific resource utilization and cost and provides tangible evidence for justification of resource levels. WLM provides a readily accessible information base to assist with management decision making such as staff allocation and deployment, and serves as one tool in the evaluation of personnel performance. Workload systems were initially developed as a discipline-specific reflection of activity. However, changes in healthcare delivery have resulted in the development of workload measurement systems that allow standardized recording and reporting.

Service Plans

Ensuring that others understand the work of child life specialists is a constant challenge for the profession. Changes in healthcare staff are constant due to staff shortages, rotations of medical personnel and the reality of learner placements. The key to fostering an understanding of child life among others is to provide a clear definition of the basics of child life service, including who, why, what, when and where. Clearly written service plans contribute to understanding and valuing child life service. Service plans, such as those for a school-age child who requires preparation (see Appendix D) or for a preschooler who has a developmental concern (see Appendix E), serve to formalize the work of child life – improving outcomes for the patient and sharing information with one's colleagues. The service plans are concise and efficient for the child life specialist to use, and yet they accomplish a great deal. The service plan documents pertinent assessment information, service provided and outcomes of intervention. Although most service plans will not be part of the permanent record, they are valuable for the child life specialist to manage the care of the child, and refer to on subsequent admissions.

Conclusion

Professional work is based upon a clear system of assessment, interventions and outcomes. Child life specialists follow this process as well. However, because child life is still a relatively new profession, it is critical for child life specialists to formalize this process and share it with other team members. The results of documentation of the professional child life process are an improved understanding of the rationale for specific interventions and an increased appreciation for the possible outcomes of child life work. Solid assessment of patients and documentation of services provided will result in increased support for child life services.

REFERENCES

Bayley Scales of Infant and Toddler Development – Third Edition (Bayley-III) (2007). Retrieved March 28, 2007 from http://harcourtassessment.com

Denver II (1989). Denver Developmental Materials Retrieved March 28, 2007 from http://www.denverii.com/DenverII.html

Francis, S. (1990). *Child life education series: Child life theory into practice.* Dallas: Children's Medical Center Dallas, TX.

Gaynard, L., Wolfer, J., Goldberger, J., Thompson, R. H., Redburn, L., & Laidley, L. (1998). *Psychosocial care of children in hospitals: A clinical practice manual.* Rockville, MD: Child Life Council.

Hawaii Early Learning Profile – HELP Retrieved March 28, 2007 http://www.vort.com/

Rollins, J. A., Bolig, R., & Mahan, C. C. (2005). Meeting children's psychosocial needs across the health-care continuum. Austin, TX: PRO-ED, Inc.

Skinner, L., & LeBlanc, C. K. (2002, June). *The complete picture: Assessment, documentation and outcomes.* Paper presented at the Child Life Council's Twentieth Annual Conference on Professional Issues, Orlando, FL.

Thompson, R. H., & Stanford, G. (1981). *Child life in hospitals: Theory and practice.* Springfield, IL: Charles C Thomas.

Walsh, E. (2003). Get results with workload measurement. *Nursing Management, 34,* 16.

Watts, J (1986). Workload measurement systems: Their applications and limitations. *Dimensions in Health Service, 63,* 44-46.

Appendix A

CHARTING

IWK HEALTH CENTRE

HALIFAX, NOVA SCOTIA

Child Life Policies
CHARTING

Responsibility of: All Child Life Staff	Effective Date: April 2002
Last Review Date: April 2002	Next Review Date: April 2004
Cross-References:	Document Number:
Target Audience: All Child Life Staff	Form Number: 113
Pages: 2	Approved By: Chief, Child Life &
	School Services

POLICY I:
Child life specialists will record relevant information in the patient record.

GUIDELINES:
1.   Consults
      • All written consults will be answered in a reasonable time frame on either the NCR consult form
        or the child life consult form
      • All consults will record assessment information and a child life plan of care. Outcomes of care will
        be recorded in progress notes.
      • Consults may be initiated by child life staff using the assessment criteria of the Child Life
        Assessment & Intervention Plan.
      • Copies of Child Life Consult & Intervention plan may be given to parents with explanation by the
        CLS.
      • Copies of the completed Child Life Consult & Intervention Plan may be retained by the CLS in a
        secure location.

2.   Brief Note
      Brief notes will be used to record the involvement of the patient in the child life service if a consult
      form is not used.

3.   Comprehensive Note
      A comprehensive note will include data (subjective/objective), an assessment and a plan. A follow-
      up note will include evaluation / outcome information.
      A comprehensive note will be entered in the patient chart in order to record child life
      information/concerns/issues. The comprehensive note will include all elements of the SOAP for-
      mat, and *may* be entered using the SOAP headings. Other formats may be used as well.

The comprehensive note *may* (but is not limited to) address the following:

Coping
      • hospital stay – problems or no problems
      • chronic illness/repeated admissions – response to, coping well, not coping well
      • intrusive procedures – response to
      • interventions to promote coping – medical play, preparation, routine, transitional/security objects,
        importance of play/activity, privacy, independence

- parent concerns about – long term effects, separation, life threatening illness, prognosis
- staff concerns about – cooperation with procedures, "depression"
- observed coping skills – activity, medical play, verbalization, security object
- behaviors to encourage – verbalization, manipulative play
- response to separation – what happens, what helps
- response to sensory environment – e.g. ICU, isolation
- significance of behavioral changes – decreased talking, regression, aggression
- understanding of illness/procedures – cognitive development, misconceptions, accurate perceptions
- compliance – with medication and tests, particularly with adolescents
- specific fears – needles, finger sticks, dark
- recognition of significant life-events – birthday, holidays, milestones, transition to adult care

Development
- concerns identified by staff – presence/absence of specific skills, impact of illness/hospital stay on development
- concerns identified by parents – specific skills, impact of hospital stay
- need for developmental support – long-term stay, specific disability, chronic illness (teens/peers), cognitive/psychosocial stages or progression
- importance of specific developmental activity – adaptive toys, playpen/crib, teen group, games
- skills – observed behaviors/skills, walks, talks, interacts with peers, independence
- developmental progress during hospitalization

Family Issues
- sibling coping, adjustment, understanding
- parent coping – ability to support child, siblings
- preparation for post-discharge responses
- discharge plans

4.   Format
- All entries are made in blue or black ink (not gel pens)
- All entries are signed with appropriate signature, status, printed name
- Date format is dd/mm/yy
- Time format is 24-hour clock
- Only approved health centre abbreviations may be used
- All pages (both sides of document) must be addressographed with correct patient ID in upper right-hand corner

Comprehensive notes should include behavioral outcomes of Child Life Interventions as follows:

Behavioural Outcomes of Child Life Interventions

Outcome	*Categories*	*Behaviours*
Increased knowledge of hospitalization and/or illness		• verbalize reason for hospitalization & treatment • verbalize understanding of medical procedure • demonstrate understanding of medical procedure using symbolic play • improve compliance with medical procedures

Outcome	Categories	Behaviours
Maintain developmental skills	regressive behaviour	• any repeated demonstration of behavior/skill below the child's normal developmental level
Improve developmental skills	progress in behaviour	• any repeated demonstration of behavior/skill at the next step of the child's normal developmental level
Increase in coping/adjustment	decrease aggressive behaviour	• kicks, bites, punches, hits • easily angered, grumpy • destroys property • throws things • talks of harming self
	increased sociability	• smiles • laughs • seeks physical contact • plays • helps others • shares • seeks company of others
	decrease in non compliance	• screams • refuses to take medication • refuses to eat or drink • stubborn • uncooperative with medical procedures
	decrease anxiety/distress	• cries • whines, whimpers • clings to parent • appears tense, nervous, anxious • complains about pain • nausea/vomiting before procedures • sleeps poorly • complains of being tired • worries a lot • complains of nightmares • lies • self stimulating behaviours • wets bed • soils pants

Outcome	Categories	Behaviours
	withdrawal	• refuses to speak • looks sad • withdraws from people • poor eye contact • acts like a younger child • ignores people

IWK Health Centre

Appendix B

CHILD LIFE

Consultation & Intervention Record

REASON FOR CONSULT:
Intervention Requested for Patient Who:

❑ Is developmentally vulnerable, has mental / physical challenges
❑ Displays emotional distress due to health care experience E.g. fear, confusion, apprehension

Comments: _____
_____
_____

_____   _____   _____
Signature of Staff Making Request   Print Name   Date   (dd/mm/yy)

Child Life Plan:
❑ Play/Activity Program
    -supportive play opportunities
    -developmentally appropriate activities

❑ Developmental Support
    -individual activities to support development

❑ Preparation / Procedural Support
    -cognitive and emotional preparation for procedures through play, rehearsal and/or dialogue
    -accompany child / provide comfort
    and/or other distraction during procedure

❑ Health Care Play / Therapeutic Dialogue
    -symbolic play in order to elicit concerns,
    identify coping strategies and express feelings

❑ Family Facilitation
    -emotional support
    -sibling support

_____
_____
_____
_____

_____   _____   _____
Signature of Staff Making Request   Print Name   Date   (dd/mm/yy)

Appendix C

CHILD LIFE REFERRAL INDICATORS

These indicators which appear as a drop down menu in the Electronic Health Record:

❑ Sibling issues

❑ Difficulty coping with hospitalization

❑ Difficulty coping with medical procedure

❑ New diagnosis of chronic illness

❑ Developmentally delayed

❑ Scheduled for procedure or surgery

❑ Perceived disturbance in family dynamics or recent family stressors

❑ Medication adherence

❑ Other (please enter as free text in comments section)

Source: Children's Medical Center Dallas.

IWK Health Centre Child Life

CHILD LIFE PLAN

REASON FOR PLAN: Developmental Vulnerability

CLS / UNIT: __Sandy Matthews__

DATE: ___02/08/07___

Special Needs	Neonate	Infant
_____ _____ _____ _____ _____ _____	• may have immature central nervous system • attachment may be compromised by early separation from family and inability of neonate to produce clear cues • siblings may need support to cope	• response to trauma of hospitalization is generally immediate and overt • separation is the key
Toddler • susceptible to the problems of separation • regression in development is a risk • verbal communication is limited / understand a great deal of what is said, even though may not seem to be attending to speaker / most of information is interpreted through egocentric view of world • receptive language is more developed than expressive language	**Preschool** • egocentric • limited capacity to distinguish fantasy from reality (intrusive procedures seen as hostile acts, punishment) • separation from family seen as abandonment • limited concept of time	**Schoolage** • social, capable of developing relationships • separation easier • reasoning abilities expanding • misconceptions may be revealed through play or conversation • concerned about maintaining control • fear of anaesthesia, loss of control, death and mutilation

Adolescent
• struggle with identity issues, appearance, need for privacy
• peer group is important
• 14 - 17 years biological maturation reached - concern over sexuality and independence

Objectives: *Lisa is a 13-month-old girl who will be in isolation for a minimum of 10 days. Lisa's family is unable to visit during the day, so I will ensure daily play time each am and pm to promote development. S. Matthews, CCLS*

Interventions:
❏ Basic Programming ❏ Preparation/Procedural Support ❏ Developmental Support
❏ Health Care Play/Therapeutic Dialogue ❏ Family Facilitation

Outcomes:
❏ Increased Coping/Adjustment ❏ Increased Knowledge
√ Maintains Developmental Skills √ Improves Developmental Skills

Appendix E

CHILD LIFE PLAN

IWK Health Centre Child Life

REASON FOR PLAN: Response to Health Care Variables

CLS / UNIT: Liz Smith/7 East

DATE: October 23, 2004

BEHAVIOURAL INDICATORS: This 9-year-old boy has expressed fear of needles and misconceptions about upcoming procedure.

SPECIAL NEEDS: √ NO   ❏ YES

Provide developmentally appropriate information:

Familiarize with the environment	√	Sensory Information	√√
Sequence of events	√	Anticipated Duration√	√
Post-procedural experience	❏	Other	❏

Facilitate Coping Behaviour:

Health care play	√	Expressive play√	√
Rehearsal	√	Dialogue√	√
Planning coping strategies	√	Other	❏

Procedural Support:

Accompany patient	√	Distraction	√√
Imagery	❏	Deep breathing	❏
Coaching	√	Other	❏

Post-procedural Support:

Recount events	❏	Post procedural play	❏
Expressive activities	❏	Other	❏

Procedural Support Tools:

Body Outline Doll	√	Treasure Chest	√√
Play Hospital	❏	Visual Aids	√√
Medical Play Equipment	❏	Other	❏

NOTES I will provide the above interventions in order to promote coping with needles and increase patient understanding of procedures.

P:\CLAIP\ChildLifePlan
June 2003

Chapter 8

PARADIGMS OF PLAY

PEGGY O. JESSEE AND LAURA GAYNARD

FOUNDATIONS

Play is children's most powerful tool. It helps children make sense of their world, develop new concepts, increase social skills, gain emotional support, and take responsibility for their actions through meaningful experiences. It is particularly important that children have opportunities for play when they are in stressful situations. Adults, however, often view children's play in traumatic situations as inappropriate or unnecessary. Child life specialists, therefore, often have to articulate to parents and other professionals why play is important. In doing so, they must clearly understand their own philosophy regarding play. This chapter investigates the play of children, particularly children in healthcare settings, as viewed through various paradigms.

We have all heard the statement, "Play is the child's work." Maria Montessori (1965) made this remark based on her own observations and on Groos's (1914) observations that the play of young animals mimics the survival strategies of adult animals (p. 180). This idea of defining the state of play in the language of adult work fits very nicely into our contemporary world's notion of play. Given all the unfolding research on early

brain development, windows of opportunity, and children's sponge-like abilities to learn, the idea that children's time could be best spent in useful activities that are actually "work" instead of play seems to make sense.

Montessori's motives in stating that play is a child's work are often misinterpreted and misunderstood. Her writings emphasize that children's play is a kind of fantasy preparation for adult life, not a substitute for work (Montessori, 1965). In fact, many theorists suggest that playfulness and the ability to play is a critically important characteristic of humans that promotes rapid adaptation to changing environments (Ellis, 1987; Fagen 1995; Wickelgren, 1993), allows us to psychologically cope with past and present concerns, and prepares us for our future roles as adults (Sutton-Smith, 1982; Bettleheim, 1987; Groos, 1914). For professionals who work with children, it seems obvious that play serves an important function in children's cognitive, physical, social, and emotional development and is an essential component of executing developmentally appropriate practices. Yet, as more adult occupations become technologically sophisticated, play tends to be viewed, not as a preparation for life, but as a frivolous use of time. This perspective is often taken among those who work and practice in high-tech medical environments.

A comprehensive definition of the role of play in human development and its impact on the universal human experience is very elusive. People all over the world experience a "state of play" in varying modes and degrees, yet determining what is play, and what is not, is very subjective. The topic of play in research is increasingly receiving attention. Because of recent research, we know more about the foundations of play. We know how play helps the child and, ultimately the adult, to develop; the kinds of activities that can best fit play environments; the tools are needed for play; and what play can tell us about the child's needs, problems, satisfactions, and strengths.

How does this universal, traditional, yet contemporary, phenomenon of play fit into the healthcare setting of the child life specialist? What do child life specialists need to know to internalize a philosophy of play that can be a basic guide for program planning and can be communicated to others? To begin to answer the first question, play is an arena in a healthcare setting in which children can exert power and make choices. Adults may control the space and restrict time, but children have the tools of fantasy and imagination. With these tools, play opens a window through which children can process their experiences, present and past, and grasp new meaning. The task of the child life specialist, then, is to look through this window of play with the child and help the child connect to a variety of experiences that will offer control and, ultimately, mastery. The ability to guide children through the multiple dimensions and processes of play according to their developmental and environmental needs is a competency that is core to the practice of child life.

In answer to the second question, one of the ways we can develop our own sense of the role of play in the work of a child life specialist is to form a mental framework of the various aspects of play and place it within our knowledge of child development. This chapter will offer some additional insight into these questions and will consider the varied and complex aspects of play. In so doing, we will provide a brief overview of play paradigms in the areas of enjoyment, development, learning, and therapy, and will discuss these paradigms as seen in children's ritualistic use of play as flow, comfort, and hope.

Play as Enjoyment

The radical idea that children might actually need to play was embodied in the writings of the French philosopher, Jean-Jacques Rousseau (1712-1778). Rousseau wrote in Emile, his classic book on education, that children had their own way of seeing, thinking, and feeling, and adults should allow children the innocence and freedom of childhood by not restricting them to adult ways (Hughes, 1999). However, the English philosopher, John Locke (1632-1704), whose views on the nature of children had strong influence in England and during the colonial period in America, had a different perspective. While Locke did not actually condemn play, he made it clear, in the Puritan culture of the times, that work, rationality, and discipline were the prime ingredients needed for a child's development. Even though Locke had a kindly attitude towards children, play was not part of his philosophy. Gradually, as the role of children as miniature adults changed, so did attitudes towards childhood play.

The early play theories from the latter part of the nineteenth century and the early part of the twentieth century often described play as an instinctive mechanism that leads to a number of different outcomes depending on the perspective of the theorists. For example, Spencer (1873) saw play as a way to release surplus energy. He argued that humans have a certain amount of energy that is needed for survival. As survival needs diminish, this pent-up energy must be released. Children do this through play (Hughes, 1999). Patrick (1916) suggested an opposite view of play and energy. He theorized that the purpose of play was the renewal of energy wherein children use play to avoid boredom while they wait for their energy levels to be restored (Hughes, 1999). A leading American psychologist from this period, G. Stanley Hall (1921) had a unique perspective on the role of play. Although not widely accepted in psychological circles today, Hall developed his recapitulation theory, in which each person's development reflects human evolutionary progression. A child's play framed in present experiences might be imitating behaviors of prehistoric ancestors. Another play theorist who emphasized the instinctual nature of play was Groos (1914) who suggested that play is the body's natural way of preparing for the tasks of adult life. Even though all these approaches have some elements of play as a pleasurable, recreational activity, it was not until the twentieth century that a more comprehensive view, emphasizing the intrinsic motivation of play impacting the cognitive, social, and emotional development of children along various dimensions, was articulated. As we move to more contemporary views on play, we encounter concepts proposed by many of the major theorists in human development.

Theorists have used many approaches when attempting to define, describe, or categorize children's play. When defining activities as play, there are some general characteristics that can be used to describe behaviors (Rubin, Fein, & Vandenburg, 1983).

1. *Play is intrinsically motivated.* This encompasses notions of self-directed activity and freely chosen explorations that lead to self-satisfaction.

2. *Play involves attention to means rather than to ends.* Goals are flexible, self-imposed, and changeable.

3. *Play may be nonliteral or symbolic.* Play may involve conceptualization of objects and/or roles that allow children to symbolically transform their present realities with elements of make-believe. Play may symbolically represent unconscious desires and feelings.

4. *Play may be free from external rules.* There may be rules within the imaginary context, but there is freedom to spontaneously create and change the rules, a differentiation between play and games, where rules are externally imposed.

5. *Play requires active engagement.* This may be seen in the concentration, enthusiasm, and joy of children when they play. It is also evident in the sense of mastery than can emerge from children's play (Monighan-Nourot, 1990; Thompson & Stanford, 1981).

Parten (1932), an early twentieth century play theorist, observed and identified participation with others as a four-step sequence in children's play. It begins with nonsocial activity (unoccupied, onlooker behavior, or solitary play), moves to parallel play (playing near other children but not trying to influence behavior), associative play (interacting by exchanging toys and conversation), and ends with the more advanced cooperative play (orienting toward a common goal). Piaget (1962) describes four general stages of play of children as they move from one developmental stage to another. These stages are: *functional play*, repeating actions and manipulations, imitating movements and utterances, and manipulating objects; *constructive play*, goal-directed, creating products, new manipulations of objects, and developing themes; *symbolic play*, use of dramatic situations, substitution of reality with fantasy, and social themes; *games-with-rules*, controlled behaviors within given limits, and adjustment to other's needs.

Although knowledge about play, such as typical characteristics and stages, helps child life specialists to articulate the importance of play to those who do not have this information, we must also value play because it belongs to the child and because it is enjoyable. Care must be taken not to take the joy from play or to direct and manipulate all the fun out of it with good intentions. The skill of guiding play comes while playing with a child, sometimes for a child, and always using observation to determine the next step to take.

Play as Development

Knowledge of development throughout the life span is critical for child life specialists. While many adults may recognize the importance of play in childhood, one of the roles of a child life specialist is to think of play as a developmental process that proceeds through stages that are linked to, yet separate from the areas of cognitive, social, emotional, physical, language, and gender/sex role development. In addition, this knowledge must be considered within the physical and social constraints that are present in the healthcare setting.

Infancy

There are trends in play development at each stage of life. During infancy and toddlerhood the primary mode of play is ex-

ploratory and sensorimotor. Play at this stage will center on visual and motor actions (mouthing, shaking) on objects and people. The play actions of infants and toddlers are categorized by Piaget (1962) in his sensorimotor substages of cognitive development. In Piaget's theory, children use "practice play," or repetition of motor actions, to consolidate and reorganize behaviors into symbolic play. This pretend play truly emerges during the second year of life. Children of this age gradually move practice play into purposeful manipulations of materials. As in any setting, infants in healthcare environments need toys that are responsive to their control, and by their second year, toddlers need toys, such as jack-in-the-box, shape sorter, stacking blocks, or pop-ups that also allow exploration of cause and effect.

Preschool

Between the ages of two to five, children move from on-looker, solitary, and parallel play into more associative and cooperative forms of play. Piaget also characterized this age as the "preoperational stage" with play serving as an assimilative function, allowing children to consolidate their experiences (Piaget, 1962). For example, as children move from repetitive, functional play with objects, their play shifts to assimilating the object, such as a ball, to an action scheme that they already possess, such as rolling, but they must also change or accommodate those actions to fit the nature of the object, such as size and weight of the ball. As a result, adaptation constantly takes place through the medium of play. The preschool years, termed by Singer and Singer (1979) as "the golden age of socio-dramatic and make-believe play" (p. 195) are characterized by the gradual expansion of children's play into very complex symbolic themes. Socio-dramatic play for preschoolers often has themes beginning with the simple imitation of adults and moving through intensification of real-life roles, home relationships, expression of physical and emotional needs and forbidden impulses, and the reversal of roles (Hughes, 1999). All forms of social play with peers instead of adults become more evident. Play with physical components starts to become evident. For example, rough-and-tumble play makes its appearance during the ages two to five. However, rough-and-tumble play must be distinguished from vigorous activity play. Energetic motor play can be solitary or social, while rough-and-tumble play always has a social component. Rough-and-tumble play always contains elements of mock aggression, but vigorous activity does not (Hughes, 1999).

SYMBOLIC PLAY. At the beginning of the second year, symbolic games clearly emerge. According to Piaget, this is an indication that the child is developing the ability to transform direct sensory data into abstract mental images. Children at play actively do things that represent personal images of their own experiences. For some children this may mean pretending to wrap a doll's broken leg, for others it may mean serving hamburgers at a pretend McDonald's. This sort of symbolic play action is based on similarity between the available play object and the unavailable object that it represents. Piaget links symbolic play with general intellectual growth. He states that real symbolic play develops rapidly when the child learns language, and is characteristic of the period between two and four years (Piaget, 1962).

During the years between two and seven, inner fantasy is the motivation of play. Imitation in this fantasy form reaches its highest point when symbolic play almost totally consists of personal, real-life experiences, which are channeled into the child's own subjective purposes. Such play constitutes the child's effort to recreate experiences in a way that can be dealt with, and to

repeat past experiences in order to enjoy or reframe them in acceptable and understandable ways. According to Smilansky (1968) sociodramatic play is motivated by the need of the child to model adults in their environment in their thoughts, feelings, actions, and reactions, and to view oneself as another person and act accordingly. Through symbolic dramatic and make-believe play, children of this age project and enact behaviors that are forbidden to them in real life. In this type of play, a child reconstructs frightening or painful situations, unbearable to him in reality and puts them into manageable form. Hospitalized children often find themselves in both frightening and painful situations. For this age group, and often older children as well, symbolic and pretend play is an avenue for coming to terms with the reality of difficult situations.

Although Piaget states that at a later age there appears in the child a growing sense of reality, he considers this development as a transit stage toward the next level of play. School-age children exhibit a growing concern with having things appear "real" during their dramatic play. Often, the group work and social interaction involved in planning play become the focus rather than the play itself. This shift forms the basis on which a competitive spirit in play, apparent in competitive play and games-with-rules, develops during the elementary school years. The regular development of social interaction experienced by children aged seven and older brings a gradual decrease in, and, finally an end to symbolic play (Piaget, 1962). This decrease in children's symbolic play is linked to general development and active participation in other areas to which play activity is transferred.

Not all young children are able to play at the developmental level one might expect. Cultural background and socioeconomic class may impact the level of children's play. Children from cultures that are less technologically advanced and from lower socioeconomic classes tend to engage in less complex and less sophisticated pretend play (Hughes, 1999). Smilansky (1968) suggests that the parental role and the system of social intercourse inside the family have an impact on the child's ability to engage in increasingly complex symbolic play. Higher levels of developmentally appropriate symbolic play may be fostered when parents and other caregivers reinforce imitation by teaching a step-wise versus a global approach to mastering independent activities, offer explanations of rationales supporting parental behaviors and roles, and institute active listening and responding. This type of parental interaction is most often associated with children from middle to high sociocultural backgrounds (Simlansky, 1968). Children with special needs, such as Down's syndrome, deafness, and autism may not engage in symbolic play at the level or intensity as more typical developing children (Slade & Wolf, 1994). If a basic social-communicative system is in place, varying patterns and rates of symbolic play tend to emerge. If this communicative system is not in place, the processes of symbolization are atypical and disordered.

School-age

Play of the elementary-age child moves from the central role of assimilative learning of early childhood to the less central role of accommodative learning (Fein & Schwartz, 1982). During the last half of the concrete operational stage of cognitive development, the child's thinking becomes more orderly, more structured, and more logical (Piaget, 1962). As a consequence, the school-age child's play will be more realistic and rule-oriented and will reflect a developing need for order. Complementary role games, such as construction projects, puppet shows, word games, and chants, and competitive role games, such as card, board, and computer games as well as organized physical games, become a major component of the play of school-age children (Bergen, 1987). Acceptance by peers becomes of great importance to this age group, and play often reflects a strong need to belong. Although the composition of a school-age peer group may be variable with changes made on a week-to-week basis, it has definite and often rigidly held rules. Differences of any kind may not be tolerated, and members of the group excluded if the rules are not rather arbitrarily accepted (Dodge, 1983). The Eriksonian need for industry can also be seen in school-age children's play efforts as they demonstrate to themselves and others that they are competent, have talents and skills, and abilities (Erikson, 1963; Hughes, 1999). Even though Erikson was not speaking specifically of play when defining Industry versus Inferiority in the Eight Stages of Man, the ego-building sense of mastery that can be seen in the process of play activities, such as crafts and the producing of "products," is clear.

Adolescents

As adolescents and, ultimately, adults move from concrete operations to thinking in formal operations, play's outward manifestations change and become miniaturized, socialized, and abstracted (Bergen, 1987). This is seen through doodling, daydreaming, symbolic board games, and participatory and non-participatory sports. The adolescent's quest for acquisition of skills and development of individual talents reflect this growth of self-awareness and the need for identity clarification. Csikszentmihalyi (1979) describes this adult-like play in terms of flow. Play becomes the training ground for a more adequate adult life, (i.e., living at optimal capacity, p. 275).

Play as Learning

Among those who view play as learning is Fredrich Froebel, the nineteenth century educator who gave status to play in the kindergarten movement. Froebel stated that play needs to be cherished and encouraged for it is in free play that children reveal their future minds (Froebel, 1887). In the beginning of the United States' nursery school movement in the early 1900s, play began to be accepted as a legitimate educational activity and as a potential tool for learning (Bergen, 1987). Maria Montessori observed children's play and developed an activity-based program that became know as the Montessori Method (Montessori, 1973). This method involved children playing and manipulating materials in ways that had meaning in their lives.

During the twentieth century, play came to be viewed along a variety of dimensions. An extensive treatment of play is offered by Jean Piaget, author of one of the most influential theories on cognitive development, as a tool that aids in intellectual growth (Piaget, 1962, 1972). Piaget described play as assimilation where children assimilate or solidify their existing knowledge through play activities. Children distort reality to fit their own perspective, or in other words, they incorporate new material into already existing cognitive structures. For example, children are using the process of assimilation when they decide a box is not a box, but a space ship that is capable of interplanetary travel. While play is not synonymous with learning in Piaget's cognitive theory, it can facilitate learning by consolidating newly learned behaviors (Hughes, 1999). Piaget's description of play was used by Smilansky (1968) to develop a hierarchy of cognitive play behaviors; functional, sensorimotor, constructive, dramatic (symbolic), and games with rules. Living and writing at the same time as Piaget

was the Russian psychologist, Leo Vygotsky (1962), who described play as a valuable component of young children's cognitive development and as the leading facilitator of children's ability to think abstractly within the social-cultural and historical setting of the child's world. Vygotsky suggested that Piagetian theory sometimes ignored the larger social context and was limited to his "special child milieu," and therefore, was not a universal phenomenon. Unfortunately, Vygotsky died almost fifty years before Piaget and the intellectual debate that could have been possible between these two giants of developmental theory never occurred. Play, however, was the cornerstone of cognitive development for both Piaget and Vygotsky. As children play, they build images and products that simulate reality. Piaget calls this "adaptation." This process enables the child to construct his own knowledge in present time. Vygotsky sees this process as a future-oriented phenomenon. Play moves children into the "zone of proximal development" which takes them along an oscillating continuum into higher levels of thinking (Fromberg, 2002). The "zone of proximal development" is Vygotsky's term for the distance between what a child can do without help and what a child can do through interaction with skilled helpers. It is within this zone that a child's potential for new learning is strongest (Fabes & Martin, 2001).

Brian Sutton-Smith, a contemporary researcher of children's play behaviors, maintains that play is the comfortable environment in which children learn to solve different kinds of problems. When they are faced with the more complex reality of the world, they are able to bring to bear the learning that took place during play (Sutton-Smith, 1979). This relationship between play participation and general adaptation is a way of learning (Pellegrini, 1995).

Play is one condition for learning that children can control. Quantitative, physical, social and representational knowing are separate strands of learning mastery in young children (Fromberg, 2002). Given that the human brain works in connected and integrated ways, effective teachers weave these strands into activities organized around children's dynamic themes of play. As an example, a primary tool of the stress-coping model of coping strategies for child life specialists is the "teaching" of basic information about a condition or impending procedure to children (Thompson & Stanford, 1981). A possible objective of such teaching is to provide the child with a developmentally appropriate understanding of an upcoming event. Play is the vehicle through which children can best internalize new information. The use of dolls or puppets and manipulation of the potentially threatening equipment in a "playfully serious" manner are ways that can help the child process the new material. Through play, the child is actively engaged in mastery whether it is actual cognitive accomplishment or in the sense of control and "knowing" one's environment.

Play as Therapy

A psychoanalytic interpretation of play suggests that young children use play as a medium for self-expression that can reduce anxiety caused by internal conflict. It has been suggested by many theorists that play serves as a neutralizing medium by which young children manipulate traumatic or anxiety-inducing situations in an attempt to gain mastery over the event (Axline, 1969; Csikszentmihalyi, 1975; Erickson, 1959; Freud, 1928; Moustakas, 1959). We can think of this track of therapeutic play having its beginnings in the psychoanalytic theory of Sigmund Freud (1856-1939) and his daughter, Anna Freud (1895-1982). From the psychoanalytic point of view, play allows the

child to explore unwelcome feelings or socially unacceptable thoughts without the fear of adult disapproval. Anna Freud (1928) began to use play to establish a therapeutic alliance and to build a relationship with her child patients. During the same time period, Melanie Klein (1932) proposed using play as a direct substitute for verbalizations during therapy sessions. Whether the child was normal or disturbed, Klein felt that play was the child's natural medium of expression. From Klein's point of view, play was the childhood equivalent of free association. Erik Erikson's views on play also reflect the psychoanalytic perspective. Erikson (1959) suggested that play provides young children with a way of thinking over difficult experiences and restoring a sense of mastery over the situation.

Why is play so essential for understanding the thoughts of children? Over the years, psychologists have provided several answers to this question (e.g., Axline, 1969; Guerney, 1983; Landreth, 1982; Moustakas, 1959; Schaefer & O'Connor, 1983). Some of these are:

1. Play allows children to communicate their feelings effectively and naturally.
2. Play allows adults to enter the world of children. There is mutual recognition, acceptance, and temporary power-sharing. There is less reason for the child to feel threatened by an adult.
3. Observing children's play leads to adult understanding.
4. The pleasure of play allows the child to relax and, therefore, reduces anxiety and defensiveness.
5. Play allows children to release feelings that might be otherwise difficult to express openly. It allows them to use play materials in aggressive, hostile ways without fear of reprisals.
6. Play allows children to develop social skills that might be useful in other situations.

7. Play allows children to try out new roles and experiment in a safe environment using a number of problem-solving approaches (Hughes, 1999).

The non-directive relationship approach to therapeutic play emphasizes the therapist's role in providing an environment in which the child feels accepted, with the therapist communicating a feeling of warmth, reflecting the child's feelings, giving the child time and permission to lead the way through therapy. Basic to this approach is the assumption that children have within themselves the motivation and ability to initiate positive changes in their lives (Axline, 1969).

Although child life specialists use play to achieve a number of varied goals, using play in a true therapeutic manner has three main objectives: (a) to establish contact, (b) to promote observation and collect useful data, and (c) to interpret behaviors (Esman, 1983). The play materials necessary to accomplish these goals should be simple, must lend themselves to be used in many ways, and must allow for expression of feelings. Examples would be drawing paper (not coloring books), crayons and markers, play dough or modeling clay, blocks, dolls, puppets, and cars and trucks. Additional items are useful depending on the child's needs and developmental stage. Other types of toys, equipment, and the use of crafts are used to fulfill other kinds of play objectives for a child. For hospitalized children, the efficacy of play is enhanced through the use of familiar toys that foster security and emotional support, as well as toys that are relevant to their condition and aid in the "work of worrying" (Kampe, 1990).

The symbolic material that emerges from play sessions can offer clues to the child life specialist about several aspects of the child's inner life (Irwin, 1983). Through self-presentations, enacted symbolically or more directly, children demonstrate their own views of themselves and others, including the roles they and the people around them may assume. Through watching children's play and actively listening to their stories, whether they are fantasy based or grounded in the world of reality, the child life specialist has a window that looks into children's worries, wishes, conflicts, and the defenses that are being used. During the act of pretend play, children show how they struggle with or avoid conflict. This allows the specialist to observe children's usual way of viewing the world, their habitual reasoning and thinking patterns, including intellectual capacities and problem-solving abilities (Irwin, 1983).

It is assumed that the psychologically healthy child is able to use play to organize, articulate, and master those aspects of life that would otherwise cause strain, and that play is the medium through which a child's inner world can be seen and better understood. However, some children do not engage in symbolic play. In some instances this may be due to a lack of play opportunities and stimulation for pretend play (Irwin, 1983). The child who has experienced overwhelming trauma, either sudden or continuing, may find ordinary play resources insufficient (Bolig, Fernie, & Klein, 1986). There is also the child who may be developmentally or cognitively deficient in particular areas that would enable pretend play to fully develop, specifically in language development and symbolic representation. Children may experience regression or fixation in both the form and content of their play or the child's human and physical environments may have been deficient in those factors that nourish and encourage symbolization (Irwin, 1983).

To facilitate therapeutic play, the adult may need to provide raw materials for play and help facilitate the use of these materials indirectly or more directly as a co-player (Smilansky, 1968). According to Kampe

(1990), an adult is needed to provide a context within which children's therapeutic play can flourish and be supported. To be effective, adult intervention must allow opportunities for children to be emotionally involved in the play and facilitate resolutions to the issues demonstrated in the play. This requires knowledge of child development and the impact of psychic stressors faced by children in traumatic and unfamiliar situations. This does not negate the value of families, medical personnel, and others playing with children in hospital settings. It does say that the role of the child life specialist in assessing anxiety, determining coping capabilities, and planning therapeutic play opportunities becomes more demanding.

The connections between these approaches to play, theoretical and developmental, were stated very succinctly by Petrillo and Sanger (1980). The authors observed that play was an activity that involved reason, imagination and attention on one hand, and motivated feelings on the other. The skill for the child life specialist lies in linking these elements during the observation of children's play so that the status of mental development can be interrelated with the emotional state. Oremland (2000) describes these connections as "play partnerships." She also suggests the essence of the play partnership as demonstrated by child life specialists cannot be systematically described in existing research, but evolves as each ongoing relationship progresses.

EXPANDED PARADIGMS OF PLAY

The previous portion of this chapter reflects more traditional paradigms of play as discussed in the literature. The remainder of this chapter presents additional paradigms and new ways of looking at play as related to child life professionals. These expanded alternatives are certainly not suggested as substitutes to those that form the foundation of child life specialists' play interactions with children but are offered as additional ways to view a core aspect of the specialist's professional role. The use of ritualistic modes of play, i.e., play that offers children cathartic release under guidance, will be addressed in terms of flow, comfort, and hope. In the process of considering new paradigms of play, opportunities arise to expand one's knowledge base, discover new aspects of personal growth, and enrich interactions with children, thus creating more effective child life specialists.

Play as Flow

Mihaly Csikszentmihalyi (1985), a psychologist and play researcher, found that those who get the most pleasure from play enter into a mental state that he calls "flow." This is a state in which people are fully in the moment, totally consumed with their playful pursuits and intrinsically rewarded by the spontaneous joyful feelings that accompany these experiences. Flow is a state of self-forgetfulness, the opposite of rumination and worry. Instead of being lost in nervous preoccupation, people in flow are so absorbed in the experience at hand that they lose all self-consciousness (Goleman, 1995).

This view of life and play as offered by Csikszentmihalyi (1985) is made up of different qualities of experience. He has focused his research on the experiential aspects of play. Csikszentmihalyi argues that play is too often thought of as something a person does, rather than something a person feels. In contrast to many other play researchers, he has chosen to study playfulness as a phenomenon, rather than play as an activity (Csikszentmihalyi, 1979).

Characteristics of Flow

Csikszentmihalyi (1979) maintains that an extremely high degree of concentration is, perhaps, the chief characteristic of flow. Children who experience flow are not thinking about doing something, they are simply doing it, and in the process of flow, they are unaware of challenges other than those inherent in the play situation on which they are focused (Chance, 1979). During the experience of flow, there is also a general feeling of control; a feeling of influencing whatever is happening, and a merging with the environment or process. The experience of "flow" can be momentary or long lasting and during this time the brain "quiets down" in the sense that there is a lessening of cortical arousal. This means that the brain is working very efficiently during these periods and the person is relaxed, yet focused. When the brain is operating at peak efficiency, as in flow, there is a precise relation between the active areas of the brain and the demands of the task (Goleman, 1995).

When children experience flow, they are living at their optimal capacity in that they are actively engaged in the present and are facing life with feelings of control and opportunity. It can be argued that mastery in any area is spurred on by the experience of flow, that the motivation to get better and better at something, be it playing the violin, dancing, or skiing, is, at least in part, to stay in flow while doing it. The state of flow creates a compelling, highly motivating feeling of mild ecstasy that seems to be a by-product of the heightened focus that is a requisite of flow (Goleman, 1995).

Csikszentmihalyi maintains that activities that are either too difficult or too easy, as determined by each individual, are seldom considered play. In order to be play, an activity must ordinarily be difficult enough to be interesting, but not so difficult that it is impossible. Often the challenge is clearly defined, as in card or board games. In the case of pretend and physical play, the challenge is open-ended, as much up to the player as is the solution. Play is at its best when the challenge nearly matches the skill of the individual...not too challenging but not too easy. Yet so long as a reasonable challenge exists, the activity is apt to be considered play (Sutton-Smith, 1982).

When the opportunities for action (i.e., the challenge of the activity or situation) are perceived to overwhelm the player's capabilities, the resulting stress is experienced as anxiety (see Figure 1) (Csikszentmihalyi, 1979). The state of flow is felt when the opportunities for action are in a balance with the player's abilities (skills). The experience is then autotelic, with a feeling of purpose and self-control. When skills or abilities are greater than the opportunities for using them, the state of boredom results, which again fades into anxiety when the ratio becomes too large.

Flow, as play, is always voluntary and very individually defined. It can be one of many kinds of experiences: social, kinesthetic, imagining, reading or observing (Chance, 1979; Csikszentmihalyi, 1979). Hence, the same activity for one person can be play and yet not be play for another. For example, what a 2-year old considers to be play might be considered boring for a 6-year old. Similarly, an activity may feel like play at one time for an individual and not feel like play at another time for the same individual, such as when a child's brain is working less efficiently because of nervousness or fatigue.

Given the characteristics of flow experiences reviewed here (intense concentration, merging of self with the environment and the activity/process, voluntary and rewarding nature, decreased awareness of problems and an ideal balance between tension and boredom), flow can be considered a form of

Figure 1
Model of the Flow State

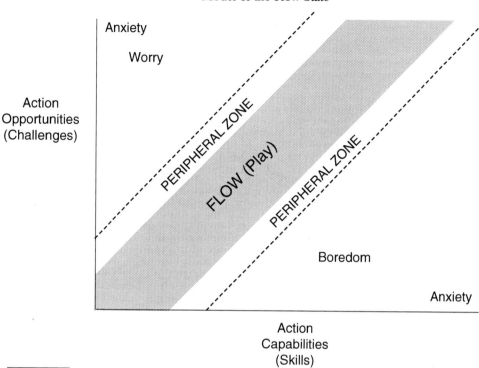

Source: Adapted from Czikszentmihalyi (1975).

escape (Sutton-Smith, 1982). However, Csikszentmihalyi (1981) questions whether play as flow can be considered totally outside of ordinary reality. He maintains that an experience is not defined as play "because it suspends or evades the rules of reality but because the players freely accept the goals and rules that constrain the actions, knowing full well that he or she need not play" (p. 19). Csikszentmihalyi also calls attention to the fact that play does not ignore reality. It is always about things that exist in reality although it usually involves a change of perspective on the part of the participant to affect a temporary transformation of some form (e.g., child playing the role of the nurse, or taking the part of the mother in separation

play). Hence, play should always be taken seriously.

FLOW AND CHILD LIFE PRACTICE. Children who cope with disability, chronic illness, frequent health care, or are recovering from some other form of trauma, need and desire avenues of escape such as that derived from flow experiences. When working with children, it is possible to watch the phenomenon of flow unfold before our eyes. For example, observing a young patient challenging himself to place a cast on a doll, watching a child learning to "pop wheelies" in a wheelchair, or seeing a preschooler intently recreating a recent separation experience with family figure dolls, can reveal children immersed in a state of flow.

One might question whether children engaged in these forms of play truly pursue them for the purpose of experiencing flow. It is possible to explain the motivation of children who are coping with stress to engage in play, such as that described above, for reasons other than to experience flow. As stated previously, we know that children in healthcare environments benefit from play by: maintaining development (Bergen, Gaynard & Hausslein, 1987; Jessee, 1992; Le Vieux-Anglin & Sawyer, 1993; Webster, 2000); providing an avenue to communicate feelings and thoughts, and gaining a sense of catharsis (Abbott, 1990; Erikson, 1963; Winnicott, 1971; Zahr, 1998); increasing positive feelings of mastery (Gillis, 1989); adjusting more easily to the hospital environment (Doverty, 1992; Hall & Reet, 2000); and improving mental processing of experiences (Abbott, 1990; Gaynard, Wolfer, Goldberger, Thompson, Laidley and Redburn, 1990; Vessey & Mahon, 1990).

It is also possible that children may sometimes play simply to immerse themselves in the experience of flow. They may seek out play experiences to escape from worries, to become one with the activity, lose themselves in the moment at hand, and forget for a brief amount of time that they are ill, injured, or otherwise stressed.

One can often observe a fine balance between tension and boredom in children's play experiences. For example, "Can I get the cast finished before it dries?" "How far can I get the wheels off the ground before I begin to fall backwards?" "How close to reality can I portray the separation experience before I feel anxious?" As Csikszentmihalyi (1979) has commented about other behaviors that are considered flow experiences, play that focuses on "serious," real-life themes (e.g., illness, health care, and other traumas) has inherent in it some degree of tension, yet lacks the "worry" (that might end the play) since "it is just pretend."

Children engaged in play as flow appear free of the problems that had so recently haunted them even though the context or theme of their play is quite serious, such as reenacting a casting experience or a traumatic separation from loved ones, or playing in a wheelchair in which one has been confined.

When observing such play, one can also observe the intensely focused attention of children and the manner in which they become one with the activity. It is in the course of such serious play that children are apt to be entirely focused on the activity, and least aware of the environment outside of the play experience (Gaynard, 1998; Oremland, 2000). This demonstrates the all-consuming aspect of play that Csikszentmihalyi maintains is central to the experience of flow.

As is also true of the characteristic of flow, children tend to find play experiences, such as those described above, rewarding and pursue them on a voluntary basis prompted by intrinsic motivation. This is the case even when children are engaged in adult-guided play, for it is never continued unless the process provides pleasure and enjoyment for the children (Gaynard, 1998a; Perez, 1989).

FLOW AND THE HEALTHY SELF. Supporting and facilitating flow experiences with children can also enhance the awareness of the "healthy self" which is essential for children who are sick, injured, disabled or traumatized (Perez, 1989). Often, children's healthy parts are buried under physical or emotional symptoms, hidden behind overwhelming feelings of helplessness, or trapped in unhealthy and disabled bodies (Sourkes, 1995). Facilitating flow experiences, via play, helps children to engage in dynamic interactions with the body, mind and spirit that can rebalance the asymmetry created between illness (physical or mental), disability and health (Sabelli, 1989). Children may connect with their healthy selves while finger painting in response to music, "dancing" with their eyes, noses and heads to their own unique rhythms, or moving their wheelchairs through the challenges of an obstacle course. In each of these peak experiences, they are reclaiming and expressing parts of themselves that continue to give them pleasure; rediscovering portions of themselves that cause delight. This can be extremely meaningful and empowering for children who may have lost touch with, or disconnected from, their healthy parts.

The physical and emotional effects of illness, disability, trauma and treatment can be children's worst enemies in their struggle to maintain a continuous sense of identity with their previous selves. By entering into the all-consuming state of flow, children can lose their self-consciousness, enjoy being one entity in body, mind and spirit, and experience a sense of overall well-being (Perez, 1989). The focus is changed from the unhealthy self, which often demands uneven attention in the lives of the children with whom we work, to the healthy self. This provides children with an increased awareness of their capacity to respond positively to others, their environment, and themselves; to create, relax and find joy in their beings. Facilitating playful flow experiences that lead to feelings of wholeness can promote a connection with children's healthy parts once again (Perez, 1989; Sabelli, 1989; Sourkes, 1995).

Play as Comfort

All humans need, and seek out, places of comfort, and we all need to return to our places of comfort on a regular basis to regroup and heal (Landreth, 1994). This is particularly true when one is stressed. On a daily basis, a place of comfort for adults may be something as simple as a favorite rocking chair or a soak in a hot bath. On a larger scale a place of comfort might be a mountain cabin tucked away from the busy, crowded city life. Many people also find places of comfort in activities such as the child who is calmed by watching a favorite video over and over, or someone who finds solace in a long, solitary walk. One's place of comfort can focus on highly idiosyncratic needs, and, therefore, be quite unique. However, what all places of comfort have in common is that they must be safe places because it is impossible to feel comfortable if we don't also feel safe.

The need for places of safety and comfort, specific to each person's needs, is clearly illustrated in the children's book, *The Kissing Hand* (Penn, 1993). In this story, a mother raccoon is preparing her child to enter school for the first time. The young raccoon worries about missing his mother while at school all day. The mother tries to reassure her child that he will be fine without her, that it is natural for children to leave their mothers and go off to school on their own. The mother devises a creative plan to support her child in his transition from home to school. As the mother raccoon tucks her child in bed on the eve of his first day of school, she takes one of his hands and places a kiss on the inside of his palm. The mother raccoon then closes her child's fingers tight around the kiss and explains that when he thinks of her or misses her he is to place his palm next to his cheek. In doing so, the young raccoon will know that his mother's love is always close at hand and he will feel comforted.

Just as the mother raccoon created a unique way for her child to return to a place of comfort while at school, we create avenues for children to return to places of safety and comfort when we facilitate their playful pursuits. Play is one of the few places of comfort that children can return to on a regular basis during times of distress. Play provides children a place where they can restore themselves, a place that has healing potential.

Intrapersonal Aspects of Comfort Play

During play children connect with themselves finding comfort not only in the process of play itself but also in the grounding of self in a familiar, safe activity. This *intrapersonal* function of spontaneous play can enable children to explore, resolve conflicts, master situations, and understand mind, body and world on their own (Loranger, 1992; Gitlin-Weiner, 1998). Carl Jung, an early twentieth century psychologist, maintained that children have within themselves the ability to heal if provided an appropriate template to do so (Allan, 1988). Since it is such a universal place of safety and comfort for all children in almost all circumstances, play creates an ideal template for children to heal themselves. Even in extremely harsh environmental contexts, such as concentration or refugee camps, children have sought opportunities to play in imaginative, creative and expressive ways (Barnes, 1998). The reason(s) that children continue to create playful experiences (alone and with others), in the face of extensive stress and challenge, are numerous and will vary somewhat depending on which theories are applied to the play behaviors. However, perhaps one reason children display the irrepressible need to play, even in the face of extreme adversity, is the intrapersonal aspect of play that compels children to return to a place of safety and comfort where they can regroup and heal themselves.

An additional value of the intrapersonal aspect of play, is that it meets a basic need to "do something" rather than remaining idle. Action in itself is soothing and can be a stress reducer for all individuals regardless of age. It gives one something to do rather than merely waiting passively for events to happen; it feels more effective and soothing than random, uncontrolled behaviors or thoughts, and is a more effective coping mechanism

(Dissanayake, 1992; Perez, 1989; Sommer, 1994). For example, we rhythmically tap toes, drum fingers, and wiggle various body parts as way of relieving impatience, energy, boredom or worry. Even non-human animals tend to use action to shape and express feelings of anxiety or despair as they pace back forth in their cages, in a seemingly endless action of "doing something" rather than remaining idle (Gaynard, 1998; Masson & McCarthy, 1995).

For children, soothing action usually takes the form of play because it is children's most familiar, comfortable medium (Bergen, 1987). Play is often the only place of comfort that children are able to bring into health care settings, and keep with them on a continual basis to confront the stresses of everyday life. In addition, the intrapersonal aspect of play allows children to engage in activities and behaviors that they can control, which is essential for children feeling overwhelmed by emotions and events. When child life specialists facilitate opportunities for play, they are creating places of comfort that help children contain feelings of worry, despair and anxiety. As children become engaged in verbal, physical or imaginative play, their feelings are shaped and expressed, via play activities and behaviors, and made manageable.

Interpersonal Aspects of Comfort Play

Children can also connect with others in the process of play if they desire. This *interpersonal* aspect of play allows for relationships to also serve as places of comfort (Landreth, 1994; Gitlin-Weiner, 1998). This is illustrated in another children's book, *The Little Prince* (Saint-Exupery, 1982). In this story the Little Prince comes from another planet to earth and meets the fox who begs the Little Prince to develop a relationship with him so the fox can teach the Prince the importance of "ties." As the fox discusses his desire to develop a relationship with the Little Prince, he refers to his safe, cozy burrow where he can hide when he hears the footsteps of the hunters. In this way, the fox's burrow provides him a physical place of comfort where he can be safe. The fox tells the Little Prince that if he develops a relationship with the fox, the Prince's footsteps will be heard differently from those of the hunters, that the tie between the Prince and the fox will call the fox out of his burrow, to the safety of their relationship.

The story of the Little Prince and the fox illustrates how interpersonal play relationships can provide us with places of comfort (Landreth, 1994). As children develop "ties" with supportive adults, via play, children are presented with opportunities to create new safe places. Through play relationships, children are able to grow in a context that is familiar. They are respected, met at their level, listened to, engaged with, not just accepted but also embraced without judgment. Play relationships can thus provide an additional template that children can use to heal themselves.

Just as the fox tended to hide in his burrow, fearful of the dangers presented by the hunters, the children with whom child life specialists work also tend to "hide" from the potential dangers of health care experiences, or the recurrence of traumatic events.

Sometimes the hiding is quite literal as the following case indicates:

> Jared, a 4-year-old patient, was found by a child life specialist hiding under a chair in the Medical Imaging Department. Jared was repeatedly whimpering, "I don't want anymore needles," while his mother sat next to him desperately trying to coax Jared out from under the chair. After the child life specialist established rapport with Jared's mother, the specialist began to quietly talk with Jared about how she could

help him make the MRI easier. During the conversation, Jared's mother and the child life specialist casually played with the toys in her basket. After a short period of observing their play, Jared came out from under the chair and reached for a toy. Before long, he was fully engrossed in inspecting the variety of toys in the specialist's basket, and the play relationship had been initiated.

Similar to the "ties" between the fox and the Little Prince, Jared had begun to trust the child life specialist, via the play relationship, and came out from under the chair to more effectively cope with the challenges confronting him.

RELATIONSHIPS DURING PLAY. Sometimes the "hiding" that children exhibit to keep themselves safe is not as concretely expressed as that observed with Jared. At times, children hide behind emotional bravado, denial, anger, or withdrawal. However, the establishment and maintenance of a play relationship can be as effective in helping these children find a place of safety and comfort. Another example is Cecelia.

> Cecelia was a withdrawn 8-year-old with Down Syndrome who was scheduled for her first clinic visit at the hospital. On arrival, the mother registered at the reception desk of the clinic and told the child life specialist that Cecelia was in the lobby with her father and would not budge. The specialist took a backpack of toys and walked with Mom to the lobby where she found Cecelia on the floor in a corner. Cecelia refused to look at the specialist even after rapport with Mom and Dad had been developed. To initiate a play relationship with Cecelia, the specialist decided to try a distal approach to provide Cecelia some extended physical space to assess the safety of the situation. The child life specialist asked Dad to sit next to Cecelia and to roll, toss, and bounce balls back and forth with

the specialist. After a bit of ball play between Dad and the specialist, they noticed Cecelia watching them. The specialist then began rolling the ball so it would gently bump Cecelia's body. Dad would show Cecelia the ball and then roll it back. Gradually, Cecelia began pushing the ball back to the specialist with her foot and then, as the child life specialist began rolling the balls so Cecelia had to reach with her arms to get them, Cecelia became quite engrossed in the play. The specialist began inching toward Cecelia until they eventually sat face-to-face moving the balls between them.

Once again, the safety and comfort of the play relationship was initiated and Cecelia was coaxed out of her familiar hiding place of withdrawal to explore, with the support and guidance of the child life specialist, playful ways to cope with her fears.

The theoretical value of the play relationship is emphasized by some play therapists who maintain that the play space created between children and therapists supercedes the value of the play content. According to these therapists, the relationship allows children to do their own processing and problem solving, and to pursue the play things and themes that will most support them in meeting their needs (Winnicott, 1971). The relationship between the therapist and child is an honoring process that allows the child to find meaning in the experience (Galligan, 2000). It is not only a working relationship, but one that is also warm, respectful, and connected with feelings of liking between the child and therapist.

Other play therapists maintain that the safety children experience in the play relationship is the key component to any successful intervention and that such a relationship can enhance a positive sense of self and minimize children's vulnerability to the effects of trauma (Gitlin-Weiner, 1998). This often allows children to generalize the safety of the play relationship to other relationships, therefore, helping children create an increased number of safe places in their lives (Gaynard & Folan Doyle, 1990; Guerney, 1983; Oremland, 2000). The therapeutic relationship can also provide children an opportunity to learn self-forgiveness and absolve inappropriate guilt. A child life specialist can help children trust in their own innocence involving their illnesses via statements such as, "You didn't make asthma happen to you," and "A bad thought did not make you sick." This release of guilt often fosters a trust of self that is claimed by many to be the foundation of hope (Fulton & Moore, 1995).

Play as Hope

Importance of Hope

Hope is about possibility, about the future, and often coexists with uncertainty. It is a potent and positive human faculty that assures us that the future is open. Hope provides a passion for the possible and is considered by many to be the strongest driving force of humans in regard to bringing about change and igniting the spirit within us to continue in the face of overwhelming challenges (Brussat & Brussat, 1996). Hope is developmental and can be evidenced in very young children most easily accessed via nonverbal mediums, such as their ability to engage with others and continuity in play behaviors. We all have a "hope history" based on current and previous life experiences, personal beliefs and our faith system (Frankl, 1972; Grossoehme, 1999; Nash, 1990).

Numerous accounts of the survival of people in World War II concentration camps seem to have rested on their ability to have a symbolic form of hope that they carried with them, a kind of portable imaginative skill, such as reciting poetry or telling stories.

Mathematicians and poets were two groups that seemed to have a unique ability to survive in these camps. Perhaps it was because they had a set of clearly ruled and structured symbolic forms that they could actually transform the camp experience into make-believe play experiences revolving around hope. They had periods of storyelling, riddling, poetry reciting, the retelling of familiar myths and other forms of imaginative play that allowed hope to remain alive for these survivors (Sutton-Smith, 1979). Our vital need for hopeful fantasies is further underscored by research indicating that when individuals lose hope (i.e., loss of a compelling, meaningful fantasy about the future) that death is not far behind (Singer & Singer, 1979).

Hope and Resilience

In recent years there has been a growing acceptance of the concept of hope as it relates to resiliency and the importance of this concept in children's development. Many children who are exposed to dangerous environments and to threatening life events continue to make positive adaptations to such stresses (Garmezy, 1991). By definition, resilient individuals possess the ability to spring back, rebound, successfully adapt in the face of adversity. They develop social competence despite the occurrence of stressful experiences and major assaults on the developmental process (Luther, Cicchetti, & Becker, 2000). Competence is demonstrated in the face of a known risk such as the presence of a disability, natural disaster, or a life-threatening, chronic illness.

Many of these recent studies indicate that there are a variety of internal and external characteristics common to resilient children. The research encompasses numerous at-risk populations, and one of the factors that most of these children and youth seem to have in common is a sense of hope. Different authors use different phrases or terms to refer to this characteristic. These include: "a sense of purpose and future" (Garmezy, 1991); "a sense of control of one's destiny and optimism" (Mandeleco & Peery, 2000); a "belief that children can influence their environment and will not be engulfed by their situation" (Bernard, 1991); a "positive outlook" (Masten, Morison, Pelligrini, & Tellegen, 1990); "a conviction that things will work out in the end despite unfavorable odds" (Werner, 1994); and the "expression of hope in fantasy"(Wyman, Cowen, Work, & Parker, 1991).

Many, if not most, of the children with whom child life specialists work can be classified as being "at risk" in regard to their physical and emotional well-being. This population of children is in need of support from others to nurture and facilitate the development of resilient characteristics so they are able to confront the stresses inherent in their lives and rebound with successful adaptation. The use of fantasy, make-believe, pretend play provides children opportunities to express and share their hopes with others, and can potentially support children in the establishment and maintenance of resilient beliefs, attitudes and behaviors.

FANTASY PLAY. Fantasy, make-believe, pretend are all words describing play that is present in all human societies (Dissanayake, 1992). This type of play is built on the foundation of symbolic play discussed earlier in this chapter. The literature on fantasy play reflects numerous schools of thought regarding the purpose and value of this form of play. Ethologists maintain that the imagination is important in the healing process, and that one's fantasies positively add to the quality of life (Dissanayake, 1992). Others have suggested that children engage in fantasy play because it broadens children's range of potential behaviors, enhances the possibility of survival in an ever-changing environment, and provides the behavioral flexibility essential for insightful problem solving (Bruner, 1972; Singer, 1994). Dramatic or fantasy play has also been explored for its potential contributions to creativity and enhancement of social and cognitive skills (Rubin, Fein, & Vandenberg, 1983). Psychodynamic theorists and practitioners maintain that fantasy play is a reflection of children's lives, a symbolic expression of their unconscious conflicts and anxieties, as well as an emotional release and a way to resolve fears (Mook, 1994; Peller, 1952). Children who engage in fantasy play also display more smiling and laughing, more cooperation with adults, and in general less evidence of anger, distress, fatigue and sluggishness than children who do not (Singer, 1998). Findings of one study that explored the impact of fantasy play on the anxiety of chronically ill children found that the fantasy activity of children had a positive effect on reducing distress and recommended the incorporation of imaginary activities into the therapeutic interventions of health care professionals (Johnson, Whitt, & Martin, 1987).Vygotsky, in contrast to Piaget who maintained that children are unable to think in the theoretical mode in early childhood, suggested that young children are capable of reasoning in a theoretical manner under certain conditions, including fantasy play (Thomas, 1985). The Russian developmentalist maintained that entering the pretend play mode enables young children to approach situations in an "as if" fashion and to consider experiences not only in the here and now (the concrete reality) but to entertain theoretical ideas. In his theory of cognitive development, Vygotsky outlined features that he viewed critical in defining make-believe play. One of these characteristics is the creation of imaginary situations that permit children to grapple with wishes that are not yet realized (Berk, 1994). Research exploring Vygotsky's assertions

that in pretend play children sometimes think and behave in a manner well beyond their age lends support to the claim that young children are able to consider numerous potential possibilities in a theoretical manner (Dias & Harris, 1988, 1990).

Hope and Fantasy Play

Vandenberg (1986) suggests that an additional way of looking at fantasy play is to view it as children "playing with hope." Vandenberg posits that perhaps children are constructing a basis for hope that may change their lives just as adults do via mental fantasy play. Common adult fantasies include imagining an upcoming vacation, winning the lottery, being free from the stresses of everyday life, and other "daydreams" of escape. Hence, fantasy play, whether merely imagined, or eventually played out, is the very stuff of life for both children and adults.

According to Vandenberg (1986) the only major difference between the hopeful play of children and adults is that children's fantasies are made public via dramatic play or expressed aloud in stories and personal monologues. As adults, most of us would be embarrassed, to say the least, if our hopes and dreams were public. However, when younger, all of us probably expressed many hopes for our future lives and roles via such public displays. Singer (1994) describes the fantasies of adults and the imaginative play of children as a process for "sustaining hope and effort" and maintains that make-believe play of children (playing that a banana is a phone, or that a doll can talk) can be regarded as a fundamental precursor of the full-blown adult imagination. Through imaginary play children take on an attitude toward the possible, explore a range of potential futures, or in effect, travel through time and space to a different or better childhood.

Many times, the problems children are confronted with seem hopeless. They may not be able to think of any possible solutions to the situations with which they struggle. In these cases, simply imagining the situation or dilemma may not be sufficient to facilitate effective problem solving or hope. Through the use of sociodrama, actual situations or problems can be enacted using physical movements, props, mental actions and mind-body interactions. For example, this can be observed as child life specialists support children in reenacting health care experiences in which children have previously been the passive recipients. The action of sociodrama can facilitate the creation of previously unconceived possibilities which can lead to more effective problem solving and coping, the reduction of distress, and the development of positive future images (Goff & Torrance, 1991)

Consider the experience of a four-year-old, in an inpatient setting, who, due to the distance the family lives from the hospital and the fact that her mother has three other children at home for which she cares, rarely receives visits from her parents.

The 4-year-old is focused on playing with a bin of animal families in the playroom with a child life specialist. The child has selected a baby giraffe from the bin and weaves a story aloud about the giraffe looking for her mommy. The child moves the giraffe around the room manipulating the giraffe to peek around corners, in cupboards, under tables and chairs, and any other place "Mommy" might be found. During the child's play, the child life specialist suggests that the giraffe might be experiencing feelings similar to those of other children who can't find their mothers (e.g., fearful, sad, mad), and receives verbal and nonverbal confirmation from the child that the baby giraffe is experiencing such feelings. The specialist also suggests reasons that the giraffe can't find its mommy ("Perhaps

Mommy had to go home to take care of the giraffe's sisters"). After looking all over the playroom in vain, the young patient returns to the bin where the rest of the animals reside. The child holds the giraffe above the bin, and looking up at the specialist asks in a woeful manner, "Is there a mommy in there for me?" (blurring the boundary between the giraffe and herself). Then, in the next instant, the child dives into the bin with the baby giraffe and pulls out the mommy giraffe squealing with delight, "Here is my mommy!" The play is concluded with the child playing the mommy's role expressing much love and concern for the baby and reassuring the young giraffe that she is very greatly missed at home.

This fantasy play appears to illustrate this patient's strongest hopes: to be happily reunited with her mother; to be certain that her mother still loves her, even when separated for long periods of time; and, that she is very much missed by all at home, all of which are realistic wishful possibilities giving rise to true hope. As the child life specialist facilitates this form of make believe play, the young patient has an opportunity to act out and express her feelings of worry and despair and then to develop a more positive image of the future and share her fantasy of hope.

It is clear there is a need for child life specialists to facilitate the fantasy play of children with whom they work in order to: enhance children's quality of life; promote problem solving skills, mental creativity and flexibility; help children express emotions and unconscious conflicts; and decrease anxiety, anger, distress and fatigue. Supporting children to maintain hope and develop resilience as they cope with illness, injury, health care, and other life stresses, should be a central focus of child life specialists. When fantasy play is viewed as a form of hope for young patients, it becomes clear that to facilitate the development and maintenance of this vital characteristic child life professionals need to maximize the opportunities for patients' imaginative play experiences. The child life specialist's own professional curiosity and willingness to share children's thoughts and pretend play can open troubled children to hopeful images via the world of fantasy. By such an approach we can support children, who are sad, lonely and despairing, in transforming a seemingly hopeless future into a world of innumerable possibilities (Singer, 1994).

Conclusion

The theories and research reviewed in this chapter are presented according to various play paradigms. It is important to realize that these are actually artificial conceptual categories imposed on the subject of play to facilitate an understanding of the different approaches that may be employed by child life specialists. However, in reality, the play engaged in by children usually reflects more than one, and sometimes many, of the paradigms presented in this chapter. Therefore, the provision of play opportunities may simultaneously benefit children in numerous ways. Play experiences may concurrently provide children with a place of enjoyment and comfort, facilitate gains in problem solving behaviors and development, encompass an experience of flow, offer an opportunity to express feelings, and foster a sense of fantasy and hope.

Play provides the child life specialist the rare opportunity to understand the child's world and allows a flow of communication when other forms of interpersonal connection are difficult or impossible. Perhaps most importantly, a playful attitude toward life allows us to keep in touch with our inner selves while we deal with the realities of our world. If we can keep this "flow" of play and work, we may be better able to help children

in our care to authentically experience their own lives.

REFERENCES

Abbott, K. (1990). Therapeutic use of play in the psychological preparation of preschool children undergoing cardiac surgery. *Issues in Comprehensive Pediatric Nursing, 13,* 265-277.

Allan, J. (1988). *Inscapes of the child's world: Jungian counseling in schools and clinics.* Dallas, TX: Spring Publications, Inc.

Axline, V. M. (1969). *Play therapy* (Rev. ed.). New York: Ballentine Books:

Barnes, D. R. (1998). Play in historical contexts. In D. Bergen & D. Fromberg (Eds.), *Play from birth to twelve: Contexts, perspectives and meanings.* New York: Garland Publishing Co.

Bernard, B. (1991). *Fostering resiliency in kids: Protective factors in the family, school and community.* Portland, OR: Northwest Educational Research Laboratory.

Bergen, D. (Ed). (1987). *Play as a medium for learning and development.* Portsmouth, NH: Heinemann Educational Books, Inc.

Bergen, D., Gaynard, L., & Hausslein, E. (1987). Designing special play environments. In D. Bergen (Ed.), *Play as a medium for learning and development.* Portsmouth, NH: Heinemann Educational Books, Inc.

Berk, L. E. (1994). Vygotsky's theory: The importance of make-believe play. *Young Children,* (November), 30-38.

Bettleheim, B. (1987). The importance of play. *The Atlantic Monthly,* 35-47.

Bolig, R., Fernie, D., & Klein, E. (1986). Unstructured play in hospital settings: An internal locus of control rationale. *Children's Health Care, 15,* 101-107.

Bruner, J. S. (1972). The nature and uses of immaturity. *American Psychologist, 27,* 687-708.

Brussat, M. A., & Brussat, F. (1996). *Spiritual literacy.* New York: Simon & Schuster, Inc.

Chance, P. (1979). *Learning through play.* New York: Gardner Press, Inc.

Csikszentmihalyi, M. (1975). Play and intrinsic rewards. *Journal of Humanistic Psychology, 15,* 41-64.

Csikszentmihalyi, M. (1979). The concept of flow. In B. Sutton-Smith (Ed.), *Play and learning.* New York: Gardner Press, Inc.

Csikszentmihalyi, M. (1981). Some paradoxes in the definition of play. In A. T. Cheska (Ed.), *Play as Context.* West Point, NY: Leisure Press.

Csikszentmihalyi, M. (1985). *Beyond boredom and anxiety.* San Francisco: Jossey-Bass.

Dias, M. G., & Harris, P. L. (1988). The effect of make-believe play on deductive reasoning. *British Journal of Developmental Psychology, 6,* 207-221.

Dias, M. G., & Harris, P. L. (1990). The influence of the imagination on reasoning by young children. *British Journal of Developmental Psychology, 8,* 305-318.

Dissanayake, E. (1992). *Homo aestheticus: Where art comes from and why.* New York: MacMillan.

Dodge, K. A. (1983). Behavioral antecedents of peer social status. *Child Development, 54,* 1386-1399.

Doverty, N. (1992). Therapeutic use of play in hospital. *British Journal of Nursing, 1,* 77-81.

Drucker, J. (1994). Constructing metaphors: The role symbolization in the treatment of children. In A. Slade and D. P. Wolf (Eds.), *Children at play: Clinical and developmental approaches to meaning and representation.* New York: Oxford University Press.

Ellis, M. J. (1987). Play and the origin of species. In D. Bergen (Ed.), *Play as a medium of learning and development.* Portsmouth, NH: Heinemann Educational Books, Inc.

Erikson, E. (1959). Growth and crises of the healthy personality. *Psychological Issues, 1*: 50-100.

Erikson, E. (1963). *Childhood and society.* New York: Norton.

Esman, A. H. (1983). Psychoanalytic play therapy. In C. E. Schaefer & K. J. O'Connor (Eds.), *Handbook of play therapy.* New York: John Wiley & Sons.

Fabes, R., & Martin, C.L. (2001). Exploring development through childhood. Boston: Allyn and Bacon.

Fagen, R. (1995). Animal play, games of angels, biology, and Brian. In A. D. Pellegrini (Ed.), *The future of play theory: A multidisciplinary inquiry into the contributions of Brian Sutton-Smith.*

Albany, NY: State University of New York Press.

Fein, G. G., & Schwartz, P. M. (1982). Developmental theories in early education. In B. Spodek (Ed.), *Handbook of research in early childhood education.* New York: Free Press.

Frankl, Viktor. (1972). *Man's search for meaning.* New York: Pocket Books.

Freud, A. (1928). *Introduction to the technique of child analysis.* (Translated by L. P. Clark.) New York: Nervous and Mental Disease Publishing.

Froebel, F. (1887). *The education of man.* New York: Appleton-Century.

Fromberg, D. P. (2002). *Play and meaning in early childhood education.* Boston: Allyn & Bacon.

Fulton, R. A., & Moore, C. M. (1995). Spiritual care of the school age child with a chronic condition. *Journal of Pediatric Nursing, 10,* 224-231.

Galligan, A. C. (2000). That place where we live: The discovery of self through the creative play experience. *Journal of child and adolescent psychiatric nursing, 13,* 169-176.

Garmezy, N. (1991). Resilience in children's adaptation to negative life events and stress environments. *Pediatric Annuals, 20,* 459-466.

Gaynard, L. (1998). Play as ritual for hospitalized children. In D. Bergen and D. Fromberg (Eds.), *Play from birth to twelve: Contexts, perspectives & meanings.* New York: Garland Publishing Co.

Gaynard, L. (1998a). *Ritualistic meanings of symbolic play in situations of illness and treatment.* San Diego: American Education Research Association.

Gaynard, L., Wolfer, J., Goldberger, J., Thompson, R., Laidley, L. N., & Redburn, L. (1990). *Psychosocial care of children in hospitals.* Rockville, MD: Child Life Council.

Gaynard, L., & Folan Doyle, C. (1990). Developing supportive relationships with patients and families. *Child Life Council Bulletin, 8,* 1-5.

Gillis, A. J. (1989). The effect of play on immobilized children in hospital. *International Journal of Nursing Studies, 26,* 261-269.

Gitlin-Weiner, K. (1998). Clinical perspectives on play. In D. Bergen & D. Fromberg (Eds.), *Play from birth to twelve: Contexts, perspectives and meanings.* New York: Garland Publishing, Inc.

Goff, K., & Torrance, E. P. (1991). Healing qualities of imagery and creativity. *The Journal of Creative Behavior, 25,* 296 - 303.

Goleman, D. (1995). *Emotional intelligence.* New York: Bantam Books.

Groos, K. (1914). *The play of man.* London: W. Heinemann.

Grossoehme, D. H. (1999). *The pastoral care of children.* New York: Haworth.

Guerney, L. F. (1983). Client-centered play therapy. In C. E. Schaefer & K. J. O'Connor (Eds.), *Handbook of play therapy.* New York: Wiley.

Hall, C., & Reet, M. (2000). Enhancing the state of play in children's nursing. *Children's Health Care, 4,* 49-54.

Hall, G. S. (1921). *Youth: Its education, regimen and hygiene.* London & New York: Appleton.

Hughes, F. P. (1999). *Children, play and development.* Needham Heights, MA: Allyn & Bacon.

Irwin, E. C. (1983). The diagnostic and therapeutic use of pretend play. In C. E. Schaefer & K. J. O'Connor (Eds.), *Handbook of play therapy.* New York: John Wiley & Sons.

Jessee, P. O. (1992). Nurses, children and play. *Issues in Comprehensive Pediatric Nursing, 15,* 261-269.

Johnson, M. R., Whitt, J. K., & Martin, B. (1987). The effect of fantasy facilitation of anxiety in chronically ill and healthy children. *Journal of Pediatric Psychology, 12,* 273-284.

Kampe, E. (1990). Children in health care: When the prescription is play. In E. Klugman & S. Smilansky (Eds.), *Children's play and learning: Perspectives and policy implications.* New York: Teachers College Press.

Klein, M. (1932). *The psychoanalysis of children.* London: Hogarth Press.

Landreth, G. (1982). Children communicate through play. In G. L. Landreth (Ed.), *Play therapy: Dynamics of the process of counseling with children.* Springfield, IL: Charles C Thomas.

Landreth, G. (1994). *Touching the inner world of children through play therapy.* Keynote Address, Texas Association for Play Therapy First Annual Conference, Dallas, TX.

LeVieux-Anglin, L., & Sawyer, E. (1993). Incorporating play interventions into nursing care. *Pediatric Nursing, 19,* 459-463.

Loranger, N. (1992). Play intervention strategies for the Hispanic toddler with separation anxiety. *Pediatric Nursing, 18,* 571-575.

Luther, S. S., Cicchetti, D., & Becker, B. (2000). The construct of resilience: A critical evaluation and guidelines for future work. *Child Development, 71,* 543-562.

Mandleco, B. L., & Peery, C. (2000). An organizational framework for conceptualizing resilience in children. *Journal of Child and Adolescent Psychiatric Nursing, 13,* 99-111.

Masson, J., & McCarthy, S. (1995). *When elephants weep: The emotional lives of animals.* New York: Bantam Doubleday Dell Publishing Group, Inc.

Masten, A. S., Morison, P., Pellegrini, D., & Tellegen, A. (1990). Competence under stress: Risk and protective factors. In J. Rolf, A. S. Masten, D. Cicchetti, K. Nuechterlein, & S. Weintraub (Eds.), *Risk and protective factors in the development of psychopathology.* New York: Cambridge University Press.

Monighan-Nourot, P. (1990). The legacy of play in American early childhood education. In E. Klugman & S. Smilansky (Eds.), *Children's play and learning.* New York: Teachers College Press.

Montessori, M. (1965). *Dr. Montessori's own handbook.* New York: Schocken. (Original work published in 1914.)

Montessori, M. (1973). *The Montessori method.* Cambridge, MA: Bently.

Mook, B. (1994). Therapeutic play: From interpretation to intervention. In J. Hellendoorn, R. van der Kooij, & B. Sutton-Smith (Eds.), *Play and intervention.* New York: State University of New York Press.

Moustakas, C. E. (1959). *Psychotherapy with children: The living relationship.* New York: Harper & Row.

Nash, R. B. (1990). Life's major spiritual issues: An emerging framework for spiritual assessment and pastoral diagnosis. *Care Giver Journal, 7,* 3-42.

Oremland, E. K. (2000). *Protecting the emotional development of the ill child: The essence of the child life profession.* Madison, CT: Psychosocial Press.

Parten, M. B. (1932). Social participation among pre-school children. *Journal of Abnormal and Social Psychology, 27,* 243-269.

Patrick, G. T. W. (1916). *The psychology of relaxation.* Boston: Houghton Mifflin.

Pellegrini, A. P. (1995). *The future of play therapy: A*

multidisciplinary inquiry into the contribution of Brian Sutton-Smith. Albany: State University of New York Press.

Peller, L. E. (1952). Models of children's play. *Mental Hygiene, 36,* 66-83.

Penn, A. (1993). *The kissing hand.* Washington, D.C.: Child Welfare League of America.

Perez, M. (1989). Music, emotions and hospitalized children. In M. H. M. Lee (Ed.), *Rehabilitation, music and human well being.* St. Louis, MO: MMB Music, Inc.

Petrillo, M., & Sanger, S. (1980). *Emotional care of hospitalized children: An environmental approach.* Philadelphia: J. B. Lippincott Co.

Piaget, J. (1962). *Play, dreams, and imitation in childhood.* New York: Norton.

Rubin, K. H., Fein, G. G., & Vandenberg, B. (1983). Play. In P. H. Mussen (Ed.), *Handbook of child life psychology: Social development.* New York: John Wiley.

Sabelli, H. C. (1989). *Union of opposites: A comprehensive theory of natural and human processes.* Lawrenceville, VA: Brunswick Publishing Corp.

Saint-Exupery, A. (1982). *The little prince.* San Diego: Harcourt Brace Jovanovich.

Schaefer, C. E., & O'Connor, K. J. (1983). *Handbook of play therapy.* New York: Wiley.

Singer, J., & Singer, D. (1979). The value of imagination. In B. Sutton-Smith (Ed.), *Play and Learning.* New York: Gardner Press, Inc.

Singer, J. L. (1994). The scientific foundations of play therapy. In J. Hellendoorn, R. van der Kooij & B. Sutton-Smith (Eds.), *Play and intervention.* New York: State University of New York Press.

Singer, J. L. (1998). Imaginative play in early childhood: A foundation for adaptive emotional and cognitive development. *International Medical Journal, 5,* 93-100.

Slade, A., & Wolf, D. (Eds.). (1994). *Children at play: Clinical and developmental approaches to meaning and representation.* New York: Oxford University Press.

Smilansky, S. (1968). *The effects of sociodramatic play on disadvantaged preschool children.* New York: Wiley.

Sommer, D. R. (1994). Exploring the spirituality of children in the midst of illness and suffering. *The Association for the Care of Children's Health Advocate, 1,* 7-12.

Sourkes, B. A. (1995). *Armfuls of time: The psychological experience of the child with a life-threatening illness.* Pittsburgh, PA: University of Pittsburgh Press.

Spencer, (1873). *Principles of psychology.* New York: Appleton-Century-Crofts.

Sutton-Smith, B. (Ed.) (1979). *Play and learning.* New York: Gardner Press, Inc.

Sutton-Smith, B. (1982). *A history of children's play.* Aukland, NZ: New Zealand Council for Education.

Sutton-Smith, B. (1994). Paradigms of intervention. In J. Hellendoorn, R. van der Kooij, & Sutton-Smith, B. (Eds.), *Play and intervention.* New York: State of University of New York Press.

Thomas, M. R. (1985). *Comparing theories of child development.* Belmont, CA: Wadsworth, Inc.

Thompson, R. H., & Stanford, G. (1981). *Child life in hospitals: Theory and practice.* Springfield, IL: Charles C Thomas, Publisher.

Vandenberg, B. (1986). Mere child's play. In K. Blanchard (Ed.), *The many faces of play.* Champaign, IL: Human Kinetics Publishers, Inc.

Vessey, J. A., & Mahon, M. M. (1990). Therapeutic play and the hospitalized child. *Journal of Pediatric Nursing, 5,* 328-333.

Vygotsky, L. S. (1962). *Thought and language.* Cambridge, MA: M. I. T. Press.

Webster, A. (2000). The facilitating role of the play specialist. *Paediatric Nursing, 12,* 24-27.

Werner, E. E. (1994). Overcoming the odds. *Developmental and Behavioral Pediatrics, 15,* 131-136.

Wicklegren, I. (1993). It's not just a game. *Current Science, 78,* 4-5.

Winnicott, D. (1971). *Therapeutic consultations in child psychiatry.* London: Hogarth.

Wyman, P. A., Cowen, E. L., Work, W. C., & Parker, G. R. (1991). Developmental and family milieu interview correlates of resilience in urban children who have experienced major life-stress. *American Journal of Community Psychology, 19,* 405-426.

Zahr, L. K. (1998). Therapeutic play for hospitalized preschoolers in Lebanon. *Pediatric Nursing, 23,* 449-454.

Chapter 9

PSYCHOLOGICAL PREPARATION AND COPING

JOY GOLDBERGER, ANNE LUEBERING MOHL, AND RICHARD H. THOMPSON

There was a child went forth every day,
And the first object he look'd upon, that object he became,
And that object became part of him for the day or a certain part of the day,
Or for many years or stretching cycles of years. . .

These became part of that child who went forth every day,
and who now goes, and will always go forth every day.

Walt Whitman

This chapter addresses the psychological preparation of children and families and the facilitation of their coping responses when confronting potentially threatening medical events, episodes, and environments. In this chapter, we review relevant theory and research and provide a framework for approaching this important component of care. As we proceed, we will encounter three children, their families, and the staff members who attempt to prepare and support them.

Ana is a four-year-old girl who will require ureteral reimplants. The child life specialist meets Ana and her mother in the surgeon's clinic. In addition to the predictable issues of typically-developing four year olds, Ana has recently experienced distressing diagnostic procedures including a VCUG.

Daniel is a seven-year-old boy in acute respiratory distress. The child life specialist in the Emergency Department hears his screams before he has a chance to meet him personally. As he enters the room he sees Daniel fighting as vigorously as he is able while staff members attempt to place an IV. Daniel's father is pleading with his son to "be good" while he assists staff in trying to hold Daniel on the treatment room table.

Jason is an eleven-year-old boy in a coma in the intensive care unit. His prognosis is poor. Jason's parents are unsure whether his eight and fourteen year old brothers should be told just how sick Jason is, and have not brought them in to visit.

INTRODUCTION AND OVERVIEW

Each of these children and families is faced with substantially different circumstances. However, each is likely to benefit from support and opportunities to enhance coping. The goal of psychological preparation is to increase children and family members' sense of predictability and control over potentially overwhelming life experiences, allowing them to proceed in these situations with a resulting sense of mastery and with the lowest possible level of distress. This, in turn, may contribute to the optimal emotional adjustment of children and families to hospitalization, health care, illness, or other potentially stressful events. Emotional readiness, or sense of being as "prepared" as possible to face impending situations, can be fostered by:

- helping individuals more accurately understand the circumstances and experiences they face
- helping them understand, identify, practice, and implement options and strategies they may use to better proceed through the experience
- helping individuals organize their emotional experience to make meaning of the events.

Ideally, the process of preparation includes support at all phases of an event in which a child and family may be challenged: before, during and after. Timing, availability of child life staff, and ability of parents and staff of other disciplines to provide support may influence the amount of direct care offered to an individual child and family. In addition, circumstances, such as the child's level of distress or the lack of time prior to an event or procedure, may dictate the relative weight that is given to enhancing understanding and facilitating coping. For example, longer lead time before an event and calm circumstances allow for a thorough approach to assessing needs and planning and rehearsing for the upcoming event. When events are imminent or in progress, efforts to provide brief explanations of components of the event as they unfold and to facilitate coping may be more prominent.

The process of providing or enhancing psychological preparation can be initiated at varying times and contexts with children and families. It may begin as soon as one knows an event is to happen (advance preparation), during the actual event (emotional support and facilitation of coping), and may even be continued after the event has concluded. After an event, a sort of debriefing, often called "post procedural play," might be the only option for a child already in a state of crisis; however, it is ideal for all children to process events that may have taxed their coping resources and to "prepare a memory" that may serve them well in subsequent situations (Solnit, 1984). In addition, support and coping options can be introduced during times of crisis, even if prior "preparation" has not been an option. While arguably no longer preparation in the sense that the child and family has not planned and rehearsed in advance, support during times of crisis or through post procedural play can be important components of preparing for the future. An important component of the role of the child life specialist in these contexts is to address issues such as: *What made it easier? What could have made it easier? What made it harder? What would you like us to do differently?*

For Ana and her mother, the child life specialist has adequate time to assess their potential vulnerabilities and to plan together for the impending surgery. The child life specialist is aware that thoughts and feelings about past difficult experiences in health care will influence responses to the upcoming surgery and, therefore, will need to be explored in preparing for the new experience.

There is no time to explore past experience with Daniel and his father, or to learn about Daniel's preferences and interests. The child life specialist must make a decision about whether to intervene in the midst of current struggles, or to offer medical play to "work through" the experience after the procedure is over.

Although time is of the essence, the child life specialist has time to learn from Jason's parents about their beliefs and concerns regarding the needs of Jason's brothers. As they are overwhelmed, and this is a dilemma with which none of them have any experience, Jason's family needs support to envision and carry through a plan of action.

OVERVIEW OF RELEVANT THEORY AND RESEARCH

Informational Approaches

Various theoretical perspectives, and a corresponding variety of clinical approaches, have shaped the practice of psychological preparation and support of children and their families for health care encounters. Initial research in this area adopted an approach primarily targeted towards children's understanding of the procedures, involving the presentation of information to children about their current or impending circumstances. This informational approach was based on the belief that "psychological upset" observed in children during or after hospitalization was due in part to the unexpectedness and unfamiliarity of events they encountered in the hospital (Vernon, Foley, Sipowitz, & Schulman, 1965).

Subsequent researchers suggested a modification of this approach, positing that the distress experienced by children is not solely a product of encountering the unknown, but rather is a result of the *discrepancy* between expectations of an event and their actual experience (Johnson, Kirchhoff, & Endress, 1975). To minimize this discrepancy, it was suggested that children be provided with "sensory" information, informing them through explanations and demonstrations of what they will see, feel, hear, smell or taste. Johnson et al. demonstrated the advantages of this approach, providing recordings of the sounds of a cast cutter for orthopedic cast removal, in comparison to explanations that simply described the procedures involved in the child's care. The use of sensory informational approaches has been frequently incorporated in preparation studies in the subsequent years with positive effect (Dahlquist, Gil, Armstrong, DeLawyer, Greene, & Wuori, 1986; Kennedy & Riddle, 1989; Siegel & Peterson, 1980, 1981).

A further elaboration of the informational approach to preparation, the introduction of play materials and techniques as a means of enhancing the communication of information, was based on developmental theory. Young children are concrete thinkers who have difficulty absorbing abstract information and who learn best when given opportunities for active involvement with the material presented (Piaget, 1962). Purely verbal descriptions, therefore, are less likely to be effective than explanations accompanied by props, pictures, and other visual displays that depict upcoming events and invite children's interaction and manipulation (Brewer, Gleditsch, Syblik, Tietjens, & Vacik, 2006; Johnson & Stockdale, 1975; Kain et al., 2007).

Behavioral Approaches

Other early approaches to preparation have their roots in behavioral theory. For example, some approaches to preparing children for events have involved the process of "systematic desensitization," in which "stimuli" capable of eliciting fearful, aversive responses in children such as medical equipment are identified and gradually introduced to children over a period of time. Research regarding this technique has occurred most frequently in dental settings, with the dental operatory and the instruments used in children's care being the objects of the introduction and desensitization (Johnson & Machen, 1973; Machen & Johnson, 1974; Sawtell, Simon, & Simeonsson, 1974).

Among the elements of the environment considered capable of contributing to children's distress was the presence of anxious parents. Research documenting a relationship between parent and child anxiety in medical settings and during medical procedures, referred to in the early literature as the "emotional contagion hypothesis" (Vernon et al., 1965), was common in the 1960s and 1970s (Johnson & Baldwin, 1968, 1969; Heffernan & Azarnoff, 1971) and continues into the present regarding parent presence during intrusive medical procedures (for example, Haimi-Cohen & Amir, 1996, regarding lumbar puncture procedures). Admittedly, this line of research has caused some to question the wisdom of "allowing" parents to be present during procedures. However, for others it suggested the necessity of including parents in preparation efforts as a means of directly addressing their own concerns and potential distress, and indirectly affecting the responses of their children (Skipper & Leonard, 1968).

Another behaviorally based technique for preparing children for medical events, the use of modeling, emerged in the research literature in the 1970s (Vernon, 1973, 1974; Melamed & Siegel, 1975). This approach, which builds upon the research of Bandura (e.g., Bandura, Grusec, & Menlove, 1967), holds that the viewing of a live or filmed model who is encountering stressful circumstances similar to that facing a child is likely to increase the probability that the child will adopt the same behaviors and, therefore, more successfully complete the procedure. Vernon (1974) found that it was important that the model express affect appropriate to the situation in order for the child to benefit from this intervention. For example, when children viewed a film of models getting injections, some showing no pain and others showing some negative reaction, the children viewing the "no pain" movie showed the greatest upset and those showing some negative reaction the least (Vernon, 1974). The value of this approach has been demonstrated for specific procedures in addition to injections, such as anesthesia induction (Vernon, 1973), as well as for the more generalized experiences of hospitalization (Melamed and Siegel, 1975). Experts surveyed by O'Byrne, Peterson, and Saldana (1997) rated modeling as among the most effective forms of preparation. On the other hand, a meta-analysis conducted by Saile, Burgmeier, and Schmidt (1988) of 75 preparation studies found modeling to be less effective than other approaches.

The Stress-Coping Framework

Much of the recent research on psychological preparation and coping has been influenced by a body of theory on stress and coping, with the most influential of the theorists in this area being Richard Lazarus and his colleagues (Lazarus & Folkman, 1984; Lazarus, 1999). Lazarus and colleagues note that not all people respond to the same set of potentially stressful circumstances in the same manner, with some experiencing extreme distress, while others are relatively undisturbed by similar circumstances. This variation is explained by the complex relationship that occurs between the potential stressor, such as a medical condition or event, and the individual's perceptions of, or appraisals about, the stressor. Psychological stress, they contend, is the product of a "relationship between the person and the environment that is appraised as taxing or exceeding his or her resources and endangering his or her well-being" (Lazarus & Folkman, 1984, p. 19).

The degree of distress one experiences in the face of potentially disrupting events is the product of a pair of "appraisals" made by the individual. One makes a "primary appraisal" about the nature of the potential threat. In this appraisal, the question asked is, "Am I in trouble?" The individual might appraise the potential threat as irrelevant, as benign or positive, or as in some way stressful. In a "secondary appraisal," the individual asks, "What, if anything, can I do about this?" (Lazarus & Folkman, 1984, p. 31). In other words, what options do I have to cope with this event or circumstance, and what is the likelihood that these efforts will be effective? It is the combination of these appraisals that results in the degree of distress one experiences. One person may appraise a situation, such as impending surgery, as highly threatening, yet manageable given available coping resources. Another may view the circumstances as being of a lesser threat, yet still experience psychological stress if coping resources are perceived as being limited or ineffectual.

"Coping," within this framework, is viewed as, "cognitive and behavioral efforts to manage specific external and/or internal demands that are appraised as taxing or exceeding the resources of the person" (Lazarus & Folkman, p. 141). Children may give themselves comforting messages or may actively deny that an event is to occur, both of which would be considered cognitive coping efforts. On the other hand, activities such as exercising prior to an examination to release tension, holding still during a procedure, or practicing useful behaviors in advance may be viewed as behavioral coping efforts.

The inclusiveness of Lazarus' definition of coping has resulted in conflicting interpretations of the framework. For example, some have *concluded* that anything one does in response to a potential threat is to be considered coping. However, this is not the case, for Lazarus specifically excludes reactions and responses that are, to use his term, "automatized" and, therefore, require no effort and do not represent attempts to manage the situation. The distinction between these automatized responses and "coping" is difficult to draw. Rudolph, Dennig, and Weisz (1995) describe the distinction by saying that, "Any response that reflects a spontaneous internal or behavior reaction to stress, rather than a deliberate attempt to cope, is referred to as a stress response" (p. 329). Even with this definition, the difference between coping and automatized stress responses is hard to pinpoint. As Rudolph et al. note, a child's crying prior to an injection may represent either a coping response, designed to relieve tension in the child or elicit emotional support, or as a spontaneous "stress response" (p. 329).

In practical terms, the distinction is more academic than actual. Certain responses, whether considered coping strategies or stress responses, run counter to the demands of the situation and to the goals one has for managing the perceived threat. Though Lazarus does not make value judgments about specific coping strategies, he does note that some efforts may not serve the individual well. For example, he suggests that "denial" may be a very effective strategy at certain points in an illness, but not for the individual who is experiencing chest pains in the early stages of a heart attack. The same would hold true for children. For example, denial that one really needs a dose of insulin would be counterproductive and dangerous for a child on a sleepover with friends. Similarly, the child who thrashes uncontrollably during a procedure may be intentionally doing so in an effort to cope, refusing to "give in" and hoping to avoid the experience altogether. Nevertheless, this choice of coping strategies may prolong the stressful situation and require firmer restraint, which may increase the pain or discomfort experienced and delay necessary care.

According to the framework, the process of making appraisals and of coping is dynamic, constantly changing, and may be influenced by one's past experiences, positive or negative, as well as changing circumstances within the environment. Because of this, child life specialists or other health care professionals have the opportunity to affect the coping process within the two levels of intervention specified by the model. First, the primary appraisal may be influenced by changing the nature of the circumstances to make them less threatening (e.g., ensuring that the procedure can be done in comforting surroundings and at a time when parents will be present) and by providing the child with accurate, accessible information about the potentially stressful circumstances. This will enable the child to make an appraisal regarding the question, "Am I in trouble?" based on the reality of the situation rather than misconceived fantasies. In addition, the child life specialist may influence the secondary appraisal ("What can I do?") by helping the child identify, practice and implement strategies that are compatible with the demands of the situation and that the child will perceive as effective.

In recent years, research on "cognitive-behavioral" approaches or instruction in "coping skills" has been common. Interventions of this type, which use cognitive strategies to alter behavioral reactions and patterns, address the secondary appraisal process, helping the child identify and practice techniques for coping with specific procedures and events. Among the approaches introduced in this research are relaxation techniques, referred to by some as "distraction" (e.g., deep and regular breathing or "blowing the feeling away"), selection of and concentration on an alternate focus (e.g., paying attention to a visually intriguing material or an imagined pleasant event or setting), and comforting self-talk (reassuring oneself that all is proceeding well and that the event will be over soon). Typically, more than one such technique is presented so that children have control over selection of the method they prefer. Instruction in coping skills has been used in combination with other techniques, such as play rehearsal and modeling (Jay, Elliott, Ozolins, Olson, & Pruitt, 1985. Jay, Elliott, Katz, & Siegel, 1987), or alone (Siegel & Peterson, 1980, 1981). This approach was found to be effective with dental patients (Siegel & Peterson, 1980, 1981), with children undergoing bone marrow aspirations (Jay et al., 1985, 1987), and for elective surgical procedures (Peterson & Shigetomi, 1982).

Another approach compatible with the stress-coping framework is stress-point preparation, which addresses both primary and secondary appraisal (Wolfer & Visintainer, 1975, 1979; Visintainer & Wolfer, 1975; Wolfer, Gaynard, Goldberger, Laidley, & Thompson, 1988). In stress-point preparation, each of a series of stress points (episodes or events during a health care encounter that are likely to be appraised as threatening) is identified. Children and their families are prepared for each stress point using a combination of interventions, including the presentation of information through play-based activities and rehearsal of coping responses to be used. For each family, preparation is ideally conducted by a single individual, who may also be present during a given stress point to provide support. This approach was found to be effective in each of the studies conducted by Wolfer and colleagues, including the Child Life Research Project sponsored by the Association for the Care of Children's Health (Wolfer et al., 1988).

Jay and colleagues (Jay et al. 1985, 1987) also used a combination of interventions, including cognitive-behavioral techniques, with success. In these studies with oncology patients undergoing bone marrow aspiration procedures, children were instructed in coping skills (breathing and imagery), were given an opportunity to rehearse the procedure and their selected coping skills, and were shown a modeling film. Children who used the techniques reported less pain, had lower pulse rates, and were observed to display less distress during the procedures.

New Perspective on Stress and Coping: Overwhelming Stress and its Impact on the Brain

Recent research has added to the body of knowledge about how memories of repeated or traumatic events are retained, even from a very early age. While not intervention-based, this body of new information lends support from a neurophysiological perspective to Lazarus and Folkman's (1984) theoretical model on which stress-point preparation is based and can also inform how we choose to emphasize components of psychological preparation.

Although it is often assumed that infants and young children will not remember early traumatic events such as painful and frightening medical experiences, more recent work informs us that these events may indeed have an impact. Infants who have undergone painful procedures, such as circumcision and heel sticks, within the first

days of life have been shown to react with more crying to subsequent routine immunizations (Taddio, Goldback, Ipp, Stevens, & Koren, 1995; Taddio, Katz, Ilersich, & Koren, 1997; Taddio, Shah, & Gilbert-MacLeod, 2002), and even to react with more facial grimacing during cleansing prior to immunization (Taddio, Shah, & Gilbert-MacLeod). Other research indicates that infants remember traumatic experiences (Fivush, 1998; Gaensbauer, 1995, 2000, 2002, 2004), specifically traumatic medical experiences (Peterson & Parsons, 2005; Peterson & Rideout, 1998), even from the first months of life. Although verbal recall of difficult medical experiences becomes more fluent and accurate over the second and third year (Peterson & Parsons; Peterson & Rideout), Gaensbauer presents case studies of children who experienced traumatic medical and non-medical experiences before they were verbal and who spontaneously acted them out with play materials even years later (1995, 2000, 2002, 2004; Gaensbauer, Chatoor, Drell, Siegel, & Zeanah, 1995). Clearly, experiences that very young children find to be overwhelming have the potential to remain with them for some time.

Refinements in technology in the last decade have allowed researchers to examine the impact of single and of repeated overwhelming painful events. There is evidence from both human research and animal research that replicates pediatric medical experience that exposure to traumatic and repeated painful procedures leads to actual changes in brain structure and neurochemistry (see Goleman, 1995; Rothschild, 2000; and DeBellis et al., 1999 for reviews). Repeatedly causing pain in a single rat pup paw as a parallel to infants' experiences with repeated heel sticks has been demonstrated to result in significantly overdeveloped afferent neural pathways from that specific anatomical structure (summarized in Gaensbauer, 2002). Children and adolescents who were maltreated and subsequently diagnosed with post-traumatic stress disorder (PTSD) were found to have detrimental changes in brain structure and size as well as problematic behavioral, emotional, cognitive, and psychological symptoms (DeBellis).

Perhaps most compelling is the summary of the components of situations that lead to PTSD, and how that corresponds closely with the stress-coping and psychological preparation model. Goleman (1995) summarizes the components and process leading to PTSD to include heightened sensitivity for fear responses at the neural level, or, in the language of the stress-coping model, sudden primary appraisal of extreme threat. In addition to the perception that the situation is extremely dangerous or threatening, the person feels overwhelmed, powerless and helpless, and feels unable to escape, change, or cope with the event. This extreme sense of danger, combined with the perceived inability to escape or cope, leads to a sudden shift of thinking from the higher order cortical areas to the primitive, lifesaving responses in the brain's limbic system. This survival mode leads the brain to secrete neurochemicals that construct more vivid, powerful, and pervasive memories and responses. These strongly engraved pathways also include more details than memories of more typical and manageable situations. Any component of these highly developed pathways that recur, even isolated and in another context, can easily trigger reentry into the state of high alarm and sense of danger.

These features are commonly recognized in veterans of war, now safely at home, who "relive" horrifying events that are triggered by a single sound or sight, or in victims of automobile accidents, who can experience a powerful memory-response at the sound of a car door slamming (Goleman). Clinically, many adults report heightened anxiety, for example, at the aroma of alcohol or hospital disinfectant, with flashbacks to their own frightening childhood experience. This recent work supports the concepts of the stress-coping and psychological preparation model: providing information to affect the primary appraisal; providing language to help the child and family remain responding from the cortical centers of the brain; and most importantly, affecting the secondary appraisal by helping the child and family plan and rehearse what they can do to manage, control, and therefore optimally cope with the potentially overwhelming event.

Current Issues Regarding Preparation

The current state of health care delivery has affected our need for information regarding the practice of preparation. With an eye to cost containment, health care providers are concerned about the effectiveness of differing approaches to preparation. In addition, changing systems of delivering care have resulted in greater use of outpatient surgery and treatment and briefer periods of inpatient care, with the latter typically experienced only by the most severely ill children. Given these changing circumstances, information on the relative effectiveness of approaches, and on the implementation of preparation interventions for patients with varying medical conditions and in varying settings, is critical. The research directly related to these questions is limited. Nevertheless, some tentative answers to these questions may be found in the research literature.

Relative Effectiveness of Preparation Approaches

The preponderance of the evidence from the scores of studies conducted on preparation of children for health care experiences over the past fifty years supports the effectiveness of the practice, although this research is not without its methodological limitations (Vernon et al., 1965; Thompson, 1985; Whelan & Kirkby, 1998; O'Connor-Von, 2000; Yap, 1998; Saile, Burgmeier, & Schmidt, 1988; Vernon & Thompson, 1993). However, information on the relative effectiveness of the forms of preparation is limited and, in some cases, contradictory. For example, a panel of experts surveyed by O'Byrne et al. (1997) judged instruction in relaxation and coping techniques as the most effective approaches to preparation, not only for surgery, but also for other procedures ranging from fingersticks to oncology procedures. The results of a meta-analysis of 75 preparation studies conducted by Saile, Burgmeier, and Schmidt (1988) agreed, finding relaxation and cognitive-behavioral approaches to be among the more effective approaches to preparation, along with interventions that emphasized the providing of information and supportive care. On the other hand, O'Byrne's experts also rated highly the use of modeling, while Saile et al. found this approach, on average, to be less effective than other forms of preparation.

Direct empirical comparisons of approaches are few. Studies making such comparisons have found the providing of sensory information (Johnson, Kirchhoff, & Endress, 1975), of detailed information about one's condition (Edwinson, Arnbjornsson, & Ekman, 1988), or a combination of information and instruction in coping skills (Campbell, Kirkpatrick, Berry, & Lamberti, 1995) to be more effective than providing basic verbal information alone. Studies directly contrasting sensory information approaches with instruction in coping skills, however, have found no significant differences (Dahlquist et al., 1986; Siegel & Peterson, 1980, 1981).

If a single form of preparation is effective (and virtually all of the approaches discussed above have been shown to be more effective

than the absence of preparation), does combining approaches increase the effect? The meta-analysis of Saile et al. (1988) suggests otherwise. Studies using single approaches were found to have a greater positive effect than combined approaches. Certainly, studies using a combination of approaches have been of demonstrated effectiveness (Wolfer & Visintainer, 1975, 1979). However, the direct empirical research examining the effects of incorporating additional components into a preparation protocol has found the marginal effects to be limited. For example, Kain, Caramico, Mayes, Genevro, Bornstein, and Hofstadter (1998) prepared children for surgery using either an operating room tour alone, the tour plus a video presentation, or the tour and video, supplemented with instruction in coping skills. Children receiving the most extensive preparation had lower anxiety in the preoperative period. However, no other significant differences were found among the groups. Robinson and Kobayashi (1991) similarly found few additional effects when preparation via modeling videotape was supplemented with instruction in coping skills for children and parents.

Effects of Preparation on Experienced Patients

A substantial number of patients come to medical events with prior experience, either because of a chronic illness or previous acute medical care. As the stress-coping framework suggests, past experiences may affect current appraisals and, in turn, children's responses to care. Research confirms this, indicating that children with prior experience may be more sensitive to medical events even very early in life (Taddio, Goldback, Ipp, Stevens, & Koren, 1995; Taddio, Katz, Ilersich, & Koren, 1997; Taddio, Shah, & Gilbert-MacLeod, 2002), and that the nature of their experience may affect their responses to preparation. For example, children with prior surgical experience reported higher levels of pre-surgical anxiety (Ellerton & Merriam, 1994) and were more aroused during preparation (Faust & Melamed, 1984) than inexperienced patients. In particular, the quality, rather than the amount, of previous medical experience may affect subsequent medical encounters. Although there was no relationship between number of previous venipunctures and anxiety or behavior during a follow-up venipuncture, Bijttebier and Vertommen (1998) found that children whose parents indicated that they had reacted negatively to a previous venipuncture were more anxious, more distressed, and less cooperative with a follow-up venipuncture than children with positive or neutral previous reactions. In addition, children with past medical experiences that were considered negative were more distressed during a physical examination and throat ·culture if they had not been prepared for the event (Dahlquist et al., 1986). Nevertheless, even among children with prior negative medical experiences, preparation may produce positive effects (Jay et al., 1985). These studies indicate the need to be aware of and sensitive to the prior medical experiences of children and families and to plan interventions accordingly.

Timing of Preparation

Given the rapid pace typical of today's health care system and the reduction in the amount of time children and families spend in health care settings, opportunities for preparation prior to events are limited. For example, with the majority of pediatric surgery conducted on an outpatient basis, formal preparation may be provided through preadmission programs or on the morning of the event. With sufficient notification, children and their families may have the opportunity to participate in preadmission programs. Research regarding the effectiveness of such programs presents a mixed picture. O'Byrne et al. contend that, despite their common use, preoperative preparation programs are among the least effective interventions. However, several recent studies provide evidence to the contrary, noting that such programs may be effective in increasing patient understanding and reducing their levels of distress (Atkins, 1987; Ellerton & Merriam, 1994; Kain et al., 1998; Lynch, 1994). Other studies find no such effect (Kain, Mayes, & Caramico, 1996).

The specific timing for offering preadmission programs or other forms of preparation has been the subject of speculation, recommendations, and a limited amount of research. The general guidance has been that younger children benefit from preparation closer to the event, while older children fair better when preparation is initiated earlier. The research addressing this question is in concert with these guidelines. Melamed, Meyer, Gee, and Soule (1976) considered children, four to twelve years of age, facing in-patient, elective surgery, showing them a modeling film either the day of admission to the hospital or six to nine days prior to admission. They found that older children benefited from preparation in advance, while younger children faired better with preparation closer to the event. In a study of day surgery patients, Kain, Mayes, and Caramico (1996) similarly found that children six and older benefited most from a preoperative preparation program if they attended it five to seven days prior to surgery and least if they attended the day before.

In the absence of preadmission programs or information provided at home via parents, children may receive information about surgery or other medical care the day of the event. Conflicting results are found in the research on the type and extent of information that should be provided to children shortly before surgery. Faust and Melamed

(1984) contrasted children hospitalized for in-patient surgery with those undergoing ambulatory surgical care, showing each group either a modeling or control film. They found that children viewing the modeling film the morning of surgery were more physiologically aroused than were children viewing a non-medical control film and suggested that presenting children with too much information immediately prior to an event may not have allowed sufficient time for processing the potentially threatening information.

In contrast to the Faust and Melamed study, Kennedy and Riddle (1989) found no significant differences in the immediate or post-hospital upset of young children (3 to 6 years of age) prepared either the morning of or the afternoon prior to day surgery through use of a photo book, explanations emphasizing sensory information, and opportunities to practice for anesthesia induction. It may be that an interactive approach such as that used by Kennedy and Riddle, as opposed to filmed modeling, may provide more flexibility to adapt to the varying needs children may have for information on the morning of the event. Nevertheless, with limited time prior to an event, it might be advisable to shift the balance of preparation from the providing of information to coping skills instruction and support.

Collaborating with Parents

Research points to a link between parental feelings, expectations and perceptions and their child's medical experience. Parents who rated themselves as more anxious about their child's medical treatment have been shown to perceive their children's fear, distress, and pain as being higher than less anxious parents (Srivastava, Betts, Rosenberg, & Kainer, 2001). In another study, anxious parents reported more changes in their children's post-hospital behavior (Small & Melnyk, 2006).

In addition to the studies relating parental anxiety to parental perceptions of their children's experiences, there is research showing that interventions can affect parents' reactions to medical events. Using positioning and distraction during venipuncture lowered parents' reports of their children's level of fear (Cavender, Goff, Hollon, & Guzzetta, 2004), using hypnosis during a VCUG led parents to report the procedure as less traumatic for their child (Butler, Symons, Henderson, & Shortliffe, 2005), and debriefing about a procedure lowered parents' reported anxiety for subsequent procedures (Chen, Craske, Katz, Schwartz, & Zeltzer, 2000). An experimental research protocol specifically designed to enhance maternal coping during and following their child's hospitalization found that mothers in the treatment group had more positive psychosocial outcomes during and post-hospitalization, and that their children had more positive behavioral outcomes, even up to a year post-hospitalization (Melnyk et al., 2004). Giving parents an active role to play in assisting their child through a difficult medical procedure may be especially useful (Blount et al., 1991; Butler et al.). Butler et al. observe that "parental involvement in . . . intervention seemed to counter the helplessness, distress, and anxiety that may come from observing one's child's discomfort and resistance" (p. 84). This evidence supports working through parents to provide supportive care. This practice may be especially useful there is too long a time between contact with the family and the planned procedure, when a child will be receiving home care, and when repeated procedures are expected.

Post-procedural Evaluation

Although it is not always recognized, post-procedural follow-up is a form of preparation for similarly stressful future experiences. According to Solnit (1984), it is important for a child to be supported in "preparing a memory" that will serve as a foundation for the future. The research of Chen and colleagues (Chen, Zeltzer, Craske, & Katz, 1999; Chen, Craske, Katz, Schwartz, & Zeltzer, 2000; Chen, Zeltzer, Craske, & Katz, 2000) supports this idea. Among pediatric cancer patients experiencing a series of three lumbar punctures, those who were debriefed by a therapist (who reviewed with each child his or her coping, distress, and levels of pain and anxiety in an attempt to increase the accuracy of their memories and emphasize the value of their coping efforts) following the first LP and again prior to the second held fewer exaggerated memories of the negative aspects of their LP, and experienced less anxiety during their subsequent LPs (Chen, Zeltzer, Craske, & Katz, 1999). This debriefing was found to be especially beneficial for younger children (Chen, Zeltzer, Craske, & Katz, 2000) and children who were assessed to be temperamentally more pain-sensitive (Chen, Craske, Katz, Schwartz, & Zeltzer, 2000).

Research on an Expanded Range of Procedures

Research on preparation in medical settings conducted in the 1970s or earlier tended to focus on children without prior hospital experience, admitted to the inpatient unit for minor, elective surgery – a group almost never encountered in today's health care system. In recent decades, research on preparation has expanded to consider a broader range of settings, conditions, and medical experiences more typical in current pediatric practice, including the research on ambulatory surgery just reviewed. In addition, studies have examined the effectiveness of providing preparation to children facing more

complicated surgical procedures, such as cardiac surgery (Campbell, Kirkpatrick, Berry, & Lamberti, 1995) or surgery performed on an emergency basis (Edwinson, Arnbjornsson, & Ekman, 1988; Mansson, Fredrikzon, & Rosberg, 1992), with each providing support for the value of the intervention.

Preparation for pediatric diagnostic procedures has also been considered. For example, Mahajan, Wyllie, Steffen, Kay, Kitaoka, Dettorre, and McCue (1998) found that children who were prepared for an endoscopy through use of a photo book and demonstration with a doll were less anxious, more cooperative, and needed less sedation during the procedure. Studies have also demonstrated the benefits of preparing children for a voiding cystourethrogram (VCUG) through interventions that included play-based explanations and coping skills instruction (Phillips, Watson, & MacKinlay, 1998; Zelikovsky, Rodrigue, Gidycz, & Davis, 2000). The beneficial effects of preparing cancer patients for the bone marrow aspirations and lumbar punctures, particularly through cognitive-behavioral techniques, have been documented (Jay et al., 1985, 1987; also, see reviews by Ellis and Spanos 1994, and Alvarez and Marcos, (1997).

APPLYING THEORY TO PRACTICE: THE PROCESS OF INITIATING PREPARATION

Knowledge of the effectiveness and appropriateness of various approaches to preparation, gained through the research literature, serves as a guide to child life specialists as they plan the most appropriate approach to the preparation process. The range and depth of a practitioner's interventions are enhanced by experience and intuition. At the same time, responsible professionals realize that one's practice should be accompanied with lifelong learning and awareness and inclusion of evidence-based practice. Professional practice includes continued education through ongoing reading of the current literature, participation in professional workshops, and clinical supervision that includes self-awareness and personal reflection, all of which promote the integration of personal and professional responses. Practitioners should be self-motivated in seeking sources of new information and seeking feedback about areas of future clinical growth. Sharing clinical stories and outcomes, as well as reflecting on past and current research that can inform practice, and getting feedback should be rewarded. It is important to facilitate a departmental process (or groups of solo practitioners) who can provide respectful clinical supervision and integration of new learning and theory.

Steps in this planning process include collaborating with members of the team, gathering basic information, assessing the demands of the situation, assessing individual variables, determining the focus of care, influencing appraisal through a variety of means, facilitating coping strategies, and re-evaluating appraisal and coping, each of which is discussed in the following sections.

Involving Team Members

Child life specialists must rely on assessment skills and teamwork for integrating the multiple factors that converge in the experiences of children and families. Assessment and collaboration facilitates decision making regarding for whom and how intervention will be provided most meaningfully. Preparation and implementation of coping strategies is ideally a collaborative effort. Interdisciplinary communication and understanding enhances this collaboration.

Optimal care is delivered when parents or other primary caregivers are primary members of the child's caregiving team. They are the best resource for understanding the child's past experience and what has been useful or disruptive in the past, as well as current needs and expectations. They will know how expectations and coping plans will resonate with their child. They are likely to be available to a child across the range of caregiving settings. Certainly, their caring is the deepest. Parents' perceptions of issues and needs (as well as children's responses) ideally guide the nature of supportive care. Thus, the role of child life is to support parents, whenever possible, as leaders in the delivery of support to their children. Some parents may be unsure of their role, and may need welcoming and guidance to participate along with the other members of the team. Others may have personal emotional or health issues or practical matters that make their presence erratic or unlikely. Nonetheless, their presence is what children desire most.

Understanding the roles, tasks and beliefs of others is an important foundation of collaborative work. Collaborative work in turn promotes an environment in which the goals of psychological preparation, optimal coping and sensitivity to individual needs can be built. As in all facets of child life care, learning from others is as important as teaching. Fellow members of the health care team are in an ideal position to provide information about the aspects of care or procedures that are the most challenging for other children and families. Whenever possible, child life staff should request formal or informal inservices about the procedures that children will experience. However, this is not always feasible for all procedures, particularly in settings where many different procedures are performed or when different health care providers may vary in their techniques. It is ideal to arrange inservices as techniques and equipment are newly developed.

Child life specialists must balance the demands of staff members' roles while intervening for the optimal psychosocial care for the child. Child life care should reflect respect and understanding of the experience, knowledge and beliefs of other members of the team, while concisely conveying relevant information regarding coping preferences and plans. In addition, it is important that child life staff be certain to offer only those coping options that will truly be available to children and families, avoiding promises that others will have to keep.

Questions related to other members of the health care team for the child life specialist to consider include:

• Are parents empowered to be central to their child's coping?
• Are all team members empowered to be appropriately involved in nurturing and supporting the child?
• Can one person serve as designated "coach" for the child so that there is less overwhelming and extraneous discussion and fewer commands to the child?
• Are we communicating and documenting what we know of children's preferred coping strategies, and enabling others to facilitate their use? What form of communication will be most effective?
• Have we rehearsed options that will truly be available to the child and family, or might a physician, nurse or technician have a differing set of preferences?

The child life specialist working with Ana in the specialty clinic has a close working relationship with the clinic team. Another child life specialist works in the presurgical area. Ana's mother will be her most consistent support and will be essential in carrying through consistent information and coping strategies. Issues and coping plans will be in the form of written communication between the child life specialists as well as documented in a formal chart note.

In addition to his father, the caregiving team involved with Daniel includes a technician, a pediatric nurse and a resident in adult emergency medicine. In the busy emergency department, there are many demands on their time. Each varies in the amount of training they have had in child development or in their experience and interest in working with children under stress. The nurse and the technician have tried their best to support and comfort Daniel, know the child life specialist and are likely to respond to his recommendations. However, the child life specialist must form a quick alliance with the doctor who is frustrated with the child's protracted distress and difficult IV access. Like the others, this doctor has tried his best with very good intentions. However, he is not only sleep-deprived and tired, but also discouraged that his usual efficient skill is not meeting with more success. Like all involved, he has other emergency situations to which he must attend. Also, the physician is not familiar with the skills that the child life specialist has to offer, and may prefer adult patients who do not have the presence of an intermediary, such as a parent, watching over interactions or skills.

Staff members working with Jason vary in their comfort level in interacting with siblings when a patient is dying. Some have strong feelings about including all members of the family; others are more reticent. Some staff members believe that parents should make an informed decision about the ways of including siblings while some believe that parents should not be "pushed". The child life specialist will collaborate with Jason's social worker and bedside nurse as she learns from and processes options with his parents. She will also learn if a member of the clergy is involved.

Gathering Information

In addition to collaboration with members of the health care team, it is important that the child life specialist gather information that is relevant to the circumstances. This information ideally will guide the content of the care that will follow.

Accurate information about sensory information, sequence of events, and the timing and duration of procedures is important for several reasons. By conveying appropriate aspects of what might otherwise be foreign and therefore frightening, child life specialists help children and families become familiar with what would otherwise be unknown, thereby decreasing distress and positively influencing their primary appraisal. Information helps in predicting potential stress points. Plans that are appropriate to the event, to the child and family, and to the staff involved can be made based on the information that has been gathered.

Whenever possible, the child life specialist should gather information about what the child and family already understand and expect. This information about individual variables is a crucial component of providing care.

The child life specialist working in the specialty clinic has learned through experience and teamwork with the surgeon about the impending sequence of events and the environment in which they will take place. However, it is impossible to predict who will provide Ana's anesthesia care; that information can be gathered on the day of surgery. Thus, most, but not all, of the impending events can be helped to be predictable.

In the emergency room, the child life specialist has little time to learn about Daniel's history or about the preferences of the resident attempting to start the IV. Most pressing questions include learning if any specific coping strategies have been introduced, and if Daniel's father and the team are amenable to supporting Daniel in other ways.

For Jason's siblings, the child life specialist needs to gather more information about the parents' perception of Jason's siblings' understanding of the current situation, what in fact the children have been told about Jason's illness, as well as learning more about the parents' desires for attention and support to for the children at home. She needs to learn from the social worker and the nurse what has already been discussed with Jason's parents. She needs to learn more from the medical team about their predictions about the course of Jason's illness. Last but not least, she must ask questions to assess the parents' current emotional ability to consider options and approaches to involving Jason's brothers at this time.

Assessing the Demands of the Situation

In health care settings or any other context in which child life specialists practice, there are challenges to child and family coping that are inherent in the situation. Experience in a given work setting helps highlight these potential stress points. A useful question may be, "Which components of this experience are likely to tax or exceed any child or family's coping resources?" (See Table 1: Examples of Situational Stressors).

Some of these stressors may be unavoidable, while others can be influenced by either case or class advocacy (see Thompson & Stanford, 1985, for a discussion of this). The sterile fields, technical equipment, medical supplies and bright lighting that may be required to ensure a safe and efficient procedure may be overwhelming for any child (or adult for that matter) and may be intensified

Table 1
EXAMPLES OF SITUATIONAL STRESSORS

- Separation from familiar caregivers
- Unfamiliar environment
- Unfamiliar caregiving routines, even if not frankly painful
- Painful and invasive procedures
- The need to stay still for an extended period of time or during a challenging point in care
- New diagnosis
- Life-threatening illness
- Transition points in chronic conditions (e.g., first hospital admission for a child with a chronic illness that has been managed at home; new need for assistive devices for mobility; need for stronger medications)
- Simultaneous or rapidly occurring contact with numerous unfamiliar adults
- Transitions to new settings (e.g., placement in foster care, transfer to a different unit within the hospital or to a rehabilitation setting)
- Altered physical appearance or ability to function
- Exposure of private body parts
- Waiting times
- Lack of privacy
- Isolation
- Dealing with the unknown
- Conflicting or unclear information about diagnosis, prognosis or care
- Change in treatment plans or discharge date if hospitalized
- Loss

for children and families who are already stressed and fearful. They may be particularly difficult for children with preexisting sensory sensitivities. It may be difficult if not impossible to alter these necessary conditions.

In any setting, and particularly with young children, restraint may be necessary during many procedures. However, positions and techniques that are both more comfortable and also more comforting may alter the otherwise unavoidable stress of being overwhelmed and feeling helpless. See Stephens, Barkey, & Hall (1999) for useful alternatives to traditional methods of restraint in these situations.

Particularly in teaching hospitals, the situational stressors may include being surrounded by a number of strangers in a setting that is strikingly unfamiliar and intimidating. Most children or adults surrounded by strangers who are talking, perhaps about them but not to them, or about entirely unrelated topics, would find the situation intimidating and demanding of coping resources. A child life specialist might work to modify the environment or caregiving protocol for a child who is uniquely and outstandingly overwhelmed (e.g., requesting a limited number of caregivers for a child with previous traumatic experience in a similar situation who remembers that "being surrounded" was one of the worst parts of that past difficult experience; collaborating with the caregiving team to be specific and conscious of what is being spoken when a child has a visual impairment and is unusually sensitive to sound). If it becomes evident that most, if not all, children and families share a certain stressor, the child life specialist might collaborate with the team to alter some aspect of caregiving (e.g., allowing children to keep underwear on until anesthesia has taken effect). Perhaps the most challenging situation to address through class advocacy is the presence of parents during procedures when staff may fear that parent parents will lose control. This condition, as well as those described above, is potentially modifiable. However, without effort and planning, these challenges will remain.

As would any child having this procedure, Ana will be waiting in a surgical setting. She will encounter many stressors that are predictable and universal for children having this surgery. For example, she will meet many people wearing surgical scrubs, caps and masks. She will need to wear a hospital gown. She will be hungry. She may have to wait for a while in the presurgical waiting area or in the "holding room" outside the operating room. She is likely to have multiple people checking her vital signs. Ana may have a premedication to drink. She and a parent will go to the operating room where they will find themselves surrounded by more people, strange furniture and a great deal of surgical supplies on shelves. She may receive her induction by mask, by IV, or even by injection, a decision that will be made by the anesthesiologist on the day of surgery. When she wakes up, she will be receiving oxygen and humidified air by facial mask. Ana will have an incision with staples or stitches, an IV, a Foley catheter, several other drainage tubes, and possibly an epidural catheter for pain control. All of these will require examination and care from both physicians and nurses. She may

go home with one or several tubes. Thus, Ana, like all children having this procedure, will have to deal with an unfamiliar environment and a rapid sequence of contacts with numerous unfamiliar caregivers, unfamiliar caregiving routines, painful and invasive procedures, and postoperative care in which private parts of her body may be exposed.

Daniel is surrounded by unfamiliar adults who are giving him suggestions and instructions. They are pinning Daniel down, despite his ardent struggles. The room is filled with all sorts of equipment. He is experiencing the pain of the needle. He will be required to keep the IV in place as well as to wear oxygen and monitoring equipment. The unpredicted need for hospital care, unfamiliar environment, multitude of staff, visible array of unfamiliar medical equipment, the need to stay still, and, last but not least, pain are among the many situational stressors for Daniel.

Neither Jason's family nor physicians predicted the sudden worsening of his illness. The intensive care unit staff and setting are all unfamiliar. Fear and anguish about Jason's illness have made it hard for them to attend to any other facet of life. Jason's appearance has changed due to medications and to the difficulties that his body is having with basic functions. Visitors to Jason's bedside see not only Jason, but also neighboring patients on ventilators who may be attached to a great deal of monitoring equipment, a variety of IV tubing and pumps, and with a range of other drainage tubes and orthopedic devices. They hear the sounds of monitors and numerous alarms. The bedside is crowded with equipment and people and there is little room to move. Thus, while needing to make decisions with the high likelihood of life-long impact for all involved, Jason's family must also contend with the situational stressors of the unfamiliar and emotionally-charged environment, unfamiliar caregivers and caregiving routines, the ambiguity of dealing with the unknown, Jason's changed appearance, Jason's life-threatening illness and his changed prognosis, and the likelihood of his death.

Assessing Individual Child and Family Variables

Each child and family brings strengths and potential vulnerabilities to challenging situations (See Table 2: Examples of Child and Family Strengths and Vulnerabilities). Thus, we consider the situational variables as they intersect with the individual variables. Developmentally, physically, temperamentally and spiritually, what capacities do the child and family have to interact with the environment? How do the challenges of the situation interface with the normally occurring developmental challenges of each stage? Has a past difficult experience sensitized this child and family to the current experience? Questions such as this lead the child life specialist to predict stress points, as well as to prioritize care in a busy work environment.

Ana, at age four, is bound by egocentric thought. She is likely to perceive pain and illness as punishments for something that she has thought or done. Her preoperational cognitive abilities will impact upon the quantity of information that she can keep in sequence. Because of concrete thinking, syringes used for IV medications may evoke distress as she may associate syringes with injections and thus with pain. She is likely to be engaged in the struggle that Erikson characterized as "Initiative vs. Guilt." At this stage, the powerful urges to master bodily functions and activities of daily life with independence make the need to be passive in response to care a particular challenge. It is developmentally predictable that she has questions, curiosity, concerns and awareness regarding genitalia; the Foley catheter and its care and the alteration in her ability to urinate may

arouse age-specific anxieties. It is likely that she makes use of fantasy, particularly to make sense of the unknown, and that she has difficulty distinguishing fantasy from reality. Past frightening and painful procedures have raised her fear and distrust of health care professionals. Her mother is attentive and thoughtful, but unsure of herself in the hospital setting. Ana's mother reports feeling "haunted" by subjecting her daughter to the highly distressing VCUG. Her mother states that Ana is a very active child, and that she is concerned about how Ana will tolerate the sedentary time after surgery. The child life specialist is aware that there are many potentially overwhelming components for this child having this procedure at this point in her life. Despite advance notice about the surgery, the need to work through past experience and to accommodate Ana's cognitive capacities and anxiety when addressing health care issues place constraints on the number of issues that can be addressed in a single play session. Given that surgery is several weeks away, the child life specialist must assess what issues can be addressed at what time.

At age seven, Daniel is likely to still make use of fantasy to fill in gaps in his understanding of events; however, he should be able to distinguish fantasy from reality. Mastering challenges successfully contributes to the sense of "Industry vs. Inferiority." The child life specialist is concerned that Daniel will interpret his overt distress as a public display of his weakness and that he will imagine that his peers would have handled it better than he did. He is at an age where many children do not like to address feelings directly and may be concerned with what is "fair." Daniel has received his primary care in a busy clinic where he has not formed any alliance with health care professionals. Thus, they are easily seen as "bad guys." His peers at home and at school would value "fighting the bad guys" and tales of bravado in persisting in a fight. The child life specialist has no way of knowing at this time that Daniel is struggling with school and beginning to compare himself unfavorably to peers. His teacher is concerned about his language skills and he has a poorer than average ability to use language to interact with others. The current situation may contribute to his sense of frustration in communicating effectively with others. While present and doing his best to modify his son's behavior, Daniel's father is primarily punitive in his style of making recommendations. The child life specialist assesses that Daniel's father could be assisted to have a more active role in comforting Daniel and in engaging Daniel in coping behaviors, but that he may feel uncomfortable doing so in the presence of hospital staff. The child life specialist is concerned about the memories that Daniel will carry into the future, particularly given the chronic nature of respiratory problems for many children. He is also aware that in Daniel's current emotional state it will be a significant challenge to engage him in new behaviors to facilitate efficient conclusion of the procedure.

Deeply religious, Jason's parents have told his brothers to pray for Jason. Jason's parents are praying for a miracle and believe hospital staff to be too pessimistic about Jason's prognosis. Thus, they have not wanted to tell Jason's brothers that doctors think that Jason probably will not survive. The child life specialist is wondering about what the boys are imagining as well as what they are overhearing from phone calls, in the conversations of the adults caring for them, as well as from their friends from school and church. She wonders if they are alone with their fears and fantasies. In addition, the child life specialist is concerned about the long-range implications for a family about keeping difficult things secret. Were Jason's brothers to visit, stress points for them likely would include seeing the changes in Jason, Jason's inability to respond, the amount of equipment they would see, knowing what to do during a

visit in that context, and dealing with the lasting memories of seeing Jason in that condition. Both boys may have guilt that they haven't prayed hard enough or often enough, or have feelings about their prayers being unanswered. In addition, an eight year old may fear "catching" something terrible and that something he did caused Jason to get so sick. A young adolescent may have thoughts and feelings about being watched or judged. There are many individual child and family variables. All involved have never faced the death of someone so young in their family. While in general they have had supportive relationships with previous health care professionals, they barely know the staff in intensive care. Their extended family and clergy are involved but as they live quite a distance away, they are minimally present. They are articulate and communicate well with those who enter their world. For Jason's parents, specific stress points are likely to include introducing the subject of how very sick Jason is, and ways of answering their boys' questions. If the parents elect for the brothers not to visit, stressors for the boys are likely to include feelings related to being excluded, the lack of opportunity to say goodbye, and fantasies of Jason being in pain or receiving adequate care.

Using Assessment of Needs to Determine the Focus of Care

All of the above factors converge into the child life specialist's assessment of what needs to be offered to each child and family. It can be difficult for the child life specialist to balance ideal care with what is realistic and possible. A reality of most child life roles is that there are numerous simultaneous demands on a child life specialist's time. Ultimately, the task is to sort through the multiple variables and address the most pressing priorities. One might ask, "Given the demands of the events and the constella-

Table 2
EXAMPLES OF CHILD AND FAMILY STRENGTHS AND VULNERABILITIES

- The child and family's degree of familiarity with and trust in staff
- Past experience with similar situations
- The child's general ability to cope with previous stressors
- The child's cognitive and developmental capacities
- Issues related to temperament and resilience
- Self-esteem
- Current physical status
- Current emotional state
- Sensitivity to pain
- Familial, social and spiritual support
- Cultural beliefs that impact upon the situation at hand
- General beliefs about healthcare providers and hospitals (or, in other settings, beliefs about the legal or welfare system, for example)
- Goodness of "fit" with the interactional style of staff
- Distance from home, with the associated impact on ability of significant people to visit, increased cost for travel and meals, and other associated stressors
- Parental ability to cope with stress.

tion of variables that the child and family bring, what components can be influenced so that the child and family will have as good a memory or experience as possible?" and "If there can be but a few goals, what would the priority goals include?"

Because Ana has had a past difficult experience and is at an age that makes her particularly vulnerable to the impending surgery, and because this surgery would pose challenges to coping in any child, she is a high priority to the child life specialist. The child life specialist will discuss with Ana's mother the possibility of an additional play session to provide preparation in a manner that Ana can accommodate given her age and attention span and her tendency to become easily distressed. The child life specialist will introduce play that the mother can continue at home. In this way, they may have the opportunity to begin to "play through" past experience. Separate play sessions will address the experiences that Ana will encounter with presurgical testing and on the day of surgery.

For Daniel, the child life specialist decides to intervene in the treatment room and focus on "things to make this easier" for Daniel as well as for his father and for the doctor and others involved. The child life specialist will make a point of framing the roles of the emergency department staff as "to do things in the way that is the fastest and easiest for children" and explore any possible avenues for forming alliances, even under these highly charged conditions. He will engage Daniel's father in specific roles of providing comfort as much as he is able. If time and Daniel's condition permit, he will also provide post-procedural play to address Daniel's perceptions, particularly the impact of the experience on Daniel's self-concept, and to plan "what will make it easier" if Daniel ever needs this kind of medicine again.

Discussing options for and ways of including his brothers, as well as sharing information about the potential effects of not including them, may help Jason's parents to begin to open doors for their increased presence. Included among the goals is for the child life specialist to suggest phrases "that other families have found helpful" that will indicate that Jason is gravely ill but will still allow for a measure of hope, enabling more honest communication among family members and inclusion of Jason's brothers in a way that will have the most positive outcome and the least traumatizing memory. The child life specialist will facilitate this process along with the social worker and Jason's bedside nurse. Clergy may be involved, as well.

PROVIDING PREPARATION WITH PLANNED COPING

Once a child and family's needs for preparation have been assessed, the task of the child life specialist is to provide information that will make events seem as predictable as possible, and realistically influence children and families' appraisal that they have adequate coping resources to manage the impending events. Simultaneously, it is ideal to plan and actually rehearse ways to cope with the anticipated stressors. This active rehearsal is at the heart of psychological preparation. The goal of this process is to influence the child and family's appraisals of their ability to manage the situation. Under ideal circumstances, practice assists coping behaviors to become vivid, familiar and accessible in advance of the situation. In order to engage in these behaviors, many children and families need coaching during the actual procedure.

Providing Information and Influencing Appraisal

As described earlier, thoughtfully presented information can influence children's and families' primary appraisal of their ability to manage impending events. The goal is to help make an otherwise unknown situation seem familiar and predictable, and for all involved to make the assessment ("appraisal") that, even if challenging at times, the event indeed will be manageable. Information can also help identify "the parts for which we should practice."

Certainly, the need for information varies based on numerous factors. For example, the need for information differs if we are interacting with children before, during or after an event. Developmental capabilities, such as expressive and receptive language and the ability to sequence information, influence the style of the interaction. Additionally, coping styles lead some children to want to gather information in advance, while the same amount of information may raise the distress of another child. Thus, quantity and style of information should be individualized to match the individual variables of each child.

Before an unfamiliar event, it is useful to help make *sensory experiences* and *sequence of events* predictable. Information should include sights, sounds, odors, tastes and tactile sensations that the child will consciously experience. Whenever possible, the child life specialist can compare these with similar situations that the child has already mastered.

As soon as young children have the cognitive and motor capacities to imitate routine tasks (around fourteen months of age in typically developing children) it is useful to actively expose them to play that familiarizes them with upcoming events. For children who are cognitively capable but have temporary or permanent challenges with motor skills, this play can be offered vicariously on their behalf. Even younger infants can explore and become familiarized with equipment and hospital garb and can play games such as peek-a-boo if separations will be involved. Indeed, for very young children for whom anxiety in unfamiliar situations and in the presence of unusual strangers is a predictable stress point, components of psychological preparation with planned and rehearsed coping can be included in interactions designed to familiarize and promote coping in the presence of these "foreigners" and foreign elements.

A child or family with past experience in a setting may have a lesser need for additional information. However, they may have a greater need to talk or play through what has happened in the past and to interpret past experiences. Moreover, the information they have about past experiences may be useful, helping them to understand the parts they can master or control, as well as the parts that might be done differently in the future. Play or discussion may also reveal fantasies and misperceptions that need to be addressed. Indeed, the balance of the information exchange should be what we learn from children and families rather than what we teach them.

There may be little time for exchanging information when intervening in the midst of a challenging circumstance or crisis. Most useful will be questions geared to assess the parts of the experience that are hardest for the child and family at that particular moment, and information about effective strategies to apply immediately.

During play about the VCUG, the child life specialist will want to learn what Ana remembers the most, what was hardest for her, and why she thought it happened (particularly searching for the fantasy and egocentric thinking common for children Ana's age). She will also be attentive to the language Ana uses to describe her experience. The child life specialist says that they will "play about things" so there should be few difficult surprises. Interventions will emphasize how this is different than before. They will play about waiting in the small room, answering questions, blood pressure and temperature like in her doctor's office,

changing into hospital pajamas and getting medicine so that she won't feel her operation.

The child life specialist asks Daniel what parts are hardest for him. He says the needles, and everybody holding him down. The child life specialist asks Daniel to draw a picture showing a boy having an IV started. The child life specialist notes that the size of Daniel's representation of the needle is larger than the entire child in the drawing. In the little time remaining, the child life specialist hopes to address both appraisal and planning for future similar situations. Time is limited, and all may not be possible. At first they explore what it's like to be a child feeling a needle, and they also compare together the size of a real needle and the tip of a pen. They wonder together which is the tiniest and joke about whether anyone could even be able to read it if someone wrote his name with the point of the needle. Next the child life specialist asks Daniel and his father if they want to learn things that many children have said make the part with the needle easier. He also asks Daniel which way he thinks it will go more quickly: if he is moving, or if he is very still. Suspecting that Daniel still will need help holding still, they quickly explore Daniel's preferences for where people should stand while helping his arm to be very still. He asks Daniel's father what he thinks is the most helpful. The child life specialist lets the doctor know that these things should make it easier for everyone.

With Jason's family, the child life specialist uses questions to explore the advantages and disadvantages of a visit and of conveying the severity of his illness. Examples of the questions include: What do you think your boys are imagining? How do you think it will be for them if they are not included? What are you most worried about if they were to see Jason now? Are you interested in hearing some ways that families have talked about difficult times in a manner that still leaves room for hope? Her goal is not to convince, but to help make things as manageable as possible for all, given the difficult circumstances.

Attention to Language

As we provide information to children and families, the language that we choose can significantly influence appraisal. The language used in play and discussion is also likely to become the language used to recall the event. Confusing terms and jargon abound in a health care setting. Words that are unfamiliar (e.g., vital signs, VCUG, catheter), that sound like other familiar words (e.g., dye vs. die, PICU vs. "pick you"), that are harsh (e.g., medicine that will burn or sting, "shoot" an x-ray) and that have more familiar meanings (e.g., "stool" collection; lie on the "table"; "broken" arm; send you to the "floor") may increase confusion and raise anxiety. Conversely, familiar and "soft" terms may positively influence children's and families' primary appraisal of the situation. This has been described in greater detail by Gaynard, Wolfer, Goldberger, Thompson, Redburn and Laidley (1990). The goal in selecting language is to account for a child's developmental level, incorporate familiar terms, make choices that are "the softest language that is honest," and to be aware of unfamiliar terms that the child is likely to overhear.

In processing her experience with the VCUG, the child life specialist talks about the place in Ana's body where her "pee" (Ana's family word) comes out and the tiny tube to help the "x-ray medicine" go in. While playing about surgery, the child life specialist uses terms such as "'medicine sleep' that makes it so that your body won't feel anything" for the state of being under anesthesia; "tiny opening" for incision; "medicine water" for IV fluids; "tiny tubes

to help her pee come out while her body rests" for the stents and suprapubic tubes; and "very sore at first, then better and better each day" to refer to the postoperative pain.

In the Emergency Department, the child life specialist remarks that it is sort of odd that people in hospitals sometimes call beds "tables" He is careful to refer to the IV catheter as the "tiny tube," the Betadine as "brown soap," and the armboard as a sort of hand-holder.

Jason's family seems comfortable with phrases such as "the nurses and doctors are using everything they know, but still Jason's body is very, very sick" and we are "very worried" as bridges to talking about the severity of his illness. The child life specialist asks the parents how they think it would be for the boys to keep their worries to themselves. The parents are encouraged to ask Jason's brothers what things they are thinking and worrying about the most, and the child life specialist explores with Jason's parents their concerns about opening up that topic. Together they rehearse some possible responses. They are assured that the child life specialist, social worker, chaplain, nurse or physician, alone or in combination, could be present to help them with this discussion if they would like. They are given recommendations for terms for what the boys would see at the bedside, such as "a machine to breathe for Jason," "tubes called IVs for medicines, blood tests and food", "different beeping sounds from machines that help the nurses and doctors know when he needs more medicine or if other things need help" and "other machines that make pictures of his heart beating and his breathing."

Tools that Facilitate Preparation

Tangible tools can assist in the task of conveying information about sensory experience and sequence of events. Photographs, dolls and actual or pretend medical equipment can enhance the degree to which an unfamiliar situation is made more predictable.

It is ideal to have a range of materials for use in preparation. Child life specialists often choose dolls and puppets to enable children and families to form a concept of a sequence of events as well as to rehearse coping behaviors. Photo albums and videotapes can be used to help make an unfamiliar setting or experience become recognizable. Audiotapes and videotapes can be used to acquaint people with unfamiliar and potentially overwhelming sounds. The most direct means of becoming familiar with aromas and manageable physical sensations such as cool alcohol wipes or bandages is to use the actual equipment. Real equipment that is proportionate to the size of a doll used in the preparation is also ideal for making health care equipment familiar.

Choosing and Using Dolls and Puppets

Vinyl dolls with appropriate anatomic features are typically most useful for play about health care with toddlers and very young preschool children. For play in preparation for broader issues, like separation from families or moving to a new location, figures of people or animals or anything that can be grouped as having the characteristics of a family can be used (mommy, daddy, baby, grandmother, etc.). For purposes of prevention of the spread of infectious disease, cloth dolls and stuffed animals are not safe to be shared among children. Blank cloth dolls, as described by Gaynard, Goldberger and Laidley (1991), are ideal for preparing children for health care procedures, as they allow the use of real needles and can be used to rehearse positions that the child will need to assume. Additionally,

children can keep these dolls, which permits repeated play and rehearsal as the child desires. The dolls can be used as puppets in the sense that they become a vehicle through which the child speaks. The child's own stuffed animals may be vested with emotional meaning, so may not be the best choice for medical play, particularly if preparation may affect the appearance of the stuffed animal. Using blank cloth dolls avoids altering or unnecessarily "hurting" something that already seems real to the child.

Puppets and puppet shows have long been used in preparation. Children will often express thoughts and feelings through puppets that they might not express directly. Puppets can be helpful in guiding children to use new coping strategies. Puppet shows, in which children are passive recipients of information, may not be as useful for preparation as the more active participation involved in using dolls for dramatic health care play. Scripted puppet shows for groups of children cannot be individualized for past or upcoming individual experiences.

Blank cloth dolls will be used with each of these children. They will be used for Ana to describe her past experience as well as to prepare for the upcoming surgery. Her mother can support Ana through this play at home, monitoring and addressing feelings and misperceptions as they arise. Daniel will be offered a "hospital doll" to work through his thoughts and feelings after the IV is placed, and to rehearse what would help if he is ever in that situation again. Alternatively, puppets would be useful and appropriate tools for Daniel to put words to his experience. If their parents elect to further involve Jason's siblings, they will be provided with a blank cloth doll to which they can be guided to attach all the equipment that they will see. Jason's teenage brother may just watch or may chose to help his younger brother.

Using Photographs and Videotapes

Visual materials can be invaluable in helping children and families gain a sense of what an otherwise unfamiliar setting will be like, and can help to convey vividly a sequence of events. Photographs should be clear and vivid, and one should consider carefully the following when using them:

* the amount of detail to show in each photograph without being overwhelming
* that the child is adequately covered
* that the affect displayed by the child and staff is appropriate
* the perspective of the camera
* the diversity in age, gender and race within a given album, if children and parents are used as models
* the diversity of staff, if they are included in photographs
* that the most likely stress points are represented so that photographs can be used as reminders of planning and rehearsing coping strategies
* that written text is minimal, so that the child life specialist is not bound by it, but rather adapts what is conveyed to individual developmental age, emotional needs and past experience of the child and family involved.

In general, carefully chosen photographs are a valuable tool. They can be particularly useful when child life specialists and other staff don't speak the same language as a child and family. Translators can assist in writing the appropriate text.

Child life specialists should consider carefully whether or not their population will be best served with photographs arranged in a photo album, or individually mounted. Many photo albums are developed with text and page decorations that are designed to appeal to a specific age group, which invariably limits their appeal for children other developmental ages. Texts often are too wordy for any but the most patient of children.

Additionally, photo albums in the hands of anyone without sufficient training may become a tool for didactic teaching or simply reading, rather than an interactive tool that emphasizes planning and rehearsing coping strategies and eliciting individual children's fears, fantasies and misconceptions. Single photos mounted with simple phrasing may help avoid that. An example might be: "Here is a picture of the operating room. Do the people look friendly? This girl wanted to sing her favorite song while she's in this room. Other kids want to look at a picture while they're falling asleep. What would you like to do?"

Videotapes can also be used to acquaint a child and family with a setting. They offer a realistic view of another child in that setting, yet they have limitations. For example, in using filmed modeling, the procedure and events must closely resemble the situation that the child will encounter, and the model must be one to whom individual children can perceive as being like themselves. Thus, a filmed videotape used in preparation for surgery would need to account for the many individual variables such as mask or IV induction of anesthesia, outpatient and inpatient recovery, and postoperative experience such as the presence or absence of incisions and drainage tubes. Staff members need to be attentive to the use of videotapes and ensure that discussion and rehearsal of coping strategies are included for each child and family.

Photographs will be available for Ana and her mother including the presurgical waiting area, doctors and nurses in surgical scrubs, the "bed on wheels" that children ride on the way to their surgery, the lights on the ceiling that they will see as they ride down the hallway, the "holding area" outside the operating room, and the actual operating room. If Ana's attention span is limited, the child life specialist may choose to use just a few, such as the waiting area, the staff in scrubs, and the operating room.

Daniel's own images are important after his ordeal. The child life specialist asks Daniel to draw a picture of what it was like for him while he was getting his IV.

Intensive care unit staff has available clear photographs of equipment. In addition, photographs of Jason taken with a digital camera are offered to Jason's parents to help his brothers be ready to see how he currently looks and to know what they will see at his bedside. If they choose to visit, additional pictures will be taken of them to keep at Jason's bedside. Finally, pictures of each of them with Jason will be taken to help them process and hold on to this important memory.

Real Equipment versus Facsimiles

In order to become familiar with, or play through, a potentially overwhelming situation, children and parents are helped if they actively acquaint themselves in advance with the unfamiliar equipment that they will consciously experience. As with all other components of the process of psychological preparation, the use of equipment is intended for familiarization, active rehearsal of coping strategies, and appraisal of the situation as manageable. They do not need to see or handle equipment that they won't feel or see.

Whenever possible, equipment chosen should be in proportion to their doll. It is more important that the equipment facilitate the perception for the child that "I can han-

dle that!" than the equipment be technically accurate. A neonatal nasogastric tube might make a better doll Foley catheter than might an actual Foley catheter, which would be very large in proportion to the doll. Tubing cut from tiny butterfly sets can portray postoperative drainage tubes.

Particularly useful and intriguing for children is the use of "doll medicine" for doll IVs. This can be made by withdrawing half the fluid from a bottle of normal saline or sterile water for injection and replacing it with food coloring. This is useful not only for conveying the image of having a number of medicines from which to choose, but also for the members of the health care team to quickly and easily differentiate the doll IV from the child's actual IV.

With children for whom any actual equipment is too threatening, commercial toy equipment can be used to help play through the impending events. Again, the focus is on finding tools that will enable the events to be predictable and to plan and rehearse coping strategies.

A tiny neonatal nasogastric tube serves as a catheter for Ana to use when playing about the VCUG. A real stethoscope and neonatal blood pressure cuff are used to "admit" her doll to the presurgical area. A neonatal anesthesia mask is used for her doll, and a child-sized mask is available for Ana and her mother to try. Tubing cut from tiny "butterfly needles" are taped to Ana's doll where her postoperative tubes will be located, and they tape "medicine water" (doll IV) to the dolls arm. If Ana's attention span will allow, they will add "doll medicine" to the doll's IV.

The child life specialist quickly shows Daniel and his father a small (24 gauge) IV catheter, and asks them if they know that the doctor will gently slide the needle out once it is in just the right place.

If Jason's brothers choose to visit, they will place electrodes on a doll for monitoring equipment, an NG tube to keep the doll's stomach empty, an endotracheal tube (cut to be appropriate in size for the doll) to help the doll breathe, and an IV to give him medicines. In this instance, if the brothers visit, the child life specialist will allow the brothers to add numerous "doll medicines" in the IV to convey the message that they are trying everything that they know.

PLANNING AND FACILITATING COPING

While conveying information, as soon as potential stress points have been identified, it is imperative to ensure that children and families have available to them coping strategies that will minimize their distress. Clearly defined coping strategies can influence the child and family's appraisals of their ability to manage impending events. The operant questions to ask in planning care include: *What will make this take the least amount of time? What will make this take longer? What can we influence so that the child and family will take from this challenging situation an enhanced sense of competence?*

When playing through stressful events with children, it is important that the ideal coping behaviors be actively rehearsed. For example, if wiggling during a procedure would increase the need for restraint or sedation or prolong the time of the procedure, then it is crucial to have the child rehearse staying still and plan what she will do if she feels like moving. The child might teach a doll by demonstrating to the doll how to stay still and teach the doll to blow if she feels like wiggling. If an anesthetic cream is going to be used to numb the area of an injection or IV start, it is important to let a child unfamiliar with the concept of numbness learn

through experience what it means so that he or she can come to trust that it will work. Ideally, this should be done in advance, at home, in a familiar or neutral hospital or clinic room, or during a play session. The child could have tiny amounts of cream placed in one or two places and have the opportunity to explore the sites and compare the difference between the pressure which will still be felt and the pain which should no longer be present.

Recognizing Naturally Occurring Coping Styles

When making choices about how much information to include and what kind of coping strategy to select, it is helpful to the clinician to recognize a child's natural preferences. One framework for conceptualizing coping styles has described people as "sensitizers" as compared to "avoiders" (sometimes also referred to as "deniers" or "repressors"). Someone who is classified as a sensitizer may articulate anticipatory anxiety, ask questions, and tend to make emotional or task-oriented plans to deal with stressful situations. Someone with an avoidant style is more likely to engage in efforts to postpone or avoid acknowledging the event for as long as possible. These styles may influence how much information and rehearsal the individual can tolerate. However, even children who prefer to avoid impending events need enough information to orient themselves to the events and rehearse a strategy for the situation that is potentially overwhelming to them. Conversely, "sensitizers" may benefit from planning and rehearsing an alternate focus from that which is overwhelming them (Smith, Ackerson, & Blotky, 1989). There is some evidence that children with a preferred coping style of avoidance are at greater risk for responding with difficulty to medical procedures (Peterson & Toler, 1986; Melamed &

Ridley-Johnson, 1988; Blount, Davis, Powers, & Roberts, 1991). Thus it is important that all children and families are provided both with core reference points that lend order and predictability to the procedure, as well as with a means of support or a strategy that has been rehearsed to "disengage" and shift focus if that becomes desirable.

Coping styles are not rigid; they can change each time a person faces a new stressor, or even the same stressor at a different time. Children may not be able to generalize the use of a previously learned strategy to a new context without support. Coping styles may change over the duration of an illness as children grow developmentally, become more or less secure in the environment, have adjustments in their understanding of the stressor, and develop a coping history and repertoire. Coping styles may also be altered by factors such as exacerbations and progression of medical condition, by changes in psychosocial support, or a wide array of other factors.

> Ana's mother has learned that Ana does best with a little information fairly close in time to the event. She needs some warning and time for questions. However, too much information, or information given too much in advance, seems to raise Ana's distress. Ana's mother must balance this with her personal tendency to gather information and engage in some "anticipatory worry," as well as her desire to protect Ana from difficult stressors. They decide to start using picture books to begin talking about hospitals a week prior to surgery but to postpone more specific preparation until a day or two before the actual surgery.

> Daniel's past history includes distress with even routine medical care. He typically plays vigorously in the waiting area, acts as if nothing is going to happen, then becomes overwhelmed during exams and immunizations. His distress in this unknown

medical situation made it difficult for him to process new information.

> Jason's parents report that their older son typically worries a great deal before exams in school or other stressful situations. His tendency has been to focus on events and ask a great deal of questions, although this diminished as he entered adolescence. Jason's younger brother is reported to be currently more active than usual, and is not asking any questions at all. Although family has believed that this younger brother is "doing fine," as they talk together they realize that his activity is likely a sign that he is avoiding the overwhelming nature of his fears and fantasies. Both boys need some relief along with some information about what is happening and how they can choose to be involved.

Selecting and Rehearsing Coping Strategies

Coping strategies, also referred to as "techniques" or "modalities," are the specific efforts to manage stressful demands (Lazarus & Folkman, 1984). They may be external, observable behaviors or internal processes such as thoughts. As stated above, it is optimal to pair coping strategies with potentially overwhelming events in a timely manner. It is essential that a child life specialist be familiar with a broad range of strategies, but offer a child and family a more focused selection of potential strategies from which to choose, allowing the flexibility to plan different strategies for different parts of the procedure. For example, children may want to focus their attention on an intriguing object during the initial phases of a procedure such as having an IV placed, but count and blow for "the part with the needle." The strategies offered should combine properties that are appropriate for the child's personality, interaction, developmental level, family beliefs and attitudes as well as the situation. Children seem to do best when they have a few solid skills on which to rely (Worchel, Copeland & Barker, 1987).

A summary of coping techniques or strategies, many of which have been discussed in this chapter, appears in Table 3. These strategies are categorized by the predominant modality used in a given approach. Techniques categorized as *sensory* rely on sound, touch, or movement to enhance the child's coping capacities. *Cognitive* approaches include those that help reframe or refocus thoughts from negative to positive, while *behavioral* approaches introduce behaviors that that are compatible with the successful completion of the threatening event. Combined cognitive-behavioral approaches are often among those employed in formal research, as described in the Cochrane Collaboration (Uman, Chambers, McGrath, & Kisely, 2007).

Included among these strategies are some that involve what is commonly referred to as "distraction." Please note that we make a distinction between the standard terminology of "distraction" and the more specific descriptor of "choosing an alternate focus." With the former, there is the implication that the caregiver is active in choosing a device for distracting and in controlling the child's attention while events unfold "behind the child's back." With the latter, more respect is implied about the child's active participation in selecting and implementing the strategy. Additionally, in our communications with other disciplines, one might argue that the phrase "supported a child's use of a planned alternate focus" reflects more skill on the child life specialist's part than does the phrase "provided distraction." Interestingly, the literature about preparation in pediatrics typically includes a host of articles reporting results of "preparation" during which the sole intervention is a tightly controlled form

of distraction. It is not surprising that results of such research are variable and typically only weakly effective. According to our theoretical foundation and orientation, "distraction" is never in and of itself preparation and certainly not what we consider "psychological preparation." The work we do includes far more focus and intention on children's and families' active roles and choices as well as range, flexibility, and skill on the part of the child life specialist.

Although this chapter has focused primarily on medical events, the practice of selecting, planning, and rehearsing coping strategies is more broadly applicable to any context in which child life specialists may work. Many of the techniques identified in Table 1 have been used in the non-pharmacologic management of pain, either alone or in conjunction with pain medication (Brown, 1996). Nevertheless, they may be similarly useful in other stressful circumstances. Just as strategies can be identified and rehearsed for coping with pain or an impending procedure, so, too, can they be applied to other stressors that children face, such as visiting with critically ill relatives, dealing with teasing, confronting the world in a body altered by injury, or facing long term separation from a family member.

For example, when visiting critically ill family members, it may help to anticipate the most difficult parts and rehearse what the child might do or say at the bedside. Children can be helped to plan the songs they will sing or select the artwork they will display. They can be helped to talk about the happy memories they will always have of the person. For children returning to school with an altered body, they can be helped by rehearsing in advance what they will say or do if other children stare, tease or question them. For a child being sent to a new foster care placement, it may be useful to plan with them what they will think and do when con-

Table 3
EXAMPLES OF COPING STRATEGIES FOR PAINFUL PROCEDURES

Sensory *NB: This may function either as an alternate cognitive focus, to provide child's sensory receptors with positive input to counteract the pain, or a combination of both*	Positioning	-Holding, such as on a parent's lap, offers a focus away from the procedure, and facilitates the ease of a procedure -Swaddling , for young infants, to provide physical security
	Movement	- rocking or patting
	Soothing Touch Massage	-coursework recommended in infant massage
	Thermal regulation -hot packs, heating pads, warm blankets -cool cloths, cold packs and ice packs	-positive touch , massage or thermal regulation may also become a cognitive strategy when a child or adolescent is encouraged to focus their attention on the positive feelings
	Music	-music that provides comfort to infants has certain properties, such as steady tempo that is at a similar rate to infant's ideal target heart rate (to hopefully entrain at a physiological level), or that replicates intrauterine experience -parent singing familiar lullaby can be ideal for infants and toddlers -toddlers and older children can choose to sing a song with a parent or other adult -hymns can be particularly comforting for some children -can become an alternate focus (cognitive-behavioral strategy) or method of timing (cognitive strategy) -music for preschool and young school age children may have either soothing or humorous qualities -music that is chosen by older school age children and teens may be disconcerting to adults; headphones should be used
Cognitive	Conscious choice of alternate focus (sometimes called "distraction")	-utilizes cognitive skills to focus attention away from painful or stressful event -may choose to perform a cognitive task such as counting, reciting the alphabet, reviewing spelling words or a vocabulary list

Table 3 – *Continued*

	-may choose to focus attention on another body part; sensory strategy may facilitate this -may choose a humorous task, such as selecting a favorite joke from a joke book or telling silly stories -may be comforted by family anecdotes -may prefer to listen and assign selected adult(s) to tell stories or jokes, or otherwise do the talking -useful visual materials on which to focus include such items as intriguing books, "magic wands," kaleidoscopes -Gameboys, videotapes and other electronic devices useful for older children and teens -virtual reality is a more all-encompassing alternate focus that may tap into sensory and behavioral strategies as well
Thought Stopping Self-Instruction	-Positive, continuous, encouraging self-talk to stop negative thoughts and promote reassurance and self-control -can help if child or teen writes positive statements on an index card
Therapeutic Storytelling	-books, often with metaphoric content (classic example: *The Little Engine That Could*) or offering avenue of emotional escape -individually invented stories with metaphoric content with successful resolution of a similar dilemma
Intellectualization	-scientific knowledge and information seeking to remove the emotion from the procedure -may be child's natural approach to new situations -if provided by staff in service of coping, should have goals of (1) positive impact on appraisal and anticipatory anxiety, (2) formal and concrete link between practice and procedure to impact appraisal of predictability and progression of events, and (3) include not only information about sequence of events, timing and duration, but also what activities and behaviors on the child's part will be most helpful
Reframing	-rethinking past experience perceived as difficult in a new light with attention to thoughts, actions that may have been overlooked but were helpful
Spirituality or prayer	-led by family member or clergy of family's choice -some children and their families have found comfort in singing hymns, reciting psalms and otherwise engaging in prayer

Table 3 – *Continued*

	Humor	-interventions may be facilitated by funny videos, joke books, a Humor Cart, child planning simple practical jokes, or commercial materials such as silly string
	Imagery	-multisensory experience using imagination and as many senses as possible -uses an image that is comforting and brings a sense of security -guided imagery led by a person other than the patient; older children with preexisting experience may use an audiotape; -REQUIRES TRAINING.
	Hypnotherapy	-REQUIRES TRAINING AND SUPERVISON -utilizes patient's imagination skills -may encourage patient to transform or dissociate from painful event -"magic glove" and "pain switch" are two useful strategies
Behavioral	Relaxation Techniques --Blowing --Deep breathing	-controlled breathing, both deep rhythmic and shallow panting, is effective to increase oxygenation and peripheral blood flow. -"blowing the feelings away", "blowing to help your veins be full", or "blowing to help your muscles be loose" also can be useful cognitive focus during procedures -bubbles and party blowers can be useful for younger children -older children can understand the physiological response and do well with coaching; can be compared to using Lamaze for childbirth
	--Muscle relaxation	-rehearse voluntarily tightening then relaxing various muscle groups -may want to focus on tightening then relaxing entire body at once, or focus on specific body parts -for general relaxation, may start at toes and work upwards with "tighten and relax" exercise
	Desensitization	-child maintains adaptive coping behaviors in a stepwise manner increasingly approximating the actual events -may include exposure to actual equipment and locations -can be useful in rehearsing for MRIs, radiation treatments, etc -medical play and art-and-craft activities with medical equipment offer additional opportunities for desensitization

Table 3 – *Continued*

Modeling	-child is shown videotape or photo album of another child mastering the same experience -model must go from a state of similar anxiety to mastery -age, gender and race of model important in having patient relate to model as credible

fronted with unfamiliar routines and with missing their parents at vulnerable times such as bedtime. This may include positive self-talk and may be assisted by pre-recorded audiotapes or pre-selected books with metaphoric themes that enhance comfort and hope for a desired outcome.

Post-Procedural Evaluation

Preparation is not a linear process with a defined beginning, middle and end. Child life specialists engage with children and families at many points in their stressful experiences. We have the opportunity to make a positive impact whether first contact with a child and family is in a treatment room in the midst of a procedure, on the day of surgery after a child has already accumulated pre-surgical diagnostic experiences, in an outpatient clinic at the time of diagnosis, or in any other context in which we work with children. It is important to learn from children and families their perception of what has helped, what has made it harder in the past, what they believe may make things go more easily in the future. Similarly, after we have facilitated the use of new coping strategies, the perceived efficacy of these interventions should be evaluated whenever possible and adjustments made in planning for future similar situations. Post-procedural healthcare play, verbal debriefing and observation all play a role. In this manner we can help children and families to create some distance from past difficult circumstances and sup-

port the appraisal that they will be able to cope effectively in the future.

In play sessions during the post-operative time in the hospital, one of the child life specialist's primary goals was to learn about Ana's assessment of the events, and her self-concept in coping with those events. Post-operatively, Ana was more eager to engage in health care play than she had been prior to surgery. In fact, it was typically the play in which she was most interested.

Although initially her play as "Nurse Ana" was notably directive and included scolding, within days her tone softened and her "nursing care" was essentially nurturing in tone, with lots of reassuring messages to her doll-patient that she was doing the best job that she could do.

When the child life specialist asked directly at different points if she and "Nurse Ana" had told the doll the right things about surgery, if they had left out some things that were important, or if they should have described things differently or used different words, Ana was alternately thoughtful and silly. She replied that there were too many people in the room where she got the medicine to help her sleep, that too many people came into her hospital room, and that people asked too many questions. Later, she said that she was more than "very, very sore" when she woke up. She did not appear to be holding back other responses, but did not offer a lot of other words to give better descriptions to help other dolls or children.

Ana's mother remained interested in taking an active role in assisting with her daughter's adjustment. They decided that her mother would help Ana make a story book about Ana's experience for other children who might need an operation, with advice about what helps the most. Although Ana started that project eagerly, she soon turned to the more novel playroom activities. The child life specialist reassured Ana's mother that this typically is a good sign that a child has mastered the stressful parts and is ready to turn her attention to a more full range of play. She asked Ana's mother to let her know if there were any changes in Ana's coping with the challenges of hospital care and routines.

When her day of discharge approached, the child life specialist made one request of Ana and her mother: Even if they didn't write any of the other pages in between, to write a last page of the story of how Ana would remember her own story of the hospital. Ana said that she had been scared and didn't want to have any operation, but that she was brave and her mommy and her nurse always helped her feel better. She ended by saying that she was going to be a nurse for children when she grows up and take care of real children and their dolls.

Daniel seemed exhausted after his IV was eventually placed. Knowing that his self-concept as a "big boy" may have been vulnerable due to his protracted crying, and that his father may have shared that perspective of how "big boys" should behave, the child life specialist chose for the first post-procedural intervention to compile a list of all specific behaviors in which Daniel had engaged that were brave and that helped make the difficult time go more smoothly. The child life specialist printed out a certificate noting Daniel's bravery, and included on the award that bravery was doing something difficult, even if it a painful or frightening thing to do. Daniel's father seemed apologetic about his son's expressions of distress, but with encouragement he was also able to help supply examples of times that were particularly difficult

during which Daniel did his best. Daniel's father and the child life specialist also remarked about the strength and agility that Daniel used to try to protect himself from the procedure, and ways that these same skills have such positive expression in his typical life, such as in sports and keeping his father on the move.

Daniel was sleepy and irritable, and attempts at learning from him what he did that he thinks made the IV placement easier and what he wished could have helped make different were met with shrugs and indifferent grunts. He did agree to make a quick drawing of what it was like to have the IV placed. He drew himself and others as scribbles but made clear drawings of very large syringes, much larger in scale than the scribble people, but drawn with developmentally appropriate skill and attention to detail. He wanted to tear up the drawing afterwards.

The child life specialist left a note in Daniel's chart regarding his concerns about Daniel's self-concept after the protracted struggles during IV placement. He also left an email for the child life specialist on the unit to which Daniel would be admitted recommending post-procedural play when Daniel was more rested. He suggested discussion and evaluation with both of Daniel's parents about concerns related to school performance and its impact on Daniel's self-concept, and recommended that Daniel's family also be referred to social work to ensure that they were positioned to make the best use of community resources.

Following through with Jason's family proves more difficult, as there are intense and complex immediate short-term outcomes as well as a lifetime of ongoing impact. Jason's parents listened to the child life specialist and social worker about word choices that might open a discussion, and agreed that in the big picture they wanted theirs to be a family in which any topic, even the most difficult, could be discussed.

Their pastor arrived and prayed with them, searching for the right path for Jason's two brothers.

As was the hospital's customary practice, a designated staff member kept in contact with the family for the first weeks following Jason's death and again about 6 weeks and then 6 months later. The family was also invited and came to the hospital's annual memorial service for the children who had died in past years, At several points, the family was asked what gave them comfort and what they wish could have been handled differently. The family reported that they appreciated being respected for their wishes in regards to Jason's final days.

Solnit (1984) notes that a child's "past" or experience serves as preparation for the present and the future. Whether there is careful advance preparation or whether the child was faced with a sudden crisis, the memories become fabric of the child's personality, identity and style of coping with life's stressors for years to come. When we prepare children, we help them not only to master an immediate challenge, but also to bring forth a coherent personality and sense of self into the future.

These became part of that child who went forth every day,
and who now goes, and will always go forth every day.

Walt Whitman

REFERENCES

Alvarez, C. B., & Marcos, A. F. (1997). Psychological treatment of evoked pain and anxiety by invasive medical procedures in paediatric oncology. *Psychology in Spain, 1,* 17-36.

Atkins, D. M. (1987). Evaluation of pediatric preparation program for short-stay surgical patients. *Journal of Pediatric Psychology, 12,* 285-290.

Bandura, A., Grusec, J. E., & Menlove, F. L. (1967). Vicarious extinction of avoidance behavior. *Journal of Personality and Social Psychology, 5,* 16-23.

Bijttebier, P., & Vertommen, H. (1998). The impact of previous experience on children's reactions to venepunctures. *Journal of Health Psychology, 3,* 39-46.

Blount, R. L., Davis, N., Powers, S. W., & Roberts, M. C. (1991). The influence of environmental factors and coping style on children's coping and distress. *Clinical Psychology Review, 11,* 93-116.

Brewer, S., Gleditsch, S. L., Syblik, D., Tietjens, M. E., & Vacik, H. W. (2006). Pediatric anxiety: Child life intervention in day surgery. *Journal of Pediatric Nursing, 21,* 13-22.

Brown, R. T. (1996). Introduction to the special series on pain: Refuting clinical folklore. *Children's Health Care, 25,* 237-251.

Butler, L. D., Symons, B. K., Henderson, S. L., Shortliffe, L. D., & Spiegel, D. (2005). Hypnosis reduces distress and duration of an invasive medical procedure for children. *Pediatrics, 115,* e77-85.

Campbell, L. A., Kirkpatrick, S. E., Berry, C. C., & Lamberti, J. J. (1995). Preparing children with congenital heart disease for cardiac surgery. *Journal of Pediatric Psychology, 20,* 313-328.

Cavender, K., Goff, M. D., Hollon, E. C., & Guzzetta, C. E. (2004). Parents' positioning and distracting children during venipuncture: Effects on children's pain, fear, and distress. *Journal of Holistic Nursing, 22,* 32-56.

Chen, E., Craske, M. G., Katz, E. R. Schwartz, E., & Zeltzer, L. K., (2000). Pain-sensitive temperament: Does it predict procedural distress and response to psychological treatment among children with cancer? *Journal of Pediatric Psychology, 25,* 269-278.

Chen, E., Zeltzer, L. K., Craske, M. G., & Katz, E. R. (1999). Alteration of memory in the reduction of children's distress during repeated aversive medical procedures. *Journal of Consulting and Clinical Psychology, 67,* 481-490.

Chen, E., Zeltzer, L. K., Craske, M. G., & Katz, E. R., (2000). Children's memories for painful cancer treatment procedures: Implications for distress. *Child Development, 71,* 933-947.

Dahlquist, L. M., Gil, K. M., Armstrong, F. D., DeLawyer, D. D., Greene. P., & Wuori, D. (1986). Preparing children for medical examinations: The importance of previous medical experience. *Health Psychology, 5,* 249-259.

DeBellis, M. D., Keshavan, M. S., Clark, D. B., Casey, B. J., Giedd, J. N., Boring, A. M., Frustaci, K., & Ryan, N. D. (1999). Developmental Traumatology Part II: Brain Development. *Biological Psychiatry, 45,* 1271-1284.

Edwinson, M., Arnbjornsson, E., & Ekman, R. (1988). Psychologic preparation program for children undergoing acute appendectomy. *Pediatrics, 82,* 30-36.

Ellerton, M. L., & Merriam, C. (1994). Preparing children and families psychologically for day surgery: An evaluation. *Journal of Advanced Nursing, 19,* 1057-1062.

Ellis, J. A., & Spanos, N. P. (1994). Cognitive-behavioral interventions for children's distress during bone marrow aspirations and lumbar punctures: A critical review. *Journal of Pain and Symptom Management, 9,* 96-108.

Faust, J., & Melamed, B. G. (1984). Influence of arousal, previous experience, and age on surgery preparation of same day of surgery and in-hospital pediatric patients. *Journal of Consulting and Clinical Psychology, 52,* 359-365.

Fivush, R. (1998). Children's recollections of traumatic and nontraumatic events. *Development and Psychopathology, 10,* 699-716.

Gaensbauer, T. J. (1995). Trauma in the preverbal period: Symptoms, memories, and developmental impact. *Psychoanalytic Study of the Child, 50,* 122-149.

Gaensbauer, T. J. (2000). Psychotherapeutic treatment of traumatized infants and toddlers: A case report. *Clinical Child Psychology and Psychiatry, 5,* 1359-1045.

Gaensbauer, T. J. (2002). Representations of trauma in infancy: Clinical and theoretical implications for the understanding of early memory. *Infant Mental Health Journal, 23,* 259-277.

Gaensbauer, T. J. (2004). Telling their stories: Representation and reenactment of traumatic experiences occurring in the first year of life. *Journal of Zero to Three: National Center for Infants, Toddlers, and Families, 24,* 25-31.

Gaensbauer, T., Chatoor, I., Drell, M., Siegel, D., & Zeanah, C. H. (1995). Traumatic loss in a one-year-old girl. *Journal of the American Academy of Child and Adolescent Psychiatry, 34,* 520-528.

Gaynard, L., Goldberger, J., & Laidley, L. (1991). The use of body-outline dolls with hospitalized children and adolescents. *Children's Health Care, 20,* 216-224.

Gaynard, L., Wolfer, J., Goldberger, J., Thompson, R., Redburn, L., & Laidley, L. (1990). *Psychosocial care of children In hosptials: A clinical practice manual from the ACCH child life research project.* Bethesda, MD: ACCH.

Goleman, D. (1995). *Emotional intelligence: Why it can matter more than IQ.* New York: Bantam.

Haimi-Cohen, Y., & Amir, J. (1996). Parental presence during lumbar puncture. *Clinical Pediatrics, 35,* 2-3.

Heffernan, M., & Azarnoff, P. (1971). Factors in reducing children's anxiety about clinic visits. *HSMHA Health Reports, 86,* 1131-1135.

Jay, S. M., Elliott, C. H., Ozolins, M., Olson, R. A., & Pruitt, S. D. (1985). Behavioral management of children's distress during painful medical procedures. *Behavior Research and Therapy, 23,* 513-520.

Jay, S. M., Elliott, C. H., Katz, E., & Siegel, S. E. (1987). Cognitive-behavioral and pharmacologic interventions for children's distress during painful medical procedures. *Journal of Consulting and Clinical Psychology, 55,* 860-865.

Johnson, J. E., Kirchhoff, K. T., & Endress, M. P. (1975). Altering children's distress behavior during orthopedic cast removal. *Nursing Research, 24,* 404-410.

Johnson, P. A., & Stockdale, D. F. (1975). Effects of puppet therapy on palmar sweating of hospitalized children. *Johns Hopkins Medical Journal, 137,* 1-5.

Johnson, R., & Baldwin, D. C. (1968). Relationship of maternal anxiety to the behavior of young children undergoing dental extraction. *Journal of Dental Research, 47,* 801-805.

Johnson, R., & Baldwin, D. C. (1969). Maternal anxiety and child behavior. *Journal of Dentistry for Children, 36,* 13-18.

Johnson, R., & Machen, J. B. (1973). Behavior modification techniques and maternal anxiety. *Journal of Dentistry for Children, 40,* 272-276.

Kain, Z. N., Caldwell-Andrews, A. A., Mayes, L. C., Weinberg, M. E., Wang, S. M., MacLaren, J. E., & Blount, R. L. (2007). Family-centered preparation for surgery improves perioperative outcomes in children. *Anesthesiology, 106,* 65-74.

Kain, Z. N., Caramico, L. A., Mayes, L. C., Genevro, M. H., Bornstein, M. H., & Hofstadter, M. B. (1998). Preoperative preparation programs in children: A comparative examination. *Anesthesia and Analgesia, 87,* 1249-1255.

Kain, Z. N., Mayes, L. C., & Caramico, L. A. (1996). Preoperative preparation in children: A cross-sectional study. *Journal of Clinical Anesthesiology, 8,* 508-514.

Kennedy, C. M., & Riddle, I. I. (1989). The influence of the timing of preparation on the anxiety of preschool children experiencing surgery. *Maternal-Child Nursing Journal, 18,* 117-132.

Lazarus, R. S. (1999). *Stress and emotion: A new synthesis.* New York: Springer.

Lazarus, R. S., & Folkman S. F. (1984). *Stress, appraisal, and coping.* New York: Springer.

Lynch, M. (1994). Preparing children for day surgery. *Children's Health Care, 23,* 75-85.

Machen, J. B., & Johnson, R. (1974). Desensitization, model learning, and the dental behavior of children. *Journal of Dental Research, 53,* 83-87.

Mahajan, L., Wyllie, R., Steffen, R., Kay, M., Kitaoka, G., Dettorre, J., & McCue, K. (1998). The effects of a psychological preparation program on anxiety in children and adolescents undergoing gastrointestinal endoscopy. *Journal of Gastroenterology and Nutrition, 27,* 161-165.

Mansson, M. E., Fredrikzon, B., & Rosberg, B. (1992). Comparison of preparation and narcotic-sedative premedication in children undergoing surgery. *Pediatric Nursing, 18,* 337-342.

Melamed, B. G., Meyer, R., Gee, C., & Soule, L. (1976). The influence of time and type of preparation on children's adjustment to hospitalization. *Journal of Pediatric Psychology, 1,* 31-37.

Melamed, B. G., & Ridley-Johnson, R. (1988). Psychological preparation of families for hospitalization. *Journal of Developmental and Behavioral Pediatrics, 9,* 96-102.

Melamed, B. G., & Siegel, L. J. (1975). Reduction in anxiety in children facing hospitalization and surgery by use of filmed modeling. *Journal of Consulting and Clinical Psychology, 43,* 511-521.

Melnyk, B. M., Alpert-Gillis, L., Feinstein, N. F., Crean, H. F., Johnson, J., Fairbanks, E., Small, L., Rubenstein, J., Slota, M., & Crobo-Richert, B. (2004). Creating opportunities for parent empowerment: Program effects on the mental health/coping outcomes of critically ill young children and their mothers. *Pediatrics, 113,* e597-607.

O'Byrne, K. K., Peterson, L., & Saldana, L. (1997). Survey of pediatric hospitals' preparation programs evidence of the impact of health psychology research. *Health Psychology, 16,* 147-154.

O'Connor-Von, S. (2000). Preparing children for surgery: An integrative research review. *AORN Journal, 71,* 334-343.

Peterson, L., & Shigetomi, C. (1981). The use of coping techniques to minimize anxiety in hospitalized children. *Behavior Therapy, 12,* 1-14.

Peterson, C., & Parsons, B. (2005). Interviewing former 1- and 2-year-olds about medical emergencies 5 years later. *Law and Human Behavior, 29,* 743-754.

Peterson, C., & Rideout, R. (1998). Memory for medical emergencies experienced by 1- and 2-year-olds. *Developmental Psychology, 34,* 1059-1072.

Peterson, L., & Shigetomi, C. (1982). One-year follow-up of elective surgery child patients receiving preoperative preparation. *Journal of Pediatric Psychology, 7,* 43-48.

Peterson, L., & Toler. S. S. (1986). An information seeking disposition in child surgery patients. *Health Psychology, 5,* 343-358.

Phillips, D. A., Watson, A. R., & MacKinlay, D. (1998). Distress and the micturating cystourethrogram: Does preparation help? *Acta Paediatrica, 87,* 175-179.

Piaget, J. (1962). *Play, dreams, and imitation in childhood.* London: Routledge.

Robinson, P. J., & Kobayashi, K. (1991). Development and evaluation of a presurgical preparation program. *Journal of Pediatric Psychology, 16,* 193-212.

Rothschild, B. (2000). *The body remembers: The psychophysiology of trauma and trauma treatment.* New York: Norton.

Rudolph, K. D., Dennig, M. D., & Weisz, J. R. (1995). Determinants and consequences of children's coping in the medical setting: Conceptualization, review, and critique. *Psychological Bulletin, 118*, 328-357.

Saile, H., Burgmeier, R., & Schmidt, L. R. (1988). A meta-analysis of studies on psychological preparation of children facing medical procedures. *Psychology and Health, 2*, 107-132.

Sawtell, R. O., Simon, J. F., & Simeonsson, R. J. (1974). The effects of five preparatory methods upon children behavior during the first dental visit. *Journal of Dentistry for Children, 41*, 367-375.

Siegel, L. J., & Peterson, L. (1980). Stress reduction in young dental patients through coping skills and sensory information. *Journal of Consulting and Clinical Psychology, 48*, 785-787.

Siegel, L. J., & Peterson, L. (1981). Maintenance effects of coping skills and sensory information on young children's responses to repeated dental procedures. *Behavior Therapy, 12*, 530-535.

Skipper, J. K., & Leonard, R. C. (1968). Children, stress, and hospitalization: A field experiment. *Journal of Health and Social Behavior, 9*, 275-287.

Small, L., & Melnyk, B. M. (2006). Early predictors of post-hospital adjustment problems in critically ill young children. *Research in Nursing and Health, 29*, 622-635.

Smith, K. E., Ackerson, J. D., & Blotcky A. D. (1989). Reducing distress during invasive medical procedures: Relating behavioral interventions to preferred coping style pediatric cancer patients. *Journal of Pediatric Psychology, 14* (3), 405 - 419

Solnit, A. J. (1984). Preparing. *Psychoanalytic Study of the Child, 39*, 613-632.

Srivastava, T., Betts, G., Rosenberg, A. R., & Kainer, G. (2001). Perception of fear, distress, and pain by parents of children undergoing a micturating cystourethrogram: A prospective study. *Journal of Paediatric Child Health, 37*, 271-273.

Stephens, B. K., Barkey, M. E., & Hall, H. R. (1999). Techniques to comfort children during stressful procedures. *Advances in Mind-Body Medicine, 15*, 49-60.

Taddio, A., Goldbach, M., Ipp, M., Stevens, B., & Koren, G. (1995). Effect of neonatal circumcision on pain responses during vaccination in boys. *Lancet, 345*, 291-292.

Taddio, A., Katz, J., Ilersich, A. L., & Koren, G. (1997). Effect of neonatal circumcision on pain responses during subsequent routine vaccination. *Lancet, 349*, 599-603.

Taddio, A., Shah, V., & Gilbert-MacLeod, J. K. (2002). Conditioning and hyperalgesia in newborns exposed to repeated heel lances. *JAMA, 288*, 857-861.

Thompson, R. H. (1985). *Psychosocial research on pediatric hospitalization and health care.* Springfield, IL: Charles C Thomas.

Thompson, R. H., & Stanford, G. (1981). *Child life in hospitals: Theory and practice.* Springfield, IL: Charles C Thomas.

Uman, L. S., Chambers, C. T., McGrath, P. J., & Kisely, S. (2006). Psychological interventions for needle-related procedural pain and distress in children and adolescents (Review). *Cochrane Database of Systematic Review.*

Vernon, D. T. A. (1973). Use of modeling to modify children's response to a natural, potentially stressful situation. *Journal of Applied Psychology, 58*, 351-356.

Vernon, D. T. A. (1974). Modeling and birth order in responses to painful stimuli. *Journal of Personality and Social Psychology, 29*, 794-799.

Vernon, D. T. A., Foley, J. M., Sipowitz, R. R., & Schulman, J. L. (1965). *The psychological responses of children to hospitalization and illness.* Springfield, IL: Thomas.

Vernon, D. T. A., & Thompson, R. H. (1993). Research on the effect of experimental interventions on children's behavior after hospitalization: A review and synthesis. *Journal of Developmental and Behavioral Pediatrics, 14*, 36-44.

Visintainer, M. A., & Wolfer, J. A. (1975). Psychological preparation for surgical pediatric patients: The effect on children's and parents' stress responses and adjustment. *Pediatrics, 56*, 187-202.

Whelan, T. A., & Kirkby, R. J. (1998). Advantages for children and their families of psychological preparation for hospitalization and surgery. *Journal of Family Studies, 4*, 35-51.

Wolfer, J., Gaynard, L., Goldberger, J., Laidley, L. N., & Thompson, R. (1988). An experimental evaluation of a model child life program. *Children's Health Care, 16*, 244-254.

Wolfer, J. A., & Visintainer, M. A. (1975). Pediatric surgical patients' and parents' stress responses and adjustment. *Nursing Research, 24,* 244-255.

Wolfer, J. A., & Visintainer, M. A. (1979). Prehospital psychological preparation for tonsillectomy patients: Effects on children's and parents' adjustment. *Pediatrics, 64,* 646-655.

Worchel, F. F., Copeland, D. R., & Barker, D. G. (1987). Control-related coping strategies in pediatric oncology patients. *Journal of Pediatric Psychology, 12,* 25-38.

Yap, J. N. (1988). A critical review of pediatric preoperative preparation procedures: Processes, outcomes, and future directions. *Journal of Applied Developmental Psychology, 9,* 359-389.

Zelikovsky, N., Rodrigue, J. R., Gidycz, C. A., & Davis, M. A. (2000). Cognitive and behavioral interventions help young children cope during a voiding cystourethrogram. *Journal of Pediatric Psychology, 20,* 535-543.

Chapter 10

PROGRAM ADMINISTRATION
AND SUPERVISION

JERRIANN MYERS WILSON AND JANET CROSS

Child life programs offer services in medical settings across several continents. A child life program may consist of one person, multiple individuals, or a staff of more than 40 people. There is no single best way to provide child life services. The goal of this chapter is to look at best practices of child life programs in the United States and Canada for various groupings of child life professionals. One-person programs, self-directed work groups, disease-based program teams, or programs based on a centralized model are all examples of organizational structures for child life practice. Whatever the organization of the program may be, it is important that its structure be in alignment with the overall goals of child life programming – that is, it should contribute to advancing the clinical excellence and quality of services offered to and for pediatric patients and their families across the healthcare system. This chapter discusses program leadership and structure, models for delivering care, staffing issues, supervision, role challenges for child life specialists, clinical advancement systems, issues of professional identity, orientation and training of staff, interns, and volunteers, program account-ability, financial issues, and program development.

PROGRAM MANAGEMENT

Child life leadership models vary widely. The individual or individuals responsible for managing the day-to-day and overall function of child life programs perform under many titles. Designations such as director, manager, supervisor, coordinator, leader, and lead child life specialist are all applicable (Child Life Council, 2003). In this chapter, the term *leader* will be used to designate any of these roles. Titles are organization specific and those used to designate child life leaders in a given healthcare setting should correspond with equivalent levels of management responsibility and supervision in other disciplines. This structure creates a parallel status with other disciplines and thus enables child life to contribute to organizational planning and decision-making.

The majority of child life programs have an identified central leader who is a child life specialist responsible for the administrative aspects and supervision of clinical practice of child life services. However, approximately one-quarter of hospitals have "one-person" child life programs. In these small programs the child life specialist is, of necessity, called upon to assume administrative duties in addition to clinical responsibilities.

Still some programs follow a "self-directed" model of leadership. Self-directed programs have no designated leader and utilize the entire clinical child life team in the management of the department by distributing, and sometimes rotating, administrative duties and responsibilities. There are advantages and disadvantages to the self-directed programs.

The Advantages of This Approach May Include:

- shared responsibility and accountability for administrative tasks, and
- variety in the job role.

The self-directed leadership model works best when the staff is small, when staff members are trained at the highest level of their profession, and when the child life program has a long-standing, proscribed and accepted service delivery.

Disadvantages of Self-Directed Programs May Include:

- the inhibition of relationship development on the management level because of increased numbers of people filling the role,
- a reduction in opportunities to develop management skills because of decreased repetition,
- lessened continuity of vision for the program, and
- decreased intimate knowledge of the evolution of the profession on a comprehensive level.

In some settings, administrative responsibilities for child life programs are shared with leaders of other departments. This may occur where child life specialists are assigned to work with teams in medical units or programs such as hematology/oncology, cardiology, or the emergency department. This is often called reciprocal or matrix management. Under this arrangement, the child life leader must collaborate with other departments to ensure quality service. The child life specialist in the assigned unit reports to the nurse manager or patient care unit manager in addition to having the child life leader as a supervisor. The child life leader may be responsible for making certain that the staff members maintain professional standards while the unit manager supervises the day-to-day work. Some child life leaders are expected to fill a part-time clinical role as part of the requirements of their job description or, in other instances, may substitute for absent staff members.

Roles of child life leaders often consist of general responsibilities determined by the institution. These include developing an environment and culture consistent with organizational mission, vision and values, achieving financial targets in support of business goals, maintaining regulatory agencies requirements, and creating and nourishing effective communication and relationships with all hospital service departments. When Theodore Hesburgh was president of the University of Notre Dame, he is reputed to have said, "The very essence of leadership is that you have to have a vision. It's got to be a vision you articulate clearly and forcefully on every occasion."

Child life leaders are responsible for developing the capability and competence of individuals and teams, and they must promote Child Life Council's *Standards of Clinical Practice* and the *Child Life Competencies*. Additionally, leaders of child life are responsible for working to enhance program integration across the institution, creating new programming areas and opportunities, and providing ongoing education for medical and healthcare professionals as well as students. In 1985, the American Academy of Pediatrics (AAP) issued the first formal position statement concluding that child life services make a difference in pediatric care. Child life leaders should possess the ability to articulate effectively and diplomatically the vision of family-centered care and the need for attention to the unique challenges children and families experience in healthcare settings. Education and advocacy information should be shared both with medical and healthcare processionals and with families consuming our services. "Children in all health-care settings will benefit if these [AAP] recommendations are followed. However, because of cost implications, this expansion is only likely to occur if families as consumers understand the importance of psychosocial support for their children and the child life specialist's ability to provide such support. Great efforts must be undertaken to educate families and healthcare professionals about the role of the child life specialist as an essential member of the child's healthcare team" (Rollins, Bolig & Mahan, 2005, p. 523).

Managing and monitoring customer service and satisfaction, developing and maintaining positive public relations with community agencies, schools and the medical community, and *benchmarking* of the department's programs are also important tasks for child life leaders. Through benchmarking, which is defined as "a continuous systematic process for evaluating the products, services, and work processes of organizations that are recognized as representing best practices for the purpose of organizational improvement" (Spendolini, 1993, p. 2), the child life leader compares ones own programs with those of other exemplary organizations. For example, a child life leader considering institution of an animal-assisted therapy program might survey programs in other hospitals regarding their policies and practices.

Organizational Structure

Just as management of child life services varies widely, so do reporting configurations. Child life programs and their staff members may report to any of a myriad of departments, including hospital administration, nursing, patient and family services, behavioral health, program teams, and individual patient care units (Child Life Council, 2003). Regardless of the hierarchical structure of the organization, the successful development of child life programs relies upon, and is enhanced by, effective collaboration between the child life leaders and their respective administrators. Regularly scheduled, individual meetings with the administrator responsible for oversight of the child life program will be beneficial. Such meetings will help the administrator to understand better the program, to articulate the program's mission and value to boards and executive committees, and to make more informed financial decisions that affect the program. Opportunities for education, program development, and support can result from these face-to-face interactions.

Teamwork across all departments is vital in today's healthcare environment. Both hospital administrators and national regulatory bodies recognize the value of interdisciplinary cooperation. The participation of the child life leader with other professionals on the management level in areas of program development and implementation can accelerate understanding and involvement of child life in overall care of patients and families. This group effort is an indication of excellence in professional and departmental management for the child life service. In addition, alignment with and contribution to the organization goals will be realized.

PROGRAM FUNDAMENTALS

Mission, Vision, and Values

Guiding principles of organizations, institutions, and professions are based on missions, visions, and values. For example, the professional organization for child life professionals, the Child Life Council, has developed mission, vision, and value statements that guide and support the work done by child life specialists (Child Life Council, 1997). The mission statement of the council helps promote success and productivity by describing the overall goals of the profession of child life, as well as the rationale for its existence (e.g., reducing stress among children and their families). The vision statement of the Council describes the tasks that are to be accomplished by the profession (e.g., that child life specialists will continue to provide therapeutic services) and is created and adhered to by members of the group. The values statement delineates the fundamental principles or beliefs of the profession (e.g., that play is essential for children and we are committed to providing opportunities for play). The mission, vision, and values influence our daily work by establishing standards for performance and specifying our operating principles (e.g., the importance of advocacy for the rights of children).

Healthcare institutions in North America are required by the Joint Commission for the Accreditation of Healthcare Organizations (JCAHO) in the United States and the Canadian Council on Health Services Accreditation (CCHSA) in Canada to have a mission statement in place (www.jcaho.org and www.cchsa.ca). Given this, it is essential for individual child life programs to create mission and vision statements, compatible with those of the institution, to define the scope of practice, guide work tasks, set goals, and effect continuous quality improvement. Policy and procedure manuals, maintained by individual child life programs, should contain the statements of mission, vision, values, and operating principles, as well as a written service plan describing the scope of the program's service (e.g., the range of services available, areas covered, hours of service, and special programs that are offered). This manual is an important tool in the promotion and development of the program.

Program Operating Principles

Policies, procedures, and program guidelines are recommended for most organizations and are mandated for healthcare institutions by the United States and Canadian accrediting agencies. Policies define the *rules* for a program and should always be adhered to without variation. For example, a program may develop policies regarding the use of "R" rated videos or what the role of volunteers is in relation to patients in isolation. Procedures are more specific and provide systematic direction for staff in carrying out tasks (e.g., the washing of toys or a visit by a therapeutic dog). Program guidelines provide more general direction for the operation of units and programs and are often open to interpretation to meet needs of patients, families, and staff. Program guidelines may be developed regarding such topics as sibling visiting or the organization of books and media for patient/family use.

Policies, procedures, and program guidelines are designed to be consistent with the program's mission, vision, values, and operating principles and provide a structure for critical thinking about important child life issues and application to the daily work.

They provide guidance for staff and expectations for performance, thereby promoting a more consistent program. Policies and procedures are helpful to child life specialists in managing day-to-day operations and in advocating for child and family-centered settings and a sensitive psychosocial culture. Policies and procedures also form a basis for communication with external customers. For example, when planning special events with outside groups, policies and guidelines developed by the program provide direction and structure for the visit.

In most cases, the hospital or healthcare agency has established administrative and clinical policies for the institution. The child life program policies are designed to be compatible with, and to complement, those of the institution. Effective policies and procedures are developed for child life programs when patient and family needs, safety issues, program operation, continuous quality improvement efforts, and available resources are analyzed. Typical categories of policies, procedures, and program guidelines include those related to clinical practice, patient care, quality improvement, financial management, safety and infection control, and program administration.

Staffing

Child life staffing must be compatible with the hospital's care delivery model. A care delivery model is a system or structure within a healthcare setting that determines the placement of patients on particular patient units. Although the nature of this system is not typically under the control of child life, one must understand the model in a given institution to distribute scarce resources. For example, inpatient care units may be set up according to ages, acuity levels, and/or diagnoses. Organization of patients by age (e.g., infants, school age, adolescents) or acuity levels (e.g., general care,

intermediate care, intensive care) is not unusual in large pediatric settings. Institutions may also choose to put together some patients by diagnoses. Grouping by diagnoses occurs when all inpatients with similar diseases are placed together (e.g., cardiology, orthopedics) or when inpatient and outpatient facilities are adjacent (e.g., hematology-oncology). Many institutions are expanding their outpatient or day treatment programs and increasing the volume of ambulatory services. This increased use of ambulatory services in hospitals requires thoughtful planning for allocation of child life services. Previously, preparation of children for procedures was performed in inpatient areas. Now many children arrive at the hospital or clinic with no advance preparation and have the potential for their first healthcare encounter to be unanticipated, painful, and negative. The preventive philosophy of child life suggests that child life services be available early in children's experience.

The decisions about where and when to provide child life services are often difficult to make, and the development of plans for targeting child life services where they are most needed is an evolving task for child life leaders and programs. As healthcare changes, it is important to assess periodically the focus of care within institutions. Staffing and scheduling of child life services are dependent upon multiple factors and require constant monitoring and assessment. Four basic factors that should be considered in staffing are needs of patients and families, volume of patients, numbers of child life staff available, and acceptance and understanding of child life service.

The needs of the patient population must be analyzed. Units or areas caring for vulnerable, high-risk populations often take precedence for child life staffing. The children in these settings may have a high emotional acuity or severity level. The child life leader should assess the emotional acuity of the patients and create staffing patterns accordingly. Factors recommended by the Child Life Council that may be considered in this assessment include the following:

- noting concentrations of the most challenging procedures and most vulnerable age groups;
- categorizing the relative severity of illness and amount of time spent interfacing with healthcare setting;
- estimating the degree to which illnesses or treatments are likely to be unexpected or unfamiliar to the child and family, thus leaving them poorly "equipped" and more likely to be overwhelmed or traumatized by events;
- identifying families who will be most helped by additional resources;
- striving for continuity of care; and
- recognizing the priority and mission of the institution. (Child Life Council, 2005)

The volume, or numbers of patients, cared for in different areas is a factor that helps determine how child life staffing decisions are made. Increase or decrease in the need for clinical child life interventions, and increased or decreased use of the playroom by patients are examples of points to consider when creating a staffing plan. The use of day treatment programs and ambulatory services again must be considered.

The number of child life staff, whether it is a one-person program, a small program with clinical leader who does direct service on a part-time basis, or a large program with multiple child life specialists available, obviously impacts the level of staffing a child life program is able to meet. The more staff that is available, the more services can be provided. Prioritization of areas or units to include in coverage must occur.

It is also crucial to consider levels of expertise in staffing and whether a child life

assistant, under the direction of a child life specialist, could expand coverage. Child life specialists must have a minimum of a bachelor's degree, whereas an associate's degree (or a diploma from a community college) in a child development or a related area is required for the child life assistant (Child Life Council, 2002). The assistant traditionally works under the direction of a child life specialist and may manage a playroom or waiting room play area with supervision from the specialist or child life leader. This pairing arrangement allows for extended coverage of child life services at a lower cost, but there must be clear role delineation.

The acceptance and understanding by the medical team of the clinical care child life provides, influence the assignment of staff. The effective, efficient, and appropriate use of child life staff and child life designated areas is an important factor. On a unit where medical, nursing, and auxiliary staffs have embraced the role child life plays, the specialist becomes an invaluable resource. In areas that present challenges with acceptance, child life services may not be as effective and will be more difficult and challenging to deliver.

Child life is beginning to use a variety of alternative staffing patterns to meet demands for increased staffing with the potential of decreasing salary dollars. The child life leader may need to develop a staffing plan based on the hours of service needed, the types of child life skills that will be required, the number of staff positions (full-time equivalents or FTEs) available to accomplish the work, vacation coverage, and the availability of on-call or backup help within the system. It is important to consider the presence of staff to work part-time versus full-time if, for instance, a presurgery unit only needs someone 6 a.m.–1 p.m. The child life leader needs the flexibility to create a position for a staff member to work on two units. For example, it might be possible for a NICU child life specialist to provide backup coverage during daytime hours to an individual trauma or emergency case when regular child life trauma coverage is not available. Child life assistants offer another alternative for extending service. The cost of using assistants is less, but the skill level is different. Child life specialists in one-person programs have the continuing challenge of prioritizing their time among all of the areas that may require their services.

Most often, child life is staffed similarly to social work, chaplaincy, and other psychosocial support departments. They are not on site 24 hours, seven days a week, but may be *on-call* to cover night and weekend hours. Accreditation regulators in the United States are beginning to challenge discharge planners and social workers to adhere to standards giving patients equal access to their services 24 hours a day, seven days a week. Child life may be called upon to respond to this need in the future.

The use of staff available on an on-call basis may also increase the variety of services offered by a program. The nature of the on-call position varies among programs. It may refer to a child life specialist who is available twenty-four hours for any child life responsibility, or one who may be called upon *after hours* for specific purposes, such as bereavement support or preparation for surgery or procedures. When implementing an on-call system, it is important that staff in other departments be fully educated about the nature and operation of the system. The child life leader should also be aware of the potential sacrifices staff members must make when on-call is provided. In making decisions about the use of this additional staffing option, the child life leader must balance the needs of areas that might otherwise go without child life services and the impact of providing those services on child life staff members' satisfaction.

In addition to planning which areas should receive child life coverage, it is important to consider *ratios* of child life staff to patients that will provide safe and effective care. These ratios should provide for day, evening (to the extent needed), weekend, and holiday coverage, and should take into account the average bed occupancy of the areas served. The Child Life Council (2002, 2005) has outlined a number of issues to consider in establishing the staffing ratios. A partial list includes age of patients, diagnosis of patients (e.g., factors of mobility, technology dependence), presence and impact of other caregivers, number of patients usually isolated, and presence of children with long-term, chronic or terminal illness. A unit with infants, technology-dependent patients, or isolated children might necessitate a smaller staff-to-child ratio while a unit that is adolescent or care-by-parents based might tolerate a larger ratio. The American Academy of Pediatrics currently recommends a ratio of one child life specialist to 15–20 inpatient pediatric patients (2005). There are no established ratios for outpatient areas.

There are additional challenges in determining appropriate use of child life staff if there are requests for child life services in alternative settings (e.g., hospice, home care, off-site or satellite clinics) or for the development of new programs within the institution (e.g., serving children of adult patients). The lack of proximity of these locations, in addition to the four basic factors for staffing listed previously, complicates the decisions.

STAFF ESSENTIALS

The child life leader has responsibility for hiring, supervising, and developing staff. Interviewing and selecting the strongest candidates are vital aspects of the process. Having a clearly written, accurate job description as a basis for beginning the hiring process is imperative. The job description should be heavily based on the Child Life Competencies and the Standards of Clinical Practice (Child Life Council, 2002) and tailored to the individual unit or healthcare situation. This will guide the human resources department in its initial identification of eligible applicants and is useful to the child life leader in the ongoing process of supervision. Human resources department personnel ensure that formal education, work experience, and professional certification have been achieved. They can also secure references and internship evaluations.

Interview questions should be based on the job competencies and may include behavior-based interview questions. Behavioral interviewing has become an important tool to discover actions and reactions of applicants in the past in job-related circumstances (Green, 1996; Still, 1997). In this form of questioning, Still notes that, "The interviewer uses examples from the candidate's past to predict future job performance" (pp. 54-55). Thus, the supervisor may ask a job candidate to provide an example of a situation in which he or she demonstrated initiative. Many times other staff members are included in the interview process – such as a senior child life specialist or interdisciplinary team members. The latter group is particularly useful for a very small program with no senior child life staff or in institutions that have program teams such as hematology-oncology or home care. It is essential to clarify in advance, however, that the child life leader must evaluate the candidate's level of knowledge and skills and will have the authority to make the final decision.

Supervision

According to Lee and Catagnus (1999), "Supervision is, put simply, a two-way relationship between two workers in which the supervisor's goal within that relationship is to empower each worker – whether employees or volunteers – to be successful in his or her work" (p. 5). Because it is a joint experience, both the supervisor and the supervisee share responsibility for the process although it is ultimately the manager's role to guarantee that this happens. Supervision begins on the new employee's first day of orientation with the discussion of the job description and continues on a regular basis thereafter through direct observation and discussion of clinical work. The process followed in a particular program may vary in terms of mechanics of the system (i.e., the actual person providing supervision), style (i.e., the evaluation tools used), and in the number of people supervised (Lee & Catagnus, 1996).

Hawkins and Shohet (2000) describe three components of supervision, these being *educative, supportive,* and *managerial.* The child life supervisor works in each of these domains, teaching staff members about skills, encouraging and supporting their therapeutic work, and providing them with feedback about the quality of their work. Hawkins and Shohet further emphasize the importance of supervision, noting that, "We believe that, if the value and experience of good supervision are realized at the beginning of one's professional career, then the 'habit' of receiving good supervision will become an integral part of the work life and the continuing development of the worker" (p. 4).

Supervision between the child life leader and child life staff can occur either in one-to-one meetings or in small groups. The advantages of the former are apparent in terms of the individual attention that can be given to the staff member. Group sessions, on the other hand, offer greater efficiency of time for the supervisor, peer support for staff, and shared staff feedback for each other. The child life leader may help staff prepare for the supervision session by asking them to list projects, committee work, challenges of difficult patients, interdisciplinary work, and the use of varied teaching techniques. This approach to structuring supervision helps the staff member to build self-evaluation skills and insight.

The annual performance appraisal or evaluation, an important part of the supervision process, is a structured, two-way exchange with responsibility for the appraisal shared between the supervisor and the supervisee (Hawkins & Shohet, 2000). It is suggested that employees complete a self-evaluation of their strengths and weaknesses to share with their supervisor. This may be supplemented with confidential appraisals from peers and other team members, a progress report on personal and professional goals for the year, and observations made by the supervisor. The tools used in evaluations (e.g., job description, performance review sheet, competency assessment forms) are part of the supervision process that are prescribed by the institution and are strongly influenced by expectations from the Joint Commission for the Accreditation of Healthcare Organizations (JCAHO) and the Canadian Council on Health Services Accreditation (CCHSA). Many institutions use a combined job description and evaluation tool based on expected standards of behavior and indicators of performance.

Healthcare institutions may establish a system of one manager supervising all child life staff members, a number that may range from one to forty, while others may appoint sub-supervisors, such as senior child life specialists or lead child life specialists. This latter method of supervision is a kind of peer supervision, which has the advantage of dividing the supervision load and insuring attention that is more individual. The disadvantages of this model of supervision can be inconsistencies occurring among the several peer supervisors, who may also have differing level of management training. Usually these supervisors also have clinical responsibility, allowing them one-quarter to half of their time for supervision.

Child life assistants require special supervision by virtue of the nature of their job description. They should receive not only formal direction from the child life leader as part of the institution's performance management process, but also may expect candid feedback from their *partner* child life specialist or the child life team. In some settings, the child life specialist partner is responsible for the supervision and evaluation of the child life assistant.

Role Challenges

As psychosocial, humanistic care providers, child life specialists help children and families experience optimal healthcare outcomes. In this work, child life specialists encounter numerous challenges related to the nature of the work they do and the perceptions of their work by others. Child life specialists often work alone, away from the support of similarly trained professionals. This may lead to a sense of isolation. Although child life is part of the healthcare team, a child life specialist might feel less valued by other members of the healthcare team (e.g., see the discussion of "Professional Issues" in Chapter 3). The need for recognition among child life professionals must be acknowledged and dealt with by the staff and managers (Bolig, 1982).

As with many in the healthcare professions, child life staff members often feel like they do not have the time or resources to meet adequately patient care needs. Staff shortages contribute to excessive workloads for many child life specialists in both small and large programs. This typically allows time only to work with the highest priority patients. In addition, relationships with patients and families are demanding because of the enormous pressures, pain, and lifestyle changes that families encounter during a healthcare experience. *Burnout* by staff members is a real possibility, and it is crucial that child life leaders work to minimize its occurrence and effects. Research conducted by Holloway and Wallinga (1990) and Munn, Barber, and Fritz (1996) indicates that burnout occurs less often among child life specialists than in other professionals. However, when it does occur, it is often associated with role ambiguity or lack of clarity about roles. Moreover, the absence of good supervisory support was found in this research to be associated with job dissatisfaction and intention to leave the position. A related concept called *compassion fatigue*, sometimes termed secondary traumatic stress disorder, is similar to post-traumatic stress except that it influences those who are emotionally impacted by the trauma of others (Figley, 1995). It was first used in relation to nurse who worked with emergency patients but obviously could apply to any healthcare professionals.

Training about professional boundaries and therapeutic relationships helps contribute to maintaining a positive morale of an individual specialist or a staff (Mc-Klindon, & Barnsteiner, 1999; Rushton, Armstrong, & McEnhill, 1996). Many healthcare professionals struggle with establishing parameters for building relationships with patients. It is essential for the child life specialist to reach and maintain a balance within the context of family-centered care that will be positive and professional without being one of over-involvement with a family. Over-involvement can lead to distress for

the child life specialist. In addition, the blurring of professional lines between staff and families can be confusing for families and patients and may encourage an increased dependency on the child life caregiver.

An additional challenge frequently faced by child life specialists relates to the pay scale for child life staff. In some institutions, child life salaries are well below those of other healthcare professionals such as social workers – a condition that may contribute to a lowered sense of self-esteem.

The child life leader should monitor each of these issues or challenges and use a variety of strategies to address them. The options available to the leader include the use of team-building exercises such as staff retreats. Staff development programs that may include clinical advancement are helpful in meeting these challenges. Policy clarification and clearly stated job responsibilities and descriptions assist in clarifying role ambiguity often experienced by child life specialists. Market salary surveys arm child life leaders with information essential in advocating for fair salaries for child life staff.

Clinical Advancement

One way of recognizing the work and accomplishments of child life specialists is through the establishment of formal *clinical advancement* systems, used by an increasing number of child life programs. These systems provide opportunities for career development within child life programs and reward child life specialists who demonstrate a high level of skill (Child Life Council, 2005). Clinical advancement is relatively new for the child life profession. It contributes to increased job satisfaction and better staff retention. In addition, an advancement program will help ensure a higher quality of services for children and families. The human resources department would post one or more mid-level child life supervisory positions that may be bid on by members of the child life staff. The child life leader interviews the child life applicants who have submitted bids and chooses the most appropriate candidate. There are usually a limited number of such openings. Under any of the systems, a pay increase should accompany the promotion.

A typical approach to formalizing clinical advancement involves the establishment of a child life career ladder (Brown & Redelheim, 2003; Gander & Varhola-Hadley, 2000). This is among the most common approaches to providing opportunities for the promotion of staff within medium and large child life programs. It is often structured with two or three steps or career levels, which are designated correspondingly as Child Life Specialist I, II, and III (CLS I, II, and III). The specialist who wishes to progress to a new level must complete a series of requirements. Extra responsibilities come with the promotion (e.g., supervisory work, preceptor or mentor role, educational presentations, and program development). There may be a limited number of places at each level, or the levels may be open to all who meet the requirements.

In a typical career ladder system, the level of CLS I is reserved for new hires with at least a bachelor's degree who meet the minimum level competencies for a new child life specialist. During their initial year of employment, they are expected to achieve professional certification while developing child life clinical skills. The CLS II level is achievable for a certified child life specialist after one or two years of employment and successful completion of core competency protocols. A letter of agreement outlining specific goals to be met may be generated or an application for promotion may be required. The CLS II accepts additional responsibilities in the program, for example, with child life interns, new hires, committee work, or utilizing skills that are more

advanced with children and families. The CLS III level, attainable after three to five years of child life work and, in some cases, the completion of a master's degree, may include a more rigorous and formal application process including journal reviews, letters of recommendation, and further evidence of clinical skills as shown through video, charting, and oral presentations. The child life leader guides a review team for this decision-making role, which may involve an interdisciplinary group.

The position of *clinical specialist in child life* is a newer concept and is similar to the well-developed model used in nursing practice. One approach to implementing this system is that the child life specialist must meet a series of requirements and make application to an interdisciplinary panel that approves the promotion. There is usually a mentor to aid with this process, and this individual is often not a child life specialist (e.g., a senior nurse or social worker). Another model for designating clinical specialists defines the position based on competency, education, and longevity and then tests the applicant who seeks to achieve the new level. Although these advancement programs are applicable in any child life program, they are particularly effective in one-person or small programs.

Professional Identity

The professional identity of the child life specialist continues to grow stronger and more clearly defined, both within and outside the profession. The stature of the child life professional and the understanding of the role have increased for several reasons. First, the role of the child life specialist has been outlined in the Child Life Competencies of the Child Life Council (Child Life Council, 2002). In addition, a formal process for certifying child life specialists has been established. This process is fully explained in the *Candidate Manual* available from the Child Life Council (2004). Nine competencies describe the minimum level of practice expected of a child life specialist in the areas of patient and family care, teaching, and administration. For each competency, the required knowledge and skills are addressed. The competencies were updated in 2001, fourteen years after they were originally published, to assure that they are contemporary.

Attaining the professional level of Certified Child Life Specialist™ (CCLS) is extremely important for the child life specialist. Many child life programs require it as a condition of employment, either at the time of hire or within one year. The certification process for the child life specialist, which had its beginnings in 1986, is now based on a validated objective test covering knowledge, comprehension, and concrete application of the theory of child life work. Eligibility requirements for the exam include completion of 480 hours in an internship, a fellowship, or a paid clinical child life experience, under the supervision of a certified child life specialist, a minimum of ten college level courses in child life and child and/or family studies, and a bachelor's degree (Child Life Council, 2004). The exam may be taken in the final semester of bachelor's work or later. The content for the exam is constantly reviewed and updated through the joint efforts of seasoned child life professionals and the experienced testing firm to guarantee that the test will continue to be an effective tool for the profession. The *Candidate Manual* describes not only the application process and eligibility requirements but also includes sample questions and other important information (Child Life, 2004).

ORIENTATION AND TRAINING FOR STAFF AND OTHERS

While most healthcare organizations provide general orientation for their new employees, opportunities should be provided for orientation and training beyond the traditional offerings of the human resources department. Refinement of existing child life skills and development of new ones need to continue for the betterment and advancement of the individuals within the child life program, and for the program as a whole. Orientation and continuing education opportunities also contribute to the ongoing professionalization of staff and are critical to improving job satisfaction, capability, and retention (Stanford, 1980).

Orientation for Staff

Orientation to a child life program for new staff members varies within institutions, but generally includes an introduction to common elements or components of the program and the institution. The human resources orientation may include an overview of the organizational structure and of institutional and individual resources. Past annual reports may be provided to the employee, and important principles, policies, and procedures discussed, including family-centered care practice, performance improvement, infection control and safety issues, and the use of information systems. Child life program orientation, which should occur before the staff member assumes patient care responsibilities, should include the scope of service provided by the program, as well as an overview of program resources, of the position the staff member is entering, and of the supervision process. In addition, the new employee should become familiar with all units of the institution and be given a thorough orientation to the assigned unit or population. JCAHO mandates that staff members have completed orientation checklists on file that include these types of elements. As supervision models differ among child life programs, all staff should clearly understand the program's direct reporting structure and accountability practices. Supervision of professional practice and clinical skill may occur by direct observation, review of documentation and statistics, or customer and peer feedback.

Some programs have adopted a mentoring system to allow the new person to have a non-supervisory colleague to meet with on a regular basis. Lee and Catagnus (1996) describe the value of this system, stating that, "The best mentors are willing to be a combination coach, confidante, sounding board, and counselor. . . . A mentor offers a 'safe harbor' where it's OK to ask naive questions. . ." (p. 70).

Training and Development for Staff

Ongoing training can be presented at staff meetings, in-services, child life rounds or staff retreats. Staff meetings usually are held on a weekly or biweekly basis for 60 to 90 minutes. Agendas, posted ahead of time, should include items that child life leaders need to communicate and issues that the staff must address as a group. This gathering provides a forum for discussing operational issues and planning necessary tasks (e.g., developing new policies, or reviewing and setting goals). All staff members are expected to attend the meeting, and minutes should be recorded, as recommended by JCAHO. These minutes serve as an informational source for those not able to attend and are required reading for all staff members, with each held accountable for this knowledge. The recording and review of

minutes helps *off-shift* staff to keep informed and documents group decisions. Child life rounds and child life in-services offer a venue for patient discussion and care plan communication. They also serve as a forum for child life staff members to present on their areas of expertise (e.g., presentations of case studies, or journal reviews).

A staff development day or retreat is a meeting that involves the entire staff and may be held only once or twice a year. The strength of a retreat is that it is often held off-site, lasts an extended period of time (i.e., a half-day or whole day), and provides an ideal setting for work and fun in a very interactive framework. It should have a carefully planned agenda with items that can be realistically accomplished within that period. A retreat appears to be a luxury, but is a very effective way for a child life staff to work on projects, reinforce team building, and focus on morale issues. Having meetings away from the hospital sometimes causes concern among staff members that patients will be left without coverage. Nevertheless, retreats must be attended by all members of the program to enhance clinical skills and promote quality programming.

Members of the child life team should also be provided with opportunities to attend hospital and professional training or workshops (e.g., pediatric grand rounds, or sessions on pain management or bereavement). Encouragement to present on topics of child life expertise, either in the hospital and community, or regionally and nationally, should also be included in a plan for staff development.

Orientation and Training for Child Life Interns

Child life internship programs exist as a part of many child life programs across the continent and offer a variety of educational experiences. As part of the process of selecting students, the child life staff and prospective interns should interview one another to ensure that their goals, needs, and expectations are congruent. The Child Life Council continues to develop the standards for internships that will lead to more uniformity in structure and content. Current requirements state that a certified child life specialist may supervise one intern at a time, and the supervisor should have completed 4,000 paid work hours as a certified child life specialist. The minimum number of hours for an internship is 480, while some are 560 to 640 hours. These hours may be completed by rotating periodically to a new patient care unit or setting within the organization, or they may be completed at more than one site.

Orientation for interns should include many of the facets that are covered in the orientation for new staff. Interns should attend pertinent parts of the hospital orientation for new employees. Clinical training, as identified in the Clinical and Academic Standards (Child Life Council, 2002), is the core of the internship experience. Ongoing education during the training is provided by daily, semiweekly, or weekly seminars or lectures covering the subject material of the Child Life Competencies and the Standards of Clinical Practice. Additionally, lectures by, or meetings with, staff members outside the child life field will enhance the content for the interns.

Internship requirements should include routine journal entries and other written assignments such as case studies, developmental assessments, and behavioral observations. Proficiency in clinical skills, including assessment, planning, providing interventions and evaluation, is also required. Periodic evaluations during the internship are imperative. Collaboration with university/college supervisors ensures clear, consistent communication between child life staff, students, and learning institutions. Child life programs should set standards for supervisors of child life interns. Supervisors should be carefully chosen and should have demonstrated skill as supervisors. In addition, they should receive ongoing education and support through seminars and student supervision meetings. Child life programs should incorporate feedback from interns in evaluating and setting goals for student internship.

Orientation and Training for Volunteers

Volunteers are usually selected in tandem by the hospital volunteer services department and the child life program (Kiley, 1992). In addition to playing a role in the orientation of volunteers, the central volunteer department usually manages recruitment, screening, suitability, recognition, and dismissal of volunteers. The institution typically is responsible for part of the orientation that includes mandatory information (e.g., policies related to standard or universal precautions and confidentiality), and may also offer child-related information, particularly if it is a children's hospital. The child life staff should provide information specific to the program's needs using a volunteer manual, job descriptions, and an on-site orientation. Other information should include discussion of the responsibilities of volunteers, age-specific competency information, tips for approaching children and parents, therapeutic boundary issues, infection control policies, safety measures, and the importance of play. The orientation to the site is also important as it gives the volunteers opportunities to locate essential supplies, meet personnel, and familiarize themselves with the needs of the children and families. Ongoing training is of benefit to volunteers, helping them improve their working skills and providing them with positive reinforcement for their work (Lee & Catagnus, 1999; MacKensie, 1988). Periodic evaluations of volunteers are suggested by JCAHO and will serve as useful tools for both the volunteers and the child life staff. Volunteer roles are diverse. They may share time individually or in groups with patients and families, and can implement recreational programs such as movie checkout, pet therapy, bingo, and parent activities. Volunteers should consider themselves members of the interdisciplinary team, sharing observations and providing feedback to child life staff.

ACCOUNTABILITY

Program Evaluation

Evaluation of programs is one way to ensure constant growth of the child life staff and program elements and to reinforce the program's mission and vision. The Child Life Council (Brown, 2003) has published the *Program Review Guidelines*, which is a useful tool to evaluate components of child life programs or the program as a whole. Information obtained through the review process, in turn, helps child life programs compile annual reports, establish annual goals, and develop three- to five-year plans, each of which plays an important role in communicating child life successes and advocating for growth of programs.

There is a variety of ways to evaluate the child life program as a whole or the components of a program, such as the animal assisted therapy or a sibling group. All of these require the use resources of time, expertise, personnel, or money or a combination. It will help discover what works or why a program does not work as well as the effectiveness of the strategies that are used (J. Thompson, 1992). The evaluation methods could utilize satisfaction surveys, data collection and analysis, a continuing quality improvement process, research, or even a cost/benefit analysis. The latter method that compares the monetary value of the benefits derived from a service (the investment) versus the costs of providing the service. This is very popular in the business community and would be a strong way to present evaluation information to administrators (R. Thompson & Stanford, 1981).

Institutional Standards

Organizational goals and structure require child life programs to meet standards in performance and service provision. Hospital or institutional policies and procedures provide many of these guidelines for establishing goals and maintaining accountability. Departments of quality assurance or continuous improvement also require child life, as well as other services, to maintain levels of accountability.

Each organization has its own risk management program, with unique reporting processes and committees. Huber (2000) defines risk management as "an organization wide program to identify risks, control occurrences, prevent damage and control legal liability. . . . Risk management is a process whereby risks to the institution are evaluated and controlled" (p. 628). Child life contributes to this effort in important ways. Safety should be of highest consideration as child life programs plan, design and staff play and activity areas, and implement child life interventions. With expertise in child development, child life can proactively influence these institution safety standards and guidelines, thus increasing the effectiveness of the risk management department.

The Joint Commission for the Accreditation of Healthcare Organizations (JCAHO), the accrediting body for hospitals and healthcare organizations in the United States, is a private, not-for-profit organization that is the principal but not the exclusive standard setter for healthcare facilities. JCAHO has integrated the use of outcomes and other performance measures into the accreditation process (Huber, 2000, p. 615). To most child life specialists, outcomes refer to the consequences of an intervention or interaction. For child life programs, participation in the JCAHO accreditation process often provides the opportunity for showcasing effectiveness of child life interventions and programs, as well as the integration of child life into interdisciplinary care. Because of the special attention that JCAHO pays to developmental issues, there are benefits for child life programs as well as the overall institution in the accreditation survey. The process gives affirmation of the contribution child life makes to developmentally appropriate patient care. Standards relevant to child life are compiled in the existing Guidelines for the Development of Child Life Programs (2005).

The Canadian Council on Health Services Accreditation (CCHSA) is the accrediting organization in Canada. Similar to JCAHO, their mission is also to promote excellence in the provision of quality healthcare and encourage the efficient use of resources in health organizations. Both accrediting agencies are forces that can influence trends in healthcare practice depending on the focus of their system of evaluation. A priority for each regulatory agency is education of healthcare professionals about best practices for efficient, effective patient care.

Another agency that mandates accountability in the United States is the Center for Medicare and Medicaid Services (CMS). This federal agency, formerly known as the Health Care Financing Administration (HFCA), is located within the United States Department of Health and Human Services. It operates the Medicare and Medicaid pro-

grams and, with the Health Resources and Services Administration, runs the Children's Health Insurance Program, a program that is designed to extend healthcare coverage to many of the approximately ten million uninsured children in the U.S. In addition to the administration of these programs, CMS conducts research on the effectiveness of various methods of healthcare management, treatment, and financing. It also assesses the quality of healthcare facilities and services and takes enforcement actions as appropriate (www.cms.gov). For programs in the United States, CMS surveys require child life leaders to collaborate with other leaders in their institutions in developing and enforcing standards and in measuring and improving outcomes of care.

In addition to the JCAHO and CMS requirements, most states in the United States have inspection requirements for healthcare institutions. These requirements tend to focus on safety, cleanliness, and maintenance of records. It is important for child life leaders and programs to be familiar with the requirements for their states or countries and to maintain declared standards.

Research

Another part of accountability is evidenced-based practice obtained through research. Although existing research indicates that many of the components of child life service are effective, there is a need for more research (AAP, 2005). Child life programs should consider conducting their own research independently or working in collaboration with colleagues from within the institution or university personnel. There are a number of resources available to help child life programs develop their own research program (Brown, Worden, Kee, Brown, & Cozby, 1998; Kachoyeanos, 1995).

FINANCE AND BUDGET

Child life leaders must play a major role in developing as well as managing the budget. Their daily child life experiences provide some of the tools necessary to understand budgetary needs and allocation of resources. It may be necessary also for the child life leaders to estimate the cost of personnel and other expenses in relationship to some standard within the hospital when establishing a budget.

Sources of Funding

A survey by Brown and Slinkard in 1990, described in a Child Life Council publication (2005), indicated that more than 87 percent of child life program budget dollars comes from the operating budget of a hospital, with the remainder coming from other sources such as grants, endowments, donations, auxiliary organizations, and telethons. It is widely perceived that *hard money* from a hospital budget indicates a strong base of support for a child life program. The survey showed that most programs had multiple sources for financial support and that at the time of the survey, only 27 percent of programs were fully supported by hospital funds. In times of fiscal constraint and contraction of hospital department budgets, some administrators take an opposing view regarding the importance of hard money, finding that there is more security for child life in *soft money*, such as endowment income, because the flow is fixed and is not likely to be taken away (Wilson & Chambers, 1996). Administrative support is necessary to motivate an institution's foundation and development staff to place child life services at a high priority for fundraising. Child life leaders must be able to effectively articulate the cost effectiveness of child life, as suggested by Wolfer, Gaynard, Goldberger, Laidley, and Thompson (1988), communicating that sig-

nificant decreases in anxiety and distress for children and parents, and more speedy return to normal activity levels, may occur when child life is effectively utilized. It is important for child life leaders to identify allies in departments such as marketing, nursing, or development, in order to be proactive in creative finance plans. The goal is to generate and maintain stable and reliable funding for the program.

There are a number of creative ways to support the funding of child life services. Following are three examples that have been successfully implemented in some healthcare settings. First, consideration of financial support from a program team, such as the oncology/hematology or emergency department, is an option. The program team may have some flexibility in spending personnel dollars because they have a larger pool of resources from which to work, and they may choose to fund a child life specialist with funds set aside for some other patient care staff use. Although the funding ultimately comes from the same institutional income, spreading of staff full-time equivalents (FTEs) over multiple cost centers may protect FTEs in the central child life budget. In other institutions, identification of specific aspects of programming likely to appeal to selected donors is helpful in securing grant funding for programs such as sibling support groups, bereavement, or music therapy (Blum, 1996; Browning, 2001). The development office will be helpful in locating these outside donors. A third possibility involves reimbursement of child life services, for example, by requesting payment for services provided in non-hospital settings or by billing adult hospitals for interventions provided for the children of adult patients.

Allocation of Budget

Staff salaries and fringe benefit expenses typically make up 85 to 90 percent of the total program budget. The survey conducted by Brown and Slinkard (Child Life Council, 2005) also determined a method for calculating the personnel cost of child life services by examining the existing ratios and salaries in a number of hospitals. They found that the average ratio of child life staff to patients was 1:28; based on salary data they secured, they reported the cost of child life coverage to be $3.29 per inpatient bed per day, assuming seven day per week coverage. Because child life services are typically neither revenue producing nor a line item on the patient bill, this figure is quite low and thus seemingly affordable. Child life does contribute to value, which is part of the decision third-party payers and families make when they seek the care of children at an institution. Usually the cost of financing the majority of child life programs is absorbed as an administrative cost of the hospital and is supported by the daily bed rate (or *per diem*). Budget categories other than personnel include equipment (toys and games), expendable art/craft materials, office supplies, funds for travel and conferences, telephone, printing, computers, dietary supplies, books and journals, teaching materials, and miscellaneous expenses.

Monetary donations to child life programs are managed in a variety of ways. There may be a special donation account established within the child life budget, or the funds may be assigned to a central fund account. Child life specialists should understand their budget allocations for materials and toy purchases. Systems for semi-annual or quarterly toy orders help manage the budget. Expenditures may be based upon volumes of patients, usage of supplies, and acuity of the patients served.

PROGRAM DEVELOPMENT

Child life programming in outpatient, inpatient, and other settings provides both developmentally appropriate play as a normalizing activity and psychological preparation as a tool to assist children and their families in understanding and coping with healthcare related procedures. In addition to play and preparation, however, there is a variety of program possibilities that could enhance the recreational and therapeutic offerings for children. These have been grouped into categories of special events, internally created projects, and programs from external sources.

Special Events

Special events have numerous values for children and their families. Not only can they offer distraction and diversion from healthcare related procedures, which may be painful and uncomfortable, but they also can provide fun and education and contribute to creating a more familiar environment. Additionally, many child life programs have found that accepting special events from the community helps create a positive way of working with those outside the hospital. The providers of special events may be local businesses, colleges and schools, grateful parents, and fraternal or philanthropic organizations, all of whom may be potential donors and supporters of the child life activities. The special events might include individuals who want to provide entertainment, casual contacts with the patients, or holiday-related activities.

Special events and holidays often require a significant amount of child life staff attention. Not all activities as proposed by the outside individuals are appropriate or desirable for the pediatric population. As a first step, it is important to create a system that works well for child life and for the donors of the activity. Putting into place a structure that effectively screens visitors and programs will begin to eliminate these challenges. Consideration of the of type of entertainment or visitor, costumes they may wear, group size, interactions with patients, food restrictions, religious content, and media should occur when scheduling special events and accepting donations (Thompson & Stanford, 1981). Child life programs have created various methods of handling the responsibility of coordinating special events. This includes the distribution of responsibilities among all child life staff; designation of one child life specialist to screen, schedule, and coordinate all activities; or the assumption of this responsibility by other departments such as volunteer services or community outreach.

Internally Created Projects

The special events listed in the previous section might occur only once. Child life programs across the continent have created numerous special programs and projects for patients and families. These offer enrichment on an ongoing basis. Some of the programs are within the pediatric setting while others occur in settings within the community. The list that follows enumerates a few ideas that may complement the program offered by the child life staff.

Camps: Day and overnight traditional camp settings for patients, siblings, and families with chronic or life threatening illness.

Closed-Circuit Television: An internal-only TV system that offers a range of subjects from educational videos to shows featuring special guests such as sports stars to live game shows like Hospital BINGO.

School re-entry: Programs to help classmates of patients who have experienced a chronic illness or a life-altering change to the body, such as cancer or burns.

Family Resource Library: A combination of a children's library for recreational reading and a family resource section with books, videos, pamphlets, and on-line research about medical, developmental, bereavement, and disability issues.

Outdoor Playdeck or Summer Garden: Outdoors play space, on rooftop or the ground, for play and relaxation and coordinated by the child life staff.

Preadmission tours: Developmentally appropriate tours for patients, siblings, and families, which include a visit to the areas a patient will experience, medical play, and a question-and-answer session for children and parents.

School: Educational activities provided by the institution-supported schoolteachers, teachers from the local school system, or volunteer tutors.

Sibling Care: An environment offering supervised care for siblings of hospitalized children and ambulatory patients enabling parents to spend time with the patient and providing siblings with an opportunity to deal with healthcare related topics.

Programs from External Sources

Many charitable organizations serving hospitalized children in North America have fashioned exciting programs that can be brought into pediatric settings to enhance the quality of the experience. They provide services ranging from donation of free electronic equipment to providing song writing or computer network services to granting wishes for gravely ill children. The list that follows is not inclusive of all of the programs available, but is a representative sample:

Animal-assisted therapy programs: Therapeutic programs, usually endorsed by the national Delta Society, which encourage the use of carefully selected and trained dogs to visit children at bedside or in an open space (www.deltasociety.org).

Clown Care Unit of the Big Apple Circus: A troop of specially trained professional clowns who work exclusively in pediatric centers (www.bigapplecircus.org).

Coalition for Quality Children's Media (Meg's Gifts): An outreach program providing free child friendly videos and CDs (www.cqcm. org).

Famous Fone Friends: A Los Angeles based organization offering free telephone calls from sports and entertainment arena celebrities to chronically ill and critically ill patients in pediatric settings (fonfriends@aol.com).

Reach Out and Read: A pediatrician-initiated literacy program, involving residents and child life staff giving children a prescription for an age-appropriate book on well-child visits with the potential accumulation of 10 books by the time they reach six years (www.reachoutandread.org).

Sabriya's Castle of Fun Foundation: A program providing a portable, self-contained, audiovisual entertainment unit (www.sab riyascastle.org).

Sib Shops: A sibling support project focusing on training of staff to provide peer support and education within a recreation context for siblings of children with special health needs (www.chmc.org/departmt/sib-supp).

Songs of Love Foundation: An organization providing one-of-a-kind songs for hospitalized and homebound children through the volunteer efforts of singers, songwriters, instrumentalists, and technicians (www.songsoflove.org).

Starbright World: A computer network program initiated by Steven Spielberg that allows patients to videoconference nationwide with other hospitalized children and teens, as well as enjoy a variety of games and educational materials (www.starbright.org).

Starlight Children's Foundation: A program supported by volunteer groups providing local activities within and outside the hospital including Fun Centers and PC Pals (www.starlight.org).

Wish granting organizations: National organizations such as the Children's Wish Foundation (www.childrenswish.org), Make-A-Wish (www.makeawish.org) and others granting *wishes* to critically ill, terminally ill, and sometimes chronically ill patients.

CONCLUSION

Through efficient program management and careful attention to program fundamentals, child life leaders are able to establish the basis for effective child life programs. Commitment to staff growth and development, as well as implementation of clear, concise accountability plans by child life leaders, are important components of a thriving program. Finally, creative funding and appropriate allocation of fiscal resources by child life leaders is crucial in the administration of successful child life programs. Although the attributes of child life programs may vary, the most crucial elements remain constant: to ensure quality services to patients and families, and to maintain professional competency and consistency of programming. Child life leaders must keep informed about healthcare trends and ensure that child life services are forward looking and innovative.

REFERENCES

American Academy of Pediatrics, Committee on Hospital Care. (2006). Child life services. *Pediatrics, 106,* 1156-1159.

Blum, L. (1996). *The complete guide to getting a grant.* New York: John Wiley & Sons.

Bolig, R. (1982). Child life workers: Facilitating their growth and development. *Children's Health Care, 10,* 94-99.

Brown, C. (2003). *Program review guidelines.* Rockville, MD: Child Life Council.

Brown, C., & Redelheim, S. (2003). *Child life resource manual.* Philadelphia, PA: Child Life and Education Department of the Children's Hospital of Philadelphia. (Policies, Clinical Advancement, Protocols, Internship, Volunteers, Community Outreach, etc.)

Brown, K. Worden, P., Kee, D., Brown, K.W., & Cozby, P. (1998). *Research methods in human development* (2nd ed.). Mountain View, CA: Mayfield.

Browning, B. (2001). *Grant writing for dummies.* Indianapolis, IN: Wiley.

Child Life Council. (1997). *The child life profession* (poster). Rockville, MD: Author.

Child Life Council. (2002). *Official documents of the Child Life Council.* Rockville, MD: Author.

Child Life Council. (2003). *Directory of Child Life Programs in North America* (13th ed.). Rockville, MD: Author.

Child Life Council. (2004). *Candidate manual.* Rockville, MD: Author.

Child Life Council. (2005). *Guidelines for the development of child life programs.* Rockville, MD: Author.

Figley, C. (1995). *Compassion fatigue: Coping with secondary traumatic stress disorder in those who treat the traumatized.* New York: Brunner/Mazel.

Gander, M., & Varhola-Hadley, J. (2000). *Clinical advancement program for child life department.* Cincinnati, OH: Child Life Department of the Cincinnati Children's Hospital Medical Center.

Green, P. (1996). *Get hired! Winning strategies to ace the interview.* Austin TX: Bard Books.

Hawkins, P., & Shohet, R. (2000) *Supervision in the Helping Professions.* (2nd ed.). Buckingham, England: Open University Press.

Huber, D. (2000), *Leadership and nursing care management.* Philadelphia: W.B. Saunders Company.

Holloway, D., & Wallinga, C.R. (1990). Burnout in child life specialists: The relation of role stress. *Children's Health Care, 19,* 10-18.

Kachoyeanos, M. (1995). Opportunities in outcome evaluation research. *MCN, 20,* 223.

Kiley, A. (1992). *Volunteers in child health: Management, selection, training and supervision.* Rockville, MD: Child Life Council.

Lee, J., & Catagnus, J. (1996). *Supervising and managing people.* Philadelphia, PA: Energize, Inc.

Lee, J., & Catagnus, J. (1999). *What we learned (the hard way) about supervising volunteers,* Philadelphia: Energize, Inc.

MacKensie, M. (1988). *Dealing with difficult volunteers.* Downers Grove, IL: Heritage Arts Publishing.

McKlindon, D., & Barnsteiner, J. (1999). Therapeutic relationships: Evolution of the Children's Hospital of Philadelphia model. *Maternal Child Nursing, 24,* 237-243.

Munn, E. K., Barber, C. E., & Fritz, J. J. (1996). Factors affecting the professional well-being of child life specialists. *Children's Health Care, 25,* 71-91.

Rollins, J., Bolig, R., & Mahan, C. (2005). *Meeting children's psychosocial needs across the healthcare continuum.* Austin, TX: Pro-Ed.

Rushton, C., Armstrong, L., & McEnhill, M. (1996). Establishing therapeutic boundaries as patient advocates. *Pediatric Nursing, 22,* 185-189.

Spendolini, M. (1993). *The benchmarking book.* New York: AMACOM.

Stanford, G. (1980). Now is the time: The professionalization of child life workers. *The Journal of the Association for the Care of Children's Health, 8,* 55-59.

Still, D. (1997). *High impact hiring: How to interview and select outstanding employees.* Dana Point, CA: Management Development Systems.

Thompson, J. (1992). Program evaluation within a health promotion framework. *Canadian Journal of Public Health, 83* (Supplement 1), S67-S71.

Thompson, R., & Stanford, G. (1981). *Child life in hospitals: Theory and practice.* Springfield, IL: Charles C Thomas.

Wilson, J., & Chambers, E. (1996). Child life can (and must) adapt to the new healthcare environment. *ACCH Advocate, 2,* 36-37.

Wolfer, J., Gaynard, L., Goldberger, J., Laidley, L., & Thompson, R. (1988). An experimental evaluation of a model child life program. *Children's Health Care, 16,* 244-254.

Chapter 11

CHILD LIFE INTERVENTIONS IN CRITICAL CARE AND AT THE END OF LIFE

Lois J. Pearson

Entering the critical care environment for the first time is most often an overwhelming experience for families. For some families, placement on a critical care unit may be a planned admission following serious surgery. In other cases, a child's condition may worsen on a general floor requiring transfer to an intensive care unit (ICU). For still other families, the admission to an ICU may be totally unexpected following the complicated birth of a new baby or the sudden illness or traumatic injury of a child or teen of any age. Regardless of the presenting circumstances, and based on a wide spectrum of coping styles and experiences, the critical care environment places unique stresses on the child and parent, siblings, and extended family. Child life programming plays an important and unique role in helping families cope with this highly technological and stressful environment.

PARENTAL STRESSORS WITHIN THE ENVIRONMENT

Several studies have identified the stresses that parents experience in the ICU setting (Miles & Carter, 1979, 1982, 1989; Carnavale, 1990). These include:

- Environmental stressors
  - Sounds of monitors, alarms, equipment
  - Visual stimulation of equipment, procedures, lighting
  - Observation of other patients
  - Procedures and surgical interventions conducted at bedside
- Communication stressors
  - Too much or too little information provided to parents
  - Few opportunities to ask questions
  - Inability to interpret staff behaviors
- Concerns about child's physical appearance, behavior and emotional coping
- Alterations or deprivations in parenting role
  - Visiting policies
  - Participation in cares
  - Inability to hold infant or young child
- Concerns about well-being of other children in family

As child life professionals, we are challenged to identify and advocate for particular policies and practices that support the family's ability to cope within the critical care setting. The presence of a dedicated child life specialist in the ICU environment helps to address the psychosocial needs of patients and families and to bring a balance to the highly technological medical environment (see Chapter 5, "Families and Family-centered Care").

Miles and Mathes (1991) identified the importance of preparing parents for the critical care setting. Most parents reported feeling well prepared for the physical environment of the ICU after touring the unit, and identified preparation as helpful in reducing their levels of stress. However, parents also reported feeling far less prepared for those aspects of the ICU stay that they identified as causing the most stress, including emotional and behavioral responses of their child as a patient and perceived changes in parental roles. Thus, when preparing parents for an ICU admission, child life professionals should address the psychosocial and emotional aspects of the critical care setting for children and families, as well as the physical setting.

STRESSES FOR THE PEDIATRIC PATIENT

The physical environment of the ICU often leads to sensory overload for patients of all ages (Baker, 1984). Research demonstrates that lighting has a profound effect on infants and children. Disturbances in blood pressure, body temperature, and sleep patterns are caused by a lack of day to night progressions. Similarly, sights and sounds of other patients, personnel, and equipment affect a patient's senses. The physical layout of the ICU adds stress for children and families in that the same open visibility that allows medical staff to be vigilant in monitoring patients also allows families to observe what is happening in nearby beds or other rooms. The death of a patient in the ICU inevitably affects the coping of other families in the unit. High noise levels affect sleep and breathing patterns. Finally, painful or disturbing touch has a negative impact on a child's ability to cope.

While environmental concerns need to be addressed by all caregivers in the critical care units, child life specialists may help to address these needs in developmentally appropriate ways. For the youngest infants, soothing music or tape recordings of a parent's voice singing or reading may bring comfort while helping to block out more disturbing noises of a busy critical care unit. Quilts placed over isolettes reduce the amount of extraneous noise, while providing diurnal lighting. For toddlers and preschoolers, videotapes may also encourage attention to familiar stimuli and distract a young child from observing the sights or hearing the sounds of surrounding patient's treatments or responses. For the school-aged child or adolescent, videotapes can help keep attention focused within an individual's room, while discouraging observation of activities taking place in other parts of the unit. Similarly, headphones may help a child or teen who has trouble resting within the ICU.

For the patient who is awake and alert, child life programming is essential to reduce the stress of the ICU environment while promoting a sense of normalcy. Even in the critical care setting, play is essential to meet the developmental needs of the recovering child and reduce the possibility of psychosocial upset. Play may be active for children or adolescents whose medical treatment may require ICU monitoring but are still able to engage in developmentally appropriate activities. For the child who is critically ill or for whom medical treatment and procedures are physically restricting, play may need to be more passive. At times, child life may play "for" a child and focus on themes that provide safe ways to express feelings of frustration or loss of control.

Medical play is often a favorite activity of patients whose frequent treatments have become stressful, as the following example illustrates.

> A toddler had become increasingly resistant to his physical cares and treatments after being in the ICU for many weeks while awaiting a heart transplant. With his mother's permission, the child life specialist provided a doll for him to care for. He easily became engaged in suctioning, bathing and feeding "his baby" while at the same time becoming more cooperative with his own treatments. The doll also became the focus of preparation and role modeling of behaviors for new situations and medical interventions.

Just as in a general unit, books, games, movies, and even video games can help to engage the child. Allowing choices encourages control and may help to motivate a child. In addition, child life specialists may use art and craft activities to encourage mastery and facilitate the expression of feelings. Activities may serve the secondary purpose of helping to decorate an ICU room to appear more childlike and hide more distressing aspects of the medical environment.

> One ten-year-old boy who had become sick quite suddenly and was now ventilator dependent, refused to communicate for several weeks, despite attempts by staff to encourage various communication techniques. When the child life intern suggested decorating his room for Halloween, this patient suddenly became interactive and engaging. With each spider, pumpkin, and friendly ghost he made of paper and paint, he become more interactive. Soon he was communicating by writing and using a

computer, two techniques he had refused before the art interventions began.

As mentioned in the above example, the ability to communicate may present a significant challenge for patients in the ICU. Some patients may be alert but unable to verbalize due to the paralyzing effects of required drugs. Other patients may be fully awake but prevented from talking because of a new tracheostomy or dependence on a ventilator. Still other patients may simply be too sick to communicate or too frightened to attempt to respond. When alternative communication techniques are necessary, child life specialists may be active participants in the healthcare team's plans for a particular patient. Mechanical speaking aids, communication boards, computer programs, writing assists, and hand and eye signals may be appropriate to meet specific needs. Yet it is often the creative work of the child life specialist that helps motivate the child to learn to use these devices and techniques through developmentally appropriate play or preparation. Collaboration with speech, physical and occupational therapists, and nursing may help to determine what methods would be most effective. A child may be more willing to use a specific speech tool or assistive device in the course of normal play activities than to answer medical questions posed by other members of the healthcare team.

The issues of privacy are often most important for older school-aged and adolescent patients. Placing these patients in areas where there is less "traffic" may help a patient retain self-esteem and positive morale. Using movable screens in areas where visibility is higher is important, especially when nursing tasks are being done. Often the child life specialist remains more attentive to these privacy needs than medical staff concentrating on procedures. Similarly it may be the role of the child life specialist to heighten awareness of particular developmental issues, for example, the child who is sedated but still sensitive to the sound of surrounding conversations or comments during treatment.

> An eight-year-old spent several months in the ICU after being severely burned in a fire, and because her mother spoke no English, many caregivers assumed that the child also did not understand English. The child life specialist who participated in her daily burn care with support and distraction techniques frequently reminded caregivers that she understood all of the conversation that took place at the bedside during these procedures.

Meeting the developmental needs of patients within the ICU can be challenging when the predominance of equipment and treatments seems to take precedence. The role of the child life specialist as part of the healthcare team may be to advocate for policies and procedures that help address both medical and emotional needs. Grouping patients of similar ages may help to normalize the environment. Scheduling caretaking activities and therapies may help a patient maintain control. A developmental care plan in the form of a dry erase board hanging prominently on the wall of each room can be helpful for children of all ages. It may be colorfully decorated with headings for the parent or child to fill in including, for example, the child's nickname, names of family and friends, favorite comfort or distraction measures, likes, and dislikes. Information about comfort measures, such as a pacifier or favorite blanket for an infant may help a caregiver or volunteer to settle a tired or anxious patient.

> A thirteen-year-old girl, frequently admitted to the ICU for IV medications while awaiting a heart/lung transplant, makes it her first priority to fill out the developmen-

tal board herself, thus making sure that everyone who cares for her will be attentive to the psychosocial needs that are most important to her.

As in other parts of the hospital, one of the ways to decrease the stress for patients and families is to provide preparation for changes that medical care or treatment may require within the ICU. The child who will awaken from surgery intubated or with a new tracheostomy needs to be prepared for changes in function and treatment procedures, as well as feelings. Preparation methods will depend upon the child's coping behaviors and ability to interact, but need to follow the same principles as traditional procedural preparation. The child life specialist will most often need to create specific teaching and preparation tools for critical care work. A doll with a tracheostomy or ventilator, photographs of medical equipment, and preparation kits for particular procedures and treatments should be part of the child life specialist's resources. Preparation programming will vary depending on the layout, policies, and procedures of the particular unit, the acuity of the patients placed there, and the demonstrated informational needs of the patient and family. In some hospitals, patients who are more responsive to preparation interventions may be placed on an intermediate care unit with the ICU being reserved for the most critically ill patients (see Chapter 8).

For the child who has recovered sufficiently to be able to leave the ICU, child life may play an important role in easing the transition from one unit to another. Transferring out of the critical care unit is often frightening to families who have established a trusting relationship with caregivers and feel supported with the small ratio between patients and nursing staff. A brief tour of the new unit by a familiar child life specialist may help in emphasizing the positive aspects of the new placement for child and family. A well-documented psychosocial plan of care may be passed from one child life specialist to another to ease the transition and increase the child's feelings of comfort in this new setting where play and developmental needs will continue to be met. Knowing how a child copes and what techniques are most helpful during particular stress points will also help the child and staff to work toward positive outcomes.

In addition to preparation and support during a child's stay in the critical care unit, and support for the transition to another unit, children and families may benefit from opportunities to visit the ICU after recovery. For a child to return to the unit and be greeted by familiar nurses, child life, and other staff who worked with him gives the child and family the experience of having managed a potentially frightening experience in a positive way. Mastery of the experience may also include special attention to those areas that the child or family has identified as most difficult. In one pediatric hospital, transport team members often visit children who have been traumatically injured. Before discharge, the child and family may be invited up to the helicopter pad to talk with the crew and take photographs. This offers another opportunity for mastery for the child while helping siblings sequence the confusing series of events surrounding a traumatic injury.

SIBLING STRESSORS

The hospitalization of a sibling represents a significant event in the life of a child, and the effects are compounded if the sibling dies or becomes permanently disabled. The bond between siblings develops before birth as a family anticipates the arrival of a new baby and the child prepares to become a big brother or sister. The sibling relationship most often lasts beyond the death of the parents (Grollman, 1995).

Siblings may experience significant distress during hospitalization if they have been separated from the parents and hospitalized sibling. They may view the parents' constant attention at the bedside of the sick child to be overprotective, and may feel guilty to have such feelings (Davies, 1999). In addition, siblings often feel responsible for the health of their ill brother or sister, especially when the treatment requires restricted social contacts and the family becomes isolated from extended family and friends.

The illness of a brother or sister is considered to be one of life's most stressful events (Coddington, 1972). Craft (1989) reports that siblings of an ill child were most concerned about being separated from their brother or sister, worried over the illness, and feared the outcome (Craft, 1989). Siblings who are denied information about the birth of a high-risk sibling may demonstrate negative behavior changes that place additional stress on the parents (Oehler, 1999). Increased knowledge of family-centered care principles has helped to identify the importance of including siblings in caring for the child in the critical care setting. Yet much controversy still exists related to whether siblings should visit the ICU.

Until the 1980s, siblings were often not allowed to visit due to the concern for the spread of infection (Murphy, 1993). However, published studies of siblings visiting in nurseries and on postpartum floors demonstrated no increased incidence of infection, even with direct sibling contact without the use of gowns or gloves (Murphy, 1993). Moreover, research began to document the potential benefits of sibling visitation. For example, studies indicated that siblings who visit their sick newborn brother or sister are better informed about their sibling and expressed feelings that imply cooperative effort in caring for the baby as part of the family (Oehler, 1990). Conroy (1990) demonstrated that a well sibling's visit to the bedside of a brother or sister following heart surgery correlated significantly with positive sibling behaviors three weeks after the patient's discharge.

Child life specialists need to continually advocate for family centered care, including sibling presence in the critical care unit. Speaking comfortably with parents under stress, answering questions, and providing support for families to be together during stressful life events may make a significant difference in a family's ability to cope. For many families, the desire to have the family together is strongly felt, but the actual process of managing a sibling's visit to the bedside of a critically ill and perhaps unresponsive child may be overwhelming. Knowing that the child life specialist has the necessary resources to implement the difficult task of preparation and can focus on the emotional and developmental needs of both the patient and siblings, may help the parent decide to have siblings visit.

If sibling visitation in critical care units is to become an accepted practice, appropriate resources must be available to assist staff in implementing this important work. Child life specialists are skilled in creating teaching tools that address the important components of preparation in a developmentally appropriate format. Many of the same resources used to prepare the patient may also be used when preparing siblings, including educational photographs, medical equipment and play. Having a safe, child-friendly play space for siblings within or near the ICU will help siblings feel welcomed and allow them to engage in play activities to encourage mastery. Role modeling language and behaviors to help siblings understand the sights and sounds of the ICU environment will help families continue to include siblings in the hospital experience. In addition to providing accessible preparation resources, it is important for child life specialists to collaborate with other members of the healthcare team to assist in supporting sibling visitation. Pastoral care, social work and nursing staff may also be trained to insure that appropriate sibling preparation is routinely provided, even when child life staff is not available.

Davies (1999) has suggested interventions that may be helpful throughout the experience of a sibling's hospitalization – interventions that may serve as a guide for best practice standards for sibling involvement

- Provide developmentally appropriate explanations to convey disease related information to siblings.
- Facilitate discussion of these feelings between parents and children when siblings are present.
- Encourage phone calls, letter writing or videoconferencing if siblings are not present.
- Remind family members to include school personnel and child care providers with information for additional sibling support.
- Include siblings in child life programming as possible.
- Provide group programming specifically for siblings in specialty units, such as oncology or NICU.
- Support parents in meeting needs of their well children.

THE DYING CHILD

A child with a life-threatening illness, and the members of his or her family, may respond in many ways and demonstrate a range of differing behaviors. Doka (1993) describes a series of phases that a family experiences when a member is diagnosed with a life-threatening illness. In the initial phase, that of prediagnosis and diagnosis, a family may face feelings of stress that are as significant as in the terminal phase or at the time of death. How the family handles this first phase may be indicative of their subsequent fears, coping patterns, and information seeking abilities. Doka refers to the time between the diagnostic or acute phase and the terminal phase of the illness, as the chronic phase. It is during this period that families realize the illness and treatment will be a continuing part of their family life. During this protracted and ill-defined phase, families may feel less supported by others and more isolated from social activities. When attention shifts from aggressive treatment to palliative care, decisions about quality of life and end of life demonstrate the realities of impending death (Doka, 1993).

In reviewing these phases, one can easily identify areas that may be addressed by child life interventions. With consideration given to the developmental needs of each age group, child life specialists help a child in the acute and chronic phases to understand the disease itself and the implications of treatment. They may also facilitate the learning of coping styles to support the child through potentially painful procedures. Involvement in child life activities helps the child ventilate feelings and fears, while learning to integrate implications of the illness into daily routines and relationships with family members and peers. Finally, in the terminal phase of illness, child life specialists may help a child prepare for death by preserving self-concepts, maintaining relationships with family and friends, and expressing feelings and fears. Through expressive art, a dying child or teen may find comfortable and developmentally appropriate ways to say good-bye

to important people in their lives. Writing is a powerful tool for many to express sincere and intimate feelings in a safe format, whether it is done through letters, journaling, poetry, or email. For others, drawing, painting, clay, or other art media may provide unique opportunities for creative self-expression. The creative thinking of the child life specialist may more easily bridge limitations in physical abilities caused by weakness or pain. For example, making audio or videotapes for family or friends may be possible when writing is no longer possible. Often the assistance of a trusted staff person rather than a family member makes this task more manageable and helps protect close family members from the emotional difficulty that these tasks may represent.

SUPPORTING THE DYING CHILD

The importance of communication between the dying child and family at end of life is well documented in the literature (Bluebond-Langner, 1978, Sourkes, 1995). Doka (1995) writes that, "Keeping information from a child is not only futile; it is also harmful. It inhibits the child from seeking support, creates additional anxiety, impairs trust and complicates the child's response to crisis" (p. 32).

The parents of a six-year-old girl in the terminal phase of leukemia refused to talk with their daughter about her impending death. When the child began to draw pictures of angels, the child life specialist asked her permission to show the drawings to her parents. After viewing their daughter's symbolic drawings, the child life specialist was able to facilitate discussion between parents and child about death.

Table 1
GUIDELINES FOR INTERVENTIONS WITH THE DYING CHILD

1. Do not underestimate the child's capacity to understand.
2. Create open communication but do not force it.
    a. Listen first, then offer support.
    b. Provide honest information.
    c. Remember that it is okay to say, "I don't know".
    d. Answer only what the child wants to know.
3. Provide creative outlets for anger, such as art.
4. Follow the child's lead.
5. Be honest with the child about impending death.
6. Allow the child time to say good-byes.
7. Permit the child to decide when he or she wants to share the pain of grief.
8. Remember the child may choose to protect the parent (mutual pretense).
9. Help the dying child to live.
    a. Make the child comfortable
        (1) Arrange physical setting for the child to be with family.
            (a) Create space for the child in family living area.
            (b) Plan family activities for the child to participate or observe.
            (c) Arrange for medical equipment only as needed.
        (2) Address pain control measures and methods.
        (3) Focus on keeping environment and routine child-focused as much as possible.
    b. Create special memorable moments.
    c. Continue some routine.
    d. Surround the child with people who mean the most to him/her.
    e. Help the child maintain peer friendships.

Note: Adapted from Wolfett (1996). From *Core curriculum for the nursing care of children and their families.* (p. 87), by M. E. Broome and J. A. Rollins, 1999, Pitman, NJ: Janetti Publications, Inc. Reprinted with permission.

Children nearing the end of life have many concerns, but may need help to express these concerns and get answers to their questions. These questions frequently focus on fear of abandonment, fear of retribution, and fear of death or dying (Huntley, 1991). Child life specialists and other trusted members of the healthcare team play a key role in addressing these communication needs. Wolfelt (1996) developed guidelines, subsequently adapted by Broome and Rollins (1999), for enhancing communication and interventions with the dying child. (See Table 1).

SUPPORTING THE DYING ADOLESCENT

The developmental tasks of healthy adolescents focus on becoming independent, acquiring social relationships, and preparing for a career and, perhaps, marriage. In contrast, some critically ill adolescents may have a childlike body appearance and face a loss of sexual development. The adolescent may also be suffering debilitating physical effects of disease and treatment and feel a strong sense of unfairness in losing everything so close to attaining adulthood (Carr-Gregg, 1997).

Considering these developmental tasks and concerns, caring for the dying adolescent may be one of the most difficult challenges for caregivers. It is also an area where little research has been done (Carr-Gregg, 1997). Caregivers may struggle with their own feelings of sadness or helplessness while hoping to meet the psychosocial needs of the adolescent patient. Addressing issues of pain control requires that pain relief options be discussed with the patient. Palliative care services, if available, may be involved.

Communication with adolescents may be challenging, but clear and straightforward conversation may never be more important than at the time of impending death. Adolescents may need time for private discussions with the medical team at a time when parents may tend to be overprotective (Carr-Gregg, 1997). These discussions must assure patient confidentiality as appropriate. Family meetings facilitated by medical staff, including patient, parents, and siblings, may help in addressing difficult or sensitive issues or concerns regarding the end of life.

Teenagers frequently choose to talk with a person with whom they feel comfortable. A child life specialist may often be the teen's choice because of the trusting and supportive relationship that has been built. In addition, the non-medical role of the child life specialist may help to support this interactional relationship. Conversations may be concrete or existential, with opportunities for the teen to express fears and anxieties. Listening requires the ability to "hear" both verbal and nonverbal cues (see Chapter 4).

Some adolescents may be more comfortable expressing feelings and thoughts through different creative outlets – music, writing poetry, or drawing, for example. With the support of child life, adolescents may write their will, plan their funeral, or make audio or videotapes for family and friends (Carr-Gregg, 1997). They may also choose to make a list of friends whom they would like notified at the time of death.

Becoming the trusted support person for a dying adolescent may be difficult, especially when a child life specialist has had a close and trusted relationship. Adolescents may choose to confide in someone whom they feel will be able to tolerate the overwhelming sadness of impending death. Knowing what to say in response to sensitive questions requires honesty and directness. Pazola and Gerberg, (1990) suggest that most adolescents want honest and direct answers to questions that may focus on the acknowledgement that death is eminent, the wish to complete unfinished business, and the desire to specify how the adolescent wants to die. Reframing the events to come, with reassurance that the patient's wishes will be honored and that the patient will not be alone, helps foster feelings of support.

SUPPORTING THE PARENTS OF A DYING CHILD OR TEEN

Parental fears at the time of impending death focus on fear of abandonment or isolation, fear of failure in their role of parent and protector, and fear of coping with a child's pain and death (Huntley, 1991). Supporting parents at this time is often hard for staff. Parents seek support, but know that absolute answers are not always possible. Interventions with parents should be specific and responsive to parents' expressed needs. Most important may be the ability to affirm parents as loving and capable of making good decisions (Huntley, 1991).

Jost and Haase (1989) documented the positive impact of the interventions by healthcare professionals at the time of a child's death. In a survey of parents which focused on helpful versus not helpful interventions at the time of the death of their child, parents demonstrated vivid recall of what was said to them and done for them by caring and supportive healthcare professionals (Jost & Haase, 1989). Parents still remembered these events and actions years after the death, despite the described emotional shock of the moment.

Worden and Monahan (2001) have identified a series of interventions that may be facilitated by child life specialists or other members of the interdisciplinary team. These include: (1) helping the family stay connected with their child until death; (2) facilitating communication; (3) helping the family develop memories they can hold and cherish long after the death; (4) helping parents negotiate the medical system; (5) helping parents with the concept of appropriate death – defined as death that is consonant with the goals, values, and lifestyle of the individual; and (6) helping parents talk about funeral plans (Worden & Monahan, 2001). Many of these interventions may be facilitated by child life specialists, especially in making memories through the creation of mementos.

PATIENT INVOLVEMENT AND END OF LIFE DECISION MAKING

"To respect a child is to acknowledge the importance of his or her world and the relationships that are central to it" (Rushton, 1990, p. 207).The role of the child as decision maker in end-of-life care is complex, because children lack the ability to make independent decisions and have not yet expressed life values or goals upon which such decisions would be made (Rushton, 1990). In addition, a child may not have reached the cognitive level to facilitate discussion in families facing critical illness or injury, or the illness or injury itself may have made the child incapable of participating in the decision making process (Voss, 1999).

For older children and adolescents, decision making involves participation of the parents and physician, but should also include the assent of the patient. The American Academy of Pediatrics (1995) states that assent requires:

- Helping the patient achieve a developmentally appropriate awareness of the nature of his or her condition
- Telling the patient what he or she can expect with tests and treatment
- Making a clinical assessment of the patient's understanding of the situation and the factors influencing how he or she is responding (including whether there is pressure to accept testing or therapy)
- Soliciting an expression of the patient's willingness to accept the proposed care

For children under the age of twelve years, it is possible to recognize the child's preferences about procedures, choices of sedatives, coping and positioning, as well as placing increased responsibility for taking oral medications, and encouraging them to ask questions during exams, tests and procedures (Rushton, 1990).

After years of treatment, multiple hospitalizations and the experience of observing the suffering and death of peers with similar conditions, adolescents with a chronic or life-threatening condition may possess a maturity like that of an adult (Weir, 1997). For this reason, physicians and parents are beginning to recognize the capacity that adolescents have to make decisions about their own healthcare options. The increased use of advance directives by adolescents would allow the adolescent to take a more active role in their life-and-death decisions and allow them to receive candid and honest information about diagnosis, prognosis, and medically acceptable alternatives. In addition, adolescents would be able to convey preferences about unwanted medical treatment and communicate choices regarding preferable location for living the remainder of their lives (Weir, 1997). Benefits of this informed relationship between adolescent and healthcare providers would also encourage improved cooperation and compliance from patients as a respected part of the decision-making team.

Practice guidelines for facilitating this increased respect for an adolescent's responsible decision making, as outlined by Weir (1997), include:

• Importance of communicating information throughout diagnosis, prognosis, evaluation, and treatment
• Comprehensible and compassionate communication
• Time for family to assimilate new information
• Opportunities for the adolescent to ask questions and respond to information, both with parents and privately with physician
• Support during emotional and physical stress
• Clarification that advance directives may be modified or reversed at any time
• Nonjudgmental attitude demonstrated by all healthcare professionals

Child life specialists may play a critical role in assessing and meeting the needs of a child or adolescent making end-of-life decisions. The relationship between patient and child life specialist is often a close and trusted relationship initiated at the time of diagnosis and supported through the course of treatment. For the family struggling with knowing the wishes of their child, it may be comforting to have the information shared in the context of play, self-expressive art, creative writing, or peer communication.

The role of child life specialist in meeting the needs of a family at the time of death requires participation as a trusted member of a multidisciplinary team that may include medical staff, nursing, social work, pastoral care, bereavement staff and other disciplines. The work of supporting immediate family, extended family, friends, and staff at the time of death requires a process of ongoing assessment and redefining of needs and concerns. Identifying a family's needs for spiritual guidance, interventional activities for siblings, financial resources for funeral planning, or simply a cup of coffee and private time to grieve, becomes the work of the team rather than particular individuals. Ongoing communication and collaboration will help identify the unique perspective and expertise of other members of the team, assuring that each family's specific needs are met in a professional, yet caring manner.

SUPPORTING SIBLINGS OF A DYING CHILD

The importance of siblings' presence in the critical care setting has already been discussed. For the child who recovers and leaves the ICU, sibling involvement assists the family in coping and returning to normal routines and lifestyle with the least disruption in development and family functioning. When a child is not expected to survive, interventions with siblings become a priority for child life. While parents may realize the implications of escalating treatments or declining medical condition of their child, children are less able to engage in anticipatory grief work and tend to believe in the sibling's improved health until the downward spiral of illness is continually demonstrated (Davies, 1999).

The factor that may have the greatest impact upon a child's ability to cope with the critical illness and potential death of a sibling is the degree to which he or she has been included in the illness and death experience (Davies, 1999). Classic theoretical work on coping by Lazarus (1966) indicates that three important principles that have direct impact upon a child's ability to cope – direct action, predictability, and affiliation. Involving siblings directly may mean encouraging their presence in the hospital setting and allowing them to participate in developmentally appropriate cares or bedside activities.

Predictability (defined as recognizing the outcome) allows siblings the ability to experience firsthand the inevitability of an impending death. Exposure to progressive sickness or weakness, for example, helps the sibling to understand the predicted outcome. In situations whereby a child is injured or suddenly becomes critically ill, a sibling's ability to visit the hospital, learn of the event, and begin processing the severity of the situation may contribute to predictability, or the realization that a brother or sister may be dying. This principle helps define best practice standards when asked to assist in preparing siblings for an anticipated death.

In the "Fetal Concerns Program" of one hospital, the child life specialist is often called upon to assist families with young children, when the prenatal diagnosis of a lethal anomaly changes the excited family's preparations for the birth of a new baby. Lauren and Alicia knew that something was wrong at home when everyone stopped talking excitedly about the upcoming birth of John. With the support of child life, their parents were able to prepare the three and five year old siblings for the birth of the baby "who will be very, very sick when he is born." This intermediate stage of preparation did not take away the family's slim hope that prenatal tests might be wrong, but still began preparing everyone for the inevitable sadness that was to come (Pearson, 1997).

Finally, research by Davies (1999) supports the importance of siblings' involvement and affiliation, indicating that siblings who are present with the family and extended family are better able to cope with a stressful event than those siblings who are not present. Siblings who do not have the support of family and are not present at the hospital often demonstrate greater emotional vulnerability and distress.

In order to plan child life interventions for children facing the impending death of a brother or sister, it is necessary to identify a child's cognitive understanding of death. Speece and Brent (1996) identified five components:

- Universality – the understanding that all things must eventually die.
- Irreversibility – once a physical body dies, it cannot come alive again. Younger children who have not developed the concept of irreversibility believe that death is temporary and reversible. Thus a dead person may come back to life spontaneously or magically. For the young child, this concept is determined by questions about how a person who has died will eat, sleep, or perform other functions such as hearing or talking.
- Nonfunctionality – the realization that when a living thing dies, all aspects of a living body cease to function. Children struggling with this concept question whether a dead person can eat or feel cold under the ground. The ability to differentiate between what is alive and what is dead defines this component.
- Causality – includes both abstract and realistic causes of death, or internal and external factors. For younger children, causes of death may be unrealistic and blamed on bad behaviors or specific causes like guns, rather than factors such as illness or old age.

• Noncorporeal continuation refers to the belief in an afterlife or some kind of communication that goes on after the death of the physical body.

Speece and Brent (1996) report that 60 percent of children develop a working understanding of these first three concepts between the ages of five and seven years. This means that for siblings under the age of seven, explanations about the impending death of a brother or sister must be presented by child life specialists in terms that identify death as final and focus on the differences between being dead and being alive. For children older than seven, for whom the finality of death may be understandable, it may still be necessary to describe dying in physiological terms, giving examples of what happens to a person's heartbeat, breathing, or brain activity at the time of death.

Parents struggle with how to communicate in ways that will help the child understand, whether they are trying to tell siblings about a dying brother or sister, or talking directly with a dying child. Talking to children using developmentally appropriate words and concepts is important for siblings to begin coping and integrating the experience of loss.

Before beginning preparation of siblings for saying good-bye, it is important to assess the situation, expected outcomes, and wishes of the family for their other children. Many families are unable to determine whether or how to include siblings at the hospital or bedside of their dying brother and sister. With guidance from child life specialists, family members may be helped to acknowledge the appropriateness of their decisions. A parent may want the other children present, but receive conflicting opinions from other family members. To encourage siblings' presence in the hospital as a first step allows an opportunity for the family to be together. Siblings may then decide if they wish to go to the bedside.

When talking with children about the impending death of a brother or sister, it is important to address the developmental needs of each child while role modeling appropriate language and behaviors. Before beginning preparation for anticipated death in the ICU setting, it may be necessary to explain to parents the importance of specific language. To use the words "dying" and "dead" might be considered insensitive by some families unless prepared for the necessity of specific and age-appropriate wording. Children need to have explanations that are clear and concise and focus on physiological facts and happenings. It may be helpful to begin such preparation by asking the children what they think is happening. Hearing their explanation of the situation will help to plan the necessary intervention. Misconceptions may be identified and areas of clarification noted. When possible, it is important to explain probable cause of death (e.g., a brain injury or heart condition) by contrasting it with the healthy state of the sibling's own brain or heart. The brother or sister of a dying child is particularly vulnerable, and to be able to reassure them of their own safety is significant if at all possible.

The environment in which sibling preparation takes place should be carefully considered. Knowing parents' wishes about what will be said and who will say it should be discussed beforehand. Sometimes parents will consider themselves emotionally unable to say the words that the other child or children need to hear. Perhaps another relative will do the talking, or the child life specialist may facilitate the communication in the presence of people the sibling trusts. Children often do not remember who said the words, but they do remember on whose lap they were sitting at the time. Limiting the number of extended family members who are present will help the sibling to feel comfortable and encouraged to ask questions. During family conversation it may also be necessary to acknowledge family beliefs that are beyond the child's developmental ability to understand. The belief that baby sister will be cared for by great-grandma in heaven may be comforting to adults, but is too abstract for young children. Supporting these beliefs with more age-appropriate words may clarify explanations without contradicting a family's belief system.

It is especially important to identify family members who will be available to the child during the periods of acute sadness and emotional inaccessibility of the parents. To point out all the people who care about the sibling provides additional support. Also, identifying a particular family member who will be responsible for accompanying the child into and out of the patient room is important, so the child is not lost in a large group of grieving adults. During preparation and bedside visits, physical touch and nonverbal comforts, as appropriate, will help the child to feel supported. Finally, a child must be prepared not only for the sights, sounds, and smells of the ICU, but also for the emotions of the surrounding adults.

Preparation for bedside visiting in the ICU should include discussion of the child's potential participation in the events, rather than simple observation, if that is the sibling's choice. For example, children should be prepared for what they might wish to do at the bedside. This might include, talking, singing, or praying with family members, touching the person if they wish to, or participating in simple caretaking routines. Clarifying what responses, if any, are to be expected of the dying child is important. Siblings need to have activities while at the bedside and between visits. Creating big brother or sister cloth dolls, memory bracelets, or blank journals will help a child

begin the work of grieving in developmentally appropriate ways. The ability to engage in expressive art activities will also add a sense of normalcy in a setting where nothing feels familiar or comfortable to the child.

Finally, child life specialists are uniquely suited to facilitate memory building by providing concrete mementoes for parents and siblings. When parents or siblings enter the ICU and notice a familiar comfort object at the child's side, perhaps that particular object will be remembered more vividly than the number of machines or IV pumps surrounding the child's bedside.

An eight-year-old was being prepared to visit the bedside of her adolescent sister who had collapsed at a slumber party they had attended together. She shared with the child life specialist that although they were technically half sisters, they had declared their sisterhood by exchanging bead bracelets that had secret meanings to the two of them and made them real sisters. Nursing staff who had removed the bracelet earlier while inserting an arterial line might easily have overlooked this fact. The child life specialist was able to go to the bedside prior to the sibling's visit to replace the bracelet so it would be obviously visible when she came to the bedside to say goodbye.

When comfort objects are not available, especially when a child is dying from traumatic injury or sudden illness, it is possible to create mementoes that help families in grieving. Giving a homelike quilt in which to hold their child at the time of death may provide family members with a sensory comfort that would not be the case with torn or stained personal objects of clothing, or the sterile whiteness of hospital linen. If siblings will be visiting, it may be possible to provide a small stuffed animal tucked in at the bedside of the dying child and then given to the sibling as a cherished personal keepsake. This helps to acknowledge the importance of each family member's need for concrete objects as mementos to assist in initiating grief work.

> When Derrick and David's two-year-old brother died after a lengthy stay in the PICU, both boys were present with the family. Each boy chose to help in creating a memory book about their brother. They chose a rainbow stamp pad to put a handprint on the front cover and a footprint on the back cover. While many family members said their good-byes at the bedside, the siblings eagerly worked on writing and illustrating their memory books in the PICU playroom with the supportive presence of the child life specialist.

CULTURALLY SENSITIVE CARE AT THE TIME OF DEATH

Families from different cultures and ethnic backgrounds may have various rituals and ways to express feelings at the time of a child's death. However, to divide families by culture into broad categories, as if all members of a certain culture believe the same thing and practice the same rituals, is inconsistent with family-centered care principles. It is generally recognized that great diversity now exists in many ethnic groups and children often represent a new and partially assimilated generation (Grollman, 1995). In addition, certain ethnic groups may have a long history of losses, including loss of homeland or native language, loss of traditions, and loss of homogeneous cultural family group. For these reasons, it is necessary to determine what each family's cultural beliefs related to end-of life care may be, especially if assertiveness in decision making in relation to medical authority is not encouraged in one's culture (Shapiro, 1994).

McGoldrick (1991) has developed a series of questions to assist in determining family beliefs and cultural practices surrounding the death of a child.

- What are the prescribed rituals for handling dying, the dead body, the disposal of the body, and rituals to commemorate the loss?
- What are the beliefs about what happens after death?
- What does the family believe about appropriate emotional expression and integration of loss experience?
- What are the gender rules for handling death?
- Are certain deaths particularly stigmatized or traumatic?

Applying culturally sensitive care principles to child life practice means developing the skills to engage the patient or sibling in appropriate anticipatory grief work within the norms for any culture. Respecting a family's beliefs at the time of death requires that we approach families with sensitivity to determine their needs and wishes. It may be necessary to ask a family directly if the interventions that might be helpful for siblings are acceptable. To create handprints or photographs may be inappropriate in some cultures. Encouraging physical touch during closing rituals may also be contrary to religious practices. A family may have strict beliefs that define which family members are allowed to be present at the time of a death.

> One child life specialist spent several hours in the ICU playroom working with two school-age siblings whose younger brother was critically ill. When it became clear that this young child was not going to survive, a discussion took place between the child life specialist and the family spokesman, the children's uncle, to determine the family's wishes and cultural expectations. The uncle

indicated that soon all of the women and children in the family would be sent home, and only the men would be present at the bedside at the time of the death. With this information, the child life specialist was able to engage the children in memory work and good-bye rituals, including making handprints, and drawing pictures to place at their brother's bedside. While the children worked on their pictures, they readily shared stories of their brother and talked about their beliefs for life after death. Their final departure from the hospital was made easier by the memory work they were able to begin. Each child left the hospital with a blank book in which to write and illustrate the stories they had begun to share about their brother's life.

Being a trusted member of the healthcare team may help to facilitate the process of determining cultural norms and practices. Working closely with social services, pastoral care, and medical staff allows for a comprehensive and culturally sensitive plan of care to be implemented. In particular instances where rituals at the time of death may appear to interfere with hospital policy, plans may be made in advance to accommodate these required rituals safely.

In one hospital, the death of a Native American adolescent many years earlier was easily recalled, as the family had attempted to perform a smoke ceremony to speed the teen's soul to the "Great Beyond." Because no one at the time knew of the family's wishes in this regard, the ritual was attempted secretly in the family lounge causing significant fire risk within the hospital. More recently, when the death of another child of a similar culture was about to occur, the staff was able to safely arrange for the ritual to take place in a safe and undeveloped shell space close to the ICU but without risk to other patients, families, and staff.

SUMMARY

In the environment of the critical care unit, where equipment and technology are the focus of so many medical advances, there is an important place for psychosocial caring. A child life presence within the ICU, NICU or Intermediate ICU confirms the growing knowledge that developmentally appropriate activities help children master medical experiences, even when critically ill or injured. In addition, attention to the needs of parents and siblings supports family-centered care principles and promotes positive coping. To master a critical care experience with supportive child life interventions may mean less disruption in family function and a child's normal development.

In the most difficult circumstances, when a child is too ill or injured to survive, the ability to provide sensitive care at the time of death to every family, regardless of cultural beliefs, socioeconomic level, family values or even differences in coping styles, presents an ongoing challenge for child life practice. Because of our unique role and the close relationships we are able to build with patients and families, we need to continually develop our knowledge base and competencies to engage in this most difficult work. We do know that our presence makes a difference, and it may be viewed as one of the reward's of this important work, that we are constantly given new gifts of understanding and compassion by listening to the families and children with whom we work.

REFERENCES

American Academy of Pediatrics. (1995). Informed consent, parental permission and assent in pediatric practice. *Pediatrics, 95*, 314-317.

Baker, C.F. (1984). Sensory overload and noise in the ICU: Sources of environmental stress. *Critical Care Quarterly, 6*, 66-80.

Bluebond-Langner, M. (1978). *The private worlds of dying children.* Princeton: Princeton University Press.

Carnavale, F. A. (1990). A description of stressors and coping strategies among parents of critically ill children – a preliminary study. *Intensive Care Nursing, 6,* 4-11.

Carr-Gregg, M. R. C., Sawyer, S. M., Clarke, C. F., & Bowes, G. (1997). Caring for the terminally ill adolescent. *Medical Journal of Australia, 166,* 255-258.

Coddington, R. (1972). The significance of life events as etiological factors in the disease of children. *Journal of Psychosomatic Research, 16,* 205-211.

Conroy, A. J. (1990). *The impact of hospitalization for cardiac surgery on well siblings.* Unpublished thesis. Yale School of Nursing, New Haven: Connecticut.

Craft, M. J., & Craft, J. L. (1989).Perceived changes in siblings of hospitalized children: A comparison of sibling and parent reports. *Children's Health Care, 18,* 42-48.

Davies, B. (1999). *Shadows in the sun: The experiences of sibling bereavement in childhood.* Philadelphia: Taylor and Francis.

Doka, K. J. (1993). *Living with life-threatening illness: A guide for patients, their families, and caregivers.* Lexington: Lexington Books.

Doka, K. J. (1995). *Children mourning: Mourning children.* Washington, DC: Hospice Foundation of America.

Grollman, E. (1995). *Bereaved children and teens: A support guide for parents and professionals.* Boston: Beacon Press.

Huntley, T. (1991). *Helping children cope when someone they love dies.* Minneapolis: Augsburg Fortress.

Jost, K. E., & Haase, J. F. (1989). At the time of death: Help for the child's parents. *Children's Health Care, 18,* 146-152.

Lazarus, R. S. (1966). *Psychological stress and the coping process.* New York: McGraw-Hill.

McGoldrick, M., Almeida, R., Hines, P. M., Rosen, E., Garcia-Prieto, N., & Lee, E. (1991). Mourning in different cultures. In F. Walsh & M. McGoldrick (Eds.), *Living beyond loss: Death in the family.* New York: W.W. Norton & Co.

Miles, M. S. (1979). Impact of the intensive care unit on parents. *Issues in Comprehensive Pediatric Nursing, 3,* 72-79.

Miles, M. S., & Carter, M. C. (1982). Sources of parental stress in pediatric intensive care units. *Children's Health Care, 11,* 65-70.

Miles, M. S., Carter, M. C., Riddle, I., Hennessey, J., & Eberly, T. W. (1989). The pediatric intensive care unit environment as a source of stress for parents. *Maternal-Child Nursing, 18,* 199-205.

Miles, M. S., & Mathes, M. (1991). Preparation of parents for the ICU experience: What are we missing? *Children's Health Care, 20,* 132-137.

Murphy, S. O. (1993). Siblings and the new baby: Changing perspectives. *Journal of Pediatric Nursing, 8,* 277-288.

Oehler, J. M., & Vileisis, R. A. (1990). Effect of early sibling visitation in an intensive care nursery. *Developmental and Behavioral Pediatrics, 11,* 7-12.

Pazola, K. J., & Gerberg, A. K. (1990). Privileged communication – Talking with a dying adolescent. *Maternal-Child Nursing, 15,* 16-21.

Pearson, L. J. (1997). Family centered care and the anticipated death of an infant. *Pediatric Nursing, 23,* 178-182.

Pearson, L. J. (1999). Separation, loss and bereavement. In M. R. Broome & J. A. Rollins (Eds.), *Core curriculum for the nursing care of children and families.* New Jersey: Jannetti Publications, Inc.

Rushton, C. H., & Glover, J. J. (1990). Involving parents in decisions to forego life-sustaining treatment for critically ill infants and children. *AACN Clinical Issues in Critical Care Nursing, 1,* 206-214.

Sourkes, B. M. (1995). *Armfuls of time: The psychological experience of the child with a life-threatening illness.* Pittsburgh: University of Pittsburgh Press.

Speece, M. W., & Brent, S. B. (1996). The development of children understanding of death. In C. A. Corr & D. M. Corr (Eds.), *Helping children cope with death and bereavement.* New York: Springer Publishing Company, Inc.

Voss, L. A., & Nelson, R. M. (1999). Ethical issues surrounding limitation and withdrawal of support in the pediatric intensive care unit. *Journal of Intensive Care Medicine, 14,* 220-230.

Weir, R. F. (1997). Affirming the decisions adolescents make about life and death. *Hastings Center Report, 27,* 29-40.

Wolfelt, A. D. (1960). *Healing the bereaved child.* Fort Collins: Companion Press.

Wordan, J. W., & Monahan, J. R. (2001). In A. Armstrong-Dailey & S. Zarbock (Eds.), *Hospice care for children.* New York: Oxford University Press.

Chapter 12

WORKING WITH GRIEVING CHILDREN AND FAMILIES

CHRIS BROWN

During the last weeks, days or moments of a child's life, and upon death, child life specialists have a unique opportunity to support children and families. As Towne (2001) notes, "Many (parents) seek someone who has been a trusted, constant influence in their child's healthcare experience, someone who has helped them in previous difficult situations related to their child's care. They look for someone who has knowledge of children and of their child as a unique individual. Often, child life specialists satisfy these needs" (p. 1). Even in cases where the family may not have previous familiarity, such as in an emergency department, the sensitivity, skills and non-medical role assumed by the child life specialist provide for effective and welcome assistance at the time of death and beyond.

Grief is a complex process, significantly impacted by many variables including the nature of the death, support system availability, and cultural norms. When a death occurs in the hospital setting it often contradicts a strong healing culture and challenges the skills and resources of individual staff members. Bereavement support services will vary depending on setting, caregiver skills and attitudes, and allocated resources.

Practices vary widely from hospital to hospital and even from unit to unit. The neonatal intensive care unit, for example, may have organized procedures for family involvement at the time of death such as making handprint molds, cutting locks of hair, taking photographs, and sharing written information to support funeral arrangements. Resources and bereavement support procedures on a general medical unit, on the other hand, may be inconsistently offered or largely unavailable. Some hospitals employ bereavement coordinators or have established bereavement committees to organize services for families and for staff. Others have professionally facilitated bereavement support groups or formal parent-to-parent support networks.

Child life specialists play an important role in assisting family members in their grief process. As noted earlier, they are often in a position to support siblings at the time of death or in providing adult family members with appropriate tools and information for communicating with and supporting children of different ages at any time during the grief process. They also play an important role when a death occurs on an inpatient unit insofar as it impacts other patients and

238

families. Child life specialists serve as integral members of an interdisciplinary team concerned with providing the most helpful and meaningful psychosocial services to families of children with life-threatening or fatal conditions, including bereavement support services.

GRIEF AS A FAMILY PROCESS

Grief is ultimately a family process and it is within the family context that grief can best be understood and support be facilitated. According to Shapiro (1994), "Grief is a deeply shared family developmental transition, involving a crisis of attachment and a crisis of identity for family members, both of which have to be incorporated into the ongoing flow of family development" (p. 12). While recognizing the diversity in individual, family, and cultural responses to loss, family systems are regarded as crucial determinants of the healthy adaptation to loss (Walsh & McGoldrick, 1991). Walsh and McGoldrick recognize two major tasks essential to family adaptation when a member dies: (1) shared acknowledgment of the reality of death and shared experience of loss, and (2) reorganization of the family system and reinvestment in other relationships and life pursuits.

Extending the tenets of family-centered care (as described in Chapter 5) to bereavement support, interventional goals must be grounded in mutually beneficial partnerships among healthcare providers, patients, and family members. Several key elements of family-centered care can be applied to effective bereavement support services (adapted from Shelton and Stepanek, 1994):

- Recognizing the family as the constant in the child's life (for example, enabling parents to bathe and dress their child after death)
- Facilitating family and professional collaboration (for example, including parents on bereavement and/or ethics committees)
- Sharing complete and unbiased information between families and professionals in a supportive manner (for example, honest disclosure of prognosis and shared decision making among child, family, and healthcare team)
- Recognizing and honoring cultural diversity, strengths, and individuality (for example, enabling culturally diverse rituals at the time of death)
- Recognizing and respecting different methods of coping (for example, offering multiple bereavement support services for families to choose from – such as memorial services, support groups, family library resources, and more)
- Encouraging and facilitating family-to-family networking and support (for example, facilitating parent and sibling support groups)
- Ensuring that services are flexible, accessible, and comprehensive in responding to diverse family-identified needs (for example, offering a variety of bereavement support services in the communities in which families live)

PARENTAL GRIEF

It is understood that the relationship between a parent and child is the most intense of all human relationships – physically, emotionally, and socially – and that the death of a child appears to result in the most intense, complicated, and long-lasting grief (Rando, 1988). Rando suggests that it is necessary to understand parents' grief in terms of their view of children as an extension of themselves and the hopes for the future that adults invest in their children. A major challenge to resolving parental grief is the assumption that the child will outlive the parent. The radical unnaturalness of a child's death forces parents into an initial state of shock and denial (Shapiro, 1994).

Parents who outlive their children often experience substantial "survivor guilt" and feelings of failure as a parent, for they have failed to protect their children from harm. Parents may hold themselves responsible for not producing a healthy child, passing on a genetic condition, or for any number of uncontrollable factors. In instances where the death was anticipated, parental grief may be lessened if the parents feel that they did "all they could" (Shapiro, 1994). In addition to the common reactions of shock and denial, some parents will experience intense anger. This anger may be directed toward the hospital or medical staff. Hostile behavior can make supportive presence by child life specialists and other staff particularly difficult, sometimes resulting in withdrawing of support or avoidance. The most important skills and behaviors of staff at this time are patience and empathy, recognizing that intense emotions are to be expected and that maintaining a supportive stance is more likely than withdrawal or confrontation to have the desired effect.

SIBLING GRIEF

Siblings generally spend more time together than with any other family member and exert a powerful influence in shaping one another's identity (Davies, 2001). Roles played by each sibling (such as the *smart* one or the *funny* one) impact the family structure and the relationship of the surviving sib-

ling(s) within that family (Bouvard & Gladu, 1988). The death of a sibling signifies the loss of a playmate, a confidante, a rival, a role model, and a friend (Davies, 1995). It also results in profound changes in family dynamics and, at least for some time, parents may be so grief-stricken that they are emotionally unavailable to their surviving children. In a sense, the child not only loses a brother or sister but also his parents (Davies, 1995; Shapiro, 1994). According to Bowlby (1980), adult defenses almost always interfere with the child's optimal mourning. This is due, he claims, to the fact that adults so often fail to provide children with complete and honest information about the death, along with their difficulty encouraging or coping with the child's direct questions and emotional responses.

Behavioral responses of children to the death of a sibling are widely variable and may include psychophysiological behaviors, such as aches and pains, sleeping difficulties, and changes in appetite. Increased anxiety, aggression, attention-seeking behavior, decreased ability to concentrate, social withdrawal and more are all seen as normal behavioral responses to the death of a loved one (Davies, 2001; Goldman, 1994; Wolfelt 1996). Parents and other concerned adults can be reassured that virtually any response to the death of a loved one might be considered "normal" for a particular individual. If a child is engaging in behaviors that might harm himself or others, or if intense responses persist without softening over time, mourning might be considered "complicated" and warrant referral to a counselor (Wolfelt, 1996).

While there are some similarities, it is understood that children grieve in some significantly different ways than do adults. Like adults, however, each child's grief is unique. As discussed in the previous chapter, children's cognitive development will influence their ability to understand the irreversibility, universality, and inevitability of death. In addition to the impact of development on initial understanding, as the child ages she will experience new perceptions and aspects of the loss.

Generally speaking, children communicate more readily through play and other creative activities than through words. We can learn more about a child's understanding and response to an event by watching and participating in their play or expressive arts than through conversation alone. Due to their limited capacity to tolerate emotional pain, children grieve in doses or sporadically. If at times the grieving child appears unaffected, such as playing or laughing with friends immediately following the funeral, this is seen as a normal defense mechanism. Children are likely to manifest grief on an intermittent approach-avoidance basis for many years (Rando, 1988).

Attig (1995) points out that among a variety of vulnerabilities, children and adolescents are vulnerable to others' intolerance of their grieving and to insensitive responses by peers. He explains that, "Not knowing what to do or say, peers may withdraw, avoid them, deal with them abruptly, make hurtful remarks, offer precious little comfort, or make them feel uncomfortably different or strange" (p. 54). Similarly, Wolfelt (1996) points out that children and teens may resist mourning due to unwanted feelings of being different from others. In addition, children, more so than adults, are reliant on those around them for help. Bereaved adults are able to seek support when it is not available, Wolfelt points out, while children who don't have family or friends supporting their need to mourn are more vulnerable to long-term difficulties.

In helping siblings grieve, and to help parents and others support a child's grief process, it is important to understand the effects of age and cognitive development, cultural and familial influences, and other variables. We also must be aware of the significance of culture, religion, family and past experiences on our own beliefs and approaches to death and bereavement. Webb (1993) developed the "tripartite" model of assessing the bereaved child, which includes individual factors such as age or past experience; death-related factors such as the type of death; and factors related to family, social supports, religion and culture (Figure 1). These response variables should be incorporated into the child life specialist's assessment of the child and family's needs for psychosocial support and resources.

It is felt that children can best manage their grief and continue healthy development if they are given accurate, factual information appropriate to their age and stage of cognitive functioning; if they are given ongoing freedom to express their many complex feelings about the illness and death; if they are included in family rituals such as the funeral; and if their caretakers continue to provide stable attention to their needs in a secure, consistent way (Shapiro, 1994).

How children are able to work through their grief is seen to depend primarily on how their parents and other adults behave and how able they are to reach out to and to support them. Child life specialists can offer guidelines and suggestions to parents and others who may be in a position to support a grieving child, such as teachers and clergy such as those in Table 1.

TASKS OF GRIEVING

The concept that grief is expressed or experienced in stages has been explored and reinforced countless times in the literature. These widely accepted stages (denial, anger,

Figure 1:
Tripartite Assessment of the Bereaved Child

Individual factors

Age
   Developmental stage
   Cognitive level
   Temperamental characteristics

Past coping/adjustment
   Home
   School
   Interpersonal/peers
   Hobbies/interests

Global assessment of functional DSM-III-R, Axis V

Medical history

Past experience with death/loss

Death-related factors

Type of death
   Anticipated/sudden
   "Timeliness" of death/preventability
   Degree of pain
   Presence of violence/trauma
   Element of stigam

Contact with the decreased
   Present at death
   Viewed dead body
   Attended ceremonies
   Visited grave/mausoleum

Expression of "good-bye"

Relationship to deceased
   Meaning of loss

Grief reactions

Family/social/religious/cultural factors

Nuclear family
   Grief reactions

Extended family
   Grief reactions

School
   Recognition of bereavement

Peers
   Response to bereavement

Religious affiliation
   Membership/participation
   Beliefs about death

Cultural affiliation
   Typical beliefs about death
   Extent of child inclusion

Note: From *Helping Bereaved Children* (p. 30) by N. B. Webb, 1993, New York: Guilford Press. Copyright 1993 by Guilford Press. Reprinted by permission.

Table 1
GUIDELINES FOR HELPING GRIEVING SIBLINGS

- Spend time with children, explaining again and again what happened and answering their questions.
- Share your own memories and feelings with children.
- Use physical touch as a way of reassuring and comforting children.
- Tell children how much the deceased child loved them.
- Reassure children that it is not likely that anyone else (particularly the parents) will also die within the near future.
- Encourage children to express their own feelings and thoughts in their own ways.
- Continue to allow the child to have responsibilities around the house as a way of normalizing life.
- Give simple directions or utilize reminder lists for things that need to be done (children, as well as adults, have a hard time remembering while they are grieving).
- Encourage children's involvement with their friends and peers.
- Recognize that there are no magic words. Avoid saying, "I know how you feel."
- Avoid comparisons between the surviving children and the deceased sibling.
- Let children know that feeling sad, angry, or scared is okay for adults and for children and that crying is okay (even for boys).
- Allow laughter and fun times, which do occur in the midst of great sadness.

Note: From "After a child dies: Helping the siblings" by B. Davies, in *Hospice Care for Children* (p. 168) by A. Armstrong-Dailey and S. Zarbock (Eds.), 2001, New York: Oxford University Press. Copyright 2001 by Oxford University Press. Reprinted by permission.

bargaining, depression, and acceptance) were developed by Elisabeth Kübler-Ross (1969) based on interviews with 200 dying adults. Her research concluded that dying adults tended to progress through these stages as they advanced toward death. However, these stages were not intended to be universally applied to the grief process of individuals experiencing the death of a loved one, nor did the research conclude that to be the case.

Tasks of grieving have been used in more recent conceptualizations of bereavement and in the goals of intervention, both for adults and for children. Thus, bereavement is not seen as falling into orderly stages or even into predictable phases. Instead, the grief journey can be seen as involving tasks to be accomplished. These tasks do not necessarily occur in a specific order, and can be reworked at various times depending on the needs and characteristics of the individual (Worden & Monahan, 2001).

Early tasks are those that begin as soon as the child learns of the death. They involve the developing understanding of what has happened while protecting oneself against the full emotional impact of the loss. *Middle-phase tasks* include accepting and processing the loss, including the intense psychological pain. *Late tasks* include the integration of a new identity and continuing developmental progress (Wolfe & Senta, 1995).

Incorporating several similar models (Fox, 1988; Wolfelt, 1996; Worden, 1982), the tasks of grieving or reconciliation needs include:

1. Understanding and acknowledging the reality of the death
2. Grieving or "feeling the feelings" associated with the loss
3. Commemorating or keeping alive the memory of the loved one; converting the relationship with the deceased from one of presence to one of memory

4. Adjusting to a life from which the deceased is missing; developing a new self-identity based on life without the loved one
5. Relating the experience of the loss to a context of meaning
6. Going on (e.g., going on with fun activities; developing loving relationships with others, etc. This does not mean forgetting the person who's gone.)

These models all include cognitive tasks (understanding what death is, understanding that a loved one is gone forever, etc.), emotional or affective tasks (grieving, feeling the feelings associated with loss, expressing emotions), and faith-based or future-oriented tasks (incorporating the loss in a way that allows personal growth and loving relationships with others, finding meaning, enjoying positive life-affirming experiences, etc.). Because these activities obviously take place over time, leading up to and following an experience with death, child life specialists in traditional hospital-based roles are rarely in a position to provide interventions that will support the sibling's long-term progress toward reconciliation of their loss. We can, however, provide information and resources to family members, either before they've left the hospital or in follow-up communication. As illustrated in the previous chapter, interventions with siblings can support the child's understanding of death and include initial grief expression activities.

In some cases child life specialists are involved in ongoing bereavement support activities such as sibling support groups, memorial services, or educational sessions for extended family members. In these cases, activities and interventions should be consistent with the tasks of grieving identified above.

Parents may struggle with decisions around how and to what extent to involve their other children in the circumstances surrounding their child's death. This uncertainty will often lead parents to seek and respect the advice of the child life specialist. Webb (1993) advocates that children be permitted to have personal contact with the deceased, including at the time of death, viewing the body, attending ceremonies, and visiting the grave or mausoleum. Experts universally agree that children, even as young as preschool age, be prepared for all rituals and observations surrounding a loved one's death and be given the choice to participate (Anderson, 1995; Grollman, 1995; Rando, 1988; Wolfelt, 1996). Rationale includes that:

• Funerals serve to confirm and reinforce the reality of the death
• Funerals are an important occasion in a family's life (like weddings, graduations, etc.) and provide a framework for family support
• Funerals are an important source of ritual, providing an opportunity to remember the loved one's life and to say goodbye

As preparations were made to remove eleven-year-old Holly from life support following a motor vehicle accident, the child life specialist worked for several hours with her three siblings, ages four, six, and seven, preparing them to visit and say good-bye to their sister. Among the many conversations held with Holly's insightful parents that day, the child life specialist suggested that the siblings be prepared for the funeral, including the presence of an open casket, the likelihood of people crying, etc. Additional recommendations included that the siblings be accompanied by a close relative who could focus attention on their needs and remove any one of them from the room if need be, and that the siblings be given some role in the planning of the funeral. The parents and child life specialist discussed the funeral with the children and they all agreed they wanted to attend. The child life specialist attended the memorial service at a nearby funeral home the following day. Upon arrival the six-year-old sister ran to welcome the child life specialist and immediately asked her if she needed to go to the bathroom. A bit puzzled, the child life specialist reported that she did not, whereupon the child took her by the hand and showed her where the bathroom was located "just in case." As it turns out, this was the "job" the child had chosen to perform during the visiting hours. The specialist was then escorted to the viewing room and was instantly approached by another sibling with a box of tissues, tearing several from the box and offering them to the specialist "in case you need to cry" (another "job"). All three siblings proudly took the child life specialist by the hand to stand beside the casket, pointing out several pictures and letters they had placed inside. The seven-year-old sister explained that she had chosen Holly's clothes. The children's parents expressed much appreciation to the child life specialist for the time she had spent with the siblings and pride in their remarkable involvement in the entire process.

CULTURAL AND RELIGIOUS INFLUENCES

How individuals, families, and groups mourn – what they believe, feel and do – varies widely from person to person, family to family, and, certainly, culture to culture.

Different cultural traditions approach the following social and personal issues of bereavement differently: defining the relationship between the dead and the living, describing the nature of life after death, and enabling the social reconstruction of the ruptured relationships within family and community. Each culture defines the processes of bereavement and reconstruction in ways that are consistent with its beliefs regarding life,

death, and an afterlife, emphasizing certain aspects of the broad range of human experience while diminishing the importance of others (Shapiro, 1994, p. 220).

Cultural influences on how members of a family grieve include the meaning a death has for the group; the customs surrounding death and funerals; and family-life patterns, such as the lines of authority, the roles of various family members during periods of grief, and the amount of help available (Lawson, 1990).

While there is considerable diversity within any ethnic or religious group, and it is important not to assume generalized cultural norms to the exclusion of individual beliefs and behaviors, it can be helpful to ascertain cultural influences on the bereavement process. The predominant culture of mourning in the U.S., for example, is restrained and largely expected to be resolved quickly and quietly. For the most part, death is denied in our culture, not openly discussed and even considered a taboo subject. Public composure and what many experts would say is an unrealistically short mourning period represent "appropriate" or "expected" expressions of grief in mainstream American culture. On the contrary, individuals from other cultures may tend to express grief "loudly" or with more outward manifestation, such as some African Americans, Mexican Americans, and Arabs.

Rituals observed by members of certain ethnic or religious groups may challenge not only caregiver skills but also hospital policy and community resources. While recognizing the fact that differences exist within cultures as well as between cultures, and acknowledging the incomplete nature of these examples, Table 2 illustrates some of the culturally distinct customs related to death and mourning.

As is the case in any work with children and families from a variety of ethnic and religious backgrounds, the best way to deter-

Table 2
EXAMPLES OF TRADITIONAL RITUALS AND MOURNING

- A Hmong funeral may last up to ten days or more. Customs include bathing, dressing, the sacrifice and eating of a chicken and other animals, reciting of text, and prescribed roles for various family and community members (Bliatout, 1993).
- When the member of a Jewish family dies, the family sits Shiva for a week after the funeral. As Lanton (1991) wrote in her book for children about a Jewish funeral tradition, "Shiva means seven. For seven days we stay home. We sit on low benches to show that we are feeling low. We don't wear leather shoes of party clothes because they are for happier times. And the black ribbon I'm wearing is another symbol of my sadness." (p. 15).
- Upon the death of a Muslim, Islamic tradition holds that the family must immediately turn the body to face Mecca; have someone sit nearby reading the Koran; close the mouth and eyes of the deceased and cover the eyes and face; straighten both legs and stretch both hands by the sides; announce the death immediately to all friends and family; and quickly bathe the body and cover it with white cotton (Gilanshah, 1993).
- The Vietnamese strongly believe that death should occur at home, surrounded by family. Medical care may be sought at a hospital but all efforts are made to get the person home before the moment of death (Truitner, 1993).
- More so than probably any other religion, Quaker and Unitarian-Universalist groups have incorporated guidance and education around dying, death and mourning into their way of life (Irish, 1993). Brochures, manuals, audiovisuals and checklists have been developed for use in the church community to prepare for and mourn losses.
- If a Hindu child dies the family is particular about who touches the body. The priest pours water into the child's mouth, ties a thread around their neck or wrist to signify blessing, and the family washes the body (Gabbert, 1994).

mine cultural influences is usually to ask questions, listen, and adapt interventions to accommodate individual differences and needs. An openness and active acceptance of a broad range of reactions to death and grief behaviors will allow the child life specialist to respond appropriately and supportively despite individual or cultural differences. Literature, experts, and community resources can also support the health care team as they strive to provide culturally sensitive and appropriate care.

CHILD LIFE SPECIALIST COMPETENCY DEVELOPMENT

There is a good deal written in the bereavement literature suggesting caregiver

skills and techniques helpful in working with grieving children (Brown, 2001; Edwards & Davis, 1997; Goldman, 1994; Grollman, 1995; Rando, 1984; Webb, 1993; Wolfelt, 1996; Worden, 1982). Most, if not all, of these skills are consistent with child life work in any setting and provide the basis for primary and advanced competency development.

Play Facilitation Skills

A fundamental competency for child life specialists is the ability to provide opportunities for and facilitate "a variety of play, activities, and other interactions which promote self-healing, self-expression, understanding and mastery" (CLC, 2002, p. 23). As in supporting a child's adaptation to the hospital setting or facilitating the expression of anger over needle sticks, for example, play is a most appropriate means to support a child's grief work. Play and other creative activities provide opportunities for the expression of feelings in naturally therapeutic and developmentally appropriate ways.

As children attending a bereavement support group played with Play-Doh®, mashing and pounding the clay to express feelings, Brian meticulously created a scene of cars, telephone poles, and ambulances. As the child life specialist sat closely by, supporting his animated reenactment, Brian smashed the model cars into each other and described his conception of the drunk driving accident that had taken his father's life.

The provision of play and other expressive activities to support children's grief is primarily a facilitative role. As facilitator it is generally the child life specialist's role to allow and encourage the child to lead or direct the play. Using the example above, the child life specialist did not direct Brian to recreate his experience with Play-Doh®; he determined for himself that this activity would support his own unique needs. She did, however, provide an emotionally safe environment for him to explore his experiences and feelings.

Play also presents opportunities for the child life specialist to detect and clarify misperceptions or to therapeutically support the child's grieving.

As Maria played at the sand table, repeatedly burying a plastic female figure in the sand, she shouted down toward the buried figure, "Are you okay?! Can you breathe down there??" The discovery of Maria's misconception allowed the child life specialist to clarify that when someone dies they no longer eat or breathe or hear. The

sand table remained one of Maria's favorite activities throughout her support group attendance.

While therapeutic play and expressive arts facilitation skills are fundamental to virtually every child life specialist's practice, the ability to design activities to support the grief process in particular presents some unique opportunities. Play therapy education and skills development are seen as greatly enhancing traditional child life training in working with children in crisis. A variety of specific activity ideas can be found in publications sited in this chapter, including Brown (2001), O'Toole (1989) and Whitney (1991).

Communication Skills

Probably the most essential skills for supporting the grieving child, as can be argued for child life work in general, involve communication. The primary goals of communication are to build a trusting relationship, to convey information, and to receive information (including facts, feelings, perceptions, etc.). As child life specialists we often think of our effectiveness as communicators with children to rely largely on our command of child development and our abilities to convey information in a developmentally appropriate manner. Equally, if not more, important may be our *listening* skills, particularly in our efforts to support grieving children. Effective listening involves active listening skills (being present, reflection, mirroring, perception checking, clarifying, etc.) and attending behaviors (such as eye contact, tone of voice, rate of speech, facial expression, body posture, and proximity/posture of involvement).

An important skill for child life specialists to develop is the prudent use of questions. Questioning not only tends to direct the child's thoughts and actions but also implies that the objective is for the adult to gain knowledge about the child. Supportive techniques (reflection, paraphrasing, clarifying) sustain the child's *own* process, self-understanding, and mastery. Consider the following conversation with a grieving sibling during medical play:

> Child, dressed as a doctor, is engaged in medical play with a baby doll. . . . The child life specialist is seated nearby, on the child's level, and is attentive in posture, eye contact and tone of voice.

Child: *Quick, he needs an operation, his heart isn't working!*

CLS: *Sounds like an emergency . . .*

Child: *Quick! His heart isn't beating! Cut him open!*

CLS: *The doctor is working very hard to help. . . .*

Child: *Nurse! Tell the parents their baby is very, very sick.*

CLS: *. . . the baby is very, very sick.*

Child: *Get more doctors in here! Give the baby all the medicine we have!!*

CLS: *The doctor thinks maybe more medicine and more doctors will help.*

Child: *This is bad, it's really bad.*

CLS: *(nods silently)*

Child: *I'm afraid it's too late. The medicine is not helping. Nurse, tell the parents their baby is dead.*

CLS: *The doctors tried very hard to help the baby, but the baby was very sick and he died.*

Group Facilitation Skills

Given the playroom supervision/facilitation responsibilities of most child life specialists, the ability to "balance group process with individual needs" (CLC, 2002, p. 14) is an important skill. The ability to effectively facilitate a peer support group, such as a cancer support group or a group for bereaved siblings, calls on a related but unique set of skills. Most child life specialists receive little to no formal training in group facilitation, phases in group development, group interaction processes, etc. Specialized training in the provision of bereavement support groups for children or for adults is highly recommended.

Empathic Response Skills

Another essential skill for child life specialists is the ability to empathize effectively. Empathy is identified as a basic helper attitude and characteristic in counseling children (Edwards & Davis, 1997).

This is often described as the ability to step inside someone's shoes and experience the world from their perspective. We can never totally achieve this or fully understand how another person feels, but we can try to reach a fairly accurate view of the other person's model or way of conceptualizing the world. To be effective, empathy has to be conveyed to the child, and this requires being able to communicate some understanding of the child's thoughts and feelings back to them. It does not necessarily mean agreeing with the child, but involves trying to put aside one's own views and feelings and to focus one's thoughts on the experience of the child. Coming to an understanding of a child's world can be difficult for an adult; the child's world might contain dragons, witches and magic. The helper needs to be able to put their own knowledge of the world to one side to be able to join the child in his or her world. (p. 78.)

Advocacy and Collaboration Skills

Another goal of child life specialists can be to advocate appropriate responses to and support for children's and family member's grief. Program development, committee work, policy development, and the like are often necessary to create or maintain effective bereavement support systems for children and families. Child life specialists need to develop the skills necessary to participate as an active organizer, facilitator, or participant in such systems. Especially in small programs and in cases where formal systems (e.g., bereavement committees, palliative care services, etc.) do not exist, child life specialists may need to actively seek other staff members with similar goals or interests. While the need for major changes may seem daunting, manageable initiatives such as organizing the mailing of condolence cards can be the beginning of wider systemic improvements or lasting program developments.

One of the most difficult experiences for families was clearly that of spending time in the hospital's "viewing room," located just outside the morgue on the second floor. With leadership from the child life specialist a small work group was convened to determine ways in which the family's experience could be improved. Ultimately, administrative support and a modest resource allocation enabled redecoration of the area to include a rocking chair, wallpaper borders, boxes of "quality" tissues and artwork.

Self-Reflection Skills

The effective caregiver needs to be aware of her own feelings, beliefs, and values around illness, death and dying, and to process personal experiences (Irish, 1993; Rando, 1984; Sumner, 2001; Webb, 1993; Wolfelt, 1983, 1996; Worden, 1982). Worden suggests that such self-reflection is essential for the caregiver to better understand the process of mourning, to reflect on what responses are likely to be helpful or not helpful, to identify unresolved grief issues in one's own life, and to recognize one's own limitations. This self-awareness also influences the child life specialist's ability to develop therapeutic relationships within the context of effective, professional boundaries.

Implications for Training and Competency Development

Wolfelt (1983) has developed a process model for helping children cope with grief whereby the "helper" brings his or her own knowledge, experience, personal traits and a genuine regard for children to the relationship with the grieving child. Wolfelt concludes that it is within the context of a caring relationship and the helper's utilization of identified skills that the desired outcomes for the grieving child can best be achieved. The knowledge base suggested for working with grieving children is largely consistent with the training and expertise of child life specialists. For example, child development knowledge, a family-centered approach, and skills in using play and other forms of communication with children are of paramount importance in effective bereavement support and are typical strengths of the child life professional.

Additional training and experience may be indicated in order for the child life specialist to understand common grief reactions of children and teens, to offer appropriate helping responses, to facilitate the "tasks of grieving" discussed earlier, and to facilitate effective support groups. The adaptation and development of skills to meet the needs of special populations (e.g., developmentally delayed, culturally diverse, hearing or speech impaired, etc.) or special circumstances (e.g., suicide, murder, AIDS, local or national tragedies) ought to be pursued. In addition, child life specialists should become aware of available resources and mechanisms for referral to other experts, such as in cases where suicidal thoughts or actions, chronic depression, eating disorders, drug or alcohol abuse, or inappropriate sexual behaviors are suspected.

BEREAVEMENT SUPPORT SYSTEMS

Several programs and practices can be identified that serve to support children and families, as well as the staff who work with dying or grieving children and families. In most cases child life specialists can and should be represented and involved in these supports, whether as leader, advocate, participant, teacher, or consumer. The development and availability of services for either families or staff members depend upon factors such as the number and types of deaths typical of the particular setting; the presence, number and expertise of certain professionals (as well as the level of interdisciplinary collaboration versus territoriality of these groups); the predominant philosophy and culture of the particular hospital or unit; and the allocation of resources.

Until a few years ago child life services in a large children's hospital were only extended to the pediatric intensive care unit upon the rare request by nursing staff for play interventions with certain long-term patients. Once a full-time child life specialist was hired, the role evolved over time to the extent that the interdisciplinary team relies heavily on the clinical skills of the child life specialist to work with the sickest patients and their families, including regular and active participation at the time of death and leadership in the establishment of a unit-based bereavement committee. Consequently, siblings are now regularly and effectively prepared for the death of a brother or sister, child life consultation is sought in off-hours via an on-call system, and families consistently have access to keepsakes and follow-up supports.

Family Support Systems

In many pediatric healthcare settings systems have been designed to support families at the time of a child's death and/or for a time following the death. Typically, several disciplines are involved in such activities including nursing, pastoral care, social work, and child life. These practices vary widely, however, and often would benefit from further development, organization, or expansion. Examples include written information for families (such as information on autopsies, funeral planning, grief responses, community resources, etc.), keepsakes (such as locks of hair, handprints or photographs given prior to or at the time of death), support groups, workshops, or memorial services, and follow-up mailings to families (such as sympathy cards, grief literature, invitations to hospital or community events.

One of the most useful roles the child life specialist can play to support bereaved children and family members is the identification of appropriate resources. There are many excellent books, websites, brochures, and community resources available – too numerous and too variable for a family to navigate at a time of great shock and grief. The child life specialist should be familiar and up-to-date with the best resources to meet various needs, and provide for the timely and appropriate dissemination of such resources for families as well as other professionals. Short annotated bibliographies are essential if families are to easily take advantage of available resources. Having specific materials available, for example in a family resource library or as a timely gift, demonstrates a true commitment to sensitive, responsive care.

The strength of a multifaceted approach to family support services is that the families, and even individuals within a family, can choose which type of service will best meet their unique needs. Some will participate in and appreciate an ongoing support group while others will more readily take advantage of an annual memorial service or an online support network.

Depending on circumstances surrounding a death (or multiple deaths) and on available community resources, child life staff may be sought out to provide support to schools or other community-based groups. Such support may be initiated by the child life specialist or members of the healthcare team, as in the death of a school-age cancer patient, or by the school itself, such as in response to a school shooting or the death of a teacher. Proactive planning for such requests should be undertaken to determine response policies and necessary resources, including staff training. Again, child life skills may be consistent with the skills needed for such interventions and can result in very effective supports for teachers, parents, classmates, and others. There are some excellent resources available to support the child life specialist in addressing the needs of classmates and school staff in the event of a catastrophic event or the death of a classmate (Fox, 1988; Gliko-Braden, 1992; Metzgar, 1995; Pitcher & Poland, 1992). Even in the case of limited staff resources or long-distance requests, appropriate print materials and other supports can be made available to schools and communities.

Staff Support Systems

Equally important are the systems and programs in place to support staff in their skills development and stress management relative to working with dying or grieving children and families. Edwards and Davis (1987) offer that "In order to ensure that the quality of services remains at a high level, it is important to acknowledge the stresses and strains that are experienced by all staff working in this area. To enable them to cope effectively, they require appropriate support, ongoing supervision, and their further training needs should be identified and met" (p. 193). The stresses most commonly identified by healthcare professionals relate to witnessing children in physical and emotional pain and distress, a perceived lack of available resources (including time), and difficulties in staff communication and interrelationships (Edwards & Davis, 1987). Burnout, chronic grief, and staff turnover due to "vicarious traumatization" (Webb, 1993) are recognized in the literature as common problems in end-of-life caregiving (Rando, 1984; Sumner, 2001; Worden, 1982). Ethical issues (such as do-not-resuscitate orders and artificial life support) along with the perceived "unfairness" of a child's death and feelings of vulnerability as a parent oneself, all compound the emotional stress of this type of work. It is essential that child life specialists and other team members have a healthy self-awareness of their loss experiences and grief responses, have opportunities and success in resolving their own grief, and maintain effective support systems.

Supervision, debriefings, memorial services, support groups, stress management activities and educational opportunities are all examples of useful strategies to improve and maintain a professional's abilities to provide competent and effective care to children and families in highly emotional and challenging circumstances.

Worden (1982) suggests three guidelines to avoid burnout. First, to know one's limitations; second, to practice active grieving; and third, to know how to reach out for help. Sumner (2001) suggests several systems and personal strategies to manage the stresses common in hospice work:

- Fostering optimal team functioning – whereby interdisciplinary team members trust and support one another, have clearly defined role boundaries, and are supported by hiring practices that promote effective team functioning
- Successful orienting and precepting of new employees – characterized by immediate availability of support, mentoring, and supervision to develop confidence and self-sufficiency of new staff
- Ongoing training and resources for experienced staff – including conflict resolution training, memorial activities, team meetings, and employee assistance programs

In one child life department, "stress-buster" sessions are offered on a monthly basis to assist staff in dealing with the intense emotions of working with dying children and other difficult experiences. Sessions are facilitated by child life or interdisciplinary team members, such as the hospital bereavement coordinator, chaplain, art therapist or music therapist, and by outside experts. Staff voluntarily attend the sessions they feel will best meet their needs, with many of the activities designed to facilitate the expression of feelings, promote healthy coping, and generate an atmosphere of team support.

Several child life departments have established on-call systems to make child life services available in off-hours or in areas not covered by a dedicated staff member. In this case, one of the biggest stressors reported by "on-call" specialists was their uncertainty and lack of comfort in being called to the bedside of a dying or deceased patient to assist with sibling support or in making keepsakes. In order to promote competence and reduce stress, a cabinet of key resources (Table 3) was created in the child life office and a series of inservices was developed including a "hands-on" workshop to practice the challenging art of handprint molds.

Table 3
BEREAVEMENT SUPPORT SUPPLIES

- Materials for hand and/or foot molds
- A variety of papers, inks and brayers for hand and footprints
- Containers for locks of hair
- Digital and instant cameras
- Booklets and brochures for parents (such as *What Will I Tell the Children* by Bell and Esterling, 1986)
- Memory boxes (blank craft boxes for siblings to decorate)
- Blank books or journals
- A variety of books for children about loss, death, grief, and feelings
- Grief support activity manuals (for example, those by O'Toole, 1989 and Whitney, 1991)

FACILITATING PEER GRIEF IN THE HOSPITAL SETTING

It is not uncommon for children and teens with similar conditions, such as cystic fibrosis or those awaiting organ transplants, to develop strong attachments to each other. As a result, there are emotional repercussions on the unit or in the clinic when a child dies (Edwards & Davis, 1987). Such instances often result in a complex combination of patient fears and concerns, staff member responses, family stress, and policy/procedure questions (e.g., around disclosure, confidentiality, or hospital-sponsored activities to recognize the death.)

Several thirteen to seventeen year old female patients, all hospitalized on the cardiac unit for over six months developed strong friendships and a "three musketeer" reputation. All awaiting heart/lung transplants, they played together, attended school together, ate holiday meals together, and shared virtually every aspect of their lives with each other (as, to a large extent, did their parents). Their relationships with the child life specialist also grew strong and trusting. When Dorothy, the oldest girl, was transferred to the Cardiac ICU the girls expressed a great deal of fear and concern. Communication was facilitated by the child life specialist, including some not entirely successful advocacy on the specialist's part that the healthcare team be honest with the girls about Dorothy's condition. When Dorothy died two days later, the child life specialist and transplant psychologist were immediately called in to support the girls. Parents were called to come to the hospital and were assisted in telling their daughters the news. To put it mildly, the girls were devastated. Throughout the weekend the child life specialist supported the girls' repeated questions about Dorothy's death, while respecting confidentiality and maintaining contact with all the girls' parents,

including Dorothy's. The girls spent hours decorating the playroom, one of Dorothy's favorite activities, and pouring over digital photos taken over the past several months of the "three musketeers" enjoying child life activities and celebrating various holidays. With the sensitive support of the child life specialist, the girls used the digital photos to make each of them a memory book, all the while telling stories about their shared adventures and recalling Dorothy's sense of humor. Because they would be unable to attend the funeral, the child life specialist assisted in plans with one of the hospital's part time chaplains to hold a memorial service in the girls' room at the same time as Dorothy's funeral two days later.

BEREAVEMENT SUPPORT GROUPS

One of the most effective models for facilitating children's grief is the peer support group. The benefits of the support group approach are described by Webb (1993) as: facilitating normalization; providing peer support; breaking the sense of isolation; and creating a safe place to share taboo issues. Comprehensive information on the facilitation of bereavement groups for children is beyond the scope of this chapter. However, the following program components should be considered:

- A family-centered approach (it is recommended that groups be available for parents as well as for children)
- Open-ended versus a finite number of sessions (Grief is a long-term versus short-term process. If ongoing weekly/biweekly sessions are not possible, children should be permitted to attend a succession of groups if desired or have access to other programs – e.g., grief camp, "reunion" activities with group members, phone follow-up, etc.)

- Child-directed play and creative arts based sessions are most appropriate for children of all ages (versus scripted, structured sessions addressing pre-selected issues)
- Facilitation by professionals (e.g., child life specialists, creative arts therapists, social workers) and/or volunteers with specific bereavement training
- Grouping by age/developmental level and type of death (e.g., sibling versus parent versus pet death)

(Note: Children's bereavement support group programs can be found in many communities. One of the most effective models is that created at the Dougy Center in Portland Oregon, and replicated in centers throughout North America. The Dougy Center and its sister programs make excellent training and material resources available.)

A wide variety of common play, creative arts, and literature-based activities have proven useful in facilitating children's grief work. Popular choices among children attending bereavement support groups include arts and crafts, medical play, puppet play, sand play, and physical or gross motor play. The following examples of actual support group sessions demonstrate the value of these activities to grieving children and will hopefully serve to generate additional ideas.

The "Volcano Room" became Michael's favorite place. Outfitted with punching bags, boxing gloves, pillows, and a large wall for drawing, Michael could be loud and aggressive. Initially, when Michael began to demonstrate out of control behavior during group, the child life specialist would take him to the Volcano Room to let off steam and express his strong emotions. Eventually, Michael himself recognized those times when he needed that particular outlet and would tell the staff or volunteers that he needed to have some "angry play time."

One of the group's favorite storybooks was Badger's Parting Gifts (Varley, 1984). The story follows a group of friends recounting the many gifts left behind by their deceased friend, Badger -- gifts in the form of skills, memories, and stories. After reading and discussing the story as a group, the children set about drawing pictures about gifts their loved one had left behind for them. Luis drew a bicycle and a football, previously belonging to his brother, and a heart with a big crack down the middle. When telling about his picture, Luis described fun times riding bikes and playing football and said that sometimes his memories made his heart hurt.

Another popular storybook about friendship prompted a lively discussion of new and trusted friends found at the support group. Later, during art time, Jodie made certificates for several friends and family members for helping her with her sad feelings.

After weeks of starting each support group session with a book about feelings or death, seven-year-old Shawna enthusiastically accepted the idea of making a book to tell her own story. For two complete sessions, nearly four hours, Shawna painstakingly worked on the cover of her book, never getting to the pages inside. Upon completing the cover she declared her book done and entitled it The Nightmare Before the Understanding. Shawna's brother had committed suicide.

SUMMARY

The child life profession has grown and developed to represent a unique collection of skills and practices in support of the psychosocial needs of children and families in healthcare and other settings. These skills and practices are often called upon to address the important challenges faced by dying children, grieving families, and fellow patients of deceased children. While the experiences are sometimes daunting and frequently emotionally difficult, they can also provide for some of the most fulfilling and important work we as child life specialists might ever do.

The fundamental skills of therapeutic relationship building and play-based communication, for example, have served to position child life specialists as effective team members in the end-of-life care arena. At a time when palliative and end-of-life care is receiving more attention and development than ever, both generally and in pediatrics specifically, opportunities and resources for child life specialists are likely to increase. In order to be effective in this work, child life specialists need to establish skills in direct care provision, collaborative program development, and self-preservation.

REFERENCES

Anderson, B. (1995). Do children belong at funerals? In D. W. Adams & E. J. Deveau (Eds.), *Beyond the innocence of children: Factors influencing children and adolescents' perceptions and attitudes toward death* (Vol. 1, pp. 163-177). Amityville, NY: Baywood Publishing Company, Inc.

Attig, T. W. (1995). Respecting bereaved children and adolescents. In D. W. Adams & E. J. Deveau (Eds.), *Beyond the innocence of childhood: Helping children and adolescents cope with death and bereavement* (Vol. 3, pp. 43-60). Amityville, NY: Baywood Publishing Company, Inc.

Bell, J., & Esterling, L. (1986). *What will I tell the children?* Omaha, NE: University of Nebraska Medical Center Child Life Department.

Bliatout, B. T. (1993). Hmong death customs: Traditional and acculturated. In D. P. Irish, K. F. Lunquist & V. J. Nelsen (Eds.), *Ethnic variations in dying, death, and grief* (pp. 79-100). Washington, DC: Taylor & Francis.

Bouvard, M., & Gladu, E. (1988). *The path through grief.* Portland, OR: Breitenbush Books, Inc

Bowlby, J. (1980). *Loss: Sadness and depression.* New York: Basic Books.

Brown, C. (2001). Therapeutic play and creative arts: Helping children cope with illness, death, and grief. In A. Armstrong-Dailey & S. Zarbock (Eds.), *Hospice care for children* (pp. 250-283). New York: Oxford University Press.

Child Life Council. (2002). *Official documents of the child life council.* Rockville, MD: Child Life Council.

Davies, B. (2001). After a child dies: Helping the siblings. In A. Armstrong-Dailey & S. Zarbock (Eds.), *Hospice care for children* (pp. 157-171). New York: Oxford University Press.

Davies, B. (1995). Toward siblings' understanding and perspectives of death. In E. Grollman (Ed.), *Bereaved children and adolescents: A support guide for parents and professionals* (pp. 61-74). Boston, MA: Beacon Press.

Edwards, M., & Davis, H. (1997). *Counseling children with chronic medical conditions.* London: British Psychological Society.

Fox, S. S. (1988). *Good grief: Helping groups of children when a friend dies.* Boston, MA: New England Association for the Education of Young Children.

Gabbert, W. (1994). A difficult challenge: Caring for the family after a child dies. In *Nursing in pediatrics.* Fort Worth, TX: Cook-Fort Worth Children's Medical Center.

Gilanshah, F. (1993). Islamic customs regarding death. In D. P. Irish, K. F. Lunquist & V. J. Nelsen (Eds.), *Ethnic variations in dying, death, and grief* (pp. 137-145). Washington, DC: Taylor & Francis.

Gliko-Braden, M. (1992). *Grief comes to class: A teacher's guide.* Omaha, NE: Centering Corporation.

Goldman, L. (1994). *Life and loss: A guide to help grieving children.* Muncie, IN: Accelerated Development, Inc.

Grollman, E. (1995). Explaining death to young children: Some questions and answers. In E. Grollman (Ed.), *Bereaved children and adolescents: A support guide for parents and professionals* (pp. 3-19). Boston, MA: Beacon Press.

Kübler-Ross, E. (1969). *On death and dying.* New York: Macmillan Publishing.

Lanton, S. (1990). *Daddy's chair.* Rockville, MD: Kar-Ben Copies, Inc.

Lawson L. (1990). Culturally sensitive support for grieving parents. *Maternal and Child Nursing, 15,* 76-79.

Metzger, M. M. (1995). What do we do with the empty desk? In D. W. Adams & E. J. Deveau (Eds.), *Beyond the innocence of childhood: Helping children and adolescents cope with death and bereavement* (Vol. 3, pp. 167-180). Amityville, NY: Baywood Publishing Company, Inc.

O'Toole, D. (1989). *Growing through grief: A K-12 curriculum to help young people through all kinds of loss.* Burnsville, NC: Mountain Rainbow Publications.

Pitcher, G. D., & Poland, S. (1992). *Crisis intervention in the schools.* New York: The Guilford Press.

Rando, T. (1984). *Grief, dying, and death: Clinical interventions for caregivers.* Champaign, IL: Research Press Company.

Rando, T. (1988). *How to go on living when someone you love dies.* New York: Bantam Books.

Shapiro, E. R. (1994). *Grief as a family process: A developmental approach to clinical practice.* New York: Guilford Press.

Shelton, T. L., & Stepanek, J. S. (1994). *Family-centered care for children needing specialized health and developmental services.* Bethesda, MD: Association for the Care of Children's Health.

Sumner, L. H. (2001). Staff support in pediatric hospice care. In A. Armstrong-Dailey & S. Zarbock (Eds.), *Hospice care for children* (pp. 190-212). New York: Oxford University Press.

Towne, M. (2001). The role of child life in pediatric end of life care. In *Child life focus* (pp. 1-4). Rockville, MD: Child Life Council.

Truitner, K., & Truitner, N. (1993). Death and dying in Buddhism. In D. P. Irish, K. F. Lunquist & V. J. Nelsen (Eds.), *Ethnic variations in dying, death, and grief* (pp. 125-136). Washington, DC: Taylor & Francis.

Varley, S. (1984). *Badger's parting gifts.* New York: Lothrop, Lee & Shepard Books.

Walsh, F., & McGoldrick, M. (1991). Loss and the family: A systemic perspective. In F. Walsh and M. McGoldrick (Eds.), *Living beyond loss: Death in the family* (pp. 1-29). New York: W. W. Norton & Company.

Webb, N. B. (1993). Counseling and therapy for the bereaved child. In N. B. Webb (Ed.), *Helping bereaved children: A handbook for practitioners* (pp. 43-58). New York: The Guilford Press.

Webb, N. B. (1993). Assessment of the bereaved child. In N. B. Webb (Ed.), *Helping bereaved children: A handbook for practitioners* (pp. 19-42). New York: The Guilford Press.

Whitney, S. (1991). *Waving goodbye: An activities manual for children in grief.* Portland, OR: The Dougy Center.

Wolfe, B. S., & Senta, L. M. (1995). Interventions with bereaved children nine to thirteen years of age: From a medical center-based young person's grief support program. In D. W. Adams & E. J. Deveau (Eds.), *Beyond the innocence of childhood: Helping children and adolescents cope with death and bereavement* (Vol. 3, pp. 203-227). Amityville, NY: Baywood Publishing Company, Inc.

Wolfelt, A. (1983). *Helping children cope with grief.* Bristol, PA: Accelerated Development.

Wolfelt, A. D. (1996). *Healing the bereaved child: Grief gardening, growth through grief and other touchstones for caregivers.* Fort Collins, CO: Companion Press.

Worden, J. W., & Monahan, J. R. (2001). Caring for bereaved parents. In A. Armstrong-Dailey & S. Zarbock (Eds.), *Hospice care for children* (pp. 137-156). New York: Oxford University Press.

Worden, J. W. (1982). *Grief counseling and grief therapy.* New York: Springer Publishing Company.

Chapter 13

CHRONIC ILLNESS AND REHABILITATION

MELISSA HICKS AND KATHRYN DAVITT

INTRODUCTION

With advances in modern medical science, many children with chronic illnesses and traumatic injuries are living longer lives. Diseases that were once considered terminal are now viewed as more chronic in nature, with longer life expectancies for children diagnosed with diseases such as cancer, cystic fibrosis and AIDS. The distinction between chronic and acute illness is now more difficult to make. In general, there has been a shift in focus from elimination of the condition as an acute illness, to adjustment and adaptation to the illness, treatment and side effects. Further blurring the distinction between chronic and acute conditions, some acute illnesses lead to chronic conditions, and many chronic illnesses have acute phases, such as exacerbation of symptoms and periodic prophylactic medications or procedures. It is estimated that the prevalence of children in the United States living with chronic illness is between 10 and 30 percent (Bauman, Drotar, Leventhal, Perrin, & Pless, 1997). Typically, chronic illnesses are characterized by a duration of three months or longer or those which necessitate a period of continuous hospitalization for more than one month.

Often these illnesses are present for an individual's entire life, as in the case of asthma, diabetes, and sickle cell disease. Children may also present with illnesses that require extended treatment and which may have an uncertain outcome and/or degenerative processes, such as cancer, cystic fibrosis, renal and heart disease and HIV.

The most prevalent diagnoses associated with in inpatient rehabilitation programs are traumatic brain injury (TBI), spinal cord injury (SCI), cerebral palsy (CP), spina bifida, bronchopulmonary dysplasia (BPD), cerebrovascular accident (CVA), burns, orthopedic problems, and neurological problems, with TBI being the most common and disabling of these injuries (Edwards, Hertzberg, Hays, & Youngblood, 1999). Children and adolescents in rehabilitation programs were often developing typically prior to the precipitating event that created the need for rehabilitation programming. The children and youth served by acute rehabilitation programs often have experienced some type of trauma, either an accident or catastrophic illness. The importance of this area of medicine is likely to grow as technology is increasingly capable of saving lives and enhancing the recovery of those who survive (Edwards et al., 1999).

Rehabilitation and chronic illness present many challenges to children and families. Some of these pertain to both chronic illness and care in rehab settings, while others are unique to one or the other. Whether facing chronic illness or rehabilitation, children and youth confront developmental challenges throughout their lifetime. The child or teen may have limited contact with peers and increased contact with adults, presenting additional complications for social development. They confront issues of pain, grief, loss and complicated emotions. They need ongoing education related to their condition. They face extended and possibly repeated hospital admissions. Rehabilitation stays are often more continuous (two weeks to a year, with two months being an average stay), while admissions for chronic illness are more repetitive. In any case, the challenge becomes coping with the symptoms of the condition and the psychosocial sequelae. Psychosocial support becomes an important part of the child and family's healthcare regimen, with a focus on the needs of the family members.

This chapter will describe some of the challenges faced by children with chronic illness and/or rehabilitative needs and by their families. Throughout this chapter, the term "chronic condition" will be used to refer to both chronic illness and rehabilitation. Information presented in this chapter will not pertain to one particular diagnosis, but can be generalized to children with a variety of conditions, as long as the needs of the individual are the primary focus. The chapter will explore factors affecting adjustment and highlight practices that the professionals can utilize to work with the child and family to address their psychosocial concerns. It concludes with a focus on the unique professional issues that need to be evaluated and addressed when working with this population of individuals.

LITERATURE REVIEW

The impact of chronic illness on children has been well documented. This literature highlights both the potential mental health risks related to chronic illness, as well as the psychosocial resilience displayed by children and families coping with such conditions. In recent years, perspectives on chronic conditions have shifted from models of maladjustment to models considering the individual and familial factors that promote adjustment – toward a view of typical families dealing with atypical circumstances. Chronic illness in one family member has significant impact on all members of the family. Therefore, attention to the unique psychosocial needs of all family members must be considered (Cohen, 1999; Conoley & Sheridan, 1996; Eiser, 1990; Martin, 1988; Testani-Dufour, Chappel-Aiken, & Gueldner, 1992; Thompson & Gustafson, 1996; Verity, 1995).

The potential for adjustment difficulties is inherent regardless of the particular illness. Challenges among children with chronic illnesses include difficulty with peers, impaired social functioning (Meijer, Sinnema, Bijstra, Mellenbergh, & Walters, 2000), internalizing problems such as depression and anxiety, externalizing problems such as behavioral difficulties and oppositional tendencies (Bussing, Halfon, Benjamin & Wells, 1995), and concerns related to body/self image, dependency, withdrawal (Thompson & Gustafson, 1996). In addition, social and emotional issues are prevalent among children in rehabilitation settings, including loneliness, decreased self-esteem, and post-traumatic stress disorder (Abdullah, Blakeney, Hunt, Broemeling, Phillips, Herndon, & Robson, 1998; Levi, Drotar, Yeates, & Taylor, 1999; Mulcahey, 1992). These responses are often noted for several years after injury or illness (Godfrey, Knight, & Partridge, 1996). Others indicate that risks of emotional difficulty may be positively associated with age (Frank, Thayer, Hagglund, Veith, Schopp, Beck, Kashani, Goldstein, Cassidy, Clay, Chaney, Hewitt, & Johnson, 1998). Older children have the cognitive capacity to understand the implications of the illness and are keenly aware of the impact on peer relationships and other developmental tasks. Younger children appear to have more difficulty with physical tasks and school performance (Eiser, 1990).

Other perspectives focus on the resiliency of children and families in the face of chronic illness. Studies in support of this perspective note the hardiness of children and identify few risks to mental health associated with their chronic conditions (Noll, Garstein, Vannatta, Correll, Bukowski, & Davies, 1999; Soliday, Kool, & Lande, 2000). For example, Soliday et al. (2000) found no differences in behavior between children with kidney disease and their healthy peers. They concluded that a positive family environment and psychosocial support offered by treatment teams might serve as buffers to stress. Several models emphasize adaptation to chronic illness, recognizing that chronic illness is a potential stressor in the lives of children and families, that adaptation is continuous over time, and that coping strategies are important in facilitating adaptation (Moos & Tsu, 1977; Pless & Pinkerton, 1975; Thompson & Gustafson, 1996; Wallander & Varni; 1992).

While conceptualizations in the models may vary, all models acknowledge the importance of one's developmental level on adjustment to chronic illness (Brewster, 1982; Edwards & Davis, 1997; Sourkes, 1995; Thompson & Gustafson, 1996). Other variables reported to influence adjustment are social support, coping skills of the child, service support, characteristics of the condition and potential to compromise develop-

mental tasks (Edwards & Davis, 1997; Thompson & Gustafson, 1996). Family variables such as concurrent stresses, family relationships and parental stress also have significant influence on adjustment to chronic childhood illness (Edwards & Davis, 1997; Logan, Radcliffe & Smith-Whitley, 2002; Soliday et al., 2000; Thompson & Gustafson, 1996).

Psychosocial interventions for children and families to support their coping with chronic illness have proven effective (Bauman et al., 1997; Castes, Hagel, Palenque, Canelone, Corao, & Lynch, 1999). Interventions have targeted family members' understanding of the illness and treatment (Brewster, 1982; Edwards & Davis, 1997; Holzheimer, Mohay, & Masters, 1998; Sourkes, 1995; Thompson & Gustafson, 1996) and their development of coping skills (Delameter, Jacobson, Anderson, Cox, Fisher, Lustman, Rubin, & Wysocki, 2001; McQuaid & Nassau, 1999; Thompson & Gustafson, 1996). Effective techniques for facilitation of coping have included play therapy (Jones, 2002), bibliotherapy (Amer, 1999), therapeutic storytelling (Freeman, 1991), and art therapy (Fenton, 2000), as well as efforts to normalize the distress associated with chronic conditions and to minimize the impact on typical childhood experiences (Delameter et al., 2001; Thompson & Gustafson, 1996). The value of problem-solving skills has also been studied in relation to coping with a chronic illness (Heermann & Willis, 1992; Varni, Katz, Colegrove, & Dolgin, 1993).

Many studies have addressed the importance of coping strategies to cope with pain, symptom management and treatment related procedures. Some focus on cognitive behavioral techniques (Ellis & Spanos, 1994; Ross & Ross, 1984), cognitive coping strategies, such as self talk and thought stopping (Ross & Ross, 1984), and others focus on the use of relaxation and imagery techniques as pain management techniques (Castes et al., 1999; Gil, Anthony, Carson, Redding-Lallinger, Daeschner, & Ware, 2001). There are unique responses to pain in the neurologically impaired population. Staff working with patients with cognitive deficits require additional education and training to support these children and adolescents (Lahz & Bryant, 1997; McGrath, Rosmus, Campbell, & Hennigar, 1998; Oberlander, Gilbert, Chambers, O'Donnell, & Craig, 1999; Oberlander, O'Donnell, & Montgomery, 1999).

Social support interventions have proven beneficial in facilitating coping with chronic illness. Activities such as support groups (Greco, Pendley, McDonell, & Reeves, 2001; Stauffer, 1998), school re-entry programs (Bishop & Gilinsky, 1995; Hicks & Lavender, 2001; Mulcahey, 1992; Rynard, Chambers, Klinck, & Gray, 1998; Yim-Chiplis, 1998; Ylvisaker, Todis, Glang, Urbanczyk, Franklin, DePompei, Feeney, Maxwell, Pearson, & Tyler 2001), camps for children with chronic conditions (Briery & Rabian, 1999; Hicks & Lavender, 2001), and filial therapy (Glazer-Waldman, Zimmerman, Landreth, & Norton, 1992; Tew, Landreth, Joiner & Solt, 2002) are valuable. Additionally, the value of support for all family members has been investigated (Baker, 2002; Eiser, 1990; Hostler, 1999, Seiffge-Krenke, 2002; Tew, Landreth, Joiner, & Solt, 2002).

Research has also considered the question of adherence to medical regimes (Delameter et al., 2001; Holzheimer et al., 1998; Pendley, Kasmen, Miller, Donze, Swenson, & Reeves, 2002). Thompson and Gustafson (1996) indicate that several factors may impact adherence, including the degree to which the illness and treatment interferes with identity, competency and autonomy, and the chronicity and complexity of the treatment regimen. The authors advise that

adherence interventions should focus on the provision of knowledge, acquisition of procedural skills, and on a mutually negotiated treatment plan between the family and the healthcare team. Family routines and rituals (Fiese & Wamboldt, 2000), parenting styles (Davis, Delameter, Shaw, LaGreca, Eidson, Perez-Rodriguez, & Nemery, 2001) and peer support (Pendley et al., 2002) also have positive effects on adherence, supporting the notion that effective intervention should take place within the context of the family.

ADJUSTMENT TO CHRONIC CONDITIONS

When a child and family are given the diagnosis of a chronic condition, life changes forever. Families may now view their lives in two stages – before the diagnosis and after. The very nature of a chronic condition forces families to adjust to the course of the illness or condition, as well as to new challenges presented at each developmental stage in the child's and family's life.

Reactions to the diagnosis vary and are often fluid in nature. Emotions such as shock, denial, anger, guilt and sadness are experienced. Normal routines are disrupted, which can be unsettling for children who gain a sense of security and safety from predictability. Loss is experienced in many ways. Feelings of shame and embarrassment may surface as a reaction to feeling different from peers. Children coping with chronic conditions have also reported feelings of isolation, loneliness, and stress related to separation. They may become fearful about what will happen next, including fears related to leaving the watchful eye of the medical team in the hospital or clinic. As children and youth who experience these feelings are not always able to express them verbally, the child life specialist is obligated to find appropriate ways for them to express their concerns and feelings. Potential techniques will be explored later in this chapter.

Children with chronic conditions must adjust to much that is new. They are forced, in many cases, to cope with pain related to the disease process itself or procedures necessary for diagnosis or treatment. They must cope with changes in routines, meeting many new people associated with the treatment team, altered body image, managing feelings, and potentially more dependency on family members. They must accommodate medical treatments and appointments into their schedule, which can have enormous impact on peer interaction. And finally, they must cope with an uncertain future.

Families must make adjustments as well. The role played by each individual in the family may change. Parent burnout, family imbalance, fear and worry, overprotection, and depression in parents and family members may be seen (Singer, 1999). Each member may have responses to the chronic condition that are unique. Siblings are often forgotten in the crisis of diagnosis or at other times throughout the course of treatment. Brothers and sisters may experience anger, guilt (if there are misperceptions related to cause of the illness), and jealously due to the increased attention and gifts given to the child who is ill. Well children and their daily lives may also be indirectly affected by changes in family finances due to the chronic condition, a situation that is often overlooked. If there is a genetic component to the particular disease, or if there are misperceptions related to the cause of the illness, siblings may fear they will also contract the condition.

Children and families often go through a predictable set of responses, much like someone experiencing a death. Brooks and Siegel (1996) identify these stages as guilt,

anger, shame or stigma, and acceptance. Stages identified by Martin (1988) include shock, denial, and sorrow, with adaptation, rather than acceptance, as the final stage. Adaptation denotes the sense of a new normal, rather than the complacency of accepting the illness. While adapting to the diagnosis, several phases may be experienced. Fennell (2001) characterizes these phases as crisis, stabilization, resolution and integration, each with their own tasks related to adjustment. These phases are fluid and may be revisited numerous times. For example, patients and families living with chronic conditions will revisit these stages at each transition or major milestone in a child's life (Martin, 1988).

One possible response to chronic conditions and treatment is post-traumatic stress disorder (PTSD), defined by Warden, Labbate, Salazar, Nelson, Sheley, Staudenmeier, and Martin (1997) as "a psychobiologic syndrome involving reexperiencing phenomena, avoidance behavior, and heightened autonomic responses following an extremely severe stressor" (p. 18). Several indicators of PTSD that may be experienced by children and youth of all ages, including the presence of disturbing images, flashbacks, hallucinations, avoidance of reminders of the incident, and an overall decreased responsiveness or increased arousal (Levi, Drotor, Yeates, & Taylor, 1999, p. 233). Children and youth experiencing PTSD often mention frequent nightmares or exhibit extreme behavior changes. Responses vary based on developmental level (Brooks & Siegel, 1996). Children and youth may display some of these symptoms without receiving a formal diagnosis of PTSD. The frequency, duration, and intensity of symptoms and resulting disruption in daily routine will help a psychologist establish a diagnosis.

It is not uncommon to see post-traumatic stress among children in the rehabilitation setting. Although some feel that children with traumatic brain injury are protected from this condition by the post-injury amnesia that many experience (Warden et al., 1997), the literature is inconclusive on this topic (Warden et al., 1997; Levi et al., 1999). Also at risk for this disorder are children or adolescents who, although not injured, may have been involved in or witnessed the accident of a sibling. In addition, children with chronic illnesses such as cancer can experience PTSD when treatment has been completed (Goodheart & Lansing, 1997; Keene, Hobbie & Ruccione, 2000).

While there are limited studies specifically identifying the impact of particular factors on adjustment, many authors have identified some general factors to be considered (Edwards & Davis, 1997, Thompson, Gustafson, Gil, Godfrey & Murphy, 1998). These factors can be divided into three categories: condition-related factors, child characteristics, and family characteristics.

The universal factors addressed in the previous sections of this chapter hold true for most chronic conditions. However, much of the work of child life is related to the specific procedures or treatments to which the child is exposed. Therefore, it is important for child life specialists to become well versed in the particular area in which they are practicing. Identifying the challenges and concerns for children facing chronic conditions leads to more sound psychosocial practice. The following case studies highlight the unique implications of particular chronic conditions that may impact the child or adolescent. When reading them, reflect on the specific issues and concerns the child must confront related to the particular condition and on possible interventions that would be helpful.

Marco is a 17-year-old youth who experienced a traumatic brain injury in a high-speed car accident in which he was the driver. He had planned to attend college on a football scholarship; now, he is not allowed to participate in contact sports for at least a year. Upon his return to school he struggles socially because he is not involved in the same activities, has difficulty initiating conversation or activities, and is very impulsive – often saying exactly what he is thinking. Once an A/B student, he now struggles academically and has to attend special classes for his primary subjects. His mother is very concerned and talks frequently about the changes as she drives him to and from school. He often talks about how much he wishes he could be more independent, like before the accident.

Cassie is a nine-year-old who has been coping with sickle cell disease since birth. She is able to verbalize the name of her illness and the physical aspects of her disease, but cannot explain the reason for the physical effects or offer strategies for decreasing her pain or possibly preventing a sickle cell crisis. Education regarding the illness has been given to her parents by the medical team, and her father has the disease as well. Cassie has had two strokes as a result of her disease and is frequently admitted to the hospital for acute chest crises. She is admitted frequently to the hospital with pain in various parts of her body. Occasionally, staff will verbalize doubt regarding the validity of her pain.

Stephen is a five-year-old boy newly diagnosed with acute lymphocytic leukemia. Always a very healthy boy, he had just started kindergarten when his parents noticed persistent flu-like symptoms and bruising. From his pediatrician's office he was immediately sent to a children's hospital where he encountered many invasive procedures and unfamiliar people. He was admitted directly to the hospital to begin a two-and-a-half-year protocol of chemotherapy. During the lengthy treatment, Stephen had many hospital visits and frequent bone marrow aspirates and spinal taps to assess the effectiveness of treatment. He had bouts of nausea, lost his hair due to the chemotherapy and was required to stay home from school frequently when his blood counts were low and he was extremely susceptible to infection.

As illustrated by the case examples, it is important to address the stressors unique to each individual diagnosis. These elements will drive the support services and therapeutic interventions that are offered.

Many aspects of an illness can influence the adjustment of the child and family. The severity of the disease is one of these factors. The perception of the severity by the child and family is more important than the actual physical criteria (Edwards & Davis, 1997). According to Dolgin, Phipps, Harow, and Zeltzer (1990), it is the quality of health, not the particular diagnosis, that influences parents' behavior and distress. Conditions involving the central nervous system may also lead to adjustment difficulties (Thompson & Gustafson, 1996). Chronic conditions may or may not have visible signs of the disease process. Children with visible signs of disease can cope effectively with their condition, provided those people around them respond in a supportive manner. The invisible illnesses, such as diabetes, sickle cell disease, traumatic brain injury and asthma, may present coping challenges because support may not be readily available. Other illnesses, such as HIV and hepatitis, may present challenges related to issues of disclosure. The families may not want others to know about the child's illness and are, therefore, reluctant to take advantage of the support systems available to them. The age at onset of the disease may also impact adjustment. For example, older children may have a more difficult time adjusting as they are more cognitively aware of the disruption of normal activities and developmental tasks. They

also may have a more mature understanding of the illness and its potential consequences.

All chronic conditions present a degree of unpredictability. However, some may have more unpredictable courses. The more unpredictable the course of the illness, the more likely the child and family may experience difficulty adjusting. Finally, the nature of the treatment must be considered. The more the treatment disrupts normal developmental tasks and activities, the greater the potential for coping challenges.

Frank et al. (1998) contend that adaptation to chronic illness is more dependent on individual characteristics than on common characteristics of the illness, suggesting the importance of attention to the individual characteristics of the child, including developmental level. Progress at each level of development can be impeded by the diagnosis, treatment and progression of the illness. Attention should also be paid to the predictable, developmental changes in children's understanding of their conditions (Bibace & Walsh, 1980; Brewster, 1982). It is important to acknowledge the perceptions the child may have based on his or her developmental level and match this with information given. Failure to do so may lead to misperceptions and adjustment difficulties.

As stated previously, adjustment is a continuous process and will be approached differently by children at each stage based on their developmental capacity. Throughout their lifetime, children will be forced to reprocess the impact of their illness within the framework of their understanding and developmental level at that particular time.

Other characteristics of the child that may impact adjustment are the child's protective factors (Edwards & Davis, 1997). These are qualities such as confidence, high self-esteem and self-reliance. Attitude toward illness has also been reported to have significant impact on adjustment (Briery & Rabian, 1999). In most cases, knowledge of coping skills already in place and ready to be deployed by the child and family during this crisis time is extremely helpful to the child life specialist. Capitalizing on these positive individual assets are important for intervention.

The degree to which parents successfully cope with an illness also has significant impact on the child (Frank et al., 1998; Soliday et al., 2000). Children take cues from their parents and respond accordingly. Families that exhibit open communication related to the condition may cope more effectively, as a trusting relationship is maintained. Decreased family conflict, improved family closeness and improved expression of emotions are related to more positive adjustment to chronic childhood illness (Thompson & Gustafson, 1996).

Canam (1993) has summarized the goals of family adaptation as the following:

- Accept the condition and manage it on a daily basis
- Meet normal developmental needs
- Cope with ongoing stress and crisis
- Manage feelings
- Educate others
- Establish support systems

These goals are achievable, for many families do adjust and cope effectively with chronic childhood illness. The work of the child life specialist can be extremely supportive and valuable in reaching each of the goals.

When assessing a child and family's adjustment it is important to evaluate their knowledge of the disease, their role in treatment, their ability to integrate into normal routines and their available support systems. These tasks and the possible skills exhibited to evaluate the accomplishment of the task are described in Table 1. For each task indicated, the clinician should evaluate whether

or not the skills indicated below the task are exhibited by the child and family. Skills that are not exhibited should be incorporated into the team's goals.

STATE OF THE ART PRACTICE

Promoting Developmental Tasks

Children diagnosed with a chronic condition are put into situations very different from their peers. In some ways, coping with a chronic condition forces children to grow up faster, and in other instances, parents may maintain a sense of dependency in their child. Child life specialists are in the unique position to refocus attention on normal developmental tasks. While important for all hospitalized children, children with chronic conditions may be at particular risk because the condition frequently spans multiple developmental levels. The child life specialist has a responsibility to promote developmental tasks at each stage. The impact on developmental tasks will need to be reassessed frequently as the child matures.

Regression is a common reaction among children of all ages when confronting chronic conditions. The regression may be related to the stresses of hospitalization and treatment or to the effects of their condition on cognitive development. On the other hand, many children and youth say that their experiences make them feel much older than their peers (Mulcahey, 1992) and that they are forced to relinquish the "invincibility fable" that is characteristic of adolescents at an early age.

Rehabilitation creates its own set of "unique developmental milestones" (Molnar, 1999, p. 30). These include things such as first wheelchair or AFO (ankle/foot orthotic), first time to self-catheterize, or first time to cut food using one hand. Families need education on these milestones.

Table 1
PSYCHOSOCIAL ADJUSTMENT EVALUATION POINTS

Task	Knowledge of Disease	Role in Treatment	Integration into Normal Routines	Support Systems in Place
Skills Exhibited	**Can the child and family, on a developmentally appropriate level...** Name the disease Describe how disease works Describe effects of disease Identify how the disease is treated Discuss possible side effects of treatment Describe the etiology of disease Understand the future expectations related to the illness	**Do the child and family...** Understand the need for treatment Use coping skills effectively Participate in self care as appropriate Receive opportunities for realistic choices Know hospital routines Adhere to treatment regimen Include the child in decision making as developmentally appropriate	Is/Are... The child attending school when possible An appropriate education plan devised for returning student Siblings included Roles in family maintained Open communication exhibited in family Limits and discipline maintained and consistent Roles, environment and/or activities modified as needed Roles in community maintained	Is/Are... Social support services, such as camps and support groups, engaged as necessary Medical information communicated clearly (misperceptions clarified) Extended family educated about condition Peers/community educated about condition Opportunities for emotional expression and validation available Important relationships outside the family maintained

Mastery

Mastery is of great significance for the developing child and opportunities to achieve are important. Potentially, the child with a chronic condition can achieve a sense of mastery through scholastic, physical, or creative accomplishments, by accepting household responsibilities, and through con-trolling their behavior (McCollum, 1975). Child life specialists can focus on areas where the child can succeed and can empower the child or adolescent to be successful through preparation, clearly identifying expectations, reinforcing the use of coping skills and providing information to help them understand their illness. For example, when provided with the proper education and support, children with diabetes can aid in effectively managing their illness by making proper food choices, understanding situations that may impact blood sugar levels, doing their own finger sticks for blood glucose checks, and even administering their own insulin. Participation in the management of the illness can lead to an enhanced sense of control for children with chronic illnesses.

Competency

Closely related to mastery, competency is the sense of accomplishment perceived by the child. Children need to succeed in order to feel competent; part of that success is mastering their environment. Children who feel self competent may have the internal resources to deal with whatever challenges they may face. It is essential for healthcare professionals to facilitate this process. However, child life specialists must be mindful to not create a sense of dependency on themselves, especially in the treatment room, but rather seek to promote self-efficacy in children and families. Helping children to establish effective coping skills to manage their anxiety and pain during procedures instills a sense of competency. This use of coping skills in an effective manner should be positively reinforced to encourage use during subsequent procedures in the future. Though child life specialists may verbally espouse the concept of mastery and competency, their actions can support or refute that notion. Examples include directing questions to parents that children can answer for themselves, or completing activities of daily living for children that can complete them on their own.

Autonomy/Independence

Chronic childhood conditions throw children and youth into a world in which they may become more dependent on their parents or other adults to care for them. Adults place additional constraints on these children and youth in an attempt to keep them safe and well. Parents may monitor treatments, be present at all times in the hospital and during social activities, and become overprotective. Child life specialists can help make parents aware of developmental tasks that may be impacted by the condition. For example, a teenage patient who has experienced a spinal cord injury will require assistance with many activities (e.g., bathing and toileting), but will still want to be treated in a developmentally appropriate manner. Child life specialists can help teens identify their strengths and role in the treatment process while modeling empowering behavior for the parent. This will help the teen move from a passive role to a more active role in his or her care. Advocating for privacy, inclusion in decision making, and responsibility for self-care can help to restore the sense of independence. Reassuring parents that their child or teen will be safe and cared for when apart from them will help as well.

Identity

As children and youth are trying to find a sense of who they are, a chronic condition imposes the necessity to form a new reality, as was illustrated in the case study with Marco, a teen who experienced a traumatic brain injury. Children and youth may need to reevaluate who they are and how they view themselves as individuals in relation to the life changes that the condition has imposed. Activities addressing self-exploration can be extremely helpful. One example of this may be working on boxes that the child or youth depicts the "outer me" on the outside and the "inner me" on the inside – an activity that can be done with words, drawings or pictures from magazines.

Activities such as this can facilitate conversation related to how individuals see themselves and how they want others to perceive them. Journaling is another wonderful technique for promoting self-exploration and identity formation.

Peer Relationships

Chronic conditions may change the amount of contact that children have with their peers, as in the case of a child with chronic renal failure requiring dialysis three days a week. Peers may retreat from the child with the chronic condition due to misconceptions about illness. For example, they may fear they can catch cancer, or they may wish to avoid the stigma associated with HIV/AIDS. Opportunities to educate and include peers are extremely beneficial. Providing contact with other children with chronic conditions can also help to form a second peer support network in addition to the child's already existing peer group. Formal support groups and therapeutic camp programs are effective ways to do this. In addition, technological advances have allowed children with chronic conditions to connect with others facing similar challenges who may live in another state or country.

Body Image

Many chronic conditions produce physical changes to the body. And still others, while not causing visible changes, may alter the child or teen's perception of his or her own body. In both cases the child or teen's self-esteem may be seriously affected. They may perceive their body to be defective in some way, as in the case of preschool-aged children who experience severe burns. When looking in the mirror they may have a difficult time recognizing themselves amidst the bandages. However, activities like body outline drawings and mirror projects can lead to meaningful discussions related to body image. Activities that highlight the positive aspects of the child's appearance, like a "day of beauty" with makeup and nail painting or a "muscle man" workout with hand weights, can help foster positive feelings in a child or youth. Activities that differentiate outer and inner strengths (e.g., the box activity mentioned earlier, or scratch art drawings highlighting the things that someone might not know about a child or teen just by looking at him) can also help a child maintain a strong sense of self while dealing with changes, or perceived changes, in one's body.

Facilitating Adaptation

The CLS, in conjunction with the child, family, and other members of the healthcare team, uses play, prep, and communication to promote coping/adaptation. The child life specialist, combining knowledge of development with creativity, is able to aid children in adjusting to and actually growing through their experience with a chronic condition. A proactive approach can be taken in relation to developmental tasks, and other concerns can be addressed as they arise. The primary goal of the therapeutic relationship is to "enable children (and members of their family) to develop adaptive strategies to meet the challenges of their situation, and by doing so, to prevent or ameliorate the difficulties they face" (Edwards & Davis, 1997, p. 63).

The following sections will identify some areas of child life practice that address specific goals. Many goals are similar to those of children with acute hospital experiences; however, there are some that are particularly significant for children who must cope with their condition for extended periods of time or their entire life.

Self-expression

A primary goal for child life specialists is finding ways that are most suitable for a particular child to express thoughts, concerns and feelings. In the course of their work, child life specialists conduct an ongoing assessment of the child and family's needs and formulates creative ways to address them. The creative aspect of child life is particularly important in encouraging self-expression, as many children either do not yet have the language skills or prefer ways other than talking to express themselves. Play and creative art projects help children identify feelings and concerns related to their illness and discuss potential coping strategies (e.g., allowing children to express anger in acceptable ways, not hurting themselves or others). Care must be taken when facilitating activities for children and youth who have experienced traumatic brain injury, as these patients may lack the judgment to understand the context in which an activity is appropriate. If an activity would not be safe to repeat with peers or in a different setting, it is best avoided. For example, hitting an object, even something as simple as a pillow, should be discouraged, but squeezing a squeeze ball should meet the same goal without creating risk. Sometimes just the expression of emotion and the validation of feelings alone are therapeutic.

The following activities are just some suggestions for encouraging self-expression. The opportunities are endless.

• Writing a letter to their illness, in which children can say anything they would like.

"Dear Cancer,

First, I want to know why you came into my life. I did not ask for this. But you should know that you should go ahead and give up because I have too much to live for. There are so many people that care about me. I know I am going to beat you!

Signed, _____ "

They can choose to share this letter with support people or just to seal it and keep it to themselves. Prior to writing the letter, a school aged child with cystic fibrosis reported, "I could fill the whole page." She did just that and when done stated, "It felt good just to get it out and feel like it was talking to something."

• *Engaging in a sentence completion activity, either alone or as part of another activity.* For example, a mobile of stars could be made and hopes could be written on each star. Or, worry dolls could be made and put into a box in which the child's worries were written on the lid or inside. Another variation on the theme is to design a worry box and encourage children to write their wonders and worries on paper that is placed inside.

• Creation of "feelings gardens," which can allow children to express their emotions while helping them to understand that many different feelings related to their situation, are permitted. Each flower placed in the garden represents a different feeling, an analogy that encourages discussion of the numerous feelings the child may be experiencing. This activity can be adapted for use with families. For example, a family activity might focus on creating a "strength garden" where each family member or support person is represented by a flower. On the flowers are the strengths they bring to the family when coping with challenging situations. The garden can serve as a visual reminder to draw on those strengths during times of need.

Developmentally Appropriate Education Regarding Illness

Educating children about their illness at the appropriate developmental level is essential. The child must live with this condition for extended periods of time, possibly the rest of their lives. Therefore, it is important for them to have an understanding of the specifics related to their illness – knowledge that can be extremely empowering for children and families in a situation where there are few opportunities to feel in control. It is most desirable for parents to present the information related to diagnosis to the child. However, parents often are overwhelmed and find it difficult to do so, or they may feel ill-equipped to present the information in a way in which their child will understand. Parents may be reluctant to give information for fear that they may scare their child. The child life specialist can help the parent to process this concern and point out the importance of honest, accurate information. Children typically know on some level that something is happening in their body and may have overheard others discuss their condition.

Withholding of information by the parents can impact the trust relationship between parent and child. Child life specialists can work with the parents to decide on what words to use to explain the condition to their child, or if the parents prefer, the child life specialist or another member of the healthcare team can present the information. It is important to have the parent present if at all possible. In cases where language may be a barrier, a professional interpreter should be used to present the information. Under no circumstances is it acceptable to use the child or sibling as a translator for medical teaching or information sharing

(Hicks & Lavender, 2001).

When providing information to children about any condition, it is important to remember a few basic points. First, finding out what the child knows or understands is the best place to start. This will allow the information they have picked up to be assessed for accuracy. It also acknowledges their valuable role in the process. Children may focus on the information and then appear to lose attention or give clear signals that they do not want to talk about the condition any more. It is important to recognize and respect that desire. Children have the ability to emotionally insulate themselves, taking in only what they can process or cope with at one time, and then move on to something else. Children will revisit the topic again when it is not so emotionally overwhelming. If the child is anxious or upset, it is important to validate these feelings and address the immediate concerns before continuing on with education related to the illness.

Concrete tools often help children to comprehend the information presented. Proper language choices are essential. One must bear in mind the imagery associated with the explanations that are provided. For example, when discussing cancer, using the "bad cell" and "good cell" analogy can serve to reinforce the misperception that the child got cancer because they were bad. Better word choices would be sick cells/healthy cells or abnormal cells/normal cells. Similarly, when discussing blood glucose levels and using good numbers and bad numbers, children may feel guilt or responsibility for their diabetes or their current blood glucose values. Better choices in this situation would to simply use high and low.

Information should be repeated for children and the process should be interactive. The opportunity for the child to ask questions is vital. To initiate conversation related to the information presented, one could ask children what surprised them most about what they were told or what the most important part was from their point of view.

At the conclusion of each educational session, the child's understanding should be assessed. Sometimes it is helpful to ask children what they would tell their best friend about the illness instead of simply asking them to repeat the information back to you. This will help to evaluate comprehension more effectively. Providing developmentally appropriate information related to chronic illness and treatment is a continuous process, it is not a single event. Over time the information will need to be presented again to accommodate the child's current cognitive functioning. Also, information presented during crisis is not always retained so repeating information is necessary.

Preparation

Preparation for medical events and transitions is a crucial part of a child life specialist's role in any setting. One important consideration specific to children with chronic conditions is the need for preparation over time. As is true when educating children about their illness, information needs related to procedures may change over time. As children mature, their informational needs will change. It is important to check in with children and provide some type of preparation, even if it is a simple review, regardless of how many times they have had a particular procedure.

Consideration must be taken when working with a population with cognitive deficits. For many children and adolescents, memory deficits and a decreased tolerance for stimulation make the preparation process more challenging. The degree of recovery from brain injury is described in the Rancho Los Amigos Cognitive Scales, which recently have been modified for use with children six

months and older (Savage & Wolcott, 1995). In a rehabilitation setting, it is important to consider the child's Ranchos level when assessing the need for preparation. Families need support and information at all stages of the patient's recovery. Prior to the child or teen being able to respond to stimuli in a generalized manner, the child should only be told what is happening to them as it occurs: it should be concurrent, not preparatory. Memory deficits make earlier teaching ineffective. Patients should always be told when they will be touched. True preparation will not be beneficial to the child or teen recovering from a brain injury prior to this time. Medical play can also be introduced at this point. When possible, support should be provided while the procedure is occurring.

Once children progress beyond this stage (i.e., they are inconsistently oriented, able to retain some information, and can consistently follow simple directions) they can begin to learn new information and will benefit from teaching before a procedure or transition. Patients need frequent repetition of information and may not be able to generalize information to new settings. All teaching for children with cognitive challenges will need to be modified, and the following modifications should be considered:

- Use a multisensory approach (e.g., hands-on experiences, tours, etc.)
- Remove distractions, such as TV or interruptions
- If child is distracted, present one preparation tool at a time.
- Don't expect great verbal recall; assess understanding with demonstration. Allow extra time for a response.
- Document teaching in memory book or log so patient can review information as needed
- Use concrete language and avoid using humor that may be misunderstood

- Patients may be rule oriented; use this "the rule is nothing to eat in the morning"
- Use repetition; model language and encourage parents to reinforce this. Use language consistently
- Shorten the teaching sessions (no longer than 10 minutes); break it down into smaller pieces if necessary

It is important to recognize that a patient may have had a procedure numerous times, but as they move through stages of cognitive recovery their education needs change.

Play

Play continues to be the core of what a child life specialist can offer children and adolescents with chronic conditions. The following considerations are particularly applicable to the play of children in rehabilitative settings, but may apply to children with chronic illness. Initially play may not be enjoyable to a child or teen in a rehabilitation setting, but it is crucial that play be introduced as the child works to regain lost skills. An early appropriate goal in this setting is that "patient will demonstrate enjoyment in play." Also, patients will often be unable to identify activities they enjoy, so an additional goal appropriate to the early stages is that "patient will identify one activity of interest that can be completed at current level of function." As a child life specialist, it can be uncomfortable to have a child cry in the playroom or when traveling to the playroom, but this must be viewed as part of the recovery process. In addition to developmental play, several other types of play may be facilitated on a rehabilitation unit, each of which is discussed in the following sections.

POST-TRAUMATIC PLAY. This is a type of therapeutic play in which reenactment of the traumatic event occurs. It differs from other forms of play in that it "frequently lacks both pleasure and relief. It has a seriousness and intensity uncharacteristic of typical play" (Monahon, 1993, p. 34). Patients and siblings may demonstrate a need to engage in this type play. Props related to the accident or trauma are often involved. This play is very repetitious and usually self-initiated, with mastery of the events demonstrated over time. The child life specialist's role in this type play is to observe and to ensure the child's safety (i.e., watch for aggressive behavior, or overly anxious behavior; distract or redirect the child as necessary). If the child invites the specialist into this play, the child should be allowed to direct the play of the specialist. It is important that misconceptions that are identified during this play be noted, but this is not the time to correct those misconceptions. This can be done at a separate time. This type of play is sometimes used with children coping with post-traumatic stress disorder. A referral to a counselor may also be helpful for children who have experienced trauma.

ADAPTIVE PLAY. Adaptive play is defined as "play that has been altered in form, complexity, or intent to serve the needs of children with disabilities" (Musselwhite, 1986, p. xi). It includes modifying the materials, the environment or the process to meet the needs of a child or teen. The goals of adaptive play are similar to those of a child life specialist working with any child with special needs: (1) integrating the child into settings with children without disabilities, (2) providing fun play experiences, and (3) supporting of therapies or development in skills in specific areas, such as gross or fine motor skills, communication skills or social skills (Musselwhite, 1986). A child life specialist can adapt activities or materials to allow a child to experience success in a setting where his or her sense of self is already challenged. Parents can be taught to modify play to meet the needs of an individual child or teen.

FAMILY ACTIVITIES. Due to the importance of fostering independence during therapy sessions, parents are often discouraged from participating. This reduces the time they are able to interact with their children. Siblings are also restricted from participating in many therapy activities on a rehabilitation unit. Child life can create opportunities for a patient to engage in play with family members. These experiences often occur in the evenings or weekends and allow the parents and siblings to learn new activities and techniques. This involvement helps maintain a positive relationship between family members, creates a sense of community between families from diverse backgrounds, and helps solidify an open relationship between families and staff as they interact together in a play setting.

STIMULATION. Children and adolescents with brain injuries in the early stage of recovery may require a different definition of "play." These children may benefit from receiving sensory stimulation in a quiet environment with few distractions. These children may respond to reading, gentle touch, rocking, tactile stimulation, or music. Often children may benefit from one source of stimulation at a time. The child life specialist needs to be acutely aware of the behavioral signs of overstimulation.

ACTIVITY ALTERNATIVES. In conjunction with other team members, a child life specialist may serve as an educator with regards to activity restrictions following a traumatic injury. Many patients have limitations at discharge that are designed to keep them safe, such as "no contact" sports or "both feet on the ground." The child life specialist should consult with the patient and the family to identify appropriate alternatives. These may include participating in activities in a different way or identifying new activities of interest. The child life specialist is often responsible for ensuring that the patient has been taught about these restrictions and that s/he understands the reason these are in place.

Coping Skills

Children with chronic conditions are forced to cope with the effects of their disease and treatment over long periods of time. They must cope with psychological aspects of the condition itself, such as hearing the diagnosis and prognosis, as well as potential painful treatments and procedures. The establishment of coping skills can be extremely empowering for children with chronic conditions and can help to foster their resiliency (Boyd & Hunsberger, 1998). Coping activities can either be direct actions, such as changing factors in the environment, or cognitive strategies, where one changes thoughts and feelings to deal with the stressful situation (Olson, Johansen, Powers, Pope & Klein, 1993). Rehearsal and practicing of coping skills are important for their effective implementation. Modeling of appropriate coping skills by peers with chronic conditions is also extremely effective, allowing the child to perceive that getting through challenges is "doable" since someone else their age has done it. Developing a set of coping skills to draw upon can help lead to more effective adaptation to their illness. One role of the child life specialist can be to help children establish these lifelong patterns for positive, effective coping. When helping children to devise coping plans, articulating the rationale is essential. Children need to understand how employing such strategies will benefit them. Otherwise, they may be viewed as just one more thing someone else is telling them to do. Once coping preferences are identified, the child life specialist should inform other members of the team through documentation and care conferences.

A primary tool for building coping skills is allowing for control. Child life specialists are in the position to promote as many realistic choices for children with chronic conditions as possible and to remind other staff members of the importance of providing choices that are realistic. For example, rather than asking "Are you ready to take your medicine?" when it must be taken immediately, one might say "It is time to take your medicine, do you want to take it with water or juice?" These subtle changes in language can help to restore control for the child in an appropriate manner.

Child life specialists can help children to establish the skills necessary to cope with condition-related symptoms and pain. The goal of such intervention, however, is to work with the child to establish coping skills that they can put in place whenever needed, regardless of the availability of the child life specialist. Children often need someone to guide them in skill development, encourage and reinforce the use of the skills, and monitor their effectiveness over time. Carrying the skills out can build self-efficacy in children as mentioned earlier in this chapter. Many of the techniques to cope effectively with pain addressed elsewhere in this text are relevant to children with chronic conditions. It is important to be aware that preferred coping strategies might change over time, so periodic re-evaluation is mandatory. These strategies are aimed at increasing a child's feeling of self-efficacy and reducing the feelings of helplessness and lack of control over their environment or situation. Both cognitive and behavioral methods can be effective; often they are used in a package of both types of methods (Ellis & Spanos, 1994; Olson, Johansen, Powers, Pope, & Klein, 1993; Siegel & Smith, 1989). Thompson and Gustafson (1996) point out that cognitive methods often lag behind the use of behavioral methods. Relaxation, distraction

and imagery can be especially effective for pain control and symptom management, as well as treatment-related pain and anxiety (Ellis & Spanos, 1994; McQuaid & Nassau, 1999). Cognitive techniques such as positive self-talk, cognitive reframing and thought stopping (Ross, 1984) can help with anxiety and general coping with the condition (Ross & Ross, 1984).

A concrete activity to help children understand the implications of negative self-talk is "Helping Hands." In this activity, medical exam gloves (be mindful of latex allergies) are blown up and children are encouraged to write on them the things they tell themselves that are helpful, such as "I am brave," "I can do this," and "I will be proud of myself when I do this." The gloves are placed in a large garbage bag, which is then sealed. The children can hit the bag around in the air for a time, after which another glove is introduced that is filled with water. On that glove the child is encouraged to write things they think to themselves or say out loud that are not helpful, such as "It will really hurt me," "I will never be able to hold still," or "Why bother trying, I will not get better anyway." This water-filled glove is added to the bag, and the children are asked to hit the bag again. The water glove will weigh the bag down, just as negative thoughts can make it more difficult to cope with challenging situations.

Other strategies that focus on control can also be useful. For example, for children who must undergo lengthy, painful procedures, such as burn debredment, incorporating break times that they control can aid in coping. A child can be given three tokens and told that for each token they can decide when they take a one-minute "break" from the procedure. Of course, stopping in the middle of the procedure for a minute must be a medically realistic option. The child should be told that once the tokens have all been used there will be no other breaks. This should be practiced prior to the event allowing the child to experience how long the break will last and to reinforce once they are all gone the procedure will continue.

One of the greatest challenges in a rehabilitation setting is working with a child who is unable to communicate that pain is present or to independently employ coping strategies because of decreased cognition. This inability to communicate may be related to cognitive, language or physical barriers. These barriers place children and adolescents at risk for under-treatment of pain. Caregivers may view altered or blunted response to pain as an indication of insensitivity or of different physiological response to pain. Oberlander, O'Donnell and Montgomery (1999) disagree with this viewpoint, attributing the response seen in some children with special needs to the previously mentioned barriers. This condition places the burden of responsibility on the caregiver to recognize pain in this population and treat it appropriately. The challenges for the clinician include being able to identify the source and location of pain (even after its presence has been determined), as well as distinguishing actual pain from an emotional response. Oberlander et al. recommend the following guidelines while working with children with neurological deficits:

1. Allow and encourage the presence of parents and/or other familiar caregivers during assessment and management of pain. They may better recognize the signals a child is giving.
2. Ensure that the child has access to his or her means of communication (computer for "talking", vision is not obstructed if child uses eye gaze or blinking, etc.) and any comfort items or measures (seating system, transitional object, etc.) that the child or teen has used successfully in the past.

3. Advocate for children who can't advocate for themselves.
4. Encourage appropriate pharmacological interventions and the least invasive route for dosing whenever possible.
5. Ask about or document the ways the patient usually expresses stress. Do not expect the cues to be the same from child to child.

When working with children with cognitive challenges, the best approaches for coping are distraction and imagery.

Problem-solving Skills

All children benefit from the development of problem-solving skills. For children with chronic conditions it can be especially empowering as they will be cast into many situations in their lives that may require effective problem solving – situations that may be related to the disease and treatment or to social encounters. Development of effective problem-solving skills is associated with positive adjustment to chronic illness (Heermann & Willis, 1992; Thompson & Gustafson, 1996; Varni, Katz, Colegrove, & Dolgin, 1993).

Problem solving should be viewed as a process. The goal of problem solving is to help create a sense of autonomy for children. For example, providing solutions for children rather than encouraging them to identify potential options to resolve problem situations does not promote independent thought. Most models for acquiring problem-solving skills indicate a series of steps (Johnson, 1998). Basically, the steps are:

- Clarification of the problem
- Identification of potential options/solutions
- Evaluating the options
- Deciding which option to employ

- Implementing the option
- Evaluation of the effectiveness of the solution

Teaching children problem-solving skills can be done in a more conversational manner, even using books or stories for younger children. Modeling, either directly or through the stories, is also a very effective teaching tool. Once children establish problem-solving skills, they have laid the foundation for coping with challenging situation in the future.

Goal Setting and Action Plans

Children diagnosed with chronic conditions often lose hope for the future. Child life specialists can help the child or adolescent to establish realistic goals and devise the action steps to take in order to achieve them. In some cases, where life expectancy is short, achievable goals should be set to allow the child or adolescent to maintain hope "for right now." It can help them to focus on completing the things in life most important to them. For those with conditions that may not shorten the life span, goal setting can help the child or adolescent to move forward in spite of illness, instead of letting the illness hold them back.

The child and family should take the lead in establishing goals. Some concrete tools to help them achieve this may be suggested by the child life specialist. For example, using a handout with steps or building blocks can help the child to think through and visualize the action steps necessary to achieve their goals. Medical staff should be informed of these goals and provide an environment to help achieve them whenever possible.

Adherence

An important concern related to chronic illness is adherence to treatment regimens.

Historically, this topic has been referred to as compliance. However, that language in and of itself sends the message that the medical team is in a more powerful role than the child and family. Families are to be included as equal team members.

Most children with chronic conditions have difficulty following through with treatment plans at some point during their illness, for example, when their body image changes due to the effects of medication, or when their feelings of invincibility are challenged. One may hear, "I just want to be normal" or "I feel fine, so why bother?" Adherence may be affected by the parent and the child's assessment of the perceived benefits to the treatment. If benefits are seen to outweigh the inconveniences, they are more likely to adhere to the treatment plan. Edwards and Davis (1997) observe that families not adhering to treatment plans may feel that their problems are insurmountable, that the treatment plans are unreasonable, and that the plans have been imposed on them – thoughts that may lead to resentment, reduced confidence and poorer compliance.

Strategies for increasing adherence may be either educational or behavioral, as indicated in guidelines for enhancing adherence developed by Edwards and Davis (1997). They suggest that adherence can be improved through the following measures:

- Good preparation
- Rationale for treatment and consequences of not treating
- Facilitation of the child carrying out practical aspects of their care
- Negotiation of a treatment plan that is reasonable and manageable with family life.
- Reinforcing and supporting the child in taking appropriate responsibilities over their treatment.

The key to promoting adherence is open communication between the staff and the family. This should include discussions of how to realistically incorporate the necessary medical routines into the child's daily schedule. Encouraging families to employ the use of routines and rituals may prove to be especially beneficial for young children who thrive on routine and predictability. It is also important to uncover potential difficulties in maintaining the routine. To this end, the child life specialist might suggest that the child or adolescent self-monitor adherence by keeping a journal – an activity that can promote discussions of what may or may not be working. Periodic re-evaluation is important to do in collaboration with the child or adolescent and their family. Changes in the plan may be necessary and will be most effective if mutually agreed upon.

Support Systems

Family Support

Support for all members of the family is essential. Parents may find it helpful to talk with others facing similar situations, gaining valuable support as well as practical tips for managing a chronic illness. Information is extremely empowering, ensuring that parents have access to accurate information regarding their child's illness is important. Parents should be cautioned about information received from unknown sources and should check all information received with their child's doctor. Burke, Handley-Deryy, Costello, Kaufmann, and Dillon (1997) indicate that providing interventions for families in outpatient and community settings during particularly stressful times can improve coping and family functioning – a finding that may suggest a role for child life specialists in community settings, especially as medical practices shift toward outpatient care.

Brothers and sisters of children with chronic conditions have special needs, including education, support, acceptance, and time. They benefit from education related to the condition, as well as from peer support. Topics of discussion with siblings should include feelings and concerns related to the illness, communicating with others regarding the illness and their potential reactions (Powell & Gallagher, 1993). It will also be important to discuss potential role changes within the family to provide adequate preparation for the well brother or sister. Information can be shared on an individual basis or within a group setting. The child life specialist should work to create a trusting relationship with siblings to meet these needs. It is important to recognize the unique qualities of the sibling and not only focus on their importance in relation to the child with the chronic condition. When siblings live too far from the hospital to be involved in direct programming, parents need to be educated on the impact of illness on the other children in the family.

Support Groups

Support groups can be extremely beneficial for children and adolescents affected by chronic illness (Stauffer, 1998). These groups can range from closed ended to open ended and from informal support groups to more structured therapy groups. The goals of support groups vary, but most groups for children and adolescents with chronic illnesses focus on promoting a sense of universality. Many children feel that their peers are not able to understand what they are facing and express the desire to talk to others who are in similar situations. Coping skills can be strengthened and knowledge increased or reinforced through a support group (Hicks & Lavender, 2001). These groups can facilitate coping through the sharing of strategies and ideas for what has helped others experiencing similar challenges. Psycho-education can be part of these groups as well, empowering the children and adolescents with information.

Child life specialists can be effective facilitators of support groups given their knowledge of growth and development and their relationships with the children and adolescents. The goals for the group are the most important matter to consider when planning a group, as they will dictate the format. In general, groups can consist of children or adolescents with the same diagnosis or with a variety of different chronic illnesses. Each type of group has its strengths and weaknesses. Groups with the same diagnosis can more closely identify with each other. However, in a non-categorical approach the common stressors and traumas experienced by children with any type of chronic condition are the focus. The common themes among such groups are the chronicity of the illness, pain, hospitalizations, limitations, life and developmental disruptions, social stigma, life-threatening potential and the child's sense of being different (Boyd-Franklin, Steiner, & Boland, 1995). The value of this non-categorical approach has been documented (Britto, Garrett, Dugliss, Daeschner, Johnson, Leigh, Majure, Schultz, & Konrad, 1998; Garstein, Short, Vannatta, & Voll, 1999; Kibby, Tyc, & Mulhern, 1998; Meijer, Sinnema, Bijstra, Mellenbergh, & Walters, 2000; Stein, Westbrook, & Silver, 1998).

Social Interaction

Due to changes in cognitive or physical performance, as well as specific cognitive deficits (disinhibition/poor impulse control, decreased memory, increased frustration) many patients have a difficult time making and keeping friends. The child life specialist can facilitate activities that allow patients to practice skills in the group setting. This practice may be formal or informal. Modeling of social skills and reinforcement of positive social skills is an important part of programming for children with chronic conditions. Specific curricula can be purchased to reinforce this teaching. These provide exercises and activities designed to reinforce an individual skill, such as having a conversation or making friends.

Another way to help promote social interaction is to help children identify their assets, discussing and listing, for example, things about themselves that others may find interesting. According to McCollum (1975), one way to help children cope with physical challenges is to "help them develop personal characteristics, skills and talents that make a positive contribution to the group experience" (p. 101). The child life specialist can help children to focus on the abilities they do have and how to use these abilities to initiate interactions with others.

Children with chronic conditions must be prepared for reactions of others outside the hospital setting. They need to be given information related to coping with teasing. Role-playing can be a very useful interaction to help prepare children and adolescents for this type of interaction in the community setting.

Camps

Camp experiences for children with chronic conditions can have profound life-long effects. These experiences can provide a sense of hope and support like no others. Camp can be an opportunity for a child with a chronic condition to "just be a child" and perhaps develop some new skills. The supportive environment of camp can help lead to mastery for children who may feel they are no longer able to be successful at recreational activities or who have not tried new activities. Both of these can lead to an increase in self-efficacy.

Some camp programs last a week at time in the summer, while other organizations provide year-round experiences for children and families coping with chronic conditions. As with support groups, camp experiences can provide a sense of universality for children coping with a chronic illness. Bluebond-Langer, Perkel, Goertzel, Nelson, and McGeary (1990) indicate that children with cancer can come away from camp with a better understanding of their illness and its treatment. Briery and Rabian (1999) report that camp can improve a child's attitude toward illness – a benefit that was reported across diagnoses. This study also reported a decrease in self-reported anxiety after camp. The camp environment allows children to try out social skills necessary for re-integration after being diagnosed with a chronic condition. There they can practice explanations related to their illness in an informal and supportive environment with children who have faced similar challenges.

School Re-entry

School re-entry is a process that involves the hospital teacher and other hospital staff, the staff of the child or teen's home school, the patient and family, and the child life specialist. The child life specialist's role is generally to prepare the classmates for the hospitalized child's return. This may be done in person or via videotape. As technology becomes more readily accessible, videoconferencing may become a possibility. This would be preferable to videotapes because questions could be asked and answered in real time. The child life specialist often tailors a program for each individual child. Prior to the program, communication is necessary with the patient and family, as well as with the classroom teacher. At this time, consent for the program should be obtained from the parent or legal guardian.

Sometimes more than one program will be required. Classmates may need information soon after the admission to the hospital. Children or adolescents involved in rehabilitation programming will change between that point and discharge, so a program immediately prior to or following discharge will be beneficial. Students may also need additional programs at other transition points (e.g., starting a new school or joining a club with unfamiliar peers). Reentry programs may be helpful for other transitions, including return to a scout troop or a Sunday school class. Children or teens should be allowed to choose whether or not to be present for the presentation. Some may wish to be present for the entire program. If the patient elects to be present, he or she may choose to be an integral part of the program, to participate in answering questions, or to be an observer. Classmates should be prepared for the patient's role at the beginning of the program.

Classmates may ask fewer questions if the patient is present throughout. Some may choose to leave the room during the question-and-answer portion of the program. One way to address this is to allow students to write down their questions, eliminating their need to ask their question out loud. Some children and adolescents will choose to be absent for the entire program. Each of these choices is acceptable. If the patient chooses to be absent, it is important that the classmates understand that the child life specialist has the child or teen's permission to share this information.

Nothing should be revealed to classmates that can't be discussed with the patient. Questions such as "Will he die?" and "How does she go to the bathroom?" should be discussed with the child or teen. Together the patient, family and child life specialist should come up with an answer. Sometimes that answer may be "John would like that to be private." Other times the patient will want every detail shared. With many questions a range of possibilities can be offered. At times, the best response that can be offered is, "We wish we had a crystal ball, but since we don't, here are some possibilities. . . ."

Many schools will want to notify the parents of the classmates that this program will be taking place. Creating a handout for the children or adolescents to take home can be helpful. It should include the topic of the program (including the patient's name and diagnosis), some general information that will be shared with the classmates, and whom parents should contact with questions.

When creating the outline for the program, the developmental level of the participants must be considered. The length of program, selected activities, amount and type of information provided, and resources used will all vary with the age of the classmates. Remember, it is important to adapt the content to the particular child who is returning to the classroom. Active learning opportunities should be included, which might be as simple as asking questions and allowing verbal responses or as involved as creating games that the classmates can participate in to learn information. Resources, such as models and storybooks, can also enhance the learning experience and help maintain the attention of the students.

When transitioning to the question-and-answer portion of the program, it is often helpful to distinguish between "stories" and "questions." Illness and injury are such emotionally charged topics that many children and adolescents have stories they want to share about themselves or a family member. It is often helpful to review the "question words" (who, what, when, where, why, how) and establish limits prior to this session beginning.

It is important to assess the level of the classmates' understanding prior to leaving. Often a game show type review or a "thumbs up/thumbs down" assessment (with yes/no questions) allows the child life specialist to quickly verify understanding. A written evaluation or a follow-up phone call to the classroom teacher can provide additional information.

Normalcy and Redefinition of Self

As a child and family incorporate treatment and routines related to the condition into their lives, a new sense of normalcy emerges. Throughout this process, issues of loss will emerge. Providing emotional support and validating feelings is essential. Families may need support from the child life specialist as they define this "new" normal. Advocating for normalization, return to routine, school and social reintegration, discipline and household responsibility are essential (Dolgin, Phipps, Harow, & Zeltzer, 1990). The establishment of routines, rituals and schedules can help to integrate medical treatments into everyday tasks. These also provide predictability for the child.

Parents of children with chronic conditions often are reluctant to set limits and boundaries. As Sourkes (1995) notes, "The ability of parents to maintain normalcy and limits communicates the critical message, 'While the illness is abnormal, he or she is still normal in their eyes'" (p. 83). Providing support for parents as they process this notion is important.

Children and adolescents dealing with extended hospital stays and with limits in cognitive functioning, benefit from an increased amount of structure in their environment and activities. They also benefit from clear, consistent limits and behavioral expectations. The amount of structure while on the rehabilitation unit is very different than that required in other areas of the hospital. This is often uncomfortable for child life staff in a rehabilitation setting because it may feel as though they must limit the choices being offered. Some simple ways to increase structure in the environment are to use a simple kitchen timer to mark time, to create a list that a patient can use to monitor progress toward a goal, and to truly adhere to the child's daily schedule.

Adjustment over Time

Due to modern medical advances, most children with chronic conditions live long lives. Therefore, it is important to acknowledge how they adjust and change over time. A common misperception of staff is that chronically ill children have been hospitalized so often that they already have seen, heard or experienced everything. This leads many staff members to the conclusion that patients do not need further information related to their illness or procedures. This cannot be further from the truth. As children grow and gain cognitive maturity, they are able to grasp more abstract concepts. Their corresponding informational needs will increase. Concepts already taught at one developmental level will need to be readdressed in light of the new ability for the comprehension of higher-level information. Further, recurrent grief and loss may be experienced at each illness episode or stage. Key transition points such as entry into school, changing schools, puberty, adolescence and young adulthood are especially important times for checking in on individuals to update information, discuss feelings and address other concerns related to that developmental phase of life (Singer, 1999).

Transitioning care from parents to children requires assessment of the child's readiness. Among the factors to consider when assessing readiness are the developmental

level of the child and family factors (Giordano, Petrila, Banion, & Neuenkirchen, 1992). Developmental considerations include the ability to plan ahead and use judgment – both complex cognitive skills. Family factors such as parent burnout, misguided pride and busy parents may initiate the transfer of care too soon. Giordano et al. (1992) recommend the following steps for transferring responsibility for diabetes care, considerations that may equally apply to children with other conditions:

- determine the child's knowledge of disease management concepts and skills
- transfer responsibility gradually
- maintain parental supervision
- reinforce responsible behavior
- have realistic expectations related to what the child can handle

Child life specialists can help plan the transition of care from parents to the child. They can also help other healthcare staff to understand that this process is gradual and that growing pains may accompany it.

Support is also needed when adolescents transition from pediatric care to adult services – a transition can be extremely anxiety provoking. According to Edwards and Davis (1997) adolescents reported needing a year to prepare for the transition. Preparation for adult services is equally important as preparing children for painful procedures, for there will be new routines and procedures to which the adolescent must adjust.

It may also be helpful to allow opportunities for the child or adolescent to process their experience with the chronic condition over time. Making journey maps, complete with hills, bumps and signs, which outline the road they have traveled, can help to process the experience. It will allow them to mindfully reflect on the significance that each event along their journey had on their coping at that time. It is also an opportunity to evaluate the impact the condition has on who they have become as a person.

Interdisciplinary Collaboration

Children with chronic conditions typically have a team of healthcare providers addressing both their physical and psychosocial needs. This team-based focus is beneficial for the patients involved, as there are many voices and views contributing to their care. The team can take a truly holistic approach to care since there are representatives involved who focus on each area – mind, body, and spirit. This close involvement with other disciplines creates opportunities and challenges for the child life specialist.

A service delivery approach called a "co-treat" is often used in the rehabilitation setting. Due to the need for a smaller patient/staff ratio, several staff members from various backgrounds work simultaneously with one patient or with several patients. The child life specialist may be involved in several ways – planning a developmentally-appropriate activity for the session, planning an activity to recognize a holiday or special event, and/or engaging the patient in meaningful activity while the therapist facilitates a difficult skill (e.g., using distraction techniques). This treatment approach allows for the patient's needs to be met in a timely manner, helps guarantee their safety during the session and ensures that activities are developmentally or therapeutically based.

Even though there are numerous benefits, caution must be used with co-treats. Co-treats do not typically allow for parent and sibling involvement. They also do not offer children much in the way of choice, opportunities for expression of feelings, or free play. In order to build and maintain a relationship with a patient and his or her family, the child life specialist should continue to facilitate activities outside of these times as well. The child life specialist must maintain a clear sense of the goals he or she has set for a particular patient. If an activity is contradictory to these goals, that is not an appropriate co-treat.

Professional Considerations

Working with children and families facing chronic conditions presents some unique professional challenges. Relationships are developed over time or through extended hospital stays. Frequently, families refer to staff as "part of the family." The relationships formed during times of crisis are often like no others in life. There are both positives and negatives to this. The nature of chronic illness allows these relationships to be formed and maintained over time. Establishing relationships is extremely beneficial to families and also facilitates a trust in the medical team working with their family. Consistency and continuity is desirable for anyone, particularly those with much unpredictability in their life. However, long-term relationships can potentially lead to crossing professional boundaries. This balance between being supportive and professional and crossing the boundary is sometimes difficult to achieve, particularly with children who have chronic conditions.

Professional boundaries are essential for child life specialists. Boundaries can be defined as the place where one leaves off and another begins. These set each person apart from others. Professional boundaries help to delineate where staff roles begin and end. They also maintain the integrity of the family unit. The goal of professional interactions with children and families is to be meaningfully related, but professionally separate (Barnsteiner & Gills-Donovan, 1990).

All healthcare professionals working with children with chronic conditions and their families would be well served to take a close look at their professional boundaries. Not only is it helpful to the therapeutic relationship but it is self-protective for the professional.

Over involvement can lead to burnout and, eventually, ineffective interactions with children and families. Child life specialists should evaluate whether they are coming in during off times to check on particular children, seeing children and families socially outside of the professional setting, buying gifts for particular children, or showing favoritism. When experiencing burnout, some staff may curtail their involvement, decreasing their ability to be empathetic with families. Working toward a proper balance should be a professional goal.

As discussed in other sections of this chapter, the goal of work with children with chronic conditions is to build self-efficacy in the child and family. Being overly involved can breed a sense of dependency on the child life specialist, which is contradictory to the goals of empowerment of families. Child life specialists must be mindful in the support they give. One area that can lead to dependency is during invasive procedures. Certainly, the child life specialist will prepare the child for the procedure, discuss and rehearse coping strategies, and perhaps be present during the procedure. The critical consideration is that the role should be to support the child's and families' use of adaptive strategies that they are managing on their own, not to make oneself an essential piece of the plan. Rushton, McEnhill and Armstrong (1996) suggest that behaviors empowering of families are ones that facilitate goals developed with the family, support and recognize primary relationships, support the role of the parents as their child's advocates, support the child and family acting on their own behalf, and assist with providing resources necessary to make decisions.

Children with chronic conditions will experience challenging encounters throughout their lives. The best job we can do is to provide them with the tools and strategies necessary to effectively navigate difficult situations.

Child life specialists need to acknowledge that self-care is important and give themselves permission to take care of themselves. In the absence of outlets outside of the professional setting to cope with stress, anxiety and grief, professional burnout will surely follow. Professionals who experience burnout lose their effectiveness with the children and families they serve. Therefore, every child life specialist should mindfully look at what self-preservation strategies they employ to manage work-related stress. Discussing this with peers or mentors can be a helpful way to evaluate how well they are taking care of themselves.

It is the ethical responsibility of child life specialists to continue to evaluate their personal philosophy and practice. The professional should be aware of current practice considerations and their beliefs related to such practices. Remaining abreast of current literature pertinent to the field is essential and leads toward evidence-based practice. This careful self-exploration is essential in order to feel confident in one's skills, allowing both the families and the staff interacting with the child life specialist to trust the recommendations provided or skills modeled.

CONCLUSION

Children with chronic conditions are thrust into a world of uncertainty, which threatens their sense of security. No longer does their life have the predictability necessary for that sense of security. Through careful assessment and planning, the child life specialist can help children and adolescents with chronic conditions cope effectively with their illness and live life to the fullest.

REFERENCES

Abdullah, A., Blakeney, P., Hunt, R., Broemeling, L., Phillips, L., Herndon, D. N., & Robson, M. C. (1994). Visible scars and self-esteem in pediatric patients with burns. *Journal of Burn Care and Rehabilitation, 15*, 164-168.

Amer, K. (1999). Bibliotherapy: Using fiction to help children in two populations discuss feelings. *Pediatric Nursing, 25*, 91-95.

Baker, R. (2002). Support by another mother and a child-life specialist decreased anxiety in mothers of children with chronic illness. *American College of Physicians Journal Club, 137*, 28.

Barnsteiner, J., & Gillis-Donovan, J. (1990). Being related and separate: A standard for therapeutic relationships. *Maternal and Child Nursing, 15*, 223-228.

Bauman, L., Drotar, D., Leventhal, J., Perrin, E., & Pless, I. B. (1997). A review of psychosocial interventions for children with chronic health conditions. *Pediatrics, 100*, 244-252.

Bibace, R., & Walsh, M. (1980). Development of children's concepts of illness. *Pediatrics, 66*, 912-917.

Bishop, B., & Gilinsky, V. (1995). School reentry for the patient with burn injuries: video and/or on-site intervention. *Journal of Burn Care & Rehabilitation, 16*, 45-457.

Bluebond-Langer, M., Perkel, D., Goertzel, T., Nelson, K., & McGeary, J. (1990). Children's knowledge of cancer and its treatment: Impact of an oncology camp experience. *Journal of Pediatrics, 116*, 207-213.

Boyd, J., & Hunsberger, M. (1998). Chronically ill children coping with repeated hospitalizations: Their perceptions and suggested interventions. *Journal of Pediatric Nursing, 13*, 330-342.

Boyd-Franklin, N., Steiner, G., & Boland, M. (Eds.). (1995). *Children, families and HIV/AIDS: Psychosocial and therapeutic issues.* New York: The Guilford Press.

Brewster, A. (1982). Chronically ill hospitalized children's concept of their illness. *Pediatrics, 69*, 355-362.

Briery, B., & Rabian, B. (1999). Psychosocial changes associated with participation in a pediatric summer camp. *Journal of Pediatric Psychology, 24*, 183-190.

Britto, M., Garrett, J., Dugliss, M., Daeschner, C., Johnson, C., Leigh, M., Majure, M., Schultz, W., & Konrad, T. (1998). Risky behavior in teens with cystic fibrosis or sickle cell disease: A multicenter study. *Pediatrics, 101*, 250-256.

Brooks, B., & Siegel, P. M. (1996). *The scared child: Helping kids overcome traumatic events.* New York: John Wiley & Sons, Inc.

Burke, S.O., Handley-Deryy, M. H., Costello, E. A., Kaufmann, E., & Dillon, M. C. (1997). Stress-point intervention for parents of repeatedly hospitalized children with chronic conditions. *Research in Nursing & Health, 20*, 475-485.

Bussing, R., Halfon, N., Benjamin, B., & Wells, K. (1995). Prevalence of behavior problems in US children with asthma. *Archives of Pediatric and Adolescent Medicine, 149*, 565-572.

Canam, C. (1993). Common adaptive tasks facing parents of children with chronic conditions. *Journal of Advanced Nursing, 18*, 46-53.

Castes, M., Hagel, I., Palenque, M., Canelone, P., Corao, A., & Lynch, N. R. (1999). Immunological changes associated with clinical improvement of asthmatic children subjected to psychosocial intervention. *Brain, Behavior, and Immunity, 13*, 1-13.

Cohen, M. (1999). Families coping with childhood chronic illness: A research review. *Families, Systems & Health, 17*, 149-164.

Conoley, J. C., & Sheridan, S. M. (1996). Pediatric traumatic brain injury: Challenges and interventions for families. *Journal of Learning Disabilities, 29*, 662-669.

Davis, C., Delameter, A., Shaw, K., LaGreca, A., Eidson, M., Perez-Rodriguez, J., & Nemery, R. (2001). Brief report: Parenting styles, regimen adherence, and glycemic control in 4 to 10 year old children with diabetes. *Journal of Pediatric Psychology, 26*, 123-129.

Delameter, A., Jacobson, A., Anderson, B., Cox, D., Fisher, L., Lustman, P., Rubin, R., & Wysocki, T. (2001). Psychosocial therapies in diabetes. *Diabetes Care, 24*, 1286-1292.

Dolgin, M., Phipps, S., Harow, E., & Zeltzer, L. (1990). Parental management of fear in chronically ill and healthy children. *Journal of Pediatric Psychology, 15,* 733-744.

Edwards, M., & Davis, H. (1997). *Counselling children with chronic medical conditions.* Leicester, England: The British Psychological Society.

Edwards, P. A., Hertzberg, D. L., Hays, S. R., & Youngblood, N. M. (1999). *Pediatric rehabilitation nursing.* Philadelphia: W. B. Saunders Company.

Eiser, C. (1990). Psychological effects of chronic disease. *Journal of Child and Adolescent Psychology and Psychiatry, 31,* 85-98.

Ellis, J., & Spanos, N. (1994). Cognitive-behavioral interventions for children's distress during bone marrow aspirates and lumbar punctures: A critical review. *Journal of Pain and Symptom Management, 9,* 96-108.

Fennell, P. (2001). *The chronic illness workbook.* Oakland, CA: New Harbinger Publications, Inc.

Fenton, J. (2000). Cystic fibrosis and art therapy. *Arts in Psychotherapy, 27,* 15-25.

Fiese, B., & Wambolt, F. (2000). Family routines, rituals and asthma management: A proposal for family based strategies to increase treatment adherence. *Families, Systems & Health, 18,* 405-418.

Frank, R., Thayer, J., Hagglund, K., Vieth, A., Schopp, L., Beck, N., Kashani, J., Goldstein, D., Cassidy, J., Clay, D., Chaney, J., Hewett, J., & Johnson, J. (1998). Trajectories of adaptation in pediatric chronic illness: The importance of the individual. *Journal of Consulting and Clinical Psychology, 66,* 521-532.

Freeman, M. (1991). Therapeutic use of storytelling for older children who are critically ill. *Children's Health Care, 20,* 208-215.

Garstein, M., Short, A., Vannatta, K., & Noll, R. (1999). Psychosocial adjustment of children with chronic illness: An evaluation of three models. *Journal of Developmental and Behavioral Pediatrics, 20,* 157-163.

Gil, K. M., Anthony, K. K., Carson, J. W., Redding-Lallinger, R., Daeschner, C. W., Ware, R. E. (2001). Daily coping practice predicts treatment effects in children with sickle cell disease. *Journal of Pediatric Psychology, 26,* 163-173.

Giordano, B., Petrila, A., Banion, C., & Neuenkirchen, G. (1992). The challenge of transferring responsibility for diabetes management from parent to child. *Journal of Pediatric Health Care, 6,* 235-239.

Glazer-Waldman, H., Zimmerman, J., Landreth, G., & Norton, D. (1992). Filial therapy: An intervention for parents of children with chronic illness. *International Journal of Play Therapy, 1,* 31-42.

Godfrey, H. P. D., Knight, R. G., & Partridge, F. M. (1996). Emotional adjustment following traumatic brain injury: A stress-appraisal-coping formulation. *Journal of Head Trauma Rehabilitation,* December, 29-40.

Goodheart, C., & Lansing, M. (1997). *Treating people with chronic disease: A psychological guide.* Washington, DC: American Psychological Association.

Greco, P., Pendley, J., McDonell, K., & Reeves, G. (2001). A peer group intervention for adolescents with type 1 diabetes and their best friends. *Journal of Pediatric Psychology, 28,* 485-490.

Heermann, J., & Willis, L. (1992). Effect of problem solving instruction and health locus of control on the management of childhood asthma. *Children's Health Care, 21,* 76-83.

Hicks, M., & Lavender, B. (2001). Psychosocial practice trends in pediatric oncology. *Journal of Pediatric Oncology Nursing, 18,* 143-153.

Holzheimer, L., Mohay, H., & Masters, I. (1998). Educating young children about asthma: Comparing the effectiveness of a developmentally appropriate asthma education video tape and picture book. *Child: Care, Health and Development, 24,* 85-99.

Hostler, S. L. (1999). Pediatric family-centered rehabilitation. *Journal of Head Trauma Rehabilitation, 14,* 384-393.

Johnson, K. (1998). *Trauma in the lives of children* (2nd ed.). Alameda, CA: Hunter House.

Jones, E. M. (2002). The efficacy of intensive individual play therapy for chronically ill children. *International Journal of Play Therapy, 11,* 117-140.

Keene, N., Hobbie, W., & Ruccione, K. (2000). *Childhood cancer survivors. A practical guide to your future.* Sebastopol, CA: O'Reilly & Associates.

Kibby, M., Tyc, V., & Mulhern, R. (1998). Effectiveness of psychological intervention for children and adolescents with chronic medical illness: A meta-analysis. *Clinical Psychology Review, 18,* 103-117.

Lahz, S., & Bryant, R. A. (1997). Pain coping strategies following traumatic brain injury. *Journal of Head Trauma Rehabilitation,* June, 85-90.

Levi, R. B., Drotar, D., Yeates, K. O., & Taylor, H. G. (1999). Posttraumatic stress symptoms in children following orthopedic or traumatic brain injury. *Journal of Clinical Psychology, 28,* 232-243.

Logan, D., Radcliffe, J., & Smith-Whitley, K. (2002). Parent factors and adolescent sickle cell disease: Associations with patterns of health service use. *Journal of Pediatric Psychology, 27,* 475-484.

Martin, D. A. (1988). Children and adolescents with traumatic brain injury: Impact on the family. *Journal of Learning Disabilities, 21,* 464-470.

McCollum, A. (1975). *The chronically ill child.* New Haven: Yale University Press.

McGrath, P. J., Rosmus, C., Canfield, C., Campbell, M. A., & Hennigar, A. (1998). Behaviours caregivers use to determine pain in non-verbal, cognitively impaired individuals. *Developmental Medicine & Child Neurology, 40,* 340-343.

McQuaid, E. & Nassau, J. (1999). Empirically supported treatments of disease-related symptoms in pediatric psychology, *Journal of Pediatric Psychology, 24,* 305-328.

Meijer, S., Sinnema, G., Bijstra, J., Mellenbergh, G., & Walters, W. (2000). Social functioning in children with a chronic illness. *Journal of Child Psychology, Psyciatry & Allied Disciplines, 41,* 309-317.

Molnar, G. E., & Alexander, M. A. (1999). *Pediatric rehabilitation* (3rd ed.). Philadelphia: Hanley & Belfus, Inc.

Monahon, C. (1993). *Children and trauma: A guide for parents and professionals.* San Francisco: Jossey-Bass Publishers.

Moos, R., & Tsu, U. (1977). The crisis of physical illness: An overview. In R. H. Moos (Ed.), *Coping with physical illness,* (pp. 3-21). New York: Plenum.

Mulcahey, M. J. (1992). Returning to school after a spinal cord injury: Perspectives from four adolescents. *The American Journal of Occupational Therapy, 46,* 305-312.

Musselwhite, C. R. (1986). *Adaptive play for special needs children: Strategies to enhance communication and learning.* Austin, TX: Pro-Ed, Inc.

Noll, R., Garstein, M., Vannatta, K., Correll, J., Bukowski, W., & Davies, W. (1999). Social, emotional, and behavioral functioning of children with cancer. *Pediatrics, 103,* 71-78.

Oberlander, T. F., Gilbert, C. A., Chambers, C. T., O'Donnell, M. E., & Craig, K. D. (1999). Biobehavioral responses to acute pain in adolescents with significant neurologic impairment. *The Clinical Journal of Pain, 15,* 201-209.

Oberlander, T. F., O'Donnell, M. E., & Montgomery, C. J. (1999). Pain in children with significant neurological impairment. *Developmental and Behavioral Pediatrics, 20,* 235-243.

Olson, A., Johansen, S., Powers, L., Pope, J., & Klein, R. (1993). Cognitive coping strategies of children with chronic illness. *Developmental and Behavioral Pediatrics, 14,* 217-223.

Pendley, J. S., Kasmen, L., Miller, D., Donze, J., Swenson, C., & Reeves, G. (2002). Peer and family support in children and adolescents with type 1 diabetes. *Journal of Pediatric Psychology, 27,* 429-438.

Pless, I., & Pinkerton, P. (1975). *Chronic childhood disorders: Promoting patterns of adjustment.* Chicago: Year-Book Medical Publishers.

Powell, T. H. & Gallagher, P. A. (1993). *Brothers & sisters: A special part of exceptional families* (2nd ed.). Baltimore, Maryland: Paul H. Brooks Publishing Co.

Rushton, C., McEnhill, M., & Armstron, L. (1996). Establishing therapeutic boundaries as patient advocates. *Pediatric Nursing, 22,* 185-189.

Ross, D., (1984). Thought-stopping: A coping strategy for impending feared events. *Issues in Comprehensive Nursing, 7,* 83-89.

Ross, D. & Ross, S. (1984). Stress reduction procedures for the school-age hospitalized leukemic child. *Pediatric Nursing,* Nov/Dec, 393-395.

Rynard, D., Chambers, A., Klinck, A., & Gray, J. (1998). School support programs for chronically ill children: Evaluating the adjustment of children with cancer in school. *Children's Health Care, 27,* 31-46.

Savage, R. C., & Wolcott, G. F. (Ed.) (1995). *An educator's manual: What educator's need to know about students with brain injury.* Washington D.C.: Brain Injury Association, Inc.

Seiffge-Krenke, I. (2002). "Come on, say something, dad!": Communication and coping in fathers of diabetic adolescents. *Journal of Pediatric Psychology, 27,* 439-450.

Siegel, L., & Smith, K. (1989). Children's strategies for coping with pain. *Pediatrician, 16,* 110-118.

Singer, A. (1999). *Coping with your child's chronic illness.* San Francisco: Robert D. Reed Publishers.

Soliday, E., Kool, E., & Lande, M. (2000). Psychological adjustment in children with kidney disease. *Journal of Pediatric Psychology, 25,* 93-103.

Sourkes, B. (1995). *Armsful of time: The psychological experience of the child with a life-threatening illness.* Pittsburgh: University of Pittsburgh Press.

Stauffer, M. (1998). A long-term psychotherapy group for children with chronic medical illness. *Bulletin of the Menninger Clinic, 62,* 15-32.

Stein, R., Westbrook, L., & Silver, E. (1998). Comparison of adjustment of school-age children with and without chronic conditions: Results from community-based samples. *Journal of Developmental and Behavioral Pediatrics, 19,* 267-272.

Testani-Dufour, L., Chappel-Aiken, L., & Gueldner, S. (1992). Traumatic brain injury: A family experience. *Journal of Neuroscience Nursing, 24,* 317-323.

Tew, K., Landreth, G., Joiner, K., & Solt, M. (2002). Filial therapy with parents of chronically ill children. *International Journal of Play Therapy, 11,* 79-100.

Thompson, R., & Gustafson, K. (1996). *Adaptation to chronic childhood illness.* Washington, D.C.: American Psychological Association.

Thompson, R., Gustafson, K., Gil, K., Godfrey, J., & Murphy, L. (1998). Illness specific patterns of psychological adjustment and cognitive adaptational processes in children with cystic fibrosis and sickle cell disease. *Journal of Clinical Psychology, 54,* 121-128.

Varni, J., Katz, E., Colegrove, R., & Dolgin, M. (1993). The impact of social skills training on the adjustment of children with newly diagnosed cancer. *Journal of Pediatric Psychology, 18,* 751-767.

Verity, P. A. (1995). Burn injuries in children: The emotional effect and psychological effects on child and family. *Australian Family Physician, 24,* 176-180.

Wallander, J., & Varni, J. (1992). Adjustment of children with chronic physical disorders: Programmatic research on a disability-stress-coping model. In A. LaGreca, L. Siegal, J. Wallander, & C. Walker (Eds.), *Stress and coping with pediatric conditions,* (pp. 279-298). New York: Guilford Press.

Warden, D. L., Labbate, L. A., Salazar, A. M., Nelson, R., Sheley, E., Staudenmeier, J., & Martin, E. (1997). Posttraumatic stress disorder in patients with traumatic brain injury and amnesia for the event? *Journal of Neuropsychiatry, 9,* 18-22.

Yim-Chiplis, P. K. (1998). The child with traumatic brain injury returns to school. *Pediatric Nursing, 24,* 245-248.

Ylvisaker, M., Todis, B., Glang, A., Urbanczyk, B., Franklin, C., DePompei, R., Feeney, T., Maxwell, N. M., Pearson, S., & Tyler, J. S. (2001). Educating students with TBI: Themes and recommendations. *Journal of Head Trauma Rehabilitation, 16,* 76-93.

Chapter 14

THE EMERGENCY DEPARTMENT AND AMBULATORY CARE

VICKIE L. SQUIRES AND KIM EURY ALLEN

INTRODUCTION

Child life practice in emergency department and ambulatory care settings differs greatly from that of the traditional inpatient unit, differing in the priorities of the child life specialist, the strategies used to provide care, the acuity levels of patients served and the overall pace of the setting. Establishing a therapeutic relationship in outpatient settings represents a challenge and the results often do not reach the level that is common to inpatient service.

The practice of child life in the emergency department and ambulatory care setting is rooted in the tradition, experience and training of inpatient practice, based on a "linear" model of developing therapeutic relationships and implementing care strategies over time a period of days, weeks, or even months. Although the average length of inpatient stay has declined substantially in recent years, the amount of time available to the inpatient child life specialist for the development of therapeutic relationships is still typically greater than that available during outpatient visits. In inpatient settings, therapeutic relationships grow through repeated contact and opportunities to build trust. The therapeutic process evolves as objectives, care plans and outcomes roll out and are redefined as patients and families are re-assessed, progress in their care, and prepare for discharge. In outpatient settings, the care and practice strategies can be characterize as "vertical" instead of linear, with children and families sometimes served a single time, never to be seen again. Patients are served in shorter units of time, often as little as 10 or 15 minutes. Interdisciplinary team care may be limited to a single patient problem or complaint and not involve the more integrated needs such as coping support, developmental assessment, dietary needs or spiritual care. Nevertheless, in ambulatory care settings, the need for therapeutic relationships exist and may build slowly over a period of several appointments or through opportunities to collaborate with inpatient colleagues during a hospital admission.

Despite the differences inherent to practice in inpatient and outpatient settings, the practice of child life in ambulatory settings shares the same guiding principles of inpatient care – that the child's developmental capabilities define the strategies used to assist coping, that family centered care is essential, and that play is the therapeutic glue that ties care together for all into a meaningful outcome.

LITERATURE REVIEW

The literature related to child life interventions in an emergency department and ambulatory care settings is limited. Little aggregate data exist comparing the relative frequency of inpatient pediatric admissions versus ambulatory pediatric encounters in the United States. Nevertheless, what is clear is that the vast majority of pediatric healthcare for any given child is provided on an outpatient basis, be it an emergency department or, more commonly, in any of a wide variety of ambulatory care settings.

This situation has required the child life profession to continually re-evaluate and adapt to patient care priorities. Nevertheless, Krebel, Clayton, and Graham (1996) reported that relatively few emergency departments offered child life services at the time

of their study. Of the hospitals contacted that served pediatric patients in the emergency department, 72 percent reported that no child life services were made available in the area. Only 14 percent reported that at least one full-time child life specialist was devoted to the service. The situation observed by Krebel et al. has improved somewhat in the past ten years. The 2006 Directory of Child Life Programs (Child Life Council, 2006) lists 382 programs in the traditional hospital-based settings in the United States. Of these programs, 27 percent provided child life service in emergency departments, with 35 percent serving ambulatory clinics. The extent of child life service allocated in these areas is indicated by the number of full-time equivalent positions (FTE's) devoted to the area. Generally, FTE's ranged from .5 to 3 in both emergency departments and ambulatory clinic programs. Similar patterns of involvement of child life programs in emergency and ambulatory departments are found in hospitals in Canada and other countries reported in the directory (see Table 1).

Table 1

PROPORTION OF CHILD LIFE PROGRAMS STAFFING EMERGENCY DEPARTMENTS OR AMBULATORY CLINICS

2006 Directory of Child Life	Total Number of Hospital-based Child Life Programs	Emergency Department Programs with Allocated FTE(s) Includes Full & Part Time, Not On Call	% of Hospitals with Emergency Department Child Life Programs	Ambulatory Clinic Programs with Allocated FTE(s) Includes Full & Part Time, Not On Call; Primary & Specialty	% of Hospitals with Ambulatory Child Life Programs
USA	382	106	27%	134	35%
Canada	41	5	12%	18	43%
International Programs	22	3	13%	5	22%

The few studies that exist on the value of child life services suggest that when appropriately utilized in the emergency department, they help increase patient and parent satisfaction, are effective in reducing a child's verbal fear responses, and may decrease the need for medication – results that may apply to other ambulatory settings, as well. Approaches used in these studies included the providing of play and developmental stimulation, offering information regarding the procedure, and acknowledging of fears and concerns related to the health-care setting or contributing accident. (See Chapter Three for a fuller discussion of this research.)

SCOPE OF OUTPATIENT CHILD LIFE SERVICE AND IMPLICATIONS

In 2007 we sampled several of the emergency department and ambulatory care child life programs from the United States listed in the 2006 Directory of Child Life Programs. These programs were informally surveyed regarding the scope of child life service in the emergency department and ambulatory areas. Programming priorities and aspects of care were also discussed. Through this inquiry we noted that the child life profession has moved greatly, but not proportionally, with the healthcare industry's trends toward increased outpatient service. In particular, we observed the following:

• Each respondent noted that the majority of the child life department's staff served inpatient units.
• No one reported the availability of child life service 24 hours per day, seven days per, unlike other disciplines in the emergency department.

• Most provided one shift of emergency department child life service with coverage emphasizing Thursday through Sunday on the late afternoon through evening shift.
• The majority of hospitals reported that staffing of the outpatient surgical unit had priority over the emergency department and other ambulatory settings.
• A portion of the respondents reported that child life services were provided to some of their specialty clinics; however, none provided direct child life service to the majority of their facility's clinics.

Trust and therapeutic relationship building remain an integral component of outpatient child life service, even though they must be addressed in a briefer period of time. Preparation, treatment support, emotional support, advocacy for family involvement, and the provision of developmentally appropriate play are the focus of child life practice in all outpatient settings. Emergency department child life specialists work quickly to assess and provide therapeutic interventions to patients to relieve fear and pain. Most of the interventions come in the form of emotional support and preparation for an immediate treatment or procedure. Providing developmentally appropriate play opportunities and family interventions are also priorities in the hectic emergency department environment. Child life specialists in other ambulatory settings may provide short, single-visit interventions with similar focus as the emergency department, such as surgical or procedural preparation. In some settings, the child life specialist may develop long-term patient and family care plans based on assessed needs. These may be implemented over a period of time such as a week as in a hematology clinic or over as much as a month or year in a rehabilitation or dialysis setting. A single visit for the purpose of completing a standardized assessment such as a Denver Developmental Screening Test to complement the healthcare team's knowledge about a child may be completed in a "well child" or specialty clinic setting.

Significant changes in practice in outpatient healthcare services in the past decade have changed child life care and focus. These changes can be attributed to healthcare costs, reimbursement and governmental interventions imposed on the healthcare industry, as well as many technological advances. When the early child life professionals began assisting children in hospitals, it was not uncommon for children to be isolated from their families and admitted, at times for lengthy admissions for diagnosis and treatments. Child life specialists were well-suited to assist children with their separation from parents, helping them build trusting relationships with their healthcare providers, understand and master their healthcare experiences and supporting their ego development through these life-changing events.

However, in the first decade of the twenty-first century, economic pressures altered many of the practices and routines of outpatient care. An example of this is the practice of "cohorting" patients in the emergency department for as long as 23 hours. Cohorting refers to the practice of placing several patients together in the single room. It is more efficient and cost effective to serve multiple patients within a close proximity. Many hospitals have also created parallel observation units staffed by emergency department personnel to decrease lengths of stay and, therefore, costs. Observation care costs and reimbursement is significantly less than that of emergency department and inpatient care admissions. As a result, cohorting patients in well-managed observation units within emergency departments can significantly drive down hospital expenses.

Outpatient surgical units provide a variety of surgical and procedural interventions under conscious sedation, reducing the need for inpatient hospitalization. Surgeries that once would have necessitated hospital admission (e.g., non-ruptured appendectomies, hernia repairs, and some cardiac procedures) now result in same-day discharges. An increasing number of invasive interventions such as Botox injections and renal dialysis are provided in pediatric outpatient clinics in an effort to curb costs and support family needs. Pediatric home healthcare routinely includes the providing of IV fluids and medications, wound care, catheter interventions, and palliative care.

Many currently practicing child life specialists or other healthcare providers were in training or in the early stages of their careers when these treatments and procedures were provided in inpatient settings. When now provided in outpatient settings, children and families must rapidly absorb confusing technical information, interventions, pain and body alteration, and other life changes, then return to their homes to sort out and manage their follow-up or maintenance needs. As care increasingly moves to the outpatient setting, child life specialists are challenged to adapt their practice to meet the needs of children and families in the ambulatory environment.

Type of Services

Regardless of the outpatient care setting, child life practice must be structured around clear goals and, ideally, be monitored by a certified child life specialist with considerable experience. As with inpatient care programs, goals should include the following:

- To assess coping responses and needs of children and families to healthcare experiences
- To minimize stress and anxiety for the child

- To prepare children and families for healthcare experiences
- To provide essential life experiences that are relevant to the child's developmental needs, and their family and community values
- To create opportunities that strengthen self-esteem and independence
- To communicate effectively with other members of the healthcare team

The adaptation, implementation and emphasis placed on these goals may vary with outpatient setting. Specific activities associated with them may be delivered all or in part by a child life specialist. However, in larger settings it may be desirable to incorporate others under the direction of the child life specialist to deliver portions of the plan of child life care. Child life practice may be provided directly, indirectly or through ancillary means – for example, through play or care delivered by volunteers and prescribed by child life specialists. Direct services such as trauma support and bereavement support, treatment support, and developmental assessment will remain the domain of the child life specialist. Indirect and ancillary service can be delegated to child life assistants or trained volunteers to complement and add efficiency to child life care. Waiting room activities, special events, animal visits, infection control practices, and education programs can all be enhanced under the direction of the child life specialist.

Most outpatient child life programs offer educational components. Injury prevention education, child development and parenting topics are useful information for the "captive audience" in busy waiting rooms or during the longer waits or stays in treatment rooms. Education is best received when related to the area or issue at hand and when relayed in an engaging, interactive manner. For example:

- Providing waiting and treatment areas with programmed TV viewing. Alternating children's entertainment with short parenting topics is effective.
- Creating fact sheets for children and families. Many of these are available for purchase and can be reprinted with the hospital's logo at a reasonable cost. It might be helpful to include a short quiz, a "draw-a-picture" opportunity or some other mechanism to measure or evaluate the participant's understanding of the topic. Fact sheets and newsletters can be displayed on waiting room bulletin boards or counter brochure stands. Child life and nursing staff can also hand them out during visits or during the education and instruction portion of discharge.
- Drawings or raffles may increase participation in education events.
- Guest speakers from local public service agencies (e.g., libraries, fire and police departments, utility companies) can be invited to provide presentations in waiting areas and to healthcare team members. Many community agencies have educational programs or departments interested in providing programs in well-populated, child-focused areas.

Staffing Plans and Service Hours

Staffing organization in outpatient areas differs greatly from standard inpatient units where the majority of treatment and procedures occur during business hours. Staffing plans must be organized and maintained in correspondence with patient flow. Clinic business hours, outpatient surgical schedules, and regional emergency department patient flow patterns must be evaluated to provide optimal child life service. Studying the flow of patients (i.e., the high and low census volume periods during a designated time frame) will identify the periods when child life services should be available to assist the majority of patients. If, for example, this information indicates that Sunday and Monday evenings are peak periods in the emergency department, staffing the area during this time frame would prove to be most effective. The "vertical care" model of outpatient services lends itself well to the work preferences of part-time, or "flextime" child life staff allowing them to work during these peak times. Staffing plans should be reviewed periodically to offer and support quality patient and family education programs. Providing adequate coverage is not a simple task, but it is one that warrants careful attention. Many children's first and lasting impressions are formulated in emergency departments or through single experiences in outpatient settings. The task of scheduling coverage or substitutions is lessened when experienced child life specialists are cross-trained and skilled in implementation of pain and fear management techniques.

Outpatient surgical centers often open and receive patients before 6:00 a.m., Monday through Fridays. Ambulatory and specialty clinics more often revolve around common community business hours. It is not uncommon, however, for many clinics to offer evening and weekend services in response to consumer demand. The emergency department, by definition, is always open and ready to respond to urgent and emergent patient needs. Many hospitals offer ancillary programs entitled "Fast Track" or "Walk-In Clinic" staffed by the emergency department for non-urgent, common illnesses when most primary care provider offices are closed for business. Priority for child life staffing in all of these areas must consider patient need and maximum patient contact.

The bulk of emergency department patient volume again may be regional and not exclusively within a given city or locality. Hospitals may have contracts with rural or other area hospitals creating business partnerships for service. Some hospitals are assigned geographic regions by state or local governments, stipulating the areas they must serve. Pediatric emergency department peak volumes tend to be afternoons and nights, on weekends through Tuesday. Ideally, child life staffing in the emergency department staffing would provide daily service between the hours of 3:00 p.m. and 2:00 a.m. If staffing and budget are more restricted, then service between the hours 3:00 p.m. and Midnight, Friday through Monday, is suggested for maximum patient and family benefit. An exemplary emergency department child life staffing plan would include daily programming between 10:30 a.m. to midnight, for a minimum of ten hours, with some variability to accommodate hospital obligations. Because of the intense and stressful nature of the emergency department setting, we recommend a three- or four-day workweek with ten- or twelve-hour shifts to afford emergency department child life specialists ample time for emotional recovery each week.

Optimal staff-to-patient ratios have not been formally evaluated or reported in the literature. However, based on our experience, we recommend that outpatient surgical units or conscious sedation settings provide a minimum of one child life specialist for each ten to fifteen patients served daily. Specialty clinics settings can offer quality child life service with one child life specialist for each 25 scheduled patients. In a primary care setting, our recommended ratio would be one child life specialist per 30 scheduled patients. Emergency department settings need to consider patient volume, peak census periods and accredited level of care when planning staff to patient ratios. For example, in an emergency department serving 10,000 pediatric patients annually during peak hours, one child life specialist can provide a basic standard of psychosocial care to the bulk of that program's patients. In "level one" trauma centers, where the most acute and critical patients are routed or airlifted by emergency medical services, more child life support would be required. On-call child life specialists may be beneficial in extending coverage in the emergency department in response to episodic trauma and tragedies or sporadic high census periods. On the other hand, rural emergency departments (where the level of care is less acute and more like that of an urgent care pediatric setting) will require less child life support.

Other Service Tasks and Assignments

PAIN ASSESSMENT. Pain assessment is a multidisciplinary responsibility. Child life specialists play a significant role in the assessment of pain in children. They can assist their units in posting approved, standardized pain scales in treatment rooms and other important patient care areas. Child and parent education in the use of these tools can also be implemented during routine child life interventions. A child life specialist's report of a child's pain during a treatment or moment of diversion can offer the team important information regarding the child's coping.

Child life specialists often serve as advocates for pain reduction measures such as the use of topical anesthetics. They can also be instrumental members of pain management teams bringing a significant perspective on children's coping and responses.

NON-ACCIDENTAL TRAUMA. Non-accidental trauma patients (i.e., those who have been abused or assaulted) are another population that child life specialists encounter in their routine service in both emergency department and ambulatory care settings.

Some, but not all, states have specific programs for assisting this patient population. State governments may license registered nurses specifically to obtain and maintain the criminal evidence of sexual assaults, both actual and potential. These practitioners, often referred to by the acronym SANE (sexual assault nurse examiner), are required to complete specialized training for assisting this population and to follow specific protocols incorporated into the plan of care. A child life specialist can assist in this care as an advocate and figure of support for patients who may have been abused. Working as part of the team, the child life specialist may perform such functions as preparing the child for the examination, assisting the child during the examination by providing coping or distraction interventions, and providing families with necessary information and support.

DISASTER PREPAREDNESS. Child life specialists assigned to specific outpatient settings may be asked to serve on Disaster Preparedness Teams. In this role they draw upon their keen knowledge of the healthcare facility and may be assigned specific duties when an alert is activated.

DOCUMENTATION. Documenting in outpatient medical records presents a challenge, regardless of the setting. Patients are seen and discharged at a pace that makes it difficult for all team members to manage. There are, however, priorities that must be respected. Physicians and nurses must complete all documentation requirements to meet minimal regulatory standards. It is not uncommon to observe a waiting line for a patient paper chart. Electronic charting might alleviate this, but it too brings a set of challenges that have yet to be fully addressed. Many facilities continue to rely on the paper medical record. Standardizing patient care chart notes and the use of stickers or stamps based on child life practice priorities and key interventions (e.g., procedural preparation, treatment support, injury prevention education, developmental and play support, family interventions) can expedite the process.

Most productivity measures and process improvement plans require ambulatory child life specialists to maintain some form of statistics. The minimum data recorded may include the number of patients receiving child life interventions, their priority level, and the types of interventions provided per shift. This information may be used or reported in a variety of ways depending on the program and institution. Data may be compiled annually for budget planning or used when proposing additional positions. Missed opportunities may also be tracked. For example, a child life specialist working with a trauma patient and family in the emergency department or with a patient in the clinic facing complicated issues may be unavailable to work with other patients during this interval. Reporting the number of patients not served may provide justification for new or expanded child life coverage.

NEW DIRECTIONS. Healthcare is becoming increasingly technological, fast-paced and decentralized, with care provided in homes and community settings. As a result, children and families must frequently process and cope with new information, interventions, pain, body alterations, and other life changes with minimal support. This changing reality of healthcare offers a challenge to the profession of child life to find innovative ways of supporting children and their families. Child life clinical practice should broaden its focus to address these needs, for example, becoming a developmental case manager to assure that children's needs do not fall into the cracks of cyber healthcare. Developmental evaluations followed by play prescriptions, child and family education and home-based therapeutic interventions may become the humane link to healthcare in the future.

Child life specialists will need to consider the home care needs of medically fragile children in foster care, group homes and other institutional settings. In addition, the coping and bereavement needs of children of adult patients will also require consideration by child life. Child life specialists may need to partner with funeral homes, local police, or emergency medical services to address the needs of a broad range of children and families in the community.

One aspect of human healing and healthcare that has not, and will not, change in spite of economics, regulations or technological advances is the need for human connection, trust in others and hope. This is the foundation of child life clinical practice. Trust gives children and families the hope that drives their healing process and carries them through their experience.

Emergency Department Specific Issues, Patient Assessment and Prioritization

At the beginning of a day the only people who think that they will end up in the emergency department of their local hospital are the staff who work there. Patients and families do not plan emergency service visits. Therefore, the experience of the emergency department, simply by the unexpected nature of the need for a visit, is stressful. The perceived stress by a family is directly related to the intensity of the injury or illness of the patient. An unexpected visit, often accompanied by a wait to receive services, can lend itself to an anxiety-provoking and sometimes highly volatile experience. Child life can assist in this aspect of the emergency department in many ways. Often the child life specialist, or a designee under his or her supervision such as a child life assistant or volunteer, is responsible for providing "normalizing" activities and interventions in the lobby and waiting space for patients and families. This may be in the form of volunteer programs that may include play assistance or entertainment. Play materials or wall-mounted play equipment available for children to view and manipulate are essential. A child who enters the emergency department and finds a fish tank, for example, may calm down while waiting to be seen. Child-friendly environments begin to tell children that the emergency department is an "okay" place for them. It says that other children have been there and are welcome. The skilled child life specialist will take the unpredictability of the environment and address it with the patient. It is helpful to ask patients what experience they have had with the hospital, clinic, or a doctor's office in order to assess how they are coping with this specific visit.

Often children are exposed to things that are quite scary in the emergency department. A child who is in for a broken arm may see a child who requires sutures and immediately think that he or she will receive the exact same treatment. By its very nature, the emergency department serves children with a variety of ages, diagnoses and treatment needs at any given time. For children, this is an open invitation to misconception and fertile ground for false fantasies. It is very important for the child life specialist to take an active role in clarifying the sites and sounds of a busy emergency department. Children's overt cues, eye contacts, visible upset behavior, and clinging are all signals that a child life specialist can read and address.

An emergency department can quickly become a hostile environment, due to circumstances including trauma and sudden injury, as well as the treatments required. Parents and patients can become upset or volatile upon hearing "bad news." They may be forced to remain in the area for extended periods of time, waiting for treatment or the availability of a room if hospitalization is required. The presence of a child life specialist can be critical in helping children and families deal with these circumstances. Child life staff can be instrumental in maintaining open communication with the family and the healthcare team, as well as providing normalization activities for children to help them bide time.

Perhaps one of the most challenging aspects of the emergency department is the variety of diagnoses, treatments and procedures that one encounters. The child life specialist must be ready for the unpredictable. Most child life specialists rely on their own assessment procedures when seeing a patient. Different doctors may treat the same injuries in different ways. The child life specialist must adapt interventions to suit each situation. For example, a child in the emergency department with a laceration on the arm may receive sutures from one doctor, while another may try a different method of addressing the same diagnosis. This flexibility, which is one of the most interesting aspects of emergency medicine, is also one of the most important lessons to be learned by the emergency department child life specialist. A child life specialist in the emergency department must be familiar with a repertoire of treatments and how to educate the patient in the one that will be experienced. Open communication with the medical staff is essential in this process.

A superstition among emergency department personnel is to never say the word "slow." Once said aloud, the environment has a tendency to change. The unpredictability of patient volume, types of complaints, and acuity levels is truly the only given in an emergency department environment. High-volume emergency departments often have after hours or walk-in clinics where patients can be seen in order to reduce the number treated in a main emergency department. In busy seasons, patients may be triaged in and sent to other areas. High volumes of patients present a unique challenge for child life. Prioritization is essential when a slow night suddenly becomes a very busy one.

A child life specialist must be able to meet and establish rapport with a patient and family very quickly, and a well-balanced bag of tricks is required. Entering a room with, for example, a toy or coloring sheet sends important nonverbal information to children and families that the staff wants to make their stay more comfortable. A silly sticker on a nametag or bubbles communicates to a scared patient that the child life specialist is trying to make this experience more kid friendly. In a fast-paced, intimidating emergency department, which causes many patients to "shut down," simple steps such as these speak volumes in the precious seconds that the child life specialist has to establish a relationship and treat a patient.

Another important skill for the emergency department child life specialist is to be able to hold a one-sided conversation. Some patients may not respond to the child life specialist. Essentially, the child life specialist is yet another stranger coming into the patient's room. Not having the luxury of time to establish a trusting relationship with the patient, the child life specialist needs to be able to prepare the patient for what is about to happen via a one-way conversation. The patient may not acknowledge the effort, but the child life specialist can provide needed information while seemingly talking to the wall. There is, however, risk in the use of this therapeutic technique. A child may not want, need or be able to tolerate all of the information that is provided, becoming overly excited or threatened. Because of this, it is imperative to continually monitor the

child and parents for responses that indicate that this technique should either continue or stop. Affect, eye contact, breathing patterns, muscle tension, responsiveness to commands and emotional behaviors can be the critical observations for assessing the positive or negative response to this technique. The child life specialist should periodically ask the child or a family member whether this technique is useful or helpful and should continue.

The child life specialist must be available to the medical staff in order to be effectively utilized. Because of the rhythm and pace of procedures and treatments, the child life specialist cannot expect the rest of the medical team to afford them luxury of time for procedural preparations, education and coping strategies. Ideally, the child life specialist should be available whenever needed for patient care. This requires careful consideration of the staffing patterns. The visibility of the child life specialist also contributes to effective use of the service. It may be important for the child life specialist to "hang out" during the down times at the desk, setting the stage for involvement in the next case. This can also result in opportunities for advocacy, as well as informal staff training on topics such as children's perceptions or strategies for enhancing coping.

The environment can change in the blink of an eye, and it is not always appropriate to expect that medical staff will page and wait for child life. Being visible and showing the value of child life interventions will help "sell" the importance of preparation, procedural support and coping to those who may be skeptical. Actions are worth a thousand words, and the medical staff may need to see child life services to believe in the possibilities and understand. An orthopedic surgeon who witnesses a patient being prepped by child life for a conscious sedation and proceeds with a more cooperative, less anxious patient will be more receptive to child life interventions with future patients. Physicians and administrators may observe that calmer patients require less pain medication and sedation and recover more quickly, saving medical staff and time, room utilization and other resources – not to mention improving patient and family satisfaction.

Perhaps one of the biggest lessons for any emergency department child life specialist is the need for multiple plans. Flexibility in thinking and planning is essential. Not only must emergency department child life specialists have a plan B, but they must also have a plan C, D, E, and F. When walking into a room to provide procedural support for a patient having an IV, the child life specialist may anticipate using bubbles as an initial distraction and coping intervention. Two minutes into the procedure the patient no longer pays attention to the bubbles and begins to become restless. Plan B may be a hide-and-seek book. The patient does not even look twice at this intervention. Plan C may be a stress ball that the patient may squeeze. This may work fine for a few minutes, but the nurse starting the IV is having a hard time finding a vein, so it is taking a little longer than usual. Plan D may be a party blower, given to the patient. The child life specialist encourages the patient to "blow away the pain" or "scary feelings," which works for a couple minutes before the patient becomes disinterested. Plan E may be to recite the ABC's. The same patient, who may return the very next day, may decide to look at the hide-and-seek book. Flexibility is, above all, the most essential trait for the clinical practice of the emergency department child life specialist.

Educating staff on a variety of topics from the child life role to teaching child development is an ongoing opportunity. Especially in a teaching hospital, where various staff members rotate through each department, education occurs daily and is the responsibility of many staff. Emergency department child life specialists may conduct staff in-services, speak at rounds, or individually introduce themselves to staff in the emergency department. It is difficult to reach every staff member at one designated time because of the large and rotating shifts. Recordings of in-services, in-service outlines, newsletters, participation in team meetings, and informal after-hours visits are all pathways used by successful child life specialists to educate their staff as to what is important for children and families and the role the team can play.

Environmental maintenance can be a major piece of an emergency department child life program. Typically, toys are cleaned in between every patient due to the nature of the population – an essential, yet time-consuming task. Each hospital adheres to its own guidelines on infection control and toy cleaning, but all child life specialists must address this issue. Child life assistants, interns, nursing students, volunteers and others can assist in this tedious process. Another component of environmental maintenance is providing a kid-friendly environment. Decorating for a season or a holiday can brighten an area and let patients and families know that the emergency department is a welcoming place for children. Because of the transient nature of the areas, material retention is a big issue. Supplies and materials must be replenished frequently.

Volunteers are especially helpful to the emergency department child life program, extending the services provided in wait spaces and lobbies, offering much needed diversional activities for patients and family members. Volunteers can also assist families in meeting their basic needs, providing directions, information regarding conveniences (i.e., restroom, food, phone facilities) and activities for siblings. Due to the nature of the emergency department, volunteers must be adequately trained and have demonstrated competence in providing services to patients and families. Emergency department programs may require volunteers to work in other areas of the hospital prior to working in the busy and stressful emergency department. Many large corporations have volunteer corps that contribute significant volunteer hours to community charities and nonprofit organizations.

A difficult reality for the emergency department child life specialist is the need to help a family that has suffered a loss. A death that occurs in the emergency department is most often unexpected, sudden or traumatic. The raw emotion of a grieving family can be difficult to digest and understand. Every family has its individual ways of coping. A child life specialist may be a sounding board, a listener, an advocate, an educator (especially with siblings) and a child-oriented "friend" in these unfortunate circumstances, and may be involved in a variety of tasks. Some create handprints, footprints or other memory items for family keepsakes, although many of these legacy activities may be prohibited in some areas by the medical examiner prior to a patient's autopsy. Others work with siblings helping to explain, comfort and work through their emotions. Some assist families with logistics such as bathroom, drink and phone locations and availability. All in all, the child life specialist is part of the multidisciplinary team consisting of doctors, nurses, social workers and chaplains in helping to meet the needs of the family during this extremely difficult time. Child life specialists are also members of stress debriefing teams at institutions that support staff in processing patient deaths.

Yet another challenging aspect of work as a child life specialist in an emergency department is the assessment and prioritization of patients. The pace of an emergency department often dictates that multiple and con-

current patient needs be addressed simultaneously. There is no magic formula to determine which patient needs child life interventions the most. There are, however, pieces to the puzzle that the child life specialist can extract from many different sources to best determine needs and develop a plan of care.

The first piece is the triage code. This is a measurement of patient acuity assigned to each patient by a nurse upon entry to the emergency department. A child life specialist can use this information to understand how sick or injured the patient is and consider the priority level for administering the medical attention. A patient who is triaged and immediately seen by the medical staff may require immediate child life attention. Treatment may be administered very quickly and, if circumstances allow, the child life specialist can explain what is happening to the patient and family in developmentally appropriate terms. Family intervention can be an important component of care for the urgent patient. The child life specialist can assist the family by explaining or interpreting what the medical team is doing, offering support and suggestions for coping, providing information regarding roles of team members and other hospital personnel, as well as the locations of telephones, restrooms or other needed services. In addition, support can be provided to siblings.

A second piece of the puzzle is the "chief complaint," which aids the child life specialist in determining the procedures and treatments that may be forthcoming. A laceration, for example, may require sutures, glue or staples. Once familiar with the emergency department, the child life specialist will be able to anticipate the treatments that typically happen for specific diagnoses and patient complaints. However, circumstances often change. Therefore, it is important that the child life specialist have excellent communication with nursing and medical staff to determine the most appropriate supportive interventions to address each patient's individual needs.

Patients who will require invasive procedures are given higher priority by the triage nurse and may receive team services sooner. Also given higher priority are patients who come to the emergency department via ambulance service, or are accompanied by the police or child protective services, as well as those with lacerations, bone reduction needs, and those who have experienced sexual assault or will require surgery or admission. It is essential for the child life specialist to attempt to prepare these patients for what they may experience. Strategies for preparation may include the use of admission or surgical photo books, videos, and medical play with stuffed animals or dolls to demonstrate what is going to occur.

The child's developmental level is another important piece in completing the emergency department service puzzle and is integral in planning child interventions. Infants need to remain with their primary caregivers whenever possible in order to maintain a sense of trust. Child life can assist in this by remaining with an infant whose parent is unavailable, providing a safe, less-threatening presence. A toddler may experience difficulty in autonomy secondary to being restricted in an exam room, for example. A child life specialist can provide developmentally appropriate interventions to help the child feel in control. Preschool children, whose understanding of events in the world is characterized by magical thinking, may feel as though a trip to the emergency department is punishment. Child life can provide the opportunity for medical play, or procedural explanations that focus on the reason for the visit to clarify their misconceptions. School-age patients may experience a lack of control in this stressful, often chaotic environment. Child life can provide

choices for these patients and, when possible, educate and involve them in the process of the emergency department visit. Adolescents may try to exert their control over the situation and be concerned about their privacy. Child life can provide support for this age group, carefully guiding them through the emergency department process without taking away their sense of independence. The child's age, complaint and name are, at times, the only information a child life specialist may have before meeting a patient. It is essential that the emergency department child life specialist be well versed in child development in order to assess whether a patient is developmentally appropriate and responding to the stresses encountered within or beyond normal ranges of their age. A two-minute assessment of developmental level is sometimes all that is afforded the child life specialist in this fast-paced environment before a procedural support is performed.

Although age can sometimes be a clue, it is not always the best way to assess child life priority. Sometimes the teen who has just been involved in a car accident is much more anxious than the toddler who has injured her arm. This is where the expertise of the child life specialist comes into play. Overt cues such as crying, decreased eye contact or visible upset are indications that the child be given priority.

Parental support, or absence thereof, is another factor in assessing and prioritizing patients. Children whose parents are also being treated by medical personnel in another facility or another room are a priority. These children, who typically have come into the emergency department due to a trauma, are scared and surrounded by an unfamiliar environment and strangers. The child life specialist can become the trusted, non-threatening liaison between the patient and the medical staff.

Parents serve as a secure base for children in an unfamiliar environment. However, some experience extreme discomfort in the emergency department environment and, therefore, are unable emotionally to participate in procedures and treatments that their child may undergo. If the parent elects not to be present during procedures and treatments, a child life specialist may accompany and support the child. Alternatively, the child life specialist may prioritize the parent over the patient, teaching, coaching and supporting parents, enabling them to better support their child.

Length of time a child is likely to spend in the emergency department is another important consideration for the child life specialist. Frequently, patients remain in the emergency department for extended periods. The child life specialist can use this time wisely, ensuring that the patient and family understand what is happening, preparing them for the next step in the process and helping to make the environment as normal and comfortable as possible, for example, by providing developmentally appropriate activities. If a child life specialist knows that he or she has the luxury of time with a patient, that time can be utilized accordingly.

Assessment and prioritizing will routinely leave some patients without experiencing the direct benefit of child life service. A child life specialist must continually ask this simple, yet complex question – Where is my expertise and service most needed at this moment? One can't be everywhere at once. A child life specialist may spend two hours with a trauma patient and miss several patients who were admitted and discharged from the emergency department during that same time span. The trauma patient and family were the priority of the child life specialist at that time. Once the priority is made and the intervention has begun, the child life specialist must then let go of the other seemingly high-priority needs within the emer-

gency department – a concept often difficult to reconcile in practice.

Ambulatory Care Setting Specific Issues

Other ambulatory care settings provide the child life specialist with a broad range of opportunities for interventions. There is often a captive audience waiting patiently, or perhaps not so patiently, for what may be a considerable amount of time to receive care. The patient is typically accompanied by a caregiver and often other family members, as well. Unfortunately, outpatient services are all too frequently designed to accommodate the business of healthcare and the convenience of providers, rather than the comfort of the ones receiving care. This is evident in the use of multiple open cubicles for patient triage, which allow children to observe or hear the reactions of others to care, triggering anxious responses in the observing child. Waiting rooms may be crowded with uncomfortable chairs and have limited materials for play during lengthy waits. Child life interventions will be dictated by the setting and will differ greatly depending on the nature of the children served. In an orthopedic clinic, for example, a child life specialist may be involved extensively in preparing patients for a casting, cast removal, radiological procedures or surgery, while in an allergy/immunology clinic the focus may be on preparation for, and support during, skin tests. A child life specialist in a high-risk infant clinic may focus more on developmental assessment and parent education. Child life roles and practices differ with each ambulatory setting, even within a single institution, and continue daily to be created and defined.

There is no standard method of organizing pediatric ambulatory clinics, although the tendency is to organize them by specialty based on the child's medical or developmental diagnosis. Children's hospitals and larger research university hospitals sponsor a large number of specialty clinics (e.g., renal dialysis, endocrinology, mental health, and wheelchair or prosthesis clinics). Some specialty clinics may actually have subspecialty clinics – for example, an orthopedic clinic with subspecialty hand or scoliosis clinics. Some settings include primary care clinics, also known as "well baby" or "sick child" clinics, monitoring infants and young children for normal childhood illnesses and immunizations. Each hospital or institution has its own system, and the logistics of providing child life coverage for clinics can be challenging. Clinics may meet on different floors, in different buildings and, in some instances, on a different campus or cities. The physical space for a clinic may remain constant with the program or service utilizing the site changing from day to day. A clinic environment may at first seem overwhelming to the child life specialist. Typically the number of patients alone, excluding the family members accompanying each patient, is staggering.

The appropriate use of child life services can be a challenge in these settings. It is therefore important that healthcare staff be aware of the child life specialist's appropriate role for their clinic, the range of services they can provide, and how to contact a child life specialist when needed. Traditionally, the numbers of child life specialists assigned to ambulatory care services and clinic areas are disproportionately low compared to the number of patients served. Therefore, the child life specialist must prioritize clinic areas and interventions to adequately and appropriately provide coverage and service. When setting priorities, the following should be considered:

- The type of disease or disability of the population served

- Acuity levels or the intensity of their illness
- The type or invasiveness of procedures and treatments given in a setting
- The average number of procedures in each area
- The likelihood that patients from the clinic will be admitted for inpatient care
- The average age of the patient
- Scheduling patterns and patient volume

Child life services may be initiated in a given area for specific reasons that may dictate the nature of the service provided. For example, a program manager may realign staff positions, convert a nursing or other team positions into a child life specialist position, with the goal of enhancing clinic service and improving patient satisfaction. As the need for child life services will likely exceed the capacity to deliver those services, it is imperative that child life specialists stay focused and realistic about what they can provide. The child life specialist must clearly define the work to be accomplished and avoid the urge to be distracted by competing needs.

The clinic child life specialist must be proficient in patient assessment and knowledgeable about multiple medical and nursing procedures. Many of the techniques used to assess and prioritize patients in clinics are identical to those used in the emergency department. Age and developmental level of the patient, his or her coping skills, the availability of family support, and the child's familiarity with procedures and processes all are important considerations. One difference, however, in the outpatient clinic is the nature of the clinic itself. Patients and their families typically know that they are going to the clinic to see the doctor on a given day and, therefore, have the opportunity to prepare for the visit.

Child life specialists working in certain clinics, such as those serving children with chronic illnesses, may repeatedly interact with patients over time. This offers a distinct advantage in assessing patient needs and coping skills. For these patients, continuity of care can be maintained and follow up can be offered to the patient and family when the child is admitted for inpatient care or seen in the clinic for subsequent visits. Clinic child life specialists can also provide important information to inpatient child life specialists and healthcare team members regarding coping styles and preferred methods of procedural supports, as well as social and developmental issues. Referrals to benevolent organizations, camps, home-based school services, parent education, and respite care can also be valuable component of child life service in these settings.

The ambulatory surgical center has long been a focus of child life interventions. Preparation of children for surgery was among the earliest primary responsibilities of inpatient child life specialists. As surgery began to move to the outpatient setting, so did child life. The routine within ambulatory surgery centers may be similar to that of clinics. Surgical centers often schedule specific types of surgeries or procedures on certain days by particular physicians. These may even be labeled as "clinics," such as a circumcision clinic or biopsy clinic. Child life specialists may prepare patients and families, sometimes days ahead of time or, perhaps, just minutes before the surgery or procedure. Tours and orientations of the surgical area are often provided prior to surgery to prepare the patient and family for the experience, clarify misconceptions and address fears.

Waiting spaces present an ongoing challenge to the clinic child life specialist. Routinely, a large number of people may wait a considerable time in one space, with a variety of age groups utilizing it. Children, most often siblings, may wait unsupervised, as well. Providing a kid-friendly, safe and inviting environment is an obvious and essential goal, yet achieving it is often problematic. Clinic wait spaces need adequate seating and the opportunity for play. Secured, wall-mounted toys and play structures help keep children meaningfully occupied. When outfitting a waiting area with play materials, the child life specialist must be aware of the challenge of keeping materials clean and replenishing them as a result of loss or damage. Budgets should be planned with this in mind. Volunteers can serve an essential role in monitoring the use of equipment and in providing normalizing activities. Ancillary programming, such as literacy programs, child safety and injury prevention sessions, and animal visitation programs have been implemented with success in large wait spaces of ambulatory settings.

Tools and Techniques

The basic child life tools of outpatient setting, that is, toys and equipment, can be grouped into three functional categories – fixed, consumable, and therapeutic. Regardless of category, the equipment selected for use by the child life specialist must facilitate play, education or personal support and reflect the cultures, interests and needs of children and families in the region.

Quality "fixed" tools (i.e., those attached or secured in the setting) can be an extremely valuable. These may include wall-mounted toys, climbing or maze areas for exploration, interactive educational exhibits, electronic games with varying levels of sophistication, and televisions with prescribed viewing. These materials offer an indirect avenue for child life staff to influence the experiences of children in outpatient settings. Given staffing realities, the provision of these materials may represent the only service child life can provide for some children in high-volume outpatient settings.

Consumable child life tools vary greatly and represent the bulk of materials used in most child life programs. These items may be intended for a single use or are given to the child to take home. Consumables also include less expensive items that multiple children may play with in treatment rooms, but tend to disappear or may not be constructed to withstand extended play. Items in this category include such staples as common, developmentally appropriate toys, books, and electronic games. Materials used by multiple children must be cleaned and inspected routinely for infection control and safety, following policies and procedures that are developed under the guiding eye of infection control professionals. Other consumables may include diapers, clothing or hygiene items that support the immediate comfort and dignity needs for children away from their home. Each setting must make selected consumables such as· coloring sheets, small cars and underwear accessible to all team members. Lockable storage is necessary for child life service to ensure the continuing availability of these items.

Therapeutic tools used for focusing and redirecting attention, promoting relaxation, or teaching specific information must be maintained for use by the child life specialist. While many consumable tools may be used in child life clinical practice in a therapeutic manner and may be more readily accessible, certain tools must be held exclusively by the child life specialist to assure their availability when needed. Examples include:

- Kaleidoscopes, magic wands
- Electronic props that feature flashing lights, movement, sound, music
- Small electronic games
- Books that require a child to search and find or manipulate objects
- Teaching dolls and procedural preparation kits

- Virtual reality systems for enhanced redirection of attention and greater diversion

Child life specialists in outpatient settings, as well as inpatient settings, may use coping kits. These kits are collections of toys and other items intended for therapeutic use only. They may be kept in bins strategically placed in the treatment areas or in packs or bags carried by the child life specialist throughout the shift. As procedures and treatments can occur in multiple areas, often concurrently, specific therapeutic tools must be readily accessible. Coping kits for preschoolers may include:

- Small talking electronic games
- Paper party blowers
- Wands filled with glitter or interesting shapes or objects
- Hide-and-seek books
- Squeeze balls, clay or another malleable substances
- Pinwheels
- Music-producing devices
- Bubbles with multiple blowing wands

These items can be used to focus attention or to induce imagery, helping a child cope with fear and pain. The gold standard of developmental care in any healthcare setting would include all professional team members utilizing coping kits, positioning for comfort and multiple psychotherapeutic interventions in the treatment of children. Professionals providing this care should be trained in the use of props and imagery techniques, measured for competence and annually evaluated using quality assurance standards set by the facility. This is a worthy target when we consider that the volume of patients served in outpatient settings is great and the healthcare dollar is not, and when we recognize that ill and injured children are treated every second of every day.

A number of authors have provided useful guidelines for assisting children and families in coping with healthcare experiences (e.g., Kuttner, 1996, 1989, 1988a & 1988b; Acterberg & Lawlist, 1980; Acterberg, 1985; Klein, 2001; Olness, 1981). The most useful techniques for emergency department and other ambulatory care settings include those that are quick in focusing attention and utilize imagery, redirecting attention away from the associated fear or pain of the healthcare experience.

The use of selected props, imagery, and coached breathing are most effective in helping a child to cope with a procedure when applied in a planned order, progressing from the least restrictive to most restrictive interventions, following this pattern:

1st   The child is coached, with self-control
2nd   The child is coached, with self-control and physical assistance
3rd   The child is coached, with self-control and physical restraint

Whenever possible, even in situations deemed urgent or emergent, children and families should be afforded self-control options prior to implementation of more restrictive measures.

Recommendations for distraction and focusing strategies by age include the following:

• *Birth to 2 years*
  Use of positioning and alignment, a secure or firm touch, stroking, patting, rocking, music, mobiles or other visual props
• *Ages 2 to 4 years*
  Play, storytelling, reading, breathing, and blowing
• *Ages 4 to 6 years*
  Same as previous age adding talking and sharing interests

• *Ages 6 to 11 years*
  Same as previous age, and adding counting, chanting, singing and/or humor
• *Ages 11 and older*
  Same as previous age, and adding multi-sensory imagery, and/or progressive relaxation

Hypnotherapeutic techniques or "tricks" are very effective in engaging and redirecting children's attention to address their fear and pain. Training in these techniques is essential and is offered in multimedia formats. Professional instruction, coaching, and supervision are recommended prior to engaging children in these techniques. Kuttner (1996) provides a particularly rich resource for healthcare professionals and parents in comforting and guiding children through frightening or painful healthcare experiences. In addition, Solomon (1998) presents a training course for professionals on multiple techniques and strategies used during invasive procedures, and Sugarman (1997) provides a practical, in-depth introduction to mind-body methods for pediatricians and other healthcare providers.

These techniques can be powerful in engaging children's imagination and are easily taught to, and coached by, parents and others. They focus the child's imagination on an action, feeling or sensation, and provide "anchoring" statements labeling or identifying the child's experience, suggesting that they are comforted, experiencing less pain or fear. Examples of anchoring statements include the following.

• You feel more and more calm
• You are aware of others talking, but you are relaxed by listening only to my voice
• You are aware of what is going on, but you are not bothered by it

- You are comforted by your own calm feelings
- You know just how to help yourself

Other techniques that are useful include progressive muscle relaxation and coached breathing experiences. The simple tension and release of the hands can be effective, but the experience is powerfully amplified when applied to the entire body from head to toe, resulting in a total relaxed state. Coached breaching techniques are enhanced when applied in combination with props and other techniques. A cleansing breath, blowing a cloud away, or inhaling and exhaling at desired rates are all effective techniques that readily change a patient's breathing patterns, and ultimately their physiological status, to a more relaxed state. A forced exhale is one of the most useful coached breathing techniques. It is particularly effective when the exhalation is forced in a fast, hard, and long push manner, as during a pulmonary function test. It can be easily coached and repeated whenever the patient experiences anxiety or pain, resulting in a fast-acting relaxed sensation.

A "countdown" is another technique that is very helpful. The child life specialist simply counts from five to zero while lessening the tempo and intensity with each number spoken. When the coach's voice finally arrives at zero, a whisper quality produces a calming affect for all involved. The countdown can be repeated to gain an even more relaxed state, if desired.

PROFESSIONAL ISSUES

Educating staff is particularly challenging in each of these transient healthcare environments. It is rare that an opportunity presents itself to include all staff at a single meeting. The child life specialist can address this issue by providing in-services, newsletters, and games to increase awareness of, and knowledge about, child life services. Visibility is the most important factor in advocating for child life utilization and philosophy. When the nurse or doctor sees a child life intervention in progress and witnesses firsthand the difference it makes with the patient, education has occurred. Actions speak louder than words, and so does the impact of child life when witnessed by a skeptical staff. Education is an ongoing process, especially with an ever-changing team of players.

It is not uncommon for outpatient healthcare team members to "flex," cross duties and assist each other in multiple tasks to assure quality and efficient care. Child life specialists must continually keep in mind that this flexing of duties and tasks must never be done *instead of* their child life patient care priorities. Before engaging in certain tasks such as patient transport, hospitals may require competency training. Hospital policies will also stipulate that some tasks are reserved for designated personnel. The child life specialist must be aware of these limiting factors when offering assistance.

Nevertheless, with this in mind, it is also clear that the goal for all involved is to move children and families through the healthcare visit as quickly as possible, thus decreasing the stress of being in the facility and away from more normal family routines and comforts. Assisting others with their tasks may facilitate this goal. For example, child life specialists may consider paging or calling doctors, radiology or the lab to expedite service for trauma patients when all team members are in a response mode. A child life specialist may assist a busy nurse by collecting supplies needed for a laceration tray, cleaning a room or helping move waiting patients to designated exam rooms or treatment areas. Transporting and escorting patients to radiology may also be of assistance to the team and contribute to the care of the patient and family. Similarly, child life specialists contact ancillary services, such as chaplains and social workers, when necessary. Most facility policies do not state that only a single discipline can contact a physician or set up a procedure tray.

Courtesy and teamwork are qualities that make or break a team. The ability and willingness to flex from the traditional role of the child life specialist to indirectly assist patients and support team members can be a value-added service that supports advocacy efforts and patient care. Many of these flex moments provide valuable opportunities for time with the patient and family – time to build therapeutic rapport, assess anxiety or pain and, perhaps, to offer a quick preparation or hospital orientation in the scurry of an acute situation. These are valuable moments that maximize use of time and demonstrate child life's responsiveness and team orientation. It is often these actions that become the catalyst for cultural change on a unit.

Healthcare teams have personalities that are often characterized by the nature of the work. Emergency department teams in particular can be demonstrative and known for their intense, sometimes-unforgiving nature. These caregivers have had firsthand experience and responsibility that most people only glimpse on the television or on a theater screen. They routinely encounter throngs of patients with minor to life-threatening problems. Patients and families want to enter an emergency department, be seen, receive treatment and be sent on their way as quickly as possible – a goal shared by members of the healthcare team. Child life specialists must support this goal. They must be able to assess a developmental level and provide normalizing activities, education

and coping support strategies, sometimes in a matter of minutes. Time is of the essence, and the effective child life specialist in the emergency department or ambulatory surgery center must be able to assess and implement interventions at this very rapid pace.

On the other hand, in certain ambulatory settings such as dialysis or cystic fibrosis clinics, the pace can be slow, even arduous, at times. The opportunity to know patients and families intimately over a long period of time and deal with their potentially complex issues requires the child life specialist to master a very different set of professional skills. They must become adept at the development of long-term relationships and skilled at task analysis, developmental assessment and the sequencing of care plans over a period of years or even decades. The unique demands of each of these areas of healthcare suggest that only seasoned, skilled and experienced child life specialists be placed in these settings.

It has been repeatedly noted that the work of the child life specialist brings softness or a more human and natural flow to the work of the healthcare team. The work of child life adds fun, humor and play, as well. These qualities, as well as the patient advocacy role of the child life specialist, can shape and change the care priorities and personalities of the healthcare team in each of these areas.

Self-care is essential in outpatient work, especially in emergency department settings. Practicing in isolation by shift, population or location is very common. The child life specialist can become a team leader in difficult situations – as bereavement support for trauma patients, as emotional support during difficult or painful procedures and events, or as advocates for unpopular points of view. The stress associated with this work must be managed or it will take its toll on the child life specialist, the team, and ultimately the children and families that are served. It is recommended that all child life specialists receive clinical supervision to maintain boundaries and quality of care. Personal supervision, similar to that characteristic of other mental health professions, is recommended. Periodically, crisis management defusing or debriefing sessions can be extremely helpful for the emergency department or child life staff. Models for stress management sessions, such as those offered by the International Critical Incident Stress Foundation (ICISF), are effective in addressing the chronic or acute stress of staff members. Debriefing sessions are not, however, psychotherapy. They are short group opportunities to release stress and minimize the wear and tear of the secondary and chronic crisis that is common in emergency medicine. These brief sessions are designed to discuss the circumstances of a recent incident, as well as staff members' reactions to it. Such sessions may also identify and address symptoms the staff may be experiencing and the forms of therapeutic assistance available to them as they re-enter their setting. Occasionally a temporary unit reassignment can also relieve chronic stress, supporting the skills and longevity in the child life professional.

CONCLUSION

The child life profession has celebrated more than a half a century of service to children and families during a period of unprecedented change in the history of healthcare. Child life foundations, practices and training continue, however, in a tradition that is largely based on the systems and needs of inpatient children and families. Families that experience a life-changing episode in a matter of hours, as well as those that raise their children with healthcare teams as the extended members of their families, need greater commitment from our profession. We must celebrate our great success in facilitating humane, child and family-oriented practices in inpatient settings. However, we must continue to extend our care and strategies to those areas and individuals not yet influenced by the presence of child life service. Too many children leave the healthcare setting frightened or confused because child life practices were not afforded them. Ambulatory care settings and the emergency departments are challenging environments for the child life specialist. Each offers opportunities to provide much-needed child life interventions for a rapidly-changing patient population. Each area serves as a gateway to the entire healthcare system. The patient experience in either of these areas may set the tone for future healthcare encounters.

The greatest catalyst for expansion of outpatient child life service will come at the grass roots level, through each child life specialist and department and in each facility and community. Greater resources must be allocated to the outpatient arena – resources of seasoned child life specialists, time, and money. In extending services to these areas, especially when all resources are finite, we may need to investigate alternative delivery systems and practices. This may include reexamination of child life skills and role definitions including, perhaps, a model analogous to that of a clinical nurse specialist. As we move into the future of child life, we must remain cognizant that outpatient healthcare is not only the gateway into inpatient care but, more often than not, is the sole healthcare service that children experience. These children need and deserve child life intervention and service in order to grow and flourish.

REFERENCES

Achterberg, J., & Lawlist, G. F. (1980). B*ridges of the mind.* Champaign, IL: Institute for Personality and Ability Testing.

Achterberg, J. (1985). *Imagery in healing.* Boston: Shambhala.

Alcock, D., Berthiaume, S., & Clarke, A. (1984). Child life intervention in the emergency department. *Children's Health Care, 12,* 130-136.

Alcock, D., Felman, W., Goodman, J. T., McGrath, P. J., & Park, J. M. (1985). Evaluation of child life intervention in emergency department suturing. *Pediatric Emergency Medicine, 1,* 111-115.

Boie, E. T., Moore, G. P., Brummett, C., & Nelson, D. R. (1999). Do parents want to be present during invasive procedures performed on their children in the emergency department? A survey of 400 parents. *Annals of Emergency Medicine, 34*:1.

Brunnquell, D., & Kohen, D. P. (1991). Emotions in pediatric emergencies: What we know, what we can do. *Children's Health Care, 20,* 240-247.

Bush, J. P. (1987). Pain in children: A review of the literature from a developmental perspective. *Psychology and Health, 1,* 215-236.

Bush, J. P., & Harkins, S. W. (Eds.). (1991). *Children in pain: Clinical and research issues from a developmental perspective.* New York: Springer-Verlag.

Child Life Council. (2006). *Directory of child life programs.* Rockville, MD: Child Life Council.

Child Life Council. (2002). *The official documents of the Child Life Council.* Rockville, MD: Child Life Council.

Gardner, G. & Olness, K. (1981). *Hypnosis and hypnotherapy with children.* New York: Grune and Stratton, Inc.

Hemmelgarn, A. L., Glisson, C., & Dukes, D. (2001). Emergency room culture and the emotional support component of family-centered care. *Children's Health Care, 30,* 93-110.

Klein, N. (2001). *Healing images for children.* Waterton, Wisconsin: Inner Coaching.

Kohen, D. (1986). Applications of relaxation/mental imagery (self-hypnosis) in pediatric emergencies. *The International Journal of Clinical and Experimental Hypnosis, 34*: 283-294.

Krebel, M. S., Clayton, C., & Graham, C. (1996). Child life programs in the pediatric emergency department. *Pediatric Emergency Care, 12,* 13-15.

Kroger, W. (1977). *Child clinical and experimental hypnosis in medicine, dentistry, and psychology.* Philadelphia: J.B. Lippincott Co.

Kuttner, L. (1996). *The child in pain: How to help and what to do.* Berkeley, CA: Hartley and Marks.

Kuttner, L. (1989). Management of young children's acute pain and anxiety during invasive medical procedures. *Pediatrician, 16*: 39-44

Kuttner, L. (1988a). Favorite stories: A hypnotic pain reduction technique for children in acute pain. *American Journal of Clinical Hypnosis, 30*: 289-295.

Kuttner, L. (1988b). Psychological treatment of distress, pain and anxiety for young children with cancer. *Journal of Developmental and Behavioral Pediatrics, 9*: 374-381.

McGrath, P. A. (1990) *Pain in children: Nature, assessment and treatment.* New York: Guilford, 1990.

McGrath, P. J., Finley, G. A., & Turner, C. J. (1992) *Making cancer less painful: A handbook for parents.* Halifax, Nova Scotia: Dalhousie University.

Olness, K. (1981). Hypnosis in pediatric practice. *Current Problems in Pediatrics, 12*: 1-46.

Orstein, R., & Sobel, D. (1989) *The healing brain.* New York: Simon & Schuster, Inc.

Ornstein, R., & Sobel D. (1989) *Healthy pleasures.* New York: Addison-Wesley Publishing Co.

Resnick, R., & Hergenroeder, E. (1975). Children and the emergency room. *Children Today, 4,* 5-8.

Sacchetti, A., Lichenstein, R., Carraccio, C., & Harris, R. H. (1996). Family member presence during pediatric procedures. *Pediatric Emergency Medicine, 12,* 268-271.

Schechter, N. L., Berde, C. B., & Yaster, M. (1993). *Pain in infants, children, and adolescents.* Baltimore, MD: Williams and Wilkins.

Schechter, N. L., Blankson, V., & Pachter, L. M. (1997). The ouchless place: No pain, children's gain. *Pediatrics, 99*: 890-894.

Simonton, C. (1982). *Getting well again.* New York: Bantam Books.

Solomon, R., & Saylor, C. (1998) *Pediatric pain management: A professional course.* East Lansing: Michigan State University.

Spiegel, H., & Spiegel, D. (1978). *Treatment.* New York: Basic Books.

Zeltzer, L., & LeBaron, S. (1982). Hypnosis and non-hypnotic techniques for reduction of pain and anxiety during painful procedures in children and adolescents with cancer. *Journal of Pediatrics, 101*: 1032-5.

RECOMMENDED VIDEO REFERENCES

- "No Fears, No Tears: Children with Cancer, Coping with Pain." (1986), Dr. Leora Kuttner
- "No Fears, No Tears, 13 Years Later." (1995), Dr. Leora Kuttner
- "Imaginative Medicine – Hypnosis in Pediatric Practice." (1997), Dr. Laurence Sugarman, M.D.

Chapter 15

CHILD LIFE AND EDUCATION ISSUES: THE CHILD WITH A CHRONIC ILLNESS OR SPECIAL HEALTHCARE NEEDS

PATRICIA L. WEINER, MAGGIE HOFFMAN AND CYNTHIA ROSEN

INTRODUCTION

Approximately six million children ranging from newborn to seventeen years of age are hospitalized for a variety of conditions in the United States each year. Many children who are hospitalized have some type of a chronic illness. The estimated number of children in the United States with a chronic illness ranges from 13.7 percent to 17 percent (Stein & Stein, 2002), yet the number may be as high as 20 percent (Bauer, Duitch, & Birenbaum, 2003).

As medical research and technology continue to advance, more and more children are living into adulthood and entering the schools. These children are spending less time in hospitals and more time at home, in their communities and at school. At the same time, trends in education are bringing more diversity into the classroom. Children with special healthcare needs and other forms of disabilities are attending their neighborhood schools in growing numbers. When hospitalized, they stay for shorter periods of time than when hospital school programs were

instituted over thirty years ago. The average length of a hospital stay today is approximately 3.5 days (Owens, Thompson, Elixhauser, & Ryan, 2003). Nevertheless, school services in the hospital continue to be important for both children and their families, and the words of Emma Plank (1959) still apply: "Learning takes on a very different meaning when a child is hospitalized. Going to school in the hospital can be a link to the past and the future. It reassures a child that his parents, his home, school and the hospital believe in getting well" (p. 47). Some twenty years later Jerriann Wilson (1979), Director of Child Life at Johns Hopkins Children's Center, cited the continuing need for educational programming, "School programming in the hospital serves to emphasize the healthy part of a child during his/her confinement" (p. 64). All children are entitled to develop to their full potential through the benefits of healthcare and education. Psychologically, school connotes normalcy and familiarity. Developmentally, school offers the opportunity to be industrious and develop a strong sense of self. Academically,

310

skills are mastered. At school, children meet new friends, discover how to interact with other children and adults and learn about themselves. In her book, *Educating the Chronically Ill Child*, Susan Kleinberg (1982) recommended that educational planning for children with specific chronic conditions be implemented in the hospital and when they return to school. Children in elementary school through high school are mandated through federal, state and local laws to receive hospital and home instruction with appropriate medical documentation. Parents should work with the child life specialist, educator or social worker at the hospital and their local school district to find out their district's specific local regulations. For children and their families, a smooth transition back to school is the key to quality of life.

In order to ease the transition from the hospital to home and eventually back to school, an educational discharge plan needs to be in place, similar to a hospital roadmap, to help families find their way from one place to another. In the hospital setting, child life specialists can take the lead role in guiding families on this journey. This chapter presents information necessary for child life specialists to help facilitate the educational needs of the children with whom they have contact. Through reading of this chapter, the reader will:

- Develop an understanding of the integration of child life and education services.
- Become familiar with the educational issues specific to children with special healthcare needs in the United States.
- Be able to locate resources in Canadian law as it relates to special education. In Canada, the education laws are referred to as "human rights." Many Canadian child life programs have been leaders in school reentry programs for children who have been hospitalized.

- Become familiar with special education law and related documents.
- Become familiar with the types of educational services available to children with chronic illness, developmental disability, physical disability and mental illness in the United States.
- Develop an understanding of the multiple ways child life specialists can assist children and their families with educational discharge planning (through school reentry programs, as well as by acting as the liaison from the hospital advocating for the specific needs of each child).

CHILDREN WITH SPECIAL HEALTHCARE NEEDS

Gaps in Educational Services

As mentioned earlier some estimate that 20 percent of American children have a chronic illness (Bauer et al., 2003). There are many definitions of a chronic illness. Pless and Pinkerton (1975) describe chronic illness as a condition that lasts at least three months during the year, has intermittent impact on daily functioning, may require in-home health services or frequent hospitalizations, and limits age-appropriate play, school performance or educational activities. Some examples of chronic illness are asthma, sickle cell disease, brain and spinal cord tumors, leukemia and other forms of childhood cancer, muscular dystrophy, gastrointestinal and cardiac disorders, genetic conditions, diabetes and AIDS.

The number of children to consider increases when we include those with developmental disabilities, children who have health and cognitive impairments due to an injury, children who are physically disabled, or those with a psychiatric disorder. Some children have multiple needs, such as a chronic illness, a physical challenge and learning disabilities. Beyond healthcare, parents of children with special healthcare needs want what all parents want for their children, including acceptance and understanding by their peers, a positive school experience, and a successful social life.

Parents have told us in advocacy groups, support groups, at conferences and, ultimately, in their children's hospital rooms that there is a lack of appropriate school planning and that neighborhood schools overall are unprepared for their children. Upon discharge from the hospital, through the course of outpatient treatment, at home during acute episodes of chronic illness and even at school, many children are not receiving the educational services they need and are entitled to.

Since the groundbreaking Vanderbilt Study, which began in 1980 (Hobbs, Nicholas, Ireys and Perrin, 1983), it has been known that significant educational gaps exist for children with special healthcare needs. Some of the difficulties associated with educational services are:

- Lack of communication from the healthcare team to the school staff.
- Parental difficulty in navigating the education system.
- School absence which, unless the school district is willing to provide additional home and hospital instruction, makes it more difficult for these children to learn.
- Limited availability of nursing coverage in schools.
- Little or no training for school personnel in providing healthcare services.
- Lack of information about illness and its impact on education, the family and society.
- Inflexible attendance policies.

More recently, national attention has focused on the value of linking health and education services to improve the well-being of children and families. Many national organizations support school-health partnerships in a variety of ways. Some of these organizations include: the American Academy of Pediatrics (AAP), the National Association of Children's Hospitals and Related Institutions (NACHRI), the Child Life Council (CLC), the Council for Exceptional Children (CEC), and the Association for the Education of Children with Medical Needs (AECMN).

Judith Palfrey (1992) documented similar gaps in educational services in the Project School Care study and went on with a multidisciplinary team to create the Project School Care program at Children's Hospital in Boston, MA. This program addresses the educational needs of children with special healthcare needs as they return to school. A major component of the program and materials are aimed at improving communication and the sharing of information between the healthcare team and the school. Bridging the gap from the hospital to home to school has become an integral part of education planning; actually, it is an integral part of life planning for pediatric patients.

UNDERSTANDING THE EDUCATION LAW

In order to best serve children and their families, child life specialists should develop an understanding of the educational rights of children with disabilities. Until 1969, most children in need of specialized services were not able to attend school. There were few options available to them. Finally in 1975, a landmark piece of legislation was passed by Congress to ensure that children with special educational needs could attend school and receive appropriate educational services. This was known as the Education for All

Children Act, Public Law 84-142. At the heart of education reform were parents who wanted their children educated in the public schools.

Today, we know that all children with special needs in all 50 states are entitled to a free and appropriate education (FAPE) in the least restrictive environment (LRE), yet the type of services they receive may vary greatly depending on their locale. When educational laws are passed by Congress they are interpreted and implemented by the United States Department of Education. State departments of education, in turn, further interpret these laws and develop regulations to be followed by school districts in their state. The actual interpretation of federal law can vary from state to state. Adding to the confusion of professionals and parents, the laws are further interpreted at the local level resulting in variation of the special education supports and services from district to district. The Education for All Handicapped Children Act of 1975 (P.L. 94-142), which created special education services the way we know it today, was a major step in education as the first law requiring free, appropriate, public education to be provided to all children from 5–21 years of age regardless of their disability. This legislation included the stipulation that Individual Education Plans (IEPs) be developed for children in special education – a practice still in effect today (Wright & Wright, 2004b).

INDIVIDUALIZED EDUCATION PLAN (IEP)

Once a child is identified as needing special education services, the parents, student (when old enough), teachers, school administrators and related service providers collaborate to develop a plan that will improve the child's educational results. The IEP is the cornerstone of a quality education so that all children with disabilities will receive an appropriate education.

We may see various forms of IEPs, but what is important is that they all contain the same information in the most clear and concise way. The IEP should be an educational tool that is easy to use. Information included in the IEP is the following. The child's:

- Current performance.
- Annual goals.
- Special education and related services (transportation, speech, counseling, health services, nursing, language and speech, occupational and/or physical therapy, etc.) provided to achieve these goals.
- The child's participation with non-disabled children, or a statement why this will not occur.
- The provision of assistive technology evaluations, appropriate equipment and training, as needed.
- The provision of supplementary aids (e.g., an FM trainer, communication board).
- Participation in state and district-wide tests and modifications in the administration of these tests, depending on the unique needs of the child.
- Program modifications and support services.
- Dates and places of when services will begin, how often they will be provided, where they will be provided and how long they will last.
- Transition services – a statement of the transition services that are needed to help the child become a productive member of society.
- How the child's progress towards the annual goals is measured and how the parents will be informed.

This landmark piece of legislation didn't include infants, toddlers and preschoolers – a condition that was changed with the passing of P.L. 99-457 in 1986. The new law also mandated that Individual Family Service Plans (IFSP's) be created for infants and toddlers in Early Intervention programs, serving children from birth through two years, eleven months. Each county in each state has designated a lead agency to run its Early Intervention (EI) program, but EI is mandated through Federal legislation. Children three to five years of age are provided with special education services through the Committee on Preschool Special Education (CPSE) by their local school district. Children ages five years and up are referred to the Committee on Special Education (CSE).

The next important step in special education was the development of the Individuals with Disabilities Education Act of 1990 (P.L. 101-476), also known as IDEA. This legislation, which superseded the previous Education of Handicapped Children's Act (EHA) and its amendments, mandated major philosophic changes including the replacement of the word *handicap* with *disability*, the requirement of transition planning to begin at an earlier age, that assistive technology evaluations are to be considered when planning for the educational needs of the child, and that sensitivity to ethnically and culturally diverse children with disabilities be exercised. The U.S. Congress periodically reauthorizes IDEA, most recently in December 2004.

IDEA requires public schools to locate and identify children with disabilities who may be in need of special education. These children will " have available to them a free, appropriate public education that emphasizes special education and related services designed to meet their unique needs and prepare them for further education, employment and independent living" [20 U.S.C.

{1400(d)]. The statute includes specific requirements about eligibility for service and the components of the IEP, designates the IEP team members, and outlines the comprehensive procedural requirements related to disputes and complaints. However, the law is always changing and evolving. To better understand IDEA you need to read the statute, the regulations, and cases that have interpreted the statue (Wright & Wright, 2004a).

Section 504 of the Rehabilitation Act of 1973 (P.L. 93-112) and the Americans with Disabilities Act of 1990 (P.L. 101-336) are both civil rights provisions barring discrimination against persons with disabilities and are very helpful in the education of children who may have special needs but don't require specialized education. Under these laws, individuals must have an impairment that substantially limits one or more major life activities such as seeing, walking, breathing or learning to be designated a "person with a disability." If institutions that receive federal financial assistance, including schools, don't comply with Section 504, they are in jeopardy of losing that assistance (www.insideschools.org). In contrast, the mandates of the Americans with Disabilities Act (ADA) apply to all institutions of learning, regardless of Federal funds.

Under Section 504, an Accomodation Plan is developed that outlines reasonable accommodations and services that children need to fully participate in all activities of school. The plan may include such accommodations such as preferential seating, a second set of textbooks to keep at home, modifications for testing or intermittent home instruction. School district teams, with parents and sometimes other professionals, develop IEPs and Accommodation Plans. Special education law and 504 plans offer due process rights to families (Wright & Wright, 2004b).

As professionals who work with children with special healthcare needs, it is important to keep up with the new provisions in the law. Resources listed in the reference section will help you understand the relevant legislation.

As a result of the laws described above, students in special education now participate more fully in the general education curriculum and the role of their parents has been strengthened. In order for children to receive special education services, they must be evaluated at school or privately, and be found to have a physical, cognitive or behavioral impairment that substantially interferes with their ability to benefit from general classroom curriculum. The following is a list of disabilities that require either special education or accommodation plans:

1. Mental retardation
2. Hearing impairments
3. Deaf-blindness
4. Speech or language impairments
5. Visual impairments
6. Emotional disturbance
7. Orthopedic impairments
8. Autism
9. Traumatic brain injury
10. Other health impairments
11. Specific learning disabilities
12. Multiple disabilities
13. Deafness

THE ROLE OF CHILD LIFE

Hospital staff members usually consider a discharge "well done" if a child goes home and a treatment regimen is recommended. Medications are prescribed, medical equipment is ordered and, when necessary, therapeutic treatments are continued (e.g., speech, occupational therapy, physical therapy).

Clearly, a positive health outcome, the adaptation to an ongoing illness, is the most important part of any inpatient experience. Families and children, however, do not see a cure of an illness nor a comfort measure as an end in itself. Returning to school and enjoying the company of friends is the goal for most children. It is important to look at the child as a whole child, not a disease by itself.

Although the healthcare team is a collaboration of many disciplines, the child life specialist knows the child well, is often in contact with the schools and listens to families about school issues. Yet, education advocacy often seems to fall outside the realm of child life services. In actuality, child life specialists are uniquely qualified to advocate for children in schools as they have advocated on behalf of children in the hospital setting for decades. Having child life specialists take a lead role in educational planning for children with special healthcare needs makes perfect sense. In the United States and Canada there are over 450 child life programs. Many child life programs already have existing hospital-schools under their domain. Even if a child life program is small, an approach that truly includes family-centered care can and should include school planning.

School reentry begins when a child is admitted to the hospital. When a child is hospitalized or has a chronic illness, daily routine is changed and contact with friends, family, and school is interrupted. The presence of school in the hospital allows a child to keep up with his studies, participate in the education process, and maintain continuity with normal experiences. When school-age children are hospitalized, contact with their school is important. In addition, emotional support from friends at school can help children adjust to health issues more easily. Child life specialists can encourage the following: cards, letters, emails and pictures from the entire class or individuals; photos of the class; tape-recorded messages; video of the class; phone calls to the patient; and visits from classmates and school staff, only with parental permission.

When students return following an illness or hospitalization, they often have cognitive, physical, and psychosocial difficulties meeting the demands of school. Key to a smooth transition is making sure that the necessary supports are in place to maximize social and academic success. The student, the family, the school, and the student's classmates should all be prepared for the student's return to school.

Going back to school means "back to normal," and careful planning has to take place to ensure a successful return. Who is involved in this planning process varies from place to place. Some hospitals have education resource teams consisting of a child life specialist, a nurse, a social worker, a special educator, a psychologist and sometimes a physician. Families are referred to the team by the child life specialist or another member of the team. This individual speaks with the family to assess the child's needs and, in turn, shares that information with the team. Plans are then made to help the family access educational services for their child upon discharge or during treatment. This team approach is especially important in chronic situations where the child's medical condition fluctuates. Changes in mobility, for instance, require a change in services and service delivery. Because the resource team includes members from the many disciplines involved in the ongoing care of the patient, communication among the team members facilitates the child's needs being met in a timely manner.

The essential ingredients of a school reentry program are:

- Early and ongoing communication with the parents, healthcare providers, and school personnel to facilitate reentry back to school. A child life staff member can be designated to serve as the contact person for the healthcare team. This can be communicated to the parent upon discharge, in case the parent has questions or additional need for support.
- Before the child is discharged, develop a parent information packet. Include a consent form and any additional pertinent medical information that is necessary for the child to return to school. Explain to the family what a school reentry program is and how it can be tailored to meet the needs of their child. Let parents know that school reentry services are optional. They can make the decision now or at a later date. Often school reentry is needed at different critical points in the child's education. Discuss the laws with the parents and the rights of children with special healthcare needs. Refer families to local support groups and other agencies for advocacy and information, parent support groups, sibling programs, school referrals, respite care, socialization groups and summer programs.
- Plan for coordination of services (e.g., school visits, in-services for school staff, and/or a child's classmates). Parents should be included on the team to support family-centered care.
- Discuss this plan with the school team. Parents are a critical part of the healthcare team and must be involved in the developments of their child's school reentry plan, because they are the experts in knowing what their child needs. Everyone's input is important so that the child can reach his/her full academic potential.
- Plan for a review of the student's progress.
- Check again before the child is discharged to see if the school requires any

medical documentation to facilitate the return to school.

- Recognize and acknowledge sibling issues and the need for support. Let the parents know that a child life specialist is available to provide sibling support.
- Acknowledge that ongoing care is often needed to assist families after they return home. It is helpful to call parents to see how their child is managing the return home and back to school, continue to offer support to the child and the family, and ask if they have any questions. Reaching out to the child's family might be helpful. Also, a note to a child might brighten his/her day. This way of systematically reaching out to families may send a positive, caring message and may help support them during the school reentry process.

A child life program can initiate a school-health-parent task force or a community advisory board and include several members from various disciplines, staff from local school districts, administrators and parents whose children are either frequently hospitalized or have a chronic medical condition. It is always helpful to have a physician and local state representative on your task force. Once school district personnel understand the challenges that chronically ill children and their families face on a daily basis, they often listen and respond appropriately. This is one of many models that will strengthen ties among schools, parents and healthcare providers. Sharing information can help to develop mutual respect for one another. School district administrators need to hear the issues, and healthcare providers must know what is realistic for schools to provide. Parents bring to the table their experience and knowledge, which will help foster true parent-professional partnerships – partnerships that are pivotal in the education of chil-

dren with special healthcare needs. This type of collaboration can close gaps provided for all children in the community.

The child life specialist can encourage the family to speak to members of the healthcare team regarding their child's needs at school. Usually medical documentation is needed to access services. Parents should be informed of medication effects, and letters documenting possible behavior changes, written by physicians, can be given to the schoolteachers. Helping families obtain this documentation is another way child life specialists can make the transition back to school an easy one.

Child life specialists encourage families to be proactive. While most school districts have policies that grant tutors to students who have been out of school for two or three weeks consecutively, educational plans may be written for weekly extra help so that the student does not fall behind. There needs to be coordination and communication among parents, school personnel and healthcare providers. Child life specialists can facilitate this by acting as a liaison between the family and the medical team once the child is discharged from the hospital.

Child life specialists can also assume the responsibility for teaching families how to advocate for their children outside of the hospital. Offering informational sessions on the unit or in the outpatient setting on topics such as parent-school communication, special education law and due process, and other related issues can provide support to families even after their children are discharged. You can post information about these meetings in pediatric clinics and Family Resource Centers. Meeting regularly with parents helps child life specialists understand the needs of families and children in school and the community. Child life can then refer families to appropriate programs and agencies to help them access needed services for their children. Becoming a parent advocate begins with understanding and accepting that parents know their children best (reinforcing family-centered care) and then supporting them as they speak with other professionals such as school personnel. Listening to parents and encouraging them to speak out for their children is an important role for child life specialists in and outside of the hospital.

Federal education laws insure all children access to free educational services through the public school programs, but it is critical that families are put in touch with local and regional advocacy groups to help them navigate a very complex educational system. It is essential that child life specialists are able to refer families to the appropriate services available for their children. Child life specialists can serve as the transition liaison for the family. Now laws are in place to protect the rights of children who may have limitations or disabilities because of an illness at birth, an injury, or an acquired illness.

Unfortunately, many parents/caregivers are not informed of the laws and aren't sure whether their child qualifies for special services. Parents can have their child evaluated by their local school district at no charge, but families need to know who to contact for an evaluation. This is where child life specialists can make a huge impact in the lives of these children. Helping families to understand their children's educational rights and to learn what supports and services are available requires extensive research in your community. There are many organizations and parent groups that can help you along the way. Referrals to such groups can actually save the day for so many families. Organizations, schools and hospitals have free educational booklets with school guidelines available for families. In addition information may be obtained from special education directors, members of the Parent Teacher Association (PTA), members of the Special Education Parent Teacher Association (SEPTA), pediatricians, school principals, the state education department where you reside, regional advocates, members of the school board and friends.

Researching the problem a child and family may face, and finding corresponding solutions, is important. A good way for parents to start is by asking the following questions:

1. What is the problem/s that my child may have upon going to school, returning to school or staying at home? (e.g., How will my child attend school now that he can no longer walk? Does my child need an individual healthcare plan on file with the school nurse? Will my child be able to attend school for part of the day and receive homebound services?)
2. What are some of the solutions? (Special busing, barrier-free schools, a 1:1 aide).
3. Who should I call to assist me? (Who is the school district contact for these services?)
4. What is the plan? How do you refer a child for an evaluation? What is the referral process? What is the length of time from the referral of a child for evaluations to the implementation of services? What if a child doesn't meet the criteria for special education but still has special needs? What other options are there?
5. How do we implement the plan? (Who is in charge of his program? Who will monitor his progress?)

SOCIALIZATION AND SCHOOL

If school and play are a child's "work," then a hospitalization has not had a successful outcome if we haven't created a plan for school reentry and supported a child's ability to socialize with friends. Child life specialists are uniquely positioned to assess children's play skills in therapeutic groups as well as during playroom and teen room activities. Many children experience social-emotional changes caused by feeling ill or exhausted. Pain also has a huge impact; a child in pain withdraws from social contact and has great difficulty engaging with peers or attending to schoolwork. Child life specialists can identify children who are experiencing a change in play or study skills and inform the medical staff and the child's family.

Healthcare providers have become very sophisticated in communicating diagnoses and prognoses to parents, offering explanations of tests, sharing written materials about specific diseases and even providing referrals to homecare. Those same providers, however, focused on the treatment and possible cure of illnesses, often do not address children's ability to integrate with peers. Additionally, healthcare professionals are often reluctant to highlight the unfortunate secondary effects of medications, treatments and procedures.

For example, a child being treated for asthma may become hyperactive or aggressive while being treated with steroids. These side effects can be distracting in a classroom, and the behavior is off-putting to peers. Long-term steroid use may increase a child's weight, lowering self-esteem, as well as making the child "stand out" among friends. The asthma and weight gain combine to become an obstacle to participation in gym class and after-school sport activities. Lastly, that child makes frequent visits to the emergency room, and so misses a day of school every week. Inability to keep up with schoolwork accelerates the loss of self-esteem. Each day of school missed further separates the child from other children. The child starts to be left out of the easy banter that other kids effortlessly enjoy and, in effect, has been sidelined.

Neurological illnesses (e.g., seizures, meningitis), brain and spinal cord tumors, organ transplants, HIV, sickle cell anemia and many genetic disorders cause profound behavioral, social and academic changes in children. Chemotherapy may result in some learning and social deficits. These changes may be temporary, of a few weeks' or months' duration, or they may be permanent. Just as child life staff help prepare children and their families for physical changes, so too they need to encourage the medical staff to inform parents about neurological changes.

A child's peers may be as distressed as the child who is ill. Physical and cognitive differences may upset children, making them reluctant to approach their sick or recovering friend. Child life specialists can help families design social reentry plans. Classmates can be educated about a friend's hair loss from chemotherapy. A child who is feeling weak may still help manage a soccer team. A best friend's parents, once they understand a specific situation, can bring their child to visit or schedule phone calls to keep "the patient" in the loop. Socialization sessions, a form of "play therapy," can be part of a discharge plan. An IEP or accommodation plan can direct the teacher, school social worker or guidance counselor to invite a few peers to play sessions with the recently discharged child.

Information and preparation are the best medicine. It is unfair to have a child experience school and social failure before hastily cobbling together a plan. Social reentry anxiety is a foremost concern for children who have been ill. They just want to get back to school, to blend in without a fuss. Their friends and teachers are frequently unaware of the impact illness has on a child. The former patient has felt sick and experienced pain or fatigue. Most likely, the child has been afraid. School lessons, holiday celebrations and the latest movie releases have been missed. The re-entering child has to hide a newly acquired knowledge base (IVs, catheters, surgery, medications) and try to slip back into school culture, fast.

Parents need documentation from physicians, psychologists, child life specialists, social workers and other relevant professionals in order to create new school programs or adapt existing ones. Child life staff can be the liaisons between families and the medical team, helping to collect the assessments and specific orders necessary to convince school personnel to adjust schedules and work load, and provide extra academic help and social support.

A healthy body is just part of what children and their families seek through medical care. They will only feel well served if, in addition, they are successful in school and have a rewarding social life.

CASE STUDIES

The following cases illustrate the many issues facing children with special healthcare needs at school and how child life professionals can play a role in helping children and their families develop an appropriate plan to achieve a positive school experience.

Randy

Randy's story illustrates:

• Impact of chronic illness on education
• Application of Section 504
• Interdisciplinary collaboration
• Family support

Randy was a fourteen-year-old female diagnosed with Crohn's disease when the child life specialist met her in the fall of her sophomore year of high school. This was only her second hospitalization, the first being the winter before when she was initially diagnosed. Like most adolescents, Randy was anxious about missing school while in the hospital. Upon interviewing her and her family, the child life specialist discovered that despite frequent absences and little support from teachers or her guidance counselor, Randy was an honors student with an A average. Currently, however, Randy was experiencing difficulty keeping up with assignments and was receiving negative feedback from her teachers regarding her frequent absences.

Over the past year, Randy had missed more than forty days of school, yet had received fewer than five days of home tutoring services. Like many children with chronic illness, Randy experienced frequent intermittent absences. Mostly absent less than a week at a time, she never met the length of absence necessary to qualify for home tutoring services under her school district's policy. According to the policy, a student must be absent for fifteen school days before a request for home tutoring could be initiated. Add an average of five days to process a request and arrange for a tutor, and the time out of school is closer to a month before actual services are received. In addition, once Randy returned to school for even one day, the process began all over again. Because of the gaps in Randy's schooling, she was constantly learning new material and trying to catch-up at the same time. Without the support and understanding of her teachers, this led to the nearly impossible expectation that Randy could complete assignments and prepare for exams on time. Teachers were becoming frustrated with Randy and impatient with her requests for time extensions and make up exams. This all added to the stress over Randy's illness presenting a difficult situation for Randy and her family. Working together with Randy's family, school district personnel, and the medical team, her school issues were addressed using a two-pronged approach.

First, the district's policy regarding home instruction was inappropriate to meet the needs of a student with Crohn's disease or any chronic illness. As a chronic medical condition, a diagnosis of Crohn's disease categorizes one as a person with a disability entitled to accommodation under Section 504 of the Rehabilitation Act of 1973. An early ancestor of the Americans with Disabilities Act, Section 504 of The Rehabilitation Act of 1973 bars any institution or agency receiving federal funding from denying access to any of its activities to persons with disabilities. In this case, the home instruction policy was denying Randy access to educational services. The act also requires agencies to "reasonably accommodate" persons with disabilities through changes in policy, facility or through other means so that they may benefit, thereby requiring the school district to provide "reasonable accommodations and/or services" in order for Randy to benefit fully from her educational program. These accommodations are written in the form of an individual plan, developed with input from the student, parents and the treating physician. The plan is implemented by the school district and building personnel and provides support for a student with disabilities. In Randy's case, the plan allowed for home tutoring services to begin immediately following the tenth absence of the school year. From then on, tutoring was delivered at the rate of two hours for each school day missed. Once hours were "earned," they remained available, even after Randy returned to school allowing her to receive the services to which she was entitled when she was well enough to receive them. This is not special education, but equal access to all of the educational activities already available to students in the district.

Secondly, communication between the school, Randy's family and the medical team needed to improve regarding Randy's illness and her educational needs. There appeared to be little understanding in the school community about the symptoms of Crohn's disease and its effect on a young person's ability to manage the school environment, with or without additional support. With the help of the director of a local support group for children with Crohn's disease, the child life specialist gave a presentation to Randy's teachers, principal and other school staff on living with Crohn's disease. Randy's parents attended the meeting and were able to speak on the impact of this illness on their family. They expressed concern over the way their daughter was viewed by her teachers and about her fear of school failure. Randy chose not to be at this meeting. The representative from the support group suggested ways the school could support Randy by allowing her access to a private bathroom, time to rest in the nurse's office and counseling if needed. Because the disease affects stamina, Randy would be given a second set of books to keep at home so she wouldn't have to carry a heavy backpack back and forth to school. This was also put in the written accommodation plan. The child life specialist and other members of Randy's care team hoped that by raising awareness, they would increase sensitivity allowing Randy to receive more emotional support at school.

Consulting with Randy's family regarding her educational rights as a person with a disability, providing disease-specific information to school personnel and supporting the patient and family through the educational process, facilitated the transition for Randy from the hospital, home and back to school.

Joey

Joey's story illustrates the importance of:

- Appropriate referrals for educational services
- Early Intervention services
- Physician involvement
- Nursing in schools
- IDEA '04
- Assistive technology communication

Joey is a 12-year-old male diagnosed with a rare genetic neurological disorder. His condition, a progressive and degenerative disease, leads to a loss of milestones. His mom often describes him as a child trapped within his own body – something that many parents of physically disabled children feel. His illness causes body movements that are difficult for him to control. He could possibly hurt himself or others unintentionally. Yet, he deserves to be able to go to school like other children his age.

All children are entitled to a free, appropriate, public education (FAPE) in the least restrictive environment because of the education laws that have been passed (e.g., IDEA '04). From birth to age 2 years, 11 months, Joey received early intervention services at home. Joey is a delightful youngster, confined to a wheelchair, yet able to benefit from all types of assistive communication. When he answers a question correctly in class, he is just as excited as any other child. When he smiles, you know that he belongs in school with his peers. Joey attends a private, state-approved school at the present time. He needs a 1:1 nurse with him on the bus and during school so that he will be able to attend school.

Nursing is considered a related service under IDEA and is documented on Joey's Individual Education Plan (IEP). A 1:1 nurse is very expensive and, until recently, parents were often made to provide this service through their insurance program or by other means. The Supreme Court has ruled that in cases where 1:1 nursing is required, children should go to school and the home school district should be financially responsible for this service (Garrett Frey v. Iowa City School District, 2000). However, this decision is interpreted differently by states and individual school districts across the country. In addition, each state has its own Nurse Practice Act which governs what tasks must be performed by a nurse and which may be performed by other personnel.

For Joey and his family, the process of obtaining school-funded nursing services was long and frustrating. They required extensive documentation from their physician supporting Joey's need for nursing during the school day. Joey's family had to advocate extensively for their child's right to this service along with his right to attend school. There are still problems to iron out. What if the nurse is sick? Is the school responsible for providing a substitute? Who is responsible for training the nurse and who deems her competent?

Joey's story suggests the need for child life specialists to help families develop an educational roadmap and to provide families with appropriate referrals so that wherever they reside they will know how to begin to obtain the necessary educational services for their children.

Max

Max's story illustrates:

• Change in functioning brought on by illness/injury
• Team approach
• Long-term educational planning
• Family support
• Social issues

Max arrived at the hospital in May of his sixth grade year. He had been experiencing headaches and nausea, and within 24 hours of his admission Max was diagnosed with a brain tumor. After surgery, Max began a course of chemotherapy. He did not respond well to the treatment suffering significant side effects. After additional surgery and a serious infection, Max ended up in intensive care for a long admission. It was now October of Max's seventh grade year, and he had not been to school since his diagnosis.

As Max's medical condition stabilized, it was time to attend to his educational needs. During his stay in intensive care, he had not been well enough to receive regular instructional services from the hospital-based teacher, although she read to him often and encouraged communication between Max and his classmates. Prior to his illness, Max attended a parochial school in his neighborhood. They had been in touch with Max and his family over the past few months offering much needed support and encouragement. Unfortunately, due to his illness and the nature of his treatment, Max would be unable to return to school on a regular basis.

A child life specialist referred Max to the education resource team on the unit. The team considered his current medical status and treatment plan. Although well enough to be discharged, Max would not be able to return to school until he was stronger. He was referred to his school district for home instruction services. In addition, he now had mobility issues, speech and language difficulties and other special learning needs. These needs had to be addressed, and appropriate referrals needed to be made. Medical documentation of Max's illness was obtained from the treating physician. A member of the team met with Max's family to discuss special education law and the services available in their community. Max was referred to the Committee on Special Education in his local school district. Evaluations would be made, and an Individualized Education Plan would be developed.

Confronting Max's change in functioning was very difficult for him and his family. His cancer had been treated successfully, but he now faced a whole new set of challenges. Because of his mobility and learning needs, Max would be unable to return to his old school. Finding a new school would require a lot of research. In the meantime, Max would be tutored at home. The Committee on Special Education will recommend a type of placement for a child, but it is important for families to be informed of the different programs available in order to make the best choices for their children. Max would require a bar-

rier-free school (not all schools are accessible) with special education classes and on-site physical therapy – a pretty tall order. Of equal importance to Max and his family was the need for social activities at school. Like all kids, Max wanted to have friends to eat lunch with, clubs to join and even sports opportunities. He wanted to feel included.

Navigating the complex special education system and researching programs takes a lot of time and effort. Family support sometimes means staying in for the long haul. Max had been receiving home instruction for two years and his care team was committed to helping him go to high school. Remembering that a school health coordinator from the hospital's School-Health-Parent task force worked in Max's district, the child life specialist called her to ask her opinion regarding an appropriate school for Max. She had the reputation from professionals, parents and students of being an advocate for kids with special needs in the schools. She made a recommendation and provided the name of the special education coordinator there. Max's mom made an appointment to visit and, at her request, the child life specialist went along to speak about Max's illness and its impact. Mom didn't want Max to come until she knew it would be a good choice. She didn't want him to be disappointed.

Max returned to school in September of his ninth grade year. His Individual Education Plan allowed for some of his time to be spent in general education, while still receiving special education services for the majority of the day. He also received occupational and physical therapies and had a 1:1 aide to help him with mobility. He attended a social skills group once a week with a guidance counselor for kids with similar needs and joined a special computer club. If his plan needed revising, there was a team in place in the building to work with Max and his mom to better meet his needs. And of course, he could always call a member of the hospital's education resource team.

CONCLUSION

The profession of child life can play an important role in the transition of children with special healthcare needs from the hospital, to home and eventually back to school. If child life specialists take the lead and assist families in navigating the complex educational system, more children would receive the services they need and to which they are entitled. School is the main activity of childhood. Allowing children to participate in it to their fullest potential enhances their quality of life. A comprehensive school reentry plan and an ongoing care program should be put in place in each hospital where children are served. The ongoing care team is available to assist parents at critical points, and with critical issues, they and their children face with a chronic illness. These include: (1) the initial time of diagnosis, (2) the weeks, months or years after the diagnosis, (3) socializing with their peers, (4) developmental and emotional milestones, (5) returning to school with academic, cognitive or social disabilities at various times throughout their illness; and (6) difficulty obtaining ongoing services for their children and themselves. Continuing services that may be provided include: medical referrals and coordination of school services, consideration of psychosocial concerns, referrals to sibling and parent support groups, discussion of financial entitlements, socialization and respite care. The more informed physicians are about the total needs of their patients, the better advocates they can be. The role of child life specialists collaborating with other disciplines is critical in helping to inform school personnel about the current needs of children with chronic conditions. Comprehensive care should continue even when patients are discharged from the hospital to ensure a successful school and social reentry.

With more children with chronic conditions being served in outpatient settings, and a decreased length of hospitalization for school-age children, perhaps now is the time to revisit how and where we deliver educational services to this unique population of children. It is the time to look at our hospital-school policies and how we use the financial resources available to best serve these children. At the same time, we should investigate more cost-effective ways of funding hospital-school teachers so that children with chronic medical conditions have their educational needs met, both in the hospital and when they return to school. We are in the midst of changing times. Children who once died before they reached school age are surviving into adulthood, attending our schools and becoming productive members of society. Now is the time to look closely at how we deliver educational services to these children in a comprehensive, ongoing and cost-effective way when they are hospitalized and upon their return to school.

Appendix

TIPS FOR CHILD LIFE SPECIALISTS

1. Develop a comprehensive school reentry program that includes other disciplines from within the hospital.
2. Know the education laws and regulations in your state.
3. Be familiar with IDEA '04, Section 504 and the ADA.
4. Know the referral process for early intervention (birth–2.11), preschool (3–5) and school-age children (5–21).
5. Know the guidelines for a school district evaluation, reevaluation.
6. Become familiar with special education and related documents such as Individual Education Plans, Individual Family Service Plans, Section 504 Accomodation Plans, Health Care Plans and Transition Plans.
7. Understand due process rights and parental consent.
8. Become familiar with the educational leaders in your community and network whenever possible.
9. Ask the family before they are discharged if they feel their child might need any specialized services in school. Make sure to include the child if appropriate. Talk with the multidisciplinary team about the impact of the child's medical condition on their education, now and in the future.
10. Speak to the family about how child life could be helpful in the schools.
11. With parental permission, contact the school district. Find out who the key people are.
12. Help obtain necessary medical documentation that the family and school will need.
13. Set up an informal meeting with school, parents and child life to discuss meeting the educational needs of the child.
14. Become involved in medical education – teaching medical students and residents about the impact of health conditions on a child's education.

REFERENCES

Advocates for Children. (n.d). Retrieved August 22, 2005 from http://www.advocatesforchildren.org

Bauer, T., Duitch, S., & Birenbaum, A. (2003). *Children with special health care needs: Next steps for New York.* United Hospital Fund and the Foundation for Child Development for the New York Forum for Child Health.

Canadian Council for Exceptional Children. (n.d.). Retrieved August 22, 2005 from http://www.canadian.cec.sped.org/

Hobbs, N., Perrin, J., & Ireys, H. (1983). *Public policies affecting chronically ill children and their families.* Tennessee: Vanderbilt University Institute for Public Policies, Center for the Study of Families and Children.

Kleinberg, S. (1982). *Educating the chronically ill child* (1st ed.). Rockville, MD: Aspen Systems Corporation.

Liptak, G., & Weizman, M. (1995). Children with chronic conditions need your help at school. *Contemporary Pediatrics, 12,* 64-80.

McCormick, D. (1986). Social acceptance and school reentry. *Journal of the Association of Pediatric Oncology Nurses,* 13-25., Vol. 3, No. 3.

Owens, P., Thompson, J., Elixhauser, A., & Ryan, K. (2003). *Care of children and adolescents in U.S. hospitals.* Rockville, MD: Agency for Healthcare Research and Quality; HCUP Fact Book No.4; AHRQ Publication No. 04-0004.

Plank, E. (1959). *Working with children in hospitals.* England: Tavistock Publications.

Pless, I. B., & Pinkerton, P. (1975). *Chronic childhood disorder: Promoting patterns of adjustment.* Chicago: Yearbook Medical Publishers.

Porter, S., Burkley, J., Bierle, T., & Lowcock, J. (1992). *Working toward a balance in our lives: A booklet for families of children with disabilities and special health care needs.* Boston: Harvard University.

Stein, R., & Silver, E. (2002). Comparing different definitions of chronic conditions in a national data set. *Ambulatory Pediatrics, 2,* 63-70.

Stuart, J., & Good, H. J. (1996). From hospital to school: How a transition liaison can help. *Teaching Exceptional Children,* 58-62.

Wilson, J. (1979). School as part of a child life program. *The Australian Nurses Journal, 8,* 64-67.

Wissler, K., & Proukou, C. (1999). Navigating the educational system: A practical guide for nurse practitioners. *Journal of Pediatric Oncology Nursing, 16,* 145-155.

Wright, P., & Wright, P. (2004a). *From emotions to advocacy.* Hartfield, VA: Harbor House Law Press, Inc.

Wright, P., & Wright, P. (2004b). *Wrightslaw: Special education law.* Hartfield: Harbor House Law Press, Inc.

Chapter 16

CHILD LIFE: A GLOBAL PERSPECTIVE

MELODEE MOLTMAN, PRITI P. DESAI AND LEEANN DERBYSHIRE FENN

There is no trust more sacred than the one the world holds with children. There is no duty more important than ensuring that their rights are respected, that their welfare is protected, that their lives are free from fear and want and that they grow up in peace.

Kofi A. Annan
Secretary-General of the United Nations
(UNICEF, 2000, foreword)

INTRODUCTION

The threefold purpose of this chapter is:

1. to familiarize the reader with the universality of the needs of children, youth and families, no matter where or how they may live;
2. to explore psychosocial practices in child healthcare settings in different parts of the world; and
3. to examine how child life specialists may become involved in international activities.

Familiarity with international perspectives will strengthen clinical practices with children, youth and families, and help us become clearer in our values and expectations for all children equally, at the local, national, and international levels. As our sensitivity to and understanding of a wide variety of social, economic and cultural contexts is increased, we can become more responsive clinicians and better advocates for the needs of a wider circle of children, youth and families.

In expanding our knowledge and understanding, we may be challenged in our expectations. Values we hold as universal, such as accessibility to healthcare, are not universally attainable; there are many children and youth worldwide whose health is compromised both before and after their birth because healthcare services are not readily available to them. Other values, such as access to opportunities for play and learning, may be unattainable for children in various parts of the world, or even in our own countries, as a result of social, economic or political factors. Thus, the resources that we expect to be available to us as clinicians of child health and positive psychosocial development may, in fact, not be available in a variety of settings and locations throughout the world. We can learn about the practices of colleagues who work in widely varying circumstances, thereby enriching our own practices and professional adaptability.

Many factors alert us to the fact that our world is "shrinking". Our communities are becoming more ethnically diverse. The media bring daily reports of challenges and heartbreak faced by children, youth and their families around the globe. Growth in technology, such as the Internet and e-mail, and opportunities for communicating with people at great distance are an accepted and expected aspect of our personal and professional activities. International travel is widely accessible to individuals.

Some of these factors have contributed to increasing interest expressed by child life professionals to learn how children and youth are being cared for in the world, especially with regard to their health and psychosocial needs. There is also an expressed interest in collaborating with like-minded caregivers around the world, to share knowledge about health and psychosocial practices, to develop ideas for delivering services, and, as a result, to learn from each other. We can increase our reach as more child life professionals become involved in a variety of international roles and activities and communicate these experiences professionally.

Each culture has values, beliefs and practices that are supportive of its children, youth and families. It would not be possible to describe each strength and barrier to the provision of care to children in all the cultures and countries of this world, but we can learn about them by becoming open and inquisitive. Most importantly, we can learn what advocacy tools are available to help build and strengthen sound, effective and proven health and psychosocial supports for

children and youth living in a variety of cultural milieus and economic conditions.

To this end, this chapter explores a range of facts and issues that affect the health and psychosocial care of children, youth and families internationally. Our discussion is divided into four distinct sections.

Part I examines the current healthcare status of children around the world; a definition of health and identification of some factors that contribute to health; the universal rights of children; and the evolution of children's rights in healthcare.

Part II focuses on selected worldwide attitudes and practices in the delivery of health and psychosocial care to children, youth and families.

Part III reviews a number of international programs and efforts currently in place for the delivery of psychosocial care in child health.

Part IV focuses on global opportunities and challenges for child life practice; suggestions for preparing for international work; and a brief chapter conclusion.

PART I: CHILDREN OF THE WORLD

Global situations and struggles continue to produce many alarming events and trends, which have negative impacts on children's development, health and opportunities for a productive future. Child life specialists can have a role within the global call for the promotion and advocacy of children's rights. Awareness is our first step.

There are 197 countries in the world at the time of writing. How countries care for their children, especially for children with healthcare needs, may vary significantly between countries. In general terms, our world's countries reflect a range of rich (developed) or poor (developing) economies, which in turn directly affect the lives and health of their people, especially their children and youth.

There are more than 6.1 billion people in the world: more than 1.1 billion live in more developed regions, greater than 4.9 billion live in less developed regions, and approximately .675 billion live in the world's least developed countries (United Nations Population Fund, 2001). Healthcare availability, accessibility and quality are all affected by the widely divergent economic conditions of developed and developing nations. Within each country, there are discrepancies in healthcare received in urban and rural sectors, and oftentimes gender differences exist. Indeed, where some countries have achieved remarkable outcomes in healthcare for their children, there are many countries where children and youth are suffering from preventable illnesses and who face significant challenges accessing even the most basic amenities of living. There is wide divergence in the availability and delivery of health and psychosocial care both within and between countries around the world.

The Current Health Status of Children Around the World

The most accurate indicator of the status of child health in a given country is the "under-5 mortality rate" (U5MR), which defines the probability of a child dying between birth and five years of age per 1,000 live births. Table 1 examines the mortality rates for the years 1990 and 2000. This table illustrates the global disparity that exists. The situation for young children in rich countries continues to improve, but progress is much slower in poorer countries. A number of factors, including inequitable economic levels, poverty-related problems, and limited access to healthcare for many families in poor countries, result in high rates of mortality and morbidity in their children.

Every year nearly 11 million children in developing countries die before they reach their fifth birthday, many during the first year of life, and primarily as a result of preventable causes (UNICEF, 2001a, 2001b). The most common causes of death include: diarrhea, acute respiratory illnesses (mostly pneumonia), measles, malaria, HIV/AIDS, perinatal conditions, and malnutrition. Malnutrition is a multidimensional problem, which affects the overall health status of children often resulting in secondary infections (UNICEF, 2001a, 2001b). Malnourished children suffer recurrent illness, do not grow well, are more lethargic and apathetic, and less interested in play, exploration and learning.

Table 1

CHANGES IN UNDER 5 MORTALITY RATES FROM 1990 TO 2000

U5MR	1990	2000	Reduction
Most advantaged (richest) countries	9/1000 live births	6/1000 live births	32%
South Asia	128/1000 live births	100/1000 live births	12.8%
Sub-Saharan Africa	181/1000 live births	175/1000 live births	3%

Source: Data compiled from UNICEF (2001a).

It is evident that for many of the world's children and youth, their futures are severely jeopardized. Sadly, these preventable illnesses can be reduced, and perhaps even eliminated, through cost-effective efforts at assisting nations to develop public health interventions that provide clean water, sanitation, reliable food sources, immunizations, and permanent shelter.

A Definition of Health and Factors That Contribute to Health

We turn our attention to factors that contribute to health and illness, beginning with a definition that is applicable globally, where health is not only the absence of illness or disease. The World Health Organization (WHO) (1948) offers this definition of health: "Health is a state of complete physical, mental and social well-being, and not merely the absence of disease or infirmity." The WHO definition of health reflects a biopsychosocial model of health, as psychosocial factors have become as important as biology in our understanding of health and illness.

Health may be defined as a resource for everyday living in that it facilitates adaptability, coping and hope for individuals and groups. At the same time, health is also considered within the social, political and economic conditions of communities and countries within which people reside. The interaction between people and their social and physical environments, and the corresponding impact on health, has resulted in the identification of determinants of health. Determinants of health within communities include such factors as adequate nutritious food, clean water, childhood immunizations, good sanitation, employment, healthy work environments, adequate housing, education, and social support (London Inter Community Health Centre, 1992; World Health Organization, 2002).

What, then, are the specific determinants of health for children and youth, in addition to the basic needs for sufficient and nutritious food, clean water, good sanitation, childhood diseases immunizations, and shelter? The Canadian Institute of Child Health (Guy, 1997) identifies four determinants contributing to optimal child health and development. These include:

1. *Protection* from harm and neglect.
2. *Relationships* that nurture healthy social and biological growth and development.
3. *Opportunity and hope* including opportunities for playing, learning, exploring interests, and testing abilities, as well as hope for a healthy and productive future.
4. *Community* caring and responsiveness that provide resources, cohesion and support to families, based upon socially responsive policies and economic stability.

These factors, when available to children and youth, contribute to health, positive development, and psychosocial competence of children as they progress to maturity. They do not, in and of themselves, make healthy, well-adjusted children, but they do create the potential for healthy developmental outcomes. Further, when these factors are made widely available to children and youth throughout the span of childhood, a society is able to reduce the high costs and low success rates associated with treatment programs to correct childhood vulnerabilities and problems (Guy, 1997). Childhood determinants of health contribute to healthy development, resilience and positive psychosocial outcomes, and these factors are universal.

A brief overview of international research studies provides evidence of the relationship between physical and psychosocial health.

The importance of the work of child life and related psychosocially-oriented health professionals is reinforced by these studies. The determinants of child health, as outlined above, provide a model for collaborative communication within and between professional groups, as well as service delivery components for caring communities to implement effective change for their child and youth populations.

Research evidence supports the interactional relationship between health, social and physical environments, and economic opportunity. A number of studies examine the relationship between poverty and child health (Benzeval & Judge, 2001; Fentiman, Hall & Bundy, 2001; Navarro & Shi, 2001; Pattussi, Marcenes, Croucher, & Sheiham, 2001; Piko & Fitzpatrick, 2001). The research shows that political parties that enact policies to redistribute wealth will ultimately optimize the health of their populations (Navarro & Shi, 2001), and that socioeconomic factors are key determinants of health (Pattussi et al., 2001). When there is an equitable distribution of resources, the entire population benefits in overall health, development and opportunity resulting in stronger productivity, economic growth and an improved overall quality of living rating.

Maternal education is also a vital contributor to a household's health. Well-educated mothers are better able to reduce the damage to health that poverty can inflict (World Bank, 1993). An educated woman is able to benefit from health information, make better use of health services (both prenatally and following her child's birth), have smaller and healthier families, improve literacy and education levels in her children, increase her income, and enable her and her family to live better lives overall. Data from 13 African countries between 1975 and 1985 showed that a 10 percent increase in female literacy rates reduced child mortality by 10 percent, whereas changes in male literacy had little impact on child mortality rates (World Bank, 1993).

However, not only the overall wealth, literacy and related economic policies of a nation must be considered. We are reminded in a number of studies that one must also consider the impact of ethnic and cultural factors (such as language, illness beliefs, parental beliefs, and folk practices) on health and the use of healthcare services (Flores, Bauchner, Feinstein, & Nguyen, 1999; Rungreangkulkij & Chesla, 2001; Yeh, 2001; Younge, Moreau, Ezzat, & Gray, 1997). Flores et al. (1999) note that, "cultural differences can affect clinical care; a good example is *fatalismo*, or the belief among Hispanic patients that an individual can do little to alter fate" (p. 1070), which may result in a reluctance to accept healthcare interventions.

Similarly, in a study of mental illness in adult children in Thailand (Rungreangkulkij & Chesla, 2001), findings indicate that regardless of ethnicity, families of a person with mental illness experience burden. However, beliefs about causes of illness, treatments, sources of social support, and coping strategies are influenced by culture and, in this study, a number of mothers of adult children with schizophrenia responded by practicing *thum-jai*. Thum-jai creates a calm family environment by being accepting, patient, understanding, and having a sense of obligation to the ill family member. This is practiced when faced with situations that are assessed as unchangeable, and are usually explained as a result of a bad deed committed in a previous life, a belief based on Karma.

Cultural beliefs and values may influence practices of disclosing a diagnosis to a patient. Such beliefs may lead to practices very different from those in the West, where it is expected that a patient will be told his or her diagnosis to obtain informed consent for treatment. Studies of reluctance to disclose cancer diagnoses in Taiwan (Yeh, 2001) and Saudi Arabia (Younge et al., 1997) illustrate this observation. In both studies, a diagnosis of cancer was seen as a terminal illness.

Taiwanese parents considered their children too young to understand the disease, which oftentimes resulted in veiled communication contributing to non-compliant behaviors by the children, despite a cultural family value to conform to parental expectations (Yeh, 2001). Yeh (2001) recommended interventions to educate parents to be more open and comfortable when talking with their children about a serious illness, while maintaining sensitivity to the developmental stage and level of understanding of the child.

In Saudi Arabia, the relationship between doctor and patient differs from that in Western countries where it is not considered ethical to withhold information from patients who are capable and able to make decisions about their healthcare based upon honest communication (Younge et al., 1997). In Saudi Arabia, even an adult patient is seen as a member of the larger family, and the family unit holds the primary responsibility for the care and protection of that person. The family may limit the amount of information given to their ill family member, especially when it is a serious diagnosis such as cancer. The intention is to protect the patient from learning the seriousness of an illness, and to prevent a loss of hope that may lead to an earlier death than otherwise expected (Younge et al., 1997).

These studies suggest that such cultural views provide an opportunity for child life and similar professionals working in different parts of the world, to share information about differences and similarities between cultural groups. The goal for child health professionals is to reach a middle ground between cultural beliefs and psychosocial

research that documents the needs and rights of children and youth to access developmentally appropriate information pertaining to illness and treatment.

Another situation that demands our attention and understanding is that of children and youth living in areas of conflict. There are many locations globally where armed conflict exists, sometimes lasting many years or indefinitely. Some children grow to adulthood having known only conflict. Living in such conditions takes a toll on children's development, hope for the future, personal and social resources, and opportunities for health, safety and security. A study of Palestinian children living in Gaza (Miller, 2000), which examined their health risks and status, offers insight that may be applicable to children living in other countries experiencing political, social and/or ethnic conflict. Miller observed,

> broader social conditions in the form of a continuation of human rights abuses, ... high youth and adult unemployment and underemployment, a health and education system that is in need of significant material and human resource development, as well as the frustration of participating in an independence movement that has not achieved many of its goals . . . are all contributing to a level of despair felt by Palestinian people that impairs their right to higher quality, healthy living conditions. (P. 113.)

These studies reflect cultural differences, yet also suggest universal elements, such as the nature of children's responses to stressful situations. They point out the need for children, families and healthcare professionals to communicate in a manner that is culturally sensitive, developmentally appropriate, and effective in promoting healthy growth and positive coping within families and communities. We are reminded that children's health is a balance between factors that are internal to the child (e.g., development, coping, and cognitive understanding) with those that are part of the external context (e.g., social, economic, and political factors).

One very powerful and internationally recognized tool that addresses the external contexts where children live and grow is the United Nations' Convention on the Rights of the Child document. We shift our attention to this document.

The Universal Rights of Children

The twentieth century began with children having virtually no rights; it ended with children having the world's most compelling human rights instrument, the United Nations' Convention on the Rights of the Child (UN-CRC) (Bellamy, 1999). The UN-CRC (United Nations General Assembly, 1989) is a powerful advocacy tool that has the potential to transform the way children are cared for around the world. It is an international document that forms a cornerstone for the recognition and protection of children's developmentally unique human rights worldwide.

The UN-CRC has been described as the most comprehensive child human rights instrument in history. World leaders and child rights advocates reached consensus on such issues as education, healthcare, play, family life, communication and decision making, all aimed at protecting children and youth from stressful life situations, diminishing their suffering, and promoting their full development (UNICEF, 2001b). Most importantly, there was agreement on the principle that children would have the "first call" on all resources needed to secure their rights and that primacy be given to the principle of "the best interests of the child."

All but two countries (the United States of America and Somalia) of the 191 member countries of the UN (in 2002) have ratified the UN-CRC, leaving a political task for child health and welfare professionals to lobby for ratification of the Convention. The United States of America has signed the UN-CRC but not yet ratified it (a process which can take years) and Somalia, with no recognized government, is unable to proceed to ratification. With its full range of civil, political, economic, social and cultural rights, and its nearly universal ratification, the UN-CRC has positioned children squarely at the forefront of the worldwide movement for human rights and social justice.

The Evolution of Children's Rights in Healthcare

Many advocates have examined the rights of children specifically in healthcare settings. Seagull (1978) emphasized the rights of children to receive medical care administered in ways least likely to be psychologically damaging, and the need for specially trained staff to provide such care. She presented a "bill of rights" for children in medical settings, which became a key foundational document that led to the creation of institutional "bills of children's rights" in many healthcare organizations worldwide.

The UN-CRC provides a framework for the integration of the principles of children's rights into healthcare practices. More recently, based upon various articles of the UN-CRC, the Canadian Institute of Child Health (2002) created a document titled, "The Rights of the Child in the Health Care System," summarized in Table 2.

The UN-CRC and Canadian Institute of Children's Health documents clearly support the creation of opportunities in healthcare to enable children's voices to be heard, to give or withhold informed consent, and to obtain optimal pain control, among many other rights. These documents challenge tra-

Table 2

THE RIGHTS OF THE CHILD IN THE HEALTH CARE SYSTEM

1. "I have the right to live and to have my pain and suffering treated, even if I am unable to communicate my need. I have this right regardless of my age, gender or income" (based upon Articles 3, 6 and 24 of the UN-CRC).

2. "I have the right to be viewed first as a child, then as a patient" (article 3, UN-CRC).

3. "I have the right to be treated as an individual with my own abilities, culture and language" (articles 2, 23, 24 and 30, UN-CRC).

4. "I have the right to be afraid and to cry when I feel hurt" (article 12, UN-CRC).

5. "I have the right to be safe in an environment that is unfamiliar to me" (articles 9, 19, 24 and 25, UN-CRC).

6. "I have the right to ask questions and receive answers that I can understand" (articles 12 and 13, UN-CRC).

7. "I have the right to be cared for by people who perceive and meet my needs even though I may be unable to explain what they are" (articles 3 and 5, UN-CRC).

8. "I have the right to speak for myself when I am able and to have someone speak on my behalf when I am unable" (articles 12, 13 and 14, UN-CRC).

9. "I have the right to have those who are dear to me close by when I need them" (articles 3, 9 and 31, UN-CRC).

10. "I have the right to play and learn even if I am receiving care" (articles 28, 29 and 31, UN-CRC).

11. "I need to have my rights fulfilled" (article 42, UN-CRC).

Source: Canadian Institute of Child Health (2002).

ditional perceptions of children's abilities to express their own views, and encourage practices that take the views of children and youth seriously in order to facilitate their active participation in decision making. The call is for children and youth to be included with their families and healthcare professionals in healthcare decisions that directly impact them. In addition, many aspects of the empowerment of children and youth can be accomplished through education and changes in social practices, structures, and professional attitude, rather than by spending extra resources. This model of practice requires the education and active partnership of children, youth and families with the interdisciplinary healthcare team in order to create healthcare environments that are responsive to the needs and rights of children. This may be accomplished at the local level through to international projects.

The necessity and value of collaborative leadership in child health was explored in an article by Southall, Burr, Smith, Bull, Radford, Williams, and Nicholson (2000). The purpose of this paper was to present plans for the development of healthcare systems, monitored by the Child Friendly Healthcare Initiative (CFHI) in six countries, which focus on the physical, psychological, and emotional health of children. The goal of the development of comprehensive child healthcare is,

> To develop in consultation with local healthcare professionals and international organizations, globally applicable standards that will help to ensure that practices in hospitals and health centres everywhere respect children's rights, not only to survival and avoidance of morbidity, but also to their protection from unnecessary suffering and their informed participation in treatment. (Southall et al., 2000, p. 1054)

The authors list four areas for improvement in the delivery of child healthcare worldwide, in poorer countries, as well as those with greater resources. These include:

1) Health Facility (including security; cleanliness; safety policies; and basic drugs and medical supplies to provide a minimal standard of care)
2) Performance of Staff (including basic medical and nursing training on the needs of children)
3) Medical Practices (including effective pain control; effective hand washing practices; and reduction in the indiscriminate use of powerful antibiotics)
4) Respect and Sensitivity for the Child (including implementation of family-centred care practices that encourage parental participation in care and reduction of separation of children from parents, especially during painful and invasive procedures; respect of the child's need for privacy; explanation of the illness and its treatment to the child and family; and creation of environments that reduce fear) (Southall et al., 2000, p. 1055)

The authors note that even in well-resourced countries, technological advances in healthcare are not always accompanied by attention to children's overall well-being and concern for their anxieties, fears, and emotional suffering. Even wealthy, well-resourced and knowledgeable nations are unable to lay claim to the elimination of negative childhood psychosocial responses to healthcare experiences. Children, youth and families continue to be traumatized by healthcare experiences and practices that are unresponsive to the developmental, informational, emotional and family support needs of children and youth. Southall et al. (2000) provide discussion and guidelines that are applicable to any children's healthcare setting in any country of the world.

The UN-CRC has led to the development of many international projects; some of these are briefly highlighted below. More detailed information about the organizations, their activities, projects and services are available from a number of sources including related professional organizations, published literature, the Internet, as well as on the Child Life Council website (www.childlife.org) which maintains a list of international organizations.

The Child-Friendly Healthcare Initiative (CFHI) is an exemplary pilot initiative implemented by Child Advocacy International (CAI) based in the United Kingdom (UK). The pilot initiative is based on the principles of the UN-CRC, and it aims to support local healthcare professionals to improve the standards of healthcare received by children in state hospitals of poorly resourced countries, such as Uganda, Nicaragua, Afghanistan and Bosnia.

In the UK, the Action for Sick Children (formerly the National Association for the Welfare of Children in Hospital or NAWCH) has, since 1961, advocated for the improvement of the psychosocial care of children receiving healthcare and established a number of initiatives worldwide. Similar organizations exist in a number of European countries as well as in other parts of the world such as Romania (the Romanian Children's Relief Fund) and Kuwait (KAACH – Kuwait Action for the Care of Children in Hospitals).

Additional European organizations that advocate on behalf of children in healthcare settings include the European Association for Children in Hospitals (EACH) and the National Association of Hospital Play Specialists (NAHPS) in the UK. In North America, the Institute of Family Centered Care and the Child Life Council carry on advocacy and leadership initiatives.

In order to empower child health personnel to provide care in a child and family-friendly manner, one must consider the conditions under which professionals work and the curriculum or training medical personnel receive. In developed countries, nurses and physicians caring for children receive some formal education and have opportunity for continuing education on the developmental and emotional needs of hospitalized children. They also have opportunities to collaborate with colleagues, such as child life specialists, hospital play specialists, social workers and psychologists, who keep child psychosocial aspects of care in the forefront.

In many developing countries, this may not be the case. Kaur (2000) evaluated nursing curricula in India for content specific to child development and behavioral aspects of care. The study noted a few topics within the curriculum related to psychosocial care and child development, but overall found the child and family health related content to be minimal and inadequate. The author suggests that the curriculum and training of physicians and nurses be strengthened to address the psychosocial needs of children, youth and families.

The training suggested by Kaur would likely be favorably received, according to anecdotal accounts. A child life specialist visiting Kenya, Bolivia and India found that nurses were interested in education on the provision of psychosocially supportive care, as long as the resultant care did not demand more of their time. There is opportunity for child life educators and academicians to be involved in curriculum enhancement of psychosocial aspects of child and youth healthcare for pediatric practitioners.

And, of course, there is a need for child life specialists to share their expertise with learners and entry-level child life specialists throughout the world. This can occur even when language presents a barrier, as in the experience described below:

A visiting child life consultant was responsible for the clinical supervision of students in a child life training program in Kuwait. While the students were all fluent in Arabic and English, the consultant knew only English and most of the families spoke only Arabic. The consultant's belief that "play is a universal language" was reinforced. Children, parents, and the consultant communicated through play even when students were not available to translate.

To solve the language barrier during clinical training on medical play and preparation, the child life students and consultant developed the following approach:
- Upon arrival on the unit, the consultant and students spoke to the nurses and determined which children and families would require child life support, care and intervention.
- A student would approach each child and family regarding their desire to participate in medical play and preparation, speaking Arabic.
- The students and consultant would privately develop the approach to take in each preparation session, speaking in English.
- One student would carry out the preparation while another student and the con-

sultant observed, but far enough away so as not to interfere; the observing student translated into English the details of the interaction, for the consultant.
- The students and consultant then met as a group to debrief and evaluate the preparation sessions, speaking English.

Child life specialists and colleagues with similar interests around the world can be effective advocates for child health practices. As practitioners of health and psychosocial care we can share our knowledge and expertise in all parts of the world. There is much work to be done.

PART II: THE UNIVERSAL NATURE OF SUPPORTIVE PSYCHOSOCIAL SERVICES IN HEALTHCARE

Settings throughout the world where health professionals may provide psychosocial care are numerous and diverse. Whatever the setting, the elements that reflect quality care remain constant. These include:

- Parental presence with their children in health and psychosocial care and in family-centered care
- Psychological preparation for stressful events and situations
- Play, developmentally appropriate activities, and educational opportunities
- Pain management, including nonpharmacologic techniques
- Practices that are based on respect and dignity of the individual, family and all aspects of diversity
- Environments that are safe, clean, and child-oriented
- Staff training that supports the delivery of child and family oriented, quality, comprehensive health and psychosocial care

We believe that professionals like child life specialists can play a cost-effective role in providing support, education and interventions that address child development, typical behavioral responses of children, parental anxieties, coping strategies and parent-child interactions. Mallya (1986) initiated child development student placements in a general hospital in India and reported on the success of psychosocial interventions for parents, which included parenting education, support groups, and recreational activities. The interventions resulted in increased participation by parents in their child's play, rather than just in caregiving routines; increased social networking with other parents and an ability to express their feelings; better comprehension of their child's illness; and increased ability to ask for information about their child's illness, as well as about play and parenting roles. It was also noted that the children coped better and displayed more positive behaviors after the interventions, which resulted in decreased levels of verbal threat or indifferent behavior toward the ill child by the parents (Mallya, 1986).

Studies from Australia, Haiti and India report on parental needs for information about child development and behavior and the positive outcomes for families when this is provided (Goodfriend, 1999; Hall, Johnson, & Middleton, 1990; Mallya, 1989a, 1989b; Ramritu & Croft, 1999). These studies identified a need for family support and social re-integration services, and found that when needs of parents were met, they were better able to care for their sick children and cope with the health problems and possible attendant disabilities. Goodfriend (1999) noted that parents in Haiti benefited from guidance regarding developmental milestones of children and how these can be reached. When provided with information, parents were better able to follow through on suggested interventions with their children.

Studies from diverse geographical settings indicate that children's reactions to illness and hospitalization are universal, and the need for preparation and acquisition of coping skills is reinforced. Children and youth in any part of the world may find illness and healthcare experiences stressful and some behavioral changes may be expected as a result. Education of families and support of children and youth can promote the acquisition of effective coping skills. Health professionals can provide a range of care and psychosocial interventions that are both responsive to this need and, at the same time, reflective of the cultural and social expectations of the country. The knowledge and practices of child life professionals are well-suited to fulfill these roles and needs.

For example, a study of hospital patients in Jamaica aged 3 to 13 years found that those with a history of previous hospitalization appeared to be significantly more distressed than patients without previous hospitalization, displaying more uncooperative, anxious, and immature behavior patterns (Pottinger & Ehikhametalor, 2000). This study underscores the need for children to be better prepared for hospitalization, for greater parental involvement in the management of their children's behavior, and for the provision of programs that address the informational and emotional needs of children and families.

Recognition of the potential long-term emotional effects of hospitalization on children and youth and of the need for advocacy for children's rights in healthcare have led the staff of the Schneider Children's Medical Center of Israel to make changes in nursing care on pediatric surgical wards (Zelikovsky, 1996). Policies were revised to allow parents to accompany children through induction of anesthesia, whenever possible. This action was credited with decreasing anxiety and fear in both children and parents. Zelikovsky

(1996) concludes that parental participation during surgical induction plays an important role in helping children cope with potentially traumatic experiences.

The importance of procedural support and intervention is evident in the experience of a visiting child life specialist's work with a surgical mission in Kenya, where a young child needed to have sutures removed from his tongue.

A nurse held a small pair of scissors in her hand, and approached the terrified child who was screaming, flailing his arms, and not allowing the nurse to come close to him. The child's mother looked embarrassed and appeared helpless. The child life specialist took the help of an attending nurse to interpret and encouraged the child's mother to hold the child in her lap, and put her arms supportively around the child in a comfort hold. The mother complied and the child, although still frightened, was in a more secure position. The child life specialist also asked the nurse interpreter to let the child know that the scissors in the nurse's hand were just to loosen the "string" and would not touch his tongue. The child calmed down considerably and the procedure was concluded.

Following this experience, the child life specialist discussed with nurses the power of including parents in procedural support. This was reported to be novel for them, indicating they would not have thought to ask for parental participation in this type of situation. They noted that they eventually would have strapped the child down, and perhaps even sedated him, if he had not complied, but acknowledged that using the mother's support was a much kinder and more effective way to deal with the situation.

The nurses were also impressed with the value of providing stress-point preparation and comfort positioning to a child about to undergo a medical procedure. The nurses expressed interest in learning more about such interventions when caring for their patients. They reported that the observed approach did not take extra time, but enabled them to perform the procedure in a more child-friendly and family-centered manner.

Concerns about the developmental and healthcare needs of children, youth and families are wide-ranging and the need for inclusion of sound psychosocial practices in support of their health experiences is evident. Children and youth who are prepared for healthcare experiences in a developmentally appropriate manner demonstrate more positive outcomes in their behavior, recovery and strengthened ability to cope with stressful events. These outcomes are well documented in the child life literature and provide a solid foundation for child life interventions (see Chapter 9).

How, then, can child life specialists become involved? What follows are descriptions of ways that child life specialists have become involved in international activities that promote opportunities for professionals and learners to share their skills with children, youth and families in our global community.

PART III: INTERNATIONAL EFFORTS TO PROMOTE PSYCHOSOCIAL CARE IN HEALTH

Taking Stock: Current Programs and Efforts

In this section we take a brief look at some psychosocial programs and services around the world. Before we begin, however, we want to acknowledge the work of

Muriel Hirt and Peg Belson. These two individuals are child life role models who, in the late 1970s, collaborated to initiate an international experience for child life students called the "Wheelock Summer in London" exchange, a program that continues to this day. Even before this collaboration, Muriel Hirt, founder of the Wheelock College Child Life program, had advocated for the psychosocial care of child patients during her travels to India. Peg Belson was a founding member of the National Association of the Welfare of Children in Hospital (NAWCH) in the United Kingdom (now the Action for Sick Children) where she is currently an advisor to this organization.

Over the years Belson has coordinated the Wheelock summer exchange program and lectured on the psychosocial healthcare of children and families in countries around the world including China, Bosnia, the Netherlands, Poland, the United States, and Australia. Belson initiated the development of play programs in Kuwait, Bosnia, the Netherlands, Malta and the Czech Republic, and developed the initial curriculum for the child life training program in Kuwait in the early 1990s. Belson and Hirt have opened their homes to guests from around the world who have traveled to their respective countries to observe psychosocial practices in action. These are two of many child life leaders who have contributed to the development of our profession; they have encouraged us to learn from and work with all who are striving to provide psychosocial and healthcare to children and families around the world.

Development of programs that promote the psychosocial care of children has occurred throughout the world, but we will highlight only four countries: the United Kingdom, New Zealand, the Philippines, and Kuwait. Development of such programs is typically an interdisciplinary effort based on collaboration among child advocates in pediatrics, nursing, social work, psychology, education, and child development fields. The funding for psychosocial programs may vary, from hospital funds to government budgets. The philosophies of the programs may vary, from informal play programs provided by untrained volunteers to highly structured psychosocial support programs provided by qualified child life and hospital play staff. Each program reflects the social, cultural and economic conditions of its country of origin.

The United Kingdom (UK)

Hospital play specialists, a term coined in the UK, now work in about 17 countries throughout Europe as well as in Australia, New Zealand and Hong Kong, China. Barnes (1995) reports significant advances since 1965 in providing for the medical and emotional needs of hospitalized children. The role of hospital play staff in the UK and elsewhere is similar to the role of child life specialists in North America. In addition, hospital play specialists have begun to extend their role to community care. UK hospital play staff has been successful in gaining government recognition, as evidenced in a Department of Health document that outlines a pay scale for hospital play specialists that hospitals are advised to implement. In addition, advocacy that every pediatric ward have trained hospital play specialists has been supported by a 1991 Department of Health recommendation, and re-emphasized in 1993 by the National Service framework for hospital services for children. These are notable accomplishments.

New Zealand

In New Zealand, there is a commitment to biculturalism with recognition of the culture of the indigenous Maori people. A multidisciplinary reference group including pediatricians, child health nurses, hospital play specialists, and child advocacy groups, is developing New Zealand's Standards for the Wellbeing of Children and Young People in Healthcare Facilities. Hospital play programs are funded by both the Ministry of Education and hospital budgets and are chartered as early childhood services, which must incorporate New Zealand's early childhood curriculum. This curriculum is conceptualized as *Te Whaariki* or "precious woven mat," which is defined as all experiences, activities and events, both direct and indirect, which children experience in the environment. When considering the hospital environment, the curriculum requires that the environment be structured so that health and development is promoted, emotional well-being is nurtured, children are kept safe from harm, and are psychosocially supported in order to develop trust, attachment and self-esteem. This is accomplished through the delivery of healthcare that includes play, preparation, parental involvement in care, and trained staff (Kayes, 2000, 2001). The Hospital Play Specialist Association of New Zealand is a professional body that publishes a journal called *Chapters*, advocates with hospital administrators and government policymakers, and liaises with comparable agencies internationally including the Child Life Council.

Philippines

In some countries, child life program initiatives are limited to a single institution serving a specific patient population. For example, in the Philippines, a country of 76 million people, an organization called Kythe Inc. has the first and possibly the only formal child life program which focuses specifically on children with cancer (Garcia, 2000). The program was the vision of a pediatric oncologist who invited professionals with training in psychology to implement a psychosocial program for her pediatric patients. This organization is registered as a non-profit organization, and its members include parents and professionals. Their child life plan of care has five progressive components: (1) preparation; (2) stress relief and therapeutic play during treatment; (3) transition support (support groups and camps); (4) hospice care; and (5) bereavement support. There are also outreach and research programs. Kythe Inc. promotes a holistic approach to the care of children with cancer. Building upon the core program in one hospital, similar programs may be developed in other hospitals in other parts of the country, and programming may be expanded from the care of children with cancer to other pediatric health conditions.

Kuwait

In Kuwait, a vision of more comprehensive psychosocial care can be seen in an organization called Kuwait Action for the Care of Children in Hospital (KACCH), founded and directed by Margaret Al-Sayer. "KACCH is a voluntary organization devoted to improving the ways in which the healthcare community in Kuwait responds to the unique emotional and developmental needs of children in hospitals" (Coleman, 1999). At the time of writing, there were teams of one or two child life specialists and one or two play leaders in six of the country's hospitals. The teams work on pediatric wards and provide services to other areas such as outpatient departments, same-day surgery units, and pediatric accident and emergency units. Students interested in acquiring child life skills enroll in training courses at Kuwait University supported by KACCH. The goal is to continue to intro-

duce child life care to hospitals throughout the country, as well as to create a children's hospice in three phases by 2007 and a children's hospital by 2010. A further goal is for graduates of the postgraduate program to attain professional certification like that offered by the Child Life Council (M. Al-Sayer, personal communication, fall 2001, summer 2004). In 2005, one student trained by KACCH came to the United States to take the Child Life Certifying exam and was subsequently certified – the country's first CCLS.

PART IV: CHILD LIFE INVOLVEMENT

The Opportunities and Challenges for Child Life Practice Internationally

Portions of the Mission, Vision, Values and Operating Principles statements of the Child Life Council's Official Documents (2002) support an expanded role for child life professionals on the international stage. For example, statements note that child life practices "will be applicable to any healthcare setting and transferable to other environments or situations in which the potential for infants, children and youth to cope, learn and master is placed at risk" (p. 4) and that our "philosophy and identity [will be] accepted on an international level" (p. 5). The Child Life Council's vision-to-action initiative in 1996 challenged child life professionals to consider settings and countries where they can offer their knowledge and skills, and to identify settings where children are facing stressful life events. This includes children and youth around the world living through stressful life events and conditions including war, refugee camps, poverty, epidemics such as HIV/AIDS, and orphanages, to name a few. These professional documents and activities lead us to dream, plan and implement new roles in which we can apply the rich knowledge, skills and experience we possess.

Opportunities for involvement may include activities that are broad in scope, affecting change of policy at governmental levels, while other activities may involve more direct service at a grassroots level. In addition, it is not always necessary to travel the world to effect change; we offer examples of opportunities for participation in affecting changes for children, youth and families without leaving your community. The world has truly become a global village as a result of technological advances. And we must remember that our own "back-yards" also need attention and change in order to create better futures for our children and youth.

As child life specialists and as a profession, we can contribute by learning and advocating for child and youth rights at all levels. There are many activities that can facilitate this goal, and yet there are also many barriers to work through. We recognize the many opportunities and challenges to our participation in international activities; sometimes it takes courage and commitment to become involved and to meet or discover individuals and organizations that share common interests and goals. We offer the following examples and ideas to stimulate your thinking about ways you might become involved in international activities.

Advocacy

We can advocate and lobby for a variety of issues affecting children's health and well-being, including ratification of the UN Convention on the Rights of the Child (UN-CRC) by the United States of America. When a number of professional groups advocate for the rights of children and youth, including access to healthcare and comprehensive psychosocial services based upon the principles of the UN-CRC, the strength and viability of the message increases and political pressure is more likely to succeed.

Collaboration

As members of professional organizations, we can join hands with other agencies to set standards and promote the rights of children in healthcare settings and in other potentially detrimental circumstances. Non-governmental organizations (NGOs) with similar service goals offer excellent launching points for establishing international partnerships. Long-term initiatives to address economic, social and political issues of countries in need are another option for collaborative work. The challenge is to define roles for child life specialists, train for those special circumstances, and work within interdisciplinary teams.

Education

In many countries, people involved in child healthcare may not have specific education or training available about childhood psychosocial and health needs or the needs of children living in difficult or potentially detrimental circumstances. As an example, many pediatric residency curricula do not include information or training in psychosocial aspects of child health. Even psychology and child development curricula may have little focus on the psychosocial issues of childhood health. Child life specialists, working with interdisciplinary child health professionals, can facilitate the development of minimal standards for inclusion of psychosocial principles in all spheres of child health training. The Child Friendly Healthcare Initiative (CHFI) is an example of a program that is advocating that psychosocial interventions move from a position of "extras" in mainstream treatment, to full integration, acceptance and expectation of these interventions in all aspects of child healthcare.

Professional Membership and Involvement

We need to remove barriers to membership and professional participation at an international level. An example is the need to explore credentialing options whereby child life specialists are able to train under the supervision of hospital play specialists or other related professional groups and vice versa. Alternative educational models will ultimately enrich the care we provide children, youth and families. As such, our professional bodies need to embrace diverse models of providing services, support, education, and credentialing opportunities to professionals around the world.

International Research and Information Sharing

Studying trends from international public health models for the care and reduction of childhood illnesses worldwide provides an understanding of practices that are successful and why. Maternal and child health programs, implemented worldwide, offer models for learning and collaboration. Communication and discussion with international strategists can lead to integration of psychosocial care into the various models of healthcare delivery to children and youth. Researching and documenting the practices of parents and professionals in countries that reflect excellence in the psychosocial healthcare of children can provide opportunities for collaborative work to develop and strengthen practices in a variety of settings.

Use of the Internet

Internet websites provide an effective method for connecting with like-minded professionals and groups, as well as accessing information about child health practices worldwide. Internet search engines make it easy to access information by typing in key words, names of countries, and/or organizations of interest. In addition, research papers and reviews of literature on a wide range of topics are available through a number of university and community libraries.

International Consultation and Student Exchange

Excellent learning opportunities are made possible by the ease of global communication and travel coupled with interest expressed by students and professionals to travel for educational, consultative, and job exchange experiences in children's psychosocial and healthcare environments. As individuals, we can participate in professional exchanges, arrange seminars about child life in various countries, and encourage international student exchanges in internship and academic programs. Exchanges have occurred in countries such as Sarajevo, Kuwait, India, China, Bolivia, New Zealand, and Britain.

Medical Missions

Medical missions, with a variety of goals and activities, have become more visible and accessible to individuals with a range of skills and experience. Working with medical missions in developing countries in Africa and South and Central America have revealed that the concept of play and preparation for hospitalized children was primarily a novel idea, especially in rural areas, very poor communities, and in most public hospitals. It has been noted by professionals working on these missions that preparation of children for medical procedures was well received by parents. Parents often expressed appreciation for the information and asked questions concerning their children's behavioral and emotional responses (Desai-Joshi, 2000). It has been observed by the writers that children in any country respond positively to toys or an opportunity to play.

Preparing for International Work

There are a number of considerations to be made related to international work. This section discusses some of the components international travelers and workers should consider as part of their preparation. To begin, at a personal level, the challenges one may face in another country are mainly overcome by one's attributes of flexibility, caring, compassion, an ability to relate to others, to work with an interpreter, and to maintain a sense of humor and wonder. These interpersonal skills help to smooth the challenges that are sure to be encountered in international work and will also increase the experience of success and reward.

In addition, when a professional works in another country and does not address the prevailing cultural issues, the work will likely not be sustained over time. Professionals must remain sensitive to their role as guest. A colleague, George Lang (personal communication, spring 2000), reminds us, "always remember it's their program, not ours." If these words are carried with us, we can best appreciate the privilege of sharing in another culture and then returning home to share what we have learned.

The example below speaks to these points.

In Kuwait, a child life consultant visited a hospital unit for children with leukemia.

Child life students wanted the consultant to see a hallway playroom in action.

As the consultant entered the unit, a young teenage boy was seen standing in his hospital room doorway. The consultant greeted him and to the surprise of the consultant, he responded in English. The consultant stopped for a brief chat and invited him to join the activities in the play area. As the consultant proceeded down the hallway, she stopped to admire a beautiful well baby sibling in a walker in the middle of the hallway. Siblings and mothers or maids may room-in during hospitalization in Kuwait; family-centered care, in that sense, seemed natural and commonplace here. A short time later, in the play area, the teenager arrived and chatted with the consultant as the younger children played. When the teenager was asked if the consultant could have a photograph taken with him, he graciously agreed. He and the consultant posed and a student was preparing to take the picture. Suddenly, all the children in the play area gathered around for the picture, with their mothers or maids watching from nearby; the students joked and told the consultant the moms wouldn't join the picture because they didn't have their makeup on yet. What a wonderful shared experience. Then out of no-where, the healthy infant sibling whom the consultant had been admiring a short time earlier was thrust into the consultant's arms for the photo shoot. What a beautiful picture; what an incredible memory!

The consultant will always remember the feeling of honor and privilege she felt as someone handed her their baby, their most cherished possession, to her a total stranger, a foreigner in this land. At that moment the consultant says she knew what it felt like to bridge cultures. Many reading this chapter may also have such amazing experiences.

How does this all relate to child life and psychosocial care? The consultant hopes that it is evident from this story that respect can be conveyed by one's manner, behavior, love and compassion, and a desire to learn. The reciprocated sharing, exchanging and learning began to blur the distinction between learner and consultant and one must ask, "Who was really learning the most here?"

Whether one is preparing for a short-term medical mission or work on a longer project in another country, the following guidelines may be helpful. In all instances, it is important to explore the following points:

- The purpose of your travel
- The country you will visit, including the language, geography, economy, political system, educational and healthcare systems, culture(s), foods, clothing, behavioral expectations
- Developing cultural sensitivity
- The varied roles of child life specialists in a variety of settings and cultures
- General travel tips

Purpose of the Travel

First and foremost, explore in detail the purpose of the travel. Become informed about your role on the specific project. There are a number of international activities that have varying goals and purposes, including medical missions, student exchanges, faculty or professional exchanges, consulting work, and other opportunities, such as conference participation. Be familiar with the purpose and objectives of your travel activities.

The Travel Destination

Learn as much as possible about the country, and the specific region of the country, where you will be traveling. Read and

talk with people from that country. Contacting a cultural center or college/university in your area may be helpful, as both often have people from many different countries who would be willing to talk with you. Also, consider contacting the Child Life Council to find out if they know of anyone who has been to the country you will visit or check the website (www.childlife.org) to locate related organizations in the country of your destination. A contact person will be an invaluable source of information.

Learning will continue when you arrive at your destination by talking with the local people. In our experience, people are willing to share information about their country and culture if the traveler is interested and respectful. Aspects of a country to inquire about may include:

- Geography and weather
- Language, foods and clothing
- Religion, ethnic groups and culture(s)
- Economic and political systems
- Education and healthcare systems
- Healthcare beliefs and psychosocial practices
- Education of healthcare providers
- Common childhood health concerns in the region/country.
- Demographics and health indicators
  a. Population, including the child population
  b. Infant Mortality Rate (IMR) or the Under 5 Mortality Rate (U5MR), and fertility rates
  c. Literacy rates and indicators
  d. Gross National Product and other economic indicators

Cultural Sensitivity

Familiarity with the culture will promote a timely transition. Learning phrases and greetings used in the local language will convey respect for the people and their culture, and your desire to learn. If there is time before your departure, you might enroll in a conversational course in the language the children and their families will be speaking. If this is not possible, try to learn basic greetings and farewells and common phrases. Remember, too, that "play is a universal language" and it will open doors to building trusting relationships with children and families the world over.

You may be working with interpreters. Avoid language with jargon and slang forms of words. Use basic, common language so an interpreter will have an easier time finding a similar word in their language to convey your message. One author experienced difficulty presenting a paper on child life in Beijing, China. Translators were available and helpful, but at times it was difficult translating professional jargon or vocabulary you, as a healthcare professional, may take for granted. Have colleagues from outside your field read prospective papers and give feedback before you travel so you can minimize the possible confusion poorly translated jargon may cause.

Space, touch and eye contact all vary widely from culture to culture. One could unintentionally offend guests or be offended by them. Once again, contact someone at a cultural center or college in your area for help with these questions, or ask your host about expected behaviors. Accept the customs of the country you are visiting; don't expect people to change their customs for your comfort.

Time concepts vary widely from culture to culture. In industrialized Western culture, work and everyday activities tend to center around the clock. In many other parts of the world, "clock time" appears less important. For instance, a visiting consultant found students arriving late for class, but they were willing to stay beyond the scheduled class

time. Initially, the consultant was concerned that the students were not interested in what she had to offer and felt frustrated that the students did not arrive on time, yet expected her to stay longer than intended. She later learned that the students were celebrating a religious holiday that included fasting and preparation of special foods for when the fast was broken. As a result, they were staying up much later than usual. It was clear in this case that what might be considered tardiness in Western culture was not a lack of interest or desire but due to religious and cultural obligations.

Gender roles and respect for the elderly may hold primary importance in many cultures. In some cultures, males or elders are viewed as the decision makers for the family, and questions must therefore be addressed to them. A mother may feel "lost" if she is asked to make an important medical decision about her child if her husband is not present, as this is part of his culturally designated role. Similarly, in other cultures, women may hold the primary responsibility for children and their overall care, including health matters, and be primary decision makers.

Review common healthcare beliefs of the country you are visiting. The hosts can be very helpful in answering questions. In some countries, as discussed in this chapter, there may exist a strongly held belief that the word "cancer" is not used with a patient or family, or that a patient is not told of his or her diagnosis. Knowing these beliefs and values is very important when working with children and families in healthcare settings.

Similarly, determine what is acceptable clothing. Be culturally sensitive and respectful. Find out what is typically worn by people in the area, and dress according to local expectations. In general, and especially when working with children and families, it is best to dress conservatively; for example, women should wear longer length skirts, and blouses and sweaters with sleeves.

Be prepared and willing to try a variety of foods. People the world over use food to welcome and nurture. Be a gracious guest and try the range of foods presented. Before a trip, you might also inquire about the accessibility of the ingredients of one of your own favorite recipes; how wonderful if you can make your favorite dish and share it with new friends.

The Role of the Child Life Specialist

The four main functions you will most likely be asked to address as a child life specialist working in another country include:

- Providing play opportunities
- Providing psychological preparation for children and families
- Advocating and facilitating parental participation and family-centered care
- Completing an educational or work exchange

Review the job description for the trip. Consider carefully what people will want and expect of you. At the same time be prepared to remain flexible. Prepare for your work, but know that you may need to adjust your plans to respond to the circumstances or needs and interests of your hosts.

PROVIDING PLAY OPPORTUNITIES. When providing play opportunities, it may not always be possible to carry toys or play supplies with you. If, however, you are able take supplies, a suggested list follows. Be aware of cultural issues in toy and play material selection.

Consider cost-effectiveness. If possible, find out about popular local games in advance (the Internet is a good source of information for this), or learn about these once you arrive at your destination. Learn cultural beliefs about play. For example, many Muslim families (but not all, remembering that each family and country is unique) believe personification of a life form is not acceptable in toys or drawings. That may mean one may not be able to use infant mobiles with animals or dolls. Older children should not be asked to draw themselves or their families. If planning medical play with a hospital soft doll, explain to the caregiver what you are about to do and ask if it is permissible to do so.

You should plan to take with you materials that are simple, easily transportable, and reusable. This may include arts and craft supplies (crayons and markers; glue sticks; paper; scrap materials; a play dough recipe; string; needle and thread; stickers), dolls and puppets, picture books or books in the language of the country, basic toys and activities (playing cards; magic wands; blocks; bubbles; matchbox type cars; plastic animals), baby toys such as rattles and mobiles and a toy medical kit.

PROVIDING PSYCHOLOGICAL PREPARATION FOR CHILDREN AND FAMILIES. If involved in psychological preparation activities, consider bringing your own supplies, if possible and appropriate. In developing countries, it would be considered wasteful to use expensive medical equipment for medical play and preparation. Consider group preparations. Take pictures of medical equipment in the country of your visit, in order to prepare children for procedures; do not use pictures of equipment from your own country. Include parents of all children during preparation, especially parents of infants and toddlers. Don't take pictures of children and families or any local people, unless they give their permission. If your request is denied, be gracious and accept the fact.

ADVOCATING FOR AND FACILITATING PARENTAL PARTICIPATION AND FAMILY-CENTERED CARE. When advocating for family-centered care and parental participation, model behaviors to encourage parents to participate in their child's routine care, and provide a supportive presence during procedures. This process may include educating medical staff as well. Encourage parents to ask questions about their child's medical care as well as their child's developmental and emotional needs. Encourage parents to be supportive of each other.

COMPLETING AN EDUCATIONAL OR WORK EXCHANGE. For an educational exchange, plan your lectures, presentations or discussions recognizing that you will need to be very flexible. Be prepared to put lecture notes and plans aside, so you can talk with students or professionals about their interests and concerns, which may not be part of your prepared text. Work side-by-side with local staff especially pediatric nurses and other front-line staff to increase the likelihood of sustainability of the child life philosophy.

Consider bringing small gifts to give to your hosts. Children's books that don't require language to read, something special made in your area of your country, and special candies are all good possibilities. Of course the gift of sharing yourself is most important, but some remembrances will be highly prized. Bring a package of thank you cards from home since you may not find them easily or have the time to search for them in local stores.

Travel Tips

It is important to be well prepared and informed about your personal needs when you travel. The following are some items you may need. Some are essential and other items may be beneficial to have with you:

Essential Travel Documents

1. Passport and Visa

- Be sure to make a photocopy of your passport and keep it separate from the original copy of the passport.
- Leave photocopies of all key documents at home in a place known to someone, in case the documents you take with you are lost.
- Check travel advisory updates. You will want to go to government websites for this information. In addition, you may want to take a small short-wave radio along with you so you can have access to breaking news from around the world.
- Determine whether you will need an International Driver's License; this may or may not be essential.
- Prepare emergency contact information. Your itinerary and contact information should be left with family and friends at your home, and you should carry information on your person about whom to contact in case of an emergency.

2. Health Information and Immunization Record Card

- Contact your physician several months prior to your travel, to find out what inoculations you will require prior to travel, for a general health examination, and to determine any health-related issues you need to consider prior to traveling.
- Check the Centers for Disease Control website (http://www.cdc.gov), which has a wealth of information on disease protection, places to avoid, and other health-related information. This site may be helpful even to those not living in the USA. Your local health department may also provide health-related information of benefit to you.
- Foreign travel can be stressful. Sometimes people become ill with colds,

viruses, or intestinal infections. Take along your own medicines for diarrhea, upset stomach, aches and pains, mild fever, and skin irritations. Be sure to pack sanitary supplies.
- Don't drink the tap water; use bottled water, even to brush your teeth.
- Dehydration and diarrhea may occur; consult your physician for medication to take with you for diarrhea. But remember, if possible, you should allow the infection to "run its course" and completely leave your system.
- Take toilet paper and disposable towels with you.
- Take your regular medications with you.
- If you wear glasses, take an extra pair.
3. Money Questions
- Take enough cash to get by for one or two days; sometimes it is difficult to get to a bank right away. Ask your hosts to give you an idea of how much money you should bring.
- Take traveler's checks in U.S. dollars rather than the currency of the country you are visiting; the United States currency is accepted for exchange in many banks around the world.
- Take a credit card or ATM card with a pin number; you should be able to access your account from most places around the world.
4. Other items to be aware of:
- Electricity:
Find out what the voltage is in the country you will visit. Remember that hair dryers, VCRs, computers and other electrical appliances do not all run on the same voltage around the world; you may need an adapter. If you plan to use videotapes, you will need to have them transposed to the format of the country you will be traveling to or have an international player available that can transpose

them. Most of Europe uses PAL, the USA uses NTSC, and Russia and South America use yet another format. There are approximately five different formats. Contact someone who works in your media center, as they should be able to assist you with this matter.
- Local country time; be sure to learn the 24-hour clock for time, as most travel will be displayed this way. Having an international watch or clock is helpful but not necessary.
- Telephone system; check your phone card for any restrictions before you leave.

Always remember your incredible ability to remain flexible. Use that ability now. Your combined warmth and generous heart, personality and sense of wonder will take you far in international experiences. Have fun, share yourself, and learn! (Adapted from Moltman, Giardina-Auten & Lang, 2000; Desai-Joshi, 2000).

CONCLUSION

Earlier in the chapter we asked the question: How can child life help to promote the psychosocial health of children and youth worldwide? It has been our intent to provide the reader with information necessary to begin the learning process and to identify a range of challenges and opportunities that exist. Our goal has been to share information that provides a "point of entry" into our ever-shrinking global community. There is a role for child life specialists in many parts of our world, especially where illness, conflict, deprivation and upheaval exist.

One of our colleagues, Marianne Kayes, Hospital Play Specialist in New Zealand, poses a challenging question by asking:

Do we take a stand regarding decisions made by our governments, where it is clear that our countries are worsening the situation of children, and of civilian populations in general [for example, embargoes on medicine and food to a given country or the waging of war], or do we just keep going out and picking up the pieces? (M. Kayes, personal communication, November 2001.)

This is a difficult question with no easy answers. Hopefully, questions of this type will spark in us a challenge to connect and dialogue with each other in order to broaden our knowledge and understanding of global issues, cultures, and resources in relation to the psychosocial needs of our children and youth globally.

There are many voices of children and youth calling for our action. Responding to this call is vitally important. As it has been said so many times, our children are the future of this planet. We encourage you to join us, as we have joined Muriel Hirt and Peg Belson, pioneers and mentors in international work, in accepting the challenge. Most exciting is the prospect that there is as much to gain as is given as we joyfully embrace the diversity of our planet.

REFERENCES

Barnes, P. (1995). Thirty years of play in hospitals. *The International Journal of Early Childhood, 29*: 48-53.

Bellamy, C. (1999). *The progress of nations 1999.* New York: United Nations Children's Fund.

Benzeval, M., & Judge, K. (2001). Income and health: The time dimension. *Social Science and Medicine, 52*: 1371-1390.

Canadian Institute of Child Health. (2002). *The rights of the child in the health care system.* Ottawa, ON: Canadian Institute of Child Health.

Child Life Council. (2002). *Official documents.* Bethesda, MD: Child Life Council.

Coleman, D. (editor) (1999). KAACCH's mission statement. *KACCHWORD, 2*: 2.

Desai-Joshi, P. (2000). *Medical missions: Role of a child life specialist.* Presentation at the Eighteenth Annual Conference on Professional Issues. Child Life Council, Boston, MA.

Fentiman, A., Hall, A., & Bundy, D (2001). Health and cultural factors associated with enrollment in basic education: a study in rural Ghana. *Social Science and Medicine, 52*: 429-439.

Flores, G., Bauchner, H., Feinstein, A. R., & Nguyen, U-S.D. (1999). The impact of ethnicity, family income and parental education on children's health and use of health services. *American Journal of Public Health, 89*: 1066-1071.

Garcia, F. O. (2000). Caring for children in hospitals: Philippine style. *Child Life Council Bulletin, 18*: 6,12.

Goodfriend, M. (1999). The importance of psychosocial paediatrics in the developing world. *Tropical Doctor, 29*: 90-93.

Guy, K. (Ed.) (1997). *Our promise to children.* Ottawa: The Canadian Institute of Child Health.

Hall, D., Johnson, S., & Middleton, J. (1990). Rehabilitation of head injured children. *Archives of Disease in Childhood, 65*: 553-556.

Kaur, R. (2000). *Towards a child life programme at the children's hospital: A focus on nurses.* Unpublished master's thesis. Department of Human Development and Family Studies, M.S. University of Baroda, Baroda, India.

Kayes, M. (2000). Tonga treasures unique to New Zealand. *Bulletin: Child Life Council, 18*: 3,10.

Kayes, M. (2001). *Te Whaariki in hospital settings: Supporting well-being of children and families.* Paper presented to Children's Issues Centre Conference, Dunedin, June 2001.

London InterCommunity Health Centre. (1992). *Culture, health and you.* London, Ontario: London InterCommunity Health Centre.

Mallya, I. P. (1986). Child in the hospital: A traumatic experience for parents and children. *Social Welfare, 33*(9).

Mallya, I. P. (1989a). Child life programme, an innovative approach in health care setting: Issues and strategies for parent/family involvement (Report). Baroda, India: Department of Human Development & Family Studies, M.S. University of Baroda.

Mallya, I. P. (1989b). *Towards a viable child life programme in a hospital setting (Final report submitted to Indian Council of Social Sciences Research).*

Baroda, India: Department of Human Development & Family Studies, M.S. University of Baroda, Baroda, India.

Miller, T. (2000). *Health of children in war zones: Gaza child health study.* Hamilton: McMaster University Printing Services.

Moltman, M., Giardina-Auten, P. & Lang, G. (2000). *International nuts and bolts: Child life in a global community.* Presentation at the Eighteenth Annual Conference on Professional Issues, Child Life Council, Boston, MA.

Navarro, V., & Shi, L. (2001). The political context of social inequalities and health. *Social Science and Medicine, 52*: 481-91.

Pattussi, M. P., Marcenes, W., Croucher, R. & Sheiham, A. (2001). Social deprivation, income inequality, social cohesion and dental caries in Brazilian school children. *Social Science & Medicine, 53*: 915-925.

Piko, B., & Fitzpatrick, K. M. (2001). Does class matter? SES and psychosocial health among Hungarian adolescents. *Social Science and Medicine, 53*: 817-830.

Pottinger, A. M., & Ehikhametalor, ʹO. (2000). Children's responses to hospitalization at the University Hospital of the West Indies. *West Indian Medical Journal, 49*: 47-51.

Ramritu, P. L., & Croft, G. (1999). Needs of parents of the child hospitalized with acquired brain damage. *International Journal of Nursing Studies, 36*: 209-216.

Rungreangkulkij, S., & Chesla, C. (2001). Smooth a heart with water: Thai mothers care for a child with schizophrenia. *Archives of Psychiatric Nursing, 15*: 120-127.

Seagull, E. A. W. (1978). The rights of the child as a medical patient. *Journal of Clinical Child Psychology, fall*: 202-205.

Southall, D. P., Burr, S., Smith, R. D., Bull, D. N., Radford, A., Williams, A., & Nicholson, S. (2000). The child-friendly healthcare initiative (CFHI): Healthcare provision in accordance with the UN convention on the rights of the child. *Pediatrics, 106*: 1054-1064.

UNICEF. (2000). *State of the world's children 2000.* New York: United Nations Children's Fund.

UNICEF. (2001a). *Progress since the world summit for children: A statistical review.* New York: United Nations Children's Fund.

UNICEF. (2001b). *We the children: Meeting the promises of the world summit for children.* New York: United Nations Children's Fund.

United Nations General Assembly. (1989). *Convention on the rights of the child.* New York: United Nations.

United Nations Population Fund. (2001). *UNFPA: The state of world population 2001.* New York: United Nations.

World Health Organization. (1948). *Definition of health.* Geneva, Switzerland: World Health Organization. (Preamble to the Constitution of the World Health Organization as adopted by the International Health Conference, New York, 19-22 June, 1946; signed on 22 July 1946 by the representatives of 61 States [Official Records of the World Health Organization, no. 2, p. 100] and entered into force on 7 April 1948.)

World Health Organization. (2002). *Investment for health: A discussion of the role of economic and social determinants.* Copenhagen: WHO Regional Office for Europe.

World Bank. (1993). *World development report 1993: Investing in health.* New York: Oxford University Press.

Yeh, C. (2001). Adaptation in children with cancer: Research with Roy's Model. *Nursing Science Quarterly, 14*: 141-148.

Younge, D., Moreau, P., Ezzat, A., & Gray, A. (1997). Communicating with cancer patients in Saudi Arabia. *Annals: New York Academy of Science, 809*: 309-316.

Zelikovsky, N. (1996). Parental participation during the induction stage of children's anesthetic procedures in Israel. *Seminars in Perioperative Nursing, 5*: 213-217.

INDEX

A

AAP (*see* American Academy of Pediatrics)
Abuse/assault (*see* Trauma, non-accidental)
ACCH (*see* Association for the Care of
    Children's Health)
Accommodation, 26
Action for Sick Children, 335–336
Administration (*see* Programs)
Age
    assessment, 121
    play paradigms
        adolescent, 141
        infancy, 139
        preschool, 139–141
        school-age, 141
    see also Development
Allness errors, 83–84
Ambulatory care
    clinical settings, 40
    disaster preparedness, 293
    documentation, 293
    issues
        future, 294
        professional, 305–307
        specific, 300–302
    literature review, 288–289
    outpatient services, 289–305
        other tasks and agreements,
            293–294
        staffing, 291–293
            proportion of child life, 288
        types, 290–291
    pain assessment, 293
    tools and techniques, 302–305
        consumable items, 303
    trauma, non-accidental, 293
    waiting rooms, 302

see also Emergency department
American Academy of Pediatrics (AAP), 98,
    201
Americans with Disabilities Act (ADA, 1990),
    314
Angela's Ashes (McCourt, 1996), 4
Antibiotics, use of, 6
APIE (Assessment, Plan, Intervention,
    Evaluation), 125
Appearance, physical, 85–86
Assessment
    benefits for other disciplines, 122–123
    consistency, programs for, 109
    developmental variability, 120–121
        example, 134
    emergency department, 294–300
    models, 118–123
        age, 121
        culture and language, 121
        family support, 121
        mobility, 121
        social and family status, 121
    pain, 293
    stress potential assessment process, 33,
        118–119
    tools, formal, 122
    variables, response to, 119–120
        example, 135
    see also Documentation
Assimilation, 25–26
Association for the Care of Children's Health
    (ACCH), 5, 13–14, 97
Association for the Well-Being of
        Hospitalized Children and Their
        Families, 14
Attachment theory, 28–29

B

Bakwin, Harry, 6–7
Barker, Larry, 92
Bayley Scales of Infant and Toddler
        Development, Third Edition
        (Bayley-III), 122
Belson, Peg, 339
Bereavement (*see* Grieving)
Big Apple Circus, 217
Bolig, Rosemary, 70–71
Bowlby, James, 10
Bronfenbrenner, Urie, 31–33

C

CAI (*see* Child Advocacy International)
Camps
        illness, chronic, 277–278
        programs, 217
Canadian Council on Health Services
        Accreditation (CCHSA), 202, 207,
        214
Candidate Manual (CLC, 2004), 210
CCLS (*see* Certified Child Life Specialist)
Center for Medicare and Medicaid Services
        (CMS), 214
Certified Child Life Specialist (CCLS), 18,
        210
        see also Staffing
CFHI (*see* Child-Friendly Healthcare
        Initiative)
Chapin, H. D., 6–7
Child Advocacy International (CAI), 335
Child and Adolescent Service System
        Program, 97
Child-Friendly Healthcare Initiative (CFHI),
        335, 342
Child Life Council (CLC)
        Conference on Professional Issues
                (2005), 73
        history, 15–16
        mission, vision and values, 21, 57, 202
Child Life movement (*see* History)
Child Life Position Statement (1979), 15–16
Child Life Specialist (CLS) (*see* Staffing)
Children's Health Care (journal), 14, 17
Children's Hospital (Boston), 100–101, 312
Children's Medical Center (Dallas), 126, 133

Children's Memorial Hospital (Chicago), 8–9,
        12
CLC (*see* Child Life Council)
Cleveland Metropolitan Hospital (Ohio),
        10–13
Clothing, 86
Clown Care Unit, 217
CLS (*see* Staffing)
CMS (*see* Center for Medicare and Medicaid
        Services)
Coalition for Quality Children's Media
        (Meg's Gifts), 218
Cognitive theories
        information processing, 26
        Piagetian, 25–26
        Vygotskian, 27
Comfort
        aspects
                interpersonal, 150–152
                intrapersonal, 150
        play paradigms, 149–152
        see also Play
Communication
        complexity of, 79–82
                context, 81
                process, 79–80
                symbolic, 81–82
                transaction, 80–81
        and grieving, 247–248
        journals, 79
        listening, 91–93
                misconceptions, 92–93
        literature review, 78–79
        nonverbal, 85–91
                appearance, physical, 85–86
                clothing, 86
                facial expression, 86–87
                gaze, 87–88
                gesture, 88–89
                space, 90–91
                touch, 89
                voice, 89–90
        and relationships, therapeutic, 67
        verbal, 82–85
                allness errors, 83–84
                confusion
                        fact inference, 82–83
                        word-thing, 84
                jargon, 84–85

Compassion fatigue (*see* Stress)
Confusion
    fact inference, 82–83
    word-thing, 84
    see also Communication
Coping
    definition, 164
    evaluation, post-procedural, 192–194
    family strengths and vulnerabilities, 179
    "helping hands," 273
    illness, chronic, 272–274
    kits, 303
    and painful procedures, 189–192
    planning and facilitating, 186–194
        selecting and rehearsing, 187–192
    with preparation, 180–186
        information, providing, 180–182
        language, attention to, 182
    styles, naturally occurring, 186–187
    see also Preparation, psychological;
        Stress
Countertransference, 68–70
    see also Transference
Critical care (*see* End-of-life care)
Crossing the Quality Chasm (2001), 102
Csikszentmihalyi, Mihaly, 145–146
Culture (*see* Diversity)

D

Darwin, Charles, 87
Denver Developmental Screening Test
        (Denver II), 122
Development
    play paradigms, 139–141
        adolescent, 141
        infancy, 139
        preschool, 139–141
        school-age, 141
    psychosocial, 29–30
    see also Age
Developmental psychology (*see* Psychology,
        developmental)
Diversity
    assessment, 121
    and end-of-life care, 234–235
    and family-centered care, 104–106
    and grieving, 245–246
    and international work, 345–347

Documentation
    charting
        benefits
            child/family, 124
            healthcare team, 124
            profession, 124–125
            specialist, 124
        electronic, 125
        example, 128–131
    confidence, 123–124
    consult, 125–126
        example, 132
    hospital standards, 125
    information
        from child, 117–118
        from family, 117
        from healthcare team, 116–117
    outpatient services, 293–294
    referrals, 133
    role ambiguity, 123
    service plans, 127
    workload, 123
        measurement, 126–127
    see also Assessment
Dolls and puppets
    and psychological preparation, 183
    real equipment vs. facsimiles, 185–186
Dougy Center (Portland, OR), 254

E

EACH (see European Association for
        Children in Hospitals)
Educating the Chronically Ill Child
        (Kleinberg, 1982), 311
Education
    goals of, 11
    international
        professional, 342–343
        student exchange, 343
    law, 312–313
    maternal, 331
    plan, individualized (IEP), 313–315
    role of, 315–318
    and special needs, 311–312
    tips for specialists, 325
    see also Illness, chronic; Special needs
Education for All Handicapped Children Act
        (1976), 97, 312–313

Emergency department
    assessment, patient, 294–300
    clinical settings, 40–41
    literature review, 288–289
    prioritization, 294–300
    specific issues, 294–300
    staffing, proportion of child life, 288
    triage, 298–299
    see also Ambulatory care; Intensive
        care unit
End-of-life care
    culturally sensitive, 234–235
    dying child, 225–226
        adolescent, 227–228
        guidelines, 227
        stresses, 221–224
        supporting, 226–227
    and parents
        decision making, 229–230
        stresses, 220–221
        supporting, 228–229
    privacy, 222
    and siblings
        stresses, 224–225
        supporting, 230–234
Erikson, Erik, 9, 24, 29, 66, 143
Errors, allness, 83–84
    see also Communication
European Association for Children in
    Hospitals (EACH), 336

F

Facial expression, 86–87
Fact inference confusion, 82–83
Families (*see* Parents and families)
Families of Children with Disabilities Act
    (1994), 97
Family-centered care
    benefits, 98–102
        healthcare providers, 100–101
        healthcare systems, 102
        institutions, 101–102
        patients and families, 99–100
    core principles, 96
    definition, 95–96
    elements (nine), 97, 103–108
        collaboration, parent/professional,
           104
        comprehensive policies for support,
           106
        developmental needs, 107–108
        diversity, 104–106
        family as constant, 103–104
        family-to-family support, 108
        healthcare delivery systems, 108
        share complete/unbiased
           information, 106
        strengths and coping, 106
    history, 96–98
    legislation, 97
    strengths and vulnerabilities, 179
    see also Parents and families
Family Preservation and Family Support Act
    (1993), 97
Famous Fone Friends, 218
Federation for Children's Mental Health, 97
Flow
    and healthy self, 148–149
    play paradigms, 145–149
        characteristics, 146–149
        and practice, 147–148
    see also Play
Foundations, charitable, 217–218
Freud
    Anna, 143
    Sigmund, 62, 65, 69, 143
Froebel, Fredrich, 142

G

Gaze, 87–88
Gender and hospitalization, 43
Germ theory, 6
Gesell, Arnold, 66
Gesture, 88–89
Global perspective
    children of the world, 328–337
    children's rights
        evolution of, 333–337
        universal, 333
    education, maternal, 331
    health status
        current, 329–330
        definition, 330–333
    international work, 341–344
        preparation, 344–349
    involvement, 341–349

mortality rates (U5MR), 329
NGOs, 342
see also History
"Goodness of fit," 29
Grieving
    bereavement systems, 250–252
        cultural and religious influences,
            245–246
            rituals and mourning, 246
        peer grief, facilitating, 253
        supplies, 252
        support
            family, 250–251
            groups, 253–254
            staff, 251–252
    competency development, 246–250
        advocacy and collaboration, 249
        communication, 247–248
        empathic response, 248–249
        facilitation
            group, 248
            play, 246–247
        self-reflection, 249
        training, implications for, 249–250
    as family process, 239
        parental, 239–240
        siblings, 240–241
            guidelines, 243
        "survivor guilt," 240
    tasks of, 241–245
    tripartite model, 241–242
Groos, Karl, 136, 138
*Guidelines for the Development of Child Life
    Programs* (1984), 17
    see also Program Review Guidelines

H

Hall
    Edward T., 90–91
    G. Stanley, 138
Hawaii Early Learning Profile (HELP), 122
Hirt, Muriel, 339
History
    family-centered care, 96–98
    healthcare, 5–10
        changing role, 20
        hospitalization, 4–5
        nature of, 19

pediatrics, 5–6
    Vision to Action, 20–21
"hospitalism," 6–8
movement (child life), 10–16
    academic programs, 16
    credentialing, 17–18
    credibility, 17–19
    defining the tasks, 16–17
    environments, 12–13
    of name (child life), 12
    relationships, therapeutic, 61–63
Hope
    and fantasy play, 154–156
    importance of, 152–153
    play paradigms, 152–156
    and resilience, 153–154
    see also Coping; Play
"Hospitalism," 6–8
Hospitalization, children's response, 42–45

I

ICISF (*see* International Critical Incident
    Stress Foundation)
ICU (*see* Intensive care unit)
IDEA (*see* Individuals with Disabilities
    Education Act)
IEP (*see* Individualized education plan)
Illness, chronic
    adaptation, facilitating, 267–279
        adherence, 275–276
        coping, 272–274
        education, developmentally
            appropriate, 269–270
        goal-setting and action plans, 275
        play, 271–272
        preparation, 270–271
        problem-solving, 274–275
        self-expression, 268–269
    adjustment, 260–264
        over time, 280–281
        psychosocial evaluation, 265
    collaboration, interdisciplinary, 281
    developmental tasks, 264–267
        autonomy/independence, 266
        body image, 267
        competency, 266
        identity, 266–267
        mastery, 265–266

peer relationships, 267
literature review, 258–260
normalcy and self, 279–280
and parents, 48
professional considerations, 281–282
support systems
    camps, 277–278
    family, 276
    school re-entry, 278–279
    social interaction, 277
    support groups, 276–277
see also Rehabilitation; Special needs
Individual family service plans (IFSP), 314
Individualized education plan (IEP), 313–315
    see also Education
Individuals with Disabilities Education Act
    (IDEA, 1990), 97, 314
Industrial Revolution, 3
Infant (term), 9
Information processing theory, 26
Intensive care unit (ICU), 40, 220–221
    pediatric (PICU), 49–50
    see also Emergency department
International Critical Incident Stress
    Foundation (ICISF), 307
Internet and international practice, 343
Interns (*see* Staffing)
Interventions
    effectiveness, 45–48
    play, 45–47
    preparation, 47–48
IWK Health Centre (Halifax, Nova Scotia),
    118–119
    documentation (examples), 128–132,
        134–135

J

Jacobi, Abraham, 5
Jargon, 84–85
Joint Commission on the Accreditation of
    Healthcare Organizations
    (JCAHO), 109, 125, 202, 207,
    213–214

K

The Kissing Hand (Penn, 1993), 149
Klein, Melanie, 143

Korzybski, Alfred, 83
Kuwait, 341

L

Language
    and assessment, 121
    and psychological preparation, 182
Lazarus, Richard, 31, 163–164
Learning, play paradigms, 142–143
Listening, 91–93
    misconceptions, 92–93
    see also Communication
The Little Prince (Saint-Exupery, 1982),
    150–151
Locke, John, 137

M

Management (*see* Programs)
McCourt, Frank, 4
Medical College of Georgia (Augusta),
    101–102
Medical missions, 343–344
Medicare/Medicaid, 214
Mobility, assessment, 121
Modeling, 27–28
Montagu, Ashley, 89
Montessori, Maria, 136, 142
    Montessori Method, 142

N

Networking, family-to-family support, 108
"New morbidity," 19
New Zealand, 340
Newborn Individualized Developmental Care
    and Assessment Program
    (NID-CAP), 101
Non-governmental organizations (NGO), 342

O

Outpatient services (*see* Ambulatory care)

P

Parents and families
    assessment, 121

end-of-life care
   decision making, 229–230
   stresses, 220–221, 224–225
   supporting, 228–230,
   grieving, 239–241
   and healthcare, 19–20
   preparation, psychological, 170
   presence and participation, 48–50
      anesthesia induction, 49
   sibling care, 217, 224–225
   see also Family-centered care
Parten, Mildred, 24, 138
Pediatrics, history of, 5–6
Philippines, 340–341
Phoenix Children's Hospital (Arizona), 18, 42
Photographs and video
   closed-circuit television, 217
   and psychological preparation, 184–185
Piaget, Jean, 9–10, 138–140, 142
   Piagetian theory, 24–26, 139
PICU (*see* Intensive care unit)
Plank, Emma, 10–13
Play
   adaptive, 271
   alternatives, 272
   developmentally appropriate, 25
   expanded paradigms, 145–156
      as comfort, 149–152
      as flow, 145–149
      as hope, 152–156
   family activities, 272
   fantasy, 153–156
   foundations of, 136–145
      as development, 139–141
      as enjoyment, 137–139
      as learning, 142–143
      as therapy, 143–145
   and grieving, 246–247
   as healing modality, 23–24
   and illness, chronic, 271–272
   medical, 222
   outdoor space, 217
   programs and healthcare, 8–9
      as intervention, 45–47
      post-procedural, 161
      post-traumatic, 271
   relationships during, 151–152
   stimulation, 272
   symbolic, 140–141

terminology, 12
Post-Hospital Behavior Questionnaire, 43–44
Post-traumatic stress disorder (PTSD), 167,
   261
   see also Stress
Practice
   clinical settings
      ambulatory clinic, 40
      emergency department, 40–41
      ICU, 40
   community-based programming, 41
   family-centered care, 95–112
   and flow, 147–148
   foundations, theoretical, 23–34
   international, 341–344
      advocacy, 342
      collaboration, 342
      consultation, 343
      cultural sensitivity, 345–347
      education, 342–343
      Internet, 343
      medical missions, 343–344
      preparation, 344–349
      research, 343
      role of, 347–348
   travel
      purpose of, 345
      tips, 348–349
   see also Programs
Preparation, psychological
   approaches
      behavioral, 162–163
      informational, 162
   coping, planned, 180–186
      language, attention to, 182
      providing information, 180–182
   current issues, 167
      research, 171
   effectiveness
      on experienced patients, 168–169
      relative, 167–168
   evaluation, post-procedural, 170–171
   illness, chronic, 270–271
   initiating, 171–180
      assessment
         situation, 174–177
         variables, individual, 177–178
      focus of care, determining, 178–180
      information, gathering, 174

team members, involving, 172–173
overview, 162–171
parents, collaborating with, 170
preadmission tours, 217
stress-coping framework, 163–166
    overwhelming stress, 166–167
    "stress-point" preparation, 48
timing, 169–170
tools that facilitate, 182–186
see also Coping
Privacy, 222
Professionals (*see* Staffing)
Program Review Guidelines (1985), 17, 213
Programs
    accountability, 213–214
        evaluation, 213
        institutional standards, 213–214
        research, 214
    assessment, for consistency, 109
    culturally competent care, 109–111
        implications, 111
        incorporating, 110
        spirituality, 110–111
    development, 216–218
        external sources, 217–218
        internally created, 217
        special events, 216–217
    family resource library, 217
    finance and budget, 215–216
        budget, allocation of, 215–216
        funding, sources of, 215
    fundamentals, 202–205
        mission, vision and values, 202
        operating principles, 202–203
        staffing, 203–205
    future, 111–112
    management, 199–202
        benchmarking, 201
        leadership, 199–200
        organizational structure, 201–202
    outdoor play space, 217
    school re-entry, 217
    staff essentials, 205–210
        orientation and training, 210–213
    wish-granting organizations, 218
    see also Practice
Psychology, developmental, 9–10
Psychosocial care
    current programs, 339–341

Kuwait, 341
New Zealand, 340
Philippines, 340–341
United Kingdom (UK), 340
development, 29–30
promoting, international efforts,
    339–341
universal nature, 337–339
PTSD (*see* Post-traumatic stress disorder)
Puppets (*see* Dolls and puppets)

R

Rainbow Babies' and Children's Hospital
    (Cleveland), 101
Ranchos Los Amigos Cognitive Scale, 270
Reach Out and Read, 218
Rehabilitation, 258–260
    see also Illness, chronic
Rehabilitation Act (1973), 314
Relationships
    boundaries, 67–68
    clinical/non-clinical, 60, 72
    communication skills, 67
    countertransference, 68–70
    developing, 75–76
    foundations, theoretical, 65–66
    phases, 64–65
    during play, 151–152
    professional, 59–60, 71–72
    supportive, 60, 72
    therapeutic, 60–61, 72–73
        concepts, 63–70
        definition, 57–58
        history, 61–63
    transference, 68–70
    trust, 66–67
    types, 63–64
    and typology, 71–75
Religion (*see* Diversity; Spirituality)
Research
    clinical settings, 39–41
    efficacy, 41–42
        interventions, 45–48
    hospitalization
        children's response, 42–45
            stress-coping response, 44–45
    methodological problems, 51–52
    parent presence, 48–50

professional
  development, 37–38
  international, 343
  issues, 38–39
  specific, 37–42
Robertson, James and Joan, 10
Rogers, Carl, 62–63, 65
Rousseau, Jean-Jacques, 137

S

Sabriya's Castle of Fun Foundation, 218
Scaffolding, 27
Schneider Children's Medical Center (Israel),
  338
Sib Shops, 218
Siblings (*see* Parents and families)
Smith, Anne, 8–9
SOAP (Subjective, Objective, Assessment,
  Plan), 125
Social learning theory, 27–28
Songs of Love Foundation, 218
Space (personal), 90–91
Special needs
  case studies, 320–323
  educational services, gaps, 311–312
  socialization and school, 318–320
  tips for specialists, 325
  see also Education; Illness, chronic
Spirituality, 110–111
  see also Diversity; Family-centered care
Spitz, René, 6
Staffing
  advancement, clinical, 208–209
  burnout, 208, 251–252
  CCLS, 18, 210
  essentials, 203–210
  outpatient services, 291–293
  professionals
    challenges, 207–208
    identity, 209–210
    membership, 343
    role of, 102–103
  supervision, 206–207
  training and development, 211
    interns, 211–212
    orientation, 210–211
    volunteers, 212–213, 297
*The Standards for Academic and Clinical
  Preparation Programs in Child Life*
  (CLC, 1992), 16
Stanford, Gene, 15
Starbright World, 218
Starlight Children's Foundation, 218
Stress
  compassion fatigue, 208
  and coping theories, 31
  end-of-life care, 221–224
    for parents, 220–221
    for siblings, 224–225
  overwhelming, 166–167
  post-traumatic stress disorder (PTSD),
    167, 261
    secondary traumatic stress disorder,
    208
  preparation, psychological, 163–166
  "stress-point," 48
  stress-coping response, 44–45
  stress potential assessment process, 33,
    118–119
  stressors, situational, 174–175
  see also Coping
Supervision (*see* Programs)
Support systems
  end-of-life care, 226–234
  grieving, 250–254
  illness, chronic, 276–279
  psychosocial services, 337–339
Sutton-Smith, Brian, 142
Systems theories
  ecological, 32–33
  family systems, 32

T

Temperament theory, 29–30
Theoretical foundations
  attachment theory, 28–29
  cognitive theories, 24–27
  development, psychosocial, 29–30
  social learning theory, 27–28
  stress and coping theories, 31
  systems theories, 31–33
  temperament theory, 29–30
Therapy
  animal-assisted, 217
  hypnotherapy, 304–305
  play paradigms, 143–145

relationships, therapeutic, 57–77
tools, therapeutic, 303
"T.L.C." (tender loving care), 6
Touch, 89
Transference, 68–70
    see also Countertransference
Trauma, non-accidental, 293
Trust and therapeutic relationships, 66–67
A Two-Year-Old Goes to the Hospital
    (Robertson, 1953), 10
Typology
    of child life, 70–71
    and relationships, 71–75

U

U5MR (*see* Global perspective)
United Kingdom (UK), 340
United Nations' Convention on the Rights of
the Child (UN-CRC), 333–334, 342
Universal rights of children, 333
    see also Global perspective

V

Video (*see* Photographs and video)
Vision to Action, 20–21
Voice, 89–90
Volunteers (*see* Staffing)
Vygotsky, Leo, 142, 154
    Vygotskian theory, 24, 27

W

Winnicott, D. W., 7, 12
Wolfer, John, 18
Word-thing confusion, 84
Working with Children in Hospitals (1962),
    10–11
Workload measurement (WLM), 126–127
    see also Documentation
World Health Organization (WHO), 330

Z

"Zone of Helpfulness," 68–69
Zone of proximal development (ZPD), 27,
    142